Scots Commercial Law

Scots Commercial Law

2nd edition

Edited by Ross G Anderson

EDINBURGH
University Press

Edinburgh University Press is one of the leading university presses in the UK. We publish academic books and journals in our selected subject areas across the humanities and social sciences, combining cutting-edge scholarship with high editorial and production values to produce academic works of lasting importance. For more information visit our website: edinburghuniversitypress.com

First edition published 2014 by Avizandum Publishing Ltd

Edinburgh University Press Ltd
The Tun – Holyrood Road
12(2f) Jackson's Entry
Edinburgh EH8 8PJ

Typeset in 10/11 Plantin by
by Cheshire Typesetting Ltd, Cuddington, Cheshire, and
printed and bound by CPI Group (UK) Ltd,
Croydon, CR0 4YY

A CIP record for this book is available from the British Library

ISBN 978-1-4744-9418-2 (hardback)
ISBN 978-1-4744-9419-9 (paperback)
ISBN 978-1-4744-9420-5 (webready PDF)
ISBN 978-1-4744-9421-2 (epub)

Contents

Preface

Commercial law, it is sometimes said, is the application of the general principles of contract and property law in particular practical contexts. This edition, like its predecessor, builds on those general principles. We set out how contracts are concluded (often by agency) by particular parties (often juristic persons, such as partnerships) on classic commercial subjects (such as sale, insurance, partnership, caution). Other chapters address some of the basic legal structures used to ameliorate risk (as with security); and what can happen when the risks undertaken do not provide the anticipated rewards: possible alternative dispute resolution methods (ADR) and enforcement, whether by conventional security or by diligence. Fundamentally, since risk must often be measured against the benchmark of a counterparty's insolvency, there are also chapters on the detail of the law of bankruptcy (for individuals and partnerships) as well as an introduction to the Scots law of corporate insolvency.

The first edition of this textbook was a collaboration between various colleagues then teaching at the Glasgow Law School, all under the editorship of Professor Iain MacNeil. Due to other commitments Iain was unable to continue as general editor. My enthusiasm for a second edition reflected in part my admiration for the way Iain brought the first edition to fruition. That enthusiasm has not always been matched by any confidence in my ability to emulate Iain as editor. But I am grateful to Iain for giving those of us who embarked on the first edition the opportunity to do so and, having himself disembarked, for encouraging the rest of us on to a second edition. We hope we have done justice to his brainchild.

The present volume is a student textbook. The chapters that follow contain introductions to their respective subjects, not the last word. The views expressed are not designed to be definitive commentary. The university teacher, like the advocate, for the purposes of presentation and exposition, must often simplify material that is inherently complex. Whether we have succeeded in our modest presentational aims is for others to judge.

I am grateful to all the contributors for their industry and enthusiasm: to the surviving members of the original team, some of whom are no longer in Glasgow or even in Scotland; and to those from outside the Glasgow Law School who have been so willing to join in the preparation of this edition.

I thank Laura Williamson and Sarah Foyle at Edinburgh University Press for their assistance and, indeed, their patience in dealing with an editor often preoccupied with the pressures of professional life. Above all, however, I thank my wife, Veronika, without whose support I could not have had any involvement in the second edition at all.

The law is stated as at 30 April 2021, although some later references have also been included.

R G Anderson

Edinburgh

19 July 2021

Table of statutes

Table of statutory instruments

Table of EU Legislation, International Documents and Soft Law

Soft Law

Table of cases

List of contributors

Ross Anderson is an Advocate and Honorary Research Fellow in the University of Glasgow.

Mat Campbell is Lecturer in Law in the University of Glasgow.

Katarzyna Chałaczkiewicz-Ładna is Lecturer in Commercial Law in the University of Glasgow.

David Fox is Professor of Common Law in the University of Edinburgh.

Bobby Lindsay is Lecturer in Private Law in the University of Glasgow.

John MacLeod is Senior Lecturer in Private Law in the University of Edinburgh.

Frankie McCarthy is a Scottish Law Commissioner and Professor of Private Law in the University of Glasgow.

Paul McClelland is IP Faculty member, IPOS International, Singapore.

Dot Reid is Senior Lecturer in Private Law in the University of Glasgow.

Elisabeth Roxburgh is an Advocate.

Cameron Smith is an Advocate.

Matteo Solinas is Senior Lecturer in Commercial Law in the Victoria University of Wellington, New Zealand.

Alexander Sutherland is an Advocate.

List of abbreviations

Institutional Writers

Bankton, *Institute*	A McDouall, Lord Bankton, *An Institute of the Laws of Scotland in Civil Rights with the Observations upon the Agreement or Diversity between them and the Laws of England* (1751–1753, Stair Society edn by W M Gordon, Vols 41–43, 1993–1995).
Bell, *Commentaries*	G J Bell, *Commentaries on the Law of Scotland and on the Principles of Mercantile Jurisprudence* (7th edn by J McLaren, 1870) 2 vols.
Bell, *Principles*	G J Bell, *Principles of the Law of Scotland* (4th edn 1839, reprinted with an introduction by K G C Reid, 2010).
Erskine, *Institute*	J Erskine, *An Institute of the Law of Scotland* (1777, reprinted with an introduction by K G C Reid, 2014).
Stair, *Institutions*	J Dalrymple, Viscount Stair, *Institutions of the Law of Scotland* (2nd edn 1693 reprinted in Tercentenary Edition by D M Walker, 1981).

Court Rules

OCR	Act of Sederunt (Ordinary Cause Rules) 1993 (SI 1993/1956).
RCS	Act of Sederunt (Rules of the Court of Session 1994) 1994 (SI 1994/1443).

Chapter One

Introduction to Juristic Persons

Ross Anderson with Cameron Smith

INTRODUCTION

The law of persons

'All our law is about persons, things and actions.'[1] In other words, *who* has rights, *what* rights they have and *how* they are enforced.[2] The law of persons is one of the fundamental pillars of private law. It is not possible in the short space available here to sketch the entire law of persons and to explain, for example, how the University of Glasgow was originally founded by Papal Bull; how the Aberdeen Harbour Board is considered to be the UK's oldest commercial corporation;[3] or why unincorporated associations do not, in Scots law, generally enjoy legal personality.[4] For present purposes, suffice it to say that, in commercial law – as well as many other areas of legal practice – the law of persons is of fundamental importance, not least because, more often than not, the parties to commercial transactions are juristic rather than natural persons. It is thus necessary to identify certain fundamental principles of legal personality before turning to consider the particular rules that apply to the juristic persons considered in this book: partnerships, limited partnerships and limited liability partnerships. **1.01**

GENERAL PRINCIPLES OF LEGAL PERSONALITY

Legal personality

The concept of legal personality is central to any legal system.[5] Only a legal person can enter into legal transactions or hold patrimonial rights. Natural persons – human beings – acquire, on being born alive, legal personality. With **1.02**

1 Gaius, *Institutes* I, 8.

2 G L Gretton and A J M Steven, *Property, Trusts and Succession*, 4th edn (London: Bloomsbury Professional, 2021), para 1.14.

3 J Micklethwait and A Wooldridge, *The Company: A Short History of a Revolutionary Idea* (London: W&N, 2003), p.23 confer upon the Aberdeen Harbour Board, which can trace its origins to at least 1136, the accolade of the oldest UK corporation.

4 Cf C Hemström, 'Associations' in *International Encyclopaedia of Comparative Law*, Vol.III/2, Ch. 8 (2006).

5 D N MacCormick, *Institutions of Law: An Essay in Legal Theory* (Oxford: Oxford University Press, 2007), Ch. 5; MacCormick, 'General Legal Concepts' in *Stair Memorial Encyclopaedia* (Reissue) (2008).

legal personality comes, normally, at least passive legal capacity: an infant can benefit from juridical acts even if, at that stage, an infant has no active transactional capacity. So fundamental is legal personality to vindicating legal claims, that the very right to be recognised as a person is enshrined in the UN's Universal Declaration of Human Rights[6] and, for similar reasons, some national constitutions tightly regulate the related issue of the withdrawal of citizenship.[7] In Scotland, one of the most extreme sanctions historically imposed on a natural person was where that person was declared an 'outlaw' or a rebel, resulting in limitations on civil legal personality and forfeiture of assets.[8]

1.03 Not all associations of natural persons create juristic persons. Unincorporated associations, such as sports and social clubs, do not have legal personality and cannot, therefore, hold patrimonial rights or be a party to juridical acts.[9] In contrast, commercial undertakings formed as partnerships, limited partnerships, limited liability partnerships or companies are all juristic persons and may enter into juridical acts and hold patrimonial rights. Death by liquidation and dissolution of juristic persons presents special problems. A paradigm situation involves the dissolution of a company that still holds assets. The effect of dissolution is that the assets pass to the Crown.[10]

Capacity

1.04 Recognition as a legal person does not in itself define that person's legal capacity. Capacity determines whether, and to what extent, a legal person can enter into juridical acts, hold patrimonial rights and incur liabilities. The legal capacity of a child, an adult, a company and a partnership may each be different. The differences can be clarified by examining legal capacity in its active and in its passive sense.

1.05 Active capacity focuses on two characteristics of a legal person. The first aspect is the ability to enter into juridical acts, the paradigm example of which is a contract. This ability to enter into juridical acts is sometimes known as 'transactional capacity'. Transactional capacity may vary. For instance, the capacity of a child to enter a contract is limited compared to that of an adult.[11] A person suffering from mental illness or infirmity may also have limited active transactional capacity.[12] The second aspect relates to the ability of a person to commit legal wrongs, such as delicts.

6 Universal Declaration of Human Rights, art. 6: 'Everyone has the right to recognition everywhere as a person before the law'.
7 As in the German *Grundgesetz*, art. 16.
8 Cf *Lord Advocate v Marquis of Zetland* 1920 SC (HL) 1 at 27 per Lord Shaw of Dunfermline.
9 But compare an 'owners Association', created where the development management scheme applies, which is a body corporate created at the time specified in the registered deed: Title Conditions (Scotland) Act 2003, s. 71 and Title Conditions (Scotland) Act 2003 (Development Management Scheme) Order 2009 (SI 2009/729) art. 4(2).
10 Companies Act 2006, s. 1013 onward. See, further, Chapter Fourteen: Corporate Insolvency.
11 Age of Legal Capacity (Scotland) Act 1991, s. 1(1)(a) and s. 2 (transactional capacity); Children (Scotland) Act 1995, ss. 9 and 10 (property).
12 There are detailed provisions in private law for dealing with natural persons lacking transactional capacity: Adults with Incapacity (Scotland) Act 2000, for which see generally A D Ward, *Adult Incapacity* (Edinburgh: W. Green, 2003).

A person may have no active legal capacity, but may nonetheless have passive legal capacity. Passive legal capacity is the ability to benefit from unilateral juridical acts[13] or to benefit from the protection of the law of delict. At the simplest level, this form of capacity identifies the capability of an entity to fall within the protection of the law. A related and controversial question is whether juristic persons (as opposed to natural persons) fall within the protection of human rights legislation.[14] **1.06**

Mortality

All natural persons are mortal and legal personality ends with death. But Scots law does not provide for an automatic universal succession of the deceased's assets to successors. Legal personality ceases with death, but, between death and the confirmation of executors, there is a legal limbo (the *haereditas jacens*): a patrimony but no person to represent it.[15] A major difference between juristic and natural persons is that juristic persons are not subject to the laws of mortality: they are potentially immortal. Historically, with some exceptions, only the Crown or Parliament could create bodies corporate. The University of Glasgow, founded by Papal Bull, is recognised as a body corporate by virtue of Acts of Parliament. The Faculty of Advocates is a common law corporation. **1.07**

Juristic persons in commerce

Company law is a specialist area on which there are many excellent introductory texts.[16] Company lawyers tend to focus, understandably, on a paradigm vehicle in order to illustrate the general principles. That paradigm is normally the private company limited by shares. But that is only one of a number of different possible vehicles available either under the Companies Acts and related legislation. In summary, the following are possible: **1.08**

- An unlimited company.[17]
- A company limited by guarantee (Ltd).[18]

13 Bilateral juridical acts, by definition, require the consent of both parties. A person with no active legal capacity cannot give consent.

14 Juristic persons, as a general principle, benefit from the European Convention on Human Rights: R G Anderson, 'Fundamental Rights of Juristic Persons' in E Reid and D Visser (eds), *Private Law and Human Rights in Scotland and South Africa* (Edinburgh: Edinburgh University Press, 2013).

15 For all this, see L Smith, 'Scottish Trusts in the Common Law' (2013) 17 Edin LR 283.

16 P Davies, *An Introduction to Company Law*, 2nd edn (Oxford: Oxford University Press, 2002); P Davies and S Worthington, *Gower and Davies Principles of Modern Company Law*, 11th edn (London: Sweet & Maxwell, 2021); R Kraakman et al, *An Anatomy of Corporate Law: A Comparative and Functional Approach*, 3rd edn (Oxford: Oxford University Press, 2017).

17 Companies Act 2006, ss. 3 and 102. An unlimited company can reregister as a limited company, although it may do so only once: s. 102(3) and s. 105(2). The name of a company with unlimited liability does not contain a suffix indicating its status. Unlimited companies are more common than might be imagined, not least because they are not subject to rules on capital maintenance. Take, for example, *Re Lehman Brothers International (Europe) (in administration)* [2012] UKSC 6. Lehman Brothers International (Europe) (registered number 02538254) was an unlimited company.

18 Not all companies limited by guarantee need to include 'Limited' or 'Ltd' in their name: Companies Act 2006, s. 60 (which also contains a small number of exceptions for companies limited by shares).

- A private company limited by shares (Ltd).
- A public company (plc).
- Community Interest Companies (CIC).[19]

1.09 Only a public company can apply to be listed on a regulated exchange. It is worth emphasising, however, that not all public companies are listed. Otherwise, of the entities listed above, only the private company limited by shares (Ltd) and the public limited company (plc) are commonly encountered in commercial life. Following the UK's exit from the EU, it is no longer possible to incorporate a Societas Europa (SE) in the UK. In addition to companies, three other juristic persons, which are covered in this book, are common:

- A limited liability partnership (LLP).
- A limited partnership (LP).
- A partnership.

1.10 With this limited knowledge of the law of juristic persons, it should in principle be possible instantly to verify the vehicle adopted by a business to pursue its commercial activities: companies, like LPs and LLPs, have to publicise their status on all their business documents, including emails and websites. The designation plc, Ltd, LLP or LP is a mandatory part of the registered name for these respective vehicles – it is not an optional suffix. The plc, Ltd, LLP or LP designation is as part of the company name as a natural person's surname.

Limited liability

1.11 All persons, natural or juristic, are liable for their debts without limitation. In this sense, the liability of everyone is *unlimited*. What, then, is the concept of 'limited liability'? In historical terms, it is a relatively recent private law development. In Roman law every juristic person (*universitas*) had limited liability in the sense that only the *universitas* was liable for debts. But the Roman law business organisation, the partnership (*societas*), was never a *universitas*: juristic persons existed only in public law. The revolution in the modern world was to fuse *societas* (business but not person) with *universitas* (person but not business), thus creating the modern company (both business and person), with explosive consequences.[20] Today, 'limited liability' means that the liability of a *member* of a company or an LLP, or a limited partner in a limited partnership, for the debts of the company, LLP or LP as the case may be, is limited by reference to the capital that is contributed by the member of limited partner.[21] The limitation of the liability of the member or limited partner carries no implications for the liability of the juristic person. The juristic person's liability for its own debts, like the liability of a natural person for his or her own debts,

19 Companies (Audit, Investigations and Community Enterprise) Act 2004, Part II.

20 This insight is gratefully acknowledged to be that of the Lord President Reid Professor of Law Emeritus in the University of Edinburgh, Professor G L Gretton.

21 Cf *J H Rayner (Mincing Lane) Ltd v Department of Trade and Industry* [1990] 2 AC 418 at 479H–480A per Lord Templeman and at 508D–508E per Lord Oliver of Aylmerton. In the case of companies limited by guarantee, members' liabilities are limited to the guarantee provided in the memorandum of association.

is unlimited.[22] Scottish partnerships, as we will see, are unusual. Not only is the firm as a juristic person liable for its own debts, the partners are expressly held by statute to be secondarily liable – essentially guarantors – for the firm's debts.[23]

PERSONALITY AND PATRIMONY

The concept

Every person has a patrimony. A patrimony contains the totality of that person's assets.[24] Assets are a person's patrimonial rights: real rights, personal rights and intellectual property rights. The general principle of personal liability (whether of a natural or a juristic person) is that a creditor may look to all the debtor's assets to satisfy the creditor's claim, by way of diligence or, ultimately, through bankruptcy. It is for this reason that a personal obligation granted by a juristic person with plentiful assets (relative to its liabilities) may often be more valuable than a real right in security in a thing that is of fluctuating value or for which there is no ready market. A bank guarantee (a personal obligation) is commercially preferable to a standard security (a real security) over an owner-occupied residential property. **1.12**

But although all assets in the debtor's patrimony are available, it is *only* the debtor's patrimony that is available: assets held in a separate patrimony are not available to the debtor's personal creditors. The classic example for explaining this distinction is the trust. A trustee is bound to segregate trust assets from their personal assets. The trust assets are thus considered to be held in a patrimony that is separate from the trustee's personal patrimony. The significance of the distinction is that trust assets are not available to the personal creditors of the trustee; nor are the trustee's personal assets available to creditors who have contracted with the trustee on the basis that only the trust assets shall be available to satisfy the creditor's claim.[25] **1.13**

Asset partitioning: juristic persons

Every person, natural or legal, has a patrimony but, ordinarily, only one patrimony. The creation of a juristic person as a vehicle for a business involves the creation of a new person and thus a new patrimony. Assets acquired by the business vehicle, let us suppose a company, are held in the company's patrimony, not the patrimony of individual shareholders. Two aspects of asset partitioning between the company and its shareholders are worth **1.14**

22 *Muir v City of Glasgow Bank* (1878) 6 R 392 at 401 per Lord President Inglis. The decision was affirmed by the House of Lords: (1879) 6 R (HL) 21.

23 *J H Rayner (Mincing Lane) Ltd v Department of Trade and Industry* [1990] 2 AC 418 at 479H–480A per Lord Templeman and at 508D–508E per Lord Oliver of Aylmerton.

24 G L Gretton and A J M Steven, *Property Trusts and Succession*, 4th edn (2021), paras 1.9–1.12. Sometimes the word 'estate' is used as a synonym for patrimony, as in 'trust estate', 'bankrupt estate', 'deceased's estate'.

25 *Gordon v Campbell* (1840) 2 D 639, affd (1842) 1 Bell's App 428. Where a trustee commits a breach of trust, the beneficiaries may seek to satisfy their claim from the trustee's personal assets.

highlighting.[26] The first, sometimes known as *entity shielding*, exists for the benefit of the company. The personal insolvency of a shareholder does not – at least directly[27] – affect the company's assets. The second aspect (*asset partitioning*) arises by virtue of the company's separate legal personality and the idea of limited liability: individual shareholders are not liable to the company's creditors on the company's insolvency. The shareholders may, however, be affected in other ways, for if a company cannot pay its creditors, then shareholders will not receive back the money they originally invested in the company.

1.15 But sometimes asset partitioning for particular purposes is more specifically intended. A special purpose vehicle (SPV) or special purpose entity (SPE) is, normally, a juristic person whose only purpose is to hold particular assets. An SPV is often incorporated to hold assets rather than to trade. The assets are partitioned in theory because they are held by a separate juristic person; but that partition is reinforced in practice because the basic premise of the SPV is that it holds rather than trades; it is an entity that does not incur debt; and, because the entity has no debts, it has no creditors who can enforce court judgments against the vehicle's assets.

Asset partitioning: trusts

1.16 Another possibility for asset partitioning is the trust.[28] A trust is *not* a legal person, but gives rise to the creation of a separate patrimony.[29] A trust must have trustees. The trustees must be natural or juristic persons, for only persons enjoying legal capacity can enter into juridical acts. A trustee is in an exceptional position because the trustee has more than one patrimony. The first patrimony is that in which their personal assets are held. The additional patrimony is that in which the trust assets are held. In principle, a trustee, can contract on such terms as to choose which patrimony is benefited and burdened by the contract. What, then, if the trustee becomes insolvent? The general principle is that assets held by a trustee in their capacity as trustee may not be attached by the trustee's personal creditors.[30]

Trust companies

1.17 A 'unit trust' may be a trust; but more usually it is a juristic person subject to some sort of trust deed. A REIT (a real estate investment trust), despite its name, cannot be a trust and must be a UK company whose shares are traded

26 The ideas are well explained in R Kraakman et al., *The Anatomy of Corporate Law*, 3rd edn (2017), para. 7–11.

27 It may do so indirectly because the shareholder's insolvency administrator may be able to take control of the shares and, thus, the company. Once in control of the company the insolvency administrator could, in principle, wind up the company.

28 Gretton & Steven, *Property, Trusts and Succession*, Ch. 23.

29 G L Gretton, 'Trusts without equity' (2000) 49 ICLQ 599; K G C Reid, 'Patrimony not equity: the trust in Scotland' (2000) European Review of Private Law 427, cited with approval in *Ted Jacobs Engineering Group Inc v Robert Matthew Johnson-Marshall and Partners* [2014] CSIH 18, 2014 SC 579, [90] per Lord Drummond Young.

30 Bankruptcy (Scotland) Act 2016, s. 88(3).

on a recognised stock exchange.[31] A 'trust company' is normally a company acting as a trustee.

PUBLICITY

Juristic persons

In the case of companies, LLPs and LPs, registration with the Registrar of Companies[32] is essential to the creation of these entities as juristic persons.[33] Registration serves the purpose of providing a central public record of information relating to the entity for the benefit of creditors, members and others who may have dealings with the entity. In theory, a contractual creditor of a corporate entity should be able to inform itself of the nature of the entity with whom a prospective contract is to be concluded.[34] In the case of companies and LLPs they must have a registered number, a registered name and a registered office. The registered number does not change even if the name of the company or LLP changes. In addition to the publicity required for incorporation, a company or LLP has continuing reporting requirements, the most of important of which is the public filing of annual audited accounts.[35] A company must disclose to the Registrar of Companies its directors and its members; it must also keep registers of this information at its registered office, which registers are, essentially, open to public inspection.[36] **1.18**

Most ordinary partnerships are not subject to registration in any form. An ordinary partnership may be formed simply by the conduct of persons carrying on a business in common with a view of profit,[37] which means that, in contrast to registered business structures, its very existence may not always be clear. There is no easy way for third parties to establish, from an independent source, whether a partnership has been constituted, who the partners are and where it does business. There are, however, specific registration requirements at Companies House for 'qualifying partnerships', namely partnerships the partners of which are juristic persons.[38] **1.19**

31 Corporation Tax Act 2010, s. 528.

32 The Registrar of Companies for Scotland is based in Edinburgh. There are separate Registrars for England and Wales (in Cardiff) and Northern Ireland (in Belfast).

33 See Companies Act 2006, s. 16; Limited Liability Partnerships Act 2000, s. 3; Limited Partnerships Act 1907, s. 8C.

34 Some creditors, however, are involuntary: delict victims, for instance, do not choose their wrongdoer.

35 Companies Act 2006, s. 394.

36 Companies Act 2006, s. 116 now imposes a 'proper purposes' test on applicants wishing to consult the registers kept at the company's registered office. For discussion, see *Burry & Knight Ltd v Knight* [2014] EWCA Civ 604, [2014] BCC 393.

37 See Partnership Act 1890, s. 1.

38 Partnership (Accounts) Regulations 2008 (SI 2008/569), reg. 3. See further Chapter Five: Partnerships, LPs and LLPs below.

Trusts

1.20 Trusts may be latent. There may be no way of telling whether particular assets are held in trust.[39] But although trusts may be used for all kinds of legitimate purposes, they may not be used for purposes that are contrary to public policy. A trust which has only one purpose – to ring-fence assets from the trustee's lawful creditors – is not a valid trust.[40] The point is important to emphasise because, in the corporate and financial world, where there are no statutory prohibitions on exclusion of trustee duties,[41] constant recourse is made to trusts that often have few, if any, legitimate trust purposes and in which the normal duties of a trustee are largely excluded. Some English decisions have allowed sophisticated parties to exclude almost all of the duties of a trustee without invalidating the trust.[42] But it may be questioned whether a trustee with no fiduciary duties is a trustee at all.

Persons with significant control

1.21 Despite publicity requirements for companies, LLPs, LPs and some partnerships, there are additional disclosure requirements in relation to publication of the identities of persons with significant control over the juristic person.[43] The provisions are detailed but, in broad terms, persons with significant control are those who hold, directly or indirectly, more than 25 per cent of the shares or voting rights; or hold the right to appoint or remove the majority of the board. The entities subject to these provisions must keep available for public inspection a register of those exercising control,[44] or elect to provide the information to the registrar.[45] The information must be kept up-to-date. The entity is subject to duties to find out and identify registrable persons or registrable legal entities; similarly registrable persons or legal entities have a duty to notify the company of their status.[46]

Beneficial owners

1.22 There is extensive and very detailed legislation on anti-money laundering. Those subject to anti-money laundering legislation (including solicitors)

39 There are, however, extensive anti-money laundering rules that apply to trusts: see para. 1.22 below.

40 G L Gretton and K G C Reid, *Conveyancing 2004* (Edinburgh: W. Green, 2005), p. 81. A striking English example is *Midland Bank v Wyatt* [1997] 1 BCLC 242.

41 There are various statutory prohibitions on exclusion of duties by trustees of occupational pension schemes, of issues of debentures, of unit trusts, or of contractual structures: see I MacNeil, *An Introduction to the Law of Financial Investment*, 2nd edn (Oxford: Hart Publishing, 2012), p.178.

42 Cf *Spread Trustee Co Ltd v Hutcheson* [2012] 2 AC 194. The leading Scottish case is *Lutea Trustees Ltd v Orbis Trustees Guernsey Ltd* 1997 SC 255.

43 Companies Act 2006, Part 21A, s. 790A onward and Sch. 1A. For LLPs: Limited Liability Partnerships (Register of People with Significant Control) Regulations 2016 (SI 2016/340); for partnerships and limited partnerships: Scottish Partnerships (Register of People with Significant Control) Regulations 2017 (SI 2017/694).

44 Companies Act 2006, ss. 790M–790N.

45 Companies Act 2006, ss. 790W–790X.

46 Companies Act 2006, ss. 790D–790H.

are often required to obtain information about the 'beneficial owners' of bodies corporate, partnerships or trusts with whom a business relationship is established.[47]

JURISTIC PERSONS AND BODIES CORPORATE

All 'bodies corporate' are juristic persons, but not all juristic persons are bodies corporate. Of the three vehicles with which this book is concerned (partnerships, LPs and LLPs), all are juristic persons, but only one – the LLP – is a body corporate. Companies are also bodies corporate. Bodies corporate enjoy what is known as 'perpetual succession': that is to say, their legal personality continues without reference to its members. A change in membership of a body corporate has no effect on the body's legal personality. Neither partnerships nor LPs, in contrast, automatically enjoy this attribute.[48] All other things being equal, a change in the constituent partners of a partnership – whether by death, resignation, bankruptcy or assumption of new partners – may result in dissolution of one, and reconstitution of a new, juristic person.[49] **1.23**

FORMS OF BUSINESS ORGANISATION

Sole trader

A sole trader is a natural person who trades in that capacity without using a juristic person as a business vehicle. The 'sole' descriptor emphasises the solitary nature of this form of business organisation: it is possible for a sole trader to have employees and agents but if there is more than one person engaged as a principal (contributing capital and entering contracts) it is likely to be considered as a partnership. The sole trader bears full liability for all debts incurred in the business and faces the risk of bankruptcy if those debts cannot be paid.[50] **1.24**

Partnerships and limited partnerships

A partnership is 'the relation which subsists between persons carrying on a business in common with a view of profit'.[51] Partnership is primarily an owner-manager form of business entity in which the owners (partners) themselves manage the business. Before the introduction of the limited company **1.25**

47 See Money Laundering, Terrorist Financing and Transfer of Funds (Information on the Payer) Regulations 2017 (SI 2017/692). The provisions are complicated and cannot be further discussed here.

48 'Person', in terms of the Interpretation Act 1978, Sch. 1 and the Interpretation and Legislative Reform (Scotland) Act 2010, Sch. 1, includes bodies *unincorporate*. We read '*unincorporated* associations' and reason that they have no legal personality. But 'unincorporated' does not equal 'no legal personality'. Scottish partnerships and LPs are perhaps the classic example of bodies with juristic personality but that are not bodies corporate.

49 See para. 5.40 below.

50 Cf *Accountant in Bankruptcy v Butler* 2007 SLT (Sh Ct) 200.

51 Partnership Act 1890, s. 1.

in Scotland in 1856,[52] and for some time thereafter, partnership was the dominant form of business organisation. The limited partnership (LP) differs from the LLP in that it is not a body corporate. The LP's main commercial application is as a vehicle for investment management in which limited partners (investors) contribute capital to be managed by a professional manager (the general partner).

1.26 All partnerships in Scotland are juristic persons. General partnerships are governed by the Partnership Act 1890.[53] The 1890 Act comprises both default provisions which are capable of modification by the partnership agreement (the relations of partners to one another) as well mandatory provisions (relations between the firm and third parties). The Limited Partnerships Act 1907 (the 1907 Act) made available the limited partnership, which combined aspects of the traditional partnership (legal personality, privacy) with limitation of liability (for limited partners). But except in so far as inconsistent with the terms of the 1907 Act, the 1890 Act applies also to limited partnerships.

Limited liability partnerships (LLPs)

1.27 The Limited Liability Partnerships Act 2000 was introduced largely in response to demand from professional firms for protection from the potential liability to which their partners were exposed under the general law of partnership. An LP under the 1907 Act was not satisfactory since it did not provide limited liability for partners involved in management (and partners in professional firms are involved in management); nor did it clearly provide for perpetual succession on death or resignation of general partners. Since the 2000 Act, most professional firms have adopted the LLP model. And so too have many commercial firms who see it as an alternative to a company, especially with regard to the different approach to taxation applied to partnerships compared to companies.[54]

Companies

1.28 Companies represent the dominant form of business organisation. While limited liability and corporate status is also now available in the form of the LLP, the company still has a number of attractions that are not available in other business structures. They include the separation of ownership (members) and control (the board of directors) that enables external investors to contribute capital to be managed by others. The availability of a detailed and well-tested legal regime offers certainty for investors. In the case of public companies there are also the attractions of access to public capital markets, enabling large projects to be financed, and a liquid market in shares enabling investors to sell their shareholding in a regulated market.

52 For further discussion, see Chapter Five: Partnerships, LPs and LLPs.

53 See Partnership Act 1890, s. 46, preserving the common law except so far as inconsistent with the Act.

54 Partnerships are generally taxed according to the 'look-through' principle whereby profits are treated as earned by the individual partners (which may be companies) whereas companies pay corporation tax as separate entities from their members.

Companies are governed by the Companies Act 2006. Earlier Companies Acts have been largely repealed. But companies incorporated under previous Companies Acts remain subject to the model articles prescribed by the Act under which a company was formed.[55] 1.29

TRUSTS

Introduction

A Scottish trust is *not* a legal person but gives rise to the creation of a separate patrimony.[56] A trustee is in an exceptional position because the trustee has more than one patrimony. An important patrimonial question arises on the trustee's insolvency. The general principle is that assets held by a trustee in their capacity as trustee may not be attached by the trustee's personal creditors.[57] It is possible for one patrimony held by a trustee to be insolvent while the trustee's private patrimony remains solvent. A trust patrimony can be sequestrated, or can have a judicial factor appointed to administer it. 1.30

Contractual liability of trustees

As a general rule, creditors who have contracted with the trustee on the basis that only the trust assets (the trust patrimony) are liable, cannot attach assets held in the trustee's personal patrimony. There are conflicting cases on this extremely important practical issue. In *Gordon v Campbell*,[58] signature of a bond by trustees '*qua* trustees only' was held by the House of Lords as sufficient to limit the creditors' rights to the trust funds; the trustees had no additional personal liability. In two subsequent decisions of the House of Lords,[59] however, registration of trustees as shareholders 'as trustees' was held, in terms of the relevant companies legislation, to be insufficient to prevent an imposition of personal liability on the trustees (the shares in question being held in banks with unlimited liability). As a matter of civil procedure, a decree against defender in a representative capacity ('as judicial factor') has been held sufficient to limit the holder of the decree to recourse against the trust patrimony.[60] As a general rule, therefore, a decree against a representative, as representative, imposes no personal liability; a decree, without qualification, imposes personal liability but accords to the representative a right of relief against the fund held; and a decree against a representative 'personally' imposes personal liability and excludes a right of relief.[61] There is no equivalent of the *ultra vires* 1.31

55 Companies Act 2006, s. 20(2).

56 Gretton, 'Trusts without equity' (n 29); Reid, 'Patrimony not equity' (n 29).

57 Bankruptcy (Scotland) Act 2016, s. 88(3).

58 *Gordon v Campbell* (1840) 2 D 639, affd (1842) 1 Bell's App 428.

59 *Lumsden v Buchanan* (1864) 2 M 695 (Whole Court), revd (1865) 3 M (HL) 89, 4 Macq 950 and *Muir v City of Glasgow Bank* (1878) 6 R 392, affd (1879) 6 R (HL) 21, (1879) 4 App Cas 337, discussed in *Investec Trust (Guernsey) Ltd v Glenalla Properties Ltd* [2018] UKPC 7, [2019] AC 271. See too *Brown v Rysaffe Trustee Company (CI) Ltd* [2011] CSOH 26.

60 *Craig v Hogg* (1896) 24 R 6 at 21 per Lord M'Laren following the decision of the House of Lords in *Gordon v Campbell* (n 58).

61 *Kilmarnock Theatre Co v Buchanan* 1911 SC 607; *Dyer v Craiglaw Developments Ltd* 1999 SLT 1228.

rules for creditors contracting with Scottish trustees. Third parties acting in good faith are protected even where the trustee has acted in breach of trust.[62]

1.32 The trust did not evolve as a business structure and is not often employed in Scotland for that purpose. But it may be that a trust is created in association with a specific transaction or course of dealing. For example, trusts are commonly used in various forms of financing because they offer the following benefits: separation of title and benefit (for example, a pool of financial assets held and managed by professionals for investors); privacy; and insolvency effect (the pool of assets is ring-fenced on the insolvency of the trustees). The formal requirements for creating a trust are minimal.[63] There are no compulsory public registration requirements (although many trusts are in fact registered in the Books of Council and Session). In the case of shares in a Scottish company held in trust, the existence of the trust may be publicised on the company's register of members, whereas in the case of shares in English companies, there is a prohibition against trusts appearing on the register.[64]

JURISTIC PERSONS AND CONTRACTS

Overview

1.33 Transactional capacity is a necessary prerequisite for a natural or juristic person to enter into juridical acts. A juristic person, in addition, can act only through human agents. In those cases, it is necessary for the agent to have the requisite authority to bind the juristic person. Two separate issues thus arise for contracts to be concluded by juristic person: (a) does the juristic person as principal have capacity to enter the contract; and (b) does the juristic person's agent have authority to bind it to the contract?

Capacity

1.34 Historically, the contractual capacity of a company was linked to the objects clause (found in the memorandum of a company formed prior to the entry into force of the Companies Act 2006). The objects clause defined the permissible business activity of the company. Acts outside those objects, such as purported contracts, were held to be *ultra vires* and void.[65] The underlying rationale of this approach was that members and creditors could better estimate the risk to which they were exposed if there was a clear limit to the activities of the company. The problem with the *ultra vires* doctrine was that it created uncertainty for creditors, especially as companies began to adopt broader objects clauses so as to permit a wide range of activities. The Companies Act now provides that the validity of an act done by a company shall not be called into question

62 Trusts (Scotland) Act 1961, s. 2. The trustee's personal patrimony will, however, be available to satisfy any losses brought about by their breach of trust.

63 Only so-called 'truster-as-trustee' trusts (where the truster declares a trust over their own assets in which they also act as trustee) require to be in writing: RWSA 1995, s. 1(2)(a)(iii).

64 See Companies Act 2006, s. 126 for the prohibition.

65 *Ashbury Railway Carriage and Iron Co Ltd v Riche* (1875) LR 7 (HL) 653, applied in *Piggins & Rix Ltd v Montrose Port Authority* 1995 SLT 418.

on the ground of lack of capacity by reason of anything in the company's constitution.[66] Any objects clause in the company's constitution does not limit the company's capacity so far as third parties are concerned, but it will operate internally: any contract concluded for and on behalf of the company by a director who has exceeded their powers may leave the director liable to the company for any losses the company incurs.

Authority and agency

Juristic persons, being creations of the law, can act only through human agency.[67] The common law of agency enables an agent to bind the principal to a third party.[68] In relation to commercial transactions, the law of agency allows juristic persons to enter into juridical acts. Suppose Alpha Limited wishes to enter into a contract with Bravo Limited. Alan, a director of Alpha Ltd acts for and on behalf Alpha Ltd; Brian, a director of Bravo Ltd, acts for and on behalf of Bravo Ltd. On conclusion of the agreement, the parties to the contract are the principals, namely Alpha Ltd and Bravo Ltd. **1.35**

PRACTICALITIES: SUBSCRIPTION AND SIGNING

General requirements for writing[69]

As a general rule contracts may be formed in Scots law without formality. There are four major practical exceptions to that rule: (1) writing is required for the creation, transfer, variation or extinction of a real right in land; (2) for the creation of a gratuitous unilateral obligation undertaken other than in the course of business; (3) for the creation of a truster-as-trustee trust;[70] and (4) for wills.[71] Where writing is required, the document must be subscribed by the granter of it, or, if there is more than one granter, by each of the granters.[72] Subscription means signing at the end of the last page of the document, excluding any annexations. **1.36**

Execution by juristic persons

Juristic persons can act only through human agency. The Requirements of Writing (Scotland) Act 1995 (the 'RWSA 1995') sets out who can properly execute written documents for and on behalf of a juristic person. Many, perhaps most, commercial contracts do not *require* to be in writing. But corporate **1.37**

66 Companies Act 2006, s. 39.
67 Companies Act 2006, s. 155 requires a company to have at least one director who is a natural person.
68 See generally L J Macgregor, *The Law of Agency in Scotland* (Edinburgh: W. Green, 2013) and Chapter Four: Agency below.
69 See generally Gretton and Steven (n 2), Ch. 31; G L Gretton and K G C Reid, *Conveyancing*, 5th edn (Edinburgh: W. Green, 2018), Ch. 18.
70 RWSA 1995, s. 1(2)(a).
71 RWSA 1995, s. 1(2)(b) and (c).
72 RWSA 1995, s. 1(7) and 2(1) respectively. In the case of contracts constituted by separate offer and acceptance documents, each must be subscribed (s. 2(2)).

lawyers spend their professional lives drafting detailed contracts that the law does not require to be in writing at all. The RWSA 1995 distinguishes between 'traditional' documents and 'electronic documents'. Each will be considered in turn.

Traditional documents: valid subscription

1.38 Part 2 of the RWSA 1995 applies to traditional documents. Valid execution in terms of s. 2 requires only subscription by the granter: that means signature by the granter 'at the end of the last page'.[73] In practical terms, therefore, in order to ensure a contract complies with the RWSA 1995, the page on which the first signatures appear should also contain the last clause of the agreement. It should be mentioned that a 'deed' is not a term of art in Scots law.[74]

1.39 Where the granter of a traditional document is:

(a) A company: the document is signed by the company if it is signed on its behalf by a director or by the secretary or by a person authorised to sign on its behalf.[75]
(b) An LLP: the document is signed by the LLP if it is signed by a member of the LLP on its behalf.[76]
(c) A partnership: the document is signed by the partnership if it is signed by a partner, or by a person authorised to sign on its behalf.[77]
(d) Some other body corporate (other than a company or a local authority[78]): the document is signed by the body if it is signed on its behalf by: (a) a member of the body's governing board or, if there is no governing board, a member of the body; (b) the secretary of the body by whatever name they are called; or (c) a person authorised to the document on behalf of the body.[79]

Traditional documents: probative execution

1.40 In addition to ensuring that the document is formally valid, it is standard practice to have the documents executed in such a way as to confer probative status in terms of s. 3 of the RWSA 1995. Probativity refers to the evidential presumption that the document was executed by the granter and, if the document included a date and a place of execution, that the document was indeed executed on that date and at that place.[80] Probativity is about form rather than substance: the presumption allows reliance to be placed on a document without recourse to extrinsic evidence. The presumption is rebuttable.[81] But even if the document is formally and probatively executed, the document may

73 RWSA 1995, s. 7(1).
74 Cf *Walker v Whitwell* 1916 SC (HL) 75 at 79 per Lord Dunedin and *Low & Bonar plc and Low & Bonar Pension Trs Ltd v Mercer Ltd* [2010] CSOH 47, at [21] per Lord Drummond Young.
75 RWSA 1995, s. 2 and Sch. 2, para. 3(1).
76 RWSA 1995, s. 2 and Sch. 2, para. 3A(1).
77 RWSA 1995, s. 2 and Sch. 2, para. 1.
78 For which, see RWSA 1995, s. 2 and Sch. 2, para. 4.
79 RWSA 1995, s. 2 and Sch. 2, para. 5(2).
80 RWSA 1995, s. 3(1) and 3(8).
81 RWSA 1995, s. 3(4) and 3(5).

nonetheless be invalid: subject to the general law of agency, the party who bears to have signed as an authorised signatory of the granter company, for instance, may not, in fact, have been authorised to sign.[82] The general rule for achieving probative status is that the subscription of someone authorised to sign on behalf of the company must be witnessed;[83] and the witness must be designed by name and address. This means, in the case of companies, that signature by a director and a witness is sufficient. There is, however, an alternative method, which is that the document may be signed by a second signatory. There are three permitted combinations:

(1) two directors;
(2) a director and the secretary of the company; or
(3) two persons bearing to have been authorised to subscribe the document on the company's behalf.[84]

LLPs execute documents by a member signing for and on behalf of the LLP 1.41
in the presence of a witness; or by two members signing for and on behalf of an LLP.[85] Partnerships execute documents by a partner, or other authorised signatory, signing for and on behalf of the firm in the presence of a witness.[86] Uniquely among juristic persons, a partnership can validly subscribe a document by the partner or authorised signatory signing the name of the partnership rather than his or her own name.[87]

Counterpart execution

The parties to a commercial contract governed by Scots law may be spread 1.42
out around the world. Careful thought needs to be given to how such documents can be executed remotely. Under the Legal Writings (Counterparts and Delivery) (Scotland) Act 2015, it is possible for parties to subscribe separate but identical copies (counterparts) of a transactional document and deliver the document (electronically) to the other parties or to an agent appointed for that purpose.[88] Once executed by all parties the counterparts are treated as a single document.[89]

Electronic signatures and documents

Electronic signatures exist in one of three different categories – simple, 1.43
advanced and qualified – with each carrying different levels of security and, thus, legal effect.[90] Electronic documents are defined as documents that,

82 RWSA 1995, s. 3(1C) as substituted by Sch. 2, para. 3(5)(a).
83 RWSA 1995, s. 3(1)(b), as substituted by Sch. 2, para. 3(5)(a).
84 RWSA 1995, s. 3(1A) as substituted by Sch. 2, para. 3(5)(a).
85 RWSA 1995, Sch. 2, para. 3A(1) and (4) and (5). Curiously, no reference is made, in the case of LLPs, to signing by an authorised signatory. But the ordinary principles apply and there is nothing to prevent an LLP specifically authorising a non-member, such as an employee, to sign on its behalf. Such a document would be validly executed.
86 RWSA 1995, Sch. 2, para. 2(1).
87 RWSA 1995, Sch. 2, para. 2(2).
88 Legal Writings (Counterparts and Delivery) (Scotland) Act 2015, ss. 1 and 2.
89 Legal Writings (Counterparts and Delivery) (Scotland) Act 2015, s. 1(3).
90 Law Society of Scotland, *Guide to Electronic Signatures*, Version 8, section 2.

rather than being written on paper are created in electronic form.[91] All of those documents falling within s. 1(2) of the RWSA 1995 can be generated electronically.[92] In order to be validly executed, an electronic document must be authenticated by the granter in terms that meet the regulations.[93] A document is authenticated by a person if the electronic signature of that person is incorporated into, or logically associated with, the electronic document; was created by the person by whom it purports to have been created; and is of such type, and satisfies the requirements (if any), as may be prescribed.[94]

1.44 At present, the only regulations that have been made are the Electronic Documents (Scotland) Regulations 2014.[95] For documents which require writing under s. 1(2) of the RWSA 1995, those regulations require an advanced electronic signature (AES).[96] That term is defined[97] under reference to the EU 'eIDAS' Regulation as 'data in electronic form which is attached to or logically associated with other data in electronic form and which is used by the signatory to sign'.[98] In practice, only solicitors can utilise an AES.[99] In order for an electronic document to be self-proving in terms of s. 9C the document must be authenticated by the granter with an AES and certified with a certificate in terms of art. 3(15) of the eIDAS Regulation.[100] Electronic documents may be delivered electronically or by such other means as are reasonably practicable; but such a document must be in a form, and such delivery must be by a means, the intended recipient agreed to accept.[101]

Electronic documents in commerce

1.45 Outside of commercial property transactions or truster-as-trustee trusts used in some financial transactions, most commercial documents do not need to be in writing. The mere fact that a document has not been executed in terms that comply with the RWSA 1995 does not prevent the documents being used as evidence in relation to a right or obligation to which the document relates.[102] In that context it is important to recall that simple electronic signatures are

91 RWSA 1995, s. 9A. As such, a document that has been executed in traditional wet ink, scanned and then delivered electronically (as under the Legal Writings (Counterparts and Delivery) (Scotland) Act 2015) is not an electronic document.
92 RWSA 1995, s. 1(2) as amended.
93 RWSA 1995, s. 9B(1).
94 1995 Act, s. 9B(1) and (2).
95 SI 2014/83.
96 Electronic Documents (Scotland) Regulations 2014 (SSI 2014/83), reg. 2.
97 Electronic Documents (Scotland) Regulations 2014, reg. 1.
98 Regulation (EU) No 910/2014 of the European Parliament and of the Council of 23 July 2014 on electronic identification and trust services for electronic transactions in the internal market and repealing Directive 1999/93/EC. Following the UK's exit from the EU in December 2020, the eIDAS Regulation has been incorporated into UK law pursuant to the European Union (Withdrawal) Act 2018, in terms of the Electronic Identification and Trust Services for Electronic Transactions (Amendment etc.) (EU Exit) Regulations 2019 (SI 2019/89).
99 K G C Reid and G L Gretton, *Conveyancing*, 5th edn (2018) para. 18–30.
100 RWSA 1995, s. 9C and Electronic Documents (Scotland) Regulations 2014, reg. 3.
101 RWSA 1995, s. 9F.
102 RWSA 1995, s. 2(3) and s. 9B(5).

admissible in evidence in relation to any question as to the authenticity or integrity of an electronic communication.[103]

JURISTIC PERSONS AND DELICT

Introduction

A juristic person may have rights to claim damages in delict or it may be liable to pay damages for delicts. Juristic persons have to act through the medium of human agents and workers, so the issue will regularly arise of how the acts and intentions of human beings are to be treated as the acts and intentions of the juristic person.[104] **1.46**

Vicarious liability

Under the law of delict an employer is vicariously liable for the wrongdoing of another when: (i) the wrongdoer is an employee (or is in a relationship sufficiently akin to employment);[105] and (ii) when the wrongdoing occurs within the scope of their employment. An important distinction is drawn between employees who are employed under a contract of employment (and for whose acts or omissions the employer is normally vicariously liable);[106] and independent contractors who are employed under a contract for the provision of services (and for whose acts or omissions the employer is not normally vicariously liable).[107] The test for determining if the wrongful acts occurs within the scope of the wrongdoer's employment is whether the wrongful acts were so closely connected with acts that the employee was authorised to do that they may be fairly and properly regarded as done by the wrongdoer in the ordinary course of their employment.[108] Vicarious liability may also arise in the case of principal and agent. Employment and agency may well overlap in circumstances where scope of employment is linked to the authority granted by an employer to an employee. **1.47**

Corporate structures

A fundamental principle of the law of juristic persons is that of separate legal personality.[109] In the same way that a company is a separate legal person from its members, so too are parent companies separate legal persons from their subsidiaries. The courts have consistently held that it is legitimate to use the corporate form to structure matters in such a way that effectively limits the **1.48**

103 Electronic Communications Act 2000, s. 7.

104 *Singularis Holdings Ltd (In Liquidation) v Daiwa Capital Markets Europe Ltd* [2019] UKSC 50, [2020] AC 1189.

105 *Various Claimants v Catholic Welfare Society* [2012] UKSC 56, [2013] 2 AC 1.

106 *Wilsons & Clyde Coal Co Ltd v English* 1937 SC (HL) 46.

107 *Barclays Bank plc v Various Claimants* [2020] UKSC 13, [2020] AC 973.

108 *WM Morrison plc v Various Claimants* [2020] UKSC 12, [2020] AC 989; *Mohamud v Wm Morrison Supermarkets plc* [2016] UKSC 11, [2016] AC 677; *Vaickuviene v J Sainsbury plc* [2013] CSIH 67; *Lister v Hesley Hall Ltd* [2002] 1 AC 215.

109 The classic case is *Salomon v A Salomon & Co Ltd* [1897] AC 22.

claims of involuntary creditors – such as employees who are victims of delicts – to claims against a subsidiary company that has contracts with the workers, but which has few assets.[110] The parent company, however, may owe duties of care directly to those workers also owed duties of care by a subsidiary.[111] And, in appropriate cases, the courts may look behind the corporate veil.

Claims against third parties

1.49 A juristic person may pursue remedies for injury or loss suffered as a result of delicts committed by third parties. So companies may recover for damage caused to the company's property,[112] reputation[113] or creditworthiness.[114] A clear distinction should be drawn between: (a) loss suffered by the company as a juristic person; and (b) loss suffered by other persons related to a company. Members, directors or employees have no rights to sue for damage to the company's assets. In respect of shareholders, where loss has been suffered by a company as a result of a wrong committed against it, the shareholders of that company are prevented from bringing a claim in damages for any consequential diminution in the value of their shares as a result of that wrongdoing in circumstances where the company has a cause of action against the same wrongdoer.[115] One exception to this principle arises in the case of derivative actions.[116]

1.50 The board of directors of a public or private company has responsibility for the management of a company's business and the board may exercise all powers of the company. This responsibility, subject to the company's articles, extends to the control of litigation by the company.[117] Any action the board elects to pursue is pursued in the company's name. In the case of a general or limited partnership, the default rule is that the decision to bring or defend an action is taken by the majority of (general) partners.[118]

110 *Adams v Cape Industries plc* [1990] Ch 433. The principles on which the courts may ignore formal corporate structures are set out in *Petrodel Resources Ltd v Prest* [2013] UKSC 34, [2013] 2 AC 415.
111 *Okpabi v Royal Dutch Shell plc* [2021] UKSC 3, [2021] 1 WLR 1294; *Chandler v Cape plc* [2012] 1 WLR 3111.
112 *Macaura v Northern Assurance Co Ltd* [1925] AC 619.
113 *Jameel v Wall Street Journal Europe Sprl (No. 3)* [2007] 1 AC 359.
114 *Downtex plc v Flately* [2003] EWCA Civ 1282.
115 This is the so-called rule in *Foss v Harbottle* (1843) 67 ER 189. See *Prudential Assurance Co Ltd v Newman Industries Ltd* [1982] Ch 204; *Sevilleja v Marex Financial Ltd* [2020] UKSC 31, [2021] AC 39.
116 These are briefly discussed in para. 5.64 below.
117 Companies (Model Articles) Regulations 2008 (SI 2008/3229), Model Articles for private companies limited by shares, art. 3, Model Articles for public companies, art. 3.
118 Partnership Act 1890, s. 24(8).

JURISTIC PERSONS AND CRIMINAL LIABILITY

Introduction

A juristic person may commit a criminal offence or be the victim of a criminal offence.[119] The criminal liability of juristic persons, however, poses particular problems of attribution. Not only must conduct (*actus reus*) be attributed to the juristic person, but also criminal intent (*mens rea*). The following section deals with the attribution mechanisms employed by the criminal law. **1.51**

Attribution

The doctrine of vicarious liability is also utilised in the context of criminal law in order to attribute criminal liability to juristic persons in respect of wrongdoing carried out by their employees or agents. Vicarious liability for criminal offences in Scots law arises only under statute rather than as a matter of common law. Many statutory offences are strict liability offences, whereby proof of *mens rea* – whether that be intent, recklessness or negligence – is not part of the *corpus delicti* of the offence, thus alleviating some of the difficulties in attributing criminal liability to juristic persons. In the main, prosecutions of juristic persons in Scotland arise in relation to regulatory offences. **1.52**

The 'identification doctrine' has been developed in the context of companies but, in principle, applies also to other juristic persons.[120] That doctrine identifies those individuals (in principle an open category) who stand above the company's employees and agents and who may be considered the embodiment of the company.[121] Such individuals are sometimes referred to as the 'directing mind and will' of the company. The actions and intentions of such individuals are therefore considered to be attributable to the company. The individuals likely to be considered a company's embodiment must, of their nature, be senior management. The identification doctrine is narrower in scope than the principle of vicarious liability; but as in the case of vicarious liability, the manager's personal culpability must be established in order to attribute it to the company he or she manages. **1.53**

In addition, various statutory offences have been created, which utilise attribution models designed specifically to attach liability to juristic persons. Under the Corporate Manslaughter and Corporate Homicide Act 2007, the statutory model of attribution is based on management failure within the organisation and not on the action/intent of a single individual.[122] Additionally, **1.54**

119 Some criminal offences which can be committed only by an individual because it is not possible to attribute the act and intent to a juristic person: they include murder (but not culpable homicide) and rape. Similarly, a juristic person cannot be a victim of crimes against the person (e.g. murder, assault, rape).

120 Scottish Law Commission, *Discussion Paper on Criminal Liability of Partnerships* (DP No. 150, 2011), Ch. 3.

121 *Tesco Supermarkets Ltd v Nattrass* [1972] AC 153 at 170 per Lord Reid, applied in *Transco plc v HM Advocate* 2004 JC 29; *Meridian Global Funds Management Asia Ltd v Securities Commission* [1995] 2 AC 500; *Singularis Holdings Ltd (In Liquidation) v Daiwa Capital Markets Europe Ltd* [2019] UKSC 50, [2020] AC 1189.

122 Corporate Manslaughter and Corporate Homicide Act 2007, s. 1.

the attribution model adopted by the Bribery Act 2010 is broader than the common law approach because it holds a juristic person liable for failing to take action (no *mens rea* is thus required) to prevent bribes being paid by its employees (as well as attaching liability to employees who arrange bribes).[123] Similarly, liability under the Criminal Finances Act 2017 arises as a result of the failure of a juristic person to prevent the facilitation of UK or foreign tax evasion.[124]

1.55 Beyond senior managers, other individuals within a corporate structure may incur criminal liability in two ways. In the first place, individuals may be found to have acted 'art and part' in the commission of an offence committed by others within the company, or the company itself, or both. Secondly, individuals may commit the secondary offence of assistance in respect of the commission of a primary offence.[125]

Effect of dissolution

1.56 Termination of legal personality poses similar problems for criminal law as in the law of delict since there is no longer a legal person that can be prosecuted. In *Balmer v H M Advocate*[126] a prosecution under the Health and Safety at Work etc. Act 1974 was brought against a partnership for breach of duties that had caused the deaths of fourteen people in a fire. Prior to the indictment being served, however, the partnership had been dissolved. As a result, it was held that the indictment was incompetent.[127] The Scottish Law Commission subsequently investigated the matter and its report has led to a change in the law whereby a partnership can be prosecuted for a criminal offence committed within five years of its dissolution.[128]

Criminal sanctions

1.57 The most serious sanction for conviction of a criminal offence is imprisonment. Juristic persons, however, cannot be imprisoned. The common sanction, therefore, is to apply financial penalties to juristic persons or their officers. When determining the appropriate level of any financial penalty the court can have regard to multiple factors, including the annual turnover of the juristic person.[129] Ordinarily, any financial enquiry will be focused solely upon the juristic person before the court, however, where it can be demonstrated that the juristic person is situated as part of a group of companies, then the court may, in exceptional circumstances, decide to lift the corporate veil and take into account the finances of a linked organisation.[130] In the case of a partnership, a fine is a debt owed by the partnership and may be recovered

123 Bribery Act 2010, s. 7.
124 Criminal Finances Act 2017, ss. 45 and 46.
125 For example, the Health and Safety at Work etc. Act 1974, s. 36.
126 2008 SLT 799.
127 There was no charge brought against the partners 'art and part' or under the accessory liability provisions of the Health and Safety at Work etc. Act 1974. For the prosecution of trustees, see *Aikenhead v Fraser* 2006 JC 231.
128 Partnerships (Prosecution) (Scotland) Act 2013, s. 1.
129 *Scottish Power Generation Ltd v HM Advocate* 2017 JC 85.
130 *R v NPS London Ltd* [2019] EWCA Crim 228.

from the personal assets of the partners if the firm's assets are inadequate.[131] Companies cannot exempt or indemnify directors for liability arising from a fine (and, indeed, civil liability for negligence, default, breach of duty or breach of trust) imposed on directors personally.[132] The rationale for that approach is that an indemnity would effectively shift the cost of mismanagement onto members.

131 Scottish Law Commission, *Criminal Liability of Partnerships* (Scot. Law Com. No. 224, 2011), para. 3.1. The principle of limited liability prevents a fine levied on a juristic person being recovered from the personal assets of company shareholders, LP limited partners or LLP members.

132 Companies Act 2006, s. 232. Under s. 233, however, a company may obtain insurance for its directors against such liabilities.

Chapter Two

General Principles of Contract Law

Dot Reid, Mat Campbell and Bobby Lindsay

INTRODUCTION

2.01 Contracts are quintessentially about relationships. In the usual case, two (or more) parties enter into an agreement in which they commit themselves to certain obligations to each other. The relationship between the parties is of relatively little importance in over-the-counter sales or even in the high-value world of financial trading, where transactions are concluded instantaneously. However, commercial parties often enter into contracts that last for many years and the provisions of the contract are the backdrop against which they do business with each other. At the beginning of the life of a contract both parties optimistically hope that the courts need never be involved and in most cases the content of the contract remains a private matter which regulates their business relationship without contention. It perhaps seems strange that the law should intervene at all in private commercial agreements and in the common law world there has traditionally been reluctance for either governments or courts to interfere with the operation of commerce. That reluctance stems from the belief that individual and commercial freedom creates the best environment for business to flourish and for the economy to grow. However, when things go wrong it is important for business confidence and commercial certainty that the agreement the parties have made with each other is enforceable and that the remedies it provides can be relied on. Commercial contracts, therefore, have two principal functions: to provide certainty by setting out clearly and concisely in advance the parties' respective rights and obligations; and to provide a solution when things go wrong through application of the default rules of contract law.

2.02 Much of what we refer to as commercial law is founded on the application of the law of contract in a corporate and business context. Contract is at the core of the law of agency (Chapter Four); it provides the basis of the relationship between partners to a partnership (Chapter Five); it regulates the seller's obligations towards the buyer, and vice versa, in the sale of goods (Chapter Six); the institution of insurance depends on a contractual relationship between the insurer and the insured (Chapter Seven); contract is the primary means through which a commercial debt may be created and enforced (Chapter Eight); and it provides a mechanism by which one party undertakes to guarantee the performance of another's obligation (Chapter Ten). Whilst the core principles of contract law will not vary, each of these areas has its own specific rules applicable to the particular type of contract in question. The objective of this chapter is to provide a selective overview of the general principles of Scots contract law which are most relevant in a commercial context.[1] Attention is also given to the content of commercial contracts and some of the most commonly used contract terms. A more comprehensive treatment can be found in specialist textbooks.[2]

FUNDAMENTAL CONCEPTS IN CONTRACT LAW

Freedom of contract

The most important theoretical principle in contract law is *freedom of contract.* **2.03**
The development of contract law coincided with a period when Scotland's economy changed from being largely agrarian to one that was industrial and commercial. By the end of the nineteenth century contract cases dealt less often with transactions concerning horses and cows and more frequently with obligations incurred by banks, shareholders and company directors. In this period of transformation entrepreneurs and investors were needed to oil the wheels of commerce and the role of law was not to impede progress by placing obstacles in their way. Hence, within certain limits, businesspeople were free to decide both whom they wanted to conduct business with and the terms on which they entered into contractual relationships. Unless the contract had been entered into using deceit, force or under a fundamental error,[3] or it dealt with illegal or immoral activities,[4] the rules of contract law would not interfere with what the parties had agreed. The purpose of contract law was to facilitate commerce and the growth of wealth for the benefit of society as a whole, as encapsulated in Jessell MR's well-known statement:[5]

> 'If there is one thing which more than another public policy requires it is that men of full age and competent understanding shall have the utmost liberty of contracting, and that their contracts when entered into freely and voluntarily shall be held sacred and shall be enforced by courts of justice.'

Legal certainty

What then was the role of the courts, if not to interfere with commercial bargains? The second part of the quotation tells us that it was to ensure that contracts were enforced. It expresses the related principle of *sanctity of contract* and the idea that the law will respect commercial bargains, holding them as 'sacred', and will ensure that the parties perform the obligations they have freely entered into. Contracts are entered into against the backdrop of legal enforcement and legal sanctions which in turn give both parties the legal certainty required in **2.04**

1 The assumption is made that the parties to a commercial contract are businesses, unless otherwise stated. No attempt will be made to outline the growing body of rules which apply to consumer contracts (see generally the Consumer Rights Act 2015). The law of promise is also excluded from this chapter.

2 W W McBryde, *The Law of Contract in Scotland*, 3rd edn (Edinburgh: W. Green, 2007); H L MacQueen, *MacQueen and Thomson on Contract Law in Scotland*, 5th edn (London: Bloomsbury Professional, 2020).

3 See paras 2.54–2.68.

4 See paras 2.75–2.80.

5 *Printing and Numerical Registering Co v Sampson* (1875) LR 19 Eq 462 at 465 per Jessell MR.

the commercial world. If you cannot be sure that the agreements you make have the support of the law, you cannot plan with certainty the future of your business. And when businesspeople enter into high-value contracts they need reassurance that if the other party fails to deliver they have recourse to the courts to protect their assets and investment. Freedom and certainty go hand in hand to create the best commercial environment for economic growth in that once the parties have exercised their freedom, they are legally bound by the obligations they have undertaken. It is therefore good for the state and for society as a whole as a matter of legal policy. Certainty is particularly important since the commercial world is inextricably linked to the operation of credit. Loans and other credit transactions are the day-to-day business of banks, financial institutions and many businesses, but they are only possible because the law of contract stands behind them as both a carrot and a stick.

Limitations on freedom of contract

2.05 Freedom of contract was the legal equivalent of economic liberalism, or *laissez-faire*, which had its heyday in the nineteenth century.[6] However, freedom has its limits and in some circumstances may be illusory, particularly where the parties are not on an equal footing. Even in a commercial context a small business may find itself subject to harsh contract terms when dealing with a much larger enterprise: for instance, a local newsagent dealing with a multinational company for the supply of goods may be bound by that company's standard terms and conditions with no opportunity to negotiate a deal. In those circumstances it cannot be said in reality that the newsagent has true freedom of contract to decide the terms on which any purchase is made. Freedom of contract is most meaningful where the parties enter into contracts on relatively equal terms, where both parties can negotiate about the terms and can tailor the contract to their specific needs. Over the course of the last fifty years judges and legislators have intervened to place limits on the parties' freedom where there was an imbalance of power and particularly if one of the parties was a consumer dealing with a business.[7] In 2005 the Law Commission and the Scottish Law Commission acknowledged that a similar regime was needed to protect small businesses,[8] but these proposals have not yet been implemented.[9]

Good faith and fair dealing in a commercial context

2.06 Another underlying, although not uncontested, concept in contract law is good faith. The modern debate on the subject began after Lord Clyde referred in *Smith v Bank of Scotland* to 'the broad principle in the field of contract law

6 For a fuller discussion see P S Atiyah, *The Rise and Fall of Freedom of Contract* (Oxford: Clarendon Press, 1979).

7 For instance, the Unfair Contract Terms Act 1977 (see paras 2.115–2.122) and the Consumer Rights Act 2015.

8 See *Joint Report on Unfair Contract Terms* (Scot. Law Com. No. 199, 2005), Part 5.

9 The most recent consideration (*Protection of Small Businesses when Purchasing Goods and Services: Government Response to the Call for Evidence* (February 2016)) suggested that the UK Government's focus going forward would be on microbusinesses, but there has been no further consideration.

of fair dealing in good faith',[10] which sparked a flurry of academic writing reflecting a broad range of views as to whether or not such a principle existed.[11] Some argued that good faith was indeed an underlying principle and appeared throughout the law of contract in various guises; others were sceptical about the development of a concept which was ill-defined and could lead to uncertainty. It was later affirmed at the highest judicial level that 'good faith in Scottish contract law . . . is generally an underlying principle of an explanatory or legitimating rather than an active or creative nature',[12] and yet the Scottish judiciary remained resistant to the development of any general principle, as this statement from the Outer House demonstrates:[13] '[i]t is, of course, no part of Scots law that, in the absence of agreement, parties to a contract should act in good faith in carrying out their obligations to each other'.

English law is similarly resistant to a general principle of good faith[14] but the courts have been willing to uphold duties to act in good faith (either express or implied) in particular commercial contracts.[15] Commercial parties often expressly contract to act in good faith towards each other.[16] If further proof were needed of its value, two of the world's most successful market economies, the US and Germany, do not appear to have suffered for doing business under a legal regime that places good faith at its core.[17] **2.07**

PRE-REQUISITES TO FORMATION OF CONTRACT

Agreement: *consensus in idem*

Contracts are voluntary obligations entered into by the parties of their own free will. The core idea behind contractual agreement is that of consent or *consensus in idem*, a meeting of the minds. The parties' intentions must coincide about the mutual rights and obligations they are about to undertake towards each other. Establishing whether or not agreement has been reached is often analysed by reference to the offer and acceptance framework. Besides the central notion of agreement there are certain other prerequisites which must **2.08**

10 *Smith v Bank of Scotland* 1997 SC (HL) 111 at 121.

11 See contributions in A D M Forte (ed), *Good Faith in Contract and Property* (Oxford: Hart Publishing, 1999).

12 *R v Immigration Officer at Prague Airport, ex parte European Roma Rights Centre* [2004] UKHL 55, [2005] 2 AC 1 at [60] per Lord Hope; *Van Oord UK Ltd v Dragados UK Ltd* [2021] CSIH 50, 2021 SLT 1317 at [19]–[20].

13 *EDI Central Ltd v National Car Parks Ltd* [2010] CSOH 141, 2011 SLT 75 at [23] per Lord Glennie; affd without reference to this point [2012] CSIH 6, 2012 SLT 421.

14 *MSC Mediterranean Shipping Co SA v Cottonex Anstalt* [2016] EWCA Civ 789, [2017] 1 All ER (Comm) 483 at [45] per Moore-Bick LJ.

15 See, e.g. *Unwin v Bond* [2020] EWHC 1768 (Comm) (express duty of good faith); *Al Nehayan v Kent* [2018] EWHC 333 (Comm), [2018] 1 CLC 216 at [167]–[176] per Leggatt LJ (recognising a duty of good faith as a term implied in fact).

16 One of the world's most important standard contractual documents – the English law-governed International Swaps and Derivatives Association (ISDA) Master Agreement – contains various clauses that expressly impose duties of good faith on the counterparties. For further discussion of good faith and endeavours clauses see below at paras 2.104–2.107.

17 Bürgerliches Gesetzbuch [BGB] (German Civil Code) § 242; American Uniform Commercial Code § 1–304. Cf developments elsewhere: *Beadica 231 CC v Trustees for the time being of the Oregon Trust* [2020] ZACC 13, 2020 (5) SA 247.

be satisfied before a contract comes into existence: the parties must have legal capacity to transact; they must intend to enter into a legal relationship; and the essential terms of their agreement must be ascertainable. It should be noted that a bare agreement is sufficient to conclude a contract in Scots law, unlike English law where a contract is binding only if supported by consideration. This means, broadly speaking, that there must be reciprocity or *quid pro quo* and that each party must receive something in return for giving something.[18] The term consideration is sometimes found in Scottish case law but not as a term of art and it is not a prerequisite for formation of contract. Indeed, Scots law recognises the enforceability of unilateral or gratuitous promises.[19]

Legal capacity

2.09 In every legal transaction there is a requirement that the party or parties concerned must have the legal capacity to transact, that is, they must be legally capable of entering into obligations. Where individuals are concerned they may be deemed to lack capacity because they are too young[20] or because they lack sufficient understanding or mental capacity to enter into legal obligations. The consequence of entering into a contract with a party lacking capacity is that the contract will be treated as void, as if it never existed, and no rights or obligations can arise for the parties in such circumstances.

2.10 In a commercial context, artificial legal entities such as companies and partnerships also require legal capacity,[21] which arises when they are constituted as legal persons under the relevant legal framework. If such a body acts outwith the powers conferred on it, it will be acting *ultra vires*, that is, it will lack legal capacity and any contract entered into will be void. The Companies Act 2006 has significantly altered this position in order to prevent such situations arising and to protect all parties to a contract involving a company.[22] The requirement of capacity to contract also applies to other bodies (like local authorities or trades unions) which act under statutory authority. For instance, in *Morgan Guaranty Trust Co of New York v Lothian Regional Council*[23] a local authority acted beyond the powers prescribed in the Local Government (Scotland) Act 1973 with the result that the contract it had entered into was void. If money or other assets have changed hands there is no remedy in contract law (because no contract exists) but there may be in the law of unjustified enrichment.

Intention to create legal relations

2.11 A second prerequisite for entering into a contract is that the parties must seriously intend the transaction to be a legally enforceable obligation, sometimes known as the doctrine of 'intention to create legal relations'. Here context is

18 For further detail see E Peel (ed), *Treitel on the Law of Contract*, 15th edn (London: Sweet & Maxwell, 2020), Ch. 3.

19 *Regus (Maxim) Ltd v Bank of Scotland plc* [2013] CSIH 12, 2013 SC 331; H L MacQueen, 'Unilateral Promises: Scots Law Compared with the PECL and the DCFR' (2016) 24 ERPL 529.

20 Age of Legal Capacity (Scotland) Act 1991.

21 See Chapter One: Introduction to Juristic Persons.

22 See paras 1.35–1.36.

23 1995 SC 151.

important and there is a presumption that agreements made in a commercial context are intended to be legally binding while those made in a social content are not.

Social and domestic agreements

Obligations undertaken in a social or domestic context are presumed not to create legal obligations, especially between family members. However, this is only a presumption and there are likely to be many exceptions, for instance separation agreements between couples or loans between family members. In *Robertson v Anderson*[24] an agreement between two friends to share their bingo winnings was held to be a legally enforceable obligation. Lord Reed explained that the presumptions do not amount to 'watertight compartments', rather 'it is . . . essential to look at the particular facts to discover whether those facts reveal an intention to conclude a contract'.[25] **2.12**

Commercial agreements

Conversely, in a commercial context the parties are presumed to intend their agreements to be legally binding. The presumption can be rebutted by clear indications in words or conduct that any agreement reached is not intended to have legal force. Phrases such as 'subject to contract' suggest that the parties are still at the negotiating stage prior to reaching a final agreement.[26] In *Wick Harbour Trs v The Admiralty*[27] an agreement was held to be binding despite the use of the words '*ex gratia*', Lord Sands taking the view that '[i]f he has agreed to a payment it does not matter what he calls it'.[28] The courts will consider individual facts and circumstances in determining whether or not the parties intended their agreement to be binding. In a commercial context the court will take an objective approach and consider what would have been the reasonable expectations of sensible businesspeople in the position of the parties.[29] **2.13**

Particularly problematic are cases where the parties have ostensibly reached agreement but the final step of embodying that agreement in writing has not yet been taken. The question that arises is whether or not there is an enforceable contract without that final stage. There is no doubt that freedom of contract demands that the parties can stipulate when the contract comes into force and prior to that they retain the right to withdraw (*locus poenitentiae*), but the words used must be clear and unambiguous.[30] In *W S Karoulias SA v The Drambuie Liqueur Co Ltd*[31] the two companies had a long-standing business relationship and a number of previous contracts. When their agreement came to be renewed the negotiations between them were concluded in an email **2.14**

24 2003 SLT 235.
25 2003 SLT 235 at [13].
26 For discussion see, e.g. *Joanne Properties Ltd v Moneything Capital Ltd* [2020] EWCA Civ 1541.
27 1921 2 SLT 109.
28 1921 2 SLT 109 at 112.
29 *Morgan Utilities Ltd v Scottish Water Solutions Ltd* [2011] CSOH 112 at [52] per Lord Hodge.
30 Such a right was recognised in *Van Laun v Neilson* (1904) 6 F 644 and *Stobo Ltd v Morrisons (Gowns) Ltd* 1949 SC 184.
31 2005 SLT 813.

attaching the 'final draft' of the agreement with confirmation that two copies would be sent for signature if everything was in order. However, it transpired that Drambuie was in negotiations with another distributor and did not intend to sign the final contract. The court held that both parties had intended to be bound only when the agreement was signed. By contrast, in *Royal Bank of Scotland plc v Carlyle*[32] a bank was held objectively to have committed itself to loaning several million pounds to a customer in a telephone conversation, even though the parties knew that formal documents were to be prepared. Though the parties' detailed obligations remained to be specified, the bank was held to have communicated not simply a decision in principle but a promise to provide funding, to which it was bound.

Agreement on essential terms

2.15 The exercise of drafting a contract is an attempt to look into the future, to cover all eventualities and to provide remedies if things should go wrong. However, even if all the details are not settled, the parties must agree on the *essential* terms before a contract can come into existence and those vary depending on the type of contract:[33] '[a]s a matter of the general law of contract all the essentials have to be settled. What are the essentials may vary according to the particular contract under consideration'.

2.16 In a contract of sale the subject matter and the price, or method of fixing a price, must be agreed.[34] For a lease to be enforceable the essential terms are the parties, the rent, the subjects to let and the duration or *ish*. It has been held that an agreement to pay 'a reasonable or fair market rent', absent stipulations as to how to arrive at such a figure, was too vague to establish consensus on this essential term.[35]

2.17 However, where parties clearly intend to be bound the courts approach problems of contract formation robustly with the reasonable expectations of sensible businesspeople in mind.[36] Situations have arisen where, though important elements of a transaction have not been agreed initially, a contract has been held to exist. In *R & J Dempster Ltd v Motherwell Bridge & Engineering Co Ltd*[37] the parties were contracting against the backdrop of a steel shortage. Such was the demand for the product that the industry was operating an 'open order' system whereby work was carried out on the basis that the price would be worked out later. The court concluded that price was a secondary issue to supply: 'in the market conditions operating when this contract was made, all the essentials were settled'.[38] As well as operating in unusual market

32 [2015] UKSC 13, 2015 SC (UKSC) 93.

33 *May & Butcher Ltd v The King* [1934] 2 KB 17 at 21 per Viscount Dunedin.

34 *Grant v Peter Gauld & Co* 1985 SC 251 (subjects); *MacLeod's Executor v Barr's Trustees* 1989 SC 72 (price); the Sale of Goods Act 1979, s. 8(2) allows for payment of a reasonable price if it has not been determined by the parties.

35 *Gray v University of Edinburgh* 1962 SC 157.

36 *R & D Construction Group Ltd v Hallam Land Management Ltd* [2009] CSOH 128 at [39] per Lord Hodge; affd [2010] CSIH 96, 2011 SC 286.

37 1964 SC 308.

38 1964 SC 308 at 329 per Lord President Clyde.

conditions, it was relevant that the parties were already performing the contract and the open order system was standard trade practice at that time.

2.18 Another important exception can be found in *Avintair Ltd v Ryder Airline Services Ltd*[39] where one party was already providing services to the other without having agreed a rate of commission. Despite the apparent lack of an essential term the court did not find the contract invalid but instead implied a term that a reasonable sum should be paid for work done. The fact that parties have started to perform their contractual obligations will be highly relevant to the issue of formation where all of the essential terms have not been agreed.[40] Some commentators have been critical of the decision in *Avintair*, arguing that a term should only be implied where it is clear the parties intended the matter to be settled at a later date, but not where it was the very issue on which they could not agree.[41]

Uncertainty of expression

2.19 Despite believing they have reached agreement, there may in fact be no contract between the parties if the words used are too vague or if there are contradictory terms which would undermine consensus. The contract may be 'void from uncertainty'. For instance, a description of a share in a partnership as being 'a substantial interest' was too vague to be enforceable;[42] likewise a description of property as 'the ground at present being quarried by our clients and the surroundings' with no identification of the boundaries.[43] The key is whether or not the contract can be enforced as it stands, in which case some uncertainty can simply be ignored. Alternatively, if the uncertainty arises from an error in drafting the offending term can be rectified under s. 8 of the Law Reform (Miscellaneous Provisions) (Scotland) Act 1985. A ruling that an agreement is void from uncertainty when parties intended that their bargain be enforceable is a last resort. The courts strive to give effect to the parties' intentions by interpreting their agreement in a manner which gives it practical meaning.[44]

FORMATION OF CONTRACT

2.20 The idea of predicating the formation of a contract on the agreement of the parties derives from a will theory of contract, so-called because the parties are deemed to have intended and chosen the obligations they enter into. However, there is a philosophical as well as a legal difficulty with this theory in that it leads logically to an enquiry into the state of mind of the parties at the time of contracting, an entirely subjective matter. This would be unworkable in

39 1994 SC 270.

40 *Wells v Devani* [2019] UKSC 4, [2020] AC 129 at [18]; *RTS Flexible Systems Ltd v Molkerei Alois Müller GmbH & Co KG* [2010] UKSC 14, [2010] 1 WLR 753.

41 MacQueen, *Contract Law* (2020), paras 1.41 and 2.20.

42 *McArthur v Lawson* (1877) 4 R 1134.

43 *Grant v Peter Gauld & Co* 1985 SC 251.

44 *Novus Aviation Ltd v Alubaf Arab International Bank BSC(c)* [2016] EWHC 1575 (Comm), [2017] 1 BCLC 414 at [60].

practice. Whilst maintaining agreement as the central concept in the formation of a contract, the law will ascertain the existence and the terms of that agreement *objectively*. Instead of conducting an investigation into subjective intentions the question for the court is not whether the parties actually consented but whether they *appeared* to consent. This is assessed according to what they say and what they do rather than what they think, according to the standards of a reasonable person: '[c]ommercial contracts cannot be arranged by what people think in their inmost minds. Commercial contracts are made according to what people say'.[45]

The offer and acceptance framework

2.21 The principal technique used by the courts to determine whether or not agreement exists is the offer and acceptance framework. The conduct or words of the parties are analysed objectively as an offer or an acceptance until the point of agreement is reached. A contract is formed when the terms of the offer are met with an unqualified acceptance. A contract comes into existence at the moment the offer is accepted: 'an offer accepted is a contract, because it is the deed of two, the offerer and the accepter'.[46]

Limitations of the offer and acceptance analysis

2.22 Despite being the dominant analysis of contract formation, the offer and acceptance framework does not adapt well to every contractual situation and it is not the only way in which a contract can be formed.[47] Where formation of contract and its performance are instantaneous, for instance in over-the-counter sales, it is somewhat artificial to say that a shop 'offers' goods for sale and that one accepts by completing payment. Similarly, at the other end of the spectrum where there are long and complex negotiations with multiple drafts of documentation it can be difficult to ascertain which version is an offer and which an acceptance. Many, perhaps most, commercial contracts involve such a process and the parties are free to stipulate, for example, that the contract will come into existence only when negotiations on particular matters are concluded, or when they have signed the final draft of their agreement.[48] To deal with cases involving a mix of written and oral communications, which may further challenge the traditional offer and acceptance analysis, greater emphasis may be placed on evidence of intention to create legal relations.[49] Technological advances may bring further challenges, such as where

45 *Muirhead and Turnbull v Dickson* (1905) 7 F 686 at 694 per Lord President Dunedin; *Coal Authority v Pegasus Fire Protection Co Ltd* [2019] CSIH 12, 2020 SLT 279 at [29]–[30] and [71]–[72].

46 Stair, *Institutions* 1.10.3.

47 Scottish Law Commission, *Report on Review of Contract Law: Formation, Interpretation, Remedies for Breach, and Penalty Clauses* (Scot. Law Com. No. 252, 2018), para. 4.7 (henceforth 'SLC Report 252').

48 See SLC Report 252, paras 4.12, 4.20 and 4.52.

49 *Moorgate Capital (Corporate Finance) Ltd v Sun European Partners LLP* [2020] EWHC 593 (Comm) at [81]–[82].

contracts are formed on algorithmic trading platforms with no direct human involvement.[50]

Coincidence of offer and acceptance

In order for there to be *consensus in idem* the terms of the offer and the terms of the acceptance must coincide. In *Mathieson Gee (Ayrshire) Ltd v Quigley*[51] Quigley contacted the company, MG, about having mould removed from a pond on his property. MG wrote offering 'to supply the necessary mechanical plant for the excavation and removal . . . of the mould' to which Quigley replied 'confirming my verbal acceptance of your offer to remove the silt and deposit from the pond'. In retrospect it was clear that the parties were at cross purposes, one offering to supply machinery, the other believing he had a contract to carry out the work of removing mould from his pond. The House of Lords held that this was a case of *dissensus* and that no contract existed. However, the case was litigated through the Scottish courts without such a conclusion and with differing interpretations of what the contractual obligations of the parties were, thus demonstrating that applying the offer and acceptance analysis is not always straightforward. **2.23**

Offers

One of the difficulties in contract formation is classifying whether a communication from one of the parties amounts to an offer. **2.24**

Pre-contractual statements not amounting to an offer

Often people will, by their words or their actions, indicate that they are willing to do business without intending to begin the process of contract formation. These types of pre-contractual statements or actions are sometimes referred to as 'invitations to treat' and must be distinguished from offers. Indeed the response to an invitation to treat is usually an offer, thus beginning the contractual process. A key distinction is that a willingness to do business does not involve an intention to enter into a legal obligation: it merely invites offers. As a general rule the following are considered invitations to treat: **2.25**

- Advertisements are generally regarded as 'trade puffs' whose purpose is to generate business, even if they use the wording 'special offer'.[52]
- Mail order catalogues are not offers even if they invite customers to place orders.[53] This also accords with business sense, for if every order placed amounted to a concluded contract the supplier could find themselves in breach of contract if stock was in short supply.

50 *Quoine Pte Ltd v B2C2 Ltd* [2020] SGCA(I) 02.
51 1952 SC (HL) 38.
52 *Fenwick v Macdonald Fraser & Co Ltd* (1904) 6 F 850; *Philp v Knoblauch* 1907 SC 994.
53 *Grainger & Son v Gough* [1896] AC 325 at 334 per Lord Herschell.

- Window and shop displays are equivalent to advertising and are not offers.[54] It may be that a similar analysis would apply to websites offering products for sale, although there is little authority to date.[55]
- Inviting tenders to be submitted amounts to an invitation to treat, the response to which is to make an offer by submitting a bid.[56]

Characteristics of an offer

2.26 An offer is a proposal to enter into an agreement which invites acceptance. It is therefore implicit that if the party to whom the offer is made accepts, a binding contract is formed. The terms of the offer must be sufficiently definite to create legal obligations and the offeror must intend to be legally bound. For an offer to be effective it must be communicated to the offeree and, logically therefore, acceptance cannot take place or be inferred prior to the offer being communicated.

2.27 An offer is usually made to a specific offeree, particularly in a commercial context. However, it is possible for an offer to be open to the general public. In an exception to the general presumption that an advertisement does not constitute an offer, one placed in a newspaper advertising a reward of a specific sum of money to anyone who complied with its terms was held to constitute an offer 'open to the world', which was sufficiently specific in its terms to show an intention to be legally bound upon acceptance.[57] Likewise, automatic ticket and vending machines have been held to amount to 'standing offers' open for acceptance by anyone.[58] Notices displayed in private car parks that impose parking charges are also considered to be contractual offers.[59]

Revocation of offers

2.28 An offer can be withdrawn at any time prior to acceptance. The offeror can change their mind and has the right to withdraw the offer (*locus poenitentiae*) unless the offer contains within it a promise to keep it open for a specific period (a 'firm offer').[60] Withdrawal or revocation of an offer must be communicated before it is effective.[61] In exceptional circumstances the offeree may be deemed to have been notified that the offer has been withdrawn because communication is assessed objectively. In *Burnley v Alford*[62] the fact that the

54 *Fisher v Bell* [1961] 1 QB 394.

55 But see the tentative invitation to treat characterisation of one website (though the point was not squarely in issue) in *O'Donnell v On the Beach Ltd* 2021 SLT (Sh Ct) 70 at [62]. See SLC Report 252, paras 4.50 and 5.12–5.16.

56 Though the express or implied terms of an invitation to tender may commit the tenderer in some way. See *Harvela Investments v Royal Trust Co of Canada* [1986] AC 207 (express terms of invitation entailed that bids not in round figures could not be considered); *Blackpool and Fylde Aero Club v Blackpool BC* [1990] 1 WLR 1195 (implication that conforming bids would at least be considered).

57 *Carlill v Carbolic Smoke Ball Co* [1893] 1 QB 256.

58 *Thornton v Shoe Lane Parking Ltd* [1971] 2 QB 163; *National Car Parks Ltd v Revenue and Customs Commissioners* [2019] EWCA Civ 854, [2019] 3 All ER 590.

59 *Vehicle Control Services Ltd v Mackie* [2017] SC DUN 24 at [14].

60 *A & G Paterson Ltd v Highland Railway Co* 1927 SC (HL) 32 at 38.

61 *Thomson v James* (1855) 18 D 1.

62 1919 2 SLT 123.

solicitor was on a shooting trip and not in his office to receive a telegram withdrawing an offer did not prevent the withdrawal being deemed to have been communicated. A modern equivalent may be a business that does not take care to check emails on a regular basis or fails to deal with an inbox that is full.

Lapse of offers

Where a time limit has been specified in the offer it must be accepted within that time period or it lapses. The wording of the offer will determine whether or not it can be withdrawn before the time period ends. An offer stating that it was open for acceptance for three days was held to contain a promise to keep the offer open and it could not be withdrawn;[63] however, an offer stating that it must be accepted within three days had a different semantic meaning and could be revoked during those three days.[64] If no time limit is specified an offer will lapse within a reasonable time.[65] What is considered reasonable may be influenced by factors such as trade practice; market fluctuations; and the mode of communication adopted by the parties.[66] **2.29**

If an offer is rejected by the offeree it will lapse. Rejection is implied if the offeree makes a counter-offer in response to an offer. Whilst the offeror's insolvency will by itself have no effect on an offer,[67] death or insanity will likely bring the offer to an end.[68] More generally, a material change of circumstances may render an offer ineffective.[69] **2.30**

Acceptances

Once an offer is met with an unqualified acceptance indicating assent to its terms a contract is formed. Offers and acceptances are generally made verbally, either orally or in writing, and if the offer prescribes a certain mode of acceptance, for instance that it must be in writing, the acceptance must be in the prescribed form. The law is fairly relaxed on this question and if no mode of communication is stipulated the acceptance can take any form, though normally it will follow the form in which the offer is made. An offer can also be accepted by conduct if actions imply consent to the offer.[70] Drivers who park their vehicles after being made aware of charges imposed by parking management companies are deemed to have accepted the terms displayed in the car park (the offer).[71] However, silence does not by itself amount to acceptance: **2.31**

63 *Littlejohn v Hadwen* (1882) 20 SLR 5.
64 *Heys v Kimball and Morton* (1890) 17 R 381.
65 *Pinecraven Construction (Guernsey) Ltd v Taddei* [2012] CSOH 18.
66 See McBryde, *Contract* (2007), paras 6–49–6–50.
67 SLC Report 252, paras 6.25–6.29.
68 SLC Report 252, paras 6.11–6.24.
69 *Davidson v Clyde Training Solutions Ltd* 2020 SLT (Sh Ct) 302; SLC Report 252, paras 6.5–6.10.
70 *Carlill v Carbolic Smoke Ball Co* [1893] 1 QB 256; *Bank of Ireland (UK) plc v Knight Frank LLP* [2015] CSOH 157 at [34]–[39].
71 *University of Edinburgh v Onifade* 2005 SLT (Sh Ct) 63; *Vehicle Control Services Ltd v Mackie* [2017] SC DUN 24 at [14].

there must be some positive indication by words or conduct of consent to the offer.[72]

Qualified acceptances

2.32 If an acceptance attempts to alter material terms of the offer it amounts to a qualified acceptance,[73] with two dramatic results:

(a) it rejects the original offer which then lapses and is no longer open for acceptance;[74] and
(b) the qualified acceptance in itself becomes a counter-offer that is open for acceptance.

2.33 This analysis can pose difficulty for the parties involved and highlights one of the limitations of the offer and acceptance framework. The parties may believe they are negotiating to the point of agreement, but imposing a legal analysis which categorises their communications as either offers or acceptances can lead to unintended consequences. For instance in *Wolf and Wolf v Forfar Potato Co*[75] an offer to supply potatoes was made by FPC to WW and it included terms relating to delivery, carriage, inspection and payment. The response from WW 'accepted' the offer but made alterations in relation to some of the terms (hence it was a counter-offer). A phone call then took place between the parties subsequent to which WW sent another response accepting the original offer. However, the court held that the original offer had been struck down by the counter-offer and was no longer available for acceptance, contrary to the expectations of the parties. Where two cross-offers are made without knowledge of or reference to each other, both have been held to amount to offers open for acceptance.[76]

Standard form contracts and the 'battle of the forms'

2.34 The rule relating to counter-offers is particularly problematic in a commercial context where parties may use standard form contracts, that is, pre-printed forms containing detailed terms of the contract which are standard for the business in question and are not individually negotiated. Indeed both parties to a commercial contract may have their own standard terms and conditions and the question in those circumstances is which set of terms will regulate the contract.

2.35 On a strict application of the counter-offer rule the party who sends their standard terms last will prevail. This is known as *the battle of the forms* and the rule boils down to the fact that whoever fires the last shot wins.[77] For instance, Company A makes an offer subject to its standard terms. Company B accepts

72 *Shaw v James Scott Builders & Company & Co* [2010] CSOH 68 at [50] per Lord Hodge.
73 *Pinecraven Construction (Guernsey) Ltd v Taddei* [2012] CSOH 18.
74 Mere inquiries or requests for further information in response to an offer will not have this effect: *Stevenson Jacques & Co v McLean* (1880) 5 QBD 346.
75 1984 SLT 100.
76 *Findlater v Maan* 1990 SC 150.
77 *Grafton Merchanting GB Ltd t/a Buildbase v Sundial Properties (Gilmerton) Ltd* 2013 GWD 17-349.

subject to Company B's standard terms, which amounts to a counter-offer and Company A's offer would lapse. If Company A then performs the contract, B's counter-offer is impliedly accepted and Company B's terms will prevail. This application of the offer and acceptance framework is known to be problematic in practice, and can work against the fundamental principle of freedom of contract.

Forty years ago Lord Denning suggested a different approach:[78] **2.36**

> 'In many of these cases our traditional analysis of offer, counter-offer, rejection, acceptance and so forth is out of date . . . The better way is to look at all the documents passing between the parties – and glean from them, or from the conduct of the parties, whether they have reached agreement on all material points – even though there may be differences between the forms and conditions printed on the back of them.'

His suggestion has not been adopted, but the problem continues to attract the attention of law reformers and academics. The Scottish Law Commission has suggested that it is for the courts to develop this area further, relying particularly on the implication of terms. It noted cases in which the courts were prepared to analyse the parties' intentions and dealings to discern which terms had been incorporated into their contracts, and to imply terms if necessary.[79]

Communication of acceptances

An acceptance is ordinarily effective when on an objective analysis it has been communicated to the offeror. This general rule is subject to the express or implied provisions of a given offer, established practice between parties, trade usage,[80] and a special rule applicable to acceptances by post. **2.37**

The postal acceptance rule

An important exception to the general rule that offers and acceptances must be communicated to the other party is the postal acceptance rule, which provides that where an acceptance is sent by post a contract is concluded at the point of sending, rather than the point of receiving, the letter. The rationale behind the rule is that the acceptor has done everything possible to accept and has no control over the postal service or any delays that may occur.[81] **2.38**

The rule applies only to *acceptances* by post.[82] A postal acceptance can, therefore, defeat the withdrawal of an offer that has been sent but has not yet reached the acceptor.[83] In *Thomson v James*[84] one of the negotiating parties posted an acceptance on 1 December and on the same day the other party **2.39**

78 *Butler Machine Tool Co Ltd v Ex-Cell-O Corporation (England) Ltd* [1979] 1 WLR 401 at 404.
79 See, e.g. *CR Smith Glaziers (Dunfermline) Ltd v Toolcom Supplies Ltd* [2010] CSOH 7; *Transformers and Rectifiers Ltd v Needs Ltd* [2015] EWHC 269 (TCC).
80 SLC Report 252, paras 2.3, 4.56–4.71, 4.95–4.99.
81 *Dunlop, Wilson & Co v Higgins & Son* (1848) 6 Bell's App 195.
82 And not, for example, to the exercise of an option: *Carmarthen Developments Ltd v Samuel James Pennington* [2008] CSOH 139; or to acceptance by email: *Greenclose Ltd v National Westminster Bank plc* [2014] EWHC 1156 (Ch), [2014] 1 CLC 562 at [138].
83 Unless non-receipt of a withdrawal is the acceptor's fault: *Burnley v Alford* 1919 2 SLT 123.
84 (1855) 18 D 1.

posted a withdrawal of the offer – both letters arrived on the same day. The court had to decide what the priority was between one party's wish to accept and the other's wish to withdraw from the contract. It was held that a contract had been concluded at the point of posting the acceptance, applying the postal acceptance rule, and that an offeree was entitled to assume that an offer was open until he heard otherwise.

2.40 Though the rule will apply even if there is a long delay in the letter arriving,[85] a postal acceptance must ultimately reach its destination to be effective.[86] It should also be noted that it is open to parties to disapply the rule by providing that all communications between them must be received before they are effective to conclude a contract.[87] In practice the rule is commonly excluded in offers.[88]

Other modes of communication

2.41 Acceptances not sent by post take effect on communication to the addressee. Acceptances in face-to-face conversation and by other instantaneous means such as telephone pose no difficulty albeit there is a general duty on the party communicating to take reasonable steps to ensure the other party has heard and understood the communication, for instance if a mobile phone signal is lost.[89] Acceptances by other methods such as telex and fax have also been held to be effective upon communication.[90] It is suggested that email, regularly employed by contracting parties without incident in the commercial context,[91] is generally to be treated in the same way so that, subject to considerations such as the intentions of the parties, business practice and possible misdirection, an acceptance by email will be taken to be communicated when it is available to be read.[92]

Proposed abolition of the postal acceptance rule

2.42 The rule serves to protect an offeree against withdrawal of the offer, but arguably tips the scales too far in favour of the acceptor. Under the current law if an acceptance is posted the acceptor has full knowledge of the risks whereas the offeror will usually be unaware that a contract has come into existence until the acceptance arrives. The acceptor could carry out certain activities in performance of the contract, but the offeror has no such advantage. The Scottish Law Commission has proposed that the postal acceptance rule should

85 *Jacobsen, Sons & Co v Underwood & Son Ltd* (1894) 21 R 654.

86 *Mason v Benhar Coal Co Ltd* (1882) 9 R 883 at 890 per Lord Shand.

87 As discussed in *Carmarthen Developments Ltd v Samuel James Pennington* [2008] CSOH 139 at [17] per Lord Hodge.

88 SLC Report 252, para. 4.87.

89 *Entores Ltd v Miles Far East Corporation* [1955] 2 QB 327.

90 *Entores Ltd v Miles Far East Corporation* [1955] 2 QB 327 (telex); *JSC Zestafoni G Nikoladze Ferroalloy Plant v Ronly Holdings Ltd* [2004] EWHC 245 (Comm) at [75] per Colman J (fax).

91 See, e.g. the undisputed formation of a contract by email in *Trilogy Power Solutions Group v Hawick Plant Auctions Ltd* [2021] CSOH 27 at [13].

92 The general rule and possible complications were discussed *obiter* in *Thomas v BPE Solicitors (A Firm)* [2010] EWHC 306 (Ch) at [85]–[90] per Blair J. For detailed discussion see SLC Report 252, paras 4.69, 4.71–4.85.

be abolished. Subjecting postal acceptances to the general communication requirement 'would better accord with the reasonable expectations of most, in particular those of the commercial community in Scotland'.[93]

Contracts and writing

As a general rule, contracts do not need to be in writing in order to be valid.[94] However, commercial contracts are often detailed written documents, running to hundreds of pages and, once finalised and signed, they mark a transition from negotiations to the contract proper. The terms of a well-drafted contract can usefully be referred to in case of doubt, and relied upon in any dispute, which many commercial parties and their advisors will look to resolve informally if possible. **2.43**

The Requirements of Writing (Scotland) Act 1995

The rules on writing and formal validity of contracts are set out in the Requirements of Writing (Scotland) Act 1995 (the 'RWSA 1995'), which begins by stating the general rule.[95] The main exception to the general rule is that writing is required for contracts relating to real rights in land.[96] This includes missives for the sale of heritable property, standard securities and leases of more than one year,[97] as well as other contracts which create, transfer, vary or extinguish any of the fixed list of real rights.[98] Such contracts must be 'subscribed' (signed at the end of the last page) by each granter in order to be valid either as traditional paper documents, subscribed in pen and ink,[99] or electronic documents authenticated by an electronic signature.[100] The Scottish Law Commission has pointed out that in modern life many if not most traditional documents start out in electronic form but are later printed and signed in the usual way. It appears that the character of a document, whether traditional or electronic, will be determined at the point of execution according to the type of signature used.[101] Contracts relating to a real right in land do not, therefore, exist unless they are in the form prescribed in the RWSA 1995 and the parties are free to withdraw from negotiations. **2.44**

However, in certain circumstances the parties are personally barred from denying that a contract exists even if it is not in writing when it ought to be. Four conditions must be satisfied:[102] **2.45**

93 SLC Report 252, paras 4.86–4.94.
94 Statute sometimes requires it. See, e.g. the Consumer Credit Act 1974, ss. 61(1), 105(1); or the Employment Rights Act 1996, ss. 1, 13(1)(b).
95 RWSA 1995, s. 1(1): '... writing shall not be required ...'.
96 RWSA 1995, s. (1)(2)(a)(i).
97 RWSA 1995, s. 1(7).
98 See para. 3.22.
99 RWSA 1995, s. 2(1).
100 RWSA 1995, s. 9B(1); Electronic Documents (Scotland) Regulations 2014 (SSI 2014/83).
101 Scottish Law Commission, *Discussion Paper on Formation of Contract* (Scot. Law Com. DP 154, 2012), para. 7.9.
102 RWSA 1995, s. 1(3)–(4).

(a) There must be a *prima facie* contract, i.e. the parties must have reached agreement on all the essentials and must intend to be legally bound.[103]
(b) One party ('the first person') must have acted in reliance on the putative contract.
(c) Those actions must be carried out by the first person with the *knowledge and acquiescence* of the other party ('the second person').
(d) The first person (who has acted in reliance) must be affected to a material extent by their actions, for instance by having incurred expenditure, and must also be adversely affected to a material extent if the second person were to withdraw from the agreement.

If all of these conditions are satisfied, the second person cannot withdraw from the obligation. A contract would exist despite it not being in writing.

Execution in counterpart and remote transactions

2.46 In a global economy commercial contracts are often entered into by multiple parties who may be spread across Scotland, the UK or the world. To identify definitively the binding final terms of their agreement, parties commonly set them out in a single document or set of documents which are signed by the parties. The ability to conclude a contract remotely is convenient and reduces transaction costs where parties are based in different locations.

2.47 The Legal Writings (Counterparts and Delivery) (Scotland) Act 2015 provides a clear legal basis for contracts to be executed in counterpart, whereby each party signs an identical copy of the contract, then delivers it to the other parties or to a nominee.[104] Once executed, the counterparts are treated as a single document. In terms of contract formation, it is only once each counterpart has been signed and delivered to the other parties that a contract is formed unless the parties have agreed an alternative.

Third party rights

2.48 The parties to a contract may agree that a third party should be given rights or benefits under their contract. The most obvious example is a life assurance policy, which is a contract between the insured and the insurance company but which will usually stipulate that in the event of the insured's death the proceeds of the policy go to a family member. That person will have a legally enforceable right in the contract although not a party to it. A third party right may also be desirable in the construction context: a developer may agree with the primary contractor that the contractor owes duties to the financiers of the project, the intended purchasers, or prospective tenants. Until recently, this was achieved by the doctrine of *jus quaesitum tertio*. However, the practical utility of the doctrine was limited by the need for the third party right to be irrevocable, which precluded the ability of the contracting parties to restructure or renegotiate arrangements.[105]

103 *Aisling Developments Ltd v Persimon Homes Ltd* 2009 SLT 494.
104 2015 Act, s. 2.
105 See generally *Review of Contract Law: Report on Third Party Rights* (Scot. Law Com. No. 245, 2016).

The Contract (Third Party Rights) (Scotland) Act 2017 (the 2017 Act) replaces the doctrine of *jus quaesitum tertio* for contracts entered into, or varied, on or after 26 February 2018.[106] It provides that a third party ('C') may enforce a third party right where: 2.49

(a) there is a valid contract between A and B, containing an undertaking that either party will do, or refrain from doing, something for C's benefit;[107]
(b) the contracting parties intended that C should be able to enforce that undertaking;[108] and
(c) C is clearly identifiable from the terms of the contract,[109] even if they were not in existence or within the stipulated class at the time of the contract's constitution or variation.[110]

Crucially, this regime has no irrevocability requirement,[111] and a third party right may be revoked or altered by agreement between A and B at any time.[112] However, in recognition of the detriment this may cause to a third party, the 2017 Act provides for exceptions to the freedom to revoke: where the third party right has arisen on the basis of the third party's fulfillment of a stipulated condition;[113] where the third party has been notified of the undertaking in their favour;[114] and where the third party has acted in reliance on that undertaking with the acquiescence or reasonable foresight of the contracting parties.[115] The third party enjoys the same remedies that would available to a contracting party in respect of a breach of the undertaking,[116] and also is subject to the same defences that could be pled by a contractual party in relation to a breach of the undertaking.[117] In practice, it will be common to see contractual provisions purporting to exclude the operation of the 2017 Act, which presumably will be effective.[118]

INVALID AND UNENFORCEABLE CONTRACTS

Introduction

This section will consider situations in which contracts are either invalid or unenforceable and are, therefore, ineffective. The first part examines ways in 2.50

106 2017 Act, ss. 11 and 12.
107 2017 Act, s. 1(1)(a). This may be a conditional undertaking: s. 2(2).
108 2017 Act, s. 1(1)(b). The intention may be express or implied: s. 2(3).
109 2017 Act, s. 1(3).
110 2017 Act, s. 1(4) and 1(5). So, to return to the construction example, if the contract provides for a right to be enforceable by an 'eventual tenant' of the property, it is no objection that the third party in question only became a tenant *after* the constitution of the primary contract.
111 2017 Act, s. 2(4).
112 2017 Act, s. 3.
113 2017 Act, s. 4(1); however, this can be disapplied by the contractual parties: s. 4(2).
114 2017 Act, s. 5(1)–(2); note the limited exceptions in s. 5(3)–(4).
115 2017 Act, s. 6(1)–(2); this can be disapplied by the contractual parties if C knew, or should have known, about their ability to vary or revoke the third party right: s. 6(4).
116 2017 Act, s. 7(1)–(2). The parties may, however, provide otherwise in the contract: s. 7(2).
117 2017 Act, s. 8(1)–(2). This, again, is subject to contrary contractual provision: s. 8(3).
118 This is because such a clause demonstrates the parties did not intend for any undertaking within their agreement to be enforceable by a third party, i.e. it negates requirement (b) above.

which a contract can be nullified because there is deemed to be no consent or flawed (vitiated) consent and as a result the contract is essentially invalid. Three classic vitiating factors are examined: fraud, error and force and fear. The second part examines situations in which a contract may become unenforceable, that is, the contract remains valid but it cannot be enforced usually because of external events outwith the control of the parties or on grounds of public policy. These two categories clearly have different conceptual underpinnings but they are treated together since both have the effect of bringing performance of the contract to an end.

Void and voidable contracts

2.51 A void contract, sometimes referred to as being *null ab initio*, is one that has no legal effect and contractual remedies are thus not available to the parties. Usually a contract will be void because there is a flaw in the consent of one or both parties that is so severe that the law deems there to have been no contract from the outset. By contrast, a voidable contract is one that has come into existence but is retrospectively set aside because a vitiating factor, such as misrepresentation, has later come to light with the result that consent turns out to have been flawed. A voidable contract exists up to the point when it is rescinded at which point the parties are obliged to restore each other to their original starting positions (*restitutio in integrum*) by undoing any effects of the contract, for instance by returning money or property that has already changed hands.

Implications for third parties

2.52 Usually it will be of little consequence to the contracting parties whether a contract is deemed to be void or voidable. However, it is a crucially important distinction where third parties are involved. The distinction is illustrated in the well-known cases of *Morrisson v Robertson*[119] and *MacLeod v Kerr*.[120] In both a plausible rogue pretending to be someone else tricked the owner of goods into selling them to him: in the first case, on the credit of the party for whom the rogue was pretending to act; in the second, by paying with a cheque from a stolen chequebook which was subsequently dishonoured. In both cases the rogue sold the goods on to a good faith third party (and in both the rogue was later convicted of the crime of theft). In both cases there was a competition for the goods between the original owner/seller and the third party who had bought in good faith. In *Morrisson* it was held that an essential error as to the identity of the buyer rendered the contract void, that the rogue had therefore never acquired title to the goods and so neither did the good faith third party. The owner regained his cows. In *MacLeod*, by contrast, the owner was held to be the victim of fraud, the contract was voidable and, therefore, the good faith third party was entitled to keep the car in question.

119 1908 SC 332.
120 1965 SC 253. For comment see D Reid and H L MacQueen, 'Fraud or error: a thought experiment?' (2013) 17 Edin LR 343.

In such a scenario the law has to make a policy choice. There are two innocent parties: the seller and the innocent third party buyer who has no knowledge of any deception. Who should be protected? Normally the law favours the innocent third party and this is indeed the rule where a contract is voidable, on condition that the third party has given value and is in good faith (i.e. has no actual or constructive knowledge of the defect). However, if a contract is void the third party is not protected and cannot acquire property or other rights. This will be a relatively rare occurrence and only if the flaw in consent is so serious that no contract has come into existence in the first place. A contract can be void where there is dissensus, incapacity, force and fear and, in some cases, error. In all other cases it will be voidable. 2.53

Fraud

Historically fraud had a broad meaning in Scots law encompassing a spectrum of behaviour ranging from deliberate deceit to simply taking advantage of someone in an unscrupulous way.[121] Under the influence of the important English case of *Derry v Peek*[122] the meaning of fraud narrowed so that in modern Scots law fraud amounts to intentional or reckless deceit, traditionally 'a machination or contrivance to deceive'.[123] Within this narrow definition it has been said that 'the categories of fraud are never closed'[124] and any behaviour which is designed to deceive will amount to fraud. Fraud renders a contract voidable and, as it also amounts to an intentional delict, damages can be claimed. The principal manifestation of fraud in the modern law is in the law of misrepresentation.[125] 2.54

Misrepresentation

A misrepresentation is any inaccurate statement of fact which would have resulted in any reasonable person refraining from entering into the contract had that statement not been made. Advertisements are not generally presumed to be statements of fact unless they claim to have a factual basis, for instance in scientific research. Nor are statements of opinion or statements of future intent. Although misrepresentations generally are to be found in written or oral statements, they can also take the form of positive misleading conduct. Deliberately placing reproduction furniture that had been distressed to make it look old among genuine antiques amounted to a misrepresentation because of the seller's positive misleading conduct.[126] In a recent case involving a fake antique table (described as being 'designed to deceive') which was offered at 2.55

121 See D Reid, 'The doctrine of presumptive fraud in Scots law' (2013) 34 *Journal of Legal History* 307.
122 (1889) LR 14 App Cas 337.
123 Erskine, *Institute* 3.1.16.
124 McBryde, *Contract* (2007), para. 14–03.
125 It should be noted that many commentators regard misrepresentation as an aspect of the law of error, MacQueen, *Contract Law* (2020), para. 4.27; for discussion see Reid and MacQueen (n 120).
126 *Patterson v Landsberg* (1905) 7 F 675.

auction the court held that in order for it to amount to a misrepresentation there must be intention to deceive, i.e. fraud.[127]

2.56 A misrepresentation cannot generally be constituted by silence unless there exists a duty of disclosure,[128] for instance where there is a fiduciary or quasi-fiduciary relationship between the parties or in the special category of contracts which are considered of the utmost good faith (*uberrimae fidei*) such as insurance contracts or partnership agreements.

2.57 Four conditions must be satisfied for a misrepresentation to be operative:[129]

(a) The misrepresentation must be made by the other contracting party – or their agent – and not a third party to the contract.
(b) It must be made prior to formation of the contract, generally in the course of negotiations between the parties.
(c) The misrepresentation must cause the other party to be under a material error.
(d) There must be a causal link between the error and the reason for entering into the contract.

Consequences of a misrepresentation

2.58 An operative misrepresentation will render a contract voidable and it can be rescinded if *restitutio in integrum* is possible. In *Boyd & Forrest v Glasgow & South Western Railway Co*[130] the contract could not be annulled even though an innocent misrepresentation was established because construction work had already been carried out: 'unless the railway is obliterated, *restitutio in integrum* is impossible'.[131] Despite the fact that the House of Lords has advocated a more flexible approach[132] the Scottish courts continue to apply this condition strictly.

2.59 Misrepresentations can be made fraudulently, negligently or 'innocently' (i.e. without intention or negligence) and the distinction is important in relation to remedies. A fraudulent misrepresentation involves making an inaccurate statement intentionally or recklessly without regard to its truth. As well as rendering the contract voidable damages can also be claimed in delict, since fraud is an intentional delict. A misrepresentation may also made negligently, most notably by professional or expert advisers whose opinions are likely to be relied on.[133] For such negligence damages can be claimed in addition to any contractual remedy.[134] However, if a misrepresentation is made innocently, i.e. where a person honestly believes in the statement they are making but it is

127 *Lyon and Turnbull v Sabine* [2012] CSOH 178. For discussion of this point see M Hogg, 'A Regency drama: misrepresentation by appearance, reduction and *restitutio in integrum*' (2013) 17 Edin LR 256.
128 *Broatch v Jenkins* (1866) 4 M 1030.
129 *Ritchie v Glass* 1936 SLT 591.
130 1915 SC (HL) 20.
131 1915 SC (HL) 20 at 36 per Lord Shaw.
132 *Spence v Crawford* 1939 SC (HL) 52 at 70 per Lord Thankerton.
133 This is an exception to the rule that statements of opinion do not constitute a misrepresentation: *Esso Petroleum v Mardon* [1976] QB 801.
134 Law Reform (Miscellaneous Provisions) (Scotland) Act 1985, s. 10.

false nevertheless, the only remedy is contractual (rescission) and no damages can be claimed.[135]

Error

'Error arises when there is a discrepancy between reality and a party's belief.'[136] 2.60

One of the most complex areas that contract law must deal with is the situation when people make mistakes. If I have entered into a contract under some kind of error, how should the law deal with that error? Subjectively, if I have made a mistake it would appear to be unfair to insist on performance of the contract. On the other hand, setting aside the contract on the grounds of my error may be equally unfair to the other party, not to mention the difficulties of proof, and contracting parties need to be able to rely on obligations that have been undertaken. Much of the confusion which can be found in decisions involving error comes back to the familiar tension between the subjective and the objective approach. The application of objective criteria to an essentially subjective problem is the heart of the error dilemma.

There are three basic types of error that may arise in contracts.[137] First, 2.61
there may be an error in expression where the terms of a written contract do not match the agreement of the parties.[138] Such errors can be rectified.[139] Secondly, there may be an error in performance, for instance if money is paid in error or goods delivered to the wrong person. The remedy in these cases usually lies in unjustified enrichment if it was not caused by the fault of either party.[140] Thirdly, there may be an error in the consent of one or both parties, consensual error.

Consensual error

The historical approach to consensual error was that for the contract to be 2.62
reduced the error must be in 'the substantials' of the contract, sometimes referred to as essential error. Traditionally an essential error had to fall within Bell's five pre-defined categories:[141] the subject of the contract; the identity of the debtor in the obligation; the price; the quality of the thing bargained for; or the nature of the contract. Such an error in theory is so fundamental that it prevents formation of a contract with the result that any putative contract will be void.[142] It remains the case that an operative error not caused by the other contracting party (an uninduced error) must 'go to the root of the contract'.[143]

135 *Boyd & Forrest v Glasgow & SW Railway Co* 1915 SC (HL) 20.
136 McBryde, *Contract* (2007), para. 15–36.
137 McBryde, *Contract* (2007), para. 15–01.
138 *Anderson v Lambie* 1953 SC 94.
139 Law Reform (Miscellaneous Provisions) (Scotland) Act 1985, ss. 8, 9.
140 *Morgan Guaranty Trust Co of New York v Lothian Regional* Council 1995 SC 151.
141 Bell, *Principles*, § 11; *Stewart v Kennedy* (1890) 17 R (HL) 25.
142 *Morrisson v Robertson* 1908 SC 332.
143 MacQueen, *Contract Law* (2020), para. 5.37. MacQueen suggests that in the modern law of error Bell's categories may be illustrative rather than definitional (as above). For a historical analysis see J MacLeod, 'Before Bell: the roots of error in the Scots law of contract' (2010) 14 Edin LR 385.

Shared error

2.63 The effect of such a fundamental error is to prevent *consensus* between the contracting parties. They may be mistaken as to the same thing,[144] for instance the extent of boundaries in the sale of property, or they may be at cross purposes (sometimes called a mutual error).[145] Both types of error will prevent formation of a contract and can be considered examples of *dissensus*. Both will also be rare.

Unilateral error

2.64 The most problematic case is where only one of the parties is labouring under an error, that is, a unilateral error. A key question to ask is whether the error was induced or not by the other contracting party. If it was induced, this amounts to a misrepresentation and the contract will be voidable.[146] Furthermore, the error need not be fundamental or essential, although it must be material.[147]

2.65 An uninduced unilateral error will not be sufficient to annul a contract.[148] However, if such an error is combined with an additional factor it may be operative:[149]

(a) if the contract is gratuitous;[150] or
(b) if the other party is aware of the error and takes advantage of it.

The second category has both older and more recent authority in Scots law and amounts to punishment of bad faith and sharp practice. In *Steuart's Trs v Hart*[151] a contract was reduced on grounds of an uninduced unilateral error because the seller knew about the purchaser's error and took advantage of it, Lord Deas holding that 'the purchaser is not fairly entitled to take advantage of such an error'.[152] More recently in *Angus v Bryden*[153] and *Wills v Strategic Procurement (UK) Ltd*[154] the courts have confirmed that *Steuart's Trs v Hart* remains good law.

144 *Hamilton v Western Bank of Scotland* (1861) 23 D 1033.
145 *Mathieson Gee (Ayrshire) Ltd v Quigley* 1952 SC (HL) 38; *Raffles v Wichelhaus* (1864) 2 H&C 906.
146 There is some discussion to the effect that an induced error (i.e. a misrepresentation) which falls within one of the five categories of error in the substantials ought to lead to a void contract, as in fact was the case in *Morrisson v Robertson*. There is little authority on this issue, but see the English case of *Shogun Finance Ltd v Hudson* [2004] 1 AC 919.
147 *Ritchie v Glass* 1936 SLT 591 at 594 per Lord Carmont.
148 *Steel v Bradley Homes (Scotland) Ltd* 1972 SC 48; *Royal Bank of Scotland plc v Purvis* 1990 SLT 262; *Spook Erection (Northern) Ltd v Kaye* 1990 SLT 676.
149 This borrows from McBryde's 'error plus' analysis, see McBryde, *Contract* (2007), para. 15–23, an approach that was affirmed in *Wills v Strategic Procurement (UK) Ltd* [2013] CSOH 26, 2016 SC 367 at [2] and [14] per Lord Malcolm.
150 *Hunter v Bradford Property Trust Ltd* 1970 SLT 173.
151 (1875) 3 R 192.
152 (1875) 3 R 192 at 200.
153 1992 SLT 884.
154 [2013] CSOH 26, 2016 SC 367. See also *Parvaiz v Thresher Wines Acquisitions Ltd* 2009 SC 151.

Force and fear

2.66 Force and fear or extortion was one of the earliest grounds of challenge to a contract in Scots law. The terminology is misleading in that it suggests that to be a valid ground of challenge two elements are required, namely force and fear. It would be more accurate to call this ground of challenge force or fear since either may be sufficient depending on the circumstances:[155] 'although we couple together force and fear as one ground of reduction, the act of force is truly only one means of inducing fear, the true ground of reduction being extortion, through the influence of fear induced in [the] various ways'.

2.67 Force and fear will be a relevant ground of challenge where some form of coercion or pressure is applied to induce fear and to secure consent. The essence of the challenge is that a deed was granted or a contract entered into without consent because it was induced by fear and often threats. Force and fear is historically regarded as being such a serious matter that consent is excluded completely and any contract will be void.[156]

2.68 The force or threat must be sufficient to annul consent, therefore futile or empty threats will not be sufficient. In addition, the threat itself must be illegitimate,[157] for instance threatening assault or harassment of a family member but not a threat to report illegal behaviour to the police, which would not be unlawful. In a commercial context English law has developed the concept of economic duress. However, legitimate commercial pressure, no matter how unpleasant it may be, to undercut a competitor's prices or create other financial difficulties for them, will not be sufficient to constitute duress as the law currently stands in Scotland. Generally the law of contract will accept that, in a capitalist system, economic pressures are a legitimate part of the operation of the free market.

Unenforceable contracts

2.69 Contracts may become unenforceable because of events outwith the control of the contracting parties which they have not foreseen or on grounds of public policy. It is important to note that, unlike contracts which are void or voidable, the contract is not nullified retrospectively. The contractual relationship between the parties still exists and transactions that have already taken place, such as payment, are not invalidated. However, parties are freed from any outstanding or subsequent obligations under the contract, and any subsequent performance is ventured without the backstop of judicial remedies: the court will not lend any support to policing an agreement which has been declared unenforceable. Frustration and illegality are two situations that render contracts unenforceable.

155 *Priestnell v Hutcheson* (1857) 19 D 495 at 499 per Lord Deas.

156 Stair, *Institutions* 1.9.8. For discussion see J E du Plessis, *Compulsion and Restitution* (Glasgow: Stair Society, 2004) Vol. 51, para. 6.2.2.

157 *Earl of Orkney v Vinfra* (1606) Mor 16481.

Frustration of contract

2.70 Frustration of contract arises where some external event 'supervenes' between the time when the contract is formed and the time when performance is due that renders performance illegal or impossible or radically different in nature from what the parties had contemplated when they entered into the contract. The criteria for a frustrated contract have been held to be the same in both Scots and English law,[158] and include the following:

(a) The supervening event must be such as to render performance of the parties' obligations fundamentally different from that which was within their contemplation when initially contracting.[159] Mere increase in the difficulty or cost of performance will not suffice.[160]
(b) The supervening event must not have been foreseeable,[161] except in exceptional cases.
(c) Frustration cannot be self-induced: it must be caused by an external act beyond the control of the party contending that the contract is frustrated.[162] Furthermore, if the consequences of that act could have been avoided, then a party cannot rely on their own indolence to argue frustration.[163]

Frustration is a relatively rare occurrence and most commercial contracts will contain *force majeure* clauses which allocate risk if certain events occur. These may provide for the continuation or termination of the contract or may provide either party an option as to how to respond to the event. Such agreements represent a private ordering of the consequences of unforeseen events and take precedence over the default rules of frustration.[164]

Supervening illegality

2.71 Supervening illegality arises where there has been a change in the law[165] between the time a contract is formed and the time when performance is due. Many of the cases on frustration deal with the impact of the outbreak of war on contracts.[166] Often supervening illegality is caused by emergency legislation: for instance when a wartime ban on importing pine wood rendered a contract

158 *James B Fraser & Co v Denny Mott & Dickson* 1944 SC (HL) 35, 41; *Robert Purvis Plant Hire Ltd v Brewster* [2009] CSOH 28 at [12]–[13].
159 *National Carriers v Panalpina Ltd* [1981] 1 AC 675.
160 *Davis Contractors Ltd v Fareham Urban District Council* [1956] AC 696.
161 See *Flying Music Company v Theatre Entertainment SA* [2017] EWHC 3192 (QB) (contract to tour show in Greece not frustrated by Eurozone crisis riots as civil unrest was foreseeable).
162 *Taylor v Caldwell* (1863) 3 B&S 826.
163 *Maritime National Fish Ltd v Ocean Trawlers Ltd* [1935] AC 524.
164 For a *force majeure* clause triggered by the COVID-19 pandemic, and subsequent repurposing of the SEC in Glasgow as the NHS Louisa Jordan, see *Billy Graham Evangelical Association v Scottish Event Campus Ltd* 2021 SLT (Sh Ct) 185 at [25]–[33].
165 Supervening illegality under foreign law, e.g. the law of the place where the contract is to be performed, may also bring the contract to an end: *Ralli Bros v Compañia Naviera Sota Y Aznar* [1920] 2 KB 287.
166 See W W McBryde and I Scobbie, 'The Iraq and Kuwait conflict: the impact on contracts' 1991 SLT (News) 39.

for the supply of wood illegal;[167] or where a Scottish company found itself trading with an enemy alien (an Austrian company) after the outbreak of the First World War, thus rendering any future supply of marine engines illegal.[168] A more recent example is the emergency legislation passed in response to the COVID-19 pandemic which had the effect of rendering the operation of some businesses illegal. This supervening illegality may, in certain circumstances, have had the effect of frustrating leases of commercial premises held by such businesses.

Supervening impossibility

Supervening impossibility arises where performance of the contract has become impossible, not simply more difficult or more expensive, because of a supervening event. For instance, the subject matter of the contract may have been destroyed (*rei interitus*)[169] or it may be held *constructively* to have been destroyed if it has become impossible to use it for its original purpose, such as a property that became impossible for a tenant to live in because it had been requisitioned by the military.[170] The same principle would apply where the qualities of a person are essential to the contract (*delectus personae*), for instance cancellation by a concert pianist or a particular artist with unique and irreplaceable skills. Some changes may make performance impossible, for instance a strike by workers, but a frustrating event must be outwith the normal range of risks that the parties impliedly undertook when they entered into the contract. **2.72**

Supervening radical change of circumstances

The third category of events that can frustrate a contract are those which amount to a radical change of circumstances. In this case the supervening event does not render performance impossible or illegal but instead it destroys the basis of the agreement between the parties, i.e. performance would be radically different from what the parties had envisaged. It is not enough for performance to be more difficult or less profitable,[171] rather it must destroy the common assumptions of the parties at the point when they entered into the contract. It is important that the alleged frustrating event is identified at the right level of generality: while a very specific event may not have been in the contemplation of the parties at the time of contracting, that event may be a particular instance of a wider class of event that may have been foreseeable at the time of contracting.[172] **2.73**

167 *James B Fraser & Co v Denny, Mott & Dickson* 1944 SC (HL) 35.
168 *Cantiere San Rocco SA v Clyde Shipbuilding and Engineering Co Ltd* 1923 SC (HL) 105.
169 *Cantors Properties (Scotland) Ltd v Swear & Wells Ltd* 1978 SC 310 (subject of lease destroyed by fire).
170 *Mackeson v Boyd* 1942 SC 56.
171 *Tzakiraglou & Co v Noblee & Thurl GmbH* [1962] AC 93 where the cost of shipping increased because of the closure of the Suez Canal but although the contract was less profitable it was not held to be frustrated; see also *Davis Contractors Ltd v Fareham Urban District Council* [1956] AC 696.
172 See *Canary Wharf (BP4) T1 Ltd v European Medicines Agency* [2019] EWHC 335 (Ch) (while the UK's vote to leave the EU was not foreseeable at the time of an EU agency

The consequences of frustration

2.74 Frustration renders a contract unenforceable (not void or voidable) with the result that future performance is suspended and the parties are freed from their obligations after the supervening event has occurred. Frustration only has *future* effect, so that any contractual effects which have occurred before the supervening event took place will survive and are not struck down. If one of the parties has already incurred costs, for instance by having paid for a service that becomes impossible to render, in principle the losses lie where they fall and no damages are payable. Where the effects of frustration are inequitable the courts have been willing to grant a remedy in unjustified enrichment.[173] More recently, the Supreme Court has acknowledged that there may be scope in future for an alternative approach based on 'equitable adjustment' of the contract where it has been frustrated,[174] but this has yet to be applied in a reported decision.

Illegal contracts

2.75 In all areas of private law court decisions are sometimes made not on the grounds of a specific rule of law but on the grounds of public policy and this is clearly illustrated in the area of illegal contracts, sometimes referred to as *pacta illicita*.[175] As in the case of frustrated contracts, if a contract is set aside on grounds of being illegal it is neither void nor voidable, but it becomes unenforceable and any future performance simply stops.

2.76 Some contracts are illegal from the outset because they are in explicit contravention of either a rule of common law or a statutory provision, for instance entering into a contract with someone to commit a theft or an act of deception. Others may be implicitly illegal in that they do not directly contravene a rule of law but the illegality is to be found in the way in which the contract is performed. For instance, in *Jamieson v Watts Trs*[176] under wartime regulations it was necessary to obtain a license to carry out construction work. Mr Jamieson, a joiner, had the necessary license to carry out work up to the value of £40 but he exceeded the permitted value. His contract with his customer was not in itself illegal but the way in which he had performed it was and as a result the court would not 'lend its aid in any way to one who has to found on what he has illegally done or on his own turpitude'.[177] In *Jamieson*, the presence of any form of illegality was seen as sufficient to bar any attempt to enforce the contract. However, the modern approach to contractual illegality is a more

entering into a lease for London headquarters, it could be foreseen that for some reason the agency might have to leave the premises before the expiry of the lease).

173 *Cantiere San Rocco SA v Clyde Shipbuilding and Engineering Co Ltd* 1923 SC (HL) 105.

174 *Lloyds TSB Foundation for Scotland v Lloyds Banking Group plc* [2013] UKSC 3, 2013 SC (UKSC) 169 at [46] per Lord Hope; for further comment on equitable adjustment following the Outer House decision in *Lloyds* see L Macgregor, 'Long-term contracts, the rules of interpretation and "equitable adjustment"' (2012) 16 Edin LR 104.

175 For a more extensive treatment see McBryde, *Contract* (2007), Ch. 19. Immoral contracts would also come into this category but are not dealt with in this chapter.

176 1950 SC 265.

177 1950 SC 265 at 279 per Lord Jamieson.

flexible one. The court should ask whether enforcing the contract would be an affront to the public interest, taking into consideration:[178]

(a) the purpose of the prohibition allegedly infringed by the contract, and whether this purpose also mandates the denial of contractual enforcement;
(b) other public policy factors that are relevant to the question of whether to deny enforcement; and
(c) whether, in light of (a) and (b), non-enforcement is a proportionate response to the alleged illegality.

Illegality and fault

The consequences of operative contractual illegality vary depending on the degree to which the parties are to blame for the illegality either through their behaviour or their state of knowledge. Where the parties are equally to blame (*in pari delicto*), i.e. where both parties intend to commit or have knowledge of an illegal act, the courts will refuse to implement the contract or to allow damages for its breach. Any losses will lie where they fall.[179] On the other hand where the parties are not equally blameworthy, in principle an innocent party can sue under the contract to recover losses. In *Dowling & Rutter v Abacus Frozen Foods Ltd*[180] illegal workers were supplied by Dowling to work in Abacus' fish processing factory. However, since the company had no knowledge that the workers were illegal the court considered it would be inequitable to deny them payment under their contract with Abacus. Even where the parties are *in pari delicto* a remedy in unjustified enrichment may be allowed if there is 'no moral turpitude' and the court considers it equitable to do so.[181] **2.77**

Illegality and restraint of trade

A restrictive covenant or a covenant in restraint of trade is perhaps the most common type of illegal contract and an early example of the operation of competition law. Any contract, or clause within it, that unreasonably restricts a person's freedom to trade is potentially illegal and therefore unenforceable. Attempts by employers to restrict the future employability of employees will be carefully scrutinised. Commonly employees may be asked to agree not to reveal the employer's trade secrets or not to work for a competitor. As a general rule if a contract or term of a contract restricts a person's economic freedom to an unjustified extent, in light of what is reasonable in a market economy, that term will be illegal and unenforceable. **2.78**

In deciding whether or not a restraint of trade clause is reasonable there are some general principles: **2.79**

- It must be reasonable between the parties at the time the contract is formed and in the public interest.[182]

178 *Patel v Mirza* [2017] AC 467 at [120] per Lord Toulson JSC, cited in *A&E Investments Inc v Levy & McRae Solicitors LLP* 2020 SLT 133 at [84] per Lord Doherty.
179 *Cuthbertson v Lowes* (1870) 8 M 1073.
180 2002 SLT 491.
181 MacQueen, *Contract Law* (2020), para. 7.20.
182 *Nordenfelt v Maxim Nordenfelt* [1894] AC 535.

- It must be necessary to protect a legitimate interest and the question to be asked is whether a lesser restriction would reasonably have protected that interest. Factors such as the duration of the restriction, its geographical extent, the range of people it applies to, the nature of the business and the status of the employee within that business are relevant.[183]

2.80 If a restraint of trade clause is shown to be unreasonable it will be unenforceable. However, where possible, unreasonable elements may be severed from reasonable ones or from the rest of the contract (the 'blue pencil' rule).[184]

CONTRACT TERMS: THE CONTENT OF A CONTRACT

2.81 This section considers the content of the contract and what the parties have agreed to, that is, the contract terms which will determine their respective rights and duties. First, we examine the *express terms* of the contract, namely those which have actually been agreed by the parties. Questions may arise as to the precise scope of those terms, the relationship between the terms of the agreement and the prior negotiations of the parties and whether additional terms may have been incorporated into the agreement (incorporation of terms). Secondly, we will consider the circumstances in which terms not expressly stated are *implied* into a contract by the courts. Many contracts consist of a mixture of express terms, including terms incorporated by reference, and implied terms. This section will also examine the approach of the Scottish courts to the interpretation of contracts. Finally, consideration is given to particular types of clause: good faith and endeavours clauses, suspensive and resolutive conditions and exclusion clauses.

Express terms of the contract

2.82 The terms of a contract can derive from a number of different sources and, since contracts generally do not need to be in writing, some terms may arise from the parties' conduct or have been agreed orally. Even when a contract is in writing the express terms may be found in several different documents. For instance, when negotiating a property sale offers and counter-offers are likely to go back and forth between the parties as they make concessions and demands about the terms and conditions of the sale. The express terms will be in writing between the parties but may be found across multiple documents. There are three principal sources of express contract terms: in a written document, in exchanges between the parties or in an external written source.

Terminology

2.83 It is worth noting that Scots law generally conceives of the provisions of a contract as *contract terms* without substantive distinction.[185] This can be

183 For a recent application, see *Apex Resources v McDougall* [2021] CSOH 40.

184 *Hinton & Higgs (UK) Ltd v Murphy* 1988 SC 353; *Egon Zehdner Ltd v Tillman* [2019] UKSC 32, [2020] AC 154.

185 *Trilogy Power Solutions Group v Hawick Plant Auctions Ltd* [2021] CSOH 27 at [23] per Lady Wolffe. For details, see MacQueen, *Contract Law* (2020), paras 4.14–4.19, 4.55–4.60.

contrasted with English law which classifies terms as *conditions* (material terms which go to the root of the contract) and *warranties* (less fundamental terms), a distinction which is important when identifying remedies for breach of contract.

Express terms in a written document

If there is a written agreement that will be the starting point for determining the rights and obligations of the parties, but it may not be the end point. The safest way to be sure of the content of an agreement is to reduce the terms to writing and the presumption will be that the express terms of the contract are to be found only in the written document(s):[186] **2.84**

> 'Where a document appears (or two or more documents appear) to comprise all the express terms of a contract or unilateral voluntary obligation, it shall be presumed, unless the contrary is proved, that the document does (or the documents do) comprise all the express terms of the contract or unilateral voluntary obligation.'

This presumption can be rebutted if it can be shown that the parties agreed additional terms not found in the written agreement, for instance if they reached agreement orally on specific details.[187]

Where a contract contains an 'entire agreement' or 'entire contract' clause no evidence can be led of additional express terms.[188] An entire agreement clause serves to prevent the other party from relying on anything outwith the written document, for instance prior statements made, the conduct of the parties or any other communication between them.[189] However, unless such a clause clearly excludes an implied term, or the basis on which the term is sought to be implied,[190] it will not prevent the implication of terms into a contract.[191] Nor will such a clause bar the remedy of rectification, prevent consideration of surrounding circumstances for the purposes of interpreting an agreement,[192] or preclude a search for its commercial rationale.[193] Furthermore, an entire agreement clause is not generally effective to exclude liability for **2.85**

186 Contract (Scotland) Act 1997, s. 1(1); see also *Macdonald Estates plc v Regensis (2005) Dunfermline Ltd* 2007 SLT 791 at [126] per Lord Reed.

187 Contract (Scotland) Act 1997, s. 1(2).

188 Contract (Scotland) Act 1997, s. 1(3).

189 *Rock Advertising Ltd v MWB Business Exchange Centres Ltd* [2018] UKSC 24, [2019] AC 119 at [14].

190 *Burnside v Promontoria (Chestnut) Ltd* [2017] CSOH 157 at [55]–[57] per Lord Clark.

191 See the authorities cited and explanations in *Zahid v Duthus Group Investments Ltd* [2018] CSOH 59 at [13] per Lord Doherty; and *NHS Commissioning Board v Vasant* [2019] EWCA Civ 1245, [2020] 1 All ER (Comm) 799 at [51].

192 *Macdonald Estates plc v Regenesis (2005) Dunfermline Ltd* 2007 SLT 791 at [131], [138] and [178] per Lord Reed. But see *Gillespie Investments Ltd v Gillespie* [2010] CSOH 113 at [60] per Lord Hodge.

193 *Gatsby Retail Ltd v Edinburgh Woollen Mill Ltd* [2019] CSOH 49, 2020 SLT 122 at [29] per Lady Wolffe.

pre-contractual misrepresentations;[194] nor, as with any contractual provision, can it operate to exclude liability for fraud.[195]

Negotiations and express contract terms

2.86 We have previously encountered the principle that while the parties are still negotiating their agreement they are entitled to withdraw and are under no legal obligation to enter into the contract. However, negotiations are not completely irrelevant to establishing contract terms. Indeed, in a commercial context there may be many meetings, telephone calls, emails and letters which pass between the parties addressing particular contractual issues. The question may arise as to which statements concerning the negotiations can be regarded as terms of the contract. Some statements made in the course of negotiations have no legal effect; others may amount to representations; some will amount to terms of the contract (such terms are sometimes called warranties for the purpose of distinguishing them from representations).[196]

2.87 Statements which only amount to an invitation to treat, advertising puffs, bargaining positions adopted by the parties and expressions of opinion or future intention – none of the above are deemed to have legal effect unless it is proved they were intended to be part of the contract. Statements made which may have induced or influenced the other party to enter into the contract are known as representations. These may have legal effect in a negative sense in that there may be a right of action if they amount to an inaccurate statement of fact, i.e. they engage the law of misrepresentation. If so the contract may be reduced if *restitutio in integrum* is possible and there will be a remedy in damages if the representation has been made fraudulently or negligently. Statements of fact made in negotiations which become part of the contract are express terms.

2.88 There is little judicial guidance in Scotland on how to decide whether a statement is a representation or a contract term. 'It is difficult to state any test other than the presence or absence of contractual intention as objectively disclosed by the wording of the statement.'[197] The timing of the statement will be relevant and the nearer it is to the point of formation of the contract the more likely it is to be a term.[198]

Incorporation of terms

2.89 Some express terms are not discussed at length or at all in negotiations between parties. Commonly, such terms are *standard terms*, introduced at the point of

194 *Axa Sun Life Services plc v Campbell Martin Ltd* [2011] EWCA Civ 133, [2012] Bus LR 203, in which Stanley Burnton LJ also confirmed, at [49]–[50] (with the agreement of Wilson and Rix LJJ on this point at [76]–[77]), that in appropriate cases, entire agreement clauses may be subject to the Unfair Contract Terms Act 1977.

195 *Boyd & Forrest v Glasgow & South-Western Railway Co* 1915 SC (HL) 20 at 35–36 per Lord Shaw; *H & J M Bennett (Potatoes) Ltd v Secretary of State for Scotland* 1988 SLT 390.

196 It should not be inferred from this terminology that Scots law draws substantive distinctions between different kinds of contract term. See para 2.83.

197 MacQueen, *Contract Law* (2020), para. 4.17.

198 *Malcolm v Cross* (1898) 25 R 1089; *Paul & Co v Glasgow Corp* (1900) 3 F 119.

contract formation. They can be incorporated into the contract by signature, by reference or by a prior course of dealing between the parties.

Incorporation by signature

Contracts do not need to be in writing, nor do they need to be signed in order to be valid. However, where parties have freely put their signatures to a contractual document they are bound by its terms and the express written terms are deemed to have been incorporated by signature. A signature is taken to be 'conclusive'[199] and to indicate agreement regardless of whether the parties have taken the time to read the terms and conditions carefully. **2.90**

Incorporation by reference

Sometimes a contract may refer to an external document which contains additional terms in an attempt to incorporate those terms by reference. Many of these cases concern tickets in various forms. For instance, the purchaser of a train ticket in Scotland will find on the reverse of the ticket that it is 'issued subject to the National Rail Conditions of Carriage', which are available either on the National Rail website or from staffed stations. Few are likely to make any effort to find those conditions, far less read them, and yet a contract of carriage with the rail company is subject to those terms. The courts apply a three-stage test to determine whether or not such terms have been effectively incorporated into a contract: **2.91**

(a) *Is the document itself contractual in nature?* Tickets are generally deemed to have contractual effect, particularly travel tickets and tickets of deposit, but in some situations they merely function as a receipt showing that the customer has paid.[200] The function of the document will be relevant, hence invoices, receipts and delivery notes do not generally have contractual effect.
(b) *Are the terms and conditions known to the parties prior to formation of the contract?* Consistent with the principle that consent is required, terms contained in an external source must be known to the parties prior to formation of the contract. Notices or documents containing contract terms must therefore be displayed in such a way that they can be read and understood when the contract is entered into. For instance, a notice in a car park excluding liability for any damage caused must be displayed prior to taking a ticket from an automatic machine and entering the car park.[201] Similarly, online transactions usually require an act of consent to indicate acceptance of the seller's terms and conditions prior to payment.
(c) *Has sufficient notice been given?* The party seeking to incorporate terms by reference must establish that the other party has reasonably sufficient notice of those terms. This depends on all the circumstances, including the nature of the business and the position of the parties to the transaction.[202]

199 *McCutcheon v MacBrayne* 1964 SC (HL) 28 at 40 per Lord Devlin.
200 *Taylor v Glasgow Corporation* 1952 SC 400.
201 *Thornton v Shoe Lane Parking Ltd* [1971] 2 QB 163.
202 *United Central Bakeries Ltd v Spooner Industries Ltd* [2013] CSOH 150 at [57] per Lord Hodge.

Where contract terms are particularly unusual or onerous, they must be drawn to the other party's attention:[203]

> 'The question really is whether a particular condition is of such an unusual nature that it should specifically be drawn to the attention of the other party rather than being left simply as part of a large collection of other terms and conditions which are of a fairly standard nature.'

Clauses excluding liability or imposing a personal cautionary obligation are sufficiently onerous to warrant attention being drawn to them in a specific way.[204]

Incorporation by a prior course of dealings

2.92 The final means of incorporation noted here is incorporation by a prior course of dealings between the parties. For a term to be successfully incorporated by this method there must be a consistent pattern of transactions on the basis of the term, sufficient either to establish actual knowledge of it, or to lead all parties reasonably to believe that the term has been incorporated into the parties' instant contract.[205] Whether a given course of dealings suffices depends on the facts of the case.[206] It is relevant that terms of a particular or similar type to those sought to be incorporated are known to be used in a given commercial sector.[207]

Implied terms

2.93 Terms not expressly included in a contract are called implied terms, so called because they are *deemed* to be part of that contract. These are of two general kinds. First, terms implied in law apply to all contracts in more or less general fashion, often those of a particular type (for instance, sale or employment). Secondly, terms implied in fact are imposed into individual contracts between specific parties where the express terms are silent on a particular question. In general, commercial parties will not wish to rely on implied terms, aiming for their contracts expressly to deal with all matters of importance to them.

2.94 Whichever type of implied term is under consideration the common intention of the parties is a priority: terms implied in law are included *unless* the intentions of the parties is otherwise indicated in the contract; terms implied in fact will only be implied if the court deems it would have been the intention of reasonable parties to agree to those terms had they considered them.

203 *Montgomery Litho Ltd v Maxwell* 2000 SC 56 at 59 per Lord Sutherland.

204 *Hood v Anchor Line (Henderson Bros) Ltd* 1918 SC (HL) 143.

205 *McCutcheon v MacBrayne* 1964 SC (HL) 28; *Bank of Ireland (UK) plc v Knight Frank LLP* [2015] CSOH 157 at [40]–[46] per Lord Woolman, *obiter*.

206 Compare *Hollier v Rambler Motors (AMC) Ltd* [1972] 2 QB 71 with *Henry Kendall & Sons v William Lillico & Sons Ltd* [1969] 2 AC 31.

207 See *British Crane Hire Corporation Ltd v Ipswich Plant Hire Ltd* [1975] QB 303, though this was not a course of dealing case.

Terms implied in law

2.95 Terms can be implied into contracts by statute. The most common example is the Sale of Goods Act 1979, which contains a number of implied terms, for instance that goods sold must be of satisfactory quality.[208] Terms can also be implied at common law, as where a contract for sale is silent as to the time for performance, and an obligation to perform within a reasonable time is implied;[209] or where mutual obligations of trust and confidence are implied into a contract of employment.[210] Terms may also be implied from custom and trade practice within a particular commercial sector,[211] but this is a relatively rare occurrence.[212]

Terms implied in fact

2.96 The court will only imply a term in fact if it would be reasonable to do so in a specific sense. The analysis is objective, and depends on what would have been the intentions of reasonable persons in the position of the parties to a particular contract at the time it was made.[213] If asked, and knowing the provisions of the contract and the surrounding circumstances, would they have considered that the term sought to be implied is necessary to give the agreement business efficacy, or legal and practical coherence; or that its inclusion is so obvious that it goes without saying?[214]

2.97 Any implied term must be capable of clear expression. It must also be consistent with the express terms of the parties' contract.[215] Furthermore, whilst an implied term must be fair,[216] this is insufficient on its own: the court will not rewrite a contract in a way it considers reasonable or preferable.[217]

Interpretation of contracts

2.98 One of the most important areas of commercial contract law, contractual interpretation is relevant to the drafting and performance of transactions and the disputes to which they give rise.

2.99 The general approach to contractual interpretation is established by many Supreme Court and Inner House decisions.[218] The task is objectively to deter-

208 Sale of Goods Act 1979, s. 14(2).
209 *Burnside v Promontoria (Chestnut) Ltd* [2017] CSOH 157.
210 *Macari v Celtic Football & Athletic Co Ltd* 1999 SC 628.
211 *William Morton & Co v Muir Bros & Co* 1907 SC 1211.
212 See further MacQueen, *Contract Law* (2020), paras 4.45–4.47.
213 *J & H Ritchie Ltd v Lloyd Ltd* [2007] UKHL 9, 2007 SC (HL) 89 at [14]–[19] and [37].
214 *Granton Central Developments Ltd v Len Lothian Ltd* [2021] SAC (Civ) 7, 2021 SLT (Sh Ct) 101 at [22]; *Tarmac Trading Ltd v Network Rail Infrastructure Ltd* [2018] CSOH 33 at [61], [68]–[70], and the authorities cited, particularly *Marks & Spencer plc v BNP Paribas Securities Services Trust Co (Jersey) Ltd* [2015] UKSC 72, [2016] AC 742.
215 *Unicorn Tower Ltd v HSBC Bank plc* [2018] CSOH 30 at [71] per Lady Wolffe.
216 See *Mayfly Containers Ltd (In Liquidation) v Monument Containers Ltd* [2018] CSOH 115, 2019 SCLR 438 at [32].
217 *Ali v Petroleum Company of Trinidad and Tobago* [2017] UKPC 2, [2017] ICR 531 at [7].
218 See *Scottishpower Energy Retail Ltd v Equorium Property Company Ltd* [2021] CSOH 98 at [20]; *Crimond Estates Ltd v Mile End Developments Ltd* [2021] CSIH 60 at [18].

mine the meaning of the words used by the parties by reference to how their intentions would be understood by a reasonable person with the background knowledge reasonably available to the parties at the time the contract was made. A contract term is considered in its documentary and wider factual, legal and commercial context in light of its ordinary meaning; other relevant contract terms; its purpose(s) and the purpose(s) of the whole contract; the facts and circumstances known or assumed by the parties at the time of the contract; and commercial common sense. Where a term has more than one meaning, a commercially sensible interpretation may be preferred. The weight placed on text or wider context depends on matters such as the nature, formality, and coherence of the contract. Suggested interpretations are checked against the contract itself and indications appearing from the wider context. It is also to be remembered, for example, that some provisions may be the product of failures to agree, or negotiating compromises: contractual interpretation is not a means to protect parties against bad bargains or to penalise astuteness.

2.100 The Inner House favours objective, contextual, and purposive contractual interpretation, repeatedly emphasising these very general matters of technique, along with recourse to commercial common sense.[219] Objectivity entails a search for the intention attributed to all parties to a contract. Considering the meaning of words in context is consistent with how we generally understand language and filter out ambiguity. Purposive interpretation is said to entail prioritising the fundamental objectives of reasonable persons in the parties' position at the time of the contract over 'niceties of wording' and poor drafting.[220]

2.101 Perhaps more controversial is the Inner House's strong endorsement of commercial common sense as an aid to contractual interpretation. It may assist with vague contract terms where what is commercially sensible is clear.[221] However, the notion plainly has its limitations. Most obviously, and apart from the fact that it may add nothing of significance to careful textual analysis,[222] what is commercially sensible is often not apparent;[223] and different parties can plausibly argue that their preferred interpretation is the more businesslike.[224]

2.102 It should be noted that there are limits to the wide range[225] of background and context admissible in aid of interpretation. Statements made in pre-contractual negotiations are irrelevant.[226] So, more generally, is all evidence

219 See lengthy discussion by Lord Drummond Young in *Ashtead Plant Hire Co Ltd v Granton Central Developments Ltd* [2020] CSIH 2, 2020 SC 244. Also *British Overseas Bank Nominees Ltd v Stewart Milne Group Ltd* [2019] CSIH 47, 2020 SC 24; *Ardmair Bay Holdings Ltd v Craig* [2020] CSIH 21, 2020 SLT 549.

220 In so far as the objectives can be determined, see *Somerville v McGuire* [2020] CSOH 70 at [46]–[49].

221 See *Coal Pension Properties Ltd v Technip UK Ltd* [2021] CSOH 39, 2021 SLT 1224.

222 As in *Buchan Biogas Ltd v BSG Civil Engineering Ltd* [2020] CSOH 42 at [28].

223 As noted in *Wood v Capita Insurance Services Ltd* [2017] UKSC 24, [2017] AC 1173 at [28].

224 As in *Scottishpower Energy Retail Ltd v Equorium Property Co Ltd* [2021] CSOH 98 at [28].

225 See especially *Ashtead Plant Hire Co Ltd v Granton Central Developments Ltd* [2020] CSIH 2, 2020 SC 244 at [10] and [19]–[21].

226 *Somerville v McGuire* [2020] CSOH 70 at [42]–[45].

of the parties' subjective intention or understanding.[227] There is also a well settled general rule that a contract cannot be interpreted by reference to the parties' post-contract conduct.[228]

Particular contract terms

Three particular types of contract terms are considered in more detail below, namely good faith and endeavours clauses, suspensive and resolutive conditions and exclusion clauses. **2.103**

Good faith and endeavours clauses

Since the decision in *Smith v Bank of Scotland*[229] lawyers in Scotland have become increasingly familiar with the idea of good faith and its role in domestic legislation[230] as well as in international instruments.[231] But it remains uncertain whether Scots law recognises a general principle of good faith,[232] and there is little Scottish authority or academic writing on what it means to deal in good faith.[233] Based on what sources exist, a similar approach to that adopted in the more numerous English authorities may emerge. **2.104**

The content and breadth of obligations of good faith depend on their context and true construction.[234] Generally, they entail that parties act honestly and openly towards each other; refrain from conduct which reasonable people would regard as commercially unacceptable; adhere to their common purposes as evidenced by their agreement and refrain from undermining their bargain; not use their powers for ulterior purposes; and have regard to their counterparties' interests, even though they need not subordinate their own interests to them.[235] Although contractual duties of good faith have been little litigated in Scotland it is not uncommon for parties to commercial contracts expressly to agree to act in good faith or equivalent terms.[236] There is no reason to believe that Scottish courts would not enforce sufficiently certain contractual provisions[237] requiring, for example, good faith performance, dispute resolution or **2.105**

227 *Scot Roads Partnership Project Ltd v The Scottish Ministers* [2019] CSOH 113 at [38] and [41].

228 *SI 2016 Ltd v AMA (New Town) Ltd* [2019] CSOH 99 at [50].

229 *Smith v Bank of Scotland* 1997 SC (HL) 111 at 121.

230 For instance, the Commercial Agents (Council Directive) Regulations 1993 (SI 1993/3053).

231 Draft Common Frame of Reference, art. III–1:103.

232 *Unicorn Tower Ltd v HSBC Bank plc* [2018] CSOH 30 at [72]; cf *Van Ourde UK Ltd* (n 12) at [19].

233 But see *EDI Central Ltd v National Car Parks Ltd* [2010] CSOH 141, 2011 SLT 75 at [23] per Lord Glennie; affd without reference to this point [2012] CSIH 6, 2012 SLT 421; H L MacQueen and S O'Byrne, 'The principle of good faith in contractual performance: a Scottish-Canadian comparison' (2019) 23 Edin LR 301.

234 *Mid Essex Hospital Services NHS Trust v Compass Group UK and Ireland* [2013] EWCA Civ 200, [2013] BLR 265.

235 *Al Nehayan v Kent* [2018] EWHC 333 (Comm), [2018] 1 CLC 216 at [175]; *Faulkner v Vollin Hollings Ltd* [2021] EWHC 787 (Ch) at [365]–[368] (decision under appeal).

236 See, e.g. *J H & W Lamont of Heathfield Farm v Chattisham Ltd* [2018] CSIH 33, 2018 SC 440 at [3] and [45].

237 *Beaghmor Property Ltd v Station Properties Ltd* [2009] CSOH 133 at [22] per Lord Hodge.

negotiation,[238] whilst avoiding any extension of such provisions beyond their stated terms.[239]

2.106 If commercial parties wish good faith to form part of the contractual backdrop to their working relationships, it is preferable for them expressly to provide for this,[240] addressing both the nature and scope of any relevant obligation. It does, however, also seem clear that parties might persuade a Scottish court that a sufficiently certain[241] obligation of good faith should be *implied* into a commercial contract. Obligations of good faith will not be implied where inconsistent with the express terms of the contract,[242] or the other incidents of the parties' relationship.[243] They are 'unlikely to arise by way of necessary implication in a contract between . . . sophisticated commercial parties negotiating at arms' length'.[244] But they may be implied on occasion if the stringent test for the implication of terms in fact is satisfied,[245] including to bridle the exercise of expressly agreed contractual discretions.[246]

2.107 Whilst the Scottish courts have given little guidance on duties of good faith in contracts, they have considered the content and effect of what are known as endeavours clauses. These are commonly employed where absolute obligations are considered too onerous. For example, what must be done to achieve an objective may be difficult to agree upon, incapable of precise definition, or outwith the control of the parties. Endeavours clauses oblige parties to *attempt* to bring about a specified result.[247] The courts will enforce such clauses, provided the object of the endeavours is sufficiently certain and there exist sufficient, generally objective, criteria by which to judge a party's efforts.[248] In *Mactaggart & Mickel Homes Ltd v Hunter*[249] the contract provided that one of

238 For English cases see *Health & Case Management Ltd v The Physiotherapy Network Ltd* [2018] EWHC 869 (QB) (performance); *Emirates Trading Agency LLC v Prime Mineral Exports Private Ltd* [2014] EWHC 2104 (Comm), [2015] 1 WLR 1145 (dispute resolution); *Knatchbull-Hugessen v SISU Capital Ltd* [2014] EWHC 1194 (QB) (negotiation, but refusing to imply an obligation beyond that expressly agreed).

239 *Mid Essex Hospital Services NHS Trust v Compass Group UK and Ireland* [2013] EWCA Civ 200, [2013] BLR 265; *UTB LLC v Sheffield United Ltd* [2019] EWHC 2322 (Ch) at [207] and [213].

240 *Chelsfield Advisers LLP v Qatari Diar Real Estate Investment Co* [2015] EWHC 1322 (Ch) at [80].

241 *Russell v Cartwright* [2020] EWHC 41 (Ch) at [90].

242 *Unicorn Tower Ltd v HSBC Bank plc* [2018] CSOH 30 at [70]–[71] per Lady Wolffe.

243 *UTB LLC v Sheffield United Ltd* [2019] EWHC 2322 (Ch) especially at [209]–[209], [212]–[213].

244 *Greenclose Ltd v National Westminster Bank plc* [2014] EWHC 1156 (Ch), [2014] 1 CLC 562 at [150].

245 *Unicorn Tower Ltd v HSBC Bank plc* [2018] CSOH 30 at [71] per Lady Wolffe; *Cathay Pacific Airways Ltd v Lufthansa Technik AG* [2020] EWHC 1789 (Ch) at [212]–[217] and [218](c)–(f).

246 As in *Equitas Insurance Ltd v Municipal Mutual Insurance Ltd* [2019] EWCA Civ 718, [2020] QB 418 at [148]–[162]; compare *TAQA Bratani Ltd v Rockrose UKCS8 LLC* [2020] EWHC 58 (Comm).

247 See, e.g. the provision referred to and construed in *David MacBrayne Ltd v Atos IT Services (UK) Ltd* [2018] CSOH 32 at [6] and [44].

248 For discussion, see *R & D Construction Group Ltd v Hallam Land Management Ltd* [2009] CSOH 128; affd [2010] CSIH 96, 2011 SC 286; *Astor Management AG v Atalaya Mining plc* [2017] EWHC 425 (Comm), [2018] 1 All ER (Comm) 547 at [62]–[72]; affd without reference to this point [2018] EWCA Civ 2407.

249 [2010] CSOH 130.

the parties should 'use reasonable endeavours' to obtain planning permission for a development. Lord Hodge suggested that there was a hierarchy in the standard of behaviour expected: a requirement to use 'reasonable endeavours' is less onerous than requiring 'all reasonable endeavours' (which raises the question whether there were any reasonable steps that could have been taken but were not), which in turn is less onerous than the even higher standard of 'best endeavours', which 'requires a party to take all the reasonable courses he can'. [250] However, such obligations do not mean that a party must act completely altruistically or disregard their own commercial interests in the process. Lord Glennie in *EDI Central Ltd v National Car Parks Ltd*[251] aligned with the prevailing international view that there is ordinarily no practical difference between an 'all reasonable' or a 'best' endeavours obligation,[252] a distinction that was 'likely to be metaphysical rather than practical'.[253] A 'prudent' party under such an obligation must consider their own interests; need not continue with endeavours once it becomes clear they are unlikely to be successful; and if difficulties are encountered should inform the other party.[254] The Inner House has confirmed that there is a difference between 'reasonable' and 'all reasonable' endeavours, and that it would be a defence to an action for breach of an endeavours clause to show that taking particular steps would not have been successful in achieving the desired result.[255]

Suspensive and resolutive conditions

Obligations may be contingent, that is, their existence may be conditional on some future event happening or not happening. It is possible for a condition to delay the contract coming into being, for instance a stipulation that the parties' agreement must be embodied in a written document and signed by both.[256] This should be distinguished from the situation where the contract exists but *performance* of the parties' obligations is conditional on some other event. In Scots law there are two principal types of condition: suspensive and resolutive. The former suspends performance of an obligation. The latter resolves (or dissolves) it.[257] **2.108**

A suspensive condition (sometimes called a condition precedent) is the most common type of condition where the parties agree to delay performance until a future event has happened or not happened. For instance, A and B are respectively the buyer and seller of property that A plans to develop into **2.109**

250 [2010] CSOH 130 at [63].
251 [2010] CSOH 141, 2011 SLT 75. This case concerned an obligation to 'use all reasonable endeavours', linked to an obligation to act in good faith.
252 *EDI Central Ltd v National Car Parks Ltd* [2010] CSOH 141 at [20]; approved subject to details on this point with several other authorities in *KS Energy Services Ltd v BR Energy (M) Sdn Bhd* [2014] SGCA 16.
253 [2010] CSOH 141 at [20].
254 [2010] CSOH 141 at [20]–[21].
255 *EDI Central Ltd v National Car Parks Ltd* [2012] CSIH 6, 2012 SLT 421.
256 Such a term may be contained in a preliminary agreement, such as 'heads of terms', used to record the outcome of negotiations for the sale of a business.
257 For a fuller discussion see J Thomson, 'Suspensive and resolutive conditions in the Scots law of contract' in A J Gamble (ed), *Obligations in Context: Essays in honour of Professor D M Walker* (Edinburgh: W. Green, 1990).

a block of flats. A and B may have agreed all of the essential terms of the missives but they may also agree that the sale will only go ahead if planning permission for the block of flats is granted by the local authority. The contract between A and B exists but the respective obligations to transfer title to the property and to pay the price will not be triggered unless the condition is fulfilled or 'purified'. If planning permission is not granted the contract will effectively come to an end because performance is unenforceable. If no date is specified, performance cannot be suspended indefinitely and the condition must be fulfilled within a reasonable time.

2.110 By contrast, a resolutive condition is one which, when fulfilled, brings an obligation to an end. The condition is often a time period or date. This is a relatively uncommon term but, for instance, A and B entered into a subletting agreement that was conditional on obtaining the head landlord's consent by a certain date otherwise either could resile from the contract. However, the letter of consent was not obtained until eight days after the date stipulated. Lord Sutherland held that this was a resolutive condition and failure to obtain consent by that date brought the contract to an end.[258]

2.111 There is another subdivision in that suspensive and resolutive conditions can be either potestative or casual conditions: a potestative condition is one which is within the power of one or both parties to fulfil; by contrast, a casual condition is not within the power of the parties, but fulfilment depends on a third party or on chance. If one party has it within its power to fulfil the condition, it must not to anything to prevent it being fulfilled. Otherwise, on grounds of fairness, the condition will be held to be fulfilled.[259] The character of particular conditions, and the mix of obligations present in more detailed agreements, depend on their true construction but it plainly makes good business sense as well as good legal sense for the parties to act reasonably in fulfilling conditions that are within their power to fulfil unless they are clearly optional.

Exclusion clauses

2.112 Finally, in addressing the terms of a contract consideration must be given to the way in which the law exercises control over exclusion clauses, i.e. clauses designed to avoid (an exclusion clause proper) or reduce (a limitation clause) liability. Such clauses are commonly used in commercial contracts to allocate risks, including those arising from parties' own fault or negligence. This practice may be commercially sensible and is not necessarily unfair. The courts are now more accepting of exclusion clauses, at least in commercial contracts between parties of broadly equal bargaining power.[260] However, a number of legal controls exist to subject them to further scrutiny. First, the rules of incorporation of terms still determine whether an exclusion of liability has been effectively incorporated into the contract.[261] Secondly, the Unfair Contract Terms Act 1977 (the UCTA) places statutory controls on exclusion clauses.

258 *Ford Sellar Morris Properties plc v E W Hutchison Ltd (No. 4)* 1990 SC 34 at 37.
259 Bell, *Principles*, § 50; *Smith v Stuart* 2010 SCLR 131, affd 2010 SC 490.
260 *Interactive E-Solutions JLT v O3b Africa Ltd* [2018] EWCA Civ 62 at [14].
261 See paras 2.89–2.92 above.

Interpretation of exclusion clauses

There is a considerable body of authority on the interpretation of exclusion clauses.[262] The cases suggest, for example, that liability for negligence is more difficult to exclude than liability for mere breach of contract;[263] and that a limitation of liability is interpreted less strictly than a total exclusion of liability.[264] **2.113**

It remains a rule of law that a party can never exclude liability for their own fraud.[265] However, the courts' lesser hostility to exemption clauses, the availability of statutory controls, and the establishment of the modern general approach to contractual interpretation, mean that the future of many principles specific to the construction of exclusion clauses is now a matter for debate.[266] Opinions divide on whether those principles still serve a useful purpose.[267] However, while it may be the case that the *contra proferentem* rule of interpretation, by which the court will resolve any ambiguity against the interests of the party attempting to rely on the clause, is less significant in modern commercial cases than in older decisions, it will apply in 'a case of genuine ambiguity or real doubt as to the meaning of the words used'.[268] **2.114**

The Unfair Contract Terms Act 1977

The intervention of Parliament to control contract terms runs contrary to the principle of freedom of contract, and it does so for policy reasons. The Unfair Contract Terms Act 1977 is a UK-wide statute, Part II of which, along with Sch. 2, applies to Scotland. As its name suggests, there was governmental concern at the potential for abuse of contract terms, particularly where there is a risk of unfairness in the terms of contracts and where contracts are drawn up in advance on the basis of standard terms. However, in another sense the name is misleading in that UCTA does not regulate 'unfair' contract terms generally, only those attempting to avoid liability, i.e. exclusion clauses. **2.115**

The scope of UCTA

UCTA applies to clauses inserted by businesses (widely defined to include companies, firms, professions, sole traders, government departments, local and public authorities)[269] into contracts with another business.[270] Its scope is wide in that most types of contract (and non-contractual notices[271]) are **2.116**

262 See McBryde, *Contract* (2007), paras 8–60–8–97.
263 *Boomsma v Clark & Rose Ltd* 1983 SLT (Sh Ct) 67.
264 *Bovis Construction (Scotland) Ltd v Whatlings Construction Ltd* 1995 SC (HL) 19.
265 *HIH Casualty and General Insurance Ltd v Chase Manhattan Bank* [2003] UKHL 6, [2003] 1 All ER (Comm) 349, leaving open whether exclusion of liability for one's agent's fraud is possible.
266 McBryde, *Contract* (2007), para. 8–66.
267 See Mr Justice Foxton, 'The status of the special rules of construction of exemption clauses in commercial contracts' [2021] JBL 205.
268 *Burnett v International Insurance Co of Hanover Ltd* [2021] UKSC 12, 2021 SC (UKSC) 1 at [29] per Lord Hamblen.
269 UCTA, s. 25(1).
270 Related protection for consumers is now provided for by the Consumer Rights Act 2015, see Part 2 on unfair contract terms.
271 Also called disclaimers of liability. See UCTA, ss. 16(1)–(1A) and (3), 24(2A)–(4), and

included except for insurance contracts, contracts relating to the creation or transfer of a real right in land and contracts setting up or dissolving corporate entities such as companies and partnerships.[272]

Statutory controls

2.117 Two different control mechanisms are used in UCTA depending on what type of liability the business is attempting to exclude in a given contract clause: the first declares the clause to be void; the second subjects it to a fair and reasonable test. The broadest provision of UCTA, s. 16, applies to any clause, negotiated or not. It concerns attempts to exclude liability for any breach of duty[273] (which would include a duty arising from contract or from delict, including liability for negligence) 'arising in the course of a business' or 'from the occupation of business premises'.[274] Section 16(1)(a) states that clauses that attempt to exclude or limit liability for personal injury[275] or death will always be void. Section 16(1)(b) states that attempts to exclude or restrict liability for any other loss or damage will be effective only if they are fair and reasonable.

Standard form contracts

2.118 Section 17 concerns exemptions in standard form contracts. It protects one party to a contract, called 'the customer', on whom the 'written standard terms of business of the other party to the contract' are imposed,[276] by subjecting to the fair and reasonable test any attempt to exclude liability for breach of contract (either non-performance or performance that was substantially different from what could reasonably have been expected).[277] To come within the scope of s. 17 the relevant terms must be in a pro forma document and the same terms must invariably be imposed on customers.[278]

The fair and reasonable test

2.119 The party attempting to rely on an exclusion clause must establish that the test is satisfied.[279] In determining whether an exclusion clause is a fair and reasonable one to incorporate into a contract, 'regard shall be had only to the

25(1), defining a notice to include 'an announcement, whether or not in writing, and any other communication or pretended communication'.

272 UCTA, s. 15.

273 UCTA, s. 25(1)(a)–(c); s. 25(2): the act or omission giving rise to a relevant breach of duty may be inadvertent or intentional, and the liability arising from it may be direct or vicarious.

274 UCTA, s. 16(1).

275 Defined to include 'any disease and any impairment of physical or mental condition': UCTA, s. 25(1).

276 UCTA, s. 17(2).

277 UCTA, s. 17(1)(a)–(b).

278 *Border Harvesters Ltd v Edwards Engineering (Perth) Ltd* 1985 SLT 128; *Langstane Housing Association Ltd v Riverside Construction (Aberdeen) Ltd* [2009] CSOH 52, 2009 SCLR 639 at [48]. For discussion of the scope of the equivalent English provision (UCTA, s. 3), see *African Export-Import Bank v Shebah Exploration & Production Company Ltd* [2017] EWCA Civ 845, [2018] 1 WLR 487.

279 UCTA, s. 24(4).

circumstances which were, or ought reasonably to have been, known to or in the contemplation of the parties to the contract at the time the contract was made'.[280] Some guidance is given on what is to be regarded as 'fair and reasonable' both in UCTA and in subsequent case law.[281] The following factors are relevant:

(a) the parties' knowledge when the contract was concluded of, e.g. the purported exemption, and the risk and extent of any potential loss;
(b) equality of bargaining power: the extent to which the parties are on an equal footing in matters such as commercial experience, and have negotiated the terms of the agreement;
(c) availability of goods and services elsewhere, the extent to which there is freedom of contract in the particular market, and whether a given exemption is in common use;
(d) the complexity or bespoke nature of the tasks to be performed;
(e) the practical consequences of not allowing the exclusion, e.g. the fact that risk-bearing may determine other aspects of the parties' transaction, such as the price one party demands or is willing to pay; and
(f) insurance implications: which party can most easily insure itself against a purportedly exempted liability and what is the state of the parties' knowledge in this regard?

UCTA provides additional factors to be taken into account when assessing whether a contract term which restricts liability to a specified sum of money is fair and reasonable:[282] **2.120**

(a) the resources available to the party seeking to rely on the limitation clause; and
(b) how far it was open to that party to obtain insurance cover.

Breach of implied terms and UCTA, Sch. 2

Special provision is made in ss. 20 and 21 for any exclusion of liability for breach of implied terms in contracts of sale or hire purchase. Any attempt to exclude the obligation to pass good title will be void. Attempts to exclude other implied terms are subject to a fair and reasonable test. The range of factors to be considered in this context is set out in Sch. 2: **2.121**

(a) the parties' relative bargaining strength;
(b) whether a party received an inducement to agree to an exemption, or had an opportunity to avoid it by transacting similarly with others;[283]
(c) whether a party knew or ought to have known of the existence and extent of the exemption;

280 UCTA, s. 24(1).
281 UCTA, s. 24 and *Smith v Eric S Bush* [1990] 1 AC 831. See also discussion in *Watford Electronics Ltd v Sanderson CFL Ltd* [2001] EWCA Civ 317, [2001] 1 All ER (Comm) 696; *Rohlig UK Ltd v Rock Unique Ltd* [2011] EWCA Civ 18, [2011] 2 All ER (Comm) 1161.
282 UCTA, s. 24(3). The factors may be considered when assessing a clause drafted to exclude liability for indirect or consequential loss altogether: *Watford Electronics Ltd v Sanderson CFL Ltd* [2001] EWCA Civ 317, [2001] 1 All ER (Comm) 696 at [53], remarking on the equivalent English provision (UCTA, s. 11(4)).
283 Considered in *Denholm Fishselling Ltd v Anderson* 1991 SLT (Sh Ct) 24.

(d) where an exemption excludes or restricts a liability if some condition is not complied with, whether it was reasonable at the time of the contract to expect that compliance with that condition would be practicable; and
(e) whether the goods were specially made or adapted for the customer.

2.122 Although the legislation provides different factors for assessing what is fair and reasonable in different contexts, the above factors 'are frequently regarded as being of general application'.[284]

BREACH OF CONTRACT

2.123 The concept of breach of contract is fundamental to contract law and, along with disputes as to interpretation, is the most common reason why contract cases end up in court. The law of breach of contract provides a default set of rules setting out what constitutes a breach and which remedies are available when things go wrong. However, before examining the rules of breach it should be pointed out that the vast majority of contracts are either performed to the satisfaction of the parties or, if things do go wrong, they attempt to find a solution through negotiation or other dispute resolution processes such as arbitration or mediation. Remedies for breach are a last resort, particularly if the parties are in a long-term commercial relationship, because it is highly likely that litigation will mark the end of that relationship, not to mention the considerable time and cost involved for both sides.

2.124 There are various ways in which the parties may fail to perform their obligations under a contract. Company A enters into a contract with Company B to install a new computer system, having agreed the cost and the date for installation to begin. If B fails to appear on the agreed date it will be a breach of contract. If B gives advance notice that some of the components have not arrived and this would result in a delay, it is an anticipatory breach of contract. If B completes the installation but no one in the company can access the company's server it amounts to defective performance. If only half of the staff can access the server it amounts to a partial failure to perform. All of these scenarios constitute a breach of contract and in Scots law the type of breach is generally irrelevant as regards the remedies available for a breach of contract, although there is an important distinction between breaches that are *material* and those that are not. It is, however, important that the counterparty's conduct can be said to be in conflict with the terms of the contract before it can be said that a breach has occurred: odious or disreputable conduct which cannot be said to transgress a contract term will not found a remedy for breach.[285]

2.125 Scots law, like English law, also distinguishes between what are known as self-help remedies, which allow the innocent party to take action to defend their position, and judicial remedies that require the intervention of the courts.

284 *Shepherd Homes Ltd v Encia Remediation Ltd* [2007] EWHC 70 (TCC), (2007) 110 Con LR 90 at [90].

285 Hence the inclusion of 'good morals', 'morality', 'equality and diversity', 'modern slavery' and other similar clauses in contracts in an attempt to make such behaviour contractually relevant so as to give rise to a remedial response.

Self-help remedies for breach of contract

The mutuality principle

Underpinning the so-called self-help remedies is the idea that in most contracts there is an element of reciprocity in the obligations that the parties undertake towards each other.[286] Those obligations are often interdependent in that the performance of one party is dependent on the performance of the other. This is referred to as the mutuality principle, which has two effects in relation to a breach of contract: where obligations are interdependent if one party (the breaching party) does not perform their obligations they cannot enforce performance by the innocent party; and, as a logical counterpart, the innocent party can withhold performance and cannot be compelled to perform, with the result that the breaching party may not be entitled to a remedy. In other words, mutuality gives the innocent party a shield to suspend performance of their end of the bargain in circumstances which, absent that shield, would themselves constitute a breach of contract. In these terms, the concept clearly underlies the remedy of retention, discussed below.[287] Importantly, mutuality does not depend on the reciprocal obligations of each party being contained within the one physical contract: the Supreme Court has held that 'the unity of the overall transaction should be respected'.[288] Therefore, an obligation contained in Agreement A may be held to be the counterpart of an obligation in Agreement B, so long as it reasonably can be said that Agreements A and B form part of a single, overarching transaction. **2.126**

The materiality principle

Another key concept for the self-help remedies is that of materiality. Although its role in relation to the remedy of retention is more contestable,[289] it is central to the remedy of rescission. There is no definitive statement of what constitutes a material breach of contract but it is sometimes described as going to the root or being of the essence of the contract. It is open to the parties to agree that certain terms are fundamental to the contract and any breach thereof will be treated as a material breach entitling the innocent party to rescind. As with mutuality, materiality, where engaged, provides the innocent party a shield that justifies taking remedial action that would otherwise be contrary to the contract. This makes clear the danger for the innocent party. If they rescind in response to what they believe to be a material breach, which later is held not to be so, their action will in themselves amount to a breach of contract. **2.127**

In this regard, it must be borne in mind that, in certain circumstances, it will not be clear as to whether or not a particular breach has crossed the materiality threshold. Whether or not late performance or defective performance amounts to a material breach is a question of facts and circumstances, unless the parties **2.128**

286 On the fundamental role played by mutuality, see *McNeill v Aberdeen City Council (No. 2)* 2014 SC 355 at [20] per Lord Drummond Young.

287 Its role in the remedy of rescission is less clear: see MacQueen, *Contract Law* (2020), para. 6.13.

288 *Inveresk plc v Tullis Russell Papermakers Ltd* 2010 SC (UKSC) 106 at [42] per Lord Hope.

289 See MacQueen, *Contract Law* (2020), paras 6.12–6.13.

have so stipulated. The question is whether the consequences of such a breach are so severe that the contract has to come to an end. In most cases of late or defective performance it will be more practical to allow the party in breach an opportunity to cure the problem rather than bring the contract to an end. In relation to payment the party in breach must be given a reasonable time to pay before it can be treated as a material breach justifying rescission.[290]

Retention

2.129 Retention allows the innocent party to withhold their reciprocal performance in the event of a breach and is the most obvious application of the mutuality principle: mutuality serves as a shield that justifies the innocent party's reciprocal non-performance. Before retention can be applied it must be shown that the obligations undertaken are genuinely counterparts, which may be presumed unless there is evidence to the contrary.[291] An obvious example is withholding payment if work has not been carried out as agreed in order to persuade the tradesman to rectify the problem. Payment can only be retained for the work it relates to, i.e. the obligations must be direct counterparts. So where payments under a contract are made in instalments, an instalment can be withheld only for the breach to which it corresponds but not for obligations performed before or after the breach.[292] In an employment context the manager of Celtic football club was unable to suspend his obligation to be resident in Glasgow when he argued that it was in response to his employer's breach of the obligation of 'mutual trust and confidence' because his obligation was not a direct counterpart of his employer's obligation.[293]

2.130 Retention of performance by the innocent party does not bring the contract to an end, rather it is designed to rescue the contract by persuading the counterparty to perform their side of the bargain. The intention is to allow the innocent party to 'retain' their performance as security in order to incentivise the defaulting party to effect performance. Where retention is permissible the innocent party is not treated as being in breach of contract despite failure to perform. However, as soon as the counterparty makes good on their dereliction and performs their obligations, the once-innocent party will lose their mutuality shield, so any purported attempt to retain performance after that point will itself be a breach of contract.

Rescission

2.131 Rescission is where the innocent party brings the contract to an end or 'rescinds'. It is the functional equivalent to the English remedy of termination. Rescission is only available in response to a material breach or a repudiation by the wrongdoer (indicating that they no longer wish to be bound by the

290 *Rodger (Builders) Ltd v Fawdry* 1950 SC 483.

291 *Inveresk plc v Tullis Russell Papermakers Ltd* 2010 SC (UKSC) 106 at [42] per Lord Hope. This may not be the case in relation to employment contracts, see D Cabrelli, 'The mutuality of obligations doctrine and termination of the employment contract: *McNeill v Aberdeen City Council (No. 2)* (2014) 18 Edin LR 259. Also L Richardson, 'What do we know about retention now?' (2018) 22 Edin LR 387.

292 *Bank of East Asia v Scottish Enterprise* 1997 SLT 1213.

293 *Macari v Celtic Football & Athletic Co Ltd* 1999 SC 628.

contract). The pivotal role of materiality in the exercise of the power to rescind is demonstrated by the classic Scottish case of *Wade v Waldon*.[294] The popular comedian George Robey was hired to appear in Glasgow. Shortly before he was due to appear Robey discovered that the show had been cancelled. The manager had relied on clause 6 of the contract with Robey which provided: 'All artistes engaged . . . must give fourteen days notice prior to such engagements, such notice to be accompanied by bill matter'.

Since Robey had neither notified nor sent publicity materials the manager took this to be a material breach and cancelled the shows. However, the court found that Robey's failure to perform was indeed a breach but it did not go to the root of the contract and therefore did not constitute a material breach. The manager was not entitled to rescind the contract and, in addition, cancellation of the shows was in itself a material breach entitling Robey to damages. The manager did not have a materiality shield to protect his own actions from amounting to an anticipatory breach of contract.

A second scenario in which a party is entitled to rescind is in response to a repudiation. This is sometimes referred to as an anticipatory breach and it arises where the other contracting party has indicated their refusal to perform their obligations under the contract. Technically repudiation is not in itself a breach and only becomes one when it is 'accepted' by the other party. Acceptance transforms the repudiation into a breach and entitles the acceptor to rescind. Returning to the computer installation example above, if Company B telephones in advance to indicate that they are unable to perform the contract on the stipulated date because some of the components are not in stock, this does not necessarily amount to a repudiation. Company B may be able to procure the components elsewhere and may begin the work a few days later than planned, which may be acceptable to Company A. However, if time is of the essence, Company A may 'accept' the failure to perform, rescind the contract thus bringing it to an end and hire an alternative provider. **2.132**

The question of whether there is in fact a refusal to perform is judged objectively, and must be more than a mere threat or anticipation of non-performance that may never be fulfilled.[295] However, once refusal has been indicated it is open to the innocent party to rescind immediately for anticipatory breach, which may be of practical value and allows time to make alternative arrangements, or to wait until the date of performance and rescind for actual breach of contract. **2.133**

It is also open to the innocent party to insist on performance of the contract rather than accept repudiation. In *White & Carter (Councils) Ltd v McGregor*[296] a contract for advertising on litter bins contained an accelerated payment clause under which if there was failure to pay for one month's advertising the whole amount due under a three year contract would become payable. McGregor attempted to repudiate, indicating he wished to cancel the contract, but the company did not accept the repudiation, choosing instead to affirm the contract and implement the accelerated payment clause. The **2.134**

294 1909 SC 571.
295 *Blyth v Scottish Liberal Club* 1982 SC 140.
296 1962 SC (HL) 1.

company was entitled to payment because it had a 'legitimate interest'[297] in performance of the contract and it may also have been relevant that it was able to perform its obligations under the contract without the co-operation of the breaching party.[298]

Consequences of rescission

2.135 It is not entirely accurate to say the contract is at an end when it is rescinded for material breach. Its effect is to free the innocent party from future obligations but not from obligations, for instance payment, corresponding to satisfactory performance prior to the breach.[299] Clauses such as liquidated damages clauses, arbitration clauses, and jurisdiction clauses may also persist despite the rescission. In limited circumstances the law of unjustified enrichment may provide a remedy after a breach of contract where partial performance of a contract has taken place and the rescinding party has received a benefit under the contract,[300] although the courts tread warily so as not to undermine the rules of contract law.[301] The Scottish Law Commission has recommended the introduction of a statutory regime providing for post-recission restitution.[302]

Judicial remedies for breach of contract

2.136 Remedies for breach of contract are *cumulative* and the use of self-help remedies does not prevent the innocent party from applying to the courts for a judicial remedy, nor does one judicial remedy exclude others. The available remedies can broadly be classified as those which are designed to compel performance and those which compensate the innocent party for failure to perform.

Specific implement

2.137 Specific implement has been described as a 'primary remedy' in Scots contract law[303] in that it is always apposite for the innocent party to seek to compel performance following a breach of contract.[304] The underlying principle is that the parties should get what they contracted for and the courts will enforce performance. Non-compliance can lead to imprisonment of the party in

297 1962 SC (HL) 1 at 14 per Lord Reid.

298 See *AMA (New Town) Ltd v Law* 2013 SC 608. The SLC was previously minded to reform the *White & Carter* approach but now recommends no changes to the law: SLC Report 252, Ch. 12.

299 *Graham & Co v United Turkey Red Co Ltd* 1922 SC 533.

300 H L MacQueen, 'Unjustified enrichment and breach of contract' 1994 JR 137.

301 *Connelly v Simpson* 1993 SC 391. Later cases have preferred to conceive post-rescission restitution as a contractual remedy, see *Stork Technical Services v Ross's Executor* 2015 SLT 160 (noted Hogg (2015) 19 Edin LR 269).

302 SLC Report 252, paras 10.12–10.27.

303 Scottish Law Commission, *Discussion Paper on Remedies for Breach of Contract* (Scot. Law Com. DP 109, 1999), para. 6.1.

304 Although some doubt has been cast on its primacy given how rarely it is sought or granted (see MacQueen, *Contract Law* (2020), para. 6.6).

breach.[305] However, like all judicial remedies, it is discretionary and may be refused in the following circumstances:[306]

(a) where the decree sought is not sufficiently precise. In *Retail Park Investments Ltd v Royal Bank of Scotland plc (No. 2)*[307] the bank was under an obligation to keep the premises open for 'retail purposes' but had proposed leaving only cash withdrawal machines, which was held to breach the terms of the lease. However, in relation to specific implement it was held that the court could specify the goal (retention of premises for retail banking) but need not specify the precise means by which performance was to be achieved;
(b) where performance is impossible;
(c) where performance would cause exceptional hardship or injustice;
(d) where performance would be of a highly personal nature, for instance in contracts which depend on relationships such as employment contracts; and
(e) where replacement performance is readily available, for instance if the goods or services are readily available elsewhere.

Action for payment

An action for payment is the most common judicial remedy since the most common method of breaching a contract is failure to pay. It is procedurally distinct in that enforcement is by way of diligence to recover any sums due.[308] **2.138**

Interdict

The judicial remedy of interdict can be viewed as the reverse of specific implement in that it prevents rather than compels actions. It can be sought to prevent conduct likely to lead to a breach of contract and is therefore anticipatory in nature. It is possible to obtain an interim interdict which acts as a temporary remedy pending a full investigation of the facts and circumstances. Before granting interim interdict the court must consider whether on the balance of convenience an order should be granted. The innocent party must first present a *prima facie* case. **2.139**

An interdict cannot be granted in order to require somebody to do something. However, the distinction between positive and negative obligations may be a fine one. In *Church Commissioners for England v Abbey National plc*[309] Abbey National were in breach of a 'keep open' clause in a lease requiring them to occupy premises in a shopping centre. The landlord sought to interdict the defenders from failing to occupy the premises and was ineffective because it amounted to compelling the tenants to do something and to fulfil their **2.140**

305 Law Reform (Miscellaneous Provisions) (Scotland) Act 1940, s. 1(1).
306 This summary borrows from Scot. Law Com. DP 109, paras 6.2–6.7.
307 1996 SC 227; see also *Highland and Universal Properties Ltd v Safeway Properties Ltd* 2000 SC 297.
308 See Chapter Twelve: Judicial Security: Diligence.
309 1994 SC 651.

obligations under the lease. Lord President Hope noted that the *function* of an interdict is 'a negative one . . . namely to prevent taking of action in breach of the obligation, not to compel performance of it directly by order of the court'.[310]

Damages

2.141 The final remedy to be considered is different in nature to the other judicial remedies considered above in that it seeks financial compensation as a substitute for performance. In effect, the breaching party is permitted to pay rather than perform. However, damages must directly relate to any loss suffered by the innocent party as a result of the breach and Scots law does not allow punitive damages.[311] The aim is to put the innocent party in the position they would have been in had the contract been performed. Damages can be claimed for actual loss caused; for consequential losses, that is, losses that flow directly from the actual loss caused; and it may be possible in some circumstances to claim a 'nominal' award of damages if the innocent party has suffered 'trouble and inconvenience' as a result of the breach.[312] For instance, if Company B installs a computer system defectively with the result that none of the employees of Company A can access a computer for a period of three days, Company A will be entitled to compensation for the cost of rectifying the problem by calling in other experts (the loss caused). However, if a three-day shut-down of all computers has also led to a loss of revenue those losses can also be claimed as consequential losses. Claims for damages must not be unreasonable.[313]

Causation

2.142 A further limitation on claims for damages is the rule of causation that the loss must be caused by the breach of contract. This is sometimes expressed as asking whether 'but for' the breach the loss would have occurred. The breach may not be the only operative cause of the loss but it must be a material cause.[314]

Other limitations on claims for damages

2.143 Not all losses can be compensated and the law has developed a number of limiting devices to prevent excessive claims. The test of remoteness[315] requires that the loss must arise directly in the ordinary course of events (without special knowledge on the part of the contracting parties)[316] and must be of such a type as the parties might reasonably have contemplated.[317] In addition

310 1994 SC 651 at 660.

311 Nor has Scots law thus far provided 'gain-based' damages as English law did in *Attorney-General v Blake* [2001] 1 AC 268.

312 *Wilkie v Brown* 2003 SC 573 at [21] per Lord Justice-Clerk Gill.

313 *Ruxley Electronics and Construction Ltd v Forsyth* [1996] AC 344.

314 *A/B Karlshamns Oljefabriker v Monarch Steamship Co Ltd* 1949 SC (HL) 1.

315 *Hadley v Baxendale* (1854) 9 Ex 341.

316 *Balfour Beatty v Scottish Power plc* 1994 SC (HL) 20.

317 See H L MacQueen, 'Remoteness and breach of contract' 1996 JR 295.

the parties are under a duty to mitigate their losses and avoid incurring losses where possible. This could again be seen as amounting to a requirement that the parties act reasonably.

Agreed damages clauses

It is not uncommon for parties to agree a clause in their contract which provides for a fixed sum in damages to be awarded on the breach of stipulated contractual obligations. Such clauses – sometimes referred to as liquidated damages clauses – will generally be enforced by the courts. However, that is subject to the court's power to review 'penalty clauses', allowing it to strike down as unenforceable any clause that provides for a remedy that is 'out of all proportion to any legitimate interest of the innocent party in the enforcement' of the contractual clause breach of which has triggered the purported remedial entitlement.[318] This power only arises where the entitlement arises pursuant to a breach of contract.[319] It is, therefore, possible for parties to construct their contractual arrangements in such a way as to avoid the court's scrutiny, for instance, through use of conditions to provide for staggered entitlement to sums agreed between the parties. **2.144**

CROSS-BORDER CONTRACTS

This chapter presupposes that contractual disputes are governed by Scots law and take place before a Scottish court. However, by their nature, contracts may readily cross jurisdictions and involve connections to legal systems other than Scotland. It is, therefore, appropriate to give a brief overview of the rules of international private law that a Scottish court will use to resolve an international contractual dispute if the parties are not content to have the dispute resolved purely as a domestic matter.[320] **2.145**

Jurisdiction

The Scottish courts will have jurisdiction over a contractual dispute if the parties agree that should be the case,[321] and one frequently encounters a jurisdiction clause in the 'boilerplate' part of a contract, by which the parties **2.146**

318 *Cavendish Square Holding BV v El Makdessi* [2015] UKSC 67, [2016] AC 1172 at [32] per Lord Neuberger and Lord Sumption. This was accepted as reflecting Scots law by the Inner House in *Gray v Braid Group (Holdings) Ltd* [2016] CSIH 68, 2017 SC 409.

319 *Cavendish* at [12]–[14]; [239]–[241]. In its *Report on Penalty Clauses* (Scot. Law Com. No. 171, 1999) the Scottish Law Commission recommended the abolition of this 'breach limitation', but that recommendation was not implemented, nor was it repeated in the more recent report (SLC Report 252, Pt 5).

320 For more detail, see, e.g. E B Crawford and J M Carruthers, *International Private Law: A Scots Perspective*, 4th edn (Edinburgh: W. Green, 2015). The rules of international private law have been impacted severely by the UK's withdrawal from the EU.

321 They also will have jurisdiction if an action is raised against a defender and the defender does not object to the jurisdiction of the Scottish courts: this is the doctrine of 'submission'. See Civil Jurisdiction and Judgments Act 1982, Sch. 8, r. 7.

agree to confer exclusive[322] or non-exclusive[323] jurisdiction on a particular court. Such a provision in favour of the Scottish courts will be effective[324] and the Scottish courts will also give effect to an exclusive jurisdiction clause in favour of another legal system's courts by sisting proceedings. Exceptions exist for consumer contracts[325] and employment contracts.[326] If the contract does not contain a jurisdiction clause, then the Scottish courts will have jurisdiction where the place of performance of the obligation in question is in Scotland.[327] The 'obligation in question' refers to the obligation the performance of which is in dispute, so, for instance, in the case of non-payment of a contract governed by Scots law,[328] the courts of the place where the creditor is located will have jurisdiction, as this is the place where the debtor must make payment (i.e. where the obligation to pay under the contract is to be performed).[329] The defender may argue nevertheless that the Scottish courts should not exercise jurisdiction via the plea of *forum non conveniens*, asking the court to sist proceedings in favour of another available forum where the action could be more appropriately litigated.

Choice of law

2.147 Frequently contracts will contain a choice of law clause providing that a specific legal system will apply to the contract.[330] The court may also be able to infer that the parties intended a particular legal system to govern the contract without saying so expressly.[331] However, if the court is not able to ascertain with a degree of certainty what was the intention of the parties then the general rule is that the contract will be governed by the law of the place where the party that effects the 'characteristic performance' of the contract has its habitual residence.[332] For instance, for a sale of goods contract, this will be the place where the seller is based.[333] This, however, may be displaced where the contract as a whole is manifestly more closely connected with another legal system.[334]

322 That is, to the exclusion of jurisdiction of courts in any other legal system.
323 That is, with the effect of conferring jurisdiction on the chosen court, without excluding any other available jurisdiction.
324 1982 Act, Sch. 8, r. 6; Sch. 4, r. 12 (intra-UK cases); Hague Convention of 30 June 2005 on Choice of Court Agreements, art. 5.
325 1982 Act, Sch. 8, r. 3.
326 1982 Act, Sch. 8, r. 4.
327 1982 Act, Sch. 8, r. 2(b); Sch. 4, r. 3(a) (intra-UK cases).
328 If the contract is governed by a different law, then the court must look to the applicable law to ascertain where the obligation in question is to be performed.
329 See, e.g. *Fisher Services Ltd v All Thai'd Up Ltd* 2013 SLT (Sh Ct) 121. The situation would be slightly different if the UK is able to accede to the Lugano Convention 2007, art. 5(1) of which contains a similar rule based on the place of performance of the obligation in question, but provides a specific rule for sale of goods and supply of services contracts.
330 Regulation (EC) No 593/2008 of the European Parliament and of the Council of 17 June 2008 on the law applicable to contractual obligations (Rome I), as retained in terms of the European Union (Withdrawal) Act 2018, and as modified by the Law Applicable to Contractual Obligations and Non-Contractual Obligations (Amendment etc.) (EU Exit) Regulations 2019 (SI 2019/834) ('Rome I'), art 3(1).
331 Rome I, art. 3(1). Such an implied choice must be 'clearly demonstrated by the terms of the contract or the circumstances of the case', so the bar for implication is a high one.
332 Rome I, art 4(1)–(2). A limited definition of habitual residence can be found in art. 19.
333 Rome I, art. 4(1)(a).
334 Rome I, art. 4(3).

Foreign law is presumed to be the same as Scots law unless the contrary is proved.[335] It is open to either party to argue that the law of another legal system should apply to the contract. But the content of the foreign law must then be averred and proved by leading evidence of witnesses with expertise in that foreign law. Even if foreign law is applicable, the Scottish court may still refuse to apply foreign rules that conflict with its public policy,[336] and may apply essential rules of Scots law as 'overriding mandatory provisions'.[337] **2.148**

335 *Bonnor v Balfour Kilpatrick Ltd* 1974 SC 223 at 228 per Lord President Emslie.

336 Rome I, art. 21.

337 Rome I, art. 9(1)–(2). See also, where there has been a choice of foreign law and that choice is the only factor not to connect the contract to Scots law, art. 3(3).

Chapter Three

General Principles of Property Law

John MacLeod

WHY DOES PROPERTY LAW MATTER FOR COMMERCIAL LAW?

3.01 Commercial law is to a large extent the law of trade. Trading assets involves buying and selling them. This is often financed by loans which are secured against other assets. Buyers will not be content merely to have a contract obliging the seller to make them owners of goods, they want that contract to be fulfilled. A lender may only be willing to lend if the borrower gives a right in security that allows the lender to sell some of his or her property if the debt is not paid.

3.02 Trade also involves risk. Things may not work out as parties hope. If commercial transactions do not work out as parties hope, they may find that their assets are not sufficient to meet their obligations. That means that the debtor will not be able to pay every creditor in full. This situation is known as insolvency and it is handled through processes such as sequestration and liquidation, which are discussed later in this book. Crudely put, they involve selling off the debtor's assets and sharing the proceeds between the creditors. No one gets all that they are entitled to because there is not enough to go round.

3.03 In this situation, property rights in the debtor's assets are much more valuable than contractual rights against the debtor. They give direct access to the assets without the need to share with other creditors. Imagine that Susan has four tonnes of wheat and no other assets. She gets a bit confused and makes contracts for the sale of a tonne of wheat with six different people. She does not have enough wheat to fulfil all of the contracts. Insolvency processes are about sharing the four tonnes of wheat between the six buyers. None of the buyers will get a whole tonne (or its value) from the insolvency official.

3.04 If, however, Susan has transferred a tonne of wheat to Brenda (one of the buyers) before the insolvency process starts, then Brenda won't have to share her wheat with the other buyers. The insolvency process is about sharing Susan's assets between her creditors. Brenda's tonne is no longer one of Susan's assets. It belongs to Brenda and she does not owe any obligations to Susan's creditors. Of course, this means that the others now have to share three tonnes between five buyers. Brenda received full performance but that makes things worse for everyone else.

3.05 Cases like this show that a sound grasp of the basic principles of property law is essential for the commercial lawyer. This chapter is intended to give a brief outline of these principles. For reasons of brevity, citation of authority will be kept to a minimum. For a more detailed account, texts devoted to property law should be consulted.[1]

KINDS OF RIGHTS

Real and personal; absolute and relative

The key distinction in property law is between personal and real rights.[2] Personal rights are the 'correlative' or mirror image of obligations. If David has borrowed £100 from Colin, then he owes Colin £100 (and perhaps some interest as well). That, in turn, means that Colin has a personal right against David for payment of the £100 (and the interest). Colin's personal right against David and David's obligation to Colin are two sides of the same coin. Put another way, a personal right is a right that somebody does or refrains from doing some action. The person against whom the right is held is obliged to act or refrain from acting in that way. **3.06**

Personal rights are so called because they are enforceable against a certain person or group of persons (whoever owes the relevant obligation) and only them. Colin can sue David for enforcement of the right to the £100 but he cannot sue anyone else because only David owes the obligation. Contracts are the most important source of personal rights in commercial law, but personal rights can also arise from delict, unjustified enrichment, *negotiorum gestio* (benevolent intervention in another's affairs) and trusts. Personal rights are sometimes said to be relative because they express the specific relationship between particular persons. Whatever the origin of a personal right, it behaves in much the same way once it has been created. **3.07**

Real rights are different from personal rights. Where a personal right is a right against a person or group of persons for the fulfilment of a particular obligation, a real right is a right 'in' a thing. The term 'real right' is derived from the Latin word for thing: *res*. Because the object of the real right is a thing rather than conduct by a particular person, it is valid against the whole world. Most importantly, it can usually be enforced against whoever is in possession of the thing. Because they can be enforced against the whole world, real rights are said to be absolute rather than relative. **3.08**

Thus, if Olivia owns a car and it is stolen, she can recover it from the person in whose possession it is found, irrespective of how that person got hold of the car. This can be contrasted with the position of someone with a contractual right to the car. Imagine that Olivia contracts to sell the car to Brian. Before ownership is transferred to Brian, the car is stolen. The thief "sells" the car to Peter. Peter had no idea it was stolen. Olivia can sue Peter to recover the car because she owns it. Brian, on the other hand, has a personal right to the car arising from the contract of sale but he has no real right. His personal right means that he can sue Olivia for breach of contract seeking damages (or, if she **3.09**

1 G L Gretton and A J M Steven, *Property, Trusts and Succession*, 4th edn (London: Bloomsbury Professional, 2021); K G C Reid, *The Law of Property in Scotland* (London: Butterworths Law, 1996).

2 See the judgment of Lord Hope in *Sharp v Thomson* 1995 SC 455, especially at 461–475.

has recovered the car, delivery of the car itself). Peter, however, is not a party to the contract of sale so it cannot be enforced against him.

3.10 Some rights, particularly intellectual property rights such as copyright, patents and trademarks are enforceable against the whole world without there being an obvious 'thing' for the right to be in. In relation to these, it might be suggested that they are absolute rights (i.e. rights which are good against the whole world) but not real rights because there is no *res* (thing). Although copyright can protect an artistic work such as a picture, it does not concern the physical picture itself. Rather, it relates to the expression of ideas found in the picture.

3.11 However, it is also possible to see the intellectual products that are covered by the intellectual property right (whether that be a picture, song or work of literature protected by copyright, an invention covered by a patent or an image, phrase or sound protected as a trademark) as incorporeal things and the relevant intellectual property rights as real rights in these things. Some care must be taken with this approach. If a song is a thing that can be the subject of real rights, we might expect that it is possible to own the song. That, however, is not the case. The greatest right that the law admits in the song is copyright, which is not the same as ownership.

3.12 Intellectual property rights work by conferring a monopoly on the right holder: the holder of a patent over an invention is the only one who is allowed to manufacture the relevant product. Thus they can be said to be exclusive privileges. Historically, there were other types of exclusive privilege, such as the monopoly rights of royal burghs in respect of trade. In the modern era, however, intellectual property rights are the only important rights of exclusive privilege as a result of the general hostility to monopolies.

Ownership and the subordinate real rights

3.13 Scots lawyers explain a person's relationship with his or her corporeal property in terms of ownership: the principal real right. The concept appears to be a simple and familiar one. If a car belongs to Oliver, he is said to own that car. The aspiration to own a home is a regular topic in news reports.

3.14 Various attempts have been made to define ownership: it is sometimes said to be the exclusive and absolute right of use and enjoyment of the thing.[3] Others feel that this does not capture everything that an owner can do and simply say that it is 'the most complete right a person can have in a thing'[4] or 'the main real right'.[5] Some present it as the 'residual' right in a thing;[6] still others are sceptical about the possibility of, or need to offer, a definition of ownership.[7] To some extent, the scepticism about a definition and the idea of ownership

3 Erskine, *Institute* 2.1.1; Bell, *Principles*, § 1284. This is sometimes expressed with the Latin expression *ius utendi fruendi abutendi*.

4 For example, Draft Common Frame of Reference art. VIII–1:202.

5 Stair, *Institutions* 2.1.28.

6 S J Grossman and O D Hart, 'The costs and benefits of ownership: a theory of vertical and lateral integration' (1986) 94 Journal of Political Economy 691.

7 S R Simpson, 'Towards a definition of "absolute ownership": II' (1961) 5 Journal of African Law 145.

as a residual right spring from a common root: the grant of subordinate real rights.

The owner of a thing can grant subordinate real rights in it. For instance, if Lionel owns some land, he might grant a lease to Teresa and a standard security to Calum. Once he has granted these rights, the freedom that Lionel has to deal with his property is limited. Teresa, rather than Lionel, is entitled to possess the property and he can only transfer it subject to Calum's standard security. The rights which Teresa and Calum enjoy can be enforced against someone to whom Lionel transferred the property because they are real rights. **3.15**

In some sense, Lionel's rights in respect of the property are diminished. For this reason subordinate real rights can be described as encumbrances on Lionel's right of ownership. On one view, Lionel has carved out a bit of his ownership and transferred it to someone else. This has led some scholars, particularly in the French legal tradition, to describe subordinate real rights as dismemberments of ownership. **3.16**

We might think of ownership as being a bit like a box of chocolates: as the owner grants subordinate real rights they give away chocolates. Even after all the chocolates have been given away, the owner is still holding the box and is therefore still the owner.[8] Even if Lionel has burdened his property with so many subordinate real rights that he has no meaningful freedom to decide what happens to it, he is still the owner just as much as he was before he granted the rights. For this reason, it is difficult to define ownership in terms of what the owner can do since that can vary quite a lot from case to case. Thus some consider ownership to be a residual right. **3.17**

We should be conscious that ownership is not as simple as first appears but it is important not to overstate the difficulties. The concept of ownership in civilian systems such as Scots law has been worked out over thousands of years and it helps us to analyse many of the most important property law problems. We can be relatively confident in saying that ownership establishes a default rule: in the absence of any rule or right to the contrary, the owner gets to decide what happens to his or her property. It is up to someone who wants to object to the owner's conduct in respect of the property to point to the rule of law or right that restricts his or her freedom. **3.18**

Ownership is the right that a person has in his or her own things. Subordinate real rights are the rights that a person can have in other people's things. **3.19**

Scots law recognises a fixed list of types of subordinate real rights. This is known as the principle of *numerus clausus*. Attempts to create real rights outside this list will be ineffective. This principle is one of the major features which distinguish the law of property from the law of contract. The reason for the principle is the third party effect of real rights. Since contracts do not impose obligations on third parties, third parties have little or no interest in being able to discover the content of the contract. Therefore, the contracting parties are generally entitled to craft their contracts as they wish, creating **3.20**

8 The analogy is not completely accurate since, in theory, is always possible to grant further subordinate real rights so the box of chocolates is never empty.

bespoke regimes which fit their needs. The position is somewhat different for real rights.

3.21 As explained above, real rights affect everyone. They are particularly important to singular successors: those who acquire the property from a former owner. Therefore, third parties (particularly those who are considering acquiring the property) have a strong interest in discovering which real rights affect an asset. This process is made much easier if there is a limited number of potential real rights to consider and if the creation of these rights is attended by some publicity.

3.22 The subordinate real rights are:

- Rights in security: which allow the security holder to realise the value of an asset in order to satisfy a debt due to him or her and/or to retain possession until payment.
- Proper liferent: which allows the liferenter to possess property for his or her lifetime.
- Lease of land:[9] which allows possession for a specified period of time on condition of payment of rent.
- Servitudes: which allow the right holder to make some use of the property burdened by the servitude, typically for the benefit of neighbouring property. The classic example is a right of way.
- The right to enforce a negative real burden: which allows the right holder to veto certain uses or modifications of property by the owner.

Some would also suggest that being in possession confers a real right not to be forcibly dispossessed, which is a distinct real right.[10] This view might be contested on the basis that a bare possessor could not be maintained in possession in the face of a judicial challenge by the owner, while the other real rights would remain. It has also been suggested that rights held by the public, such as public rights of way, are real rights because they are generally enforceable.[11]

3.23 As noted above, some would see intellectual property rights and other rights of exclusive privilege as real rights because they are enforceable against the whole world. Others would suggest that they are absolute but not real because there is no *res*.

Common ownership

3.24 The potential for the grant of subordinate real rights shows that more than one person can have a real right in a thing. Can more than one person own a thing? They can. Indeed they can do so in two different ways: common ownership and joint ownership. The most important instance of the latter is the trust and joint ownership is discussed along with the rest of the rules on trusts below.

9 The position of leases is slightly more complex than that of other subordinate real rights. In many civilian systems, a lease is considered as a contract which transfers to successors with or without their consent rather than as subordinate real rights.

10 K G C Reid, *The Law of Property in Scotland* (1996), para. 5.

11 Reid, *The Law of Property in Scotland*, para. 5.

In common ownership, the right of ownership is shared reflecting each person's share of the property. Each common owner is entitled to make normal use of the property, transfer his or her share and grant rights in security over it. Acts which would affect other owners, such as leasing the property or granting servitudes, can only be done with their consent.[12] Each common owner is entitled to raise an action for division and sale under which the action the property will be sold and each common owner will receive his or her share of the proceeds.[13] If property is transferred to more than one person, the assumption is that they will have equal shares but it is possible to vary this so that one party has 75 per cent and another 25 per cent or one 60 per cent and another 40 per cent. **3.25**

Competing rights

One of the most important differences between real and personal rights is the way in which they compete with other rights. There are three basic principles: personal rights rank *pari passu*; real rights trump personal rights; and competing real rights rank by date of creation. **3.26**

Personal rights rank pari *passu*

An earlier personal right does not normally enjoy priority over a later one. Each creditor is entitled to seek satisfaction without worrying too much about other creditors. If the debtor does not have enough assets to satisfy all creditors, insolvency law will usually compel each one of them to take a proportionate cut. **3.27**

Imagine that Gary has a gambling problem. He borrows £3,500 from Frances on Monday and loses it on the horses. On Tuesday, he borrows £4,500 from Serena, which he loses in the casino. Chastened by his losses, he goes home to stay with his mum who gives him free board and lodgings. After some time, he is sequestrated. After gathering in Gary's assets, the insolvency official finds that Gary has £5,000 of assets but £8,000 worth of debts. The *pari passu* principle means that Frances cannot claim full payment on the basis that her debt was constituted first. Instead each of them will be entitled to 5/8ths of their debt: so Frances would get £2,187.50 and Serena would get £2,812.50. **3.28**

Real rights v personal rights

Since a real right is good against the world, it is good against the holders of any personal rights with which it is in conflict. Peggy concludes a contract with Harriet under which Harriet has the right to use Peggy's car every Tuesday. Peggy then pledges the car to Cathy in security for a debt that she owes her. When property is pledged, the pledgee (Cathy) is entitled to possession until the debt is paid.[14] Harriet's right and Cathy's right appear to be in conflict: when Tuesday comes, Harriet's contract says she is entitled to take the car but **3.29**

12 Bell, *Principles*, §1072–1075.
13 Bell, *Principles*, §1079.
14 See para. 11.29.

Cathy's pledge says she is entitled to hold onto it. In such a situation, Cathy wins. Her right of pledge is a real right, which is enforceable against Peggy, Harriet and anyone else. Harriet's personal right, on the other hand is only enforceable against Peggy and so is no use in a dispute with Cathy. Harriet would, however, be able to sue Peggy for breach of contract.

3.30 The most common cause of a conflict of rights is insolvency and it is here that rights in security come into their own. Consider the following case. Widget Co Ltd has four creditors, each of whom is owed £100,000. It owns a factory worth £200,000 and other assets worth £100,000. Total assets are therefore £300,000 and total liabilities are £400,000. If expenses are ignored, each unsecured creditor would get around £75,000. If, however, two of the creditors (Al and Betty) had secured their debts by way of standard securities over the factory, the picture would be different. Al and Betty would be entitled to sell the factory and share the proceeds between themselves, taking £100,000 each. The two unsecured creditors would be left to share the remaining £100,000 worth of assets, leaving them with £50,000 each.

3.31 This story is a little bit like that of Susan, Brenda and the wheat which was discussed earlier. But the secured creditors' preferential treatment cannot be explained on the basis that the factory belongs to them and not to Widget Co Ltd. Although the company has granted standard securities, it remains the owner. Rather, the result is explicable on the basis that a standard security is a real right and may therefore be invoked in disputes with the other creditors just as much as it can be used against the company.

3.32 The rule that personal rights are trumped by real rights means that holders of personal rights are very vulnerable in insolvency situations: they have to share the assets equally and the assets only start being shared out after those with real rights have taken their entitlement.

Real rights rank by date of creation

3.33 The rule that real rights rank ahead of personal rights in respect of the item of property which they affect governs the interaction of real rights and personal rights. Since it is possible for more than one real right to exist in an asset, a rule is also needed to regulate the relationship of these rights to one another.

3.34 Al and Betty both had a standard security which burdened the factory. Since the value was enough to satisfy both of them, their respective priority did not matter. If, however, the factory was only worth £150,000, then its sale would not be enough to satisfy both Al and Betty. Unlike personal right holders, Al and Betty will not rank *pari passu*. They will rank according to the date of creation (sometimes expressed in the Latin phrase *prior tempore potior iure*[15]). Therefore, if Al's standard security was created first, Betty would not receive any of the proceeds of the sale of the factory until Al had been paid in full.[16] It is possible for Al and Betty to make an agreement between themselves which

15 Which means first in time, stronger in right.

16 Conveyancing and Feudal Reform (Scotland) Act 1970, s. 27(1).

alters this, so that both rank together (and thus take a proportionate cut in the case of the assets being of insufficient value). Alternatively, Al may agree to give up his prior rank so that Betty ranks ahead of Al.

TRUSTS

Under normal circumstances the owner of property uses it for his or her own benefit. There is one important exception to this, however: the trust. The basic idea behind the trust is that property is owned by a trustee or trustees but not used for their benefit. Rather they administer it for the benefit of other parties known as beneficiaries in accordance with a set of aims known as trust purposes. The situation is set up by a truster who transfers the property to the trustee and imposes the duty to administer it for the benefit of beneficiaries.[17] In the typical case, there are at least three parties: a truster, a trustee and a beneficiary. Tracey might transfer a number of buy to let properties to Trudy in trust for Bertie. Trudy owns the properties but profits arising from rental income should go to Bertie (although his precise entitlement would depend on the terms of the trust). Bertie and Tracey have personal rights against Trudy which they can use to compel her to act in accordance with the trust. **3.35**

It is also possible for one person to perform two roles. So Tracey might transfer the properties to Trudy to be held for Tracey's benefit. In that case, she would be both truster and beneficiary and Trudy would be the trustee. Alternatively, Tracey might declare that, from now on, she would hold the properties for Bertie. This needs to be done in writing and intimated to Bertie[18] but once these steps have been fulfilled, Tracey is the trustee in respect of those assets and Bertie is the beneficiary. The only combination that is not possible (because it would be pointless) is being a trustee and beneficiary. In that situation, the trustee would be obliged to administer the property for his or her own benefit but that is what a normal owner does anyway. **3.36**

Where there is more than one trustee, the trustees are said to have joint ownership. In contrast to common ownership, individual trustees have no share of the property that they can deal with individually and where a trustee ceases to perform that role, he or she ceases to be owner of the trust property automatically. Where a new trustee is assumed, he or she acquires joint ownership automatically. **3.37**

Trusts have one characteristic which has given rise to extensive use of the trust in commercial contexts: trust assets are protected from the trustee's personal creditors.[19] This means that the beneficiaries under the trust enjoy exclusive access to these assets held in trust for satisfaction of their rights. This has led some to question whether the beneficiaries' rights can be said to be truly **3.38**

17 Bell, *Principles*, § 1991.

18 Requirements of Writing (Scotland) Act 1995, s. 1(2)(a)(iii); *Allan's Trs v Lord Advocate* 1971 SC (HL) 45.

19 *Heritable Reversionary Co Ltd v Millar* (1891) 19 R (HL) 43; Bankruptcy (Scotland) Act 2016, s. 88(1)(c).

personal and others to doubt whether it is possible to properly rationalise the trust in Scots law.

3.39 The trust can be explained without abandoning the principle that the beneficiaries' rights are personal by the separation of patrimonies. As discussed in Chapter One, a patrimony is the totality of a person's assets.

3.40 A patrimony can be thought of as a suitcase, into which all your property is put. Your creditors are entitled to seize and sell items from the suitcase in order to satisfy your debts to them. A trustee has two suitcases: a personal patrimony which contains their own assets, which is liable for their personal debts and a trust patrimony which is liable for the trust's debts (most importantly the personal rights of beneficiaries). The beneficiaries do not have to share these assets with the personal creditors of the trustee but that is because the assets are in a different patrimony, not because the beneficiaries' rights are stronger than any other personal rights. They do not have access to the second suitcase.

3.41 We can see that separation of patrimonies rather than some special quality of the beneficiaries' rights explains the trusts' insolvency effect by comparing the position of creditors of the trust. Trust creditors are entitled to payment in priority to the beneficiaries.[20] An example might be a plumber who does work on the buy-to-let properties that Trudy holds in trust for Bertie. Bertie's entitlement under the trust is subject to the claims of trust creditors, such as the plumber.

3.42 The fact that a trust estate can be sequestrated independently of sequestration of any of the trustees also points to the trust being a separate patrimony.[21] As discussed in Chapter Thirteen, in personal insolvency sequestration is the mechanism by which the assets of a person whose liabilities outweigh the contents of his or her patrimony are gathered in, sold off and distributed to the creditors. In the same way, the creditors of the trust can petition for the sequestration of the trust. If the trust merely consisted of some special right against the trustee held by the beneficiary, it is difficult to see how such an insolvency treatment could make sense.

3.43 The idea of the trust as a separate patrimony also helps to explain the operation of the trustees' joint ownership. The asset is in the trust patrimony, which is a single patrimony controlled by multiple trustees. Since it is a trust patrimony, power over the patrimony is vested in the trustees because they are trustees. If someone resigns as a trustee, he or she necessarily gives up authority over the trust patrimony.[22] This contrasts with common ownership where each common owner has his or her own right of ownership in his or her personal patrimony. The contrast between joint and common ownership can thus be illustrated in these diagrams.

20 *Lamond's Trs v Croom* (1871) 9 M 662.
21 Bankruptcy (Scotland) Act 2016, s. 6(1)(a).
22 Trusts (Scotland) Act 1921, s. 20.

Common ownership:

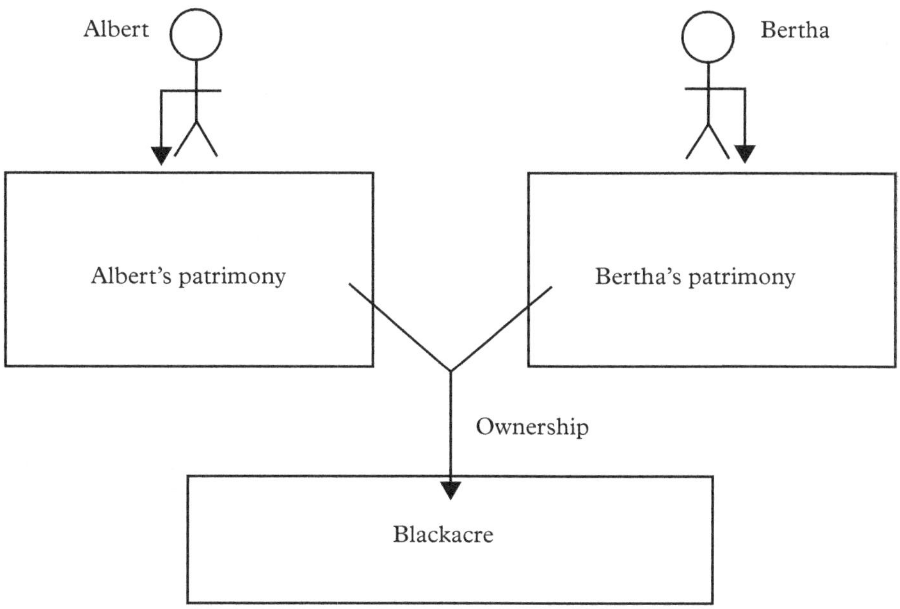

Trustees' joint ownership:

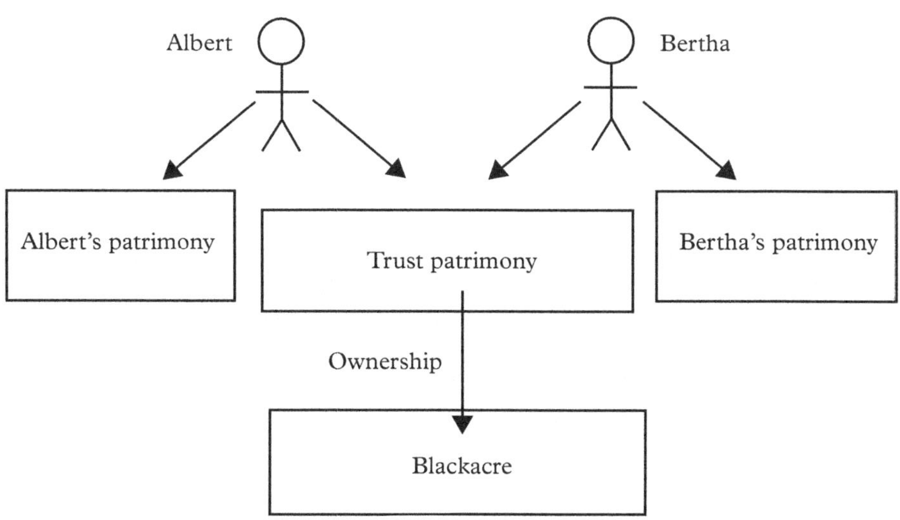

KINDS OF PROPERTY

Rights as rights and rights as things

3.44 Real rights and personal rights do have one very important thing in common, however. They are ways in which the law conceptualises relationships between persons and the 'real world'. Personal rights express the relationship between persons. Saying Christine has a right to payment against Debbie expresses something about the relationship between Christine and Debbie that is relevant to the law: Debbie is obliged to pay a sum of money to Christine and the courts will give Christine aid in her efforts to secure that payment. Real rights express something about a person's relationship with a thing. Saying that Brian has a servitude of access over a piece of land expresses something about Brian's relationship with that piece of land and (by virtue of that fact) his relationship with everyone else: namely Brian is entitled to take access to his property (e.g. his house) across that piece of land and that everyone else must refrain from obstructing Brian's efforts to do this. Rights express the relationship between persons and the real world but the law must also find a way of expressing the relationship between a person and their rights.[23]

3.45 This is important because rights themselves are important assets which can be traded. In fact, many of a business's more important assets will be rights: real rights such as leases or standard securities, personal rights against debtors, intellectual property rights such as copyright, patents and trademarks. These rights can be transferred in more or less the same way as physical things. Transfer of a right has a special name. It is known as assignation.

3.46 The traditional approach to conceptualising the relationship between a person and their rights in Scotland, as in the rest of Europe, is based on a scheme presented by the Roman jurist Gaius in his *Institutes*. He proposed a general class of things, which he subdivided into corporeal and incorporeal things:

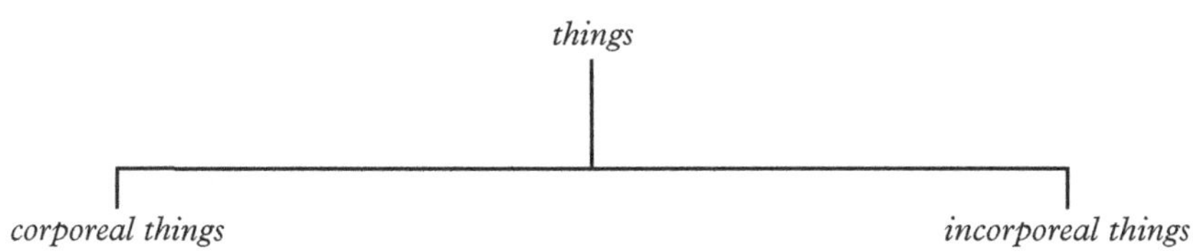

3.47 The corporeal things are items with a real, physical existence such as plots of land, cars, lorries, sacks of coal and so on. Incorporeal things, on the other hand, are assets which cannot be touched. The main items in this class are rights. Since all things can be owned, the real right of ownership expresses the relationship between a person and his or her assets. Christine owns her personal right against Debbie or a lease over another plot in much the same way as she owns a plot of land. On this model, a person's patrimony comprises

23 Strictly speaking, where this chapter says 'his or her', it should say 'his, her or its' since juristic persons such as partnerships, companies and limited liability partnerships can have personal and real rights in just the same way as natural persons.

of things which he or she owns. Christine's affairs may be illustrated in the following way:

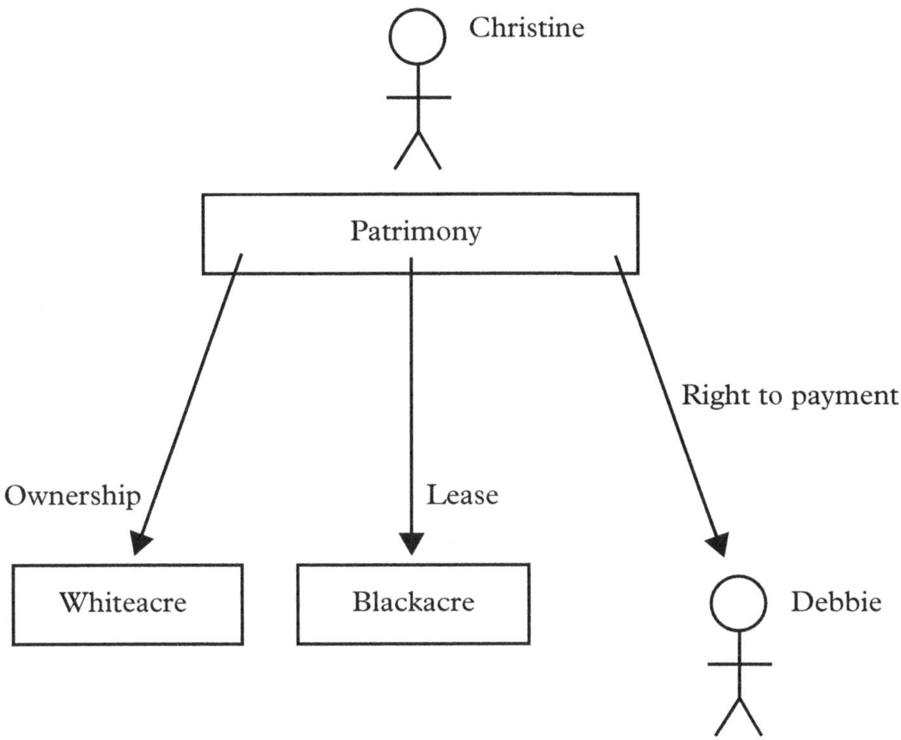

This approach makes it easy to explain why rights are transferable and to apply principles developed in the context of corporeal property to incorporeal assets. Just as the owner of a plot of land can transfer it so can the owner of a right to payment. In every case, what is transferred is ownership of the relevant thing. In one case the thing is the plot of land; in the other it is the right to payment. Further, if subordinate real rights (such as rights in security) are conceptualised as burdens on or dismemberments of ownership, then it is easy to understand which subordinate rights might be granted in incorporeal things. **3.48**

It does, however, face one major challenge: ownership is generally recognised as a real right. Indeed, it is the principal real right. If real rights are things, and ownership is a real right, then it appears that it should be possible to own ownership. That, however, sets up a problem of perpetual regression, since the same thing could be said regarding the ownership of the right of ownership, so the ownership of the ownership of the ownership would be owned, and so on. **3.49**

There are various possible responses to this problem. One is to suggest that ownership is a special kind or real right which cannot be owned.[24] Another is **3.50**

24 Reid, *The Law of Property in Scotland*, para. 16.

to suggest that ownership is not a real right.[25] Both of these approaches can be seen as efforts to retain the Gaian scheme or a modification of it. A further alternative is outright rejection of the Gaian scheme. This rejection is most closely associated with German scholars, in particular to the Pandectist school but it is also adopted by some modern scholars in Scotland.[26]

3.51 Key to the Pandectist approach is the idea that a patrimony rather than ownership is the mechanism which explains the relationship between a person and his or her rights. On this view, the patrimony contains a person's rights but nothing else. Rights reach out from the patrimony to things in the real world.

3.52 This approach avoids the problem of perpetual regression in the ownership of ownership. It is possible to apply principles of transfer developed in relation to land or corporeal moveables to dealings with rights to payment or leases because each case involves moving a right from one patrimony to another. If Christine assigns her right against Debbie, it moves from her patrimony to that of the assignee. If she transfers ownership of Whiteacre, the real right of ownership over Whiteacre moves from her patrimony to that of the transferee. On the Pandectist view, nothing more need be said.

3.53 The Pandectist approach faces greater challenges with subordinate rights in rights. If Christine wants to grant a right in security over the lease of Blackacre, it is relatively easy for the Gaian scheme to explain it: the lease is a thing and can therefore be the object of a real right in security. The fact that Christine owns the lease explains why she should be able to burden it. Should Christine become insolvent, the security holder's real right explains the priority over unsecured creditors.

3.54 The Pandectist can say that she should be able to deal with the lease because it is part of her patrimony, but there is more difficulty in explaining the nature of the subordinate right which she grants. Similarly, the right in security's status as a real right is more difficult to invoke to explain any insolvency protection. Explanations of how this may be are possible but they are rather complex and, in the view of the writer of this chapter, a little awkward.[27] The other, more pragmatic problem with the Pandectist approach is that most lawyers in the western tradition have been using Gaian language for a very long time and it would take a significant intellectual effort to displace that tendency.

3.55 Both views of the relation between persons and their rights are respectable. Each helps to explain one part of the law and struggles with another. They have implications for the language used in discussions of assignation and rights in security but few, if any, implications for the substance of the rules used. Once the basics of both systems are properly grasped, it becomes possible to translate from one view to the other without too much difficulty. The

25 The most famous statement of this view is S Ginossar, *Droit réel, propriété et créance: Élaboration d'un système rationnel des droits patrimoniaux* (1960). In addition to being in French, this work is very difficult to locate. A good summary of Ginossar's views and those of his later interpreters can be found in G Gretton, 'Ownership and its objects' (2007) 71 *Rabels Zeitschrift für ausländisches und internationales Privatrecht* 802 at 810–815.

26 Most notably Gretton, 'Ownership and its objects' and R G Anderson, *Assignation* (Edinburgh: Edinburgh Legal Education Trust, 2008), para. 1–09. See para. 8.01 below.

27 See further Gretton, 'Ownership and its objects', at pp. 840–844.

rest of this chapter and the chapters on rights in security are written from a Gaian perspective, although the alert reader will have noticed the Pandectist approach in the diagrams at para. 3.43.

Kinds of property: heritable and moveable; corporeal and incorporeal

As well as recognising different kinds of rights, Scots law recognises different kinds of property. The distinction between corporeal and incorporeal things has already been discussed. There is a further distinction between heritable and moveable property. **3.56**

The heritable-moveable distinction is basically a distinction between land and rights in land on the one hand and everything else on the other. In many systems, the equivalent of heritable property is called immoveable property because land cannot really be moved. Of course, it would be possible to dig up a lot of the soil from a plot of land, put it in a lorry and drive it away but the digging up of the soil would separate it from the land. This separation of the soil from the earth would mean it was no longer part of the land and therefore no longer heritable. As well as land itself, rights in land are heritable: so servitudes or rights in security over land are examples of incorporeal heritable property. **3.57**

The term heritable derives from the old Scots law of succession, under which the land passed to the heir, while the moveable property passed to an executor who administered it either according to the deceased's will or to the law of intestate succession. There are some examples of heritable property not connected to land,[28] but they are not important for the purposes of this book. **3.58**

Combining the two divisions of types of property gives four possible categories: **3.59**

Corporeal heritable	Incorporeal heritable
Corporeal moveable	Incorporeal moveable

While the basic principles remain the same, the details of the rules about how property is dealt with vary depending on which of the four categories a right falls into.

ACQUIRING AND DEALING WITH PROPERTY

Publicity principle

Since property rights affect third parties it is important that they are discoverable by third parties, particularly potential purchasers. For that reason, some public act is usually required for the constitution or transfer of real rights. Until that act is completed, the grantee will not acquire the real right. **3.60**

28 Erskine, *Institute* 3.2.6.

3.61 Publicity benefits third parties but it imposes costs on the parties to the transaction because it means doing something extra for the sake of notifying others. There is a balance to be struck between the effectiveness of the notice and the burden it puts on the transacting parties. Where this balance lies varies depending on the type of property and the nature of the transaction (as will be discussed below). The principal means of publicity are registration and change of possession.

Specificity principle

3.62 The other general principle which plays an important role in the rules on acquiring and dealing with property is the principle of specificity. Since real rights are rights in particular things, it is important to know which thing is being burdened or transferred. For this reason, a disposition[29] of 'some of my land' could not effectively transfer anything. The Keeper of the Register would not know which plot was being transferred. This principle explains why s. 16 of the Sale of Goods Act 1979 (the 1979 Act) requires goods to be ascertained before ownership can pass. Like the publicity principle, the specificity principle is not always strictly adhered to. The main exception is found in s. 20A of the 1979 Act and it is discussed in Chapter Six below.

Original acquisition

3.63 Most property which is relevant to commercial life is already owned by someone and is acquired by a grant from that person. However, it is possible to acquire property without the involvement of any prior owner, indeed, without there being any prior owner at all. This is known as original acquisition of property. It is so called because the owner acquires a fresh right to the property rather than having someone else's right transferred to them.

3.64 There are a number of different mechanisms for original acquisition. The key common factor is that, in every case, the legal effect results from some physical act done to the property, which explains the irrelevance of any prior owner. The terms for the various mechanisms by which this occur may look rather puzzling. They are derived from Latin and this area of property law draws very heavily on Roman law.

Occupation

3.65 The simplest method of original acquisition is occupation. If property is ownerless, anyone may acquire it by taking possession of it with the intention of becoming owner. This principle derives from Roman law and is expressed in the maxim *quod nullius est fit occupantis*. However, it is of very limited relevance because ownerless property is very unusual.

3.66 Land is rarely ownerless. Under the now-abolished feudal system, the Crown was considered to have the ultimate right to all land. Grants by the Crown were the ultimate basis of private persons' rights in land. Therefore, any

29 The special term for the voluntary transfer of land. The deed by which land is disponed is known as a disposition.

residual land, over which no one else had acquired a right of ownership, remained with the Crown. Secondly, occupation will not usually apply to property that has been owned. If property has been owned and is then lost or abandoned or where the owner ceases to exist it is considered *bona vacantia*. Another maxim applies to such property: *quod nullius est fit domini regis* – what is owned by no one belongs to the Crown. This means that the Crown has the right to administer ownerless property: either taking ownership itself or granting it to another.[30]

Wild animals form a slight exception to what has just been said. It is impossible to tell whether a wild animal has never been captured or has been captured and escaped. Therefore, wild animals are treated as capable of occupation even if they have been owned and then escape and no regard need be had for the Crown's right to administer *bona vacantia*. **3.67**

Specification

Where items are taken and used to make a new thing (a *nova species*: thus the name) specification occurs. Of course, if the items belong to the person who makes them, there is no issue. If Spencer bakes bread using flour, yeast and water which belong to him then the ingredients are his and so is the loaf. The law of specification addresses what happens when a new thing is made from someone else's property, as where Spencer uses Olivia's flour and yeast to make his loaf. The rationale for the rule is that the raw materials have ceased to exist and that the person who made the new thing is entitled to it, although the owner of the raw material is entitled to compensation from the acquirer.[31] **3.68**

Where the process is irreversible and the manufacturer is not aware that the property belongs to another, the manufacturer becomes the owner of the new thing.[32] Where, however, the process can be reversed, ownership remains with the owner of the raw materials. So Spencer owns the loaf, even if he uses Olivia's ingredients. If, however, he had made a salad by adding some cherry tomatoes to some mixed leaves which belonged to Olivia, she would remain owner of the leaves because it would be easy enough to pick out the tomatoes and thus return things to their former state. **3.69**

Accession

A similar logic is apparent in accession. This applies where one thing becomes attached to another in such a way as to be subsumed into it. The thing which is subsumed (the accessory) becomes part of the other thing (the principal). The result is that the accessory ceases to have an existence independent of the principal. This in turn means that, if the accessory belongs to one person and the principal to another, the owner of the accessory will lose his or her right of ownership because the object of the right will disappear. As a matter of law, nothing new is acquired by the owner of the principal: the whole point of the **3.70**

30 *Joint Liquidators of Scottish Coal Co Ltd v Scottish Environment Protection Agency* [2013] CSIH 108, 2014 SC 372 at [108].

31 *International Banking Corporation v Ferguson, Shaw & Sons* 1910 SC 182.

32 Bell, *Principles*, §1298; *McDonald v Provan (of Scotland Street) Ltd* 1960 SLT 231.

doctrine is that the identity of the principal remains the same. Thus where paint is used to paint a wall, the paint becomes part of the wall. However, the operation of accession may significantly increase the value of the principal.

3.71 There are three elements to accession: attachment, functional subordination and permanence.[33] All must be present in some degree for accession to take place. The need for attachment is obvious: without it there would still be two separate objects. Functional subordination is important because it provides guidance as to which of two objects is the principal and which is the accessory. In some cases this is obvious: moveables accede to land rather than the other way around. Where there are two moveables, however, working out which has acceded to the other is important because it is the former owner of the principal who becomes owner of the item. Functional subordination is not the same as value. A diamond may be worth very much more than the ring it sits in but it is nonetheless functionally subordinate to it.[34] The better view is that the parties' intentions are not relevant to the operation of accession. Unless the attachment has some degree of permanence, one object can hardly be said to become part of the other. If the three elements of attachment, functional subordination and permanence are present, the fact that the person who did the attaching did not intend that accession should operate is irrelevant.

3.72 Where an object is productive, the items produced by the object belong to its owner. So, if Bob owns a cow and it has a calf, the calf belongs to Bob. If he has an apple tree, the apples belong to him. This is sometimes said to be accession by fruits. This title is somewhat perplexing since these processes are the opposite of accession: one thing is coming out of another rather than being subsumed by it.[35] Nonetheless, the rule has common sense appeal. It is difficult to see who else could reasonably be owner of the new thing.

Confusion and commixtion

3.73 In specification and accession, one right of ownership is lost because its object has disappeared. Commixtion and confusion cover the case where property belonging to two different people are mixed together in such a way that it is impossible to separate what belongs to one owner from what belongs to another. In both cases, the result is that the 'contributing' owners become common owners of the result of the combination.[36]

3.74 Confusion applies to liquids: so if 600 litres of petrol belonging to Enid are mixed with 300 litres of petrol belonging to Freddy the resulting 900 litres are owned in common by Freddy and Enid. Enid has a two third share and Freddy gets a one third share. Commixtion applies to solids: so if five tonnes of wheat belonging to George are mixed with five tonnes that belong to Helen, the resulting ten tonnes of wheat are owned in common by George and Helen. Each has a half share.

33 Reid, *The Law of Property in Scotland*, p. 571.
34 Stair, *Institutions* II.i.39.
35 Stair, *Institutions* II.i.34.
36 Bell, *Principles*, §1298.

Prescription

3.75 The methods of original acquisition discussed so far operate more or less instantaneously. They are the law's response to an action which fundamentally affects the physical state of the thing in question. There is, however, another method of original acquisition which only happens after a long period of time: positive prescription. Positive prescription only affects land and the requirements vary slightly depending on whether ownership or a subordinate real right is being acquired.

3.76 To acquire ownership of a piece of land, it is necessary to have a foundation writ and to possess it as of right, 'openly, peaceably and without judicial interruption' for ten years. A foundation writ is a registered deed (usually a disposition) which would have entitled the possessor to the land had it been effective.[37] From this it becomes evident that the effect of positive prescription here is to cure a void transfer. This process is, however, excluded in cases where the deed is forged and the grantee is aware of that fact.[38] Suppose that Bob forges Bill's signature on a disposition to Carol (who is unaware of the forgery). Carol registers the disposition and takes possession of the property. These things will not make Carol the owner because the disposition was not granted to her by Bill, the owner of the property. If, however, she possesses the land for ten years after registering the disposition, she will become the owner of the plot instead of Bill.

3.77 The possession requirements are designed to ensure that the owner has opportunity to challenge the prescriptive acquirer's right. The possession needs to be as of right so that someone who only possesses the plot because the owner lets them do so will not acquire it by prescription. The possession needs to be open so that the owner is alerted to the need to challenge the possessor's right to the plot. Possession is peaceable and without juridical interruption if no one challenges the possessor's right to possess. Taken together, the requirements mean that the possessor is behaving as owner and no one with a relevant interest has questioned this for ten years. That being the case, it makes sense to bring the legal situation into line with the facts on the ground.

3.78 In the majority of cases where it operates, positive prescription cures voidness of which the grantee is not aware. However, it also plays a role in bringing land whose owner cannot be traced back into circulation. This is done by registering an *a non domino* disposition (that is, a disposition by a non-owner) and waiting for the clock to run out. Of course, for this to operate, the Keeper must be willing to accept the *a non domino* disposition. The Keeper will only accept such a disposition if the land has been in possession of the *a non domino* disponer and/or the grantee for at least a year counting back from the application to register the deed. Further, the Keeper will only accept the registration if notification of the application to register has been given to the person who is currently entitled to the property or, if no such person can be traced, to the Crown.[39] If the Keeper decides to accept the deed for registration, they must

37 Prescription and Limitation (Scotland) Act 1973, s. 1(1).
38 Prescription and Limitation (Scotland) Act 1973, s. 1(2)(b).
39 Land Registration etc. (Scotland) Act 2012, s. 43(3)–(4).

notify the person entitled to the property or the Crown, if this is reasonably practicable.[40] These requirements are designed to ensure that the property is truly out of circulation before the *a non domino* disposition can be registered and that, even after this happens, the owner has every opportunity to step in and assert their right to the property.

3.79 It is also possible to acquire subordinate real rights by positive prescription.[41] Possession still requires to be open, peaceable and without judicial interruption and as of right but requires to be for twenty years rather than ten.[42] In practice, the most important subordinate real rights acquired by prescription are rights of way, which are a type of servitude that allow the holder to access their property by passing over the burdened property. In contrast to other subordinate real rights, it is possible to acquire a servitude by prescriptive possession without founding the prescriptive possession on a deed.[43] For servitudes, the notion of possession is somewhat difficult: the servitude is not a thing which can be held. However, exercise of the right is taken to be equivalent to possession.[44]

Voluntary grant of real rights

3.80 Since most property which is commercially significant is already owned by someone, the most important methods for acquisition of property or of a subordinate real right is by a grant from someone else (usually the owner of the property). This is sometimes known as derivative acquisition because the acquirer's right derives from someone else's right. Thus where Olivia grants a disposition of a piece of land to Albert and he registers it, Albert's right is derived from Olivia. Similarly, if Albert then grants a standard security to Bank of Alba Ltd, the bank's right is derived from Albert's.

3.81 The basis for recognition of these grants is the owner's freedom to deal with property as he or she wishes. For the same reason, the holder of a subordinate real right is entitled to discharge the right and thus to disencumber the property.

3.82 The fact that the acquisition derives from the granter's act implies three requirements for an effective grant: the granter must intend to bring the transfer about; since real rights are being transferred or created, this intention must usually be expressed in some formal, external act to give third parties notice of the right; and the granter must have the power to make the relevant grant (usually because they own the property which is transferred or encumbered).

Intention

3.83 From the requirement of intention, it follows that if Victoria is physically forced to sign a deed which purports to transfer property to William, that

40 Land Registration etc. (Scotland) Act 2012, s. 45(1)–(2).
41 Prescription and Limitation (Scotland) Act 1973, ss. 2, 3.
42 Prescription and Limitation (Scotland) Act 1973, ss. 2(1)(a) and 3(1) and (2).
43 Prescription and Limitation (Scotland) Act 1973, s. 3(2).
44 For more detail on prescriptive acquisition of servitudes, see A Peterson, *Prescriptive Servitudes* (Edinburgh: Edinburgh Legal Education Trust, 2020).

deed will be ineffective. Ineffective grants are typically said to be void. Even if William complies with the requisite formalities, he will not become owner because Victoria did not consent to the transfer. Similarly, if Ivor intends to transfer a cow to David but delivers it to Daniel, who knows of this, Daniel will not acquire the cow because there was no intention to make him the owner.[45]

In most cases, the property which is being dealt with has some value. For that reason, the main focus of discussion is on the granter's intention. However, there may be situations where someone tries to make a grant to someone who does not want it. For instance, the property in question might be very expensive to maintain. Therefore, the consent of the acquirer is also required for a valid transfer. Since both granter and acquirer must consent to a transfer, it is commonly said that a transfer or real agreement is necessary. **3.84**

Often, however, the acquirer's intention is less formally expressed than that of the granter. Thus, where land is disponed, the transferor's intention to the transfer must be expressed in formal writing. The acquirer's intention on the other hand, is inferred from their accepting delivery of the deed and presenting it for registration. Similarly, an assignor must express his or her intention to transfer a personal right to the assignee but very little is required of the assignee in terms of indicating consent to the transfer. It is even open to the assignor to make the intimation which completes the transfer. **3.85**

Formalities: heritable property

The intention to grant a real right usually requires some formal expression. In the case of heritable property, the formalities are quite extensive: the grant must be made in formal writing[46] and the written grant must usually be registered in the Land Register.[47] This writing can be either traditional writing on paper, subscribed with pen and ink[48] or an electronic document authenticated by an electronic signature.[49] This serves to preserve the terms of the grant in a durable medium and as an 'indication of seriousness', which helps to ensure that grants made are truly intended. Registration is in a public register and is thus a mechanism for giving notice to third parties. The requirement of registration is an application of the publicity principle. **3.86**

Failure to register can have serious consequences if the seller resells the property or becomes insolvent. Until registration, the seller remains the owner and thus retains the power to transfer the property. As discussed below, the fact **3.87**

45 Illustrated by the facts and result but not the reasoning in *Morrisson v Robertson* 1908 SC 332.

46 Requirements of Writing (Scotland) Act 1995, s. 1(2)(b).

47 Registration of Leases (Scotland) Act 1857, s. 20B; Conveyancing and Feudal Reform (Scotland) Act 1970, ss. 11 and 14–17; Land Registration etc. (Scotland) Act 2012, ss. 50, 51. There are some exceptions to the requirement for registration. Constitution of a lease of less than twenty years is completed by taking possession: Registration of Leases (Scotland) Act 1857, s. 1. Where a servitude is granted, it may be completed by exercise of the servitude right rather than by registration: *Campbell's Trs v Corporation of Glasgow* (1902) 4 F 752 at 757 per Lord Kinnear.

48 Requirements of Writing (Scotland) Act 1995, s. 2(1).

49 Requirements of Writing (Scotland) Act 1995, s. 9B(1). An electronic signature is a mechanism similar to the chip and PIN devices used for payment by debit or credit card.

that the seller is still the owner also means that the property is open to seizure by the seller's creditors.

Formalities: corporeal moveable property

3.88 There is no general register of corporeal moveable property.[50] The main reason for this is that corporeal moveables have tended to be of less value than land. For the same reason, there was less concern about preserving the terms of any grant or making sure that grants were seriously intended. At Scots common law, the only applicable formality was delivery. Both constitution of rights in security and transfers of ownership were effected by delivery accompanied by intention on the part of granter and grantee.[51] This remains the main rule for Scots law: where corporeal moveables are transferred as a gift or bartered, ownership will not pass before delivery. It is, however, subject to one very significant exception.

3.89 Victorian legislative reforms which are now embodied in the 1979 Act removed the requirement of delivery for transfers which are made in pursuance of contracts of sale. Section 17 of the 1979 Act provides that, where goods are sold, ownership will pass from seller to buyer at the moment when the parties intend as long as the goods are specific or ascertained (i.e. as long as the principle of specificity is satisfied). This means that ownership can pass before delivery or, if the parties prefer, at some point after delivery (usually when the price has been paid). An agreement to delay transfer until the price or other debts owed by the buyer to seller have been paid is known as a retention of title clause.

3.90 Often, there will be no discernible intention regarding the moment of transfer. If that is the case, then s. 18 supplies five rules which effectively create presumptions about when ownership is to pass. They are discussed in Chapter Six.

Formalities: incorporeal moveable property

3.91 Incorporeal moveable property cannot be delivered because there is no physical thing which can be handed over. Of course, intention to transfer still requires to be expressed and, in the case of intellectual property rights, this requires to be done in writing.[52]

50 The register of keepers of vehicles kept by the Driver and Vehicle Licensing Authority does not have property law effect because it is a register of keepers rather than owners. There is a register of ships, and dealings with ships are effected by registration in that register: Merchant Shipping Act 1995, Sch. 1, para. 1. There is also a Register of Aircraft Mortgages in which security rights over aircraft may be registered: Mortgaging of Aircraft Order 1972 (SI 1972/1268). The Scottish Law Commission has proposed the creation a register of statutory pledges as part of its moveable transactions project. This would allow the creation of non-possessory security over many classes of moveable property by registration. It is discussed further in Chapter Eleven: Non-judicial Real Security.

51 Bell *Commentaries* II, 11.

52 Registered Designs Act 1949, s. 15B(3); Patents Act 1977, s. 31(6); Copyright, Designs and Patents Act 1988, s. 90(3); Trade Marks Act 1994, s. 24(3).

3.92 In some special cases, there is a register on which transactions can be publicised.[53] It should be noted that the existence of such a register does not necessarily imply a straightforward transfer by registration regime like the one which applies to land but even in such cases, those who rely on the register will generally be protected from unregistered dealings.[54] One of the most important instances of the use of a register to publicise dealings with incorporeal property is company shares.

3.93 Company shares can be transferred only by changing the entry in the shareholders' register maintained by the company. A share certificate (in effect an extract from the register of shareholders) is sufficient evidence, unless the contrary is shown, of the shareholder's right to the relevant shares.[55] Since it is only *prima facie* evidence, a true owner (e.g. a person from whom a share certificate is stolen by a thief who succeeds in having their name inserted on the shareholders' register) is entitled to vindicate their rights against a person wrongly recorded as the owner and have the register corrected. However, a bona fide purchaser of shares is entitled to rely on a certificate issued by the company as evidence of the seller's right to the shares. If the seller is not in fact entitled to sell the shares, the buyer cannot be registered as a shareholder but is entitled to damages from the company at the market price of the shares.[56]

3.94 Where there is no register and no possibility of delivery, another mechanism for publication must be found. For the transfer of personal rights, that method is intimation to the debtor. So, if David owes Cecil £50 and Cecil wants to transfer his right to payment to Angela, two stages are necessary: a transfer agreement known as an assignation and intimation of the assignation to David.

3.95 As with corporeal property, failure to complete the second step exposes the grantee to the risk of transfer by the assignor to a second assignee who intimates first or of the assignor's insolvency. Further, intimation plays a role in protecting the debtor from prejudice. Until intimation is made, payment to the assignor will relieve the debtor of liability. Further, the debtor is entitled to set off against the assigned claim any debt owed by the assignor to the debtor which was constituted prior to intimation.

3.96 As part of its project on moveable transactions, the Scottish Law Commission has proposed the creation of a register of assignations to facilitate the assignations of claims (i.e. personal rights to performance of an obligation). Under the scheme, publicity (and thus completion of the assignation) could be effected

53 Registered Designs Act 1949, s. 17; Patents Act 1977, s. 32; Trade Marks Act 1994, s. 63; Companies Act 2006, ss. 113 and 771. Shares in large companies are often held and traded through intermediaries (effectively bodies that hold shares in trust for those who want to invest in the companies).

54 Registered Designs Act 1949, ss. 15B(2) and 19; Patents Act 1977, s. 33(1); Trade Marks Act 1994, s. 25(3).

55 Companies Act 2006, ss. 127 and 768.

56 *Re Bahia and San Francisco Railway Co* (1868) 3 QB 584 at 594. In English law, the company's liability is based on the principle of estoppel: it cannot deny the title of the seller because the certificate issued by the company causes the buyer to believe that the seller owned the shares. It is likely that the same rule would be applied in Scotland based on personal bar (which is the Scottish equivalent of this type of estoppel).

by either intimation to the debtor or by registration of the assignation in the new register.[57]

The 'nemo plus' rule: power to make the relevant grant

3.97 As well as intention to make the grant properly expressed, it is required that the granter has the power to make it. This is sometimes expressed by the maxim *nemo plus iuris ad alium transfere potest quam ipse haberet*: no one can transfer to another a greater right than they themselves have.[58] If Ferdinand purports to dispone a field which belongs to Geraldine, his action will be ineffective. Geraldine owns the field so she is the one with power to transfer it or burden it with subordinate real rights. The rule is not without exceptions, which are discussed below, but it remains a cornerstone of Scots property law.

3.98 In the majority of cases, the only person with the power to make the relevant grant is the owner of the asset affected by the grant. However, that is not always the case. Many rights in security empower the security holder to sell the relevant property if the debt is not paid. When the security holder does so, he or she is able to transfer the property from the current owner to the buyer. What is necessary, therefore, is the power to transfer or burden the thing. The owner has that power but it can also be granted to others. When the right in security is granted, the owner grants a conditional power to transfer to the security holder. (It is conditional because the security holder will only have the power to sell if the debtor fails to pay the debt.)

3.99 The *nemo plus* rule means that it is important for potential purchasers to know that the person they are buying from owns the property (or has the power to sell it for some other reason). The general rule is that a non-owner cannot make anyone else the owner. Therefore, if you buy from a non-owner, the true owner will be able to come and demand what you bought back from you. It does not matter that you really believed that the seller owned the relevant asset. Of course, you will have a right to damages from the seller but he or she might have made off with the money by then.

3.100 It should also be borne in mind that a granter may have the power to make an effective transfer although they act wrongfully in making the transfer. Making the grant was a breach of an obligation. However, since the obligation was not owed by the grantee, they may be able to rely on the grant despite its wrongful nature.

3.101 To take a simple example: Sophie concludes a contract with Florence to sell her flat for £150,000. The next day, Gary (who is unaware of the contract) offers to buy the flat for £200,000. Sophie decides that she could do with the extra money so she quickly concludes a second contract with Gary and dispones the flat to him. Gary registers the disposition, still unaware of the prior right. Sophie's conduct is wrongful: she has breached her contract with Florence. In that sense, she was not entitled to act as she did.

57 *Report on Moveable Transactions, Volume 1: Assignation of Claims* (Scot. Law Com. No. 249, 2017) Ch. 2, especially at para. 2.4.

58 A briefer but broadly equivalent maxim is *nemo dat quod non habet*: no one can give what they do not have.

However, her grant to Gary is effective. Sophie was still the owner of the flat when she made the grant to Gary. She still had the ownership and so what she gave to Gary was no greater than what she had herself. Therefore, the *nemo plus* rule is not a problem for Gary. Sophie's breach of contract will of course make her liable to Florence in damages since the transfer does not set aside her contractual obligations. **3.102**

The 'nemo plus' rule: scope of the right

The rule says that no one can transfer a *greater* right than they themselves has. This has implications, not only for cases where a granter has no right at all but also for cases where the granter's right is limited. If Alf has a servitude over Blackacre, he can transfer the servitude to someone else. However, having the servitude does not entitle Alf to make anyone the owner of Blackacre. Similarly, if Tessa has a lease of a shop for thirty years, she may be entitled to transfer it to someone else but when she does so, she can only transfer an entitlement for so much of the lease as is still to run. In other words, no one can expand the scope of a right by transferring it to another. **3.103**

This aspect of the *nemo plus* rule is particularly important in the context of assignation where it is expressed in its own maxim *assignatus utitur iure auctoris*: the assignee uses the right of the author. The *assignatus utitur* rule (or rather, the *assignatus utitur* aspect of the *nemo plus* rule) has important implications for debtor protection. **3.104**

As noted above, rights are assets which, in the absence of any special rule, the right holder is entitled to transfer without the consent of the debtor. The justification for this is that right belongs to the right holder and persons are generally entitled to deal with their assets as they see fit. However, since the debtor does not have say in whether the transfer takes place, he or she should not be prejudiced by its occurrence. **3.105**

The *assignatus utitur* rule plays a key role in ensuring this protection. It means that any defences which the debtor had against the assignor may also be invoked against the assignee. If David owes Colin £100 under a contract for the supply of goods, David will typically be entitled to withhold payment until the goods are supplied. Colin can assign his right to Agnes before delivering the goods but if he does so Agnes will not be able to force David to pay unless Colin has supplied the goods. **3.106**

Transfer by non-owners: currency and negotiable instruments

The normal rule is that a grant by someone who lacks the power to make the relevant grant is ineffective.[59] In some circumstances, the law will protect those who deal with certain granters who lack the power to make the relevant grant. The main reason for these protections is to facilitate commerce. Were such protection not afforded, expensive and time-consuming attempts to establish sellers' rights would need to be undertaken. This would be bad for the economy as a whole. **3.107**

59 For example, the Sale of Goods Act 1979, s. 21(1).

3.108 The most common example of this kind of rule is so deeply embedded that most people do not even think about it: cash payment. If Anna sells something to Brian and he pays her in notes or coins, she will not ask him to demonstrate that he owns them. It is quite possible that Brian may have stolen them or found them on the street but in the absence of special circumstances such as notes that are stained with special ink, Anna would have no way of knowing this. For this reason, the presumption of ownership which generally arises from possession is much stronger in the case of money and the person from whom Brian stole them would not be able to reclaim them from Anna.[60]

3.109 Similar protections are afforded to recipients of negotiable instruments.[61] These are documents which embody a right to payment. One of the purposes of this embodiment is to allow the right to be transferred by transferring the document. The ease with which negotiable instruments can be transferred is enhanced by the fact that anyone who receives a bill of exchange in good faith (i.e. without knowing that the transferor does not own it) and for value is treated as the owner of the instrument.[62]

3.110 The protection afforded to those who receive cash and negotiable instruments is very extensive. Protection for those who receive other types of property is more limited. The protections cover situations where the third party is particularly likely to be misled into thinking that the granter has the power to transfer the asset in question or to grant a subordinate real right in the asset.

Transfer by non-owners: Sale of Goods Act 1979

3.111 In the 1979 Act, there are three main cases where buyers are protected in this way: where the owner is personally barred from denying the seller's authority to sell; where ownership has passed but the seller is still in possession; and where ownership has not passed but the buyer is already in possession.

3.112 The first case is addressed in s. 21(1). It sets out the basic *nemo plus* rule but then makes an exception for cases 'where the owner of the goods is by his conduct precluded from denying the seller's authority to sell'. This covers situation where the owner has given the impression that the seller had authority to sell and this has been relied on by the buyer. So, if Olivia leads Bertie to believe that her dog is in fact owned by Sidney, s. 21(1) would mean that Bertie would become owner if Sidney sold him the dog.

3.113 The other two situations, covered by ss. 24 and 25, deal with the consequences of the abandonment of the delivery requirement. As noted above, the 1979 Act removed delivery as a requirement for transfer of ownership in sale situations. Delivery was a means of giving notice to third parties of the transfer. Once it was abandoned, it became more difficult for third parties to identify the owner of the goods. Sections 24 and 25 protect third parties who are misled. In both cases, the third party acquirer needs to be in good faith

60 Stair, *Institutions* 2.1.34; Bell *Principles*, § 1333.

61 Negotiable instruments are discussed in more detail in Chapter Nine: Payment Obligations.

62 Bills of Exchange Act 1882, s. 38(2).

(i.e. to believe that the person in possession is the owner) and to have taken delivery of the goods.[63]

3.114 Section 24 deals with the case where ownership has passed but there has been no delivery. In such a situation, the seller remains in possession but a third party dealing with the seller has no way of knowing that the seller no longer owns the goods in question. A third party who buys the goods from the seller in good faith and takes delivery of them is protected. Section 24 says that such a delivery 'has the same effect as if the person making the delivery or transfer were expressly authorised by the owner of the goods to make the same'. Thus, the seller is treated as the first buyer's agent and so a transfer is effected from the first to the second buyer.

3.115 For example, Olivia sells her dog to Sidney but Sidney asks her keep it for the weekend when he will be away on holiday. During the weekend, she sells the dog a second time to Bertie who is in good faith and takes possession. The application of s. 18, rule 1 means that Sidney became the owner of the dog as soon as the contract with Olivia was concluded. However, s. 24 operates to protect Bertie so ownership passes from Sidney to Bertie.

3.116 Section 25 deals with the converse case: where there is a retention of title clause meaning that the goods are still owned by the seller but the seller has allowed the buyer to take possession of them. As with s. 24, it would be difficult for a third party to know about this arrangement.

3.117 The wording of s. 25 is a little complex but, broadly stated, it works in the same way as s. 24: the buyer in possession is treated as the seller's agent and so ownership is transferred direct from the seller to third party. So if Olivia sells the dog to Sidney but they agree that she will remain owner for a trial period of two weeks, so Sidney can see if they get along, Olivia will retain ownership although she delivers the dog to Sidney. If, however, Sidney sells the dog to Bertie after two days, Bertie will become owner provided that he is in good faith and takes delivery. Ownership would pass directly from Olivia to Bertie.

3.118 Subsection (2) of s. 25 sets out an important exception to the protection in s. 25. It does not apply where the buyer in possession had acquired the goods under a consumer credit agreement. These are defined in s. 8(1) of the Consumer Credit Act 1974 (the 1974 Act). Confusingly, the definition does not require that the credit be given to a consumer. It simply defines a consumer credit agreement as an agreement under which an individual gets credit of any amount. Equally bizarrely, the 1974 Act defines the term 'individual' as including partnerships and unincorporated associations.[64]

3.119 Since the most common reason for retention of title is that the goods have been supplied on credit, this means that s. 25 protection will usually be limited to third parties who buy from companies or limited liability partnerships. The

63 Both sections refer to 'delivery or transfer' to the third party, which seems to suggest that transfer is an alternative to delivery. However, in *Michael Gerson (Leasing) Ltd v Wilkinson* [2001] QB 514, the Court of Appeal suggested that transfer of possession was necessary in all cases, although constructive delivery (where the transferee acquires possession by the virtue of the fact that the person who has physical control of them acknowledge that they are held on the transferee's behalf) was accepted as sufficient.

64 Consumer Credit Act 1974, s. 189.

situation is further complicated by s. 27 of the Hire Purchase Act 1964. That section provides equivalent protection to that found in s. 25 of the 1979 Act for third parties who buy cars from hire purchasers or buyers in protection. Unlike s. 25 of the 1979 Act, s. 27 of the 1964 Act does not exclude consumer credit agreements but its protection is limited to third parties who are 'private purchasers'. That means that it does not extend to third parties whose business is the sale of motor vehicles or the financing of such sales.[65] It is highly unsatisfactory that the law should be so incoherent. It may be clarified somewhat by some examples below.

3.120 Edward sells some computers to Cawdors and Associates, a firm of solicitors that operates as a partnership. The computers are supplied on credit and Edward and Cawdors agree that ownership will remain with Edward until he is paid. Cawdors sell the computers on to Peterson Thirlstane, another firm of solicitors. Cawdors go bust and Edward tries to get the computers back from Peterson Thirlstane. Can Peterson Thirlstane rely on s. 25?

3.121 Cawdors were a buyer in possession and they delivered the goods to Peterson Thirlstane, who were in good faith, so all the requirements of s. 25(1) were fulfilled. However, Cawdor had received the goods on credit and as a partnership they are an individual in the terms of the 1974 Act. Since they are an individual and they received the goods on credit, this is a consumer credit agreement within the terms of s. 8 of the 1974 Act. That in turn means that the exception in s. 25(2) applies so Peterson Thirlstane are not protected.

3.122 If, however, Cawdors and Associates had been a limited liability partnership rather than a general partnership, Peterson Thirlstane would have been safe. A limited liability partnership is a body corporate[66] so it is not an individual in terms of the 1974 Act. That means that the supply of computers on credit to it would not be a consumer credit agreement in terms of s. 8 of the 1974 Act. Therefore, the exception in s. 25(2) of the 1979 Act would not apply. Since Peterson Thirlstane fulfil the requirements of s. 25(1), they would be protected.

3.123 Alternatively, if Edward had supplied cars rather than computers to Cawdors and these had been sold on, Peterson Thirlstane would be entitled to rely on s. 27 of the Hire Purchase Act 1964 since Peterson Thirlstane's business does not involve dealing in motor vehicles or financing such dealing.

Transfer and grant by non-owners: Land Registration etc. (Scotland) Act 2012

3.124 As noted above, most transactions that affect land must be registered so third parties have notice of what has happened. This might be thought to be all the protection potential purchasers would need against dealing with a non-owner who purports to sell them land or grant a subordinate real right over it. If every transaction is publicly registered, it should be possible to work out who owns each piece of land. However, mistakes occur even in the process of

65 See the definition of 'trade of finance purchaser' and of 'private purchaser' in the Hire Purchase Act 1964, s. 29(2).
66 Limited Liability Partnerships Act 2000, s. 1(2).

registration. It may be, for instance, that a fraudster has forged a disposition and managed to convince the Keeper of the Register to enter him or her as owner when in fact they are not. A third party consulting the register would then be misled.

The Land Registration etc. (Scotland) Act 2012 (the 2012 Act) contains rules which protect third parties who transact with those who appear from the register to be owners but in fact are not. This makes the register more reliable for those who are buying property and thus facilitates dealings with land. Of course, protecting the buyer who relies on an inaccurate entry on the register has a downside. If the buyer becomes owner, the former owner loses their right. This downside also exists in relation to currency and corporeal moveables but it has been taken more seriously in the context of land because land tends to be more valuable. The 2012 Act makes provision not only for the protection of those who rely on the register but also for the compensation of those who lose out as a result of that protection. **3.125**

There are two levels of protection for those who rely on the register: a money guarantee from the state and validation of void grants. For the sake of simplicity, the example of a transfer of ownership will be used as an example but the 2012 Act also protects other grantees. **3.126**

The money guarantee is known as the Keeper's warranty. When the Keeper accepts a putative transferee's application for registration, they warrant to the applicant that the register is correct in showing them as owner and that none of the subordinate real rights which should be shown on the register as affecting the property have been missed out.[67] The Keeper may exclude or restrict the warranty in circumstances where it is appropriate (usually because of doubts about some aspect of the rights claimed by the applicant).[68] If it turns out that the applicant did not become the owner, perhaps because the register was inaccurate in showing that the person who granted the disposition to the transferee was the owner, then register will be rectified to reflect the true position[69] and the transferee who made the application will be entitled to compensation from the Keeper.[70] **3.127**

Bob sees a nice house in an area he would like to move into. He checks the Land Register and finds that the owner is Frank, who was registered as owner and moved in one month ago. Frank agrees to sell the house to him. Bob pays the price, moves in and registers his disposition. Two months later, Olivia appears. She says that she is the true owner of the property and that Frank appeared on the register because he had forged her signature on a disposition and that Frank had only been in the property for six months. If she can prove that this is the case, the register will be rectified and Bob will get a payout under the Keeper's warranty. Of course, since Olivia owns the house, Bob will have to move out unless he comes to some arrangement with Olivia. **3.128**

The Keeper's liability is excluded in a number of circumstances, set out in s. 78 of the 2012 Act. The most important exceptions are set out in paragraphs **3.129**

67 Land Registration etc. (Scotland) Act 2012, s. 73.
68 Land Registration etc. (Scotland) Act 2012, s. 75.
69 Land Registration etc. (Scotland) Act 2012, s. 80.
70 Land Registration etc. (Scotland) Act 2012, s. 77(1).

(b) and (c). An applicant who knows that the register will not be accurate when his or her entitlement is entered is not entitled to compensation. Neither is an applicant who caused the Keeper to make an inaccurate entry by a failure to take reasonable care in making the application. So, if Bob knew that Frank was not the owner at the time when he registered his disposition, his right to compensation under the Keeper's warranty would be excluded.

3.130 Assuming that none of the s. 78 grounds apply, Bob may well be grateful for the money since Frank is likely to be long gone so the chances of recovering damages from him may be minimal. However, what Bob wanted was the house not the money. There are circumstances in which Bob would get the property rather than mere monetary compensation: that is the second level of protection. Of course, giving that protection to Bob involves taking the property away from Olivia, so more stringent conditions are applied.

3.131 The conditions are set out in s. 86(3) of the 2012 Act. As with the Keeper's warranty, Bob requires to be in good faith and the disposition needs to be accepted by the Keeper without excluding warranty. The extra requirement is that property had either been possessed for one year by the disponer; or, alternatively, the disponer and the applicant had possessed the property for a year between them without the inaccuracy being drawn to the Keeper's attention.

3.132 So, if Frank had acquired possession of the house eighteen months before selling it to Bob, then on registration, Bob would become the owner of the house.[71] Alternatively, if Frank had taken possession one month before the sale but more than eleven months expired before Olivia returned to challenge Bob's right, he would be safe. In that case, Bob would become owner eleven months after moving in because that would be the point when the combined possession of Bob and Frank reached one year.[72] In either case, the result is that ownership passes directly from Olivia to Bob. Frank never was and never becomes the owner. If that happens, Olivia is entitled to compensation from the Keeper.[73]

3.133 There are equivalent rules which protect assignees of registered leases[74] and grantees of servitudes.[75] Grantees of standard securities are only protected by the Keeper's warranty. The reason for this is that, unlike the other rights just mentioned, money from the Keeper can give the grantee of security complete satisfaction. All that the standard security entitled its holder to do was to sell the property for the satisfaction of a debt. It should be a matter of indifference whether the money is generated by the sale of the property or comes from the Keeper's funds, therefore, there is no good reason for curing the standard security and thus burdening the real owner's title.

71 Land Registration etc. (Scotland) Act 2012, s. 86(4)(a).
72 Land Registration etc. (Scotland) Act 2012, s. 86(4)(b).
73 Land Registration etc. (Scotland) Act 2012, s. 94.
74 Land Registration etc. (Scotland) Act 2012, s. 88.
75 Land Registration etc. (Scotland) Act 2012, s. 90.

Voidable grants

3.134 The problems discussed so far are problems which would mean that the grantee did not acquire the right at all: if there is no intention to make the grant, if the proper formalities are not complied with or if the granter did not have the power to make the relevant grant, the result is that the grant is void. That means that it is totally ineffective and no right is conferred on the grantee.

3.135 However, there is another class of cases where there is a problem with the grant but it has less drastic consequences. Some grants are said to be not void but voidable. This means that the grant is initially effective but that someone has a personal right against the grantee which entitles them to have the grant reversed. Usually, the reason for this is that the grant involved a wrong against the person who is entitled to have it reversed.

3.136 The simplest example is a fraudulently induced transfer. In that case, the transferor truly intends to transfer the property but that consent has been wrongfully obtained. For instance, Freddy might lie to Vanessa, telling her that he is her long-lost grandson. She might gift some land to him because she believes this. She really intended to transfer the land to him but that intention was induced by Freddy's fraud. Therefore the transfer is voidable at Vanessa's instance.

3.137 In many cases the granter is the person who is entitled to avoid the transaction but this is not necessarily the case. Some of the most important grounds of voidability involve cases where a third party is entitled to set the transaction aside.

3.138 If a creditor of the granter has used the diligence of inhibition against the granter, then any grant of a real right affecting heritable property will be voidable at that creditor's instance.[76] Similarly, grants made by an insolvent debtor which operate to the prejudice of his or her creditors may be voidable at the instance of those creditors or of the insolvency official acting on their behalf.[77]

3.139 Further, although a contract of sale will not prevent the seller from transferring the subjects of sale to a third party or from burdening them if the buyer has not yet become owner, the grant to the third party may be voidable at the buyer's instance under the so-called 'offside goals rule'.[78] It allows the holder of a personal right to a real right (e.g. someone with a contractual right to have property transferred or to have a subordinate real right granted) to set aside a grant made by the party obliged under that right on two conditions. The first is that the grant which is challenged must prejudice the prior personal right in some way. This is fairly obvious in the case of a double sale: if the seller has transferred the object of the sale to someone else they will no longer be in a position to transfer it to the buyer. The second condition is that the subsequent grantee must either know about the prior personal right or have received the grant gratuitously.

76 See para. 12.39 onward.
77 See paras. 13.37 and 14.114 onward.
78 *Rodger (Builders) Ltd v Fawdry* 1950 SC 483.

3.140 Sidney contracts with Bertie to sell his house and then makes a second contract with Glenda for the sale of the house. Glenda registers her disposition first so she becomes the owner. However, Bertie will be able to set aside the transfer from Sidney to Glenda if he can show that she knew of his contract with Sidney when she concluded her contract with Bertie. If the transfer to Glenda was not a sale but a gift, Bertie would be able to set it aside without the need to show that she was in bad faith.

3.141 The justification for the offside goals rule is connected to the rules allowing challenge to acts by an insolvent debtor. In each case, the actions of the granter would, if allowed to stand, defeat the interests of a prior personal right holder. Where the recipient of the second grant is in bad faith or gratuitous, this is not thought to be fair.

3.142 As far as the grantee is concerned, it makes little difference whether the grant is void or voidable: in either case challenge will lead to loss of enjoyment of the right or the property. However, the difference between a void grant, where the grantee receives no right and a voidable grant, which is effective albeit liable to be set aside, is very important for successors.

3.143 If the initial grant is void, then the *nemo plus* rule means that any attempt by the grantee to pass on what was granted will be ineffective and the owner will be able to recover the property even if it has been transferred on to a third party. If, however, the grant is merely voidable, then the grantee has the relevant right unless and until the grant is set aside. That means that they are able to transfer the right or burden the relevant property. The recipient of this further grant is not bound by the personal right which enables the first grant to be set aside. Therefore, the recipient of the further grant is safe.

3.144 So, if Glenda was in bad faith regarding the contract between Sidney and Bertie, the transfer to her would be voidable. Her right is precarious because Bertie could come along and have it set aside in court. If, however, she sells the house on to Tracy (who is unaware of any of this), Tracy will become the owner and will not be subject to any challenge from Bertie. Glenda was the owner and so she had the power to make Tracy the owner and Bertie's personal right against Glenda is none of Tracy's business.

3.145 The recipient of the further grant will find him or herself vulnerable, however, if that grant was gratuitous or if the recipient was in bad faith (i.e. knew or should have known that his or her author's right was voidable). This rule is set out for sale of goods in s. 23 of the 1979 Act but it also applies as a matter of common law to transfers of other kinds of property and to rights burdening them. So, if Tracy knew about the circumstances in which Glenda acquired the house, Bertie could set aside the transfer from Glenda to Tracy and the transfer from Sidney to Glenda. That would enable him to enforce his contract against Sidney and thus become owner of the house. Since the further grant defeats the personal right to reverse the transaction, Tracy's vulnerability as a bad faith and/or gratuitous recipient can be seen as an application of the offside goals rule.

Judicial acquisition

In certain circumstances, the court will intervene to transfer property from one person to another or to grant subordinate real rights. This is done in order to secure the fulfilment of the former owner's obligations. Although judicial acquisition occurs without the consent of, and usually against the will of, the former owner it is nonetheless a form of derivative acquisition. For that reason the *nemo plus* rule applies to judicial acquisition: the court can confer no better right on the acquirer than it takes from the former owner. 3.146

Adjudication in implement and execution by the sheriff clerk

The simplest form of judicial acquisition is adjudication in implement. It is a long-recognised but rarely used remedy by which effect can be given to an obligation to convey heritable property. It is done by raising an action in the Court of Session, the end result of which is that the relevant heritable property is declared by the court to belong to the pursuer,[79] which is then completed by registration.[80] 3.147

In practice, the pursuer often seeks specific implement of the obligation to deliver the disposition, which failing for authority to the clerk of court to execute the deed.[81] This is the method expressly provided for in s. 87 of the Courts Reform (Scotland) Act 2014, which provides that the sheriff may direct the sheriff clerk to execute the deed which should have been granted by the defender and that a deed so executed is effective as if it had been granted by the defender. 3.148

Reduction

Where a grant which affects heritable property is voidable, the personal right to reversal of the transaction is given effect by reduction. Like adjudication in implement, reduction of a transfer operates as a judicial conveyance. Reduction only takes effect against good faith third parties on registration of the decree in the public register.[82] 3.149

Insolvency officials

The appointment of a trustee in sequestration operates to vest everything in the debtor's patrimony (other than exempt assets) in the trustee in sequestration.[83] However, with regard to heritable property, this vesting requires to be completed by registration and the trustee must leave twenty-eight days from the date of publication of the sequestration proceedings before registering.[84] The purpose of this window is to allow those to whom the bankrupt has 3.150

79 J Graham Stewart, *A Treatise on the Law of Diligence* (Edinburgh: W. Green, 1898), pp.667–669.
80 Titles to Land Consolidation (Scotland) Act 1868, s. 62.
81 See further para. 12.50 below.
82 Conveyancing (Scotland) Act 1924, ss. 46 and 46A.
83 Bankruptcy (Scotland) Act 2016, s. 78. See para. 13.27 onward.
84 Bankruptcy (Scotland) Act 2016, s. 78(3)–(4).

granted real rights to register their grants. If they do not do so prior to the trustee's registration, they will not get the right which they were granted and rank as unsecured creditors in the sequestration.

3.151 Where the insolvent debtor is a company rather than a natural person, the relevant mechanism for selling off the assets for creditors' benefit is liquidation rather than sequestration. In most cases, this does not involve transfer of assets to the insolvency official: the liquidator simply takes control of the company and uses that authority to dispose of the assets. However, the liquidator may apply to the court for an order which vests the company's property in him or her.[85]

Diligence

3.151 As well as acquiring ownership as a result of judicial action, it is also possible to acquire rights in security in the debtor's assets. The general Scots law term for this mechanism is diligence.[86] However, the term diligence has a slightly broader scope than judicial rights in security. It covers both freeze diligences, which restrict the debtor's capacity to make grants affecting his or her property, and seize diligences, which give the creditor a right in security in the asset against which diligence is done.

85 Insolvency Act 1986, s. 145.

86 See generally Chapter Twelve: Judicial Security: Diligence.

Chapter Four

Agency

John MacLeod

INTRODUCTION

What is agency?

The idea that one person can transact on behalf of another is essential to modern business practice. The person on whose behalf an action is done is known as the principal, the person doing the act is known as the agent. In this chapter, for the sake of ease of expression, the principal will be referred to with the feminine pronoun, the agent with the masculine, and the third party with the neutral pronoun ('it'). So, in the typical case, a male agent will be transacting on behalf of a female principal with a third party that is a juristic person. **4.01**

The core idea is that the agent acts, but this act is attributed to the principal; the act is treated as if the principal had done it herself. If Peter is Alice's agent, and he makes an offer to buy some whisky from Teldi Ltd on Alice's behalf, then the contract which would result from Teldi's acceptance is one between Alice and Teldi. Peter made the offer but it is treated as if it was made by Alice. **4.02**

Many of the materials which discuss agency do so in terms that suggest that all agents do is conclude contracts on behalf of their principals. However, it is clear that agents can also perform other juridical acts[1] on their principals' behalf: they can transfer property,[2] appeal decisions of courts or tribunals,[3] and make or accept payments.[4] **4.03**

Many European systems have a broader notion of agency. They recognise that agents may carry out acts in the principal's name which are attributed to the latter. They call this direct agency. However, they also recognise a second category: indirect agency. In indirect agency, the agent acts in his own name but does so for the principal's benefit. Crudely put, the result is that acts done are attributed to the agent but agency rules regulate the relationship between principal and agent. **4.04**

This means that, as far as the rest of the world is concerned, the principal has no part in the transaction. However, the agent will have a duty to communicate **4.05**

1 In this chapter, the term 'juridical act' is used in a very broad sense to mean any voluntary conduct intended to affect someone's legal position.

2 For example, Factors Act 1889, s. 2(1), applied to Scotland by Factors (Scotland) Act 1890, s. 1(1).

3 *Goodall v Bilsland* 1909 SC 1152.

4 *International Sponge Importers Ltd v Andrew Watt & Sons* 1911 SC (HL) 57.

the benefit of the transaction to the principal and the principal will have a duty to indemnify the agent for any expenses associated with it. To return to the earlier example, if Peter was an indirect agent, he would make the offer to buy the whisky in his own name. That would make him a party to the contract of sale so he would be liable to Teldi for the price and Teldi would be obliged to supply the whisky to him rather than to Alice. However, Peter would be obliged to pass the whisky on to Alice (or to deal with it in accordance with her instructions) and Alice would be obliged to pay Peter the price which he paid Teldi. Lawyers in the UK have tended not to classify this kind of arrangement as agency, although agency on behalf of an undisclosed principal (discussed at paras 4.56–4.66 below) might be regarded as half-way between direct and indirect agency.

Why might an agent be used?

4.06 There are many reasons why a principal may prefer to transact through an agent rather than acting personally. The simplest and one of the most common is lack of time. If Stella owns and runs a shop and wants to keep it open when she is at the wholesaler buying more stock, she might employ Alf to look after things while she is away. Since Stella is a sole trader, a customer who buys something from the shop when she is there makes a contract of sale with her. Is it any different if Alf is manning the till when the purchase is made? No: Alf is Stella's agent, selling on her behalf. This remains so even if Alf is an employee as employees often act as agents.

4.07 Another common reason is that the agent has special knowledge or expertise that the principal lacks. This is why most people who are buying or selling a house do so through a solicitor (sometimes called a law agent). The solicitor knows what needs to be done and what problems to look out for. Similarly, a company looking to expand into a new country may employ an agent who understands the local business conditions to run its affairs there.

4.08 A company has another important reason for transacting through an agent. A company is a juristic person, with no physical body. As such, it lacks the physical presence necessary to express consent. Since expressions of consent or intention are essential to most juridical acts, this is a problem. It is addressed to some degree by the Requirements of Writing (Scotland) Act 1995, which has procedures for subscription by various kinds of juristic person.[5] They are, however, of no relevance where writing is not used. If the shop was owned by a company rather than by Stella, Alf's position as an agent would be even more important. Unlike Stella, the company could not man the tills and sell directly to customers. Its only practical means of selling is through agents.

4.09 In agency, there are three parties whose interrelationships need to be considered: the principal, the agent and the third party. If everything works properly, there should be a relationship between the principal and the third party by virtue of the agent's act on the principal's behalf. There will also be legal relations between the agent and the principal by virtue of the rules that regulate

5 Requirements of Writing (Scotland) Act 1995, Sch. 2. See Chapter One: Introduction to Juristic Persons, para. 1.37 onward.

the agent's duties to the principal and vice versa. There should be no legal relations between the agent and the third party because the agent is merely the conduit through whom the principal acts. If things go wrong, however, the agent may find himself liable to the third party. Each of the three relationships will be considered in turn.

PRINCIPAL-THIRD PARTY RELATIONS

Under normal circumstances each person transacts on their own behalf but not on behalf of anyone else. This is important because juridical acts involve the exercise of private autonomy: they are part of the way in which the law enables us to live our lives as we choose. Autonomy does not make much sense if someone else is making the decisions. If giving effect to the contracts which Alice makes is part of the law's recognition of her private autonomy, it is difficult to see how this end is served if the contract comes into existence because of Peter's actions rather than Alice's. **4.10**

Further, persons are usually entitled to choose with whom they deal. In a sense this is also part of private autonomy. When Bill decides to enter into a contract of sale he may wish to buy from Sally but not from Sophie and the law respects that choice. **4.11**

The law of agency seems to challenge both of these basic values: the agent does the act but it is the principal who is bound and the third party deals with the agent but ends up transacting with the principal. These apparent anomalies are dealt with by two concepts which are central to the relationship between principals and third parties: authority and disclosure. **4.12**

Authority

Agency involves an agent acting on behalf of the principal but that is not the first step. Peter cannot just wake up one morning and decide that he will conclude a contract on Alice's behalf with Teldi Ltd or that he will make a gift of her car to Trudy. If Peter had no authority to conclude the contract with Teldi, then Teldi will not be able to enforce the contract against Alice. If Peter had no authority to give the car to Trudy then Alice will be entitled to get it back from her. **4.13**

If Peter is to be Alice's agent, Alice must do something which gives him the authority to bind her. Without authority to bind Alice, no juridical act which Peter does in Alice's name will be attributed to her. In this way, Alice's autonomy is recognised. Peter can do things which bind Alice but his power to do so derives from Alice's actions. Alice exercises her autonomy in conferring the power on Peter. All of this means that, when trying to work out if an act of a purported agent binds the alleged principal in a question with a third party, the first question to ask is whether the agent had authority to do the relevant act. **4.14**

Scope of authority

4.15 It is rare for a principal to want to confer universal authority on the agent. The agent will usually be authorised to do some acts but not others. When Stella leaves Alf in charge of the shop, she wants him to be able to sell goods to customers but not to sell the premises to a property developer. Therefore, it is necessary to ask not just whether the person who acted was the principal's agent but also whether the act in question was within the scope of his authority. The scope of authority can vary widely: an agent may be commissioned to undertake a specific sale or purchase or to manage all of the principal's business affairs. Agents whose authority is limited to particular tasks are sometimes referred to as special agents and those with wider authority as general agents.[6] However, in every case the key question is whether the agent had authority to do the particular act in question.

Kinds of authority

4.16 There are three broad types of authority: actual, retrospective and apparent. Actual authority is authority which has been granted by the principal prior to the transaction at issue. Retrospective authority, which is usually called ratification, is granted after the fact by the principal. Apparent authority covers situations where the principal has not granted authority either before or after the agent's act but is nonetheless bound because she is responsible for the third party's belief that the agent was authorised.

Actual authority

4.17 An agent has actual authority when the principal has granted power to do the relevant act beforehand. This grant is a juridical act by the principal and it is usually done in the context of a contract between the principal and agent in which the latter takes on obligations to the principal.[7]

4.18 It is often suggested that an agent need not have active capacity since he is a mere conduit for the principal's act.[8] If this is the case, it implies that the conferral of authority may be a unilateral act by the principal since requiring the agent's consent would imply his participation in the constitution of the agency relationship.[9] Someone without active capacity would not be able to so participate and thus could not become an agent in the first place.[10] In England, it is accepted that agency may arise from a unilateral conferral of authority

6 For example, Bell, *Principles*, § 219.

7 For example, *Freeman & Lockyer v Buckhurst Park Properties (Mangal) Ltd* [1964] 2 QB 480 at 502 per Diplock LJ.

8 For example, J J Gow, *Mercantile and Industrial Law of Scotland* (Edinburgh: W. Green, 1964), p. 516; A D M Forte and J P Van Niekerk, 'Agency' in R Zimmermann, D Visser and K Reid (eds), *Mixed Legal Systems in Comparative Perspective* (Oxford: Oxford University Press, 2004), p. 240 at 245. As to the meaning of active capacity see Chapter One: Introduction to Juristic Persons, para 1.04.

9 Given that an agent needs to understand what he is doing, this does not obviate the problems entirely: see L Macgregor, *The Law of Agency in Scotland* (Edinburgh: W. Green, 2013) para. 3–18.

10 For example, Age of Legal Capacity (Scotland) Act 1991, ss. 1(1)(a) and 9(d).

by the principal.[11] Of course, explaining the basis of the agent's duties to the principal becomes more difficult if agency can come into existence without the agent having to consent.

Like most other juridical acts, the conferral of authority need not be in writing and need not take any particular form. It may be done expressly or impliedly. In the latter case, the principal does not state explicitly that he or she authorises the agent. Rather, the authority is implied from the circumstances of the case. **4.19**

Thus, where an agent is given a task, authority is given to do everything necessary to complete the task,[12] so a solicitor who is asked to purchase land on someone's behalf is authorised to have searches made of the land register to make sure that there are no problems with the seller's title. Further, appointment to some roles implies authority to enter into certain kinds of transaction: a partner in a general partnership has authority to bind the firm in its usual business relations[13] and the managing director of a company has wide-ranging authority to bind the company.[14] This authority will often depend on what is usual in the given field of activity.[15] **4.20**

Implied authority is based on the presumption that this is what the principal intends but that principle can be rebutted. So it would be open to someone instructing a solicitor to require the solicitor to get specific authority before ordering a search of the land register and s. 5 of the Partnership Act 1890 envisages that the partners may agree to limit the authority of some or all of the partners. **4.21**

Ad hoc *agency*

A line of decisions in the Outer House has suggested a further category of agency which, if it is accepted, is best considered as a type of implied authority.[16] It is known as *ad hoc* agency. The concept is the creation of Lord Drummond Young and its precise contours are not yet clear. The basic idea is that, in cases where there is a mismatch between the parties to a contract and those who are performing the obligations and enforcing the rights, the person who is acting as a *de facto* party to the contract can be considered to be the agent of the true contracting party in order to get round the mismatch. **4.22**

The usual reason for the mismatch is either that the contract has been concluded by one member of a group of companies but is then performed by another member of the group, or that a business is restructured. A sole trader may transfer their business to a limited company of which they are the shareholder and director but neglect to assign contractual rights to the company or **4.23**

11 P Watts and F M B Reynolds, *Bowstead and Reynolds on Agency*, 22nd edn (London: Sweet & Maxwell, 2020), para. 1–006.
12 *Black v Cornelius* (1879) 6 R 581.
13 Partnership Act 1890, s. 5.
14 *Freeman & Lockyer v Buckhurst Park Properties* (n 7).
15 *Black v Cornelius* (n 12).
16 *Whitbread Group plc v Goldapple Ltd (No. 2)* 2005 SLT 281; *Laurence McIntosh Ltd v Balfour Beatty Group Ltd* [2006] CSOH 197; *Stirling v Westminster Properties Scotland Ltd* [2007] CSOH 117.

secure the consent of the other parties to the delegation of the obligations to the company.

4.24 Thus, in *Laurence McIntosh Ltd v Balfour Beatty*, a contract was entered into by a partnership called Laurence McIntosh & Sons. The partners of that firm later created Laurence McIntosh Ltd and were in the process of transferring the business from one to the other. Lord Drummond Young deployed the concept of *ad hoc* agency to cover the gap between the practical moment when the company took over the business and the legal transfer of rights and responsibilities. During that gap, the company was considered to be the agent of the partnership.[17]

4.25 The basis for *ad hoc* agency appears to be that, in a given situation, the best method of making sense of what the parties are doing, in a way that keeps all the contracts running, is to assume that one person acts on behalf of another. It should be borne in mind, however, that Lord Drummond Young did not consider the inference appropriate in 'formal' situations like litigation.[18]

4.26 The idea has been subject to academic criticism[19] and has not been endorsed at appellate level so it is not clear whether it will become an established part of the Scots law of agency. The basis for the implication of authority certainly differs from classic implied authority since, in cases of the type envisaged by Lord Drummond Young, it is likely that the 'agent' would consider itself to be acting for its own benefit and thus on its own behalf rather than that of the nominal principal.

Retrospective authority (ratification)

4.27 Agents do not always remain within the bounds of the authority granted to them by their principals. The reasons why this may happen are diverse but one obvious one is a misunderstanding of the scope of the authority on the part of the agent. In more extreme cases, someone with no authority at all may purport to act as agent for another. In some cases, however, the person in whose name the act was done may be happy with the transaction that the purported agent has undertaken. In those circumstances, it is open to the 'principal' to ratify the actions. This effectively amounts to granting authority after the fact. The effect of ratification is that the act is treated as always having been authorised.[20]

4.28 The justification for allowing ratification is that everyone is getting what they want: the principal clearly wants to approve the transaction (otherwise she would not be ratifying it) and the third party thought that the agent was acting on the principal's behalf anyway. Therefore, the ratification just brings the legal situation into line with what the third party thought it was. The requirements for an effective ratification are fourfold.

17 *Laurence McIntosh Ltd v Balfour Beatty Group Ltd* [2006] CSOH 197 at [15]–[19].

18 *Stirling v Westminster Properties Ltd* (n 16) at [20].

19 L Macgregor and N Whitty, 'Payment of another's debt, unjustified enrichment and *ad hoc* agency' (2011) 15 Edin LR 57.

20 *Bolton Partners v Lambert* (1889) 41 Ch D 295; *Gray v Braid Logistics (UK) Ltd* [2017] CSOH 44.

The ratifier must make a decision

Ratification depends on the will of the ratifying party. Therefore, ratification can only occur where there is evidence that she has decided to approve the relevant transaction. This approval may be express but it is more common for it to be implied by the principal's actions. There is authority which suggests that it may even be implied by the principal's inaction for a reasonable period of time in circumstances where the principal can be expected to take steps to disown the transaction,[21] and that this evidence need not have been communicated to the third party in order to take effect.[22] **4.29**

The fact that the principal requires to make a decision means that the principal cannot be held to have ratified an agent's act merely on the basis of actions for which she had another good reason, such as recovering her property. Further, nothing done by the principal before she becomes aware of what the agent has done can imply a ratification of the agent's actions.[23] **4.30**

The principal must have had legal capacity at the time of the act which was ratified[24]

This follows from the fact that ratification is retrospective in effect. As noted above, when an agent acts within the scope of their authority, the act is attributed to the principal. Since ratification means that the agent is treated as having had authority at the time of the act, it would mean the contract or other transaction being attributed to the principal at a time when she was incapable of so acting. This would make no sense. **4.31**

The requirement that the principal has legal capacity at the time of the agent's act implies a requirement that the principal existed at the time of the relevant act since there can be no capacity without existence. The most common application for this rule relates to the formation of companies. Those behind a company may want to line business up for it before it is formed by incorporation and to have the contracts ratified once the company has been created. The retrospective effect of ratification makes this impossible. Instead, s. 51 of the Companies Act 2006 provides that those who purport to contract on behalf of the company in those cases are personally liable. **4.32**

The agent must have held himself out as acting as an agent

If part of the rationale for accepting ratification as binding on third parties is that it gives them what they thought they were bargaining for in the first place, it should be obvious that ratification can only be allowed where the third party is aware that the agent is not acting on his own behalf. Were that not the case, **4.33**

21 *Ballantine v Stevenson* (1881) 8 R 959; *Bank Melli Iran v Barclays Bank (Dominion, Colonial and Overseas)* [1951] 2 Lloyd's Rep 367.

22 *Harrisons & Crossfield Ltd v London and North-Western Railway Co* [1917] 2 KB 755; *SEB Trygg Liv Holding AB v Manches* [2006] 1 WLR 2276.

23 *Forman & Co Pty Ltd v The Liddesdale* [1900] AC 190.

24 *Boston Deep Sea Fishing and Ice Co Ltd v Farnham* [1957] 1 WLR 1051.

the third party might expect to contract with the agent and end up contracting with the principal.

There must have been no material change in circumstances between the agent's act and the ratification

4.34 This is sometimes expressed as the requirement that the ratification must be reasonable in all the circumstances. Ratification gives the principal the power to make a retrospective change. This has the potential for significant abuse. For instance, if the agent placed a bet on a football match in the principal's name, it would not be appropriate to let the principal decide to ratify the gambling contract after the match was over. However, the courts have been willing to recognise ratification of a contract of insurance after the peril against which the insurance was taken out has occurred.[25]

4.35 Thus, where an act requires to be done within a certain time (perhaps an offer made subject to a time limit), both the agent's act and the ratification must occur within the time limit.[26] Otherwise the time limit would be deprived of all effect. Similarly, if someone else has acquired a real right in the principal's property, this cannot be prejudiced by a subsequent ratification.[27] Thus, if Alf purports to pledge Phillipa's car to Terence and, in the meantime, Phillipa sells the car to Trudy, Trudy will not be affected by the pledge to Terence, even if Phillipa ratifies it. However, an attempt by the third party to withdraw an offer on learning that the agent has acted without authority can be defeated by a ratification.[28]

Apparent authority

4.36 The existence and extent of the agent's authority are the result of private dealings between the agent and the principal. As such, it is difficult for third parties to determine whether or not someone who purports to be an agent actually has the necessary authority for the transaction in question. For this reason, rules are required to protect third parties who are misled into dealing with someone whom they believe to have authority.

4.37 This protection takes two forms: the agent's warranty of authority and the validation of juridical acts performed by a person with apparent authority to do them. The former protection renders the purported agent liable to the third party and so it is considered below in the section on agent-third party relations (see para. 4.73 below).

4.38 Apparent authority (sometimes referred to as 'ostensible' authority), however, concerns the relationship between the principal and the third party. If the principal has done something which justifies the third party in believing that someone has authority to do a particular act on her behalf and the third party relies on that impression by transacting with the agent, the principal will be bound.

25 *Williams v North China Insurance Co* (1876) 1 CPD 757.
26 *Goodall v Bilsland* 1909 SC 1152.
27 *Bird v Brown* (1850) 4 Exch 786.
28 *Bolton Partners v Lambert* (n 20).

Often apparent authority results from cases where an agent is deprived of his authority but those whom the agent has dealt with in the past are not informed of the loss of authority. It can also arise where someone is appointed to a post which usually carries a certain degree of implied authority but the principal and agent agree that the latter's authority shall not extend to the usual range. 4.39

So, if Alice appoints Peter to manage her affairs and then dismisses him for misconduct, she will need to inform those with whom Peter has been dealing on her behalf. If she does not do so, they will be justified in continuing to deal with Peter on the basis that he can bind Alice. The initial appointment gave the impression of continuing authority, so the onus rests on Alice to tell people that the situation has changed. Peter will not have actual authority but he will have apparent authority and that will be enough to enable those who contract with Peter before Alice informs them of the change to enforce their contracts against Alice. 4.40

Similarly, if Stella leaves Alf in charge of her shop but tells him not to sell certain products, Alf will not have actual authority to sell these products. He will, however, have apparent authority to do so because someone who works behind the till in a shop usually has authority to sell all of the products in the shop. If Stella does not want to be bound by such sales by Alf, she would need to do something to warn potential customers such as putting up a sign in the shop. 4.41

Requirements for apparent authority

Impression given by the principal

The third party's belief must result from the principal's conduct. The justification for binding the principal to acts done by agents with apparent authority is that the principal is responsible for the misunderstanding. This can only be the case where the principal has done something which justifies the third party's belief. 4.42

Despite that, apparent authority has been held to exist on the basis of minimal action by the principal. This is illustrated by *International Sponge Importers Ltd v Andrew Watt & Sons*.[29] In that case, an agent sold sponges on behalf of the pursuer. The pursuer's terms and conditions required payment to be made by a cheque to the principal, although such cheques could be delivered to the agent. The agent induced a number of customers to pay by cheques in his name or in cash. He had no authority to do so. The agent absconded with some of the money paid to him and the principal attempted to claim the price from customers who had paid the agent in unauthorised ways. The agent was held to have apparent authority to receive payment in this way. The basis for the decision was that the agent had greater actual authority than was usual in being able to take delivery of cheques and that the pursuers had been aware of at least one of the instances of irregular payment but did not communicate any objection to the defenders. 4.43

29 1911 SC (HL) 57.

4.44 The requirement that the principal give the impression of authority means that a claim to have authority made by a purported agent will not usually give rise to apparent authority.[30] However, it should be borne in mind that a statement made by an agent with authority to communicate on behalf of the principal will be attributed to her.

4.45 The idea is well illustrated by the facts of *First Energy (UK) v Hungarian International Bank*:[31] there a company was negotiating a loan with a bank employee who acknowledged that he did not have authority to grant it. However, he then purported to contact his superiors to get authorisation (i.e. specific authority) for the relevant transaction. He told the company's representatives that he had done so, although this was not in fact the case, and the loan was agreed. The Court of Appeal held that the bank was bound by the loan agreement. While the employee did not have authority to grant the loan, he did have authority to make representations on behalf of the bank. That meant that his (incorrect) representation that the loan was approved by his superiors was attributed to the bank, i.e. it was treated as if the bank had made it. Since it gave rise to the legitimate belief that he was authorised to agree the loan, the employee had apparent authority to make the loan agreement.

4.46 The decision has been subject to criticism on the basis that it opens the door to agents creating their own apparent authority but the logic of the decision is difficult to argue with. The Court of Appeal returned to the idea that a representation by an agent with actual authority could be attributed to the principal and thus create apparent authority for a further act in an *obiter dictum* in *SEB Trygg Liv Holding AB v Manches*.[32] Further, the argument was endorsed by the Judicial Committee of the Privy Council in *Kelly v Fraser*.[33] The position therefore appears relatively well established.

Giving rise to a reasonable belief that the agent has authority

4.47 The purpose of the rule is to protect third parties who are misled into believing the agent to be authorised. Therefore, it cannot be invoked if the third party was aware of the agent's lack of authority. Furthermore, that belief must have been reasonable since the principal cannot bear the risk of unjustifiable inferences that the third party might draw.

Transaction on that basis

4.48 The third party cannot be said to rely on the representation unless a transaction has been concluded with the agent. So, a belief that the agent has authority which is not followed by a juridical act will not affect the principal. Similarly, there is no reliance on the inaccurate impression unless the agent acts in the principal's name rather than his own. If the agent acts in his own name then his lack of authority does not affect the third party.

30 *Armagas Ltd v Mundogas SA (The Ocean Frost)* [1986] AC 717.
31 [1993] 2 Lloyd's Rep 194.
32 [2006] 1 WLR 2276 at [32] per Buxton LJ.
33 [2012] UKPC 25, [2013] 1 AC 450 at [14]–[16].

Prejudice

There is some dispute about whether the third party also requires to demonstrate prejudice flowing from the principal's disavowal of the agent's transaction.[34] If such prejudice is required, however, it is thought to be satisfied in every case where the other requirements are satisfied because the loss of the benefit of the relevant transaction will be considered as prejudice. **4.49**

Rationale

In England, apparent authority has often been said to be based on estoppel[35] and some Scots lawyers have followed this by suggesting that it is based on personal bar.[36] However, the estoppels/personal bar analysis has been doubted in both jurisdictions.[37] **4.50**

There are two main reasons for this. First, the conduct on the part of the principal which can give rise to the impression of authority is not as extensive or definitive as would usually be required for personal bar. Secondly, personal bar typically requires that the party invoking the bar (the third party who dealt with the apparent agent in this case) has acted in reliance on the false impression in a way which would mean they would be prejudiced if the barred party was allowed to back out. In apparent authority, the only reliance that the third party needs to show is the conclusion of the transaction with the apparent agent and the only prejudice is the loss of the benefit of that transaction. It is open to question whether this reliance and prejudice of this kind would suffice for personal bar in another context. **4.51**

Disclosure

The requirement that the agent have authority for the relevant transaction protects the principal's autonomy. However, the third party also requires protection since it has an interest in being able to choose whom it deals with. This interest is protected by the rules surrounding disclosure of agency. **4.52**

Discussion of disclosure of the principal's identity tends to be limited to contracts. In principle, other juridical acts may be performed on behalf of an undisclosed principal but the policy issues surrounding disclosure of the principal's identity are less sharp. A transferee or payee will usually be unconcerned about the identity of the transferor as long as the transfer is effective. A transferor has few grounds to object to an agent receiving a transfer on behalf of another when it would have been open to the agent to transfer the relevant asset on. Therefore, discussion in this section will focus on contracts concluded on behalf of an undisclosed principal. **4.53**

34 *Gregor Homes Ltd v Emlick* 2012 SLT (Sh Ct) 5.

35 *Freeman & Lockyer v Buckhurst Park Properties* [1964] 2 QB 480 at 503 per Diplock LJ.

36 *Bank of Scotland v Brunswick Developments (1987) Ltd (No. 2)* 1997 SC 226 at 234 per Lord Rodger; E C Reid and J W G Blackie, *Personal Bar* (Edinburgh: W. Green, 2006), para. 13–01; Macgregor, *Law of Agency in Scotland*, paras 11–05–11–06.

37 *Gregor Homes Ltd v Emlick* (n 34); *Bowstead and Reynolds on Agency* (n 11), para. 8–028.

4.54 There are three possible levels of disclosure: where the principal is disclosed and identified; where the principal is undisclosed; and where the principal is disclosed but not identified.

Disclosed and identified principal

4.55 Where the agent discloses the identity of the principal to the third party and acts in her name, there can be no doubt that the third party intends to deal with the principal and that the contract is between the third party and the principal.

Undisclosed principal

4.56 Basic principles of private law suggest that where the agent purports to act on his own behalf the principal should be unaffected. The third party agreed to transact with the agent not with the principal. However, for pragmatic reasons, the law allows a principal who has not been disclosed to step in and enforce the contract made on her behalf by an agent despite the fact that the agent acted in his own name.[38] As might be expected, the principal can only do this where the agent has authority to act and intends to do so on behalf of the principal.

4.57 Where an agent has contracted on behalf of an undisclosed principal, the third party is entitled to choose whether to enforce its rights against the agent or the third party and can use any defence that could have been raised against the agent against the principal.

4.58 The rationale for allowing the undisclosed principal to enforce the contract is that in most transactions, people do not mind to whom they make performance. This assumption also underlies the general rule which allows assignation without the debtor's consent. If that is the case, the third party is sufficiently protected by ensuring that it can insist on having rights against the agent rather than against the principal.

4.59 If Alf concludes a contract for the sale of sheep to Trudy with Stella as his undisclosed principal, Stella can enforce the contract by bringing an action against Trudy for the price. However, if Alf owed money to Trudy, she would be entitled to set that off against Stella's claim for the price. Once Stella reveals herself, Trudy has a decision to make. She can enforce against Alf or Stella. This choice is known as an election. Once she has chosen, she cannot then go back and try to enforce the contract against the other party. So, if she decides to choose Alf as her seller and he fails to deliver, she will not be entitled to sue Stella.[39]

4.60 The choice need not be made expressly. It is implied by conduct which implies that one party or the other is liable, such as pursuing an action for enforcement of the contract to the point of judgment, or ranking in an insolvency

38 The basic principles are set out in *Siu Yin Kwan v Eastern Insurance Co Ltd* [1994] 2 AC 199.
39 *David Logan and Son Ltd v Schuldt* (1903) 10 SLT 598.

procedure.[40] If the litigation is abandoned before final judgment, however, it will not be considered as an election.

There are limits to the law's willingness to allow an undisclosed principal to step in. It is open to the third party to stipulate at the time that it is only willing to conclude the relevant transaction with the agent personally. Such a stipulation rebuts the argument that the identity of the person to whom performance must be made is a matter of indifference. Even if no such stipulation is made, if the contract is a 'personal' one, where the person to whom the performance is due is a central part of the obligation, no undisclosed principal can step in and enforce it. The standard example of such a contract is a contract to paint a picture.[41] This example is not without its difficulties. **4.61**

The difficulty arises from the fact that the rules on undisclosed principals allow the separation of rights from obligations and not all of the obligations arising from the contract are personal. In cases where the undisclosed principal intervenes, the third party can elect to treat the agent as liable and therefore demand performance from him rather than from the principal. The only effect which the intervention of the undisclosed principal has on the contract is to change the person to whom the performance is to be made. The contract to paint a picture is personal in the sense that the painter is likely to have been chosen for their particular characteristics. On the other hand, it is not obvious that the painter has particular concerns regarding the person who commissions the picture since the commissioner's obligation is to pay. **4.62**

If the undisclosed principal commissions the painting, her identity is presumed to be a matter of indifference to the painter (the third party). If, on the other hand, the third party commissions an undisclosed agent to paint the picture, it can ensure that the agent paints the picture by electing to take the undisclosed agent as its debtor in the contract rather than the principal. Although it can demand that the agent paints the picture, the third party can be forced to pay the price to the undisclosed principal but it is unlikely that this will be against the third party's interests. **4.63**

There are, however, other examples where the third party can be presumed to have taken account of the identity of the person to whom obligations are to be performed. For instance, the third party may have a contract to provide services which involve close personal contact (such as bathing or dressing the creditor) or living with her (for instance, as a nanny). **4.64**

There is also authority which suggests that the principal's intervention is excluded if the agent has concealed her identity for the purpose of deceiving the third party. The particular facts of the case were peculiar. Someone who knew he was not welcome at a particular theatre obtained a ticket for an opening night by getting an agent to apply for the ticket for him. The court held that the theatre owners were entitled to refuse him entry because the agent had been used to deceive them.[42] **4.65**

40 *Meier & Co v Kuchenmeister* (1881) 8 R 642; *David Logan and Son Ltd v Schuldt* (n 39).
41 For example, *Siu Yin Kwan* (n 38) at 210.
42 *Said v Butt* [1920] 3 KB 497.

4.66 This restriction needs to be handled with care, however. Many circumstances where the principal is not disclosed will involve a principal with some interest in concealing her identity or involvement in the relevant transaction. Such concealment necessarily implies a degree of deception. Were the restriction applied to all such cases, there would be little point in sanctioning transactions made on behalf of an undisclosed principal. Therefore, the rule ought to be read narrowly and restricted to cases where the principal is aware that the third party would be unwilling to deal with her specifically.

Disclosed but unidentified principal

4.67 The agent may make full disclosure or no disclosure at all but it is also possible that the agent will disclose the fact that he is acting on another's behalf without identifying the principal. This might be regarded as something of a midpoint between the undisclosed and the fully disclosed principal.

4.68 There has been some conflict in the authorities on the proper analysis of this midpoint. The main Scottish authorities which discuss the disclosed but unnamed principal involve an attempt by the third party to enforce the contract against either the agent or principal. Therefore they do not address whether the contract is enforceable by the principal. Given that a principal who has been neither disclosed nor identified can usually enforce the contract, it seems likely that it is. The fact that the third party knew that there was some other party behind the agent would make it difficult to argue that the contract was personal in a sense which would prevent a principal stepping forward and taking up the rights.

4.69 One approach has been to treat the situation in the same way as an undisclosed principal would be treated: giving the third party an election as to whom it wishes to hold liable under the contract.[43] The other approach is to ask whose credit the third party relied on when making the contract and to treat that person, be it principal or agent, as the party liable on the contract.[44] The expression 'giving credit' is perhaps a little obscure but it simply means asking who the third party looked to for payment under the contract.

4.70 The Inner House returned to the issue in *Ruddy v Marco*,[45] where the court stressed the responsibility of the agent to make clear to the third party that the principal, and only the principal, is liable, if the agent wants to escape personal responsibility. The fact that the third party is aware that there is a principal standing somewhere in the background is not necessarily enough to discharge this burden. If this burden is not discharged (as was the case in *Ruddy*), the general presumption that people who contract make themselves liable on the contract applies and the agent finds himself liable.

4.71 A similar analysis applies to the execution of documents by an agent. The mere fact that the person to whom the document is addressed knows that the signatory is an agent is not sufficient to release the agent from liability under the document. Rather, the signature should be qualified in such a way as to

43 *Ferrier v Dods* (1865) 3 M 561.
44 *Lamont, Nisbett & Co v Hamilton* 1907 SC 628.
45 2008 SC 667.

make clear that the document is subscribed on behalf of the principal rather than in any personal capacity.[46]

Drawing all this together, when an agent acts for a disclosed but unidentified principal, it is likely that the principal will be able to enforce the contract against the third party provided that this is not clearly excluded. Whether the agent will be liable to the third party depends on whether the agent has made clear to the third party that he accepts no personal liability on the contract. **4.72**

AGENT-THIRD PARTY RELATIONS

Since the agent transacts with the third party on behalf of the principal rather than on his own behalf, the agent will not normally find himself liable to the third party. There are three major exceptions to this: where the principal is not disclosed (discussed at paras 4.56–4.66 above); where the parties agree otherwise or the agent makes a promise to the third party; and where the agent does not have authority to do the relevant act. The fact that the agent may take on obligations to the third party by agreement or promise is a simple application of basic principles of contract or promise. A little more needs to be said, however, about the agent's liability in cases where the authority is exceeded. **4.73**

Agents acting without authority are sometimes thought to be personally bound by the relevant obligation, particularly where the purported principal does not exist. As noted at para 4.32 above, there is a special rule which makes those who contract on behalf of a company that is yet to be formed personally liable. However, the general rule is that where the agent acts outwith his authority the relevant act does not bind him personally. Instead, he is liable to the principal for breach of warranty of authority.[47] The rule was developed in England, where promise is not generally recognised as a basis for obligations, and so the warranty is described as a collateral contract between the agent and third party. In Scotland, it might have been possible to explain the rule as an implied promise by the agent but the English collateral contract analysis has in fact been followed. **4.74**

Where the agent was not authorised to do the relevant act, he is thus liable to the third party for breach of contract. The contractual basis of the obligation means that the liability is strict so it does not matter that the agent honestly believed himself authorised to do the relevant act. The contractual basis also determines the extent of the damages which the agent must pay. Contract damages usually aim to put the injured party in the position it would be in if the breach had not occurred. **4.75**

Therefore, the agent must pay the third party enough to secure the benefit of the transaction because that is what the third party would have had if the warranty had been true. So, if the third party had contracted to sell goods to the principal, the agent would usually be liable for the profit which the third **4.76**

46 *Stewart v Shannessy* (1900) 2 F 1288.

47 *Irving v Burns* 1915 SC 260 at 269 per Lord Salvesen; *Halifax Life Ltd v DLA Piper Scotland LLP* [2009] CSOH 74.

party would have made on the sale.[48] However, if the principal was insolvent and not able to pay for the goods anyway, then agent may not be liable at all since the third party would have made a loss on the sale.

4.77 From this it should be obvious that the agent only warrants that he is authorised by the principal. The agent does not warrant that the principal has any particular attributes or characteristics. In particular, the agent does not warrant that the principal owns any property over which rights are being granted or is otherwise able to perform any obligations which arise under the transaction.[49]

PRINCIPAL-AGENT RELATIONS

4.78 Principals and agents owe duties to one another. As with most personal rights and obligations, they may usually be varied by agreement between principal and agent.[50] The agent is entitled to payment for the work he does on the principal's behalf. The method of calculating how and when the agent is to be paid will usually be agreed between the parties. It is common for the agent to be employed on commission. An agent who is on commission receives a percentage of the price or the profit in transactions which he performs or negotiates on the principal's behalf, provided that the agent has made a substantial contribution to the transaction. As well as payment, the agent is entitled to relief from any liabilities and to reimbursement of any expenses which have been incurred in the course of the proper performance of his duties as agent.[51]

4.79 In some cases, the agent will agree to act for the principal without any payment. Such gratuitous agency is known as mandate. In mandate, the principal is known as the mandant and the agent as the mandatary. In such cases, the mandatary is still entitled to relief and reimbursement.[52]

4.80 The duties imposed on the agent ensure that he carries out the task or tasks with which he has been entrusted properly. For this reason, the agent is obliged to follow the principal's instructions and to exercise reasonable skill and care when acting as agent. The agent is obliged to compensate the principal for losses occasioned by breaches of these duties.

4.81 One of the most important applications of the duty to follow instructions is the duty not to exceed his authority. Of course, in many cases, an act which exceeds authority will not prejudice the principal because the act will not bind her. However, the principal may find herself bound if the act was with the agent's apparent authority. In such cases, the agent would be liable for any loss suffered by the principal in the relevant transaction.[53]

48 *Irving v Burns* (n 47).

49 *Cheshire Mortgage Corporation Ltd v Grandison* [2012] CSIH 66, 2013 SC 160.

50 An important exception to this in the case of commercial agents is discussed at paras 4.94 onwards below.

51 *Stevenson v Duncan* (1842) 5 D 167; *Tomlinson v Scottish Amalgamated Silks' Liquidator* 1935 SC (HL) 1.

52 Bell, *Principles*, § 218.

53 *Milne v Ritchie* (1882) 10 R 365.

The situation with ratification is a little more complex. The agent has strayed outwith his authority but the principal is only bound because she has decided to ratify the act. It might be argued that the principal cannot have it both ways: ratifying the transaction on the one hand and claiming against the agent for the loss occasioned by an act outwith authority on the other. In most circumstances, ratification will imply a waiver on the part of the principal of any right of recovery against the agent for exceeding his authority. **4.82**

However, the courts recognise that the principal may have good reasons, such as preservation of her commercial reputation, for ratifying a transaction though she would not have sanctioned it beforehand. In such cases, the principal is simply making the best of a bad situation and this should not bar recovery from the agent. Therefore, it is possible to ratify the agent's act without waiving the right to compensation for excess of authority.[54] If the principal wishes to retain her right against the agent, she must make this clear at the time of the ratification.[55] **4.83**

Agents are also sometimes said to have an obligation not to delegate the task entrusted to them on the basis of the maxim *delegatus non potest delegare* (one to whom something has been delegated cannot delegate it). However, this is only a general presumption and may be rebutted by evidence of the custom in particular cases.[56] Of course, where the agent has an obligation not to delegate, he also lacks the authority to create contractual relations between the principal and the delegate. **4.84**

Fiduciary duties

The duties to use reasonable skill and care and to follow instructions amount to simple duties incumbent on the agent to carry out the task or work which he has agreed to undertake. As such, they are of a type to be found in most contracts. However, agents are also subject to another class of duties which address the fact that the principal necessarily puts a lot of trust in the agent by conferring upon him the power to alter her legal position. Duties in this class are known as fiduciary duties. The law supplies default fiduciary duties but they can be varied by contract to meet individual circumstances.[57] **4.85**

Fiduciary duties are duties of loyalty to the principal. The general principal which underlies them is that, within the scope of his sphere of responsibility as an agent, he must put the principal's interests ahead of his own. This general duty of loyalty may be broken down into two broad categories. **4.86**

Duty to avoid conflicts of interest

In order to ensure that the agent puts the principal's interests first, he is obliged to avoid situations where his interests conflict with those of the principal. The most extreme version of this situation is self-dealing: where the agent deals on **4.87**

54 *Suncorp Insurance and Finance v Milano Assicurazioni SPA* [1993] 2 Lloyds Rep 225; *Wyatt v Crate* [2012] CSOH 197, 2013 SCLR 323.

55 *Wyatt v Crate* 2013 SCLR 323 at [30] per Lord Boyd.

56 Bell, *Commentaries* I, 516–517.

57 See *Kelly v Cooper* [1993] AC 205.

behalf of the principal with himself. If Alex sells goods to Paula, his principal: there is a clear conflict of interest.[58] His duty to Paula means that he should try to get the goods as cheaply as possible for her but his personal interest lies in getting as high a price as possible.

4.88 A slight variant on this case, would involve Alex acting for two principals who are both involved in the same transaction: buying on behalf of Paula and selling on behalf of Terence. Again, there is a clear conflict of interest: Alex's duty to Paula is to negotiate as low a price as possible; his duty to Terence is to negotiate as high a price as possible.[59] He cannot do both.

4.89 An agent may have a conflict of interest if he is representing multiple principals whose products are in competition. The agent cannot give his full energies to promoting one principal's products because he also has a duty to promote those of the other. For this reason, the terms of the agent's contract will often bar him from representing competing principals.[60] However, there are many common business situations where the same agent represents a number of principals, such as a solicitor or estate agent acting in the sale of a number of homes in the same street. In many cases, this is to the advantage of all of the principals because potential customers or buyers may be more likely to visit or listen to an agent who has a wide range of potential deals to offer them. Therefore, there the question must be determined according to circumstances of the case. If the principal expressly agreed that the agent could act for competing principals, or if the principal must have understood that the agent was operating on such a basis, the principal can have no complaints.[61]

Duty to communicate benefits to the principal

4.90 Since the agent is engaged to act for the principal, the agent is obliged to pass on any benefits which he receives to the principal, unless these form part of the remuneration which was agreed between agent and principal. This in turn implies a duty to account to the principal for all benefits received in the course of agency activities.[62] Together these rules are sometimes referred to as the rule against secret profits.

4.91 The most common sources of incidental benefit to the agent are use of property or information which the agent has possession of because he is an agent,[63] mistakes in payments to or from the principal[64] and payments or other benefits received from the third party with whom the agent deals on the principal's behalf.[65] The last example, sometimes referred to as a secret commission, overlaps with the conflict of interest rules because the agent may be tempted to enter into a transaction which is not beneficial to the principal as a result of his

58 *McPherson's Trs v Watt* (1877) 5 R (HL) 9.

59 *Aberdeen Railway Co v Blaikie Brothers* (1854) 17 D (HL) 20, 1 Macq HL 461, 1 Pat 394.

60 *Graham & Co v United Turkey Red Co Ltd* 1922 SC 533.

61 *Lothian v Jenolite Ltd* 1969 SC 111; *Kelly v Cooper* [1993] AC 205; *Rossetti Marketing Ltd v Diamond Sofa Co Ltd* [2012] EWCA Civ 1021, [2013] 1 All ER (Comm) 308.

62 *Trans Barwil Agencies (UK) Ltd v John S Braid & Co Ltd* 1988 SC 222.

63 *Boardman v Phipp* [1965] Ch 992.

64 *Trans Barwil Agencies* (n 62).

65 *Ronaldson v Drummond and Reid* (1881) 8 R 956; *Imageview Management Ltd v Jack* [2009] EWCA Civ 63, [2009] 2 All ER 666.

desire to secure the benefit from the third party. For this reason, the principal is entitled to set aside the transaction concluded by the agent and the third party wrongs the principal by making the payment.[66]

Consequences of breach of fiduciary duties

As with 'normal' duties, an agent who breaches a fiduciary duty must compensate the principal for any harm suffered as a result. That does not represent the limit of his potential liability. Rather, the agent is also obliged to pay over to the principal anything which he has received as a result of breach of his fiduciary obligations.[67] The agent also forfeits any right to payment or commission for the relevant transaction.[68] There is English authority suggesting that, where it is equitable to do so, the court may allow the agent to retain a proportion of the commission despite a breach of fiduciary duty.[69] The allowance is made to reflect the value of the services which the agent rendered to the principal and is usually limited to cases where the breach of fiduciary duty was an honest mistake. **4.92**

The fiduciary duties place particularly stringent demands on agents and there may be circumstances in which the principal may be content for the agent to receive an additional benefit or for the agent to supply goods which she is looking to buy. If the situation is disclosed to the principal and she consents, then there is no breach of duty. **4.93**

Commercial agents

Both Scots and English law have tended to see the regulation of the relationship between principal and agent primarily in terms of protecting the principal from wrongful conduct on the part of the agent. However, the late twentieth century saw European legislation intended to establish protection for commercial agents. This legislation was implemented in the UK by the Commercial Agents (Council Directive) Regulations 1993.[70] Like most legislation introduced to implement European Community or Union Directives, the regulations remain in force despite UK exit from the EU. **4.94**

The regulations are primarily concerned with establishing the agent's rights to remuneration, notice prior to termination of the agency and payment on conclusion of the agency relationship. Underlying these rules is a presumption that commercial agents play a role in building up goodwill for their principals for which they are entitled to appropriate reward. **4.95**

Sphere of application

The protections in the regulations only apply to commercial agents, as defined in reg. 2(1). In order to qualify as such, the agent must be: (a) self-employed; **4.96**

66 *Aberdeen Railway Co v Blaikie Bros* (n 59).
67 *Ronaldson v Drummond and Reid* (n 65).
68 *Ronaldson v Drummond and Reid*; *Imageview Management Ltd v Jack* (n 65).
69 Summarised in *Imageview Management Ltd v Jack* (n 65) at [54]–[61].
70 SI 1993/3053.

(b) have continuing authority to negotiate the sale or purchase of goods on behalf of the principal; and (c) not be excluded by the regulation.

4.97 The term continuing authority suggests that the agent must carry out more than a single transaction on behalf of the principal but it can cover a single contract where the agent has ongoing authority from the principal to negotiate extensions to that contract.[71]

4.98 The requirement that the agent negotiate might be taken to suggest that the agent has some say in the terms of the bargain between principal and third party. However, it has been read very broadly. Provided that the agent does some work to generate goodwill or drum up business, he will be considered as negotiating for the purposes of the regulations.[72] However, an agent to whom customers come without any effort on the part of the agent, such as a licensee who operated a petrol station on behalf of an oil company, did not fall within the ambit of the regulations.[73]

4.99 There are two types of specific exclusion: those based on the office held by the agent and those based on the nature of the agent's activity. Both types of exclusions are designed to focus the application of the regulations on those who were thought to require protection. The office-based exclusions cover those in posts which already have a well-established legal regime and where the protections in the regulations are not needed. Company officers such as directors, partners in partnerships and insolvency practitioners are excluded,[74] as are gratuitous agents, commodity traders and Crown Agents.[75]

4.100 The activity exclusion prevents the application of the regulations to persons whose activity as a commercial agent is secondary.[76] Guidance on when this is the case is found in the schedule to the regulations. Paragraph 2 of the schedule sets out when the commercial agent's activity will be primary: where the principal's business is the sale or purchase of a particular type of goods; where the contracts are individually negotiated; and where securing transactions is likely to build up goodwill and thus the principal's chances of further success.

4.101 Paragraph 3 of the schedule provides a number of indicators that this is the case: where the principal manufactures, imports or distributes goods, where the goods are particularly identified with the principal; where the agent's time is substantially taken up with representing the principal; where the agent is the main means by which the principal's goods are available in the relevant market; and where the parties describe the relationship as one of commercial agency. Conversely, para. 4 lists contra-indicators, which suggest that the agent's activity is secondary: where promotional material is sent to potential customers directly rather than through the agent; where the principal appoints agents without consideration of whether the relevant market is already covered by another agent; and where customers select goods themselves and merely

71 *Poseidon Chartering BV v Marianne Zeeschip Vof* (C-3/04) [2006] ECR I-2505.
72 *Nigel Fryer Joinery Services Ltd v Ian Firth Hardware Ltd* [2008] EWHC 767 (Ch).
73 *Parks v Esso Petroleum Co Ltd* [2000] ECC 45.
74 Commercial Agents (Council Directive) Regulations 1993, reg. 2(1).
75 Commercial Agents (Council Directive) Regulations 1993, reg. 2(2).
76 Commercial Agents (Council Directive) Regulations 1993, reg. 2(3)–(4).

place their orders through the agent. Further, para. 5 contains absolute exclusions for mail order catalogue agents and consumer credit agents.

The nature of the criteria in the schedule further emphasises the legislative intent to protect agents' interest in the goodwill which they build up for their principals. The greater the agent's input into building up goodwill associated with the principal's product and the more important that goodwill is to the principal's business, the more likely the agent's activities are to be considered as primary rather than secondary. **4.102**

Conduct of commercial agency

In addition to the rules on remuneration, notice of termination and payment at the end of the agency relationship, the regulations contain some brief provisions relating to the behaviour of the agent and principal. These impose an obligation to act dutifully and in good faith on both parties.[77] **4.103**

In the case of the agent, the content of this duty is further specified as making proper efforts to negotiate and conclude the transactions entrusted to him, communication of necessary information and complying with reasonable instructions.[78] In the case of the principal, it is further specified in terms of provision of necessary documentation to the agent and notification of anticipated changes to the volume of transactions and of whether she has accepted, refused or failed to comply with any transaction which the agent has procured.[79] These obligations may not be excluded by the parties[80] and the agent is entitled to a signed, written document setting out the terms of the contract,[81] but otherwise they add little to the obligations entailed by an agency relationship at common law. **4.104**

Remuneration

The regulations provide a default rule, entitling the agent to such remuneration as is customary (where there is a relevant custom in his place of operation) and to reasonable remuneration where there is no relevant custom.[82] Where remuneration takes the form of commission there are further rules detailing which transactions are to be considered as giving rise to entitlement to commission,[83] when commission is due[84] and the agent's rights to information in order to determine the commission due to him.[85] **4.105**

77 Commercial Agents (Council Directive) Regulations 1993, regs. 3(1) and 4(1).
78 Commercial Agents (Council Directive) Regulations 1993, reg. 3(2).
79 Commercial Agents (Council Directive) Regulations 1993, reg. 4(2).
80 Commercial Agents (Council Directive) Regulations 1993, reg. 5(1).
81 Commercial Agents (Council Directive) Regulations 1993, reg. 13.
82 Commercial Agents (Council Directive) Regulations 1993, reg. 6(1).
83 Commercial Agents (Council Directive) Regulations 1993, regs. 7–9 and 11.
84 Commercial Agents (Council Directive) Regulations 1993, reg. 10.
85 Commercial Agents (Council Directive) Regulations 1993, reg. 12.

Termination

4.106 The most significant provisions in the regulations relate to the agent's rights at the end of the agency relationship. First, the commission rules entitle an agent to commission on transactions concluded after termination if the order was placed prior to termination or if the transaction is mainly attributable to the agent's efforts and is concluded within a reasonable time after the termination.[86]

4.107 If the agency is for an indefinite period, either party may terminate the contract by notice. The regulations provide minimum periods of notice which vary depending on how long the agent has been in place: one month in the first year, two months in the second year and three months in the third year and thereafter.[87] However, these minimum periods do not prevent immediate termination for material breach of contract or in exceptional circumstances (e.g. frustration).[88]

4.108 Where the agency relationship comes to an end, the agent will usually be entitled to a payment from the principal.[89] The entitlement arises although the principal has not done anything wrong.[90] It even applies where the agency is terminated by the agent's death.[91]

4.109 However, the right to payment is excluded where the principal has terminated the contract for material breach, where the agent has transferred his rights and duties under the contract to a third party or where the agent has terminated the contract.[92] The last exclusion does not apply where the termination is justified by the principal's conduct or where age or illness makes it unreasonable to expect the agent to continue to perform his duties. Broadly speaking, the right to payment is excluded where the termination of the agency contract is caused by the agent's fault or free choice.

4.110 The regulations give the agent and principal two options for the payment on termination: the agent may receive either indemnity (calculated as directed by reg. 17) or compensation (calculated as directed by reg. 18). If no choice is made by the parties, compensation applies.[93] No agreement to derogate from the rules on compensation and indemnity made prior to the termination of the agency contract will be effective if it operates to the agent's detriment.[94] So the parties cannot exclude the agent's right to a payment on termination in their contract or make provision varying the rules for calculating indemnity or compensation in a way that leaves the agent with less than he would otherwise have received. However, a variation on the calculation mechanism which increases the agent's entitlement or an agreement to discharge the right made after the agency contract had come to an end would be effective.

86 Commercial Agents (Council Directive) Regulations 1993, reg. 8.
87 Commercial Agents (Council Directive) Regulations 1993, reg. 15.
88 Commercial Agents (Council Directive) Regulations 1993, reg. 16.
89 Commercial Agents (Council Directive) Regulations 1993, reg. 17(1).
90 *Cooper v Pure Fishing (UK) Ltd* [2004] EWCA Civ 375, [2004] 2 Lloyd's Rep 518.
91 Commercial Agents (Council Directive) Regulations 1993, reg. 18(8).
92 Commercial Agents (Council Directive) Regulations 1993, reg. 18.
93 Commercial Agents (Council Directive) Regulations 1993, reg. 17(2).
94 Commercial Agents (Council Directive) Regulations 1993, reg. 19.

Both indemnity and compensation are designed to give the agent some reward for his role in building up the principal's goodwill. The two methods are available because of the political process which led up to the passing of the Directive: indemnity is modelled on pre-existing German rules; compensation on pre-existing French rules.[95] **4.111**

Under the indemnity system, the extent of the payment depends on the extent to which the agent has brought new business to the principal from which the latter continues to derive benefit after the end of the agency relationship.[96] Regard is to be had to all the circumstances of the case, with particular reference to the commission the agent would have earned had the agency not been terminated.[97] The amount payable is capped by the agent's average remuneration over the last five years, unless the agent has been working for less than five years in which case the average is taken over the whole period of agency.[98] **4.112**

Compensation is calculated by reference to the damage which the agent suffers as a result of the termination of the agency relationship, in particular the loss of the opportunity to earn commission and to cover costs incurred in the performance of the agency contract.[99] After some initial doubts, it is relatively clear that damage is determined in the conventional manner: that is, by comparing the true position with what the agent's position would have been had the contract not come to an end.[100] **4.113**

95 *King v T Tunnock Ltd* 2000 SC 424 at [11].
96 Commercial Agents (Council Directive) Regulations 1993, reg. 17(3)(a).
97 Commercial Agents (Council Directive) Regulations 1993, reg. 17(3)(b).
98 Commercial Agents (Council Directive) Regulations 1993, reg. 17(4).
99 Commercial Agents (Council Directive) Regulations 1993, reg. 17(6)–(7).
100 *Lonsdale v Howard & Hallam Ltd* [2007] UKHL 32, [2007] 1 WLR 2055. This position has been subject to some criticism: Macgregor, *Law of Agency in Scotland*, paras 10–22 and 10–26.

Chapter Five

Partnerships, LPs and LLPs

Ross Anderson

INTRODUCTION

5.01 The principal juristic persons available for carrying on business in the UK are:

- A company (a 'company') incorporated under the Companies Act 2006 (the 'CA 2006').
- A partnership (a 'partnership') formed under the Partnership Act 1890 (the '1890 Act').
- A limited partnership formed under the Limited Partnerships Act 1907 (the '1907 Act') ('LP').
- Limited Liability Partnership ('LLP') incorporated under the Limited Liability Partnerships Act 2000 (the '2000 Act') and regulated by the Limited Liability Partnerships Regulations 2001 (SI 2001/1090) (the '2001 Regs').

5.02 This chapter is concerned with the general principles applicable to three of these four entities: partnerships, LPs and LLPs. Company law is considered only to the extent that it applies to LLPs.[1] The focus is on Scottish entities.

5.03 Both Scottish partnerships and Scottish limited partnerships (SLPs) have proved popular. As a result, the original words of the 1907 Act have been significantly amended, and both the 1890 Act and the 1907 Act must now be read in conjunction with a regulatory framework.[2] Scottish partnerships and SLPs may be particularly attractive because they have legal personality, limited publicity, tax transparency[3] and, in the case of SLPs, limited liability.

HISTORY

Common law companies

5.04 Scots law, like a number of other European legal systems, has long treated juristic persons as forming a major part of that fundamental first chapter of private law, the law of persons. Scots law has long recognised many common

1 Limited Liability Partnerships (Application of Companies Act 2006) Regulations 2009 (SI 2009/1804).

2 Partnerships (Accounts) Regulations 2008 (SI 2008/569); Scottish Partnerships (Register of People with Significant Control) Regulations 2017 (SI 2017/694).

3 Income Tax (Trading and other Income) Act 2005, ss. 847 and 848 (partnerships) and s. 863 (LLPs); Corporation Taxes Act 2009, s. 1258 (partnerships) and s. 1273 (LLPs).

law corporations – the Faculty of Advocates, the Society of Writers to the Signet, the Royal Faculty of Procurators in Glasgow – are just three examples from the legal profession of bodies whose status as juristic persons is recognised at common law – as well as more short-lived business associations, such as partnerships, as having legal personality.[4]

Arran Fishing Company

Perhaps the most famous case is that of the Arran Fishing Company: *Stevenson v Macnair*.[5] In that case the Court of Session appeared to hold that Scots law, following the law set down by a number of European writers on commercial law, recognised at common law a sort of limited partnership – akin to the *société en commandite* recognised in French law – whereby sleeping partners, who contributed only capital but who were otherwise not engaged in the day-to-day business of the firm, had no liability for the firm's debts beyond their capital contribution. That decision is entirely consistent with first principles. For where the law recognises a juristic person, that person alone is liable for its own debts; it is exceptional to hold other persons to be liable for the juristic person's liabilities.[6] For reasons that have never been entirely clear,[7] however, the Arran Fishing Company case was not followed in the litigation that arose out of the collapse of the Ayr Bank[8] and, although it was discussed with approval by at least one of the consulted judges in a Whole Court decision in 1834,[9] it has never been expressly followed. What the common law did allow was the establishment of firms with separate legal personality the constitutive contracts of which could permit the issuance of transferable stock and, thus, the creation of the so-called 'joint stock company', albeit that the liability of the shareholders in such firms was unlimited. The development of limited liability business vehicles, in contrast, has been almost entirely a matter for UK legislation.[10] **5.05**

Incorporation by Act of Parliament or Royal Charter

Prior to the advent of the modern form of registered company, there were three ways in which a juristic person could be brought into existence: by Act of Parliament; by Royal Charter; or by private association recognised at common law. Prior to the Union, many of the earliest trading companies in Scotland were incorporated by Acts of the Parliament of Scotland: companies such as the Company of Scotland, trading to Africa and the Indies (known to **5.06**

4 Many of the authorities and principles are canvassed in the opinions of the consulted judges in *University of Glasgow v Faculty of Surgeons* (1837) 15 S 736 affd (1840) 1 Rob 397.

5 (1757) Mor 14560 and 14667, 5 Br Sup 340, Kames Sel Dec 191 discussed in J Robertson Christie, 'Joint Stock Enterprises in Scotland before the Companies Acts' (1909) 21 *Jur Rev* 128.

6 *J H Rayner (Mincing Lane) Ltd v Department of Trade and Industry* [1990] 2 AC 418 at 508 per Lord Oliver of Aylmerton.

7 Bell mentioned *Stevenson v Macnair* for the first time only in the fourth edition of his *Commentaries* published in 1821: II, 621–623.

8 *Douglas Heron & Co v Hair* (1778) Mor 14605, 8 Fac Coll 57.

9 *Forsyth v Hare & Co* (1834) 13 S 42 at 52 per Lord Medwyn.

10 The law of business associations is a matter reserved to Westminster under the Scotland Act 1998.

subsequent students of Scottish history as the Darien Company)[11] or the better known example of the Governor and Company of the Bank of Scotland.[12] The Royal Bank of Scotland was incorporated by Royal Charter, under the Great Seal of Scotland, in 1727.[13] In 1746, the British Linen Company was formed by Royal Charter as a Scottish chartered company, and its charter also conferred note-issuing powers.[14]

Chartered companies and letters patent

5.07 Partnerships established under Scots common law were recognised as having separate legal personality. Following a detailed report to Parliament in 1837, the Chartered Companies Act 1837[15] was passed, empowering the Queen to grant, without incorporation,[16] certain privileges and immunities to 'joint-stock companies'. One such privilege was limited liability on the members and officers.[17] Letters patent issued under the 1837 Act allowed for transferable stock, with all transfers to be registered with the Lord Clerk Register.[18] The 1837 Act was described as a dead letter in Scotland, perhaps because of the uncertainty about the status of letters patent. But the Court of Session subsequently held that the effect of incorporation by Royal Charter or letters patent was the same.[19]

Separation of companies from partnerships

5.08 As has been seen, firms established under Scots law had separate legal personality and their constitutive contracts could allow for the capital contributions of partners to be recorded in stock, which was freely transferable without the need for further consent from the partners. The Joint Stock Companies Act 1844 sought to introduce this model to the laws of England and Wales and Ireland, and on the terms that the members were guarantors of the company's debts.[20] Limited liability was first introduced in England under the Limited Liability Companies Act 1855. Like the first Joint Stock Companies Act,

11 RPS 1695/5/104 (*www.rps.ac.uk/mss/1695/5/104* (last accessed 31 August 2021)).

12 RPS 1695/5/239. The Governor and Company of the Bank of Scotland came to be registered as a public limited company (Bank of Scotland plc) under the Companies Acts only in 2006 by virtue of a private Act of Parliament: HBOS Group Reorganisation Act 2006 (c i).

13 Because the charter authorised the bank to operate only in Scotland, a private Act of Parliament was required to allow the bank to open a branch in London: the Royal Bank of Scotland Act 1873, s. 2. The Natwest Group plc (formerly Royal Bank of Scotland Group plc) was incorporated under the Companies Acts in 1968.

14 The history of these banks is set out in the opinions of the First Division in *Sanders v Sanders' Trustees* (1879) 7 R 157.

15 Chartered Companies Act 1837 (1 Vict, c 73).

16 Chartered Companies Act 1837 (1 Vict, c 73), s. 3.

17 Chartered Companies Act 1837 (1 Vict, c 73), s. 4.

18 A short summary is found in Bell, *Principles*, §§ 397–403.

19 *Sanders v Sanders' Trustees* (1879) 7 R 157 at 166 per Lord Deas.

20 Joint Stock Companies Act 1844 (7 & 8 Vict, c 110), ss. 13 and 25: see discussion in *J H Rayner (Mincing Lane) Ltd v Department of Trade and Industry* [1990] 2 AC 418 at 507D–507F per Lord Oliver of Aylmerton. The 1844 Act did not apply to Scotland: see s. 2. In California, company shareholders remained guarantors of the company's debts until 1931: R Kraakman, J Armour and P Davies, *The Anatomy of Corporate Law*, 3rd edn (Oxford: Oxford University Press, 2017), para. 1.2.2, n 30.

however, the 1855 Act did not apply to Scotland.[21] Limited liability was first introduced in Scotland in 1856.[22]

Banking companies were separately regulated. They were first allowed to incorporate in England in 1844[23] and in Scotland from 1846;[24] but incorporation conferred no limitation on the liability of shareholders.[25] Under this regime, therefore, even those who held transferable shares in huge 'companies', such as international banking businesses, had unlimited liability for the company's debts. Limited liability was made available to banks from 1858.[26] The potentially ruinous consequences for investors, often as far removed from management as creditors, were highlighted in the calamitous collapse of the City of Glasgow Bank in 1878.[27] The international restructuring of this bank – it had significant positions in American railroad concerns, and in Australian and New Zealand land – dominated the pages of the Scottish law reports into the twentieth century.[28] The consequences of the collapse, immediately and painfully felt in Scotland, were much wider: within a couple of years, almost all UK banks incorporated themselves under the Companies Acts with limited liability. By then incorporation with limited liability also entailed an auditing regime introduced as a direct result of the City of Glasgow Bank collapse.[29] 5.09

FORMATION

Members

It is possible to have a one-person company – that is to say, a company with only one member and one director.[30] But that is not possible in the case of partnerships, LPs and LLPs: as the 'partnership' part of the designation suggests, these are associations that can be formed only by two or more persons.[31] If a partnership has only two partners, both of whom are natural persons, 5.10

21 Limited Liability Act 1855 (18 & 19 Vict, c 133), s. 18.

22 Joint Stock Companies Act 1856 (19 & 20 Vict, c 47).

23 Joint Stock Banks Act 1844 (7 & 8 Vict, c 113).

24 Joint Stock Banks (Scotland and Ireland) Act 1846 (9 & 10 Vict, c 75). The Joint Stock Banks (Scotland) Act 1856 (19 & 20 Vict, c 3) extended the period for which Her Majesty was able to grant letters patent to a Bank beyond twenty years.

25 Joint Stock Banks Act 1844, s. 7; Joint Stock Banks (Scotland and Ireland) Act 1846, s. 5.

26 Joint Stock Banking Companies Act 1858 (21 & 22 Vict, c 91), s. 1.

27 For which, see K G C Reid, 'Embalmed in Rettie: the City of Glasgow Bank and the Liability of Trustees' in A Burrows, D Johnston and R Zimmermann (eds), *Judge and Jurist: Essays in Memory of Lord Rodger of Earlsferry* (Oxford: Oxford University Press, 2013), p. 489.

28 In what may have been the first use of a 'good assets' special purpose vehicle, 'The Assets Company Ltd' was incorporated under the Companies Acts and it acquired the remaining assets of the bank under a local Act of Parliament: the City of Glasgow Bank (Liquidation) Act 1882 (45 & 46 Vict, c clii). The Assets Company Ltd was litigating to the House of Lords and Privy Council as late as 1905 and was finally wound-up only in the 1950s.

29 Companies Act 1879 (42 & 43 Vict, c 76), s. 7(6).

30 Public companies require two directors: 2006 Act, s. 154(2). All companies must have at least one director who is a natural person: 2006 Act, s. 155. Where the number of members in a public company falls below two, it is competent to petition for the company's winding-up: Insolvency Act 1986, s. 122(1)(e).

31 1890 Act, s. 1(1); 1907 Act, s. 4(2); 2000 Act, s. 2(1)(a).

and one dies, the partnership comes to an end.[32] LLPs are different: despite the death of its members, the LLP remains in existence. But if it remains in existence for more than six months with only one member, that member becomes jointly and severally liable with the LLP for the payment of LLP debts contracted[33] after the six-month period.[34]

Registration

5.11 It was once the case that all businesses, whether corporate or not, had to register their business name in the 'Register of Business Names'.[35] That register was abolished in 1981.[36] However, companies, LLPs, LPs and Scottish qualifying partnerships[37] must be registered at Companies House. There are separate indices of companies, LLPs and LPs. Each has a registered number, and a registered name. In the case of companies and LLPs there must also be a registered office. Companies and LLPs may be registered either in Scotland; in England and Wales; or in Northern Ireland. There is a separate registrar for each jurisdiction.[38] A company incorporated in Scotland must have its registered office in Scotland.

Registered numbers

5.12 All registered entities have a unique number. A Scottish company number is prefixed by the letters 'SC'. A Scottish LLP is prefixed with the letters 'SO'. A Scottish LP's registered number is prefixed with 'SL'. The importance of the registered number for a corporate entity cannot be overemphasised. Corporate entities can change their name by special resolution and companies do this with surprising regularity.[39] More confusing still is the situation where companies or LLPs swap names.[40] So suppose John enters into a contract on day one with Alpha Ltd (SC00001). Alpha Ltd is part of a corporate group. Another company in the group is called Beta Ltd (SC00002). On day twenty, Alpha Ltd (SC00001) resolves to change its name the same day to Beta Ltd and, simultaneously, Beta Ltd resolves the same day to change its name to Alpha Ltd. On day thirty, John wants to sue the debtor under his contract. Who should he sue? The answer is the company with whom he has a contract, whatever its name may now be. The company with whom he had a contract is that with the number SC00001, which is now called Beta Ltd. It is therefore good practice always to include, in any document where a registered entity is being referred to, that entity's registered number so that it can be unambiguously identified. It is the registered number, not the registered name, which is the entity's unique identifier, its DNA. It is not possible to register a company

32 1890 Act, s. 33(1).
33 It is not clear why the wording is limited to debts incurred by way of contract.
34 2000 Act, s. 4A(2).
35 Registration of Business Names Act 1916.
36 Companies Act 1981.
37 Scottish Partnerships (Register of People with Significant Control) Regulations 2017 (SI 2017/694), regs 2 and 58.
38 2006 Act, s. 1060.
39 2006 Act, ss. 77–81.
40 See, e.g. *FJ Neale (Glasgow) Ltd v Vickery* 1973 SLT (Sh Ct) 88.

with a name that is the same as a name already registered on the Registrar's index of companies.[41]

LPs too must be registered at Companies House and they have a registered number.[42] The application for registration of an LP must be made to the registrar for the part of the UK where the LP is to have its principal place of business.[43] The control on the names of partnerships and LPs is found in a separate part of the 2006 Act dealing with business names.[44] Partnerships and LPs must therefore comply with the detailed rules regulating the words and letters that may be used in the business's name,[45] which are applicable to all businesses, irrespective of the particular business vehicle employed. **5.13**

Most ordinary partnerships generally have no registered number, no registered office, no publicity at all and determining whether a partnership exists is an altogether more metaphysical test, which is considered below. But it is to be emphasised that even some general partnerships, whose general partners are themselves juristic persons – Scottish 'qualifying partnerships'[46] – have to register at Companies House. They are allocated a registered number and have to publicise registrable persons exercising significant control.[47] **5.14**

Regulation of business names

Companies and LLPs must publicise the fact that their members are not liable for the debts of the company or LLP. Companies and LLPs do not have limited liability; and the fact that their members are not liable for the debts of the company or LLP is entirely consistent with first principles, where the (general) partners are effectively guarantors of the juristic person's debts. **5.15**

For the purposes of the law of business names, however, there is no prohibition of founding a partnership with an identical name to another partnership; and the 2006 Act gives express authority for the use of the partners' surnames in the partnership name.[48] The only protection available to a partnership or limited partnership from another partnership trading under the same name is the common law of passing off or the law of registered trademarks. Where a firm uses a name that does not contain the surnames of all the partners, however, the firm is required to disclose in all business documents the name of each partner together with an address at which documents may be served on them.[49] Failure by companies, LLPs and partnerships to make these **5.16**

41 2006 Act, s. 66.
42 1907 Act, ss. 8, 8A, 8B.
43 1907 Act, s. 8A(1)(d). Any change to a the LP's principal place of business must be registered: s. 9(1A)(a).
44 2006 Act, Part 41.
45 Company, Limited Liability Partnership and Business (Names and Trading Disclosures) Regulations 2015 (SI 2015/17); Company, Limited Liability Partnership and Business Names (Sensitive Words and Expressions) Regulations 2014 (SI 2014/3140); Company and Business Names (Miscellaneous Provisions) Regulations 2009 (SI 2009/1085).
46 Partnerships (Accounts) Regulations 2008, reg. 3.
47 2006 Act, s. 1066 read with the Scottish Partnerships (Register of People with Significant Control) Regulations 2017 (SI 2017/694), regs 2 and 58.
48 2006 Act, s. 1195.
49 2006 Act, s. 1201.

disclosures is a criminal offence, which attracts a daily fine for every day of default. Whether there are any civil consequences for breach of the trading disclosures regulations has not been decided but would be possible in egregious cases.[50]

5.17 There is one final point to mention about business names. Sometimes third parties make speculative registrations of company names. So suppose Glaxo and Wellcome announce they are to merge. A third party, hearing this news, makes a speculative registration of Glaxo-Wellcome Ltd.[51] All other things being equal, Glaxo and Wellcome cannot now use that name because it would be the same as one already on the register.[52] The 2006 Act allows the possibility of an application to the Company Names Tribunal,[53] based at the Intellectual Property Office in Cardiff, to order a company to change its name.[54] These provisions deal, among other situations, with the problem of speculative company name registrations that are not made in good faith.[55] Indeed an application may be made by any person on the ground that the company name is the same as a business name associated with the applicant, and in which the applicant has goodwill. Once an applicant establishes that the respondent business has the same name as one in which they enjoy goodwill, it is for the respondent company to justify why the application should not be granted.[56]

Persons with significant control

5.18 The popularity of Scottish partnerships and Scottish limited partnerships – not just for carrying out business in Scotland – has resulted in additional regulation in the form of filings in relation to persons with significant control for qualifying partnerships.[57]

EXTERNAL RELATIONS

Liability

5.19 Companies, partnerships, SLPs and LLPs have unlimited liability for their own debts. Each can contract liabilities which exceed its assets; and if that leads to an inability to pay debts as they fall due the entities may be subject to insolvency: put into administration or liquidation (in the case of companies and LLPs) or sequestrated (in the case of SLPs and partnerships). Of cardinal

50 Cf *Nigel Lowe & Associates v John Mowlem Construction plc* 1999 SLT 1298.

51 The example is taken from *Glaxo plc v Glaxo-Wellcome Ltd* [1996] FSR 388, decided under the pre-2006 law.

52 2006 Act, s. 66.

53 *https://www.gov.uk/government/organisations/company-names-tribunal* (last accessed 31 August 2021).

54 2006 Act, s. 73.

55 2006 Act, s. 69.

56 2006 Act, s. 69(4). For the procedure, see the Company Names Adjudicator Rules 2008 (SI 2008/1738). See, e.g. *MB Inspection Ltd v Hi-Rope Ltd* [2010] RPC 18, which involved the name of a Scottish company.

57 See n 2 above and paras. 1.19 and 1.21.

importance, however, is the liability of those who stand behind these vehicles: the shareholders, partners and members. As is well known, in the case of a company or LLP the members have no liability beyond the amount they agreed to contribute by way of capital – the nominal value of the share (plus any premium) or the amount they have agreed to contribute under an LLP members' agreement. To that extent, therefore, there is an element of 'limited liability'. The position of partnerships and SLPs is different and, indeed, exceptional. It is a general principle of private law that each person is liable only for his or her own debts. The position of partners in a partnership, or general partners in an LP, are two well-defined exceptions to this principle, for which express statutory wording was required.[58] So, in a Scottish partnership, partners are jointly and severally liable for the debts of the partnership.[59] For SLPs, that means the general partners, if more than one,[60] are jointly and severally liable for the SLP's debts; in practical terms, anyone involved in the day-to-day management of an SLP is a general partner. It is this aspect of the law of partnership that can make partnerships unattractive to entrepreneurs; but sometimes the reasons for difficulties arise less out of the incidents of a partnership but from a lack of attention to the wording used in documentation.[61]

INTERNAL DECISION-MAKING

One of the advantages of the private company limited by shares is that, on incorporation, if the members do nothing else, the law provides a default set of terms on which the company is to conduct its affairs: the model articles. LLPs and SLPs cannot be constituted otherwise than by registration and this additional formal act is usually sufficient to focus the minds of those wishing to employ such a vehicle on the terms on which those vehicles are to conduct business. It is thus normal practice for the affairs of an LLP or SLP to be regulated by a written members' or partnership agreement. Matters may be different with an ordinary partnership. Since it is possible to get into a partnership without knowing it, partnerships are sometimes encountered which have no written partnership agreement. More common still is the written agreement the provisions of which are either difficult to interpret or say nothing about the problem in question. **5.20**

58 *J H Rayner (Mincing Lane) Ltd v Department of Trade and Industry* [1990] 2 AC 418 at 508E per Lord Oliver of Aylmerton.

59 1890 Act, s. 9. Partners in an English partnership are jointly, but not severally, liable for the partnership's debts. Confusingly, the words 'joint' and 'several' have exactly opposite meanings in Scots and English law: see W W McBryde, *The Law of Contract in Scotland*, 3rd edn (Edinburgh: W. Green, 2007), para. 11–01.

60 A limited partnership must have more than one partner, but it needs only one general partner.

61 In *AIB Group (UK) Ltd v Martin* [2002] 1 WLR 94 HL, for example, a bank (X) advanced moneys to an English firm of two partners, A and B. A and B were jointly and severally liable not just for the loan, but for any other moneys advanced to either of them by X. X subsequently advanced additional funds only to A. The House of Lords found B jointly and severally liable to repay those funds, though B had never had any benefit of those funds because A had not used the money for firm purposes.

5.21 The 1890 Act, however, confers certain basic rights and imposes certain basic obligations on the partners – such as a right to inspect the firm's books[62] – which will be considered in more detail below.

SPECIALITIES: SCOTTISH PARTNERSHIPS

Formation

General principles

5.22 No formalities are required to enter into a partnership, at least where the partners are natural persons. This is one of the attractions of a partnership. There are no prescribed formalities for formation, and no prescribed publicity. Because there are no formalities, however, it may sometimes be difficult, in the case of a UK-wide business, to determine whether the partnership is Scottish or English or whether there are separate Scottish and English partnerships.[63]

5.23 A partnership is a 'relation which subsists between persons carrying on a business in common with a view of profit'.[64] Some commercial purpose is thus required.[65] A partnership may arise because there is the carrying on of a business in common with a view of profit, though the business never advanced beyond the preparations for trading.[66] In contrast, where there is merely a prospectus setting out a proposal to enter into a partnership, but those proposals are never implemented, no partnership comes into existence:[67]

> 'Partnership is a legal status with legal implications. There are certain features which are usually to be found in a partnership. None are present here. There was no firm name, no partnership premises, no partnership employees and no partnership bank account. Nor is there any averment that steps were being taken to establish any of these. There were no partnership accounts or tax returns. None of these is fatal to the contention that there was a partnership, but the lack of any of such things points strongly against the likelihood of there being one.'

5.24 A joint venture between two or more people for single particular purpose – such as the development of a plot of land – may amount to a partnership.[68] But while all partnerships involve an element of joint venture, not all joint ventures will be partnerships. Partnerships may be formed for a fixed period of time;[69]

62 1890 Act, s. 24(9); 1907 Act, s. 6(1) (for limited partners); the 2001 Regulations, reg. 7(8) (for members).

63 See the decision of the First Division in *Mortgage Express Ltd v Dunsmore Reid & Smith* 1996 GWD 40-2295. Cf Civil Jurisdiction and Judgments Act 1982, s. 42(4).

64 1890 Act, s. 1(1).

65 *Religious Tract and Book Society v IRC* (1896) 23 R 390; *IRC v Falkirk Temperance Café Trust* 1927 SC 261.

66 *Khan v Miah* [2000] 1 WLR 2123, HL (fitting out of a restaurant amounted to a partnership though the restaurant never commenced trading).

67 *Pine Energy Consultants Ltd v Talisman Energy (UK) Ltd* [2008] CSOH 10 at [28] per Lord Glennie.

68 *White v McIntyre* (1841) 3 D 334; *Mair v Wood* 1948 SC 83 at 86 per Lord President Cooper; *University Court of the University of St Andrews v Headon Holdings Ltd* [2017] CSIH 61.

69 1890 Act, s. 27, for which see *Wallace v Wallace's Trustees* (1906) 8 F 558.

or for an undetermined period of time – the so-called partnership-at-will.[70] Where a partnership for a fixed period of time continues beyond its intended period, the terms of the original agreement may nonetheless continue as terms of the partnership-at-will.[71]

Not all joint ventures of commercially minded people, however, are partnerships. There may be another basis for the relationship, such as a company, a limited partnership or LLP.[72] In the corporate world, 'joint ventures' often, though not always,[73] use a corporate vehicle. 5.25

Indicia of partnership

Although partnership is a contract, in cases where the parties have perhaps not clearly directed their minds to the nature of their relationship, an avowed lack of any intention to share in the firm's losses does not prevent a finding that the defender is a partner, especially where there is evidence of an intention to share in profits.[74] Establishing the existence of a partnership is classically a question of substance rather than form:[75] 5.26

> 'If a partnership in fact exists, a community of interest in the adventure being carried on in fact, no concealment of name, no verbal equivalent for the ordinary phrases of profit or loss, no indirect expedient for enforcing control over the adventure will prevent the substance and reality of the transaction being adjudged to be a partnership; and I think I should add, as applicable to this case, that the separation of different stipulations of one arrangement into different deeds will not alter the real arrangement, whatever in fact that arrangement is proved to be. And no 'phrasing of it' by dexterous draftsmen, to quote one of the letters, will avail to avert the legal consequences of the contract.'

But identifying the moment a partnership has been formed, particularly in a case where there is no formal documentation, is a notoriously difficult task.[76] There is no simple or single test which can be applied in every case so as to establish or negate the existence of a partnership. All the relevant features of the parties' relationship must be examined and a view reached on the basis of all such features.[77] The 1890 Act provides some very general guidance, identifying various factors which may be indicative of a partnership. These factors are set out in s. 2 of the 1890 Act: 5.27

(1) Joint tenancy or common property does not of itself create a partnership, irrespective of what is done with profits.

70 1890 Act, s. 26(1), 'no fixed term'. Cf *Maillie v Swanney* 2000 SLT 464.
71 *M'Gown v Henderson* 1914 SC 839.
72 1890 Act, s. 1. *Chahal v Mahal* [2005] 2 BCLC 655 at [37] per Neuberger LJ; *Ilott v Williams* [2013] EWCA Civ 645 at [20] per Arden LJ.
73 See, e.g. *Emcor Drake and Scull Ltd v Edinburgh Royal Joint Venture* 2005 SLT 1233.
74 *Pooley v Driver* (1876) 5 Ch D 458 at 483 per Sir George Jessel MR followed in *Brown & Co's Trustee v M'Cosh* (1898) 1 F 52 at 60 per Lord President Robertson, affd (1899) 1 F (HL) 86; *Stewart v Buchanan* (1903) 6 F 15.
75 *Adam v Newbigging* (1888) 13 App Cas 308 at 315 per Lord Halsbury LC.
76 Two examples where the parties' relations were bedevilled by informality are *Gillespie v Gillespie* [2011] CSOH 189 and *Maritsan Developments Ltd v HMRC* [2012] UKFTT 283 (a decision of J Gordon Reid QC).
77 *Dollar Land (Cumbernauld) Ltd v CIN Properties Ltd* 1996 SLT 186 at 191 per Lord Coulsfield (affd on other grounds: 1996 SC 331 and 1998 SC (HL) 90).

(2) Sharing of gross returns of itself does not create a partnership.
(3) Receipt of a share of profits of a business is *prima facie* evidence of a partnership, but that evidence may be neutralised where the receipt is: (a) by way of repayment of a debt; (b) remuneration for services;[78] (c) by way of an annuity paid to a widow, widower or civil partner; (d) by way of repayments made pursuant to a written contract of loan;[79] or (e) by way of annuity or otherwise a share of the profits in respect of the consideration payable by virtue of a sale of the goodwill.

5.28 Section 24 prescribes various default rights which, in the absence of an agreement to the contrary,[80] each partner in a firm is entitled to exercise, including: a right to an equal share in the profits; a right to indemnity for expenses; a right to interest on loans made to the partnership (not including capital contributions); a right to participate in management of the business; and a right to sight of the firm's accounts. There is no right to remuneration for acting in the partnership business;[81] conversely a partner's entitlement to share in the profits of the firm is not conditional or dependent on that partner doing anything in particular towards generating those profits.[82] These rights are often used by the courts for descriptive purposes too: in considering whether a business relationship amounts to a partnership the exercise of any or all of the rights that would be conferred by s. 24 of the 1890 Act on a partnership is often taken as indicative of the existence of a partnership. Where someone has effective control of a business, including sharing in profits, contributing capital and having an unfettered right to appoint someone as a partner in the business, such control is indicative of that person being a partner in the business.[83] Conversely, someone who has no share of profits may nonetheless be held to be a partner and liable for its debts where, in the case of a law firm, it was necessary for them to be held out as a partner for regulatory purposes.[84] A partnership tax return is conclusive for tax purposes as to whether a person does or does not have a share in the profits or losses of the partnership for any period, and what share of any person in those profits or losses is.[85]

Trading

5.29 In terms of s. 1(1) of the 1890 Act, '[p]artnership is the relation which subsists between persons carrying on a business in common with a view of profit'. If

78 So the drowned fisherman, remunerated by a share of the boat's gross returns, in *Clark v G R & W Jamieson* 1909 SC 132 was held to have been an employee, not a partner. Cf *Sharpe v Carswell* 1910 SC 391.
79 *Buchanan v Stewart* (1903) 6 F 15.
80 For construction of an agreement held to oust the default rule in s. 24, see the decision of the First Division in *Heaney v Downie*, 11 February 1997, unreported.
81 1890 Act, s. 24(6).
82 *Sheveleu v Brown and Ducker* [2018] CSIH 68, 2019 SC 149 at [42] per Lord Brodie.
83 *Brown & Co's Trustee v M'Cosh* (1898) 1 F 52 at 60 per Lord President Robertson, affd (1899) 1 F (HL) 86.
84 *M Young Legal Associates Ltd v Zahid (a Firm)* [2006] EWCA Civ 613, [2006] 1 WLR 2565.
85 Taxes Management Act 1970, s. 12ABZB(1). A dispute between the partners about the correctness of a partnership tax return in relation to these matters may be referred to the First-tier Tribunal (Tax Chamber) for determination: s. 12ABZB(3).

a partnership is not carried on with a view of profit it will not benefit from tax transparent treatment.[86] Section 45 defines a 'business' as 'carrying on a trade, business or profession'. What amounts to a 'trade, business or profession' is of some importance to Scottish partnerships and limited partnerships that are used as vehicles for the holding of assets or investments. Investing in moveable or immoveable assets and drawing the profits from rents or dividends or capital gains, may amount to 'carrying on a trade, business or profession'.[87] Lord Justice Clerk Macdonald has formulated the question as: '[i]s the sum of gain that has been made a mere enhancement of value by realizing a security, or is it a gain made in an operation of business in carrying out a scheme for profit-making'?[88] The Law Commissions, having considered whether to legislate in this area, decided no clarification was necessary: 'it is difficult to conceive of a term wider than "business" to cover all commercial undertakings. The term seems clearly apt to include investment activities as a commercial venture'.[89] A partnership can be formed with a view of profit though it never commences trading.[90]

Agency

Because, in Scots law, partnerships and LPs are juristic persons, each of the partners is an agent of the partnership or LP as the case may be. But a 1890 Act provision says also that the partners are also agents for each other.[91] The provision is drafted with English law in mind, where a partnership has no legal personality. In Scots law, the better view is that the 'agent for each other' element of s. 5 needs to be interpreted away.[92] By way of analogy, no one would suggest that directors of a company are agents for each other. To hold that partners of a Scottish firm are agents of each other may cause all sorts of problems. Suppose Alan and Beth form a partnership (AB Partners). Charlie and David form a partnership (CD Partners). Because both entities are juristic persons, it is possible for AB Partners and CD Partners to enter into a partnership or joint venture: ABCD Partners. This structure is not possible under English law. In English law the partners of ABCD Partners are Alan, Beth, Charlie and David. In Scots law, however, the partners of ABCD Partners are two separate partnerships. If s. 5 were read literally, however, it would mean that, in the case of the Scottish partnership structure, that David was an agent of AB Partners, a partnership of which he is not a partner. 5.30

86 *Samarkand Film Partnership No. 3 v Revenue and Customs Commissioners* [2017] EWCA Civ, [2017] STC 926.

87 Cf *Glasgow Heritable Trust v IRC* 1954 SC 266; *American Leaf Blending Co Sdn Bhd v DG of Inland Revenue* [1979] AC 676; Income Tax (Trading and Other Income) Act 2005, ss. 6–12.

88 *Californian Copper Syndicate, Limited v Harris* (1904) 6 F 894 at 898, a test approved by the Privy Council in *Commissioner of Taxes v Melbourne Trust* [1914] AC 1001 at 1010 and by the House of Lords in *Ducker v Rees Roturbo Development Syndicate Ltd* [1928] AC 132 at 139.

89 Law Commission and Scottish Law Commission, *Discussion Paper on Partnership* (2000), para. 5.10. And see too the view of HMRC reproduced in Law Commission and Scottish Law Commission *Report on Partnership* (2003), para. 16.25.

90 *Khan v Miah* [2000] 1 WLR 2123.

91 1890 Act, s. 5.

92 Cf the opinion of Professor Gretton contained in *Major v Brodie* [1998] STC 491. See too P Stein, 'The Mutual Agency of Partners in the Civil Law' (1959) 33 *Tulane L Rev* 595 at 604 onward.

Property

5.31 Purchasing property for the business may itself be evidence of subsisting partnership.[93] The technical rules, which historically prevented Scottish firms from owning heritable property, no longer exist.[94] But it remains uncommon for professionally advised partnerships to take title to ownership of land in the name of the partnership: one of the reasons being that a change of partners can give rise to difficulties regarding entitlements to the partnership assets.[95]

5.32 The ordinary practice, therefore, is for the partners for the time being to take title to any heritable property in their own names as trustees for the firm. The rights of individual partners are personal rights against the firm.[96] There are thus three layers: trustees – firm (beneficiary) – partners.[97] Death, retirement or resignation of a partner under this structure does not give rise to property law problems. Trust title is the paradigm case of the elastic title found in joint ownership:[98] the departing partner's share accresces automatically to those who remain. But if the law is clear in principle, that clarity is not reflected in the decided cases. In one case, the lease was granted to the partners 'as trustees for the . . . firm and the survivors and survivor of them as trustees and trustee'. That title should have been unaffected by any change in the partners. Nonetheless it was held that the lease was terminated on a change of partners – in other words, a change in the personality of the beneficiaries of a trust to which the landlord was a stranger.[99]

5.33 In *Jardine-Paterson v Fraser*,[100] the Lord Ordinary held that a tenant under the lease was the 'business' or (trading) 'house' rather than a recognised juristic person. That may mean, in practical terms, a lease in favour of a particular person (natural or juristic) plus implied consent to assignation of the lease to associated entities of that tenant.[101] Alternatively, the idea of a trading 'house' may be no more than an ostensible holding out by the partners to the world that the business carried on by the original partnership is continuing. The wider world has no way of finding out from a public register what the basis of any 'new' partnership actually is. As a result, the partners cannot seek to rely on the provisions of the 1890 Act s. 33 to frustrate the claims of a third party creditor.[102] In the same way third parties normally do not know the actual

93 *Christie Owen & Davies plc v Raobgle Trust Corporation* [2011] EWCA Civ 1151.

94 Abolition of Feudal Tenure etc. (Scotland) Act 2000, s. 70. See generally G L Gretton, 'Who owns partnership property?' 1986 *Jur Rev* 163.

95 In *Lujo Properties Ltd v Green* 1997 SLT 225 the lease was granted to '[the firm] and [. . .] the Partners of said firm as trustees for the said firm'. It is not easy to make sense of that formulation.

96 *Revenue and Customs Commissioners v Anson* [2015] UKSC 44, [2015] STC 1777 at [39] per Lord Reed JSC; *McIrvine v McIrvine* [2012] CSOH 23 at [21] per Lord Brodie.

97 *Duncan's Exrs v The MFV Marigold PD145* 2006 SLT 975 at [16] per Lord Reed (dealing with registration of partners as owners of a fishing vessel under the Merchant Shipping (Registration of Ships) Regulations 1993 (SI 1993/3138)).

98 See K G C Reid, *The Law of Property in Scotland* (London: LexisNexis, 1996), para. 20.

99 *Moray Estates Development Company v Butler* 1999 SLT 1338.

100 1974 SLT 93 at 97.

101 Cf *Renfrew District Council v A B Leisure (Renfrew) Ltd* 1988 SLT 635.

102 Bell, *Commentaries* II, 528. Cf *IRC v Graham's Trs* 1971 SC (HL) 1 at 20 per Lord Reid.

authority of an agent, so too do third parties normally not know the actual terms of a private partnership agreement.

Relations of partners *inter se* and knowledge

Partners owe fiduciary duties to the firm.[103] Partners also owe to each other duties of good faith.[104] These duties of good faith may even arise before the partnership agreement is concluded, imposing, for instance, duties of candour and disclosure of material facts in the context of formation of the partnership agreement.[105] There are specific statutory duties to account for private profits[106] and not to compete with the firm.[107] In addition, the 1890 Act provides that 'partners are bound to render true accounts and full information of all things affecting the partnership to any partner or his legal representatives'.[108] That duty is not one, it has been said, that is owed at all times; it arises rather in specific circumstances: as when one partner seeks information from a fellow partner in the context of negotiations between the partners.[109] **5.34**

A partner of a firm (like a member of an LLP or a director of a company) is not an employee.[110] Conversely, an employee of the firm who is held out to the world as a partner (the so-called 'salaried partner') is likely to be held to owe similar duties of loyalty and good faith to the firm and to his or her fellow partners. Where partners owe duties, whether to the firm or to fellow partners, the standard of care is, today, an objective standard; looking at the matter objectively, a court will ask what an honest person would have done in the circumstances.[111] There is a detailed line of case law setting how and when a **5.35**

103 *Aberdeen Railway Co v Blaikie Brothers* (1854) 17 D (HL) 20, (1854) 1 Macq HL 461, 1 Pat 394. For modern examples in the context of solicitors' firms: see *Finlayson v Turnbull (No. 1)* 1997 SLT 613 and *Ross Harper & Murphy v Banks* 2000 SC 500.

104 *Duncan v The MFV Marigold PD145* 2006 SLT 975 at [45] per Lord Reed; *University Court of the University of St Andrews v Headon Holdings Ltd* [2017] CSIH 61 at [76] per Lord Malcolm; *O'Neill v Phillips* [1999] 1 WLR 1092 at 1098–1099 per Lord Hoffmann: 'company law has developed seamlessly from the law of partnership, which was treated by equity, like the Roman *societas*, as a contract of good faith'. See too *Helmore v Smith* (1880) 35 Ch D 436 at 444 per Bacon VC ('utmost good faith'), quoted with approval in *Sim v Howat* [2012] CSOH 171 at [39] per Lord Hodge.

105 *Manners v Whitehead* (1898) 1 F 171; *University Court of the University of St Andrews v Headon Holdings Ltd* [2017] CSIH 61 at [77], [81] per Lord Malcolm.

106 1890 Act, s. 29.

107 1890 Act, s. 30.

108 1890 Act, s. 28. For an application of that obligation to an SLP, see *Herberstein v TDR Capital General Partner II LP* [2021] CSOH 64.

109 *Sim v Howat* [2012] CSOH 171 at [40] per Lord Hodge. See too *Ferguson v Patrick & James, WS* 1984 SC 115 and *Smith v Barclay* 1962 SC 1.

110 But such a partner may nonetheless be a 'worker' for labour law purposes: *Tiffin v Lester Aldridge LLP* [2012] EWCA Civ 35, [2012] 1 WLR 1887; *Bates van Winkelhof v Clyde & Co LLP* [2014] UKSC 32, [2014] ICR 730.

111 *Royal Brunei Airlines Sdn Bhd v Tan* [1995] 2 AC 378 at 389; *Twinsectra Ltd v Yardley* [2002] 2 AC 164; *Barlow Clowes International Ltd (in liquidation) v Eurotrust International Ltd* [2006] 1 WLR 1476 at [15]. Cf *Frank Houlgate Investment Company Ltd v Biggart Baillie LLP* [2013] CSOH 80, 2013 SLT 993 at [40]–[45].

company director's knowledge may be attributed to a company.[112] Notice to a partner is deemed notice to the firm.[113]

Delicts

5.36 Section 10 of the 1890 Act provides that a firm is liable for the wrongful acts of a partner incurred in the ordinary course of the firm's business. The firm is liable for misappropriations of money made by a partner in the course of business.[114] The partners of the firm are jointly and severally liable for such delicts.[115] Wrongful acts include negligent acts or acts that amount, for example, to dishonest assistance.[116] There is, however, an exception with regard to property held by one of the partners in trust: a breach of trust by a partner does not impose on his fellow partners personal liability for those breaches of trust.[117] In the late 1940s the First Division held that a partner who suffered loss as a result of a negligent act of a fellow partner could not sue the partnership as being vicariously liable for the partner's wrongful acts.[118] That case has been followed in modern decisions. But while it may be a general principle that a principal is not *ipso jure* vicariously liable for the acts of their agent,[119] there seems no good reason in the modern law to deny a partner, injured by a negligent act of a fellow partner acting in the course of the firm's business, a claim against the firm.

Partner liability: holding out

5.37 Section 14(1) of the 1890 Act provides that:

> '(1) Every one who by words spoken or written or by conduct represents himself, or who knowingly suffers himself to be represented, as a partner in a particular firm, is liable as a partner to any one who has on the faith of any such representation given credit to the firm, whether the representation has or has not been made or communicated to the person so giving credit by or with the knowledge of the apparent partner making the representation or suffering it to be made.'

112 *Meridian Global Funds Management Asia Ltd v Securities Commission* [1995] 2 AC 500 (PC); *Singularis Holdings Ltd (In Liquidation) v Daiwa Capital Markets Europe Ltd* [2019] UKSC 50, [2020] AC 1189.

113 1890 Act, s. 16. *Zurich GSG Ltd v Gray & Kellas* 2007 SLT 917.

114 1890 Act, s. 11, for which see *New Mining and Exploring Syndicate, Limited v Chalmers & Hunter* 1912 SC 126.

115 1890 Act, s. 15.

116 *Dubai Aluminium Co Ltd v Salaam* [2003] 2 AC 366. For Scots law, see the *obiter dicta* of the Lord Ordinary (Lord Reed) in *Commonwealth Oil & Gas Co Ltd v Baxter* [2007] CSOH 198 at [197] affd 2010 SC 156.

117 1890 Act, s. 13.

118 *Mair v Wood* 1948 SC 83 at 86 and 90. But the decision in *Mair* was heavily influenced by the position of employees. A firm employee, at that time, did not have a delictual claim if injured by a fellow firm employee because of the doctrine of 'common employment'. The First Division was reluctant to confer on a partner better rights than those enjoyed by an employee. The First Division advised its opinions on 19 December 1947. The doctrine of common employment was abolished six months later: Law Reform (Personal Injuries) Act 1948.

119 In the Inner House decision of *M v Hendron* 2007 SC 556 at [131], Lord Osborne reserved his opinion on the soundness of *Mair*.

Ordinary principles of agency apply to individuals such as employees or consultants. Someone who is not a partner in the firm, but is held out to the world as such – as in the case of a 'salaried partner' – has ostensible authority on the ordinary principles of agency to bind the firm in the course of the firm's business.[120] Section 14(1) of the 1890 Act, however, is directed not to authority but to personal liability. In the ordinary course of events, an agent acting within their authority has no personal liability on a contract concluded on behalf of a disclosed principal. Section 14(1) provides that, where an individual 'suffers himself to be represented' to a creditor as a partner, that individual becomes liable as a partner to a creditor who, on the strength of that representation, gives credit to the firm.[121] **5.38**

Some circumstances, however, will place a third party creditor on inquiry: as where someone otherwise held out as a partner seeks to borrow money at uncommercial rates; or purports to grant a cautionary obligation on behalf of the firm in respect of the indebtedness of an individual who has no apparent connection to the firm. In such a case, the third party will not be able to rely on the partner's ostensible authority.[122] **5.39**

Change of partners

One of the major difficulties with a partnership is that, all other things being equal, a change of partners – whether by expulsion,[123] retirement,[124] resignation,[125] bankruptcy, death[126] – gives rise to dissolution and, if the business continues, to reconstitution of a new partnership. That may have important consequences for contracts with third parties. A third party who contracts with a firm will normally have no knowledge of the internal relationships or changes in the partners.[127] Such a third party may be prejudiced by the dissolution of the firm. For contracts that include an element of *delectus personae* a change in the personality of the firm may give the creditor an option to termination the contract.[128] There is, therefore, a fundamental tension between the rule that changes of partners give rise to successive partnerships and the perception by outsiders of the firm's business continuing as a commercial enterprise.[129] The rules set out in the 1890 Act provide that on each change in the composition of the partners there is a dissolution of the partnership, with the continuing business being undertaken by a new partnership.[130] Some of these rules are **5.40**

120 *Freeman & Lockyer v Buckhurst Park Properties (Mangal) Ltd* [1964] 2 QB 480.

121 For an example, see: *UCB Home Loans Corporation Ltd v Soni* [2013] EWCA Civ 65.

122 1890 Act, s. 7 and *Paterson Brothers v Gladstone* (1891) 18 R 403; *Fortune v Young* 1918 SC 1; *Walker v Smith* (1906) 8 F 619.

123 1890 Act, s. 25.

124 1890 Act, s. 26.

125 1890 Act, s. 32(c) ('notice to dissolve the partnership').

126 1890 Act, s. 33.

127 *Scottish Pension Fund Trustees Ltd v Marshall, Ross & Munro* [2018] CSIH 39, 2018 SC 523 at [44] per Lord President Carloway.

128 *Garden, Haig-Scott and Wallace v Prudential Approved Society for Women* 1927 SLT 393.

129 *Scottish Pension Fund Trustees Ltd v Marshall, Ross & Munro* [2018] CSIH 39, 2018 SC 523 at [61] per Lord Drummond Young.

130 In *Scottish Pension Fund Trustees Ltd v Marshall, Ross & Munro* [2018] CSIH 39, 2018 SC 523, [4] the court records that there had been some seventeen iterations of the firm in question.

expressed to be 'subject to any agreement between the partners . . .'. The effect of such agreements is addressed below.

5.41 Certain statutory provisions and common law rules address the possibility of continuity. Section 17 of the 1890 Act provides that 'a person who is admitted as a partner into an existing firm does not thereby become liable to the creditors of the firm for anything done before he became partner'.[131] That does not appear to recognise fully the ordinary effect of changes in the partnership.[132] In the law of prescription express provision is made for a series of transactions in which goods or services are sold or supplied despite a change of partners, and presumes an element of continuity.[133] The common law rules, set out in paras 5.74–5.73 below, also proceed on a view of continuity.

Dissolution

General

5.42 Winding up of the firm's affairs can be carried out by the former partners, under s. 38; or, by the court, under s. 39. In order to understand the consequences of partnership dissolution it is helpful to start with involuntary dissolution. The classic examples of involuntary dissolution provided by the 1890 Act are a partner's death or bankruptcy.[134] The provisions on dissolution in the 1890 Act, however, are expressed to be 'subject to any agreement between the partners'.[135] A partnership agreement may therefore provide that the partnership will continue notwithstanding the death or bankruptcy of one of the partners.[136] The 1890 Act is silent on the question of the effect of retirement or resignation of partner or the assumption of a new partner in the absence of notices. The general view, therefore, is that, without an express agreement to the contrary, retirement, resignation or assumption of a new partner may dissolve the existing partnership and lead to reconstitution of a new partnership. In large commercial partnerships which have traded for many years, however, such an approach would be extremely inconvenient. In such cases, the 'agreement' to oust s. 33 may be easily implied in order to reflect the commercial realities of the situation.[137]

Nature of dissolution

5.43 Whereas, with companies, the Insolvency Act 1986 envisages a winding up of the affairs of the company before the company's final liquidation and removal from the register, the Partnership Act 1890 appears to envisage that dissolution of the partnership prior to the affairs of the partnership being wound-up,

131 1890 Act, s. 17(1).
132 *Sim v Howat* [2011] CSOH 115 at [13] per Lord Hodge.
133 Prescription and Limitation (Scotland) Act 1973, Sch. 2, para. 1(3).
134 1890 Act, s. 33(1).
135 1890 Act, ss. 32, 33(1), 43 and 44.
136 *Warner v Cunninghame* (1798) Mor 14,603 approved in *Hill v Wylie* (1865) 3 M 541 at 543 per Lord Justice Clerk Inglis.
137 *IRC v Graham's Trs* 1971 SC (HL) 1 at 19–20 per Lord Reid; *Lujo Properties Ltd v Green* 1997 SLT 225 at 235 per Lord Penrose.

at least in the case of death or bankruptcy of a partner.[138] The effect of dissolution on legal personality is addressed in the following paragraph. If dissolution, followed by winding-up, is inconvenient, it is not unique, for this is essentially the position with natural persons: personality ceases with death, yet between death and confirmation of executors there is limbo, a patrimony but no person to represent it. There is a conflict of authority on the question of whether, following dissolution, the partners winding-up the affairs of the firm are to be considered as trustees.[139] On dissolution following a partner's death, it has been said to be not only the surviving partners' *right* to realise the firm's assets for the purpose of winding up the firm's affairs, but it is their *duty* to do so.[140]

Winding-up by the partners

Section 38 applies 'after dissolution of the partnership'. By that stage, the partners' s. 5 authority to bind the firm has come to an end.[141] That is why s. 38 is necessary. Following dissolution, 'the authority of each partner . . . to bind the firm . . . continue notwithstanding dissolution'.[142] A contract to which the firm is party is not necessarily brought to an end by the dissolution of the firm.[143] Where, properly construed, such a contract is brought to an end by dissolution, s. 38 does not make the surviving partners parties to the firm's contracts.[144] Notwithstanding dissolution, 'for certain purposes a partnership continues'.[145] Since, however, s. 38 applies in England and is drawn from Roman law (in both systems, partnership is a contract but not a juristic person), it may be that 'dissolution' is best considered to refer to the contractual relationship[146] rather than to the legal personality of a Scottish partnership. Moreover, even if the firm's legal personality were said to have ceased (as with death of the natural person) the firm's patrimony, including its patrimonial rights, remain and fall to be administered. The partners' secondary liabilities for the firm's debts under those contracts remain. 5.44

138 *Chahal v Mahal* [2005] 2 BCLC 655 at [27] per Neuberger LJ.

139 *Sheveleu v Brown and Ducker* [2018] CSIH 68, 2019 SC 149 at [42] per Lord Brodie (former partners who carry out work for dissolved partnership do so in the position of trustees); *Duncan v The MFV Marigold PD145* 2006 SLT 975 at [52], [65] and [67] per Lord Reed, preferring Lord Westbury's speech in *Knox v Gye* (1871–1872) LR 5 HL 656 at 675 (no trust) to Lord Dunedin's speech in *Hugh Stevenson & Sons Ltd v Aktiengesellschaft für Cantonnagen-Industrie* [1918] AC 239 at 248 (remaining partners trustees).

140 *Re Bourne* [1906] 2 Ch 427 at 431–432 per Romer LJ.

141 *Sheveleu v Brown and Ducker* [2018] CSIH 68, 2019 SC 149 at [39] per Lord Brodie. It may be observed that s. 38 does not, however, mirror the terms of s. 5.

142 *IRC v Graham's Trs* 1971 SC (HL) 1 at 4 (IH sitting as LVAC) per Lord Hunter: 'Possibly a more accurate statement may be that the surviving partners of the dissolved firm have, in such circumstances, the rights and powers necessary to enable them to wind up the affairs of the dissolved firm and distribute its assets: *Collins v Young* (1853) 15 D (HL) 35, per Lord Cranworth LC at p. 36; Bell's *Principles* (10th edn) § 379. Such rights and powers may, in appropriate cases, include the completion of depending contracts. In my opinion, the foregoing view of the law accords with the terms of section 38 of the Partnership Act, 1890, and avoids the logical difficulty of asserting that the partnership continues in existence after it has been dissolved by the death of a partner'.

143 *Sheveleu v Brown and Ducker* [2018] CSIH 68, 2019 SC 149 at [38] per Lord Brodie.

144 *IRC v Graham's Trs* 1971 SC (HL) 1 at 21 per Lord Reid.

145 *Dickson v National Bank of Scotland Ltd* 1917 SC (HL) 50 at 52 per Lord Finlay LC.

146 *Hopper v Hopper* [2008] EWCA Civ 1417 at [46] per Etherton LJ.

5.45 What, then, does s. 38 authorise? Winding up the firm, as Lord Reed said in *Duncan v The MFV Marigold PD145*,[147] may take different forms: the business may be disposed of as a going concern to a third party; or disposed of to a new firm formed by the surviving partners. In other cases, individual assets may simply be sold to different buyers. The House of Lords has held that a surviving partner has no authority 'to undertake new transactions on behalf of the firm';[148] and that 'the surviving partners have no right to bind the assets of the dissolved firm by making new bargains or contracts'.[149] But these statements cannot be read literally; if assets are to be liquidated and sold – winding-up *par excellence* – the surviving partners will have to enter into contracts of sale – new contracts – with prospective buyers. The *dicta* from the cases must therefore be read in the context of the commercial realities of the situation. And there may even be cases that warrant the continuation of the business for a limited period.[150] For, as Lord Reed has observed:[151]

> '[T]here may be practical advantages in enabling the business of a dissolved partnership to be carried on during the twilight period of winding up: a business may be realised to best advantage as a going concern, and the continuation of trading may be necessary to maintain the value of goodwill.'

5.46 The doubts expressed about the former partners' authority to enter into 'new' contracts must therefore be limited to new 'trading' contracts.[152] Contracts concluded for the purposes of winding-up the dissolved firm's affairs are expressly authorised by the section. The s. 38 power may include the power to assign a lease held by the old partnership to the partners of the old partnership, even if the lease permitted assignation only with the landlord's express written consent.[153] In the event that, in the course of an active process of winding-up under s. 38, profits are generated, s. 42 does not apply: s. 42 is concerned with the case where continuing partners seek to carry on the business. So, if following the date of dissolution, services are provided under one of the firm's contracts by some of the partners in the course of winding-up, those profits fall to be accounted for to all the partners of the dissolved firm, though some may not have performed any of the services.[154]

Voluntary departures of partners

5.47 It is in the interests of both the firm and any departing partner to agree expressly the effect of their departure, either in the original partnership agreement or in an express severance agreement.[155] But any express agreement between the partners is not of itself sufficient to bind third parties. In order

147 2006 SLT 975 at [22].

148 *Dickson v National Bank of Scotland Ltd* 1917 SC (HL) 50 at 52 per Lord Findlay LC.

149 *IRC v Graham's Trs* 1971 SC (HL) 1 at 21 per Lord Reid.

150 Cf The Lloyd's Underwriters (Scottish Limited Partnerships) (Tax) Regulations 1997 (SI 1997/2681), reg. 9(2).

151 *Duncan v The MFV Marigold PD145* 2006 SLT 975 at [43] per Lord Reed.

152 *Duncan v The MFV Marigold PD145* 2006 SLT 975 at [44] per Lord Reed.

153 *Renfrew District Council v A B Leisure (Renfrew) Ltd* 1988 SLT 635.

154 *Sheveleu v Brown and Ducker* [2018] CSIH 68, 2019 SC 149.

155 For the prescriptive periods that apply to obligations prestable on or after termination of the partnership agreement, see Prescription and Limitation (Scotland) Act 1973, Sch. 2, para. 3; and *Harper v John C Harper & Co (No. 1)* 2003 SLT (Sh Ct) 105.

to publicise that the partner no longer has ostensible authority to bind the firm, and that the partner is no longer jointly and severally liable for the firm's debts, notice of the partner's departure ought to be placed in the *Edinburgh Gazette*.[156] The departing partner's right to a share of profits made since their departure and attributable to their share of the partnership assets is a reference to net assets.[157] In the absence of agreement the preferable remedy for a departing partner is to bring an action for count reckoning and payment against the firm (if it continues) and the other partners.[158]

Expulsion and termination

The contract of partnership, as has been seen, involves implied obligations of good faith. As a result, the partners may not exclude a partner 'unless a power to do so has been conferred by express agreement between the partners'.[159] It may be a difficult question of construction of whether the agreement confers a largely unfettered power on the other partners to dismiss, or whether the power conferred requires the other parties to come to a decision on whether to expel. In the latter case, the decision may be quasi-judicial, importing rules of natural justice.[160] It is unlikely that the rules of natural justice apply where there are only two partners, since the effect of such a purported expulsion is dissolution. Where there are three partners, A, B & C, partner A cannot purport to expel B & C, the only other partners. Acceptance of a repudiatory breach of a partnership agreement, or contractual termination of the agreement, does not necessarily dissolve the firm or absolve the innocent partners of their obligations to contribute to the firm's liabilities.[161] But a partner who is themselves in material breach of the partnership agreement may lose their right to dissolve the firm based on that agreement.[162] A partner who has misused firm assets for private purposes may be liable to pay compound interest on the cost to the firm for their unauthorised use of those assets.[163] **5.48**

Dissolution by the court: s. 35

There are also provisions for dissolution to occur under the supervision of the court, on grounds of mental incapacity, prejudicial conduct, persistent breaches of the partnership agreement, business able to be carried on only at a loss; or on the basis that it would be 'just and equitable' to dissolve the partnership.[164] In practical terms, dissolution by the court under s. 35 of the 1890 **5.49**

156 1890 Act, s. 36(2). Section 37 authorises further public notices. Law firms traditionally publicised changes in the *Journal of the Law Society of Scotland*.

157 1890 Act, s. 42(1) discussed in *Sandhu v Gill* [2006] Ch 456.

158 *Green v Moran* 2002 SC 575.

159 1890 Act, s. 25.

160 *Rennie v Rennie* [2020] CSOH 49, 2020 SLT 619 at [40] per Lord Clark, considering *Green v Howell* [1910] 1 Ch 495.

161 *Hurst v Bryk* [2002] 1 AC 185; *Maillie v Swanney* 2000 SLT 464; *Golstein v Bishop* [2014] Ch 455.

162 *Hunter v Wylie* 1993 SLT 1091.

163 *Roxburgh Dinardo & Partners' Judicial Factor v Dinardo* 1992 SC 188.

164 1890 Act, s. 35(f).

Act takes place by way of a petition to appoint a judicial factor to wind down the partnership's affairs.[165] But the office of judicial factor is wider and more flexible than appointment under s. 35. A judicial factor may be appointed to any 'estate' or patrimony in cases of deadlock, incapacity or alleged illegality.[166] Because of the expense involved in appointment of a judicial factor, however, it must be 'necessary or expedient' to appoint, for instance where there is a 'danger of loss',[167] for it is a remedy of 'last resort'.[168]

Closing accounts

5.50 Section 43 provides that amounts due by surviving partners to a deceased or retiring partner are 'a debt accruing at the date of dissolution or death'. The date on which the debt becomes due is important for the purposes of the prescriptive period. But the valuation of that debt can often occur only after the firm's affairs have been wound up: the assets realised and the debts paid.[169] Section 44 provides the basis on which the partnership's closing accounts should be drawn up. Losses are paid first out of profits, then out of capital and, in the event of a shortfall of capital, by the partners individually 'in the proportion in which they were entitled to share the profits'. In other words, the partner who would have benefitted the most from the firm's success will bear the brunt of the losses as between the partners *inter se*. All assets, including work in progress, are brought into account.[170] Importantly, there is a statutory rate of interest of 5 per cent on sums outstanding to partners in the closing accounts.[171]

5.51 Following the approach of the House of Lords in *Cruickshank v Sutherland*,[172] the Court of Session has held that, unless there is a clear agreement to the contrary,[173] the valuation of the firm's assets on dissolution should be carried out at current market value rather than historic book value.[174] In England, in contrast, the Court of Appeal has held that there is no such presumption.[175]

5.52 It is important to emphasise, however, that s. 44 applies only between the partners *inter se*. Creditors may treat any partners of the firm as being jointly and severally liable for the firm's debts – even if that partner has a claim

165 *Carabine v Carabine* 1949 SC 521; *McCulloch v McCulloch* 1953 SC 189; *Mahmood, Petr* 2010 GWD 37-753.

166 *Thurso Building Society's Judicial Factor v Robertson* 2000 SC 547. A judicial factor may complete title to heritable property: Titles to Land Consolidation (Scotland) Act 1868, s. 24. Where a judicial factor is appointed and the title is in the General Register of Sasines, see Conveyancing (Scotland) Act 1874, s. 44.

167 *Gow v Schulze* (1877) 4 R 928 at 934 per Lord Shand.

168 *Rosserlane Consultants Ltd, Petr* [2008] CSOH 120 at [20] per Lord Hodge.

169 In *Duncan v The MFV Marigold PD145* 2006 SLT 975 at [51], Lord Reed described the debt as being '*debitum in praesenti, solvendum in futuro*'. See too *Purewall v Purewall* [2008] CSOH 147.

170 *Bennett v Wallace* 1998 SC 457.

171 1890 Act, s. 42(1) applied in *Dyce v Fairgrieve and Morisons Solicitors* [2013] CSOH 155.

172 (1923) 92 LJ Ch 136.

173 One example is *Thom's Exrx v Russel & Aitkin* 1982 SLT 335.

174 *Noble v Noble* 1965 SLT 415; *Shaw v Shaw* 1968 SLT (Notes) 94; *Clark v Watson* 1982 SLT 450; *Wilson v Dunbar* 1988 SLT 93.

175 *Re White* [2001] Ch 393; *Drake v Harvey* [2011] EWCA Civ 838, [2012] 1 BCLC 724.

against their fellow partners for breach of contract; the relations of the partners between themselves is not a matter with which creditors need trouble themselves.[176]

Insolvency

In England, though partnerships are not juristic persons, there are bespoke provisions for the insolvency of partnerships.[177] In Scotland, ironically, where partnerships do have juristic personality, they are nonetheless subject to the law of personal bankruptcy.[178] 5.53

SPECIALITIES: SLPs

General principle

The general principle of law regulating limited partnerships is that, unless otherwise specified, partnership law applies to them.[179] That principle is subject also to the Persons with Significant Control Regulations.[180] 5.54

Uses

SLPs have varied practical uses. One important traditional use was to hold agricultural leases; indeed, by the end of the twentieth century, nearly all agricultural leases were granted to limited partnerships.[181] As a result of legislation in 2003,[182] however, the use of SLPs in agricultural leases has become much less common. Today, one important use of the SLP is as an investment vehicle.[183] The 1907 Act has been heavily amended to provide for private fund limited partnerships ('PFLPs'): LPs which are a collective investment scheme.[184] The PFLP provisions modify the general rules. In what follows the 5.55

176 *Hurst v Bryk* [2002] 1 AC 185.

177 Partnership Insolvency Order 1994 (SI 1994/2421).

178 Bankruptcy (Scotland) Act 2016, s. 6(1)(b) (partnerships) and (e) (limited partnerships). See too *Smith, Petr* 1999 SLT (Sh Ct) 5. The Financial Services and Markets Act 2000, s. 367 allows partnerships and limited partnerships engaged in regulated activity to be wound up as an unregistered company at the instance of the FCA.

179 1907 Act, s. 7. So, for instance, the same obligations to account as arise in a partnership apply to LPs: *Herberstein v TDR Capital General Partner II LP* [2021] CSOH 64.

180 Scottish Partnerships (Register of People with Significant Control) Regulations 2017.

181 For the background to this ingenious use of the LP: see *MacFarlane v Falfield Investments Ltd* 1998 SC 14 at 29 onward per Lord President Rodger; and *Salvesen v Riddell* [2012] CSIH 26; 2012 SLT 633 at [8]–[12] per Lord Justice Clerk Gill (revd on a different point [2013] UKSC 22).

182 Agricultural Holdings (Scotland) Act 2003, ss. 72 and 73.

183 I MacNeil, *An Introduction to the Law of Financial Investment*, 2nd edn (Oxford: Hart Publishing, 2012), pp. 151–152, 184–185. See, e.g. *Inversiones Frieira SL v Colyzeo Investors II LP* [2011] EWHC 1762 and [2012] EWHC 1450.

184 1907 Act, s. 8D(3) and (4). In addition, there are further modifications to the 1907 Act where the Collective Investment in Transferable Securities (Contractual Scheme) Regulations 2013 (SI 2013/1388) or European Longterm Investment Funds Regulations 2015 (SI 2015/1882) apply. They will not be considered further here.

focus is on the general rules. Some examples of transactional structures can be gleaned from the case law.[185]

Formation

5.56 A limited partnership must have at least two partners: at least one general partner and at least one limited partner. The general partner is liable for all debts and obligations of the firm. Subject to one important exception, a limited partner must, at the time of entering into the partnership, contribute to the partnership a sum or sums as capital, or property valued at a stated amount. The limited partner is not liable for the debts or obligations of the firm beyond the amount so contributed.[186] The important exception to the requirement to contribute capital is where the SLP is a PFLP.[187] Formation of a limited partnership requires registration[188] at Companies House.[189] Its name must include designation 'limited partnership' or 'LP'.[190] Each SLP therefore has a unique registration number.[191] It is necessary in any limited partnership that at least one partner is designated the general partner. Unlike a partnership, an SLP is not automatically dissolved on the death, bankruptcy or mental incapacity of a limited partner.[192] There is no similar provision providing for continuation of the SLP on the death, bankruptcy or incapacity of the general partner. But since the general partner is often an incorporated company, which is potentially immortal, an SLP therefore comes close to enjoying perpetual succession. As with partnerships, however, the default provisions of the 1890 and 1907 Acts may be modified by express agreement between the partners. And, in practice, general partnerships or SLPs used, for example, as investment funds can avoid the consequences of death, at least, by ensuring that there are at least two partners who are juristic persons.

General partner

5.57 As has been seen, all SLPs must have at least one partner with unlimited liability for the SLP's debts. In practice, it is therefore common for the general partner to be a company.[193] These companies are sometimes easy to spot: the general partner of Alpha Bravo LP might be called Alpha Bravo (General Partner) Ltd.

185 *Greck v Henderson Asia Pacific Equity Partners (FP) LP* [2008] CSOH 5. Another example involving a Scottish LP – interesting for the facts, rather than the law – is *Berghoff Trading Ltd, GEA Holdings Ltd, Caspian Energy Group LP v Swinbrook Developments Ltd* [2009] EWCA Civ 413.

186 1907 Act, s. 4(2A).

187 1907 Act, s. 4(2A) and (2B).

188 1907 Act, s. 5.

189 1907 Act, s. 15(1).

190 1907 Act, s. 8B.

191 1907 Act, s. 8C(3)(b).

192 1907 Act, s. 6(2).

193 The 1907 Act makes express provision only for corporate *limited* partners: 1907 Act, s. 4(4). But the competence of the use of corporate general partners has never been doubted and their use is widespread.

Agency

The general partners, but not the limited partners, have authority to bind an SLP.[194] But the SLP may be bound also by an agent who has actual or ostensible authority to bind the SLP. **5.58**

Partners' relations *inter se*

The rights and obligations of a limited partner, as the designation would suggest, are limited: limited partners are not agents of the limited partnership;[195] they have no right to dissolve the partnership by notice;[196] and they have only limited voting rights. Management decisions, in the absence of any agreement to the contrary, are a matter for the majority of the general partners.[197] A limited partner does have the right to inspect the books and, in the words of the 1907 Act, 'to examine into the state and prospects of the partnership business and advise the [general] partners thereon',[198] but that right is a limited right and, in some circumstances, the general partners may be able to refuse to provide information to a limited partner.[199] But unless otherwise modified by agreement, the general principles of the 1890 Act and the common law imposing obligations to account apply also to limited partnerships.[200] Crucially, a limited partner has no ostensible authority to bind the limited partnership and they have no right to engage in management (and thus they have no right to vote on managerial decisions).[201] The 1907 Act contains a strong disincentive against limited partners attempting to participate in management decisions: the limited partner who purports to do so becomes personally liable for the limited partnership's debts as if they were a general partner,[202] without necessarily obtaining the rights of a general partner.[203] But for limited partners in a PFLP there is an extensive list of decisions in which the limited partner in such a partnership may vote without losing limited liability.[204] Importantly, a limited partner in a PFLP is not subject to a number of the duties otherwise imposed on a partner under the 1890 Act in relation to rendering accounts and not competing with the firm.[205] **5.59**

A limited partnership agreement should address partner exits, since the Act provides that, in the event that a limited partner, during the life of the **5.60**

194 1907 Act, s. 6(1) and 1890 Act, s. 5.
195 1907 Act, s. 6(1).
196 1907 Act, s. 6(5)(e).
197 1907 Act, s. 6(5)(a).
198 1907 Act, s. 6(1).
199 For limited partners' rights to see documents relating to the LP's investments, see *Inversiones Frieira SL v Colyzeo Investors II LP* [2011] EWHC 1762 and [2012] EWHC 1450.
200 *Herberstein v TDR Capital General Partner II LP* [2021] CSOH 64.
201 1907 Act, s. 6.
202 1907 Act, s. 6(1).
203 So, in *Limited Partners in Henderson PFI Secondary Fund II LP (a firm) v Henderson PFI Secondary Fund II LP* [2013] 2 WLR 1297, where the limited partners in an LP were permitted to bring a common law derivative action, the judge held that the bringing of such an action would amount to management and the limited partners would thus become liable as general partners for the LP's debts.
204 1907 Act, s. 6A.
205 1907 Act, s. 6(5)(f) disapplying the 1890 Act, ss. 28 and 30.

partnership, seeks to leave and have their capital contribution repaid, the investor attracts liability 'for the debts and obligations of the firm up to the amount so drawn out or received back'.[206] There are extensive amendments to that position for limited partners in a PFLP.[207] In practical terms, therefore, exit may often be by way of assignation of the limited partner's share, with the exiting partner obtaining their investment by way of payment from a third party as consideration for the assignation. In LPs, a limited partner can transfer their share in the LP, although, as in partnerships, the consent of the general partners (but not the limited partners) is required. In principle, therefore, although new partners can be introduced without the consent of the limited partners, the consent of the general partner will be required.[208] If the general partner is to be replaced, therefore, the replacement may need to be structured as the assumption of a new general partner by the general partner, immediately followed by the resignation of the original general partner. In addition, assignation of a limited partner's share in an SLP that is not a PFLP, requires publication by notice in the *Edinburgh Gazette* and, until that notice is published, the assignation 'is deemed to be of no effect'.[209] Since a limited partner's share is arrestable,[210] such a share probably remains arrestable by the transferor's creditors until the date of publication of the notice in the *Gazette*.

SPECIALITIES: LLPs

General principles

5.61 An LLP is a body corporate.[211] Despite its name, an LLP therefore has more in common with a company than a partnership and, unless expressly provided for in any enactment, the law of partnership does not apply to an LLP.[212] Instead large swathes of the 2006 Act and associated delegated legislation apply to LLPs:[213] corporate names; accounting; company charges; dissolution, are just four examples where the regime that applies to LLPs is the corporate regime. To incorporate an LLP, two or persons associated for carrying on a lawful business with a view to profit must have subscribed their names to an incorporation document.[214] LLPs that carry on a business with a view to profit are, in principle, tax transparent; but LLPs that are used solely for the purpose of obtaining tax reliefs but which are not otherwise carrying on business with a view to profit, do not benefit from tax transparent status.[215]

206 1907 Act, s. 4(3).
207 1907 Act, s. 4(3A).
208 1907 Act, s. 6(5)(d).
209 1907 Act, s. 10(1).
210 This is implied from 1907 Act, s. 6(5)(b).
211 2000 Act, s. 1(2).
212 2000 Act, s. 1(5).
213 Limited Liability Partnerships (Application of Companies Act 2006) Regulations 2009 (SI 2009/1804).
214 2000 Act, s. 2(1)(a).
215 *Eclipse Film Partners (No. 35) LLP v Revenue and Customs Commissioners* [2015] EWCA Civ 95, [2015] STC 1429; *Samarkand Film Partnership No. 3 v Revenue and Customs Commissioners* [2017] EWCA Civ 77, [2017] STC 926 at [71].

External relations

Each member of an LLP has ostensible authority to bind the LLP. So too does anyone else held out as having equivalent authority, such as someone who is designated as a 'partner' (as is the case with most professional services firms). But a contract purportedly concluded on the LLP's behalf by an agent before incorporation does not bind the LLP.[216] An LLP may, however, be able to sue on a negligent misrepresentation made by someone prior to its existence if reliance on those representations led to a contract to which it is a party.[217] 5.62

Members *inter se*

The default rights of LLP members are similar to those found in the 1890 Act: the right to share in profits; right to indemnification for expenses incurred in the course of the LLP business; right to participate in management; no right to remuneration; and no right to assign interest in LLP without consent of the other members.[218] Each member has a right to call other members to account for their intromissions with the LLP's assets; that right to an accounting extends to provision of 'full information'.[219] The default provision on decision-making is that of a bare majority of the members.[220] That provision appears to envisage a vote on the basis of 'one member, one vote' rather than, as is the norm in bespoke members' agreements, voting tied to capital accounts. Only two matters require unanimity (subject to the members' agreement): a decision to change the nature of the LLP's business;[221] or a decision to expel a member.[222] Members of an LLP owe their fiduciary duties to the LLP, not to each other – unless the members' agreement expressly so provides.[223] 5.63

Unfair prejudice and derivative actions

LLPs are subject to the provisions of the 2006 Act on unfairly prejudicial conduct.[224] The ability to petition for unfair prejudice is conferred on individual members. The court has a wide discretion in the orders it may make. A member's ability to petition for unfair prejudice has been described as an 'optional right'.[225] As a result, it is possible for members of an LLP by unanimous written agreement to exclude a member's remedy of petition in respect of unfairly prejudicial conduct.[226] The exercise of the remedy may be subject to 5.64

216 2006 Act, s. 51 (applied to LLPs by Limited Liability Partnerships (Application of Companies Act 2006) Regulations 2009, reg. 7); *Tinnevelly Sugar Refining Co Ltd v Mirrlees Watson and Yaryan Co Ltd* (1894) 21 R 1009; *Cumming v Quartzag Ltd* 1980 SC 276.

217 *Cramaso LLP v Viscount Reidhaven's Trustees* [2014] UKSC 9, 2014 SC (UKSC) 121.

218 2001 Regulations, reg. 7(1)–(5).

219 2001 Regulations, reg. 7(8).

220 2001 Regulations, reg. 7(6).

221 2001 Regulations, reg. 7(6).

222 2001 Regulations, reg. 8.

223 *F&C Alternative Investments (Holdings) Ltd v Barthelemy* [2012] Ch 613.

224 2006 Act, s. 994 as applied by Limited Liability Partnerships (Application of Companies Act 2006) Regulations 2009, reg. 48.

225 *Fulham Football Club (1987) Ltd v Richards* [2012] Ch 333 at [78] per Patten LJ.

226 2006 Act, s. 994(3) as applied by Limited Liability Partnerships (Application of Companies

an arbitration agreement.[227] There are no provisions in the regulations conferring on members of an LLP the right to bring a derivative action under s. 265 of the 2006 Act. But it is likely that such a right exists at common law:[228] it has been held that it is possible, in principle, for the limited partners of an LP to bring a derivative action;[229] and it has been further held in England that a member of an LLP, where the LLP was the sole shareholder in a company, could bring a derivative action on behalf of the company.[230] In Scotland it is likely that any such common law derivative action would now proceed as if it were being brought under the 2006 Act.[231]

Company charges and insolvency

5.65 The floating charge is not recognised at common law.[232] The floating charge is thus part of Scots law only as a result of the statutory provisions that permit incorporated companies and other bodies to create them.[233] The Companies Act 1985 provisions on floating charges apply to LLPs.[234] An LLP, like a company, must register any charges at Companies House within twenty-one days of creation.[235]

5.66 Partnerships and limited partnerships have no capacity to grant floating charges. One complication, however, arises where one of the partners is a company or LLP. In a limited partnership, the general partner is very often a company. In both partnerships and LPs, the normal practice is for the partners (the general partners in the case of an LP) to hold assets of the partnership or LP in trust for the partnership or LP. In that situation, where the partner or general partner holding the assets in question is itself a company or LLP, it appears possible for a corporate general partner to create a floating charge over the assets it holds in its capacity as trustee for the partnership or LP as the case may be.

Incorporation of a partnership

5.67 A partnership may agree to 'incorporate' as an LLP or limited company. There are a number of ways of doing so. Perhaps the most famous company law case

Act 2006) Regulations 2009, reg. 48 (subpara. (3) does not appear in the version of s. 994 in the 2006 Act as it applies to companies).

227 Cf *Heart of Midlothian Football Club plc v Scottish Professional Football League Ltd* [2020] CSOH 68, 2020 SLT 736. For arbitration, see Chapter Fifteen: Alternative Dispute Resolution below.

228 For which, see *Anderson v Hogg* 2002 SC 190 and *Wilson v Inverness Retail & Business Park Ltd* 2003 SLT 301.

229 *Limited Partners in Henderson PFI Secondary Fund II LP (a firm) v Henderson PFI Secondary Fund II LP* [2013] 2 WLR 1297.

230 *Universal Project Management Services Ltd v Fort Gilkicker Ltd* [2013] 3 WLR 164.

231 2006 Act, s. 266, the procedure for which is elaborated on in *Wishart v Castlecroft Securities Ltd* 2010 SC 16 and *ICE (Europe) Ltd v Ibrahim* [2016] CSIH 62, 2016 SLT 1182.

232 *Carse v Coppen* 1951 SC 233.

233 Companies Act 1985, s. 462.

234 Limited Liability Partnerships (Scotland) Regulations 2001 (SSI 2001/128), reg. 3 and Sch. 1; 2001 Regs, reg. 4 and Sch. 2.

235 2006 Act, s. 859A(4) as applied to LLPs by Limited Liability Partnerships (Application of Companies Act 2006) Regulations 2009, reg. 32.

of all time, *Salomon v A Salomon & Company Ltd*,[236] provides a useful case study for incorporating an existing business. The normal case, which the law presumes,[237] is that the business and assets of the partnership are purchased by the corporate entity, the consideration for the purchase being equity in the company. The presumption is that the partnership is thereupon dissolved. But the presumption may be rebutted.[238] There are nuances with a Scottish partnership. Sale by a Scottish partnership of its property to a corporate entity, in the absence of agreement to the contrary, would mean that the shares in the company which form the consideration for the sale would be paid to the company rather than the partners.

Dissolution

LLPs are subject to the corporate insolvency regime under the Insolvency Act 1986.[239] In the event that the liquidator fails to deal with LLP assets, the default position is that the Crown, represented by the Queen's and Lord Treasurer's Remembrancer, succeeds to them as *bona vacantia*.[240] **5.68**

BUSINESS ACQUISITIONS

Assets or equity?

Generally speaking there are two basic structures for corporate acquisitions. The first can apply only to a target business that is a body corporate: an equity acquisition whereby the shares in the target company are acquired. The second possibility is to acquire individual assets of the target business. **5.69**

There are important practical consequences as between the two approaches. As a general principle, and subject to an exception in the case of successor partnerships,[241] acquisition of individual assets means the buyer acquires only the assets; the seller's liabilities remain with the seller. But the transfer of many individual assets of large businesses is a cumbersome exercise. A buyer that acquires the equity in a company, in contrast, takes the company warts and all: the buyer acquires the shares in the company, not any rights in individual assets held by the company. The change in the company's members has no effect on the company's personality and thus no effect on the company's assets and liabilities. The value of the company to the buyer in those circumstances **5.70**

236 [1897] AC 22. In *Salomon*, the consideration was partly paid in equity, and partly in debt; the debt was secured by a floating charge in favour of the seller over the property acquired by the company. The result was not only that Mr Salomon obtained limited liability for the future; he also became a secured creditor for the balance of the purchase price.

237 *Chahal v Mahal* [2005] 2 BCLC 655 at [29] per Neuberger LJ.

238 As indeed it was in *Chahal v Mahal*.

239 2001 Regs, reg. 5. See para. 14.44.

240 See 2006 Act, ss. 1012–1013, 1020–1022, applied in amended form to LLPs by Limited Liability Partnerships (Application of Companies Act 2006) Regulations 2009, reg. 54. Assets which have been inherited by the Crown by oversight may be re-acquired, subject to agreement, by a conveyance from the Queen's and Lord Treasurer's Remembrancer: see, e.g. *Slattadale Ltd v Tilbury Homes (Scotland) Ltd* 1997 SLT 153.

241 See para. 5.71 onward below.

is only as good as the company's assets and liabilities. It is for these reasons that, in corporate acquisitions, 'due diligence' exercises are often undertaken.

Partnership acquisitions

5.71 Where a new firm acquires the assets of an old firm by sale and payment of a price, the general rule is that the new firm, as a separate juristic person, has no liabilities for the debts of the old firm.[242] But since changes in partners may not be known to the outside world, there is a fundamental tension between the rule that changes of partners give rise to successive partnerships and the perception by outsiders of the firm's business continuing as a commercial enterprise.[243] The common law rules in relation to the assumption by a new partnership that carries on substantially the same business as a predecessor partnership without interruption is thus concerned to protect those third parties. Moreover, matters are often unclear, as where there is a change of partners, no documentation, no express transfers of any assets, and the business carries on as before. As has been seen, the effect of a change in partners is, in principle, to dissolve the firm and, if the business continues, to constitute a new firm. If the new firm pays for the assets of the old firm, then the old firm's creditors are protected: they can look to the purchase price.[244] But where there has been no consideration paid, the law, in order to protect the creditors of the old firm, holds the new firm liable for the old firm's debts.[245] The doctrinal basis for the new firm's liability for the debts of the old has been said to be an implied unilateral undertaking[246] or an implied novation.[247] There are three conditions for the operation of the principle:[248]

(1) The new partnership must be 'practically the same' as the old partnership.
(2) The business must be carried on without interruption.
(3) The original partnership, if it continues to exist, should be left without assets or be left with a significant diminution in assets.

5.72 It is sometimes said that a new firm becomes liable for the old firm's debts where a new partner is assumed, creating a new firm which carries on as before, where the new partner in the firm has not contributed any capital. But a capital contribution to the new firm is of limited assistance to the creditors of the old firm.[249] A contractual provision between the old firm and the new firm, or a provision in the new firm's partnership agreement that the new firm is not liable for the debts of the old firm, may be ignored by the court where there is no evidence of payment for the assets.[250]

242 *Stephen's Trustee v Macdougall & Company's Trustee* (1889) 16 R 779; *Thomson & Balfour (A Firm) v Boag & Son* 1936 SC 5.
243 *Scottish Pension Fund Trustees Ltd v Marshall, Ross & Munro* [2018] CSIH 39, 2018 SC 523 at [61] per Lord Drummond Young.
244 *Henderson v Stubbs Ltd* (1894) 22 R 51 at 55 per Lord Adam.
245 *M'Keand v Laird* (1861) 23 D 846 (a decision of seven judges); *Heddle's Exrx v Marwick & Houston's Tr* (1888) 15 R 698; *Miller v MacLeod* 1973 SC 175.
246 *Sim v Howat* [2011] CSOH 115 at [33] per Lord Hodge.
247 *Scottish Pension Fund Trustees Ltd v Marshall, Ross & Munro* [2018] CSIH 39, 2018 SC 523, [64] per Lord Drummond Young.
248 *Scottish Pension Fund Trustees Ltd*, [65] per Lord Drummond Young.
249 *Sim v Howat* [2011] CSOH 115, [31]; *Scottish Pension Fund Trustees Ltd*, [70].
250 *M'Keand v Laird* (1861) 23 D 846 at 851 per Lord Justice Clerk Inglis.

It is worth observing, however, that the doctrine has not yet been applied by the Scottish courts to the situation where the business of a firm has been acquired by a company. One attempt to argue that the doctrine applied to the case where the transferee was a company was unsuccessful because the transferee company had paid a considerable consideration for the assets it acquired.[251] 5.73

251 *Ocra (Isle of Man) Ltd v Anite Scotland Ltd* 2003 SLT 1235.

Chapter Six

Sale of Goods

Alexander Sutherland

INTRODUCTION

6.01 This chapter concerns the law governing non-consumer and consumer contracts for the sale of goods. The former are governed by the Sale of Goods Act 1979 (the '1979 Act') and the latter, by the 1979 Act and the Consumer Rights Act 2015 (the '2015 Act'). There is considerable overlap between the two Acts. Certain sections of the 1979 Act apply to the 2015 Act. Certain sections of the 1979 Act have identical, or almost identical, equivalents in the 2015 Act. The main area of difference is the remedies available to parties in the event of breach of contract.

6.02 This chapter will not examine every provision of the Acts, confining itself to those which are most likely to be relevant to modern life and legal practice. The focus will be on the 1979 Act. The Consumer Credit Act 1974 and the Unfair Contract Terms Act 1977 fall outwith its scope. Internationally, ninety-four states have acceded to the UN Convention on Contracts for the International Sale of Goods (the Vienna Convention, 1980), which harmonises the legal rules on the international sale of goods.[1] Parties include China, the US, the Russian Federation, Canada, Australia and all EU Member States bar Ireland and Malta. The UK has not (yet) acceded.

CONTRACTS FOR THE SALE OF GOODS

The legislation

6.03 Towards the end of the nineteenth century there was a strong move towards codification of commercial law.[2] It was the spirit of the age, being promoted on all sides.[3] The legal zeitgeist resulted in the Bills of Exchange Act 1882, the Partnership Act 1890 and the Marine Insurance Act 1906. It also resulted in the Sale of Goods Act 1893 (the '1893 Act'), the first codification of the law governing contracts for the sale of goods. With the exception of the

1 The literature is extensive. See, e.g. I Schwenzer (ed), *Schlechtriem and Schwenzer Commentary on the UN Convention on the International Sale of Goods*, 4th edn (Oxford: Oxford University Press, 2016).

2 Report on the Sale and Supply of Goods (Scot. Law Com. No. 104, 1987), para. 1.5.

3 A F Rodger, 'The codification of commercial law in Victorian Britain' (1992) 108 LQR 570 at 583.

Partnership Act 1890, all these codifying Acts were drafted by Sir Mackenzie Chalmers, who became an acknowledged master of the art of codification.[4]

After the 1893 Act had received Royal Assent, a contemporary commentator declared that although it made radical changes to Scots law, it was, on the whole, 'a good measure'.[5] However, as was noted in the recent case of *Caithness Flagstone Ltd v Ballyvesey Holdings Ltd*,[6] whatever Sir Mackenzie's level of mastery, the 1893 Act had its critics. Although the drafter was aiming to state the common law of England and Wales, the 1893 Act was applied to Scotland. Professor Gow wrote: **6.04**

> 'The draftsman was Sir Mackenzie Chalmers, a county court judge at Birmingham, whose avowed purpose was to reproduce as accurately as possible the existing English law . . . Eminent English judges have described the Act an admirable, very successful and correct codification of English law. How it came to be applied to Scotland may be a mystery Scots lawyers are not anxious to have solved.'[7]

The 1893 Act was replaced by the 1979 Act, which came into force on 1 January 1980.[8] It has undergone a series of amendments since then but remains the principal statute governing non-consumer contracts for the sale of goods. Notably, the Sale and Supply of Goods Act 1994 (the '1994 Act') made a number of amendments in order to make the language of parts of the 1979 Act reconcilable with the principles of Scots law. For example, it disapplied s. 11, which makes provision about when a 'condition' is to be treated as a 'warranty', a distinction not recognised in Scots law. **6.05**

The 2015 Act consolidated the law in relation to consumer contracts for the sale of goods. It has a wider scope than contracts for the sale of goods, covering also contracts for the hire of goods, hire purchase agreements and contracts for the transfer of goods.[9] As well as goods, the 2015 Act covers digital content and services. **6.06**

Except for the final part (*buyers' remedies in consumer contracts of sale*), references to sections in this chapter are to sections of the 1979 Act. Where the section is of another Act, that will be stated. Where a section of the 1979 Act does not apply to a consumer contract of sale, that is indicated in the section.[10] A table showing the equivalents can be found at the end of this chapter. **6.07**

4 Report on the Sale and Supply of Goods (Scot. Law Com. No. 104, 1987), para. 1.5.
5 RB, 'Sale of Goods Act, 1893' (1893) 1 SLT 536.
6 [2020] SAC (Civ) 1 at [33].
7 J J Gow, *The Mercantile and Industrial Law of Scotland* (Edinburgh: W. Green, 1964), p. 75.
8 1979 Act, s. 64(2).
9 The most relevant Acts for non-consumer contracts of these types are the Sale of Goods (Implied Terms) Act 1973 (implied terms in non-consumer hire purchase agreements) and the Supply of Goods and Services Act 1982 (non-consumer contracts for the hire of goods and non-consumer contracts for the transfer of goods).
10 1979 Act, s. 1(5)–(6).

What is a contract for the sale of goods?

Non-consumer contracts for the sale of goods

6.08 Section 2(1) defines a contract for the sale of goods as 'a contract by which the seller transfers or agrees to transfer the property in goods to the buyer for a money consideration, called the price'.

6.09 Goods are 'all corporeal moveables except money'.[11] Section 61(1) defines 'property' as the general property in goods, and not merely a special property. The 'property in goods' is better expressed, in Scots law, as the ownership of goods. Ownership, or *dominium*, is 'the right of using and disposing of a subject as our own, except in so far as we are restrained by law or paction [agreement]'.[12] The general property in goods is the real right of ownership and not merely a subordinate real right, such as a right in security. This chapter refers to the ownership of goods, rather than the property in them.

6.10 In summary, a contract for the sale of goods is a contract by which the seller transfers or agrees to transfer the ownership of corporeal moveables for money. The fundamental rule is that ownership of the goods passes when the parties intend it to pass.[13] Agreements which do not effect a transfer of ownership are not contracts for the sale of goods.[14] The price is a fundamental ingredient of a contract for the sale of goods. Without it, the contract has a different character.[15] The requirement for a price distinguishes a contract of sale from barter (transfer of goods in exchange for goods), gift (gratuitous transfer of goods) and deposit (transfer of goods to a custodier for safekeeping).

6.11 Contracts for the sale of goods may be absolute or conditional.[16] Section 2 distinguishes between the contracts for the sale of goods and agreements to sell, the latter being contracts for the sale of goods where the transfer of ownership of the corporeal moveables is to take place at a future time or subject to a condition later to be fulfilled.[17]

Exclusion for transactions intended to operate as security

6.12 The 1979 Act does not apply to transactions in the form of a contract of sale which are intended to operate by way of security (including mortgage, pledge or charge).[18] The exclusion applies to transactions where a debtor sells, or purports to sell, an item to a creditor. The price is the loan. The item secures

11 1979 Act, s. 61(1). This includes crops, 'things attached to or forming part of the land which are agreed to be severed before sale' and also 'an undivided share in goods'.

12 Erskine, *Institute* 2.1.1, cited in K G C Reid, *The Law of Property in Scotland* (London: Butterworths, 1996), para. 5.

13 1979 Act, s. 17(1). See para. 6.92 below.

14 *Wilson Imports Ltd v Advance Sport SAS* [2015] CSOH 114 at [18] per Lord Woolman. For a tricky case, see *PST Energy 7 Shipping LLC v OW Bunker Malta Ltd* [2016] UKSC 23, [2016] AC 1034.

15 Commentary in *Scottish Current Law Statutes: 1979*, 54/8–54/9.

16 1979 Act, s. 2(3).

17 1979 Act, s. 2(5).

18 1979 Act, s. 62(4).

the obligation to repay to loan. As the 'sale' is intended solely to raise finance, the creditor may allow the debtor to retain possession of the item.

The 1979 Act allows ownership to pass without delivery. The exclusion in s. 62(4) means that the provisions of the 1979 Act do not operate to allow the creditor to obtain the real right of ownership. The court will examine the substance of the transaction to determine if the transaction is a true contract of sale or intended to operate as security. Under reference to s. 61(4) of the 1893 Act, the predecessor of s. 62(4), Lord Moncrieff stated: **6.13**

> '[The section] is in effect a statutory declaration that a pledge of or security over moveables cannot be created merely by completion of what professes to be a contract of sale. If the transaction is truly a sale, the property will pass without delivery. But the form of the contract is not conclusive. The reality of the transaction must be inquired into; and if, contrary to the form of the contract, and even the declaration of the parties, it appears from the whole circumstances that a true sale was not intended, it will be held that the property has not passed and that no effectual security has been acquired.'[19]

Without delivery, no effectual security can be created over moveables.[20]

Consumer contracts for the sale of goods

Much of the content of the 2015 Act is similar to that of the 1979 Act. The 2015 Act tends to deploy less legalistic language.[21] Chapter Two of the 2015 Act applies to contracts for a trader 'to supply goods' to a consumer.[22] Contracts to supply goods include contracts of sale, but also contracts for the hire of goods, hire purchase agreements and contracts for the transfer of goods.[23] All these are grouped together as contracts to supply goods.[24] **6.14**

Goods are defined as tangible moveable items. This includes water, gas and electricity if they are put up for supply in a limited volume or set quantity.[25] Chapter Three of the 2015 Act applies to contracts for the trader to supply digital content (i.e. data that are produced and supplied in digital form). Chapter Four applies to contracts for the trader to supply a service. **6.15**

Contracts of sale are defined in s. 5(1) of the 2015 Act. The definition is in substance identical to that in the 1979 Act. A contract is a contract of sale if: (a) the trader transfers or agrees to transfer ownership of goods to the consumer; and (b) the consumer pays or agrees to pay the price. Contracts for the sale of future goods are also contracts of sale.[26] A trader is a person acting for purposes relating to that person's trade, business, craft or profession, whether **6.16**

19 *Robertson v Hall's Trustee* (1896) 24 R 120 at 134 per Lord Moncrieff, cited in *Ladbroke Leasing (South West) Ltd v Reekie Plant Ltd* 1983 SLT 155 at 159 per Lord Grieve.
20 W M Gloag and J M Irvine, *Law of Rights in Security* (Edinburgh: W. Green, 1897), pp. 189, 198; A J M Steven, *Pledge and Lien* (Edinburgh: Edinburgh Legal Education Trust, 2008).
21 For example, 'tangible moveable items' rather than 'corporeal moveables'. Implied terms are dealt with in a different manner, too.
22 2015 Act, s. 3(1).
23 2015 Act, s. 3(2). A contract for the transfer of goods is one whether the consideration is not monetary.
24 2015 Act, s. 3(4).
25 2015 Act, s. 2(8).
26 2015 Act, s. 5(2). On future goods, see paras 6.18 and 6.19 below.

acting personally or through another person acting in the trader's name or on the trader's behalf.[27] The trader cannot sidestep the provisions of the 2015 Act by acting through an agent. A consumer is an individual acting for purposes that are wholly or mainly outwith the individual's trade, business craft or profession.[28] The exclusion for transactions intended to operate by way of security applies to consumer contracts of sale.[29]

A note on 'goods'

6.17 The definition of 'goods' does not embrace heritable property (i.e. land and buildings) or incorporeal moveables, such as shares in a company. The courts have occasionally had to grapple with how to classify a computer programmes/software carried on, say, a disk. In *St Albans District and City Council v International Computers Ltd* an *obiter* view was expressed that, while a computer programme, as intangible software, did not come within the definition of 'goods', a disk which contained defective software would *prima facie* be a breach of the implied terms as to quality and fitness for purpose.[30] This must be correct. If a disk containing a computer programme is supplied, it is supplied to allow the computer programme to be installed. If a defect renders that impossible, it is difficult to see how the disk could be considered as fit for all common purposes.[31] In consumer contracts of sale any conceptual difficulty is resolved by the specific provision for digital content.

6.18 Goods which are the subject of a contract of sale can be: (i) either specific (ascertained) or unascertained; and (ii) either existing or future. *Specific goods* are goods identified and agreed on at the time a contract of sale is made.[32] Despite its appearance in ss. 16, 18 and 20A, all of which deal with transfer of ownership, the expression 'unascertained goods' is not defined in the 1979 Act. *Unascertained goods* fall into three main categories: (1) goods to be manufactured or grown by the seller, which must be future goods; (2) purely generic goods, e.g. 10,000 litres of wine; and (3) an unidentified part of a specific/identified whole, e.g. ten tonnes of buckwheat out of the fifteen tonnes of buckwheat stored in the seller's warehouse.[33] The purely generic goods must also be future goods, unless the seller has sufficient goods of the description in question which can be appropriated to the contract.[34] References to goods being 'appropriated to the contract' are best understood as ascertained and identified goods being attached or earmarked for the particular contract in question.[35]

27 2015 Act, s. 2(2).
28 2015 Act, s. 2(3).
29 2015 Act, s. 3(3)(c).
30 [1996] 4 All ER 481.
31 On the implied terms as to quality, see para. 6.38 onwards below.
32 1979 Act, s. 61(1).
33 C Twigg-Flesner and R Canavan, *Atiyah and Adams' Sale of Goods*, 14th edn (London: Pearson Education, 2021), p. 56; cf M Bridge et al (eds), *Benjamin's Sale of Goods*, 11th edn (London: Sweet & Maxwell, 2021), para. 1–117.
34 *Atiyah and Adams' Sale of Goods* (n 33), p. 56.
35 *Atiyah and Adams' Sale of Goods* (n 33), p. 243. See para. 6.100 below.

Existing goods are goods owned and possessed by the seller when the contact of sale is made.[36] *Future goods* are goods to be manufactured or acquired by the seller after the making of the contract of sale.[37] **6.19**

A contract for the sale of specific goods is void if the specific goods have perished at the time of the contract without the knowledge of the seller.[38] Where there is an agreement to sell specific goods and the goods perish before risk passes to the buyer, without fault on the part of either party, the agreement is avoided.[39] **6.20**

Formation of the contract

There is nothing peculiar about the formation of a contract for the sale of goods. The general principles of the law of contract apply. **6.21**

Section 3 provides that capacity to buy and sell is regulated by the general law concerning capacity to contract and to transfer and acquire property. Persons over the age of sixteen have legal capacity to enter into any transaction.[40] Persons under the age of sixteen have capacity to enter into transactions: (a) of a kind commonly entered into by persons of their age and circumstances; and (b) on terms which are not unreasonable.[41] **6.22**

No formalities are required. The contract may be in writing (either with or without seal), by word of mouth, or partly in writing and partly by word of mouth. Equally, it may be implied from the conduct of the parties.[42] Equivalent provision is made in the 2015 Act.[43] An example of a contract implied from conduct is buying food in a supermarket. There is normally no need for parties to make clear their intentions in day-to-day transactions. **6.23**

For a contract to be formed, there must be agreement between the parties as to its essential terms. A concluded contract settles everything which must be settled.[44] In a contract for the sale of goods, the essential terms are: (i) the goods; and (ii) the price. If seller wishes to sell fifty portions of halibut for £500 and the buyer wishes to buy them for £400, there is no agreement. Agreement may also be vitiated by the other 'vices of consent', such as fraudulent misrepresentation. Section 62(2) preserves the rules of the common law in relation to, *inter alia*, the effect of fraud, misrepresentation, duress (i.e. force and fear) and mistake (i.e. error). Those are topics for a more general work on the law of contract.[45] **6.24**

36 1979 Act, s. 5(1).
37 1979 Act, ss. 5(1), 61(1).
38 1979 Act, s. 6.
39 1979 Act, s. 7. On passing of risk, see paras 6.107–6.108 below.
40 Age of Legal Capacity (Scotland) Act 1991, s. 1(1)(b).
41 Age of Legal Capacity (Scotland) Act 1991, s. 2(1).
42 1979 Act, s. 4(1). The reference to 'either with or without seal' is outdated.
43 2015 Act, s. 1(2).
44 *May and Butcher Ltd v The King* [1934] 2 KB 17 at 21 per Viscount Dunedin; W W McBryde, *The Law of Contract in Scotland*, 3rd edn (Edinburgh: W. Green, 2007), para. 5–11.
45 See McBryde (n 44), Chs 14–17; H L MacQueen, *MacQueen and Thomson on Contract Law in Scotland*, 5th edn (London: Bloomsbury, 2020), Ch. 5.

CONTENT OF THE CONTRACT I

Price

6.25 The price is an essential term of a contract for the sale of goods. Section 8(1) provides that it may be fixed by the contract, may be left to be fixed in a manner agreed by the contract, or may be determined by the course of dealing between the parties. If the price is not determined in the agreed manner, the buyer must pay a reasonable price.[46]

6.26 If there is no agreement whatsoever as to the price, there is no agreement on an essential term and, therefore, no contract. An agreement to agree at some future stage is not acceptable.[47]

6.27 Section 9(1) provides that, where there is an agreement to sell goods on the terms that the price is to be fixed by the valuation of a third party, and the third party cannot or does not make the valuation, the agreement is 'avoided'. That is subject to the proviso that, if the goods have been delivered to and appropriated by the buyer, the buyer must pay a reasonable price for them. If a third party is prevented from making the valuation by one party's fault, the innocent party can seek damages from the party at fault.[48]

6.28 What constitutes a reasonable price is a question of fact dependent on the circumstances of each case.[49] It need not be the market or current price, although that would be a sensible place to start. A reasonable price will do justice between the parties, meaning that their actings may be taken into account. As Lord Kissen stated in *Glynwed Distribution Ltd v S Koronka & Co*:

> '[a] factor which may be of considerable importance in some cases, depending on the circumstances, is that the reasonable price must be fair and just to both parties. Circumstances may require a balancing of advantages and disadvantages to the seller and buyer which arise from the sale and consideration given to the parties' actings in regard to the sale before the "reasonable price" can be fixed.'[50]

Section 9 applies to all contracts of sale.

Additional protection for consumers

6.29 Regulations afford consumers additional protections as regards the price. These Regulations implemented EU Directives, but, as domestic legislation, remain in force notwithstanding the UK's departure from the EU. They apply only to consumer contracts of sale.

6.30 There are the Consumer Rights (Payment Surcharges) Regulations 2012,[51] which implemented art. 19 of Directive 2011/83/EU of the European Parliament and of the Council on consumer rights (the Consumer Rights

46 1979 Act, s. 8(2).
47 *May and Butcher Ltd v The King* [1934] 2 KB 17 at 20 per Lord Buckmaster. Cf *R & J Dempster Ltd v The Motherwell Bridge and Engineering Company Ltd* 1964 SC 308.
48 1979 Act, s. 9(2).
49 1979 Act, s. 8(3).
50 1977 SC 1 at 8.
51 SI 2012/3110.

Directive). Strictly speaking, the 2012 Regulations relate to payment of the price, rather than to the price itself, but it is sensible to mention them at this stage. Regulation 4 provides that a trader must not charge consumers, in respect of the use of a given means of payment, fees that exceed the cost borne by the trader for the use of that means. The trader cannot charge the consumer a fee for paying by card that exceeds the cost to the trader of making payment by card an option. If a trader does charge a fee in contravention of reg. 4, any provision of a contract requiring the consumer to pay the fee is unenforceable to the extent of the excess charged. The contract is treated as providing for the excess to be repaid to the consumer.[52]

The Consumer Contracts (Information, Cancellation and Additional Charges) Regulations 2013 (the '2013 Regulations')[53] were again made in implementation of the Consumer Rights Directive. Regulation 40(1) provides that, under a contract between a trader and a consumer, no payment is payable in addition to the remuneration agreed for the trader's main obligation unless, before the consumer became bound by the contract, the trader obtained the consumer's express consent. No express consent can be inferred from the consumer not changing a default option, such as a pre-ticked box on a website.[54] As is evident from their terms, the 2013 Regulations are designed primarily to catch additional charges imposed online. For example, unless there is express consent, in the form of ticking a box, a trader cannot impose an additional charge to have goods packaged as a gift or insured. Where a trader receives an additional payment which is not payable in terms of the 2013 Regulations, the contract is treated as providing for the trader to reimburse the payment to the consumer.[55] **6.31**

Time

Section 10(1) provides that, unless a different intention appears from the terms of the contract, stipulations as to time of payment are not of the essence. Whether any other stipulation as to time (for example, as to time of delivery) is or is not of the essence depends on the terms of the contract.[56] The Court of Appeal stated in *Hartley v Hymans* that, in ordinary commercial contracts for the sale of goods, time of delivery is *prima facie* of the essence.[57] **6.32**

If a term is of the essence and is breached, that will be a material breach, allowing the innocent party to rescind the contract.[58] The consequence of s. 10(1) is that, unless a different intention appears, the seller will not be able to rescind the contract if the buyer does not pay on time. Section 10 applies to all contracts of sale. **6.33**

52 2012 Regs, reg. 10.
53 SI 2013/3134.
54 2012 Regs, reg. 40(2).
55 2012 Regs, reg. 40(4).
56 1979 Act, s. 10(2).
57 [1920] 3 KB 475 at 484 per McCardie J.
58 MacQueen (n 45), para. 6.12.

Implied term as to title

6.34 There is an implied term that the seller has the right to sell the goods. In the case of an agreement to sell, the implied term is that the seller will have the right to sell the goods at the time when ownership is to pass.[59]

6.35 The seller's duty does not stop there. There are implied terms that: (a) the goods are free, and will remain free until the time when ownership is to pass, from any charge or encumbrance not disclosed or known to the buyer before the contract is made; and (b) the buyer will enjoy quiet possession of the goods except so far as it may be disturbed by the owner or other person entitled to the benefit of any charge or encumbrance disclosed or known to the buyer.[60] The goods must not be subject to an undisclosed or unknown subordinate real right or other encumbrance.

6.36 In *Niblett Ltd v Confectioners' Materials Company Ltd* the defendants sold 3,000 tins of condescended milk to the plaintiffs.[61] The condescended milk was delivered from New York to London. A thousand of the tins were branded 'Nissly', which infringed a registered trademark held by Nestlé. Customs detained the goods. The plaintiffs had to remove the branding from the tins and sell them at a loss. They brought an action against the defendants for breach of the implied term as to title. The Court of Appeal held that the defendants were in breach of s. 12(1). Although the defendants were owners of the condensed milk, they could have been restrained by injunction from selling it. Scrutton LJ observed that if a seller can be stopped by process of law from selling, they do not have the right to sell.[62] Atkin LJ held that there was also a breach of s. 12(2), the implied term as to quiet enjoyment:

> 'It may be that possession would not be disturbed if the only cause of complaint was that the buyer could not dispose of the goods, and that the warranty is confined to disturbance of possession of the goods delivered under the contract of sale. The warranty so interpreted was broken. The appellants were never allowed to have quiet possession. They had to strip off the labels before they could assume possession of the goods.'[63]

6.37 Had the Court of Appeal not found a breach of s. 12(1), this would appear to be a clear breach of s. 12(2). There had been no quiet possession of the condensed milk. In the 2015 Act, the equivalent provision is s. 17.

59 1979 Act, s. 12(1).
60 1979 Act, s. 12(2).
61 [1921] 3 KB 387 at 395.
62 [1921] 3 KB 387 at 398.
63 [1921] 3 KB 387 at 403.

CONTENT OF THE CONTRACT II: IMPLIED TERMS AS TO QUALITY

Sales by description

Where there is a contract for the sale of goods by description, there is an implied term that the goods will correspond with the description.[64] If the sale is by sample as well as by description, it is not sufficient that the bulk of the goods corresponds with the sample if the goods do not also correspond with the description.[65] **6.38**

A sale can qualify as a sale by description even if the goods are exposed for sale and are selected by the buyer.[66] The key is that what is being bought is not the specific thing exposed, but something corresponding to that specific thing: **6.39**

> '[T]here is a sale by description even though the buyer is buying something displayed before him on the counter: a thing is sold by description, though it is specific, so long as it is sold not merely as the specific thing but as a thing corresponding to a description . . .'[67]

Lord Wright proceeds to give 'a few obvious illustrations', namely 'woollen under-garments', 'a hot-water bottle' and 'a second-hand reaping machine'. It is possible that different examples would have been selected had his Lordship been writing today. Section 13 applies to all non-consumer contracts of sale. In the 2015 Act, the equivalent provision is s. 11. **6.40**

What is a description?

The description is not all the words used to describe the goods. It is those words used to identify the goods which are the subject of the contract of sale.[68] In *Ashington Piggeries Ltd v Christopher Hill Ltd* the seller sold herring meal to mink breeders. Unknown to the mink breeders, the herring meal was poisonous to mink. Thousands of mink died. The herring meal was described as 'NORWEGIAN HERRING MEAL fair average quality of the season'. The words 'fair average quality of the season' were held not to form part of the description. The words in capitals were sufficient to identify the goods. Identification is the key. The parties can elect to have a broad description or a narrow description.[69] There was no breach of s. 13 in that case. Thankfully for the mink breeders, the House of Lords did find a breach of the implied term in s. 14. **6.41**

The decision in *Ashington Piggeries Ltd* was followed in *Border Harvesters Ltd v Edwards Engineering (Perth) Ltd.*[70] In the latter case, the pursuers bought a machine for drying grain (a Kamas dryer) from the defenders. The terms of the contract were recorded in a document. The document contained a **6.42**

64 1979 Act, s. 13(1).
65 1979 Act, s. 13(2).
66 1979 Act, s. 13(3).
67 *Grant v Australian Knitting Mills Ltd* [1936] AC 85 at 100 per Lord Wright.
68 *Ashington Piggeries Ltd v Christopher Hill Ltd* [1972] AC 441.
69 *Ashington Piggeries Ltd v Christopher Hill Ltd* [1972] AC 441 at 503 per Lord Diplock.
70 1985 SLT 128.

statement that the Kamas dryer would be capable of drying a certain amount of grain per hour. The statement as to capacity was held not to be part of the description:

> '[T]he argument was that the equipment was described as having a certain performance capacity and was therefore a sale by description within the meaning of [section] 13 of the Sale of Goods Act 1979. I disagree. What was contracted for in this case was described as a Kamas dryer; what was supplied was a Kamas dryer. What the dryer was capable of doing was . . . not part of the description of the goods supplied.'[71]

6.43 Descriptions can be conveyed through various media. In another case, the plaintiff saw an advertisement for a car (a Triumph Herald). When he was inspecting the car, he saw a metallic disc reading '1200' on it on the back of the car. On the strength of this, he believed that the car was a particular model. Unfortunately, only half of it was. The front of the car was an earlier model. The metallic disc was held to be part of the description, together with the advertisement.[72]

6.44 For a sale to qualify as a sale by description, the description must have sufficient influence on the sale for parties to have intended it to become a term of the contract. In *Harlingdon and Leinster Enterprises Ltd v Christopher Hull Fine Art Ltd* the defendants had offered for sale two oil paintings described as being the work of Gabriele Münter (1877–1962), an expressionist painter.[73] The paintings were viewed by an employee of the plaintiffs. The defendants told the employee that they knew little about the paintings and nothing about Frau Münter. It transpired that the paintings were forgeries. The plaintiffs relied on s. 13 in an action to recover the price. By a majority, the Court of Appeal dismissed the plaintiff's appeal, holding that the name of the artist had not had a sufficient influence on the sale.

Sales by sample

6.45 Section 15 applies to contracts of sale by sample. A contract is a contract of sale by sample if there is term, express or implied, in the contract to that effect.[74] Parties must intend the sale to be a sale by sample. The purpose of a sample is to present to the eye the real meaning and intention of the parties in relation to the goods, which may be impossible or difficult to express due to the imperfection of language. The sample speaks for itself.[75] In effect, the seller states that they cannot provide an adequate description of the goods and instead provides a sample to fill the descriptive void.

6.46 Contracts of sale by sample include an implied term: (i) that the bulk will correspond with the sample in quality; and (ii) that the goods will be free from

71 1985 SLT 128 at 131 per Lord Kincraig.
72 *Beale v Taylor* [1967] 1 WLR 1193.
73 [1991] 1 QB 564.
74 1979 Act, s. 15(1).
75 *James Drummond & Sons v EH Van Ingen & Co* (1887) 12 App Cas 284 at 297 per Lord Macnaghten.

any defect, making their quality unsatisfactory, which would not be apparent on reasonable examination of the sample.[76]

Section 15 applies to all non-consumer contracts of sale. In the 2015 Act, the equivalent provision is s. 13. It applies to contracts to supply goods by reference to a sample of the goods that is seen or examined by the consumer before the contract is made.[77] Section 13(2) provides that such contracts are to be treated as including a term that: (a) the goods will match the sample except to the extent that any differences between the sample and the goods are brought to the consumer's attention before the contract is made; and (b) the goods will be free from any defect that makes their quality unsatisfactory and that would not be apparent on a reasonable examination of the sample. **6.47**

Sales by a reference to a model

In consumer contracts of sale, where there is a contract to supply goods by reference to a model of the goods that is seen or examined by the consumer before entering into the contract, there is an implied term that the goods will match the model except to the extent that any differences between the model and the goods are brought to the consumer's attention before the consumer enters into the contract.[78] **6.48**

Goods to be of satisfactory quality

Section 14 begins by stating a general rule that there is no implied term about quality or fitness for any particular purpose of goods supplied under a contract of sale. That general rule is immediately qualified by s. 14(2). It provides that '[w]here the seller sells goods in the course of a business, there is an implied term that the goods supplied under the contract are of satisfactory quality'. **6.49**

As originally enacted, s. 14(2) read as follows: '[w]here the seller sells goods in the course of a business, there is an implied condition that the good supplied under the contract are of merchantable quality . . .' **6.50**

The word 'merchantable' was also in s. 14(2) of the 1893 Act. The 1994 Act followed a Joint Report of the Law Commissions.[79] The report observed that the word 'merchantable' had become obsolete.[80] The 1994 Act came into force on 3 January 1995. After being the test for more than 100 years, 'merchantable quality' was replaced by 'satisfactory quality'. Cases decided before the amendment will refer to merchantable quality.

What is 'in the course of a business'?

As the implied term applies only to sales by a seller in the course of a business, private sales are excluded. Section 14(2) does not apply to *all* non-consumer **6.51**

76 1979 Act, s. 15(2).
77 2015 Act, s. 13(1).
78 2015 Act, s. 14(2).
79 *Report on the Sale and Supply of Goods* (Scot. Law Com. No. 104, 1987).
80 *Report on the Sale and Supply of Goods* (Scot. Law Com. No. 104, 1987), para. 2.10.

sales. Where Mr Stair contracts to buy Mr Bell's car or TV, and both are acting as private individuals, there is no implied term that the car or TV will be of satisfactory quality.

6.52 The expression 'in the course of a business' has a wide meaning. It was considered by an Extra Division in *Macdonald v Pollock*.[81] In that case, both parties carried on the business of providing cruises to customers. In September 2002 the defenders sold a vessel, the *MV Monaco* to the pursuer. Defects in the *MV Monaco* emerged on a voyage from Oban to Stornoway. The defenders sought repayment of the price, having rejected the goods.[82] The pursuer contended that the sale had not been in the course of a business. The pursuer succeeded before the sheriff, but the sheriff principal assoilzied the defenders.

6.53 Before the Extra Division, the defenders argued that the concept of a sale in the course of business encompassed only three categories of sale: (i) a sale which is an integral part of the conduct of the business in question; (ii) a sale which is incidental to the conduct of the business, but which is of a kind which is carried out with a sufficient degree of regularity to bring it within the ambit of s. 14(2); and (iii) a 'one-off' venture, which is essentially the business.[83] The Extra Division rejected this interpretation. It agreed with the Court of Appeal's decision in *Stevenson v Rogers*,[84] which, it observed, was essentially indistinguishable on the facts.[85] There is no need for regularity of dealing. A one-off sale is sufficient. The Extra Division restored the judgment of the sheriff.

6.54 *Buchanan-Jardine v Hamilink* is authority for the view that the sale of the business itself constitutes a sale in the course of a business.[86] Section 14(2) applies to sales in the course of *a* business, not to sales in the course of business.[87]

Sales by agents

6.55 The implied term in s. 14(2) applies to a sale by a person who in the course of a business is acting as agent for another as they apply to a sale by a principal in the course of a business. It does not apply where the other (the principal) is not selling in the course of a business and either: (i) the buyer knows that fact; or (ii) reasonable steps are taken to bring it to the buyer's notice before the contract is made.[88]

81 2013 SC 22.
82 On buyer's remedies, see paras 6.139–6.152 below.
83 2013 SC 22 at [14]. For this interpretation, the defenders relied on *Davies v Sumner* [1984] 1 WLR 1301.
84 [1999] QB 1028.
85 2013 SC 22 at [18] per Lord Eassie, delivering the opinion of the court.
86 1983 SLT 149.
87 1983 SLT 149 at 153 per Lord Cameron.
88 1979 Act, s. 14(5).

Consumer contracts of sale

The 2015 Act follows the same scheme as the 1979 Act. Section 18(1) of the 2015 Act states the general rule: 6.56

> 'Except as provided by sections 9, 10, 13 and 16, a contract to supply goods is not to be treated as including any term about the quality of the goods or their fitness for any particular purpose, unless the term is expressly included in the contract.'

The 2015 Act's equivalent of s. 14(2) is s. 9, which provides that every contract to supply goods is to be treated as including a term that the quality of the goods is satisfactory. The 2015 Act does not use the expression 'implied term', but provides that contracts will be *treated as if* a particular term were included. With one minor exception,[89] the provisions governing how to ascertain whether goods are of satisfactory quality are the same as those in the 1979 Act. The cases interpretating s. 14 of the 1979 Act apply with equal force to s. 9 of the 2015 Act.

What is satisfactory quality?

This is an objective test. Goods are of satisfactory quality if they meet the standard that a reasonable person, one of the law's favourite fictions,[90] would regard as satisfactory. In assessing that, account must be taken of any description of the goods, the price (if relevant) and all other relevant circumstances.[91] As Lord Hodge stated in *United Central Bakeries Ltd v Spooner Industries Ltd*, the court puts itself in the position of the objective reasonable buyer with knowledge of all the relevant facts.[92] The reasonable buyer is not an expert.[93] 6.57

Unlike the 1979 Act, the 2015 provides that the relevant circumstances include any public statement about the specific characteristics of the goods made by the trader, the producer or any representative of the trader or the producer.[94] This includes public statements made in advertising or labelling.[95] There is no equivalent in s. 14. Despite the absence of specific provision in the 1979 Act, there is no reason in principle why such a public statement could not be taken into account in non-consumer contracts of sale. It may be a relevant circumstance. 6.58

The quality of goods includes their state and condition and the following (among others) are, in appropriate cases, aspects of the quality of goods: (a) fitness for all the purposes for which goods of the kind in question are commonly supplied; (b) appearance and finish; (c) freedom from minor defects; (d) safety; and (e) durability. These are considered in turn. 6.59

89 See para. 6.58 below.
90 *Healthcare at Home Ltd v Common Services Agency* 2014 SC (UKSC) 247 at [1]–[2] per Lord Reed.
91 1979 Act, s. 14(2A).
92 [2013] CSOH 150 at [73].
93 *Clegg v Andersson (t/a Nordic Marine)* [2003] EWCA Civ 320 at [73] per Hale LJ.
94 2015 Act, s. 9(5).
95 2015 Act, s. 9(6).

Factor (a): fitness for all common purposes

6.60 As originally enacted, s. 14(6) of the 1979 Act read as follows:

> 'Goods of any kind are of merchantable quality . . . if they are as fit for the purpose or purposes for which goods of that kind are commonly bought as it is reasonable to expect having regard to any description applied to them, the price (if relevant) and all the other relevant circumstances.'

Before the 1994 Act came into force, the Court of Appeal held in *M/S Aswan Engineering Establishment Co v Lupdine Ltd* that the 1979 Act had not 'revolutionised' the law and that goods were of merchantable quality if they were fit for *any* of the purposes for which they are commonly bought.[96] Academic commentary had been divided on this issue.[97] The 1994 Act removed all doubt. Goods must be fit for *all* common purposes.

Factor (b): appearance and finish

6.61 What a reasonable person would regard as satisfactory will depend, inevitably, on what is being purchased. In *Rogers v Parish (Scarborough) Ltd* the plaintiffs bought a Range Rover that proved to be defective in a number of respects.[98] At first instance the judge found that none of the defects rendered the Range Rover unroadworthy or unfit for the purposes for which a Range Rover is commonly used. The Court of Appeal allowed the plaintiffs' appeal, holding that the purposes included not just driving from A to B, but driving from A to B with the appropriate degree of comfort, ease of handling and reliability and pride in the vehicle's outward and interior appearance.[99]

6.62 In *Bernstein v Pamson Motors (Golders Green) Ltd* Rougier J commented:

> '[I]t may well be that in appropriate cases cosmetic factors will also apply depending on the description and price applied to any individual car. No buyer of a brand new Rolls-Royce Corniche would tolerate the slightest blemish on its exterior paintwork; the purchaser of a motor car very much at the humbler end of the range might be less fastidious.'[100]

The type of goods and the price will be relevant. A similar view to Rougier J's was expressed by Hale LJ in *Clegg v Andersson*,[101] a case involving a yacht, rather than a Rolls-Royce Corniche. Although Mr Bernstein was successful in his case, it appears that those purchasing 'at the humbler end of the range' will have to adjust their expectations.

Factor (c): freedom from minor defects

6.63 This is an area in which the courts' approach has softened over recent decades. In *Millars of Falkirk Ltd v Turpie* the buyer had purchased a new car (a Ford

96 [1987] 1 WLR 1 at 14–15 per Lloyd LJ.
97 [1987] 1 WLR 1 at 14.
98 [1987] QB 933.
99 [1987] QB 933 at 944 per Mustill LJ.
100 [1987] 2 All ER 220 at 227–228.
101 [2003] EWCA Civ 320 at [72].

Granada).[102] He failed to pay part of the price. The sellers raised an action for payment. The buyer argued that he had validly rejected the car on the basis that it was not of merchantable quality. The car had started leaking oil almost as soon as it was bought. The First Division did not consider that this rendered the car not of merchantable quality. It was a minor defect which could easily be cured at very small cost. The sellers were willing and anxious to cure the defect. The First Division noted that, on delivery, many new cars have some defects.[103]

A similar sentiment was expressed by Rougier J in *Bernstein v Pamson Motors (Golders Green) Ltd*, where he opined that the buyer of a new car must suffer a certain amount of teething troubles and have them rectified. No system of mass production can be perfect.[104] **6.64**

Nowadays, the reasonable person would have markedly higher expectations of how a new car will perform on delivery. A more modern approach can be seen in *Lamarra v Capital Bank plc*.[105] The buyer entered into a hire purchase agreement in respect of a Range Rover.[106] It had a number of defects: it pulled to the left; the layout of the pedals rendered it unsafe to drive; there was loud noise from the engine or transmission; there was a deep scratch on the ashtray. The buyer rejected the vehicle and raised an action for the deposit and first two instalments paid. The sheriff assoilzied the defenders. The sheriff principal allowed the buyer's appeal. An Extra Division agreed with the sheriff principal. The sheriff had placed reliance on the existence of a manufacturer's warranty. This was irrelevant. The sheriff had failed to consider the implied term of freedom from minor defects. A considerable distance away from being free from minor defects, the Range Rover was not of satisfactory quality. **6.65**

The type of goods and the price will be relevant. In *Clegg v Andersson*, a case involving the purchase of a yacht for £236,000 in 1999, Hale LJ commented: 'in some cases, such as a high priced quality product, the customer may be entitled to expect that it is free from even minor defects, in other words perfect or nearly so'.[107] **6.66**

Defects in labelling or packaging can render goods of unsatisfactory quality. They are part of the state and condition of the goods.[108] *Glen Clyde Whisky Ltd v Campbell Meyer & Co Ltd* concerned labels which had been poorly affixed to bottles of whisky: some were peeling at the edge; some were squint; and some had air bubbles.[109] Lord Doherty held that the state of the labels meant that, regardless of the drinkability of the whisky, the bottles of whisky were not of satisfactory quality: **6.67**

> 'In the whole circumstances I have no doubt that a reasonable person acquainted with all of the facts of the case . . . would not regard the bottles which had peeling

102 1976 SLT (Notes) 66.
103 1976 SLT (Notes) 66 at 68.
104 [1987] 2 All ER 220 at 228–229.
105 2007 SC 95.
106 See n 9 above. Section 10 of the Sale of Goods (Implied Terms) Act 1973 implies terms into non-consumer hire purchase agreements.
107 [2003] EWCA Civ 320 at [72].
108 *Niblett Ltd v Confectioners' Materials Company Ltd* [1921] 3 KB 387 at 395 per Bankes LJ.
109 2016 SCLR 341.

labels as being of satisfactory quality. The peeling would be noticeable to wholesalers, retailers and consumers and would tend to make the bottles concerned look more like a basic rather than a premium product.'[110]

Factor (d): safety

6.68 Goods which are *per se* safe can be rendered unsafe by misleading instructions. Goods must be considered as a whole. A leading case is *Wormell v RHM Agriculture (East) Ltd.*[111] The plaintiff was a farmer who had been prevented by inclement weather from spraying his crops to kill wild oats (weeds) until much later than usual. He asked the defendants to recommend a wild oat killer that could be used at that later time. On the defendants' recommendation, he bought a particular herbicide. The instructions stated that the herbicide ought not to be applied beyond a recommended stage of crop growth as that could damage crops sprayed at that stage. They stated that the herbicide would best control the wild oats if applied at a late stage. The plaintiff understood the instructions to mean that the herbicide could be used *at any time*, but that it might damage the crops if used after the recommended time.

6.69 Concerned about the infestation, the plaintiff sprayed the herbicide after the recommended time. It transpired that the herbicide was completely ineffective after a particular stage of crop growth. The wild oat killer killed no wild oats. The plaintiff sought damages on the basis that the herbicide was not of merchantable quality. The deputy judge gave judgment for the plaintiff. He held that the instructions were misleading.[112] It follows that 'goods' includes the goods' packaging and any instructions supplied with them.[113]

6.70 The rule that goods must be considered as whole also found application in *Wilson v Rickett Cockerell & Co Ltd.*[114] The plaintiffs bought a tonne of Coalite, a manufactured fuel, from the defendants. Unfortunately for them there was an explosive in one of the pieces of coal supplied. An explosion occurred in the grate after a fire had been set. The plaintiffs claimed for the damage to their room and furniture caused by the explosion.

6.71 In *Wilson* the Court of Appeal declined to follow the Court of Session's decision in *Duke v Jackson*, another case involving coal.[115] In *Duke* the defender supplied a bag of coal to the pursuer. The bag contained an explosive substance. There was explosion when the coal was being burned in the pursuer's kitchen. The pursuer lost his right eye as a result. He claimed damages. The Second Division held that his averments anent a breach of the 1893 Act were irrelevant. The presence of a foreign object, not the subject of the contract of sale, did not mean that the coal was not reasonably fit for domestic use. No complaint had been made about the coal itself.[116]

110 2016 SCLR 341 at [51].
111 [1986] 1 WLR 336.
112 [1986] 1 WLR 336 at 347G.
113 [1986] 1 WLR 336 at 346E–346F.
114 [1954] 1 QB 598.
115 1921 SC 362.
116 1921 SC 362 at 368 per Lord Dundas, per Lord Ormidale.

In *Wilson* Denning LJ stated that, '[w]ith all respect to the Court of Session', he could not understand the reasoning. Under reference to *Frost v The Aylesbury Dairy Co Ltd*,[117] a case involving contaminated milk, he stated: 6.72

> 'If the admixture of an injurious ingredient makes a liquid unfit for drinking, so does the admixture of an injurious detonator make coal unfit for burning. It is no answer for the seller to say that there was nothing wrong with the coal, as coal. There was a great deal wrong with the consignment as a consignment.'[118]

'Goods' means the whole of the goods supplied, including any foreign objects. The foreign object can make the whole of the goods dangerous. In *Wilson* the explosive was held to have infected all the coal.[119] 6.73

In finding against a man who had lost an eye due to a domestic explosion, it is arguable that the Second Division did not reach an especially sympathetic decision in *Duke*. Whatever its status, it is unlikely to be followed. 6.74

Factor (e): durability

This is a relative concept. Depending on the circumstances, goods may be expected to have next to no durability or a high level of durability. In *Thain v Anniesland Trade Centre* the pursuer bought a car (a Renault 19) from the defenders.[120] The car was five years old and had 80,000 miles on the clock. It became unroadworthy after two weeks of use. The pursuer raised an action. The sheriff assoilzied the defenders. The sheriff principal refused the pursuer's appeal. He observed: 6.75

> 'Even a negligible degree of durability may not represent unsatisfactory quality where the second[-]hand car supplied is as old and as heavily used as the Renault had been. The plain fact is that, given the Renault's age and mileage when supplied, its durability was a matter of luck. Durability, in all the circumstances, was simply not a quality that a reasonable person would demand of it.'[121]

This accords with the more general approach taken by the courts that a lesser standard will be expected of second hand goods than of new goods.[122]

By contrast, in *Peebles v Rembrand Builders Merchants Ltd*,[123] the sheriff found tiles of relatively high quality not to have been of satisfactory quality as certain of them had become discoloured approximately five years after installation. He held that a reasonable person would have expected the titles to retain a uniform appearance for well in excess of five years. There is a clear overlap here with factor (b) (appearance and finish). 6.76

117 [1905] 1 KB 608.
118 [1954] 1 QB 598 at 606.
119 [1954] 1 QB 598 at 609 per Evershed MR.
120 1997 SLT (Sh Ct) 102.
121 1997 SLT (Sh Ct) 102 at 106K–106L.
122 *Richford v Parks of Hamilton (Townhead Garage) Ltd* 2012 GWD 24-505 at [13].
123 [2017] SC DUN 28, 2017 GWD 15-236.

Restrictions of liability

6.77 Section 14(2C) stipulates important exclusions. The implied term does not extend to any matter making the quality of goods unsatisfactory: (a) which is specifically drawn to the buyer's attention before the contract is made; (b) where the buyer examines the goods before the contract is made, which that examination ought to reveal; or (c) in the case of a contract for sale by sample, which would have been apparent on a reasonable examination of the sample.

6.78 As for s. 14(2C)(b), the implied term will only be excluded if the defect(s) would have been revealed by the examination actually carried out by the buyer:

> '[T]he use of the words "that examination" clearly points in the direction of the particular examination which was in fact carried out. The statute does not refer to a reasonable examination but merely to "that examination". In these circumstances and looking to the terms of the regulation . . . before the seller may successfully invoke [section] 14(2C)(b) in order to limit the scope of the warranty, it has to be established that the actual examination carried out ought to have disclosed the defect or defects in issue.'[124]

6.79 The buyer is entitled to carry out no examination of the goods and rely entirely on s. 14(2). A perfunctory examination will not prevent the buyer from relying on the implied term. The same exclusion applies to consumer contracts of sale.[125]

Goods to be fit for a particular purpose

6.80 Section 14(3) inserts another implied term. Where the seller sells goods in the course of a business and the buyer, expressly or by implication, makes known to the seller any particular purpose for which the goods are being bought, there is an implied term that the goods are reasonably fit for that purpose. There is no implied term where the circumstances show that the buyer does not rely, or that is unreasonable for them to rely, on the skill or judgment of the seller.

6.81 Goods which are reasonably fit for all common purposes may not be fit for a particular purpose. It is the function of s. 14(3), not s. 14(2), to impose a particular obligation tailored to the particular circumstances of the case.[126] As Lord Shand stated, referring to a provision of similar effect of the Mercantile Law Amendment Act 1856, '[t]he provision . . . does not create or provide a warranty by the seller that the goods shall be suitable for the general purpose for which such goods are used, but for a specified and particular purpose, when that purpose is expressly stated'.[127]

6.82 To be able to rely on s. 14(3), the buyer must make sufficient communication of their purpose.[128] In *Flynn v Scott* the pursuer bought a van from the

124 *Macdonald v Pollock* 2013 SC 22 at [32] per Lord Eassie, delivering the opinion of the court.
125 2015 Act, s. 9(4).
126 *Jewson Ltd v Boyhan* [2003] EWCA Civ 1030 at [47] per Clarke LJ.
127 *Hamilton v Robertson* (1878) 5 R 839 at 841.
128 *United Central Bakeries Ltd v Spooner Industries Ltd* [2013] CSOH 150 at [76] per Lord Hodge, citing *Slater v Finning Ltd* 1997 SC (HL) 8 at 17 per Lord Steyn.

defender.[129] The van broke down seven days later. The pursuer had stated that he wished to use the van for haulage, including moving furniture and livestock. Lord Mackintosh held that this was insufficient for the then equivalent of s. 14(3):

> 'This was a van, the general purpose of which was the carrying of goods, and all that was told to the seller was that it was to be used by the buyer for that general purpose, certain examples being given of the kind of goods which might be carried in it.'[130]

At the time of those cases there was no provision that the goods would be fit for all common purposes. Mr Flynn may have fared better with s. 14(2). Unlike the term implied by s. 14(2), in s. 14(3) (reasonable) reliance (on the skill or judgment of the seller) is necessary. Reliance will seldom be express. It will usually arise by implication from the circumstances.[131] **6.83**

There is no breach of the implied term where the failure of the goods to meet the intended purpose arises from an abnormal feature or idiosyncrasy, not made known to the seller by the buyer, in the buyer, or in the circumstances of the use of the goods by the buyer. It does not matter that the buyer may not be aware of the abnormal feature or idiosyncrasy.[132] **6.84**

In *Kelly v Andersons House Furnishers (Inverurie) Ltd* the pursuer bought a suite, consisting of one sofa and two armchairs, from the defenders.[133] Areas of one of the armchairs became discoloured after about ten months. This was caused by sweat excreted by the pursuer. The sheriff rejected the pursuer's argument based on s. 14(3). The suite had been bought for general use, i.e. for sitting on. There was nothing before the sheriff to suggest that the pursuer had a particular problem with the excretion of sweat. The sheriff added that, had that been the case, and had it been drawn to the defenders' attention at the time of sale, his view might have been different. **6.85**

In the 2015 Act, the equivalent provision is s. 10. **6.86**

2013 Regulations

The 2013 Regulations[134] merit brief mention. They require the trader to provide certain information to the consumer before the consumer will be bound by particular types of contract. Before a consumer is bound by an 'on-premises' contract, the trader must give or make available the information contained in Sch. 1 to the 2013 Regulations. The information need only be provided if it is not apparent from the context. Further, the requirement does not apply contracts involving to day-to-day transactions which are performed immediately.[135] Schedule 1 sets out the information, including, *inter alia*, the main characteristics of the goods and the identity of the trader. **6.87**

129 1949 SC 442.
130 1949 SC 442 at 444.
131 *Grant v Australian Knitting Mills Ltd* [1936] AC 85 at 99 per Lord Wright.
132 *Slater v Finning Ltd* 1997 SC (HL) 8 at 14–15 per Lord Keith.
133 2012 GWD 20-422.
134 Consumer Contracts (Information, Cancellation and Additional Charges) Regulations 2013 (SI 2013/3134). See n 52 above.
135 2013 Regs, regs. 9(1)–(2).

6.88 Regulations 10 and 13 make provision in relation to 'off-premises' and 'distance' contracts. Before a consumer is bound by one of those contracts, the trader must give or make available the information contained in Sch. 2.

6.89 Section 12(1) of the 2015 Act provides that, where the trader is required to give information under regs 9, 10 or 13 of the 2013 Regulations, any information provided is treated as a term of the contract. The information about the goods mentioned in para. (a) of Sch. 1 or Sch. 2 (as to the main characteristics of the goods) is not included.

TRANSFER OF OWNERSHIP AND PASSING OF RISK

Transfer of ownership

6.90 Sections 16–19 and 20A–20B of the 1979 Act deal with transfer of ownership. These sections apply to all contracts of sale.[136]

6.91 Section 16 provides that, where there is a contract for the sale of unascertained goods, ownership of the goods cannot be transferred unless and until the goods are ascertained.[137] The exception to this rule is s. 20A, which deals with contracts for the sale of: (i) a specific quantity of unascertained goods; (ii) in an identified bulk; where (iii) the buyer has paid in advance.

Specific goods

6.92 Section 17(1) provides that, where there is a contract for the sale of specific goods, ownership of them is transferred to the buyer at such time as the parties to the contract intend it to be transferred. For the purpose of ascertaining the intention of the parties, regard is to be had to: (i) the terms of the contract; (ii) the conduct of the parties; and (iii) the circumstances of the case.[138]

6.93 Section 18 sets out five rules for ascertaining, unless a different intention appears, the intention of the parties as to the time at which ownership of the goods is to be transferred. It need only be considered if the intention of the parties cannot be ascertained. As Lord President Strathclyde observed:

> '[section 18] is only an expansion of section 17. The rules in section 18 are merely intended to be a guide in ascertaining the intention of the parties. But, if the intention of the parties is quite plain . . ., then the rules of section 18 do not come into play at all'.[139]

6.94 The rules are as follows:

Rule one

6.95 Where there is an unconditional contract for the sale of specific goods in a deliverable state, ownership passes to the buyer when the contract is made.

136 2015 Act, s. 4(2).
137 On unascertained goods, see para. 6.18 above.
138 1979 Act, s. 17(2).
139 *Woodburn v Andrew Motherwell Ltd* 1917 SC 533 at 538.

It is immaterial whether the time of payment or the time of delivery, or both, is postponed. It must be remembered that the rules in s. 18 are subordinate to s. 17. It is the intention of the parties that is paramount. Diplock LJ commented in *RV Ward Ltd v Bignall* that in modern times very little is needed to give rise to the inference that ownership is to pass only on delivery or payment.[140] If that is so, rule one will rarely determine when ownership passes.

Rule two

Where there is a contract for the sale of specific goods and the seller is bound to do something to the goods for the purpose of putting them into a deliverable state, ownership does not pass until that thing is done and the buyer has notice that it has been done. **6.96**

Gowans v Bowe & Sons is illustrative.[141] The pursuer was the trustee-in-sequestration of David Cockburn, a farmer. In August 1908 Mr Cockburn contracted to sell his potato crop to the defenders. He agreed to lift, pit and drive them to the station or harbour. He was sequestrated on 27 November 1908. At the date of his sequestration the potatoes had been lifted and pitted on the farm. The pursuer raised an action for payment of the price against the defenders, maintaining that ownership had not passed to them. His case was that the potato crop vested in him from the date of sequestration. The Lord Ordinary (Cullen) rejected this argument. Having been lifted and pitted, the potatoes were in a deliverable state. Ownership had passed in accordance with rule two.[142] **6.97**

Rule three

Where there is a contract for the sale of specific goods and the seller is bound to weigh, measure, test, or do some other act or thing with reference to the goods for the purpose of ascertaining the price, ownership does not pass until the act or thing is done and the buyer has notice that it has been done. **6.98**

Rule four

When goods are delivered to the buyer on approval or on sale or return or other similar terms, ownership of the goods passes to the buyer: (a) when they signify their approval or acceptance to the seller or do any other act adopting the transaction; or (b) if they do not signify their approval or acceptance to the seller, but retain the goods without giving notice of rejection, then: (i) if a time has been fixed for the return of the goods, on the expiration of that time; and (ii), if no time has been fixed, on the expiration of a reasonable time. The question of what is a reasonable time is a question of fact.[143] **6.99**

140 [1967] 1 QB 534 at 545.
141 (1910) 2 SLT 17.
142 (1910) 2 SLT 17 at 18.
143 1979 Act, s. 59.

Unascertained goods

Rule five

6.100 Rule five and ss. 20A–20B govern the transfer of ownership of unascertained goods. The first part of rule five applies to contracts for the sale of unascertained goods by description. Where goods of that description and in a deliverable state are unconditionally appropriated to the contract, either: (i) by the seller with the assent of the buyer; or (ii) by the buyer with the assent of the seller, ownership of the goods passes. The assent may be express or implied, and may be given either before or after the appropriation is made. 'Unconditional appropriation' means that some ascertained and identified goods must be irrevocably attached or earmarked for the particular contract in question.[144] Part two of rule five provides that where, in pursuance of the contract, the seller delivers the goods to the buyer or to a carrier or custodier for the purpose of transmission to the buyer, and they do not reserve the right of disposal,[145] the seller is taken to have unconditionally appropriated the goods to the contract.

6.101 Part three applies to contracts for the sale of a specified quantity of unascertained goods in a deliverable state forming part of a bulk and where the bulk is identified either in the contract or by subsequent agreement between the parties. Where the bulk is reduced to (or to less than) that quantity, and if the buyer is the only buyer to whom goods are due out of the bulk: (a) the remaining goods are to be taken as appropriated to that contract when the bulk is so reduced; and (b) ownership of the goods passes.

6.102 A bulk is a mass or collection of goods of the same kind which is: (a) contained in a defined space or area; and (b) such that any goods in the bulk are interchangeable with any other goods therein of the same number or quantity.[146] For an example of rule three in operation, assume that the buyer contracts with the seller to buy five tonnes of peaches out of the pile (bulk) of fifteen tonnes of peaches at the seller's place of business. If the pile of fifteen tonnes is reduced to five tonnes, and the buyer is the only person to whom peaches are due from the five tonnes, those five tonnes are appropriated to the contract and ownership passes.

6.103 Section 20A deals with the situation where there is a contract for the sale of a specified quantity of unascertained goods and: (a) the goods or some of them form part of an identified bulk; and (b) the buyer has paid the price for some or all of the goods which are the subject of the contract and which form part of the bulk. Unless otherwise agreed, as soon as conditions (a) and (b) are met, ownership of an undivided share in the bulk passes to the buyer. The buyer becomes an owner in common of the bulk.[147]

6.104 The undivided share of a buyer in a bulk at any time shall be such share as the quantity of goods paid for and due to the buyer out of the bulk bears to

144 *Atiyah and Adams' Sale of Goods* (n 33), p. 243.
145 See paras 6.109–6.111 below.
146 1979 Act, s. 61(1).
147 1979 Act, s. 20A(2).

the quantity of goods in the bulk at that time.[148] This is best illustrated by an example. The seller has 100 tonnes of rice. The buyer buys thirty tonnes of that. The thirty tonnes is a specified quantity of unascertained goods. It is impossible to tell which thirty of the 100 tonnes are the buyer's. Section 16 provides that ownership cannot pass in those circumstances. However, where the contract of sale relates to: (i) a specified quantity of unascertained goods; (ii) in an identified bulk, where; (iii) the buyer has paid in advance, the buyer acquires an undivided share in the bulk and becomes an owner in common of the bulk. In essence, the seller now has a 7/10 share in the rice and the buyer a 3/10 share.

If three others bought three tonnes of rice, meaning that 120 tonnes has **6.105** been bought, the aggregate of the undivided shares of buyers would exceed the whole of the bulk. Section 20A(4) provides that, in those circumstances, each buyer's undivided share in the bulk is reduced proportionately, so that the aggregate of the undivided shares is equal to the whole bulk. In this case, as four buyers have bought the same amount, each would have a 1/4 share in the bulk.

The general rule that common owners must consent to any dealing with the **6.106** common property is disapplied.[149] It would be cumbersome if the seller had to obtain the consent of each common owner to make a delivery to one of them.

Passing of risk

Non-consumer contracts of sale

Section 20(1) provides that, unless otherwise agreed, the goods remain at the **6.107** seller's risk until ownership is transferred to the buyer. When ownership is transferred to the buyer, the goods are at the buyer's risk, whether delivery has been made or not. Where delivery has been delayed through the fault of either buyer or seller, the goods are at the risk of the party at fault as regards any loss which might not have occurred but for such fault.[150]

Consumer contracts of sale

While the rules governing transfer of ownership apply equally to non-consumer **6.108** contracts of sale and consumer contracts of sale, passing of risk does not concur with transfer of ownership in the latter. Section 20 does not apply to consumer contracts of sale.[151] Section 29 of the 2015 Act provides that the goods remain at the trader's risk until they come into the physical possession of: (a) the consumer; or (b) a person identified by the consumer to take possession of the goods.[152]

148 1979 Act, s. 20A(3).
149 1979 Act, s. 20B.
150 1979 Act, s. 20(2). An example is *Demby Hamilton & Co Ltd v Barden* [1949] 1 All ER 435.
151 1979 Act, s. 20(4).
152 2015 Act, s. 29(2).

Retention of title clauses

6.109 Retention of title clauses (sometimes written as ROT clauses) protect the seller against both non-payment and the buyer's supervening insolvency. Section 19(1) provides that, by the terms of the contract, the seller may reserve the right of disposal (i.e. ownership) of the goods until certain conditions are fulfilled. Where this is done, ownership of the goods will not pass until the conditions imposed by the seller are fulfilled. Ownership does not pass even if the goods have been delivered to the buyer or someone acting on their behalf. The 'certain conditions' referred to in s. 19 will invariably include full payment of the price. Payment of the price is then a suspensive condition. Ownership of the goods will only pass when that suspensive condition is purified.

6.110 Section 17 provides that the parties' intention is the principal consideration when ascertaining when ownership is to pass. Section 19 makes clear that ROT clauses are acceptable. Possession can pass without ownership passing with it.

6.111 In *Armour v Thyssen Edelstahlwerke AG* the Lord Ordinary (Mayfield) and the Second Division found that a ROT clause in a contract between a Scottish company and a West German company for the sale of steel was ineffective as it was an attempt to create a right of security over corporeal moveables without transfer of possession.[153] The House of Lords allowed the West German company's appeal, holding that the ROT clause was valid: 'The contract of sale did not attempt to create a right in security in favour of the [West German company], rather did it operate to transfer possession and dominium [ownership] in two stages'.[154]

Sales by non-owners

6.112 Section 21 restates the rule of *nemo dat quod non habet*:[155]

> 'Subject to this Act, where goods are sold by a person who is not their owner, and who does not sell them under the authority or with the consent of the owner, the buyer acquires no better title to the goods than the seller had, unless the owner of the goods is by his conduct precluded from denying the seller's authority to sell.'

6.113 There are exceptions to the rule of *nemo dat quod non habet*, two of which are mentioned in s. 21. If goods are sold with the authority or consent of the owner, the buyer acquires ownership. Where the owner is personally barred from denying the authority of the seller, the buyer acquires ownership. The 1979 Act is silent on what conduct would be required to bring personal bar into operation. Reid and Blackie comment:

> 'If the common-law principles of personal bar are used as a reference point, then the buyer must identify an inconsistency in the original owner's conduct which created a false impression with regard to the seller, either to the effect that the seller was

153 1990 SLT 891 at 893I–893L.

154 1990 SLT 891 at 896B per Lord Jauncey.

155 No one gives who has not: one who has no title cannot confer a title (*Trayner's Latin Maxims*, 4th edn (Edinburgh: W. Green, 1993), p. 375). The longer version is *nemo plus juris ad alium transferre potest quam ipse habet.*

owner, or to the effect that the seller was the agent of the owner. Such false impression may be achieved either by an express representation or by conduct, including an omission to correct a misleading impression.'[156]

In *Atiyah and Adams' Sale of Goods* it is said that personal bar would operate in two cases: (1) where the owner has represented, by word or by action, that the seller is the true owner, or has the owner's authority to sell; and (2) where the owner allows the seller to appear as the true owner, or as having the owner's authority to sell, through a negligent failure to act.[157] As an express representation by the owner that the seller is the true owner is likely to be rare, personal bar is most likely to operate as a result of a failure to correct a misleading impression. **6.114**

Sections 24 and 25 provide for two more exceptions. As these exceptions are considered elsewhere in this book,[158] this chapter makes only brief mention of them. **6.115**

Section 24 concerns the situation where a person, having sold goods, continues in possession of the goods and then delivers or transfers them to another under any sale, pledge or other disposition. If the person receiving the goods is in good faith and has no notice of the previous sale, s. 24 provides that the delivery or transfer has effect as if it had been expressly authorised by the owner. In other words, the person receiving the goods acquires a good title. The person making the transfer is deemed to be the buyer's agent. The expression 'delivery or transfer' has been interpreted widely by the courts.[159] **6.116**

Section 25 concerns the obverse situation, where, having bought goods, a person obtains possession of them and, without ownership having passed, delivers or transfers them to another under any sale, pledge or other disposition. If the person receiving the goods is in good faith and has no notice of any lien or other right of the original seller in respect of the costs, s. 25 provides that the delivery or transfer has the same effect as if the person making the delivery were the mercantile agent in possession of the goods with the consent of the owner. The person receiving the goods acquires a good title. For the definition of 'mercantile agent', see s. 26. **6.117**

Section 23 provides that, when the seller of goods has a voidable title to the goods, but their title has not been avoided at the time of the sale, the buyer acquires a good title to the goods, provided that the buyer buys them in good faith and without notice of the seller's defect of title. A voidable title is valid unless and until it is avoided. It is not null *ab initio*.[160] The buyer does not obtain the protection of s. 23 if the seller's title is void, as opposed to merely voidable. That would be the case if the contract of sale which purported to transfer ownership of goods to the seller were void due to, for example, an absence of agreement on the essential terms.[161] **6.118**

156 E C Reid and J W G Blackie, *Personal Bar* (Edinburgh: W. Green, 2006), para. 11–18.
157 *Atiyah and Adams' Sale of Goods* (n 33), pp. 282–283, discussing the English doctrine of estoppel.
158 See para. 3.113.
159 *Michael Gerson (Leasing) Ltd v Wilkinson* [2001] QB 514.
160 McBryde (n 44), para. 13–21.
161 See *Shogun Finance Ltd v Hudson* [2004] 1 AC 919 at [50]–[52] per Lord Hobhouse, at [178] per Lord Phillips.

6.119 Something done honestly is deemed to be something done in good faith. It does not matter whether or not it was done negligently.[162]

DUTIES AND REMEDIES

The parties' duties

6.120 Section 27 provides that '[it] is the duty of the seller to deliver the goods, and of the buyer to accept and pay for them, in accordance with the terms of the contract of sale'.

6.121 Section 28 provides that, unless otherwise agreed, the seller must be ready and willing to give possession of the goods to the buyer in exchange for the price and the buyer must be ready and willing to pay the price in exchange for possession of the goods. These are described as 'concurrent conditions'.

6.122 The expression 'in accordance with the terms of the contract of sale' covers both express terms and those implied by the 1979 Act. Most of the terms implied by the 1979 Act impose a duty on the seller: the seller must pass good title; the seller must deliver the right quantity of goods; the goods delivered must be of satisfactory quality; the goods delivered must be fit for a particular purpose made known to the seller, etc. The 2015 Act imposes similar duties on the trader.

6.123 Before turning to the respective parties' remedies, this chapter considers the seller/trader's duty to deliver the goods. This issue of the buyer/consumer's acceptance is considered later.[163]

Delivery in non-consumer contracts of sale

6.124 Delivery is defined as voluntary transfer of possession from one person to another.[164] Whether it is for the buyer to take possession of the goods or for the seller to send them to the buyer depends on the contract between the parties.[165] In the absence of agreement, the place of delivery is the seller's place of business. If the seller has no place of business, the place of delivery is the seller's residence. However, if the contract is for the sale of specific goods, which to the knowledge of the parties when the contract is made are in some other place, that other place is the place of delivery.[166]

6.125 Section 29(3) provides that, where the seller is bound to send the goods to the buyer, but no time for sending them is fixed, the seller is bound to send them within a reasonable time. That is a question of fact.[167] Section 29(5) provides that demand or tender of delivery may be treated as ineffectual unless made at a reasonable hour. What is a reasonable hour is a question of fact. Suffice it to

162 1979 Act, s. 61(3).
163 See paras 6.139–6.141 below.
164 1979 Act, s. 61(1).
165 1979 Act, s. 29(1).
166 1979 Act, s. 29(2).
167 1979 Act, s. 59.

say that 3am may be an unreasonable hour for delivery to a hairdresser's, but not for delivery to a nightclub. The default is that the seller bears the expenses of putting the goods into a deliverable state.[168]

Delivery in consumer contracts of sale

Subject to any agreement between the parties, the trader has a duty to deliver the goods to the consumer.[169] The 2015 Act differs from the 1979 Act in terms of the timing of the delivery. It provides that, unless there is an agreed time or period, the trader must deliver the goods: (a) without undue delay; and (b) in any event, not more than thirty days after the day on which the contract is entered into.[170] **6.126**

Sellers' remedies

The seller's remedies are the same in both non-consumer contracts of sale and consumer contracts of sale. The 1979 Act provides the 'unpaid seller' with rights against the goods, or 'possessory remedies'. As would be expected, a seller of goods is an unpaid seller when the whole of the price has not been paid or tendered.[171] Section 39(1) provides that, even if ownership has passed, the unpaid seller has the following rights by implication of law: (a) a lien on the goods or right to retain them for the price while the seller is in possession of them; (b) in case of the insolvency of a buyer, a right of stopping the goods in transit after the seller has parted with possession; and (c) a right of resale, limited by the 1979 Act. As regards (b), only apparent, as opposed to absolute, insolvency is required. A person is deemed to be insolvent if they have either ceased to pay their debts in the ordinary course of business or they cannot pay their debts as they become due.[172] **6.127**

Lien (unpaid seller in possession)

A lien is a real right to retain property until the discharge of an obligation or obligations, the property not having been delivered to the retaining party for the purposes of security.[173] Section 41(1) provides that the unpaid seller in possession of the goods is entitled to retain possession of them until payment or tender of the price in the following cases: (a) where the goods have been sold without any stipulation as to credit; (b) where the goods have been sold on credit and the term of credit has expired; and (c) where the buyer becomes insolvent. The lien may be exercised even if the seller is in possession of the goods as agent or custodier for the buyer.[174] **6.128**

168 1979 Act, s. 29(6).
169 2015 Act, s. 28(2).
170 2015 Act, s. 28(3).
171 1979 Act, s. 38(1)(a).
172 1979 Act, s. 61(4).
173 G L Gretton and A J M Steven, *Property, Trusts and Succession*, 4th edn (London: Bloomsbury Professional, 2021), para. 21.58.
174 1979 Act, s. 41(2).

6.129 Where they have made part delivery of the goods, the unpaid seller may exercise their right of lien on the remainder of the goods. That is not permitted where the part delivery has been made under such circumstances as to show an agreement to waive the lien.[175]

6.130 The right of lien is lost if: (a) the unpaid seller delivers the goods to a carrier or custodier for the purpose of transmission to the buyer *without* reserving the right of disposal;[176] (b) the buyer or the buyer's agent lawfully obtains possession of the goods; or (c) the unpaid seller waives the right of lien.[177] If the right of lien is lost, it is extinct beyond revival.[178]

Stoppage in transit (unpaid seller no longer in possession)

6.131 When the buyer of goods becomes insolvent, the unpaid seller no longer in possession of the goods has the right of stopping them in transit. The unpaid seller may resume possession of the goods as long as they are in course of transit and may retain them until payment or tender of the price.[179] Section 45 provides that goods are deemed to be in course of transit from the time when they are delivered to a carrier or custodier for the purpose of transmission to the buyer, until the buyer or the buyer's agent takes delivery of them from the carrier or custodier.[180] If the buyer or the buyer's agent obtains delivery of the goods before their arrival at the appointed destination, the transit is at an end.[181] If the buyer rejects the goods and the carrier or custodier continues in possession, the transit is not deemed to be at an end.[182]

6.132 The right of stoppage in transit is exercised by the unpaid seller either taking actual possession of the goods or giving notice of their claim to the carrier or custodier in possession of the goods.[183] Section 47(1) makes clear that the unpaid seller's right of lien or stoppage in transit is not affected by any sale or other disposition of the goods which the buyer may have made. That does not apply if the seller has assented to the sale. The assent must be given in circumstances demonstrating the unpaid seller's intention to renounce rights against the goods.[184]

Limited right of resale

6.133 The contract of sale is not terminated by the unpaid seller's exercise of their right of lien or stoppage in transit.[185] Section 48(2) provides that, where,

175 1979 Act, s. 42.
176 On retention of title clauses, see paras 6.109–6.111 above.
177 1979 Act, s. 43(1).
178 Bell, *Commentaries* II, 91; cf. *London Scottish Transport Ltd v Tyres (Scotland) Ltd* 1957 SLT (Sh Ct) 48. In that case the sheriff-substitute classified a submission that the pursuers' lien was revived when the goods came back into their possession, no matter how, as a 'rather startling proposition' (at 49).
179 1979 Act, s. 44.
180 1979 Act, s. 45.
181 1979 Act, s. 45(2).
182 1979 Act, s. 45(4).
183 1979 Act, s. 46(1).
184 *Mordaunt Brothers v British Oil and Cake Mills Ltd* [1910] 2 KB 502.
185 1979 Act, s. 48(1).

having exercised a possessory remedy, an unpaid seller resells the goods, the buyer acquires a good title as against the original buyer.[186] Section 48(3) applies where the goods are perishable (e.g. Atlantic salmon) or where the unpaid seller gives notice to the buyer of an intention to resell and the buyer does not pay or tender the price within a reasonable time. In those circumstances, the unpaid seller may resell the goods and recover damages for any loss occasioned by the buyer's breach of contract.

Section 48(4) applies where the seller expressly reserves the right to resell the goods in the event of the buyer's default and where, on the buyer's default, the seller resells the goods. In those circumstances, the original contract of sale is terminated, but without prejudice to any claim the seller may have for damages. **6.134**

Action for payment (in the event of non-payment)

Where ownership of the goods has passed to the buyer and the buyer wrongfully neglects or refuses to pay for the goods according to the terms of the contract, the seller has an action against the buyer for payment of the price.[187] If the price is payable on a 'day certain', irrespective of delivery, and the buyer wrongfully neglects or refuses to pay the price, the seller has an action against the buyer for payment of the price, even if ownership has not passed and the goods have not been appropriated to the contract.[188] In *Henderson and Keay Ltd v AM Carmichael Ltd* Lord Strachan confirmed that 'day certain' means 'something of the nature of a fixed date'.[189] In that case, submission of an invoice was not a day certain, as it left it open to the seller to make the price payable at any time either before or after delivery of the goods. **6.135**

In *FG Wilson (Engineering) Ltd v John Holt & Co (Liverpool) Ltd* the Court of Appeal held that no action for payment lies with the seller unless the conditions of either s. 49(1) or s. 49(2) are fulfilled: ownership must have passed or the price must be payable on a day certain.[190] The UK Supreme Court disapproved of this approach in *PST Energy 7 Shipping LLC v OW Bunker Malta Ltd*, Lord Mance stating *obiter* that s. 49 is not a complete code of situations in which the price may be recoverable under a contract of sale.[191] For example, the price may be recoverable under an express term of the contract. **6.136**

Action for damages (in the event of non-acceptance)

Where the buyer wrongfully neglects or refuses to accept and pay for the goods, the seller has an action for damages for non-acceptance against the buyer.[192] Section 50(2) restates, perhaps unnecessarily, the standard test for the measure of damages, namely the estimated loss directly and naturally resulting, in **6.137**

186 1979 Act, s. 48(2).
187 1979 Act, s. 49(1).
188 1979 Act, s. 49(2).
189 1956 SLT (Notes) 58.
190 [2014] 1 WLR 2365 at [41] per Longmore LJ.
191 [2016] UKSC 23, [2016] AC 1034 at [58].
192 1979 Act, s. 50(1).

the ordinary course of events, from the buyer's breach of contract.[193] Where there is an available market for the goods in question, the measure of damages is *prima facie* to be ascertained by the difference between the contract price and the market or current price at time or times when the goods ought to have been accepted or (if no time was fixed) at the time of the buyer's refusal to accept.[194]

6.138 If ownership of the goods has passed, but the buyer refuses to take delivery, the seller can choose between an action for payment and an action for damages. If they refuse to take delivery *within a reasonable time*, the buyer is liable to the seller for any loss occasioned by their neglect or refusal to take delivery. The buyer is also liable for a reasonable charge for the care and custody of the goods.[195]

Buyers' remedies in non-consumer contracts of sale

When is the buyer deemed to have accepted the goods?

6.139 The buyer's primary remedy is to reject the goods and rescind the contract. This right will be lost if the buyer accepts, or is deemed to have accepted, the goods. The buyer is deemed to have accepted the goods: (a) when they intimate to the seller that they have accepted the goods; or (b) when the goods have been delivered to them and they do any act in relation to the goods that is inconsistent with the ownership of the seller.[196] The expression 'an act inconsistent with the ownership of the seller' is one with no fixed meaning, allowing the court to decide whether the buyer has the right to reject according to the circumstances of each case.[197] A valid rejection of goods can be invalidated if the buyer continues to possess and to use them.[198]

6.140 Where goods are delivered to the buyer and the buyer has not previously examined them, the buyer is not deemed to have accepted them until they have had a reasonable opportunity of examining them for the purpose: (a) of ascertaining whether they are in conformity with the contract; and (b) in the case of a sale by sample, of comparing the bulk with the sample.[199] Section 35(4) provides that the buyer is deemed to have accepted the goods when, after the lapse of a reasonable time, they retain the goods without intimating to the seller that they have rejected them. What is a reasonable time is a question of fact.[200] Whether or not the buyer has had a reasonable chance of examining the goods for the purpose stated in s. 35(2) is material to that question.

6.141 Section 35(6) provides that the buyer is not deemed to have accepted the goods merely: (a) because they ask for, or agree to, their repair by or under an agreement with the seller; or (b) because the goods are delivered to another

193 *Hadley v Baxendale* (1854) 9 Ex 341 at 355 per Alderson B.
194 1979 Act, s. 50(3).
195 1979 Act, s. 37(1).
196 1979 Act, s. 35(1).
197 *Atiyah and Adams' Sale of Goods* (n 33), p. 430.
198 *Wilson v AGCO Finance Ltd* [2018] SC EDIN 24, 2018 GWD 14-192 at [56].
199 1979 Act, s. 35(2).
200 1979 Act, s. 59.

under a sub-sale or other disposition. In *J & H Ritchie Ltd v Lloyd Ltd* the pursuers bought agricultural equipment (a modified drill and power harrow combination) from the defenders.[201] The pursuers noticed vibrations when using the harrow. They contacted the defenders. The defenders removed the harrow, investigated the issue and, without the pursuers' agreement, fixed it. Despite requests, the defenders refused to disclose what the problem had been. They refused to provide an engineer's report. The pursuers rejected the harrow. They raised an action for declarator and payment. The pursuers were successful before the sheriff, but not before the sheriff principal and an Extra Division. The House of Lords held that the defenders were bound to provide the information requested. Lords Hope and Rodger decided that to be so for different reasons but the key point is that, if a repair has already been carried out (whether or not in secret), the buyer is entitled to information as to the repair. The buyer must be able to make an informed choice about whether to reject the goods.

The right to reject must be exercised in a reasonable time. *Douglas v Glenvarigill Co Ltd* clarified that, even in the case of goods with a latent defect, time begins to run on delivery.[202] Had Parliament intended that it should run from the date of appearance of a defect, that would have been expressly provided. Commercial closure was required to permit parties to arrange their affairs on the basis that the goods have been effectively sold.[203] The pursuer was not entitled to reject the goods, but was entitled to damages. **6.142**

Where the contract is for the sale of goods comprising one or more commercial units, a buyer accepting the goods included in a unit is deemed to have accepted all the goods making the unit.[204] A 'commercial unit' is a unit, division of which would materially impair the value of the goods or the character of the unit, such as a replica set of Lewis chessmen. **6.143**

Right to reject

Section 15B(1)(b) provides that, where the seller is in breach of any term of the contract (express or implied) and that breach is material, the buyer is entitled to reject any goods delivered under the contract and treat it as repudiated. This is in addition to the right to claim damages.[205] **6.144**

The right to reject can also arise where the seller delivers the wrong quantity of goods. Where the seller delivers to the buyer a quantity of goods less than they contracted to sell, the buyer may reject them. If the buyer accepts the goods, they must pay for them at the contract rate.[206] By contrast, if the seller delivers to the buyer a quantity of goods larger than they contracted to sell, the buyer may accept the goods included in the contract and reject the rest, or may reject **6.145**

201 *J & H Ritchie Ltd v Lloyd Ltd* 2007 SC (HL) 89.
202 2010 SLT 634; see also *Combe v Pert's House Furnishers Ltd* [2018] SC FORF 28, 2018 GWD 15-207 which was decided on the basis of the necessity of 'commercial closure'.
203 2010 SLT 634 at [34] per Lord Drummond Young.
204 1979 Act, s. 35(7).
205 See para. 6.148 below.
206 1979 Act, s. 30(1).

the whole.[207] However, the right to reject can only be used if the shortfall or the excess is material.[208] Where the seller delivers to the buyer a quantity of goods more than they contracted to sell and the buyer accepts the whole of the goods, the buyer must pay for them at contract rate.[209]

6.146 Section 35A deals with the right of partial rejection. If: (a) the buyer has the right to reject the goods by reason of a breach by the seller that affects some or all of them; but (b) accepts some of the goods, the buyer does not lose the right to reject the rest.[210] Goods are 'affected' by a breach if, due to the breach, they do not conform to the contract.

6.147 If the buyer rejects the goods, there is no duty to return them to the seller. It is sufficient that the buyer intimates the rejection to the seller.[211]

Action for damages (in the event of breach of contract/non-delivery)

6.148 Section 15B(1)(a) provides that, where the seller is in breach of any term of the contract (express or implied), the buyer is entitled to claim damages. The buyer can claim damages *and* exercise the right to reject only when the seller's breach of contract is material. If it is not material, the buyer has the right to claim damages only.

6.149 Where the seller wrongfully neglects or refuses to deliver the goods to the buyer, the buyer has an action for damages for non-delivery against the seller.[212] Section 51(2) and 51(3) mirror the provisions re the measure of damages in s. 50.[213] In the event of non-delivery, the buyer may be required to mitigate their loss by buying other goods.[214]

6.150 Section 53A makes provision, more generally, for the measure of damages for the seller's breach of contract. Section 53A(1) repeats the test from *Hadley v Baxendale*.[215] Where the seller's breach consists of the delivery of goods that are not of the quality required by the contract and the buyer retains the goods, such loss (that directly and naturally arising, in the ordinary course of events, from the breach) is *prima facie* the difference between the value of the goods at the time of delivery to the buyer and the value they would have had if the seller had fulfilled the contract.[216]

Specific performance

6.151 On the pursuer's application in any action for breach of contract to deliver specific goods, the court may direct that the contract shall be performed

207 1979 Act, s. 30(2).
208 1979 Act, s. 30(2D).
209 1979 Act, s. 30(3).
210 1979 Act, s. 35A(1).
211 1979 Act, s. 36.
212 1979 Act, s. 51(1).
213 See para. 6.137 above.
214 As is stated in McBryde, (n 44), para. 22–37, '[l]oss which could reasonably have been avoided cannot be recovered from the party in breach'.
215 (1854) 9 Ex 341 at 355 per Alderson B.
216 1979 Act, s. 53A(2).

specifically, without giving the defender the option of retaining the goods on payment of damages.[217] This would prevent the seller from withholding the goods and paying damages as an alternative. The application may be made at any time before judgment or decree.[218]

Section 52(4) provides that the provisions of s. 52 are supplementary to, and not in derogation of, the right of specific implement in Scotland. As a general remedy in respect of breach of contract, whether primary or not,[219] specific implement could perhaps be used in respect of unascertained goods. Specific performance concerns specific goods only. 6.152

Buyers' remedies in consumer contracts of sale

If the goods do not conform to the contract because a breach of a term described in ss. 9 (goods to be of satisfactory quality), 10 (goods to be fit for particular purpose), 11 (goods to be as described), 13 (goods to match a sample) or 14 (goods to match a model seen or examined) of the 2015 Act, the consumer has three rights: the short-term right to reject; the right to repair or replacement; and the right to a price reduction or the final right to reject.[220] These rights are *in addition to* the 'standard' remedies for breach of contract, such as claiming damages or seeking an order for specific implement.[221] References to sections in this final part are to sections of the 2015 Act. 6.153

The short-term right to reject

The right to reject is exercised if the consumer indicates to the trader that they are rejecting the goods and treating the contract as at an end.[222] The indication may be by word or by action, but it must clear enough to be understood by the trader.[223] When the right is exercised, the trader has a duty to give the customer a refund and the consumer has a duty to make the goods available for collection by the trader or (if there is an agreement to that effect) to return them.[224] 6.154

In *Johnston v R & J Leather (Scotland) Ltd* the Sheriff Appeal Court considered whether, after rejecting them, the consumer has a duty to retain the goods.[225] A married couple bought a leather suite for their living room from R & J. It was delivered on 30 June 2017 but did not meet their expectations. They intimated rejection and sought a refund. R & J were less than responsive, refusing to collect the leather suite and refusing, more generally, to engage with the Johnstons. 6.155

217 1979 Act, s. 52(1).
218 1979 Act, s. 52(2).
219 McBryde (n 44), para. 23–08; MacQueen (n 45), para. 7.6. Neither work supports the view that specific implement is the innocent party's primary remedy on breach of contract.
220 2015 Act, s. 19(3).
221 2015 Act, ss. 19(9)–(11).
222 2015 Act, s. 20(5).
223 2015 Act, s. 20(6).
224 2015 Act, s. 20(7).
225 2019 SLT (Sh Ct) 118.

6.156 Mrs Johnston made a claim under simple procedure. It was not defended. She obtained an order for payment on 14 December 2017. Believing the matter to be at an end, the Johnstons gave away the leather suite. A charge was served to implement the order in January 2018. Only then did R & J take action. They were successful in having the order recalled. Mr Johnston became a joint claimant. After an evidential hearing, the sheriff preferred the Johnstons' version of events and granted an order for payment, excusing the failure to return the leather suite. On appeal, R & J argued that the duty to make the goods available applied without limit of time and irrespective of intervening developments and the actions of the trader(s). The Sheriff Appeal Court rejected that 'unattractive proposition'.[226] It held:

> 'The duty to make the goods available cannot be without limit of time or unqualified. In considering the nature and extent of the duty to retain goods which have been rejected, the court is entitled to take into account a number of factors, including but not restricted to: the timescale within which rejection was intimated; the nature of the goods; the practicality of providing storage; the nature, extent and frequency of communications sent by the consumers to the [traders]; any response, or lack of response, from the [traders]; the length of time for which goods were retained; and whether proceedings have been raised.'[227]

The trader must bear the reasonable costs of retuning the goods.[228]

6.157 Section 20(9)–(12) make provision in respect of the consumer's entitlement to a refund. If money was paid, the consumer is entitled (unsurprisingly) to receive back that amount of money.[229] The refund must be given without undue delay and, in any event, within fourteen days of the day on which the trader agrees that the consumer is entitled to a refund.[230] Unless otherwise agreed, the refund must be given using the same means of payment as the customer used.[231] No fee can be imposed in respect of the refund.[232]

6.158 Unless otherwise agreed, the short-term right to reject is lost if it is not exercised within the time limit for exercising it.[233] The time limit is thirty days from the day after all the following events have happened: (a) ownership has been transferred to the consumer; (b) the goods have been delivered; and (c) where the contract requires the trader to install the goods or take other action to enable the consumer to use them, the trader has notified the consumer that the action has been taken.[234] The short-term right to reject can be exercised before these events have happened.[235] If goods are likely to perish after a period shorter than thirty days, the time limit is the end of that shorter period.[236] If the consumer requests or agrees to the repair or replacement of goods,

226 2019 SLT (Sh Ct) 118 at [27].
227 2019 SLT (Sh Ct) 118 at [29].
228 2015 Act, s. 20(8).
229 2015 Act, s. 20(10).
230 2015 Act, s. 20(15).
231 2015 Act, s. 20(16).
232 2015 Act, s. 20(17).
233 2015 Act, s. 22(1).
234 2015 Act, s. 22(3).
235 2015 Act, s. 22(5).
236 2015 Act, s. 22(4).

the period within which the short-term right to reject must be exercised stops running for the length of the waiting period.[237]

The right to repair or replacement

If the consumer requires the trader to repair or replace the goods, the trader must do so within a reasonable time and without significant inconvenience to the consumer.[238] The trader must bear any necessary costs in doing so.[239] The consumer cannot exercise the right to repair or replacement if either remedy is impossible or disproportionate compared to the other.[240] Section 23(4) provides that a remedy is disproportionate to the other if it imposes costs on the trader that are unreasonable compared to those imposed by the other. The following are factors in assessing disproportionality: (a) the value which the goods would have if they conformed to the contract; (b) the significance of the lack of conformity; and (c) whether the other remedy could be effected without significant inconvenience to the consumer. 'Reasonable time' and 'significant inconvenience' are assessed taking into account the nature of the goods and the purpose for which the goods were acquired.[241] **6.159**

A consumer who requires or agrees to the replacement of goods cannot require the trader to repair them, or exercise the short-term right to reject, without giving the trader a reasonable time to replace them, unless giving that time would cause significant inconvenience to the consumer.[242] **6.160**

The right to a price reduction or the final right to reject

The right to a price reduction is the right: (a) to require the trader to reduce by an appropriate amount the price the consumer is required to pay under the contract, or anything else the consumer is required to transfer under the contract; and (b) to receive a refund from the trader for anything already paid or otherwise transferred by the consumer above the reduced amount.[243] In appropriate circumstances, the amount of the reduction may be the full amount of the price.[244] Section 20(10)–(17) apply to the consumer's right to receive a refund under s. 20(1)(b). **6.161**

The final right to reject is an alternative to the right to a price reduction. For obvious reasons, it is not possible to exercise both.[245] Either right may be exercised in one of three situations: (a) where, after one repair or one replacement, the goods do not conform to the contract; (b) where, due to their being impossible or disproportionate, the consumer can require neither repair nor replacement; or (c) where the consumer has required the trader to **6.162**

237 2015 Act, s. 22(6)–(8).
238 2015 Act, s. 23(2)(a).
239 2015 Act, s. 23(2)(b).
240 2015 Act, s. 23(3).
241 2015 Act, s. 23(5).
242 2015 Act, s. 23(7).
243 2015 Act, s. 24(1).
244 2015 Act, s. 24(2).
245 2015 Act, s. 24(5).

repair or replace the goods and the trader has breached the requirement to do so within a reasonable time and without significant inconvenience to the consumer.[246]

6.163 In *Van Gordon v Volkswagen Financial Services (UK) Ltd (t/a Audi Finance)* the claimant leased a car from a finance company under a hire purchase agreement.[247] After noticing various problems with the car, he wrote to the relevant dealership requesting a repair. As the dealership was acting as agent for the finance company, that was held to amount to a request to the trader.

6.164 If the consumer exercises the final right to reject, any refund may be reduced to take account of the use the consumer has had of the goods.[248] However, no deduction can be made to take account of use in any period where the consumer had the goods only because the trader had failed to collect them at an agreed time.[249] No deduction can be made if the final right to reject is made within the first six months unless the goods consist of a car or are of a description specified in a statutory instrument.[250] The 'first six months' is six months beginning with the first day after: (i) ownership of the goods has been transferred; (ii) the goods have been delivered; and (iii) if installation is required, the trader has notified the consumer that it has been done.[251]

6.165 The right to reject also arises where the seller delivers the wrong quantity of goods. Section 25 is the equivalent of s. 30 of the 1979 Act. If the trader delivers a quantity of goods less than they contracted to supply, the consumer may reject them. If the consumer accepts the goods, they must pay for them at the contract rate.[252] If the trader delivers a quantity of goods larger than they contracted to supply, the consumer may accept the quantity of goods contracted for and reject the rest, or may reject the whole.[253] If the consumer accepts the goods, they must pay for them at the contract rate.[254] To exercise the right to reject, the consumer must indicate to the trader that they are rejecting the goods.[255] The indication may be by word or by action, but it must be clear enough to be understood by the trader.[256] The main difference between non-consumer and consumer contracts of sale is that, in the latter, where the wrong quantity of goods has been delivered, the right to reject is not dependent on the shortfall or excess being material.

246 2015 Act, s. 24(5).
247 Nottingham County Court, 30 April 2019, unreported.
248 2015 Act, s. 24(8).
249 2015 Act, s. 24(9).
250 2015 Act, s. 24(10). As at the date of writing, no such statutory instruments have been made.
251 2015 Act, s. 24(11).
252 2015 Act, s. 30(1).
253 2015 Act, s. 30(2).
254 2015 Act, s. 25(3).
255 2015 Act, s. 25(5).
256 2015 Act, s. 25(6).

Table of sections

Table 6.1 **6.166**

Section of the 1979 Act not applicable to consumer contracts of sale	Equivalent section(s) of the 2015 Act
(*Implied terms about title, etc.*) 12	17 (*Trader to have right to supply the goods, etc.*)
(*Sale by description*) 13	11 (*Goods to be as described*)
(*Implied terms about quality or fitness*) 14	9 (*Goods to be of satisfactory quality*) 10 (*Goods to be fit for particular purpose*) 18 (*No other requirement to treat term about quality or fitness as included*)
(*Sale by sample*) 15	13 (*Goods to match a sample*) 18 (*No other requirement to treat term about quality or fitness as included*)
(*Remedies for breach of contract as respects Scotland*) 15B	19 (*Consumer's rights to enforce terms about goods*) 20 (*Right to reject*) 21 (*Partial rejection of goods*) 22 (*Time limit for short-term right to reject*)
(*Passing of risk*) 20	29 (*Passing of risk*)
(*Rules about delivery*) 29	28 (*Delivery of goods*)
(*Delivery of wrong quantity*) 30	25 (*Delivery of wrong quantity*)
(*Instalment deliveries*) 31	26 (*Instalment deliveries*)
(*Delivery to carrier*) 32	29 (*Passing of risk*)
(*Acceptance*) 35	21 (*Partial rejection of goods*)
(*Right of partial rejection*) 35A	21 (*Partial rejection of goods*)
(*Buyer not bound to return rejected goods*)	20 (*Right to reject*)
(*Damages for non-delivery*) 51 (*Specific performance*) 52 (*Measure of damages as respects Scotland*) 53A (*Interest, etc.*) 54	19 (*Consumer's rights to enforce terms about goods*)
(*Exclusion of implied terms*) 55	31 (*Liability that cannot be excluded or restricted*)
(*Payment into court in Scotland* 58	27 (*Consignation, or payment into court, in Scotland*)

Chapter Seven

Insurance

Katarzyna Chałaczkiewicz-Ładna

INSURANCE CONTRACTS

The purpose of insurance

7.01 Insurance is, in essence, a mechanism whereby risk can be transferred to an insurer. Some risks (for example, the destruction of one's home by fire) carry such severe financial consequences that it is not possible for one person to make adequate provision for the possibility of the occurrence of the risk. Insurance offers a means for a large number of people to contribute to a fund that will meet the cost of specific forms of loss or damage. As only a fraction of the contributors is likely to suffer loss in any one year, the cost can be borne more easily by a large number than by an individual. This spreading of risk across large numbers makes it possible for insurers to charge premiums which represent only a fraction of the sums that can be recovered by an insured who suffers a loss. In order for the mechanism to work fairly it is necessary that policyholders contribute to the common fund according to the degree of risk that they pose and withdraw from it according to the cover agreed in their policy. Also, since the insured knows much more about the risk they wish to have insured, they must provide all relevant information to the insurer. These objectives are reflected in the various principles of insurance law which are discussed in this chapter.[1] Much of insurance law involves the interaction of: (a) the law of contract; and (b) the regulatory regime applicable to those contracts and those authorised to engage in regulated activities.[2]

Definition of an insurance contract

7.02 The Marine Insurance Act 1906 (the '1906 Act') defines contract of marine insurance as 'a contract whereby the insurer undertakes to indemnify the assured, in manner and to the extent thereby agreed, against marine losses, that is to say, the losses incident to marine adventure'.[3] The following features of a contract of insurance were pointed out judicially in *Scottish Amicable*

1 For the history, see A D M Forte, 'Insurance' in K G C Reid and R Zimmermann, *A History of Private Law in Scotland* (Oxford: Oxford University Press, 2000) Vol. II, Ch. 13. See too N Ferguson, *The Ascent of Money: A Financial History of the World* (London: Penguin, 2008), pp. 176, 185 onward.

2 See, e.g. *Financial Conduct Authority v Arch Insurance (UK) Ltd* [2021] UKSC 1, [2021] 2 WLR 123.

3 1906 Act, s. 1.

Heritable Securities Association Ltd v Northern Assurance Co.[4] In that case, Lord Justice-Clerk Moncreiff defined insurance as a contract in which 'the insurer undertakes, in consideration of the payment of an estimated equivalent beforehand, to make up to the assured any loss he may sustain by the occurrence of an uncertain contingency'. It is essential that the insured stands to lose by the occurrence of the insured event and that the timing of the insured event is uncertain. The insured event itself does not have to be uncertain: in the case of life assurance, for example, death is a certain event, but its timing is uncertain and therefore it is an insurable risk. Uncertainty is determined at the time when the contract is concluded.[5] Nor is it necessary that the insurer agree to pay a sum of money to the insured on the occurrence of an insured event. In *Department of Trade v St Christopher Motorists Association Ltd*,[6] it was held that the provision by the insurer of chauffeur services to motorists convicted of drink-driving offences was insurance even though payment was in a form other than money. This approach was clarified in the later case of *Medical Defence Union Ltd v Department of Trade*,[7] which held that insurance was a contract for 'the payment of money or for money's worth' but that the payment of some other form of benefit could not be considered to be insurance. Following that approach, 'breakdown' cover provided by motoring organisations is considered to be a form of insurance.

Insurance contracts should be distinguished from manufacturers' guarantees and cautionary obligations. The former, in particular, can appear similar to insurance contracts, in that they provide for the manufacturer to bear the cost of an uncertain event in the future, for example the breakdown of an appliance. The law has approached manufacturers' guarantees from the perspective of the related contract for sale of goods rather than from the perspective of risk transfer.[8] Nevertheless, where a retailer offers an extended warranty to a customer covering the risk of breakdown, this may amount to a contract of insurance if the elements outlined in the paragraph above are present.[9] Cautionary obligations, by contrast, are in their nature different from insurance contracts in that they are accessory and not direct obligations:[10] thus, an insurance contract can be enforced against the insurer immediately following **7.03**

4 (1883) 11 R 287 at 303.

5 *Department of Trade and Industry v St Christopher Motorists Association Ltd* [1974] 1 WLR 99.

6 [1974] 1 WLR 99.

7 [1980] Ch 82 at 93 per Megarry V-C. The issue in this case was whether the Medical Defence Union was an insurer. It could, at its discretion, undertake or defend legal proceedings on behalf of members and could provide an indemnity in relation to awards arising from such proceedings. It was held that the discretionary power of the MDU prevented it having a contract with each member.

8 For example, as to guarantees in relation to consumer contracts for goods, s. 30(2) of the Consumer Rights Act 2015 ('CRA 2015') defines the guarantee as an undertaking to the consumer given without extra charge by a person acting in the course of the person's business (the 'guarantor') that, if the goods do not meet the specifications set out in the guarantee statement or in any associated advertising: (a) the consumer will be reimbursed for the price paid for the goods; or (b) the goods will be repaired, replaced or handled in any way.

9 In *Re Digital Satellite Warranty Cover Ltd* [2013] UKSC 7, [2013] 1 WLR 605 it was not disputed that an extended warranty was a contract of insurance at common law. An extended warranty is additional to the protection given to the customer by the terms implied into the contract of sale by the Sale of Goods Act 1979.

10 *Scottish Amicable Heritable Securities Association Ltd v Northern Assurance Co* (1883) 11 R 287 at 303 per Lord Justice-Clerk Moncreiff.

an insured event, whereas a cautionary obligation can only be enforced following the default of the debtor in the primary obligation.

TYPES OF INSURANCE

Indemnity

7.04 The most fundamental distinction is between indemnity and non-indemnity insurance. Indemnity contracts are intended to compensate the insured to the extent of their financial loss resulting from the occurrence of an insured event. Common examples are motor and home insurance. Non-indemnity contracts provide for the insurer to pay a specified amount on the occurrence of the insured event. They are used where the financial loss resulting from the occurrence of an insured event is not readily ascertainable. The most common form of non-indemnity insurance is life assurance.[11] As the loss resulting from a person's death cannot be known in the same manner as, for example, the cost of replacing a car, the sum to be paid by the insurer under a life assurance contract is specified when the contract is agreed.

First party and third party

7.05 A distinction can also be drawn between first party and third party insurance. First party cover is intended to protect against the risk of loss of or harm to the insured. Common examples of such insurance are the cover against causing damage to one's own car or having the contents of one's home stolen. Third party cover protects against legal liability arising from damage caused to a third party. Motor policies, for example, provide cover for this risk both in relation to personal injury and property damage. Where third party cover is provided, the policy wording makes clear that the insurer will only be liable in situations in which there is a legal liability to a third party. The result is that the normal principles of delictual liability apply to determine if the insured is liable to a third party and it is only if that liability is triggered that the policy provides cover to the insured.

Voluntary and compulsory

7.06 In the case of most types of insurance, the decision to insure is made voluntarily by the insured. However, there are some instances in which insurance is required by law. Two examples of this are third party motor vehicle insurance and employers' liability insurance. Section 143 of the Road Traffic Act 1988 (the 'RTA 1988') requires a vehicle to be insured in respect of death or bodily injury caused to any person or damage to property caused by the use of the vehicle on a road in Great Britain. Employers are required to insure against

11 The use of the terms 'assurance' and 'insurance' leads to some confusion. 'Assurance' is associated primarily with life assurance, as the insured event (death) is an assured event. However, it is also common practice in marine insurance to refer to the insured as the assured, despite the fact that the contract is referred to as insurance. (See the definition of a marine insurance contract in the 1906 Act, s. 1.)

the risk of bodily injury or disease sustained by employees and arising out of and in the course of their employment by s. 1(1) of the Employers' Liability (Compulsory Insurance) Act 1969.

Life assurance

In its simplest form, life assurance provides protection against the financial consequences of early death.[12] Such policies can take two forms. A whole life policy provides for a sum to be paid on the death of the assured, whenever that occurs. A term policy provides for a sum to be paid if the assured dies during a certain period (e.g. ten years) and no sum is payable if the assured survives to the end of that period. The more complex forms of life assurance are those which combine protection against early death with an investment. The most common example is endowment assurance, where part of the premium is invested by the insurer to provide the assured with a capital sum at the end of the policy term. This type of policy may be used in conjunction with mortgages and fulfils two functions: first, if the assured dies before the mortgage is repaid, the sum assured under the policy will repay the mortgage; second, if the assured survives to the end of the mortgage term, they will have a capital sum to repay the mortgage. **7.07**

SOURCES AND STRUCTURE OF INSURANCE LAW

Insurance has a long history as a means of sharing the risks faced by merchants in their trading activities. Early forms of insurance involved merchants themselves, rather than insurers, assuming the risks of ships sinking or cargoes being lost, but as trade expanded and risk assessment became more complex, it became common for insurance to be underwritten[13] by insurers. The law relating to insurance underwent its most rapid development in the latter part of the eighteenth century. The influence of Lord Mansfield, an expatriate Scot who became Lord Chief Justice of England, was particularly evident in this period. By the time of Lord Mansfield's retirement in 1788, the basic principles of the common law governing insurance contracts had been put in place. The development of the law in Scotland leant heavily on the law in England, which benefited from the emergence of London as an international centre for insurance and shipping. **7.08**

Insurance continued to be governed primarily[14] by the common law until the passing of the 1906 Act. The Act codified the law relating to marine insurance. It specifically preserved the common law governing marine insurance in so far as it was not altered by the 1906 Act.[15] **7.09**

12 The Life Assurance Act 1774 (the '1774 Act') applies to life insurance contracts and also to indemnity contracts other than relating to ships, goods, or merchandises (see s. 4); and it is especially relevant in the context of insurable interest (see below para. 7.21 onward).

13 The term 'underwrite' originates from the practice of subscribing the names of the persons bearing the risk ('underwriters') on the insurance contract.

14 As outlined below, legislation was introduced to control the abuse of insurance for the purpose of speculation.

15 1906 Act, s. 91(2).

7.10 Other types of insurance are not covered by the 1906 Act.[16] However, there has always been a tendency on the part of the courts to extend the general principles of marine insurance to other types of insurance. This resulted from marine being the major class of business in the early days of insurance. As other types of insurance, such as fire and motor, were introduced, it was natural to look to the principles which had already been established for marine insurance. In *Thomson v Weems*[17] Lord Blackburn said: 'I think that on the balance of authority the general principles of insurance law apply to all insurances, whether marine, fire or life . . . '. It follows that, to the extent that it states general principles of insurance law, the 1906 Act corresponds to the common law governing non-marine contracts.

7.11 Since 2006 the Law Commission and the Scottish Law Commission have undertaken a joint review of insurance law.[18] The Consumer Insurance (Disclosure and Representations) Act 2012 (the 'CIDRA 2012') and the Insurance Act 2015 (the 'IA 2015') are results of this review, which has produced an important reform of insurance law – a distinction between consumer and non-consumer insurance contracts being a key change. The CIDRA 2012 came into force on 6 April 2013 and applies only to consumer insurance contracts.[19] It is not possible to contract out the provisions of this Act.[20] The IA 2015 reforms insurance contract law in a number of respects and, although it focuses on non-consumer insurance contracts,[21] it affects consumer contracts as well. This Act came into force on 12 August 2016 and it allows to contract out of certain terms of a non-consumer insurance contract.[22] Also, to note in passing, insurance contracts do not fall within the scope of the Unfair Contract Terms Act 1977.[23] However, insurance contracts where a consumer is a contracting party are covered by Part 2 of the Consumer Rights Act 2015 (the 'CRA 2015') on unfair terms.[24]

REGULATION OF INSURANCE BUSINESS

7.12 A range of activities associated with insurance is regulated by the Financial Services and Markets Act 2000 (the 'FSMA 2000'). There are two regulators:

16 1906 Act, s. 2(2).

17 (1884) 11 R (HL) 48 at 51; (1884) 9 App Cas 671 at 684.

18 For the ongoing reform of Insurance Law and a list of discussion and consultation papers that have been issued so far see: *https://www.scotlawcom.gov.uk/law-reform/law-reform-projects/joint-projects/insurance-law/* (last accessed 2 September 2021).

19 'Consumer insurance contract' means a contract of insurance between: (a) an individual who enters into the contract wholly or mainly for purposes unrelated to the individual's trade, business or profession; and (b) a person who carries on the business of insurance and who becomes a party to the contract by way of that business (whether or not in accordance with permission for the purposes of the Financial Services and Markets Act 2000): CIDRA 2012, s. 1.

20 CIDRA 2012, s. 10. Also, it is not possible to contract out Parts 3 or 4 of the IA 2015 so far as relating to consumer insurance contracts: IA 2015, s. 15.

21 'Non-consumer insurance contract' means a contract of insurance that is not a consumer insurance contract. IA 2015, s. 1.

22 IA 2015, s. 16.

23 Unfair Contract Terms Act 1977, s. 15(3)(a)(i).

24 See especially CRA 2015 s. 61, for the definition of a 'consumer contract'.

the Prudential Regulatory Authority ('the PRA') and the Financial Conduct Authority ('the FCA'). The PRA is the prudential regulator of insurers. The PRA's general objective is promoting the safety and soundness of PRA-authorised persons.[25] The FCA is responsible for the conduct of insurance businesses and its operational objectives are: the consumer protection objective; integrity objective; and the competition objective.[26] An authorisation, issued by the FCA, is required by any person engaging in insurance business in the UK, including those persons who advise on insurance contracts (such as insurance brokers – persons advising on insurance contracts).[27] Before granting an authorisation, the FCA must be satisfied that the organisation will be soundly and prudently managed and that the individuals managing the organisation are fit and proper persons.[28] An authorisation brings a person within the 'regulatory perimeter' of FSMA 2000 and results in that person being bound by the regulatory rules made by the FCA under statutory authority as well as the process of supervision and enforcement associated with those rules. The FCA's regulation and supervision can be divided into two categories: prudential supervision for firms which focuses on solvency and financial stability; and conduct of business regulation for financial services firms and financial markets in the UK which focuses on the relationship between authorised persons and their customers.

Prudential supervision

Prudential supervision focuses on controlling the solvency and liquidity of participants in financial markets. There are two objectives. The first, which may be termed 'micro-prudential regulation', focuses on the solvency of individual financial enterprises and attempts to ensure that customers are not threatened by the risks to which financial institutions are exposed in the normal course of their business. In the case of insurers, the main risk faced by policyholders is that the pool of premiums held by the insurer may not be adequate to cover claims, i.e. insurer solvency. That may be the result of unexpectedly high levels of claims or a fall in the value of investments in which premiums are held by insurers. The second, which may be termed 'macro-prudential regulation', focuses on the stability of the financial system as a whole and the risks posed to it by the collapse of a financial firm and the instability that may spread across the entire financial system in those circumstances. Regulators attempt to protect customers from these risks by requiring insurers to have minimum levels of shareholders' capital (sometimes referred to as regulatory capital) and to hold a certain proportion of their assets in a liquid (readily realisable) form. This has the effect that, if the firm were to face financial difficulties, losses would be borne by shareholders before customers (policyholders) became affected. In this sense, prudential supervision uses regulatory capital to protect customers. Shareholders in financial institutions, on the other hand, like all 7.13

25 See FSMA 2000, s. 2B(2).

26 See FSMA 2000, s. 1B–1E.

27 FSMA 2000, s. 19 and s. 22(1). A firm registered in the EEA can engage in insurance business in any other EEA state through a branch or by way of freedom of services on the basis of an authorisation granted by another member state of the EEA (so-called 'passporting'). UK-based insurance firms lost this automatic right with Brexit.

28 See FSMA 2000, s. 55B and Sch. 6, para. 2E.

investors in ordinary equity capital, receive no special protection from the system of prudential regulation. Since it is they who stand to make the biggest gains if a business does well, they must face the normal risks arising from equity investment in any business if things go badly, and their interests, as at common law, are postponed behind the firm's creditors.

Conduct of business regulation

7.14 Conduct of business regulation focuses on the relationship between a financial firm and its customers and operates through rules that control the manner in which individual financial transactions are conducted. They impose different types of obligations in different circumstances. Many are, in effect, disclosure (or related) obligations, such as the rules that require disclosure of information to a customer before a transaction is agreed. Others go beyond disclosure and limit the freedom of action of authorised persons or have important implications for the structure of the market.[29] Insurance has a specific conduct of business sourcebook ('ICOBS') as well as falling under the more general rules ('COBS') which apply to all authorised persons.[30] While these conduct of business rules are essentially public law rules that do not form part of the contract between an insurer and a policyholder, they can have important implications for the contractual relationship. For example, so-called 'misselling' claims made by policyholders with regard to payment protection insurance ('PPI') are based on the failure on the part of insurers to observe conduct of business rules and have resulted in the insurance industry paying many billions of pounds in compensation to policyholders.[31]

INSURABLE INTEREST

The rationale for insurable interest

7.15 The principle of insurable interest is that only those who have a financial interest[32] in the occurrence of the insured event should be permitted to enter into and claim under an insurance policy. The origins of insurable interest

29 See further I MacNeil, *An Introduction to the Law on Financial Investment*, 2nd edn (Oxford: Hart Publishing, 2012), Ch. 6.

30 See the FCA Handbook at *https://www.handbook.fca.org.uk/handbook* (last accessed 2 September 2021).

31 For a discussion of the legal and regulatory background to PPI claims, see *R (ex parte British Bankers Association) v Financial Services Authority* [2011] EWHC 999 (Admin), [2011] Bus LR 1531.

32 See, e.g. the leading English textbook: J Birds et al., *MacGillivray on Insurance Law*, 14th edn (London: Sweet & Maxwell, 2018), para. 1–013. However, the law on insurable interest was reviewed in depth in the case of *Feasey v Sun Life Assurance Co of Canada* [2003] EWCA Civ 885, [2003] 2 All ER (Comm) 587. This case offers a new categorisation of insurable interest into the following: (1): interest in property – legal (property or contractual) or equitable right; (2): subject matter is the life of a person – life insurance with pecuniary interest in life of the person; (3): policy extends beyond a particular item of property to a project or adventure to which the property is important; (4): interests which are not strictly pecuniary: own life/ natural affection; valuable benefit; 'Pervasive interest': functional liability insurance, e.g. construction cases.

as a legal principle lie in the abuse of early forms of insurance as a form of gambling. This typically involved a person taking out a life insurance policy on a person in whose life they had no financial interest. Although gambling contracts were void under the common law in Scotland,[33] they could be enforced under the common law in England.[34] Parliament intervened to deter this abuse of insurance contracts by passing various Acts requiring insurable interest. As detailed at paras 7.16–7.24 below, the scope of these Acts does not make it entirely clear that insurable interest is a statutory requirement for all types of insurance. However, as the requirement of insurable interest is also recognised by the common law in Scotland, the problem of the scope of the statutory requirement is of limited relevance. Bell[35] refers to the common law principle in the following terms: 'It is essential to the contract of insurance that there shall be a subject in which the insured has an interest, a premium given or engaged for, and a risk run'. The scope of insurable interest is formulated in broad terms by Sheriff Guthrie, who in his edition of Bell's *Principles* states that: 'Interest is not limited to property but extends to every real and actual advantage and benefit arising out of or depending on the thing to which it refers. But one cannot insure a mere expectancy'.[36] As discussed below, the English common law and statutory formulations of insurable interest in non-life insurance have adopted a narrower approach.

Marine insurance

Legislation requiring insurable interest was first introduced in the field of marine insurance. The Marine Insurance Act 1745 made marine policies lacking interest, or with no further proof of interest than the policy itself, void. This Act was repealed by the 1906 Act, s. 4 of which makes policies lacking insurable interest void. Insurable interest is defined as 'any legal or equitable relation to the adventure or any insurable property at risk therein'.[37] The effect of that definition is to limit insurable interest to legal or equitable relations and to exclude loss suffered by a person who does not have a legal relationship with the property (e.g. a beneficiary under a will). It is not necessary that the insured has an insurable interest at the time of entering into the contract provided he has such an interest at the time of the loss.[38] **7.16**

Life assurance

The Life Assurance Act 1774 (the '1774 Act')[39] made insurable interest a statutory requirement for life assurance policies. Where there is no insurable **7.17**

33 The decision in *Bruce v Ross* (1787) Mor 9523 marked a change in the law as gambling contracts had previously been enforceable. The common law prohibition did not, however, prevent enforcement of contracts for the sharing of the proceeds of a gaming contract: see *Robertson v Anderson* 2003 SLT 235. Since the entry into force of s. 335(1) of the Gambling Act 2005 (in 2007) the fact that a contract relates to gambling does not prevent its enforcement.

34 *Jones v Randall* (1774) 1 Cowp 37, 98 ER 954.

35 Bell, *Principles*, 4th edn (1839), § 457.

36 Bell, *Principles*, 10th edn (1899), § 461.

37 1906 Act, s. 5(2).

38 1906 Act, s. 6(1).

39 1774 Act, s. 1.

interest the contract is void. The statute is silent on the issue of when insurable interest must exist. However, it was held in *Dalby v India and London Life Assurance Co*[40] that insurable interest is required only at the time of insuring and not at the time of death.

7.18 The 1774 Act does not define the circumstances in which there is an insurable interest in a person's life. However, the common law recognises that a person has an unlimited insurable interest in their own life.[41] An unlimited insurable interest in the life of a spouse is recognised both by common law[42] and by statute.[43] Provision is also made for policies effected by spouses on their own life for the benefit of their spouse and/or children to be deemed a trust for their benefit with the result that, following death, the policy proceeds do not form part of the deceased's estate but are instead paid directly to the beneficiary.[44]

7.19 In the case of all other relationships, whether within or outside a family, insurable interest can only exist where there is a financial interest in the life of the assured.[45] So in one case, a woman was held to have no insurable interest in the life of her stepmother; the policy was thus void, although she was entitled to repayment of the premiums.[46] The financial interest can arise from a contractual relationship, common examples being agency, partnership and employment. In *Turnbull & Co v Scottish Provident Institution*,[47] for example, a firm of merchants insured the life of their agent in Iceland, through whom they carried on a lucrative business, and were held entitled to recover the proceeds after his death. In such cases the sum assured is limited to the financial interest. Insurable interest can also arise from a financial interest based on an obligation of aliment. Under s. 1 of the Family Law (Scotland) Act 1985 parents owe an obligation of aliment to their children but children do not owe an obligation to their parents. It follows that parents do not have an insurable interest in the lives of their children *qua* parent[48] but may have such an interest *qua* creditor or employer.

7.20 The Law Commissions suggested that the requirement for insurable interest in life assurance might be ended or alternatively that its scope should be widened.[49] They have consulted extensively on the question of insurable interests over the years and published a draft Bill for consultation in April

40 (1854) 15 CB 365, 139 ER 465.
41 *Griffiths v Fleming* [1909] 1 KB 805 at 821.
42 *Wight v Brown* (1845) 11 D 459.
43 See, for spouses, the Married Women's Policies of Assurance (Scotland) Act 1880, s. 1; and for civil partners, the Civil Partnership Act 2004, s. 253(1).
44 Married Women's Policies of Assurance (Scotland) Act 1880, s. 2. Unlike the position in England under the Civil Partnership Act 2004, s. 70, this provision has not been extended to civil partners in Scotland.
45 The general principle is stated in Bell, *Principles*, § 457.
46 *Came v City of Glasgow Friendly Society* 1933 SC 69.
47 (1896) 34 SLR 146.
48 There is a statutory exception (limited to a sum assured of £800) in the case of policies issued by 'friendly societies' under the Friendly Societies Act 1992, s. 99.
49 See generally the Law Commission and Scottish Law Commission, *Insurance Contract Law Issues Paper 4: Insurable Interest* (2008).

2016.[50] The final draft Bill was published in 2018[51] and it adopts a relatively permissive approach to insurable interest. The draft Bill applies to contracts for 'life-related' insurance (insurance contracts relating to 'death, injury, ill-health or incapacity of an individual'). The 'life-related' insurance category has a broader character in comparison to the current term 'life assurance' as it encompasses both indemnity and contingency policies as long as they relate to a human life.[52] As explained above, under the current law, a policyholder may insure the life of another person if they would suffer a financial loss on the other's death. However, this category is extremely limited. The draft Bill sets out a broader economic interest test. It does not require a pecuniary interest recognised by law. Instead, an insured would have an insurable interest in any circumstance where they have a 'reasonable prospect' of suffering economic loss on the occurrence of the insured event (such as the death or illness of, or injury to, the person insured).[53] Clause 2 of the draft Bill also provides a non-exhaustive list of circumstances in which an insurable interest exists, which is longer than under the present law, e.g. an insured has an insurable interest in their own life, in the life of their spouse, civil partner, cohabitant (that is, an individual who lives with the insured as their spouse or civil partner), children or grandchildren.

Indemnity insurance: requirement of insurable interest

In the case of non-marine indemnity insurance, the requirement of insurable interest is recognised both by common law[54] and statute. Despite its title, the 1774 Act applies to insurance on any event with the exception of 'ships, goods and merchandises'. The Gaming Act 1845, which does not apply to Scotland, made contracts of gaming or wagering void. However, the common law principle (in Scotland) requiring insurable interest resolved any uncertainty in the application of the statutory provisions. Moreover, modern legislation has relaxed the common law rule, with financial contracts for the mitigation of risk, such as derivatives, in mind.[55] The same approach can be taken in relation to the issue of whether the 1774 Act applies to heritable property. In England, that issue remained unresolved until recent case law confirmed that it did not.[56] In Scotland it has been assumed that the general principle of insurable interest applies equally to heritable property. Thus, in *Arif v* **7.21**

50 The Law Commission and Scottish Law Commission, *Reforming Insurance Contract Law, Short Consultation on Draft Bill: Insurable Interest* (April 2016).

51 See *https://www.scotlawcom.gov.uk/law-reform/law-reform-projects/joint-projects/insurance-law/* (last accessed 2 September 2021).

52 The Law Commission and Scottish Law Commission, *Reforming Insurance Contract Law: Updated Draft Insurable Interest Bill for Review* (June 2018), para. 2.6 onward.

53 The Law Commission and Scottish Law Commission, *Reforming Insurance Contract Law: Updated Draft Insurable Interest Bill for Review* (June 2018), para. 2.24.

54 Bell, *Principles*, § 457. For the history, see L J Macgregor, 'Pacta Illicita' in K G C Reid and R Zimmermann (eds), *A History of Private Law in Scotland* (2000) Vol. II, p. 129.

55 FSMA 2000, s. 412 (the scope of application of which is, since 2007, now limited to Northern Ireland) and Gambling Act 2005, s. 335.

56 The Court of Appeal held in *Mark Rowlands Ltd v Berni Inns Ltd* [1986] 1 QB 211 that the 1774 Act did not apply to fire insurance on buildings: this decision was followed in *Siu Yin Kwan v Eastern Insurance Co Ltd* [1994] 2 AC 199.

Excess Insurance Group,[57] it was held that one partner in a hotel business could not claim under a fire policy in which he was named as the insured because the hotel was partnership property and the policy made no reference to the insured acting other than as a principal.

The scope of insurable interest in non-marine indemnity insurance

7.22 Bell's definition of insurable interest[58] clearly extends its scope beyond the ownership of heritable or moveable property. It can exist in relation to property which one does not own, subject to the existence of a financial interest. In *Fehilly v General Accident*,[59] the issue arose as to whether a tenant of a ballroom had an insurable interest in the building. A clause in the lease obliged the tenant to keep the building in good repair but gave the tenant the option of terminating the lease if major work was required. When the building was destroyed by fire the tenant claimed the full value of the building from the insurer. The insurer argued that the tenant was entitled only to recover to the extent of his loss, namely the market value of the lease. It was held that the tenant did not have an insurable interest in the full value of the building as the lease did not require the tenant to repair the fire damage. The tenant could only recover the market value of the lease. Similarly, a heritable creditor (such as a bank holding a standard security) has an insurable interest in property which is separate from that of the owner.[60]

7.23 In contracts for the sale of heritable property the purchaser has an insurable interest on conclusion of the contract (missives) and before the disposition has been recorded.[61] In contracts for the sale of goods a purchaser has an insurable interest from conclusion of the contract, irrespective of the time that risk or ownership passes:[62] the rationale being that loss of or damage to the property may diminish the value of the contractual rights of the purchaser. The general position is that it is not necessary to have a completed real right in property before there is an insurable interest; a sufficiently 'close relationship' with the property may suffice.[63] A seller of goods retains an insurable interest so long as they are in a legal position with regard to it such that any loss or damage to the property may result in loss to them. Trustees have an insurable interest in property held by them;[64] and, on one view, trustees may be bound to insure trust assets in order to discharge their duties as trustees.

7.24 Insurable interest can also exist in relation to potential legal liabilities in contract or delict. For example, if the tenant in *Fehilly* (above) had been contractually bound by the lease to reinstate the property following fire damage,

57 1986 SC 317. *Quaere* whether that approach contradicts the (limited) acceptance of the undisclosed principal doctrine to insurance contracts: see para. 7.30 below.

58 Bell, *Principles*, § 457.

59 *Fehilly v General Accident Fire and Life Insurance Corporation Ltd* 1982 SC 163.

60 *Bank of Scotland v Guardian Royal Exchange plc* 1995 SLT 763.

61 *Sloans Dairies v Glasgow Corporation* 1977 SC 223.

62 As to the transfer of risk and ownership see paras. 6. 90 and 6. 107.

63 *Cowan v Jeffrey Associates* 1998 SC 496 at 502F per Lord Hamilton (Ordinary); *Comlex Ltd (in Liquidation) v Allianz Insurance plc* [2016] CSOH 87 at [35] per Lord Doherty.

64 *Mitchell v Scottish Eagle Insurance Co Ltd* 1997 SLT 793 at 797E–797F per Lord Prosser (Ordinary).

he would have had an insurable interest in the full value of the building. Another example is the potential delictual liability which is insured under the third party section of a motor vehicle insurance policy. That form of insurance can cover both the insured and other drivers who may incur liability to third parties; and in that situation the other drivers are able to enforce the policy.[65]

FORMATION OF INSURANCE CONTRACTS

The proposal form

The normal contractual principles requiring an offer and an acceptance apply to insurance contracts. In some cases the offer is made by the proposer for insurance on the insurer's standard proposal form.[66] This asks for information about the proposer and the risk that is to be insured. The insurer then has the option of accepting the offer, or of making a counter-offer to the proposer. A potential difficulty is that the proposer is unlikely to be aware of the precise contract terms at the time of completing the proposal form. It can therefore be argued that there is no consensus at the time when the insurer accepts the proposal. This outcome is avoided by the inclusion in proposal forms of a statement that the proposer is applying for insurance on the insurer's standard terms.[67] It follows that, even if the reality is that the insured is not familiar with the standard terms, an objective analysis of contract formation will result in there being consensus when the insurer accepts the proposal.[68] 7.25

Basis of contract clauses

In the past, it was possible for some or all of the information contained in a proposal form to be converted into terms of the contract. That outcome was achieved through a 'basis of contract' clause which stated that the relevant information formed the basis of the contract. The result was that the relevant information was treated as a warranty and in the event of misrepresentation the insurer was entitled to avoid the contract regardless of the materiality of the misrepresentation.[69] While reliance on that technique had diminished in 7.26

65 The Contract (Third Party Rights) (Scotland) Act 2017 may also enable enforcement by third parties. The 2017 Act seeks to relax the formalities required for constitution of a *ius quaesitum tertio* at common law, in an insurance policy case: *Carmichael v Carmichael's Exrs* 1920 SC (HL) 195. In England, it is presumed that the insured acts as agent for other drivers: see *Williams v Baltic Insurance Association of London Ltd* [1924] 2 KB 282.

66 Completion of the proposal form can be in writing, orally or digitally. Proposal forms are not normally used for marine insurance or large commercial risks where the relevant information cannot be easily fitted into a standard format.

67 *General Accident Insurance Corporation v Cronk* (1901) 17 TLR 233. Even without such a clause, however, on first principles there will be consensus where there is agreement on the following essential terms of the contract: subject matter, risk, premium, duration and sum insured.

68 *Muirhead & Turnbull v Dickson* (1905) 7 F 686 and *Wood v Capita Insurance Services Ltd* [2017] UKSC 24, [2017] AC 1173.

69 *Dawsons Ltd v Bonnin* 1922 SC (HL) 156, discussing the importance of *Thomson v Weems* (1884) 11 R (HL) 48 above. See also para. 7.60.

the case of consumer insurance[70] as a result of self-regulation by insurers, it was ended by the CIDRA 2012;[71] however it remains possible for warranties to be expressly agreed and inserted into a consumer insurance policy. Even in non-consumer cases, s. 9 of the IA 2015, such a representation is not capable of being converted into a warranty.[72]

The cover note

7.27 Cover notes are temporary contracts of insurance issued by insurers pending the issue of an insurance policy or certificate. Their use is most common in relation to those classes of insurance where there is a statutory obligation to insure, for example, motor insurance. For such types of insurance it is important that the insured has proof of insurance (a certificate) from the outset of the period of cover. However, as technology has enabled insurers to speed up the process of issuing policies, cover notes are now much less common than they were in the past. Where they are issued, they normally incorporate, by reference, the insurer's standard policy terms.[73]

Agency and insurance contracts

7.28 The normal rules of agency law apply to insurance contracts. However, the application of these rules to the formation of insurance contracts is not always straightforward. The main difficulty is identifying the agent's principal. This problem arises from the manner in which insurance contracts are agreed. Most insurance agents who conclude insurance contracts are remunerated by the insurer. There is therefore a *prima facie* case for regarding them as agents of the insurer. However, an agent (particularly an independent broker) also advises the insured and can therefore be viewed as the agent of the insured. While it has been held that a Lloyd's broker[74] is always the agent of the insured,[75] there is no simple rule for other types of broker. In each case the position of the broker must be examined, particularly as regards the authority given by the insurer to the agent. An example of an agent being held to be the agent of the insurer is *Stockton v Mason*.[76] In that case, the insured advised his broker that he had changed his car from a Ford Anglia to an MG Midget. The broker confirmed that he would arrange for the change of car to be covered. The insured took this to mean that the existing cover for any authorised driver would apply to the MG. The plaintiff was injured as a passenger in the MG as a result of the negligent driving of the insured's son. The same day the insured received a letter from the insurers stating that only he himself was covered to drive the MG. The issue was therefore whether the insurers were bound by the broker's statement.[77] It

70 See para. 7.11 for the meaning of a consumer insurance contract.
71 CIDRA 2012, s. 6.
72 IA 2015, s. 16(1) prohibits contracting out s. 9.
73 *Re Coleman's Depositories Ltd and Life and Health Assurance Association* [1907] 2 KB 798.
74 A broker entitled to do business at Lloyd's of London (an insurance and reinsurance market located in London).
75 *Roberts v Plaisted* [1989] 2 Lloyd's Rep 341.
76 [1978] 2 Lloyd's Rep 430.
77 That issue was linked with the rule that a principal is deemed to know what their agent knows: see, e.g. *Woolcott v Excess Insurance Co Ltd* [1979] 1 Lloyd's Rep 231.

was held by the Court of Appeal that the insurers were bound as the broker had implied authority to confirm temporary cover and had clearly led the insured to believe that the existing cover had been extended.

In the case of consumer insurance, the status of an agent has been clarified by the CIDRA 2012.[78] Schedule 2 to the Act sets out the circumstances in which the agent will be the agent of the insurer[79] and provides that in other cases it is to be presumed that the agent is the agent of the insured unless, in the light of the circumstances, it appears otherwise. Examples of factors which may tend to show that the agent is acting for the insured are where an agent agrees to provide impartial advice, or the customer pays a fee. 7.29

Also relevant in this context are issues related to an unnamed or undisclosed principal.[80] In the first case, the agent discloses that he is acting as an agent but not the name of the principal. In the second case, the agent appears to act as principal but is in reality acting as agent. In the context of insurance two approaches to these situations are possible: one is to hold that the identity of the insured is material to the contract and therefore that the insurer cannot be bound to an unnamed or undisclosed principal; the other is to focus more on the insured risk and to ask whether the identity of the insured matters for that purpose. In approaching this issue the courts have tended towards the latter view, with the result that an unnamed or undisclosed principal is entitled to enforce a contract entered into by their agent.[81] In those circumstances, and contrary to the normal rule in agency law, the agent is also entitled to sue in their own name on behalf of the principal.[82] 7.30

GOOD FAITH, THE DUTY OF DISCLOSURE AND MISREPRESENTATION

The principle of good faith

The general principles of contract law do not require the parties to a contract to act in good faith towards each other either during contractual negotiations or at the time of the performance of the contract. There is a duty to avoid making misrepresentations to the other party but no duty to volunteer information or to co-operate with the other party. 7.31

Insurance contracts are one of a category of contracts in which there is an obligation of good faith imposed on the contracting parties. Lord President Inglis stated the common law in the following terms in *Life Association of* 7.32

78 CIDRA 2012, s. 9 and Sch. 2. There is no similar provision for the non-consumer contracts under the IA 2015.

79 For example, where the agent acts in the capacity of an appointed representative (aka 'tied agent') of the insurer under FSMA 2000, s. 39.

80 See para. 4.52 onward.

81 *National Oilwell (UK) Ltd v Davy Offshore (UK) Ltd* [1993] 2 Lloyd's Rep 582; *Cochran & Son v Leckie's Tr* (1906) 8 F 975. Cf *Haberdashers' Aske's Federation Trust Ltd v Lakehouse Contracts Ltd* [2018] EWHC 558 (TCC), [2018] Lloyd's Rep IR 382.

82 *Vandepitte v Preferred Accident Insurance Corporation of New York* [1933] AC 70 (although in that case there was, on the facts, no agency).

Scotland v Foster:[83] 'but contracts of insurance are in this, among other particulars, exceptional, in that they require on both sides *uberrima fides* [utmost good faith]'.[84] The same principle is to be found in s. 17 of the 1906 Act, as amended, which provides that 'a contract of marine insurance is a contract based upon the utmost good faith'. But although the duty of utmost good faith appears to be retained, it has been significantly modified by the changes made to the law of insurance by the CIDRA 2012 and the IA 2015. Importantly, s. 14(1) of the IA 2015 abolishes any rule of law permitting a party to avoid a contract of insurance on the ground that the utmost good faith has not been observed by the other party. Section 14(3) of the IA 2015 also repealed that part of s. 17 of the 1906 Act which provided that if utmost good faith is not observed by either party, the contract can be avoided by the other. Further, s. 14(2) of the IA 2015 modifies the duty of utmost good faith to the extent required by the provisions of the IA 2015 and the CIDRA 2012. It has been suggested that the extent of the duty of utmost good faith is that the insured should act honestly and not in bad faith.[85]

7.33 The obligation to act in good faith applies to the contract of insurance at all times: during the negotiations (subject to the provisions of CIDRA 2012 and IA 2015 mentioned at para. 7.32); during the period of insurance; and at the time of making a claim.[86] Both the insurer and the insured must act in good faith. Although the reported cases have dealt mainly with breaches of good faith by the insured, it is clear from the decision of the Court of Appeal in *Banque Keyser Ullmann SA v Skandia (UK) Insurance Co Ltd*[87] that the insurer can also be in breach of the principle.

The duty of disclosure: rationale

7.34 The duty of disclosure is the element of the obligation of good faith which is relevant to contractual negotiations between the insurer and the proposer. The rationale for the duty was expressed by Lord Mansfield in the early case of *Carter v Boehm*[88] in the following terms:

> 'The specific facts upon which the contingent chance is to be computed lie most commonly in the knowledge of the insured only: the underwriter trusts to his

83 (1873) 11 M 351 at 359.

84 The '*uberrima*' aspect is arguably superfluous, for it is not possible to be more honest than honest. In *Mutual and Federal Insurance Co Ltd v Oudtshoorn Municipality* 1985 (1) SA 419 (A) at 433C–433F, Joubert JA observed of the formulation 'uberrima fides' that it 'is an alien, vague, useless expression without any particular meaning in law'. This passage was quoted in *Manifest Shipping Co Ltd v Uni-Polaris Shipping Co Ltd ('The Star Sea')* [2001] UKHL 1, [2003] 1 AC 469 at [5]–[7] per Lord Clyde.

85 *The Star Sea* (n 84) at [111] per Lord Scott.

86 *Manifest Shipping Co Ltd v Uni-Polaris Insurance Co Ltd ('The Star Sea')* [1997] 1 Lloyd's Rep 360 at 372 per Leggatt L J. The House of Lords confirmed that utmost good faith does not come to an end when the contract has been made. However, it was underlined that the juridical basis for the application of the duty of utmost good faith to the later stages of the life of the contract is rather different and is of comparatively late development and there is even no general duty on the part of the assured to disclose further facts after the contract has been made: *The Star Sea* (n 84).

87 [1990] 1 QB 665 affd on different grounds, *sub nom Banque Financière de la Cité SA v Westgate Insurance Co Ltd* [1991] 2 AC 249.

88 (1766) 3 Burr 1905, 97 ER 1162.

representation and proceeds upon a confidence that he does not keep back any circumstance in his knowledge to mislead the underwriter into a belief that the circumstance does not exist, and to induce him to estimate the risk as if it did not exist.'

Thus, the essential elements which underlie the duty of disclosure are the superior knowledge of the insured in relation to the risk and the reliance of the underwriter on the information given by the insured.

What must be disclosed?

Consumer insurance

The CIDRA 2012 responded to concerns that the general law relating to disclosure was overly harsh towards consumers, who faced the risk that their insurance claims could be avoided if they did not comply with the onerous duty of disclosure.[89] The insurance industry had taken steps to mitigate the harshness of the law through self-regulatory measures, which were later incorporated into the conduct of business rules of the FCA.[90] As it was explained in para. 7.11 above, the 2012 Act applies only to a consumer insurance contract.[91] 7.35

The CIDRA 2012 Act abolishes the duty of disclosure for the purposes of consumer insurance contracts[92] and replaces it with a duty 'to take reasonable care not to make a misrepresentation'.[93] A failure by the consumer to comply with the insurer's request to confirm or amend particulars previously given amounts to a breach of this duty.[94] Importantly, the Act underlines that the duty exists only before the contract is formed or varied.[95] 7.36

The standard of care required is that of a reasonable consumer.[96] Based on s. 3(1) whether or not a consumer has taken reasonable care not to make a misrepresentation is to be determined in the light of all the relevant circumstances. The Act also refers to examples of factors that may need to be taken into account in determining reasonableness: 7.37

(a) the type of consumer insurance contract in question, and its target market;
(b) any relevant explanatory material or publicity produced or authorised by the insurer;
(c) how clear, and how specific, the insurer's questions were;
(d) in the case of a failure to respond to the insurer's questions in connection with the renewal or variation of a consumer insurance contract,

89 The CIDRA 2021 took effect generally from 6 April 2013.

90 See especially FCA Handbook, ICOBS 8.1.1 incorporating a modification of the duty of disclosure derived from the earlier (self-regulatory) Statements of Insurance Practice.

91 CIDRA 2012, s. 1. The case law issued before the CIDRA 2012 came into force is not applicable to the consumer insurance contracts.

92 CIDRA 2012, s. 2(4).

93 CIDRA 2012, s. 2(2).

94 CIDRA 2012, s. 2(3).

95 CIDRA 2012, s. 2(1).

96 Subject to two provisions: first, if the insurer was aware/ought to to have been aware of any particular characteristics or circumstances of the actual consumer, those are to be taken into account: s. 3(4); secondly, a misrepresentation made dishonestly is always to be taken as showing lack of reasonable care: s. 3(5).

how clearly the insurer communicated the importance of answering those questions (or the possible consequences of failing to do so); and

(e) whether or not an agent was acting for the consumer.[97]

7.38 The Act also modifies the remedies[98] available to an insurer following a qualifying misrepresentation. In the case of a deliberate or reckless misrepresentation[99] the insurer is entitled to avoid the contract, to refuse to pay claims and to retain the premium (unless retention would be unfair to the insured). In *Southern Rock Insurance Co Ltd v Hafeez*[100] an insurance company failed to satisfy the onus put upon it[101] to prove that a driver to whom it had granted a car insurance policy had deliberately or recklessly misrepresented his address, and it was not entitled to avoid the policy on that basis. On the other hand, in *Tesco Underwriting Ltd v Achunche*[102] an insurer was held to be entitled to avoid an insurance policy where a policyholder had deliberately and/or recklessly failed to disclose his previous motoring conviction when applying for insurance. With regard to careless misrepresentation[103] the position is more complex. If the insurer would not have entered the contract had the true position been stated, the contract can be avoided. If the insurer would have entered the contract on different terms, those terms are to apply. If the insurer would have entered the contract only at a higher premium the principle of proportionality is applied so as to adjust claims to correspond with the shortfall in the premium.[104]

Non-consumer insurance

7.39 For contracts concluded on or after 12 August 2016, the IA 2015 replaces the existing law on disclosure in non-consumer contracts[105] (including the 1906 Act, ss. 18 and 20)[106] with a new duty of a 'fair representation of the risk'.[107] This duty exists only before the contract is entered into or renewed.[108] The IA 2015 does not make fundamental changes as far as non-consumer contracts are concerned, also in non-consumer contracts it is possible to exclude the operation of the IA 2015.[109] Therefore, most of the common law remains relevant in this context.[110]

97 CIDRA 2012, s. 3(2).
98 CIDRA 2012, ss. 4 and 5 and Sch. 1.
99 A qualifying misrepresentation is deliberate or reckless if the consumer: (a) knew that it was untrue or misleading, or did not care whether or not it was untrue or misleading; and (b) knew that the matter to which the misrepresentation related was relevant to the insurer, or did not care whether or not it was relevant to the insurer: CIDRA 2012, s. 5(2).
100 [2017] CSOH 127, 2017 SLT 1159.
101 As required by CIDRA 2012, s. 5(4).
102 [2016] EWHC 3869 (QB).
103 A qualifying misrepresentation is careless if it is not deliberate or reckless: CIDRA 2012, s. 5(3).
104 Thus, if a premium of £200 were paid when it should have been £300, only two thirds of a claim will be paid.
105 A contract of insurance that is not a consumer insurance contract: IA 2015, s. 1.
106 IA 2015, s. 21(2).
107 IA 2015, s. 3(2).
108 IA 2015, s. 3(1).
109 IA 2015, ss. 16(2) and 17.
110 See paras 7.44–7.52.

A fair presentation of the risk is a presentation: 7.40

- which discloses every material circumstance that the insured knows or ought to know;[111] or failing that, which discloses enough to put a prudent insurer on notice that it needs to make further enquiries to reveal those material circumstances;
- which makes the disclosure in a manner that would be reasonably clear and accessible to a prudent insurer;
- in which every material representation as to a matter of fact is substantially correct; and
- every material representation as to a matter of expectation or belief is made in good faith.[112]

Unless the insurer makes a specific enquiry, the fair presentation obligation in s. 3(4) does not require the insured to disclose a circumstance if it: diminishes the risk; the insurer knows it; ought to know it; is presumed to know it; or it is something as to which the insurer waives information.[113]

Section 7 makes further provision about the duty of fair presentation. It contains the following definition of material circumstance and material representation: 'A circumstance or representation is material if it would influence the judgement of a prudent insurer in determining whether to take the risk and, if so, on what terms'.[114] Section 7(4) sets out three examples of things that may constitute material circumstances: 7.41

- special or unusual facts relating to the risk;
- any particular concerns which led the insured to seek insurance cover for the risk; and
- anything which those concerned with the class of insurance and field of activity in question would generally understand as being something that should be dealt with in a fair presentation of risks of the type in question.

Whether circumstances falling within these examples are in fact 'material' will depend on the facts of each case.

The IA 2015 also codifies the parties' remedies.[115] The insurer has a remedy against the insured for a breach of the duty of fair presentation only if the insurer shows that, but for the breach, the insurer would not have entered into the contract of insurance at all, or would have done so only on different terms. The breach for which the insurer has a remedy against the insured is referred to as a 'qualifying breach'[116] and the Act distinguishes between a breach that 7.42

111 IA 2015, s. 4 provides for what an insured knows or ought to know; and s. 6 clarifies what is included in an individual's 'knowledge': included is not only actual knowledge but also 'blind eye' knowledge. In *Economides v Commercial Union Assurance plc* [1998] QB 587 the value of the home contents of the insured were much higher than he stated but he genuinely thought that the information was correct. It was held the insurance company could not avoid the contract and liability as the insured has no obligation to establish the true position.

112 IA 2015, s. 3(3)–(4).

113 IA 2015, s. 3(5). Sections 5 and 6 are also relevant here.

114 The term 'material' comes from ss. 18(2) and 20(2) of the 1906 Act (now repealed) and the common law. See paras 7.44–7.52 below.

115 IA 2015, s. 8 and Sch. 1.

116 IA 2015, s. 8(4).

is either deliberate or reckless;[117] and a breach that is neither deliberate nor reckless. Where the breach is deliberate or reckless the insurer can avoid the contract, refuse all claims and need not return any of the premiums paid by the insured.[118] Where the breach is not deliberate or reckless the remedy depends on what the insurer would have done had the insurer known the true facts. If the insurer would not have entered into the contract on any terms the insurer may avoid the contract and refuse all claims but must return the premiums paid to the insured. If the insurer would have entered into the contract, but on different terms (except terms regarding the premium), then the contract is treated as if it includes those different terms. Finally, if the insurer would have levied a higher premium, the insurer may reduce proportionately the amount to be paid to the insured on a claim.

7.43 *Young v Royal and Sun Alliance plc*[119] is the first judgment to consider the duty of fair presentation. A fire occurred at the insured's property and £7.2 million was claimed from his insurers. The insurer rejected the claim on the basis that the insured failed to disclose the fact that he had been the director of four companies that had been dissolved after an insolvent liquidation in the five-year period prior to the policy. The reclaimer accepted that before a contract of insurance was entered into, the insured had to make a fair presentation of the risk to the insurer in terms of s. 3 of the IA 2015. The insured's defence was that insurer had waived disclosure of this information – in terms of s. 3 (5) of the IA 2015 – relying on the terms of an email that the insurer had sent in response to the insured's proposal (a market presentation document). The Inner House held that there was no waiver in the circumstances. This meant that the insurer was entitled to avoid the policy. To reach this decision, the court looked at the nature of an enquiry and what form that would have to take. It was found that a reasonable reader of the insurer's email would not have understood it as containing an enquiry that was to be construed as an expression of limited concern about the pursuer's past experience of insolvency such as to exclude the undisclosed information from what was required to be disclosed for a fair presentation of the risk. This case also confirms that the IA 2015 did not change the law on when an insurer waives its right to disclosure.

Pre-IA 2015 Law

7.44 As indicated above, the statutory changes introduced by IA 2015 regarding the duty of disclosure are of limited relevance for non-consumer insurance. Also, in non-consumer contracts it is possible to exclude the operation of the IA 2015.[120] Hence, most of the common law remains relevant in this context. Further, the IA 2015 does not apply to insurance contracts entered into, or varied,[121] prior to 12 August 2016. At common law, and under the 1906 Act, the duty of disclosure requires the proposer to disclose every material circum-

117 If the insured: (i) knew that it was in breach of the duty of fair presentation; or (ii) did not care whether or not it was in breach of that duty.
118 IA 2015, s. 8 and Sch. 1, para. 2.
119 [2020] CSIH 25, 2020 SC 467.
120 IA 2015, ss. 16(2) and 17.
121 IA 2015, s. 2(2)(b).

stance that is known to the proposer.[122] The insurer is required to disclose any facts known to them, but not to the proposer, which would reduce the risk.[123] A failure to observe the duty of disclosure allows the other party to avoid the contract. The proposer clearly cannot be expected to disclose information they do not know,[124] but they are assumed to know information that is common knowledge in their business.[125] The proposer is also assumed to know information which they could discover by making enquiries.[126]

The duty of disclosure lasts until the contract is agreed between the insurer and the proposer. There is no obligation to disclose information during the period in which the insurance is in force.[127] However, if the contract is renewed, the duty of disclosure revives at each successive renewal since each renewal is treated as a new contract.[128] **7.45**

The material circumstance that must be disclosed by each party to the contract was defined as follows by s. 18(2) of the 1906 Act: 'Every circumstance is material which would influence the judgment of a prudent insurer in fixing the premium, or determining whether he will take the risk'. In *Life Association of Scotland v Foster*,[129] Lord President Inglis suggested that materiality was to be judged in all forms of insurance[130] by reference to what a reasonable man would consider material. But the decision of the Inner House in *Hooper v Royal London General Insurance Co Ltd*[131] confirms that, in the case of indemnity contracts, materiality is to be judged from the perspective of the prudent insurer. In *Hooper*, the insurer refused to pay a claim on the basis of non-disclosure. The pursuer sued for payment on the basis that a non-disclosure could only be material if it would be considered as such by a reasonable person in the position of the insured. The court rejected that argument, holding that the test of the reasonable insurer was applicable to all insurance contracts with the sole exception of life cover.[132] **7.46**

Two issues have dominated judicial interpretation of the statutory definition in 1906 Act, s. 18. The first is the meaning of 'influence' in s. 18(2). Here, the focus has been on whether influence refers to a decisive influence or whether it simply refers to information that a prudent underwriter would wish to have but that would not necessarily change their mind on the decision to insure or the terms of insurance. The second major issue has been whether, in order to avoid a contract, an insurer simply has to prove non-disclosure **7.47**

122 *Life Association of Scotland v Foster* (1873) 11 M 351; 1906 Act, s. 18(1).
123 *Banque Keyser Ullmann SA*, affd (n 87) above on different grounds.
124 *Joel v Law Union and Crown Insurance Co* [1908] 2 KB 863 at 884 per Fletcher-Moulton LJ: 'The duty is a duty to disclose and you cannot disclose what you do not know'.
125 1906 Act, s. 18(1).
126 *Highlands Insurance Co v Continental Insurance Co* [1987] 1 Lloyd's Rep 109.
127 *Banque Keyser Ullmann SA*, affd (n 87) above on different grounds. A policy may, however, require the insured to report a material change of circumstances to the insurer and in some cases the cover may not extend to the new circumstances.
128 *Lambert v Co-operative Insurance Society* [1975] 2 Lloyd's Rep 485.
129 (1873) 11 M 351 at 359.
130 Although, for marine insurance, the test is contained in 1906 Act, s. 18(2) (for pre-August 2016 contracts).
131 1993 SC 242.
132 IA 2015, s. 7(3) and (5) also refer to the 'prudent insurer'.

or misrepresentation or whether it is necessary also to show that the non-disclosure or misrepresentation induced the insurer to enter into the contract.

7.48 In *Container Transport International Inc v Oceanus Mutual Underwriting Association (Bermuda) Ltd* ('*CTI v Oceanus*'),[133] the Court of Appeal held that a fact can be material even if its disclosure would not have changed the decision of the underwriter either as to the acceptance of the risk or the premium and the terms on which it would be accepted. In order to avoid the policy, an insurer simply had to show that there was non-disclosure of material information. This case formulated the law in a manner which clearly favoured insurers, in that they could avoid liability for non-disclosure of information that had no effect on their decision to insure. The matter subsequently came before the House of Lords in the case of *Pan Atlantic Insurance Co Ltd v Pine Top Insurance Co Ltd* ('*Pan Atlantic*')[134] in the form of two separate, but related, issues:

(a) Could a fact be material even if it would not have had any effect on a prudent insurer's decision to accept the insurance or the terms on which it was accepted (i.e. was *CTI v Oceanus* correctly decided on this point)?
(b) In order for an insurer to avoid liability under a policy was it enough simply to show that there had been non-disclosure of a material fact or was it also necessary for the insurer to prove that the non-disclosure had induced them to enter into the contract?

7.49 On the first point, the House of Lords (by a majority of three to two) followed the decision in *CTI v Oceanus*. On the second point, the House of Lords unanimously overruled *CTI v Oceanus*, holding that it was necessary for an insurer to show that they had been induced into making the contract by the non-disclosure. Subsequent cases have established that inducement is a question of fact and must be established by the insurer as a causal factor, albeit not the only one, for entering the contract on the relevant terms.[135]

7.50 While *Pan Atlantic* may have settled the law in England, it was by no means inevitable that the same solution would be adopted in Scotland. While the general law of misrepresentation in Scotland requires inducement[136] for the avoidance of a contract, that in itself does not resolve the issue of the role of inducement in non-disclosure (as illustrated by the uncertainty in the law in England prior to *Pan Atlantic*). However, judicial consideration of *Pan Atlantic* in Scotland has proceeded on the basis that the same principles apply to Scotland.[137]

7.51 In the case of life assurance, it was established in *Life Association of Scotland v Foster*[138] that the test of materiality in Scotland is that of the reasonable insured. In that case the insured replied in the negative to a question asking if

133 [1984] 1 Lloyd's Rep 476.
134 [1995] 1 AC 501.
135 *Assicurazioni Generali SpA v Arab Insurance Group (BSC)* [2003] 1 WLR 577 (CA); *Lewis v Norwich Union Healthcare Ltd* [2010] Lloyd's Rep IR 198.
136 *Menzies v Menzies* (1893) 20 R (HL) 108. Misrepresentation is considered in more detail below.
137 *Mitchell v Hiscox Underwriting Ltd* [2010] CSIH 18; *Gaelic Assignments Ltd v Sharpe* 2001 SLT 914; *Unipac (Scotland) Ltd v Aegon Insurance Co (UK) Ltd* 1996 SLT 1197.
138 (1873) 11 M 351.

she had a rupture. She later died from rupture and it was discovered that, at the time of making the proposal, she did have a small swelling on her groin. However, she did not appreciate that this was a symptom of rupture. Lord President Inglis, delivering the leading judgment, observed that the insured was obliged only to state such facts as a reasonable person would consider likely to influence the insurer's decision to enter into a contract.[139]

In England, the courts chose, in the context of life assurance, to follow the test of the reasonable insurer in determining materiality.[140] This resulted in the test being the same for both life and indemnity contracts. However, as far as Scotland is concerned, the decision of the Inner House in the case of *Hooper v Royal London General Insurance Co Ltd*[141] confirmed that there remains a distinction between life and indemnity contracts. Lord Justice-Clerk Ross justified the application of the reasonable insured test to life assurance on the basis that questions asked in a life assurance proposal form are 'subjective and not capable of assessment on any objective basis', whereas questions asked in indemnity proposal forms could be objectively ascertained.[142] 7.52

Disclosure to intermediaries

Insurance contracts are often entered into through an intermediary such as an insurance broker. The normal rules of agency apply in this situation but there can be some difficulty in identifying for whom an agent is acting.[143] Almost all agents are paid by the insurer in the form of a commission but, despite this, the courts have held that there are situations in which an agent is taken to be acting on behalf of the insured and not the insurer. The issue (sometimes referred to as 'transferred agency') is of considerable importance in the context of the duty of disclosure because a principal is deemed to know information known to their agent: it follows that, where an agent acts on behalf of an insurer, the insurer is deemed to know information known by the agent. Closely related to this issue is the question of whether a proposer is always bound by a signature on a proposal form. 7.53

The cases of *Bawden v London, Edinburgh and Glasgow Assurance*[144] and *Newsholme Bros v Road Transport & General Insurance Co*[145] illustrate the difficulties that can arise in agency situations. In *Bawden*, an illiterate proposer with one eye applied for accident insurance. The agent filled out the proposal form on his behalf. At the end of the proposal there was a declaration stating that the proposer had no physical infirmity. The proposer signed the proposal form and claimed under the insurance when he lost his good eye. The insurers tried to avoid liability on the basis of non-disclosure but the court held that 7.54

139 (1873) 11 M 351 at 359.

140 *Mutual Life Insurance Co of New York v Ontario Metal Products Co Ltd* [1925] AC 344.

141 1993 SC 242.

142 For a critique of this case, see Forte, 'The materiality test in insurance' [1994] LMCLQ 557. The issue was revisited in *Cuthbertson v Friends' Provident Life Office* [2006] CSOH 74, 2006 SLT 567, with Lord Eassie re-affirming the approach in *Life Association of Scotland v Foster* (n 122).

143 See paras 7.28–7.30 above.

144 [1892] 2 QB 534.

145 [1929] 2 KB 356.

the agent had acted for the insurer and therefore the insurer was aware of the insured's physical condition. In *Newsholme*, the agent entered incorrect information in the proposal despite being told the truth by the proposer. The proposer signed the proposal form in the knowledge that the information inserted by the agent was untrue. It was held[146] that the agent had acted for the insured and that the insured was bound by his signature. The result was that the insurer was able to avoid the policy on the basis of misrepresentation.

7.55 The approach adopted in *Bawden* was followed in *Stone v Reliance Mutual Insurance Society Ltd*,[147] but the *Newsholme* approach is supported by the cases of *Biggar v Rock Life Assurance Co*[148] and *McMillan v Accident Insurance Co Ltd*.[149] While these cases are not entirely irrelevant following the introduction of the provisions of the CIDRA 2012 dealing with the status of agents, they are of less direct relevance and subordinate to the statutory provisions. However, three principles derived from the cases would appear to remain good law: (1) a signature on a proposal form will normally bind the proposer whether the document has been read or not (*Newsholme*);[150] (2) an insurer's agent who acts fraudulently is acting outside their authority. Information fabricated by an agent cannot therefore be imputed to the insurer (*Biggar and Newsholme*); and (3) where the insurer's agent acts honestly but induces the proposer to sign a proposal form in the belief that it is complete and correct, the insurer cannot avoid liability on the basis of non-disclosure (*Bawden*).

Misrepresentation

7.56 Misrepresentation is the giving of false information to the other contracting party. It is in essence an act of deception and therefore different from non-disclosure which involves the withholding of information.[151] Misrepresentation can occur innocently, negligently or fraudulently. In all three instances, the general principles of contract law allow the contract to be avoided where one party has been induced by a misrepresentation into entering into the contract.[152] However, in an insurance context, misrepresentation is not particularly important as the insurer is more likely to rely on the wider duty of disclosure.

146 *Bawden* was distinguished in this case.
147 [1972] 1 Lloyd's Rep 469.
148 [1902] 1 KB 516.
149 1907 SC 484.
150 For a more recent application of this principle in the context of banking, see *Grant Estates Ltd v The Royal Bank of Scotland plc* [2012] CSOH 133 at [77] per Lord Hodge (Ordinary).
151 Despite the clear difference in principle, the distinction may be more difficult to maintain in practice. For example, if a question in a motor insurance proposal relating to previous accidents involving the insured is left blank when the insured has been involved in several, is this a non-disclosure or a misrepresentation?
152 *Menzies v Menzies* (1893) 20 R (HL) 108.

THE INSURANCE POLICY

Insured risks and exceptions

Most insurance policies contain some form of exception to the cover. They can be either general exceptions that apply to the whole policy (e.g. a motor policy that excludes the use of a car for business purposes) or specific exceptions that apply to a particular insured peril (e.g. a commercial vehicle policy that covers theft of goods from the vehicle, but not while the vehicle is left unattended overnight). The effect of the operation of an exception is that the insurer is off risk during the time that the exception operates but comes back on risk when the exception ceases to operate. For example, in *Roberts v Anglo-Saxon Insurance Association Ltd*,[153] the insurer of a van insured for business use only was held to be off risk when the van was used by the insured to drive to his golf club but was back on risk once the insured returned to his work. **7.57**

Warranties: nature, definition, identification

Warranties are fundamental terms of an insurance contract. [154] Section 33(1) of the 1906 Act makes clear the type of obligation which can be the subject of a warranty: **7.58**

> 'A warranty, in the following sections relating to warranties, means a promissory warranty, that is to say, a warranty by which the assured undertakes that some particular thing shall or shall not be done, or that some condition shall be fulfilled, or whereby he affirms or negatives the existence of a particular state of facts.'

Following this definition, warranties can be divided into two categories.

1. Warranties relating to future facts: This is the most common form of warranty. It requires the insured to conform to a certain pattern of behaviour during the period of cover. Examples of such warranties are that the insured is obliged to set a burglar alarm when premises are unoccupied (to deter burglars) or to maintain a sprinkler system in good working order at all times (to prevent the spread of fire).
2. Warranties relating to past or present facts: In this situation the insured affirms or negatives the existence of a particular state of facts at the time that the insurance contract is agreed. Where such a warranty relates clearly to the past and present, it will not be taken to apply to the future.

For example in *Kennedy v Smith & Ansvar Insurance Co Ltd*[155] a proposer for motor insurance completed a proposal form together with an 'abstinence and membership declaration' in which he stated that he was and had always been an abstainer from alcohol. However, the euphoria of victory in a bowling match led him to consume his first ever alcoholic beverage. Later, when driving home, he swerved off the road and his two passengers were killed. The insurers denied liability under the policy on the basis that, at the time of the **7.59**

153 (1927) 27 Lloyd's Law Rep 313.

154 See *Dawsons Ltd* 1922 SC (HL) 156, discussing the importance of *Thomson v Weems* (1884) 11 R (HL) 48.

155 1975 SC 266.

accident, the abstinence declaration was false as the insured was under the influence of alcohol. The court held that the warranty could not be taken to cover the future conduct of the insured (despite this being the intention of the insurer) and therefore the insurer was liable to pay the claim. If the warranty is based on the opinion of the insured, it can relate only to facts that are known to the insured. In *Hutchison v National Loan Fund Life Assurance Society*,[156] the insured warranted that she had no disease and enjoyed good health. It was held that this did not form a warranty against any latent disease which could only be discovered by post-mortem examination.

7.60 No special form of words is needed to create a warranty. It will often be the case that the word 'warranty' will be used, but this is not necessary. What is required is a form of words which makes clear that the relevant term is fundamental to the contract and that it requires strict compliance. In this context a distinction has been drawn between terms which are descriptive of the risk and those that are warranties: this is a matter of construction of the policy and turns on the issue of whether the term is intended to define the risk or to require strict compliance on the part of the insured.[157] As has been explained in para. 7.26 above, s. 6 of the CIDRA 2012 and s. 9 of the IA 2015 now prohibit consumer and non-consumer insurance contracts respectively from containing warranties created through the use of a 'basis of contract' clause.[158] The effect of such a clause was to turn all the information given in the proposal form into a warranty relating to past or present facts. Once this has occurred, any inaccuracy in the information given by the insured allowed the insurer to avoid the contract, even if the information was not material to the insurer's assessment of the risk.[159]

The consequences of breach of warranty

7.61 Prior to August 2016, the consequences of a breach of warranty were made clear by s. 33(3) of the 1906 Act:[160]

> 'A warranty, as above defined [in section 33(1)], is a condition which must be exactly complied with, whether it be material to the risk or not. If it be not so complied with, then, subject to any express provision in the policy, the insurer is discharged from liability as from the date of the breach of warranty, but without prejudice to any liability incurred by him before that date.'

Under the old law the consequences of the breach of warranty were harsh for the insured. There was no need for the insurer to show a causal connection between the breach of warranty and a loss in order to avoid the contract.[161] However, the insurer was not released from liability in relation to losses which

156 (1845) 7 D 467.

157 See, e.g. *Farr v Motor Traders' Mutual Insurance Society Ltd* [1920] 3 KB 669, where the issue turned on the interpretation of a term (incorporated into the policy via a 'basis of contract clause') stating that taxis were driven in only one shift each day.

158 An example of such a clause is: 'I hereby confirm that the information contained in the proposal form is complete and accurate and will form the basis of the contract'.

159 *Unipac (Scotland) Ltd v Aegon Insurance Co (UK) Ltd* 1996 SLT 1197.

160 Repealed by IA 2015.

161 *Geofizika DD v MMB International Ltd* [2010] EWCA Civ 459, [2011] 1 All ER (Comm) 492; *Jones & James v Provincial Insurance Co Ltd* (1929) 35 Lloyd's Law Rep 135.

occurred before the breach – the breach operated to release the insurer only from any future liability under the policy. No specific action was required on the part of the insurer in order to be released[162] and the option was open to the insurer to waive the breach and allow the policy to remain in force.[163]

Breach of warranty for both consumer and non-consumer insurance contracts is now regulated by ss. 10 and 11 of the IA 2015. Section 10(1) of the IA 2015 provides that any rule of law that breach of a warranty (express or implied) in a contract of insurance results in the discharge of the insurer's liability under the contract is abolished, which means that the insurer is not automatically discharged from liability under the contract. If there is a breach of warranty the insurer has no liability for any loss occurring after the warranty has been breached and before the breach has been remedied.[164] This does not apply if: **7.62**

- because of a change of circumstances, the warranty ceases to be applicable to the circumstances of the contract;
- compliance with the warranty is rendered unlawful by any subsequent law; or
- the insurer waives the breach of warranty.[165]

Before the IA 2015 came into force a breach of warranty allowed the insurer to escape liability even if the breach was unconnected with the loss that occurred. Now, as a consequence of s. 11, which covers terms not relevant to the actual loss, this is no longer the case. This section provides that if a loss occurs, and the warranty has not been complied with, the insurer may not rely on the non-compliance to exclude, limit or discharge its liability under the contract for the loss, if the insured shows that the non-compliance with the term could not have increased the risk of the loss that actually occurred in the circumstances in which it occurred. **7.63**

Subject to the controls and transparency requirements in s. 17, it is possible to contract out of ss. 10 and 11 in a non-consumer insurance contract: s. 16(2) IA 2015. However, it is not possible to do so in a consumer insurance contract.[166] **7.64**

Construction of insurance contracts

The normal rules for the construction of contracts apply to insurance.[167] The policy is to be interpreted objectively by asking what a reasonable person, with all the background knowledge which would reasonably have been available to the parties when they entered into the contract, would have understood the language of the contract to mean. This involves a consideration of the words used in their documentary, factual and commercial context.[168] That meaning is assessed in the light of: (i) the natural and ordinary meaning; (ii) any other **7.65**

162 *Bank of Nova Scotia v Hellenic Mutual War Risks Association (Bermuda) Ltd* ('*The Good Luck*') [1992] 1 AC 233.
163 1906 Act, s. 34(3).
164 IA 2015, s. 10(2).
165 IA 2015, s. 10(3).
166 IA 2015, s. 15.
167 *Wood* (n 68), approved in *Burnett v International Insurance Co of Hanover Ltd* [2021] UKSC 12, 2021 SC (UKSC) 1.
168 *Burnett* (n 167) at [29] per Lord Hamblen.

relevant provision of the contract; (iii) the overall purpose of the provision; (iv) the facts and circumstances known or assumed by the parties at the time that the document was executed; (v) commercial common sense; but (vi) disregarding subjective evidence of the parties' intentions.[169] The *contra proferentem* principle,[170] which requires any ambiguity in a contract to be construed against the *proferens* (the person relying on the ambiguous term), is relevant only in a case of genuine ambiguity or real doubt.[171]

Assignation

7.66 The rights of the insured or the insurer under a contract of insurance can, in principle, be assigned to a third party.[172] There are, however, limitations on the extent to which assignation can take place. First, it is possible that the policy itself will contain a prohibition on assignation. An express contractual prohibition on assignation invalidates any assignation in breach of it.[173] Secondly, it is sometimes said that rights involving *delectus personae* cannot be assigned.[174] This is true in so far as it goes. But normally what is assigned is the right to payment under the policy and, as a general principle, there is no *delectus personae creditoris* in the payment of a sum of money.[175]

7.67 Where assignation is possible,[176] it will only be effective if it is intimated to the insurer. The Policies of Assurance Act 1867 is usually cited as requiring written intimation of 'the date and purport' of the assignation to be given to the insurer at a principal place of business. But the application of the 1867 Act to Scots law is doubtful;[177] and, in any event, policies of assurance are expressly covered by s. 4 of the Transmission of Moveable Property (Scotland) Act 1862. It is therefore possible that intimation of an assignation of rights under an insurance policy may be made in the normal way. The rights

169 *Arnold v Britton* [2015] UKSC 36, [2015] AC 1619 at [15], approved in *Wood* (n 68). See, e.g. *Scragg v United Kingdom Temperance & General Provident Institution* [1976] 2 Lloyd's Rep 227, where the term 'motor racing' was held to have a technical meaning which excluded hill climbing in which each vehicle set off separately and raced against the clock.

170 For which, see *Canada Steamship Lines Ltd v The King* [1952] AC 192; *Persimmon Homes Ltd v Ove Arup & Partners Ltd* [2017] EWCA Civ 373, [2017] 2 CLC 28 at [55]–[56]; *K/S Victoria Street v House of Fraser (Stores Management) Ltd* [2011] EWCA Civ 904, [2012] Ch 497 at [68].

171 *Burnett* (n 167), [29].

172 Bell, *Principles*, 4th edn (1839), § 520, referring to a life assurance policy, states 'and as it is assignable, it is useful as a fund of credit'.

173 *James Scott Ltd v Apollo Engineering Ltd* 2000 SC 228.

174 *Cole v C H Handasyde & Co* 1910 SC 68 at 73 per Lord President Dunedin. This decision, however, confuses the contractual relationship as a whole with individual rights arising out of it. Individual rights, particularly rights to payment, are normally freely assignable (unless there is an express prohibition).

175 See R G Anderson, *Assignation* (Edinburgh: Edinburgh Legal Education Trust, 2008), para. 2–34 onward.

176 Assignation occurs most commonly in life assurance. Although it results in a change in the person to whom the sum assured is payable, the life assured/creditor, and therefore the risk, remains the same. An assignation immediately following the conclusion of a life contract can effectively circumvent the requirement for insurable interest, but the courts have not limited assignation on this basis.

177 Scottish Law Commission, *Report on Moveable Transactions, Volume 1: Assignation of Claims* (Scot. Law Com. No. 249, 2017), paras 13.21–13.23.

of the assignee are governed by the principle *assignatus utitur jure auctoris* (the assignee assumes the rights of the cedant) and priority among assignees is determined by the date of receipt of the notice. An example of this in the context of insurance is the case of *Scottish Widows' Fund and Life Assurance Society v Buist*.[178] The insured failed to disclose his addiction to alcohol at the time the contract was agreed. The policy was later assigned to a third party. When the insured died at the age of thirty, the insurer sought to avoid the assignee's claim for payment. It was held that as the assignee stood in the same position as the cedant (the insured), the insurer could avoid the policy.

Third party rights

An insurance contract imposes obligations only on the insured and the insurer and therefore, in principle, third parties are not able to enforce the contract for their own benefit. This principle holds good even when a third party has a valid claim against the insured which is covered by an insurance policy. However, there are three important exceptions to this principle. First, a pursuer with a claim against an insured party may have direct rights of action against the insurer. One example is under the Third Parties (Rights against Insurers) Act 2010(the 2010 Act),[179] which in cases where the insured is insolvent[180] allows third parties to issue proceedings directly against the insurer, by virtue of a statutory assignation of the insured's rights under the insurance contract.[181] Although those rights may now be vested without having established the relevant person's liability, the third party may not enforce those rights without having established that liability.[182] For instance, in *Burnett v International Insurance Co of Hanover Ltd*, Mr Grant died following an assault by a door steward employed by PSL (which had obtained public liability insurance coverage from Hanover). His widow, Ms Burnett claimed directly against the insurer under the 2010 Act as PSL was in liquidation. The Inner House held that Hanover was obliged to indemnify PSL and that this right vested in Ms Burnett under the 2010 Act.[183] Similarly, even outside of insolvency, it is possible for a pursuer to convene the primary wrongdoer's insurers as defenders to the action.[184] **7.68**

Secondly, in the case of compulsory motor insurance, s. 151 of the RTA 1988 requires insurers to pay directly to third parties any sums covered by a motor insurance policy. The reference to compulsory (third party) insurance under **7.69**

178 (1876) 3 R 1078.

179 The 2010 Act repealed the Third Parties (Rights against Insurers) Act 1930. The 2010 Act implements recommendations made by the Law Commissions in *Third Parties (Rights Against Insurers) Act 1930* (Consultation Paper No. 152, 1997).

180 Under the 2010 Act, s. 1 anyone who becomes insolvent for the purposes of the Act incurs a liability when damage was caused, not when a claimant established a right to compensation, see *Redman v Zurich Insurance plc* [2017] EWHC 1919 (QB), [2018] 1 WLR 280.

181 2010 Act, s. 1(2); *Cheltenham & Gloucester plc v Sun Alliance and London Insurance plc* 2001 SC 965.

182 2010 Act, s. 1(3). By comparison, under the 1930 Act the claim must have been established in legal proceedings against the insured: *Bradley v Eagle Star Insurance Co Ltd* [1989] AC 957 at 960 per Lord Brandon.

183 [2019] CSIH 9, 2019 SC 379, affd [2021] UKSC 12, 2021 SC (UKSC) 1.

184 European Communities (Rights against Insurers) Regulations 2002 (SI 2002/3061).

the RTA 1988[185] has the effect of limiting the defences which would normally be available to the insurer. In particular, s. 151 facilitates claims brought by third parties when a driver is not insured according to the terms of the policy. In those circumstances an insurer is liable to pay claims falling within compulsory insurance subject to a right of relief against any person who caused or permitted the use of the vehicle which gave rise to the liability. To benefit from s. 151, a third party must first obtain judgment against the insured and must give notice of the proceedings against the insured to the insurer, so as to allow the insurer the opportunity to defend the case.

7.70 Thirdly, persons covered by an insurance policy (such as a driver under a motor policy) are able to enforce the policy despite not being a party to the contract.[186] Further, as shown above, the Act 2010 enables direct enforcement by a third party against the insurer following the insolvency of the insured. However, even when the insured is solvent, a third party who is expressly covered by the terms of the policy (e.g. as a driver in motor insurance) is able to enforce the policy.[187]

CLAIMS

Notice of loss

7.71 A policy will normally oblige an insured to notify the insurers of a loss within a specified time limit or, if none is stipulated, within a reasonable time. In principle, non-compliance with such a term defeats a claim under the policy, at least when the term is construed as a condition precedent to the liability of the insurer. However, there are two ways in which the insured may be protected from this outcome. One is that the courts may interpret such clauses *contra proferentem*, thereby extending the time period within which notification may be made.[188] The other is that such a clause may be struck down as unfair in a consumer insurance contract under Part 2 of the CRA 2015 on unfair terms.[189]

7.72 An additional obligation often contained in a policy is that 'full particulars' – which mean the best particulars the assured can reasonably give[190] – of the loss must be given to the insurer and that the insured must co-operate with the insurer, such as by not admitting liability to, or settling with, a third party who has suffered loss. If such a clause is interpreted as a condition precedent to liability it may defeat a claim, but subject once again to interpretation *contra proferentem* and the possibility that the term may be invalid under Part 2 of the CRA 2015 on unfair terms. Conversely, if such a clause is interpreted as a standard contract term, any claim by the insurer for damages following breach must demonstrate loss resulting from the breach.[191]

185 RTA 1988, s. 145.
186 See para. 7.24 above.
187 See n 65 above.
188 See, e.g. *Verelst's Administratrix v Motor Union Insurance Co Ltd* [1925] 2 KB 137.
189 See para. 7.11 for general comment on the scope of the CRA 2015 with regard to insurance.
190 *Mason v Harvey* (1853) 155 ER 1585, at 1585–1586.
191 In *Porter v Zurich Insurance Co* [2009] EWHC 376 the insurer was unable to prove loss

Proximate cause

In order to claim under an indemnity policy,[192] the insured must show that loss or damage has been proximately caused by an insured peril. If loss or damage results from a cause other than an insured peril, the insurer is not liable.[193] The proximate cause of loss is the dominant or effective cause of that loss. It does not have to be the only cause of the loss, nor need it be the cause which operates closest in time to the loss. For example, in *Leyland Shipping Co Ltd v Norwich Union Fire Insurance Society Ltd*[194] there were two possible causes of loss. A marine policy covering a ship contained an exclusion relating to damage caused as a result of hostilities. The ship was torpedoed twenty-five miles from Le Havre by a German submarine during World War I. She was towed into port at Le Havre but subsequently ordered to anchor outside the harbour as it was feared that she would sink and block the harbour. At low tide the ship became grounded, took in water and sank. The insurers refused to pay the shipowner's claim on the basis that the proximate cause of the loss was the torpedoing, which was excluded. It was held that the torpedoing, not the grounding, was the proximate cause of loss. 7.73

Where two causes occur concurrently and it is not possible to say which is the proximate cause, there can be no claim if one of the causes is excluded. This situation occurred in *Wayne Tank & Pump Co Ltd v Employers Liability Assurance Corporation Ltd.*[195] Wayne Tank & Pump (WTP) were engineers who installed machinery in a plasticine factory. They had a public liability policy with ELA which provided cover, *inter alia*, for damage caused by WTP at customers' premises. An exception to the cover was damage caused by the nature of goods sold or supplied on behalf of the insured. The machinery was switched on by a WTP employee before installation was complete, it caught fire and destroyed the factory. WTP were held liable to the factory owners in a separate action where it was established that there were two concurrent causes of the fire: (1) dangerous plastic material used by WTP (excluded); and (2) the premature switching-on of the machinery (covered). It was held by the Court of Appeal that the insurer was not liable as the exception should be allowed to operate to limit the insurer's liability. Conversely, where two causes occur concurrently and one is covered but no mention is made of the other, the insurers are liable.[196] 7.74

The potential uncertainty in the scope of cover illustrated by these cases can be addressed by the use of appropriate contract terms. For example, in *Jason v British Traders Insurance Co Ltd*[197] Jason was a market trader who was injured in a crash when a wheel came off his van. He claimed under an accident 7.75

caused by the failure of the insured to comply with the claims co-operation clause (as opposed to loss caused by theft).

192 In the case of life assurance, it is necessary to show only that the event insured against (e.g. death) has occurred.

193 1906 Act, s. 55(1).

194 [1918] AC 350.

195 [1974] QB 57.

196 *JJ Lloyd Instruments Ltd v Northern Star Insurance Co Ltd (The Miss Jay Jay)* [1987] 1 Lloyd's Rep 32.

197 [1969] 1 Lloyd's Rep 281.

insurance policy from BTI. The policy provided cover for accidents which were, independently of other causes, the direct and immediate cause of injury. There was also an exclusion clause in respect of injuries caused by any physical defect or infirmity which existed prior to an accident. Following the accident, Jason suffered a coronary thrombosis and was disabled for about a year. The medical evidence showed that the stress of the accident had contributed to the condition but that Jason would have probably suffered this within three years in any event because of his existing medical condition. It was held that the insurers were not liable as the accident was not the independent cause of injury.

7.76 Loss caused by the deliberate act or criminal conduct of the insured is not covered by an insurance policy. The rationale lies in a correct construction of the contract[198] although there is also statutory authority for that approach.[199] In *Burnett v International Insurance Co of Hanover Ltd*[200] the Supreme Court held that in a public liability insurance policy covering injuries caused by door staff employed by a security company, an exclusion clause relating to 'deliberate acts' was interpreted as meaning acts intended to cause injury. In that case, despite the exclusion clause for deliberate acts, the liability arose as it was held that the person died out of 'accidental injury' – that is, death was not the intended objective. In the case of compulsory third party motor insurance, however, statutory intervention has provided injured third parties with a right to claim under the policy even when the injury results from the criminal act of the insured.[201]

The indemnity principle

7.77 The objective of the principle of indemnity is to put the insured in the position they would be in had the loss not occurred. Thus, in the indemnity contract, the insured must never be more than fully indemnified. For example, in *Hercules Insurance Co v Hunter*,[202] the defender insured with the pursuers certain mill machinery and materials in Glasgow for a sum of £1,450. The property was destroyed by fire but the insurers refused to pay £1,450 on the basis that the goods destroyed were of lower value. It was established that the defender had deliberately overvalued the machinery. It was decided that in a contract of indemnity it is the actual value of the property destroyed which the insured is entitled to recover and not the particular sum insured contained in the policy. The actual value of the goods was the value for which they could be sold.

7.78 There is no need for the principle of indemnity to be stated in the policy. If the nature of the policy is such that it is intended to compensate the insured to the extent of their loss, measured at the time it occurs, then the principle of indemnity applies. However, it is possible for the policy to provide that the

198 *Beresford v Royal Insurance Co Ltd* [1938] AC 586 at 595 per Lord Atkin. In that case, the insurer avoided liability under a life policy as the insured had committed suicide, which at the time was a crime.

199 1906 Act, s. 55(2)(a).

200 [2021] UKSC 12, 2021 SC (UKSC) 1.

201 See para. 7.69 above.

202 (1836) 14 S 1137.

principle of indemnity will not apply or that its application will be modified. This can occur in several ways:

(1) Agreed value policy. Agreed value policies are used for items that may be difficult to value when a loss occurs, such as works of art or antiques. The policy specifies the sum which is to be paid in the event of a total loss of the subject matter insured. Where there is a partial loss there is a pro rata adjustment made.[203]
(2) Replacement value or reinstatement policies. A replacement value policy gives the insured the cost of replacing the item that has been destroyed and a reinstatement policy obliges the insurer to restore the property to its condition before the damage occurred. Some policies may give the insurer the option of either paying the value of the property destroyed or reinstating. Once agreement has been reached on the payment of money, the insurer no longer has the option to reinstate. In *Endurance Corporate Capital Ltd v Sartex Quilts and Textiles Ltd*,[204] for an insured to recover for property loss on the reinstatement basis of indemnity, it was not necessary to show that it had a genuine, fixed and settled intention to reinstate the property. The relevant question was what had been the insured's loss, and what measure of indemnity would fairly and fully compensate (without overcompensating) the insured for that loss.
(3) Excess clause. An excess clause requires the insured to bear a certain amount of the loss but beyond this amount the insurer will be liable for the balance of the loss. It is common to find an excess clause in motor and home insurance policies because insurers regard such a clause as encouraging the insured to avoid a loss on the basis that it will not be possible to claim the entire loss from the insurer.
(4) Franchise clause. A franchise clause requires the insured to bear losses below a certain percentage of the sum insured; and where there is a loss above this percentage, it is borne in full by the insurer. For example a five per cent franchise on a policy covering goods valued at £1,000 would require the insured to bear any loss below £50, but any loss over £50 would be borne in full by the insurer.
(5) Average clause. An average clause is designed to deal with the problem of under-insurance. Where goods are insured for less than their true value, the insurer will not receive a premium that reflects the full value of the goods. For example, where goods worth £150,000 are insured for only £100,000, the insurer receives a premium based on £100,000 but is in reality exposed to the possibility of the loss of any £100,000 out of the total £150,000 of goods. An average clause prevents the insured from taking out a partial insurance and then recovering the full value of the goods which have been lost. It does this by adjusting the claim in relation to the proportion of the value of the goods which is insured.[205] The effect

203 For example, a policy states the value of goods to be £100, but the real value before loss is £60. The value after a loss is £30. The insured's claim against the insurer will be for £50 (three-sixths of £100).

204 [2020] EWCA Civ 308, [2020] Bus LR 1729.

205 In the example cited, a loss of £30,000 would result in a claim for £20,000, i.e. (100/150 × £30,000).

of this is that the insured is their own insurer for the portion of the value of the goods that is not insured.

7.79 Section 81 of the 1906 Act provides that the principle of average applies to marine policies. In the case of other classes of insurance, it is necessary for there to be a specific clause providing for the application of the principle of average. If there is not, the insurer will not be able to reduce a claim on the basis that there has been under-insurance.[206]

Subrogation

7.80 The principle of subrogation follows logically from the principle of indemnity. It operates so as to prevent the insured from recovering more than a full indemnity under the policy. The possibility of the insured gaining more than a full indemnity arises in situations where the insured may be able to recover their loss from a third party as well as from the insurer. Subrogation has the effect of allowing the insurer to exercise any rights which the insured may have against a third party who caused the loss.[207] For example, where motorist A negligently crashes into motorist B, A will be liable in delict to B. Assume that the cost of repairing B's car is £2,000. B then claims £2,000 from his insurer under his comprehensive motor policy. In this situation, B will have been fully indemnified for the loss by the insurer. The principle of subrogation would operate in this case to allow the insurer to exercise B's delictual rights against A in respect of loss caused to B.[208]

7.81 Subrogation is a common law principle and therefore applies without being referred to in the policy. It applies only to indemnity insurance and only when the insurer has paid a claim under the policy. In *Page v Scottish Insurance Corporation*[209] the insurer tried to exercise subrogation against a person who had caused damage to the insured's car. It was held that this could only be possible after the insurer had paid the insured's claim. This principle was applied in *Castellain v Preston*[210] where the insured was the vendor of a house that was burnt down between the conclusion of the contract for sale and the transfer of title. The contract provided for the risk to pass to the purchaser on conclusion of the contract. The vendor recovered the insurance money from the insurers and the purchaser then paid the price (as he was obliged to do under the contract). It was held that as the insurers had fully indemnified the vendor for his loss, the purchase price had to be passed to the insurers as they became subrogated to his rights once they had paid the claim.

206 *Sillem v Thornton* (1854) 3 El&Bl 868.

207 *Caledonia North Sea Ltd v London Bridge Engineering Ltd* 2000 SLT 1123 at 1139–1140 per Lord President Rodger (affd 2002 SC (HL) 117); *Simpson & Co v Thomson* (1877) 5 R (HL) 40.

208 In the case of motor insurance, insurers have agreed among themselves (through so-called 'knock for knock' agreements) not to exercise subrogation rights against third parties (and their insurers) because the outcome would be that the number of claims within the system would increase. In other cases (where the numbers of claims are lower or there is an imbalance in claims between insurers) the exercise of subrogation rights is more common.

209 (1929) 33 Ll L Rep 134.

210 (1883) 11 QBD 380.

7.82 In most cases the insured's rights in contract and delict will be passed to the insurer automatically.[211] However, there are circumstances where this will not occur. One is where the policy contains a contractual exclusion of subrogation. Another is where the insured's right has been excluded by contract as in the case of *Mark Rowlands v Berni Inns Ltd.*[212] A lease provided that the landlord was obliged to insure the property and that the tenant was to pay an additional insurance rent. The property was damaged by fire, the insurer paid the landlord's claim under the policy and then tried to exercise a right of subrogation against the tenant. It was held that the effect of the lease was to prevent the landlord recovering damages from the tenant for any loss covered by insurance and as the landlord had no right of action against the tenant, the insurer could have no action.

7.83 A second situation where subrogation will not apply is where the loss has been caused by the insured themselves or by a co-insured.[213] In the case of the insured causing the loss, the insurer can have no right of action because the insured has no right of action against themselves and there is therefore nothing to transfer by way of subrogation. In the case of *Simpson & Co v Thomson*[214] a ship ran down and sank another belonging to the same owner, William Burrell. The underwriters of the sunken ship paid its value to Burrell and then made a claim against him on the basis that his other ship had caused the damage. It was held that this claim was not possible as Burrell could not have sued himself and the underwriters stood in his position once they had paid the claim. Of course, had the owner of the other ship been a third party such a claim would have been possible. In *Petrofina (UK) Ltd v Magnaload Ltd*,[215] Magnaload were subcontractors involved in the construction of an extension to an oil refinery. The insurance policy provided cover for the work in progress and the construction equipment. Following the collapse of a crane, the owner of the refinery claimed on the policy for damage caused to the contract works by the crane's collapse. The insurers then attempted to exercise subrogation rights against Magnaload, who were the subcontractors responsible for the operation of the crane. It was held that as Magnaload were one of the parties insured by the policy, it was not possible for the insurers to exercise subrogation. As shown above, no subrogated claim can be made in respect of the loss caused by the insured themselves or by a co-insured. The question is less clear where the fault lies further down the contractual chain. *Gard Marine & Energy Ltd v China National Chartering Co Ltd*[216] concerned a charterparty and sub-charterers (equivalent to subcontractors) of a bulk carrier destroyed in a storm as a result of default in causing the accident by one of the sub-charterers. The Supreme Court, by a majority of three to two, held that the parties had extinguished all claims between them by agreeing to the insurance for the benefit of the vessel owner and the charterer. Therefore, since the charterer was not

211 Insurers exercising rights by way of subrogation *must* bring the action in the name of the insured: *Caledonia North Sea* (n 207).

212 [1986] 1 QB 211.

213 The reference here is to loss caused carelessly or negligently: deliberate loss caused by the insured is not covered, see para. 7.76 above.

214 (1877) 5 R (HL) 40, (1877) 3 App Cas 279.

215 [1984] QB 127.

216 [2017] UKSC 35, [2017] 1 WLR 1793.

in breach of contract, the insurer had no right to pursue a subrogated claim against the charterer (and co-insured).

7.84 Finally, insurers have informally agreed that subrogation rights will not be exercised against the employees of an insured company or firm. This avoids the harsh outcome that resulted from the decision of the House of Lords in *Lister v Romford Ice and Cold Storage Co Ltd.*[217] In that case an employee of the insured was injured negligently by a co-employee and, following the payment of damages to the injured employee, the insurer sought to exercise the right of subrogation against the employee who caused the injury. It was held that the insurers were entitled to recover but the informal agreement not to exercise subrogation in this situation recognises the dissenting view of the minority in that case, which was that it was an implied term of the contract of employment that the insured would protect the employee from liability for injury caused to third parties, thereby precluding any claim by the employer or insurer.[218]

Contribution

7.85 Contribution relates to the rights of insurers among themselves. It applies in situations in which a loss is covered by more than one policy (e.g. where a bag stolen from a car is covered both by home contents insurance and by motor insurance).[219] In this situation, an insurer who pays the insured's claim in full is entitled to recover a proportion of the claim from the other insurer (i.e. half if two, one-third from each if three). In principle the insured is free to choose which insurer to claim against in cases of double/multiple insurance but cannot recover more than an indemnity.

7.86 In order to avoid paying a claim in full in cases of double insurance, insurers often use rateable proportion clauses that provide that they are only liable for their rateable proportion of the loss. However, as was held in *Legal and General Assurance Society Ltd v Drake Insurance Co Ltd*,[220] where there is double insurance and each policy has a rateable proportion clause, any payment made voluntarily by an insurer in excess of their rateable proportion cannot be recovered from the other insurer.

Good faith and fraudulent claims

7.87 As noted earlier,[221] the duty of good faith applies at the time that the insured makes a claim under the policy. Claims made in breach of that duty have generally been characterised as 'fraudulent'[222] and raise two key issues: first, what is the standard of conduct required from the insured during the claims process; and secondly, what are the consequences of breach?

217 [1957] AC 555.

218 *Lister* was later distinguished in *Morris v Ford Motor Co Ltd* [1973] 1 QB 792, but Lord Denning's reference to *Lister* as an 'unfortunate decision' indicates that policy took priority over a strict application of the doctrine of precedent in *Morris*.

219 1906 Act, s. 80(1).

220 [1992] 1 All ER 283.

221 See above para. 7.31.

222 An insured is under an obligation not to make a fraudulent claim under the policy, see: *The Star Sea* (n 84) at [111] above.

A claim is fraudulent if it is based on substantial falsehood and is intended to secure a payment greater than the insured's entitlement. While some exaggeration in the value of a claim might be described as part of the normal process of negotiation between insured and insurer, a claim which is several times the real value of the loss is indicative of fraud. The fraudulent claim is now regulated by s. 12 IA 2015 and the same rules apply for consumer and non-consumer insurance contracts. This provision can be excluded in a non-consumer insurance contract, assuming the transparency requirements of s. 17 IA 2015 are met.[223] The effect of a fraudulent claim is that the insurer is not liable to pay the claim and may recover any sums they have paid. The insurer may also by notice treat the contract as having been terminated with effect from the time of the fraudulent act.[224] If the insurer treats the contract as having been terminated they may refuse all liability under the contract in relation to events occurring after the time of the fraudulent act and need not return any premiums paid.[225] Treating the contract as terminated does not affect the rights and obligations of the parties to the contract with respect to a relevant event occurring before the time of the fraudulent act.[226] This implies that where the insured makes a fraudulent claim, the insurer is not entitled to avoid the contract *ab initio* and they continue to be liable in respect of, for example, the occurrence of a loss, the making of a claim, or the notification of a potential claim, depending on how the contract is written, taking place before the time of the insured's fraudulent act.[227] **7.88**

The definition of a 'fraudulent' claim is not provided in the IA 2015 and is to be decided by reference to the common law. The leading authority on this issue is a recent Supreme Court case – *The DC Merwestone*[228] – where a distinction was made between a fraudulent claim ((i) where the whole claim was fabricated; and (ii) where there was a genuine claim but the amount was dishonestly exaggerated) and use of fraudulent devices or collateral lies where the claim was justified and the lie had no relevance to the insurer's liability. In *The DC Merwestone* the ship's engine room had flooded and, as a consequence, the insured ship sank. The shipowner falsely claimed that the crew had ignored a bilge alarm that had gone off some nine hours before it had been noticed that anything was wrong. In fact, the flooding was caused by a combination of the negligence of the crew, who failed to close a sea inlet valve on the emergency fire pump, the negligence of earlier contractors in failing to seal the engine room bulkheads properly and defects in the engine room pumping system. Eventually, it was established that the lie was irrelevant because the loss was caused by a peril of the seas covered by the policy. The Supreme Court, by a majority of four to one, held that a fraudulent claim did not extend to 'fraudulent devices' or 'collateral lies' as in the given case the lie turned out to have no relevance to the insured's right to recover. Lord Sumption JSC – who gave the leading judgment – stated: **7.89**

223 IA 2015, s. 16(2).
224 IA 2015, s. 12(1).
225 IA 2015, s. 12(2).
226 IA 2015, s. 12(3).
227 IA 2015, s. 12(4).
228 *Versloot Dredging BV v HDI Gerling Industrie Versicherung AG* ('*The DC Merwestone*') [2016] UKSC 45, [2017] AC 1.

> 'The extension of the fraudulent claims rule to lies which are found to be irrelevant to the recoverability of the claim is a step too far. It is disproportionately harsh to the insured and goes further than any legitimate commercial interest of the insurer can justify.'[229]

The Financial Ombudsman Scheme

7.90 An ombudsman scheme for the adjudication of consumer[230] insurance disputes has been available since the establishment in 1981 of the Insurance Ombudsman Bureau (IOB). The Financial Ombudsman Scheme (FOS) replaced the IOB when FSMA 2000 took effect and has, since then, handled a large volume of insurance-related disputes. Complaints are determined according to what is fair and reasonable in all the circumstances of the case.[231] In considering what is fair and reasonable in all the circumstances of the case, the ombudsman will take into account the relevant law, regulations, regulators' rules and guidance and standards, relevant codes of practice and, where appropriate, what they consider to have been good industry practice at the time. When a complaint has been determined[232] the ombudsman must give both the complainant and the firm a written statement of the determination, stating reasons for it. The statement will invite the complainant to notify the ombudsman in writing before the date specified in the statement whether they accept or reject the determination. If the complainant accepts the determination within the time limit set by the ombudsman, it is final and binding on both the complainant and the firm. If not, the firm is not bound by the determination and both sides are free to pursue legal remedies in court. If a complaint is determined in favour of the complainant, the determination may include:

- a money award subject to a maximum of £350,000;[233]
- a direction that the firm take such steps in relation to the complainant as the ombudsman considers just and appropriate; or
- both of these.

7.91 In the case of a money award, the ombudsman may decide to award compensation for the following kinds of loss or damage (in addition to or instead of compensation for financial loss):

- pain and suffering;
- damage to reputation; or
- distress or inconvenience.

229 [2016] UKSC 45 at [36].

230 As to the meaning of 'consumer' for these purposes and the jurisdiction of the FOS: see FCA Handbook DISP 2.

231 In the case of the compulsory jurisdiction, FSMA 2000, s. 228(2) provides a statutory basis for this approach. In the case of the voluntary jurisdiction, FCA Handbook DISP 3.6.1R provides a contractual basis for the ombudsman to determine a complaint in this manner.

232 A provisional decision, which gives both parties an opportunity to comment, is issued before the final decision.

233 With effect from 1 April 2019: for a complaint concerning an act or omission which occurred before 1 April 2019 the limit is £160,000 see FCA Handbook DISP 3.7.4R.

The limit on the maximum money award has no bearing on any direction that the ombudsman may make as part of a determination. The result is that the complainant can receive benefits in excess of the monetary limit in circumstances in which a direction has a financial benefit for the complainant. Where the ombudsman finds in a complainant's favour, they may also award an amount which covers some or all of the costs that were reasonably incurred by the complainant in respect of the complaint. A money award under the compulsory jurisdiction is enforceable through the courts in the same way as money awards made by the lower courts (the sheriff court in Scotland).[234]

No appeal to the courts is possible from a determination made by the ombudsman. The rationale for excluding a right of appeal from FSMA 2000 was that it would be inconsistent with the objective of resolving disputes quickly and with minimum formality. In principle, judicial review is available but this provides only a limited basis on which to mount a challenge. It is not normally possible to recover losses above the limit for FOS awards through subsequent court action following acceptance of a FOS award because the principle of *res judicata* applies so as to exclude the possibility of fresh proceedings based on the same cause of action.[235] 7.92

234 FSMA 2000, Sch. 17, para. 16.
235 *Clark v In Focus Asset Management & Tax Solutions Ltd* [2014] EWCA Civ 118.

Chapter Eight

Money and Debt

Ross Anderson and David Fox

PATRIMONIAL LAW

The general part

8.01 Private law is concerned with patrimonial rights: personal rights; real rights; intellectual property rights. Strictly speaking, then, it is rights, not physical things, that are properly regarded as assets:[1] 'All rights, therefore, are incorporeal; and the distinction really is not between two kinds of right, but between things which are objects of right and the legal conception of right itself'. The paradigm focus in property law on real rights in land results in a tendency to identify patrimonial rights with their objects.[2] As the famous Roman and comparative lawyer, Barry Nicholas, elegantly observed:[3]

> 'The strictly comparable statement to "I have bought a right of way over a plot of land" is not, "I have bought a plot of land", but "I have bought a right of ownership over a plot of land". In each case I have acquired a right . . . '

8.02 The relationship of a person to their rights is not their ownership (since ownership may be one of their rights), but their title.[4] Ownership is but one of the real rights and real rights are just one type of patrimonial right. Ownership is not necessary to describe the holding of personal rights. To speak of ownership of personal rights gives rise to a doubling of the rights involved and complicates unnecessarily the already difficult task of legal analysis.

8.03 In commercial law, the most important patrimonial rights are often not real rights in physical things, but personal rights to the performance of obligations.[5] Personal rights arising under the law of obligations have no physical object; their object is rather the counter-performance: to use a word of French origin, still often referred to in modern Scottish cases,[6] the object is the 'prestation'.

8.04 Obligations give rise to personal rights, whether those personal rights are born of contracts or promises or delicts or in order to prevent unjustified

1 *Burghead Harbour Co Ltd v George* (1906) 8 F 982 at 996 per Lord Kinnear.
2 See paras 3.44–3.55 above.
3 B Nicholas, *An Introduction to Roman Law* (Oxford: Clarendon Press, 1962), p. 107.
4 Cf Bankton, *Institute* I, 597, 1 'The terms Right and Title are promiscuously used in our law'.
5 Or, indeed, intellectual property rights. See, further, Chapter Three: General Principles of Property Law.
6 *Johnston's Tr v Baird* [2012] CSOH 117 at [18]–[20] per Lord Uist; *Glasgow City Council v Morrison Developments Ltd* 2003 SLT 263 at [12] and [16] per Lord Eassie; and *Allied Dunbar Assurance plc v Superglass Sections Ltd* 2003 SLT 1420 at [10] per Lord Eassie.

enrichment. Unlike real rights in land (some of which may endure forever) obligations (and thus their correlative personal rights), it has been said, are 'born to die'. This chapter will be concerned with the death of obligations, by performance or discharge; or with the maintenance of the obligation and the circulation of the creditor's position in an obligationary relationship.

Since every contract creates rights and obligations, achieving performance is the core function of all commercial contracts. The basic principles, however, are little different in a commercial case than in any other case. The detailed rules on creation, variation, discharge and transfer of rights and obligations – the lifeblood of the corporate and financial world – are the core private law rules which comprise the general part of patrimonial law.[7] **8.05**

Some vocabulary: rights and obligations

The English language has many attributes, but one major weakness is its legal vocabulary. Since this chapter is primarily concerned with 'obligations', a few words about the word 'obligation' may assist. The English word, 'obligation', focuses on the debtor, not the creditor: **8.06**

> 'Obligation is that which is correspondent to a personal right, which hath no proper name as it is in the creditor, but hath the name of obligation as it is in the debtor: and it is nothing else but a legal tie, whereby the debtor may be compelled to pay or perform something, to which he is bound by obedience to God, or by his own consent or engagement.'[8]

Or, as the leading modern writer on the civil law of obligations explains: **8.07**

> 'The substantive "obligatio" can be traced back to Cicero. As to the literal meaning of the term, its root "lig-" indicates that somebody or something is bound; just as we are all "bound-back" (to God) by virtue of our "re-ligio" . . . the English term "obligation" is merely oriented toward the person bound, not towards the person entitled. With the words "my obligations" I can refer only to my duties, not to my rights.'[9]

The point is that words like 'obligation', 'debt' and 'duty' refer to the debtor's side of the legal relationship; the creditor's position – in contrast, the positive end of the relationship – is more difficult to describe. A creditor is said to holds a 'right' or a 'claim' against the debtor. As will be seen below, a claim, held by a creditor, is normally freely transferable; a liability owed by a debtor to a creditor, in contrast, cannot normally be transferred by the debtor without the creditor's consent. This fundamental principle forms the basis of much that occurs in the financial world. **8.08**

7 The institutional writers dealt with rules of the general part in some detail. But since then the general part of Scots private law has been neglected. Compare Book One of the German Civil Code; Part One of the Swiss *Code des Obligations*; Book Three of the Dutch civil code; and Books I–III DCFR.

8 Stair, *Institutions* 1.1.22. Of this passage, A H Campbell, *The Structure of Stair's Institutions* (Glasgow: Jackson, 1954), p. 31, remarks: 'note how aptly Stair applies the metaphor of the *vinculum juris*. The chain does not, as the hasty beginner is apt to say, bind the debtor and the creditor; it binds the debtor, but the creditor's end lies freely in his hands to use or not as he pleases'.

9 R Zimmermann, *The Law of Obligations: Roman Foundations of the Civilian Tradition* (Oxford: Clarendon Press, 1990), p. 1.

Some corporate jargon

8.09 To identify rights and obligations in a corporate or financial context, however, may itself be a challenge. The term 'security' is particularly common. In this context, 'security' does not refer to a real right in security, like a standard security, which is a right additional to the creditor's principal right to payment; rather, in the corporate context, a 'security' is an instrument a company issues as an acknowledgment of investment in the company.[10] That investment may be by way of equity (shares) or debt (debentures, loan notes, bonds). In the corporate world, jargon abounds: words like 'convertible securities', 'bonds', 'stock',[11] 'debenture stock',[12] 'share warrants', etc. All of these terms describe securities issued by a company. A 'security' may be a debt instrument or a form of equity or some form of hybrid instrument (such as a debt instrument that is convertible into equity).

8.10 The security may or may not be certificated: that is to say, the security may be represented by a physical paper certificate; or the security may have been issued in dematerialised form. An 'issuer' of such security, the company, is normally the recipient of an investment, often, although not always, in money; the holder of the security is normally the investor, the creditor. A creditor who holds a corporate bond is someone who has lent money to the company and the company's obligation to repay is reified in the bond issued to the creditor. The term 'debenture' has no settled legal meaning,[13] other than an acknowledgment of indebtedness: an IOU. Determining the rights that a holder of such instruments may have, however, normally means trawling through the provisions of an overarching document (an offering circular, loan note instrument, debenture trust deed or articles of association). But the same general principles apply. And those principles essentially apply too where the issuer of the instrument is not a company, but Her Majesty's Government, which also must finance its activities on the capital markets as a company does, by issuing IOUs (government bonds, sometimes known as 'gilts') through the Debt Management Office.[14]

10 Companies Act 2006, s. 755(5): 'In this chapter "securities" means shares or debentures'; see too Financial Services and Markets Act 2000 (Regulated Activities) Order 2001 (SI 2001/544), arts 3, 76–82, 82B and 89.

11 See E Ferran and L C Ho, *Principles of Corporate Finance Law*, 3rd edn (Oxford: Oxford University Press, 2014), pp. 103–104.

12 Companies Act 2006, s. 738: '"debenture" includes debenture stock, bonds and other securities of a company whether or not constituting a charge on the assets of the company'. Companies which issue such bonds must keep a register of them: Companies Act 2006, s. 743.

13 See, e.g. Case C-80/95 *Harnas & Helm* [1997] ECR I-745, [1997] STC 364 at [AG10] and n 12 above. In English law, 'debenture' sometimes also refers to a document that not only acknowledges indebtedness, but also grants fixed and floating charges to the creditor: see *Fons Hf v Corporal Ltd* [2014] EWCA Civ 304. In Scots law, a company wishing to acknowledge its indebtedness to a creditor and grant to the creditor a floating charge does so in a document called a 'bond and floating charge'. The only difference between a 'bond and floating charge' and a 'floating charge' is that the former contains an acknowledgement of the principal debt obligation in the same document as the grant of the security.

14 United Kingdom Debt Management Office, *http://www.dmo.gov.uk* (last accessed 2 September 2021). The financial markets play a central role in contemporary society. No more can be said about them here, but three useful introductory guides are W M Clarke, *How the City of London Works*, 7th edn (London: Sweet & Maxwell, 2008); R Vaitilingham, *Financial Times Guide to*

Money: the 'universal solvent'

Obligations may arise by consent (as with contracts or promises); or they may be imposed by law (under the law of delict or unjustified enrichment); or by statute. Sometimes an obligation will require something to be done: a service performed or goods delivered. Sometimes the obligation is simply to pay money. Even in cases where the initial obligation was for some performance, the law may convert this into an obligation to pay in the form of damages. For the purposes of the law of obligations, '[m]oney is the universal solvent; everything can be turned into money that is either a gain or a loss; money is asked and damages are due for reparation of every possible suffering and injury'.[15] That is a general principle of private law, whether the basis for the liability is contract or delict or unjustified enrichment. **8.11**

DEBT AND DAMAGES

Contractual liability may be said to have primary and secondary aspects: the primary liability is performance, the secondary liability is to pay damages for breach; and that secondary liability is contractual.[16] A fundamental difference of considerable practical importance is the difference between debt and damages. A debt is a 'liquid' sum: that is, the amount owed is established. A contract or a document of debt[17] may provide for payment of a liquid sum. A claim for damages, in contrast, is the classic illiquid claim. Only on the court giving decree for the sum sued for is there a liquid sum payable. The major practical distinction between debt and damages is that a creditor in a claim for damages is required to mitigate its loss; there is no such requirement on a creditor who claims payment of a debt. The distinction is of particular importance in cases of anticipatory breach of contract where the innocent party has the option to accept the repudiation and claim damages (subject to the requirement to mitigate) or to refuse to accept the repudiation, offer to perform its side of the contract and then claim the sums owed under the contract as a debt.[18] **8.12**

Using the Financial Pages, 6th edn (London: Prentice Hall, 2011); and N Ferguson, *The Ascent of Money* (London: Penguin, 2008).

15 *Auld v Shairp* (1874) 2 R 191 at 199 per Lord Neaves.

16 It is in this sense that the distinction was tirelessly championed by Lord Diplock: see, e.g. *Moschi v Lep Air Services Ltd* [1973] AC 331 at 350; *Photo Production Ltd v Securicor Transport Ltd* [1980] AC 827 at 848–850. But as Bernard Rudden has pointed out ('Correspondence' (1990) 10 OJLS 288) the primary-secondary distinction can be traced to R J Pothier, *Traité des Obligations* (1761), § 183.

17 For which, see n 117 below.

18 *White & Carter (Councils) Ltd v McGregor* 1962 SC (HL) 1; *Geys v Société Générale, London Branch* [2012] UKSC 63, [2013] 1 AC 523.

PERFORMANCE BY PAYMENT[19]

Performance

8.13 Discharge of a contractual obligation normally involves a type of performance. What amounts to performance depends on the terms of the contract. A contract to build a tram system, for instance, is discharged by construction of the system. A contract for the sale of heritable property is discharged by delivery of a disposition which confers vacant possession.[20] In return for such a service or disposition, however, the builder or the seller, as the case may be, is entitled to payment. Payment obligations, at the risk of stating the obvious, are discharged by payment.[21]

Payment

8.14 Payment is normally conceived, by lawyers as well as laymen, to be in 'money'. But what is 'money'? Most cash is money but not all money is cash. Cash is of significance for day-to-day transactions between citizens and small businesses. But these transactions represent only tiny a fraction of what, in both law and economics, is considered to be 'money'. In recent years, notes and coins in circulation have represented only about 3.5 per cent of the total UK money supply.[22] Most money, in the commercial world, is invisible and intangible. For lawyers – especially in times of financial crisis – the law of money is a subject of considerable difficulty.[23] Today, the Bank of England refers to 'broad money' when speaking of the 'money supply'. In that context, the Bank of England's concept of money includes all sorts of important categories of money with which even the *Financial Times* subscriber may have rather limited familiarity.

8.15 For legal purposes, however, 'money' has a rather narrower meaning. A salary, a mortgage repayment, a dividend: each is rarely, if ever, paid in cash. Payments are effected rather by entries in bank accounts. Suppose a university employee is paid net of tax £3,000 in salary per month by their employer (the university). The employee, on working for a month, has a claim against the university for £3,000. In principle, the employee could ask to be paid in legal tender. But the usual practice is for the salary to be paid, net of tax, into a bank account. The employee's claim against the university is substituted for a claim against the employee's own bank (assuming the employee's bank account is in credit). Let us suppose too that the university's bank is RBS. The employee's bank is the Clydesdale Bank plc. The university would have effected the payment to the employee by instructing RBS to make a payment to the employee's bank. So there would have been a change in the debt relationship

19 See further Chapter Nine: Payment Obligations.

20 *Morris v Rae* [2012] UKSC 50, 2013 SC (UKSC) 106 at [35] per Lord Reed.

21 See generally V Dixon (ed), *Goode on Payment Obligations in Commercial and Financial Transactions*, 4th edn (London: Sweet & Maxwell, 2020).

22 Figures are available from the Bank of England quarterly statistics: *http://www.bankofengland.co.uk/boeapps/database/* (last accessed 2 September 2021).

23 See generally C Proctor (ed), *Mann and Proctor on the Legal Aspect of Money*, 7th edn (Oxford: Oxford University Press, 2012; 8th edn, forthcoming 2022).

between university and RBS. Then there would have been a change in the debt relationship between RBS and the Clydesdale; and then between the Clydesdale and the employee. No cash changes hands and, as a proportion of the funds that are transferred each day, cash payments comprise a very small proportion of daily payment operations.

Legal tender[24]

A debtor is required to pay debts in 'legal tender': **8.16**

> 'No creditor is bound to receive payment of a debt due to him by cheque or otherwise than in the current coin of the realm. A creditor may even refuse to accept Scottish bank-notes, and insist on his debtor bringing him current coin of the realm to the amount of his debt. Nevertheless, if he choose [sic] to accept these bank-notes in payment, I do not think it is capable of being disputed that he would be held, according to our law and practice, to have been paid in cash. In the same way, if he receives, although not bound to do so, a cheque from his debtor and gives him a receipt for the sum contained in the cheque, that is regarded as a payment in cash if the cheque is duly honoured, and the payment in cash is not at the date of the honouring of the cheque, but at the date of its receipt by the creditor.'[25]

Not all 'cash' is legal tender. As Lord Young points out, only 'current coin of **8.17** the realm' is legal tender. Banknotes, in Scotland, are not legal tender. Three Scottish banks have retained their note-issuing function. The present law relating to the issue of banknotes is found in the Banking Act 2009 and associated regulations.[26] Scottish banknotes are not legal tender in either Scotland or England. They are promissory notes.[27] English bank notes with a value of less than £5 are legal tender in Scotland.[28] But the only notes under £5 were £1 notes, and Bank of England £1 notes ceased to be legal tender in March 1988.[29] Gold coins and coins in denominations of £1 and £2 are legal tender for a sum of any amount; as are silver or cupronickel coins for small debts of £10 and £5 respectively; or bronze coins for debts up to 20 pence.[30]

Can a creditor in a commercial debt of millions of pounds require the debtor **8.18** to pay in £1 and £2 coins? Or can a debtor require a creditor to accept a truck-load of coins? The short answer is that Lord Young's principle that a creditor is bound to accept only legal tender applies unless the parties have not otherwise agreed, expressly or impliedly, how 'payment' is to be effected. For

24 In the US, 'legal tender' is defined in 31 US Code § 5103: 'United States coins and currency (including Federal Reserve notes and circulating notes of Federal Reserve banks and national banks) are legal tender for all debts, public charges, taxes, and dues'. The unofficial motto of the US, 'In God we Trust', has adorned US coins since the 1860s and all Federal Reserve dollar bills since the 1960s.

25 *Glasgow Pavilion Ltd v Motherwell* (1903) 6 F 116 at 119 per Lord Young.

26 Banking Act 2009, Part 6; and the Scottish and Northern Ireland Banknote Regulations 2009 (SI 2009/3056). These make important changes to the definitions of words like 'asset', 'property', 'sum' or 'fund' in Scottish insolvency legislation in the case of a bank insolvency. See too *Clydesdale Bank plc v HMRC* [2019] UKFTT 419 (TC).

27 Subject to special rules. So it is a criminal offence to deface a banknote: Currency and Bank Notes Act 1928, s. 12.

28 Currency and Bank Notes Act 1954, s. 1(2).

29 They remain redeemable as promissory notes at the Bank of England.

30 Coinage Act 1971, s. 2(1A). The legal tender status of £1 and £2 coins is fixed by the various proclamations that authorise their issue.

debts which run into tens of thousands, never mind hundreds of millions, of pounds, no sensible businessperson would expect payment other than in bank moneys.[31] 'Bank moneys' is a term used to describe credit and debit entries in the books of a bank or credit institution as opposed to physical money in coins and banknotes. Bank moneys are sometimes referred to as 'scriptural money' (*la monnaie scriptural*).[32]

Cheques

8.19 As Lord Young pointed out in *Glasgow Pavilion Ltd v Motherwell*,[33] the parties are free to agree that something other than legal tender will amount to 'payment'. It has become quite common, for example, for shops to provide that the debtor may only pay by card or contactless methods, which would exclude payment by 'current coin of the realm'. And for commercial payments the only practical solution is a 'payment' by way of replacement of the principal debtor's obligation with another obligation, normally from a bank. The key point is that, in the absence of agreement, the creditor is not bound to accept something other than legal tender.[34] A court, however, may readily infer such an agreement, particularly in payments of large sums. Traditionally, one type of payment subject to a special rule was payment by cheque:[35]

> 'Normally everyone who accepts a cheque in payment takes it in discharge of the debt. But in law, unless anything is said to the contrary, the discharge is presumed to be subject to a resolutive condition that if the cheque is dishonoured the discharge is void *ab initio*; the condition operates retrospectively so that the debt revives in its original form. I can illustrate the meaning of that by supposing that the debt carried interest. When the cheque for the principal sum and accrued interest is accepted, discharge of the obligation causes the interest to cease to accrue. But when the cheque is dishonoured and the debt for the principal sum revives, interest becomes payable for the period between the acceptance of the cheque and its dishonour so there is no question of the debt being deferred or suspended during the period between acceptance of the cheque and its presentation for payment.'

8.20 It is worth mentioning too that domestic contracts may be denominated in foreign currencies – US dollars, Euros, Swiss francs, etc. – and it is possible to sue, before the Scottish courts, for the payment of a debt – or, indeed, for damages[36] – in a foreign currency.[37]

31 See, e.g. *St Vincent European General Partner Ltd v Robinson* [2018] EWHC 1230 (Comm), [2019] 1 BCLC 706 at [61] per Males J.

32 See n 52 below.

33 (1903) 6 F 116 at 119.

34 *Child Maintenance and Enforcement Commission v Wilson* [2013] CSIH 98, 2014 SLT 46.

35 *DPP v Turner* [1974] AC 357 at 367–368. This reflects the position of Gloag, *Contract*, 2nd edn (Edinburgh: W. Green, 1929), pp. 272–273 and *Leggat Brothers v Gray* 1908 SC 67.

36 In *Fullemann v McInnes's Exrs* 1993 SLT 259, the Lord Ordinary (Cullen) calculated the damages due for personal injuries suffered by a Swiss tourist in Scotland, and awarded decree, in Swiss francs (the sum awarded was a record at the time). See further *The Despina R* [1979] AC 688.

37 See A F Rodger [Lord Rodger of Earlsferry], 'The Strange Demise of *Hyslops v Gordon*' in A J Gamble (ed), *Obligations in Context: Essays in Honour of Professor D M Walker* (Edinburgh: W. Green, 1990), p. 1 and authority there cited; and P Beaumont and P McEleavy (eds), *Anton's Private International Law*, 3rd edn (Edinburgh: W. Green, 2011), para. 12.12. For extract, see RCS, r. 7.5.

Ascription and appropriation

Suppose Dianne is indebted to Charlotte, under three separate transactions: £1,000 due under a contract for services; £7,500 on a loan; and £2,500 for goods supplied on creditor. Dianne makes a payment of £5,000. How is the payment to be treated? Payment is normally a bilateral juridical act: the payee consents, whether expressly or impliedly, to a discharge of the debt. Where only one debt is outstanding, matters are simple. Where interest runs on the debt, the creditor is entitled to payment of both principal and interest. A debtor is not normally entitled to insist that all payments are made in reduction of capital and not interest.[38] **8.21**

A creditor is not bound to accept a partial payment. A debtor may indicate, when making payment, that the payment is to be ascribed to a particular debt.[39] Where the debtor makes a so-called, 'indefinite payment',[40] the creditor may unilaterally appropriate the payment to a particular debt.[41] And the parties may, of course, expressly agree that a particular payment should be attributed to a particular debt. Where there is neither ascription nor appropriation nor agreement, the *Clayton's Case* presumption applies: that is addressed in para. 8.26 below. Ascription of payments to particular debts being often important, there are sometimes statutory rules.[42] **8.22**

The basics of bank accounts

Most debts are paid not in cash, but through the banking system. The details of bank payments are considered below. This paragraph contains some introductory general principles relating to bank accounts. A bank account represents a debtor-creditor relationship. If John pays money into his bank, and John's account is in credit, the bank is John's debtor. Similarly, if John has an overdraft with his bank and his account is overdrawn, John is his bank's debtor. An instruction to a bank to pay a sum that exceeds either the amount standing to the account holder's credit or agreed borrowing facilities, may be treated at the banker's option as a request for an overdraft. An overdraft is a loan repayable on demand. **8.23**

Working out whether the bank is a creditor or debtor, and whether the account holder is debtor or creditor, is important for matters such as the law of arrestment. For, under the law of arrestment, 'it may be stated as a rule without exception, that the arrestment will be laid in the hands of the parties who would have been defenders in an action for payment of the sum arrested'.[43] In other words, an arrestment is served in the hands of the arrester's debtor's debtor. **8.24**

The main characteristic of the current account is that sums are credited and debited. The private law principles of a current account relationship are **8.25**

38 *Wilson's Trs v Clydesdale Bank Ltd* (1900) 7 SLT 473 at 475–476 per Lord Moncreiff.
39 *China National Star Petroleum Co v Tor Drilling (UK) Ltd* 2002 SLT 1339 at [24].
40 See, e.g. Erskine, *Institute* 3.4.2.
41 *Jackson v Nicoll* (1870) 8 M 408 at 412 per Lord Kinloch.
42 See, e.g. Debtors (Scotland) Act 1987, s. 94.
43 J Graham Stewart, *A Treatise on the Law of Diligence* (Edinburgh: W. Green, 1898), p. 38.

not limited to bank accounts.[44] Suppose it becomes necessary to know, at a particular moment in time, what the state of the account is where there have been payments to account by the debtor and further advances by the creditor. The question can be particularly important where, for example, an insolvency event has occurred. According to the rule in *Clayton's Case*,[45] the presumption is that the earliest credit extinguishes the earliest debit.

8.26 The principle is illustrated by example. Suppose John carries on business as a farmer. In that business he has a running account with a supplier. John dies. At the date of his death, John was indebted to the supplier in the sum of £9,000. The supplier agrees to allow John's executor to carry on the business. Further supplies are required for the business after John's death, for which the supplier extends a further £3,000 of credit to the executor. After four years, the executor has paid some £10,000 to account. Had the debt owed by John's estate been discharged? If the principle in *Clayton's Case* applies, the answer would be yes. The additional £3,000 would remain to be paid by the executor. But it may be that the principle does not apply. The principle is merely a presumption. In a case on similar facts to the example given in this paragraph of John's executor, the court held that the presumption had been displaced.[46]

8.27 The decision of the Court of Appeal in *Re Yeovil Glove Co Ltd*[47] provides an example of the importance of the principle in modern commercial circumstances. But this decision is best discussed in the context of corporate insolvency.[48]

Payments through the banking system

8.28 The law relating to bank payments is mainly the law of interlinked mandates and payment orders. The law of bank payments is, therefore, to a large extent but a modern application of the basic principles of payment orders that have been around for millennia.[49] Much often turns on the particular wording of the contractual relationships under which cards are issued and payments processed.[50]

8.29 The common law in this area is now subject to the Payment Services Regulations 2017 (the '2017 Regulations').[51] Key definitions in the regulations

44 *McKinley v Wilson* (1885) 13 R 210.

45 The actual case name is *Devaynes v Noble* (1816) 35 ER 781. For illuminating discussion and criticism of the rule in English law, see D Fox, *Property Rights in Money* (Oxford: Oxford University Press, 2008), paras 7.62–7.64 and 8.43–8.47.

46 *Macdonald, Fraser & Co v Cairn's Exrx* 1932 SC 699.

47 [1965] Ch 148.

48 See para. 14.125 below.

49 D Fox and W Ernst (eds), *Money in the Western Legal Tradition: Middle Ages to Bretton Woods* (Oxford: Oxford University Press, 2016); B Geva, *The Payment Order of Antiquity and the Middle Ages: A Legal History* (Oxford: Hart Publishing, 2011); J S Rogers, *A History of the Law of Bills and Notes* (Cambridge: Cambridge University Press, 1995).

50 *Re Charge Card Services Ltd* [1987] Ch 150, affd [1989] Ch 497; *Mercedes-Benz Finance Ltd v Clydesdale Bank plc* 1997 SLT 905; *Duncan v American Express Services Europe Ltd* 2009 SLT 112.

51 Payment Services Regulations 2017 (SI 2017/752), implementing the revised EU Payment Services Directive 2015/2366, and all as amended by the Electronic Money, Payment Services

include 'payment instruments' and 'payment orders'. A payment order is 'any instruction by a payer or a payee to their respective payment service provider requesting the execution of a payment transaction'. A payment instrument is the procedure agreed between the payment service provider and the service user to initiate a payment order. A 'payment transaction' is the act of placing, transferring or withdrawing funds. 'Funds' is defined as meaning coins, banknotes, scriptural money and electronic money.[52] 'Payment services' include: (i) direct debits, including one-off direct debits; (ii) payment transactions executed through a payment card or a similar device; and (iii) credit transfers, including standing orders.[53] 'Payment service provider' includes credit institutions[54] such as banks.

It is not possible here to summarise these complex regulations, but certain provisions relating to 'unauthorised payment transactions' may be highlighted. Payment service users who become aware of unauthorised payment transactions are required to notify their bank without undue delay, and in any event no later than thirteen months after the debit date.[55] Failure to do so may mean they lose their rights to 'redress'.[56] But the user remains entitled to redress, though they have not notified the bank, where the bank has failed to provide the user with information about the transaction.[57] Importantly, where a payment order is executed in accordance with unique identifier provided, the order is deemed to have been correctly executed.[58] If a customer alleges that a particular payment transaction was unauthorised, the onus is on the bank to demonstrate that the transaction was authorised.[59] **8.30**

Where an executed payment transaction was not properly authorised,[60] the payment service provider must immediately: (a) refund the amount of the unauthorised payment transaction to the payer; and (b) where applicable, restore the debited payment account to the state it would have been in if the unauthorised payment transaction had not taken place.[61] There are also specific provisions for payment transactions authorised by the payee.[62] The time limits for action where the payer alleges that the amount debited was not authorised is eight weeks.[63] There are various regulatory requirements **8.31**

and Payment Systems (Amendment and Transitional Provisions (EU Exit) Regulations 2018 (SI 2018/1201). The 2017 Regulations replaced the Payment Services Regulations 2009 (SI 2009/209).

52 2017 Regulations, reg. 2(1) contains the definitions. 'Scriptural money' is a literal translation of *la monnaie scripturale* in EU Directive 2015/2366, art. 4(25). The German is *Giralgeld*.

53 2017 Regulations, Sch. 1, para. 1(c).

54 As defined in the EU Capital Requirements Regulation (No.575/2013), art. 4(1), namely 'an undertaking the business of which is to take deposits or other repayable funds from the public and to grant credits for its own account'.

55 2017 Regulations, reg. 74(1).

56 Under 2017 Regulations, regs. 76, 91, 92, 93 and 94.

57 2017 Regulations, reg. 74(2).

58 2017 Regulations reg. 90. Cf *Tidal Energy Ltd v Bank of Scotland plc* [2014] EWCA Civ 1107, [2014] Bus LR 1167.

59 2017 Regulations, reg. 75.

60 For which, see 2017 Regulations, reg. 67.

61 2017 Regulations, reg. 76.

62 2017 Regulations, reg. 79.

63 2017 Regulations, reg. 80.

for banks and other entities which issue 'electronic money'[64] to comply with, including capital adequacy requirements.[65]

Cryptocurrencies

8.32 In recent years, technology developers have invented and put into circulation a great variety of privately issued cryptocurrencies. The best-known examples are bitcoin and Ethereum. As their name implies, many cryptocurrencies were originally designed as means of payment, although in practice relatively few are now used in this way. Bitcoins, for example, are commonly bought and sold as a kind of investment.[66] The volatility in the value of bitcoins against state-issued currencies, which is the very thing that makes them unsuitable as means of payment, can make them attractive to investors who speculate on their fluctuating capital value.

8.33 Alongside these developments in the private sector, many state monetary authorities, including the Bank of England, are in the early stages of developing their own 'central bank digital currencies'.[67] These would use a technological functionality that was similar to privately-issued cryptocurrencies. They would however be denominated in the unit of account of their issuing state, such as pounds sterling or Swiss francs. The plan is that they would supplement state-issued coins or banknotes and commercial banks' reserves held at a central bank. Some central bank digital currencies may be given partial or full status as legal tender.

8.34 It is necessary to say something about the technical and legal features of cryptocurrencies that distinguish them from the usual forms of bank money held in accounts. Nowadays nearly all money in circulation is intangible. It appears only as recorded entries in an electronic ledger. Money in a bank account consists in the account holder's right to enforce payment of the bank's debt to the holder. Cryptocurrencies also consist in data recorded in electronic ledgers but their features are technically different. A cryptocurrency ledger is often

64 Which bears the same meaning in the 2017 Regulations (see reg. 2(1)) as under Electronic Money Regulations 2011 (SI 2011/99), reg. 2, which defines 'electronic money' as meaning 'electronically (including magnetically) stored monetary value as represented by a claim on the electronic money issuer which: (a) is issued on receipt of funds for the purpose of making payment transactions; (b) is accepted by a person other than the electronic money issuer'. There are various exclusions in reg. 3. Recital (7) of the Directive says: 'It is appropriate to introduce a clear definition of electronic money in order to make it technically neutral. That definition should cover all situations where the payment service provider issues a pre-paid stored value in exchange for funds, which can be used for payment purposes because it is accepted by third persons as a payment'. 'Funds' are defined in the 2017 Regulations, reg. 2 to cover: 'banknotes and coins, scriptural money, and electronic money [defined in terms of the Electronic Money Regulations 2011, reg. 2(1)]'.

65 See 2011 Regulations (n 98).

66 They are traded on specialist cryptocurrency exchanges, such as Coinbase: *https://www.coinbase.com/* (last accessed 3 September 2021).

67 See Bank of International Settlements, Committee on Payments and Market Infrastructures, "Central Bank Digital Currencies" (March 2018), *https://www.bis.org/cpmi/publ/d174.htm* (last accessed 3 September 2021); Bank of England, "Discussion Paper: Central Bank Digital Currency" (March 2020), accessible at *https://www.bankofengland.co.uk/paper/2020/central-bank-digital-currency-opportunities-challenges-and-design-discussion-paper* (last accessed 3 September 2021).

held on a distributed network rather than on a payment network maintained by a centralised entity, such as a bank. Cryptocurrencies also differ in their legal status. With many cryptocurrencies, such as bitcoin, the holder's unit of currency does not represent a legal right to performance of a monetary debt owed by another person. A unit of cryptocurrency is a notional representation of value constituted by unique data entries recording transactions on the ledger. The data entries are regarded as the unit of currency itself. Unlike bank money, they are more than records which merely evidence some other thing or a right enforceable against another person. It follows that a unit of cryptocurrency ceases to exist if the data recording it is obliterated. Similarly, a unit of cryptocurrency becomes lost and practically unspendable if the holder loses the 'private key', which is the unique digital signature enabling the holder to transact with it.

This difference in the legal status of cryptocurrencies also explains why they **8.35** do not easily fit into traditional categories of patrimonial asset in Scots law. Many cryptocurrencies are neither corporeal things nor incorporeal rights to the performance of obligations owed by another.[68] They cannot be possessed in the usual sense and it is uncertain if they can be the subject of a real right. If cryptocurrencies are to have any place in patrimonial law, it will be necessary to recognise a new category of asset, one consisting in a holder's exclusive power to control and transact with a specific locus of transferable value.[69] The emerging view in England is that cryptocurrencies are a kind of incorporeal property in common law systems.[70] The position in Scots law remains uncertain.

Cryptocurrencies can be paid as money. When paid in this way the usual rules **8.36** of contractual performance apply to them. Their precise application depends on the function that the parties attribute to the cryptocurrency in the transaction and the terms of the obligation to be performed.

If Sarah sells her car to Brian for a contract price of BTC 1.5,[71] then the parties **8.37** would treat the 1.5 units of bitcoin currency transferred by Brian as money. The transaction would be an ordinary sale of goods.[72] The completion of the transaction on the bitcoin ledger would transfer the legal right in the currency to Sarah and discharge Brian's debt to her.[73] Suppose instead that Sarah set the contract price for the car at £40,000 and Brian transferred 1.5 units of bitcoin currency to her. Brian would not get a good discharge unless perhaps Sarah chose to accept this different method of performance in settlement of the monetary obligation. It would make no difference that the market value

68 See paras 8.01–8.04 above, and D Fox and S Green, *Cryptocurrencies in Public and Private Law* (Oxford: Oxford University Press, 2019), Ch. 6.

69 See D Carr in D Fox and S Green, *Cryptocurrencies in Public and Private Law* (2019), Ch. 7.

70 *AA v Persons Unknown* [2019] EWHC 3556 (Comm), [2020] 4 WLR 35, adopting the view of the UK Jurisdiction Taskforce, 'Legal statement on cryptoassets and smart contracts', accessible at *https://technation.io/lawtech-uk-resources/#cryptoassets* (last accessed 3 September 2021).

71 'BTC' is the denomination of the bitcoin unit of value, rather as the symbols '£' or 'GBP' refer to the unit of value for the pound sterling.

72 See S Green in D Fox and S Green, *Cryptocurrencies in Public and Private Law* (2019), Ch. 2.

73 In principle, the set-off of reciprocal obligations to transfer cryptocurrency should also serve as payment and discharge of each party's obligation. For set-off, see further para. 8.51 below.

of the bitcoin units might have been exactly £40,000. The usual rule applies that the performance of contractual obligations depends on conformity with the terms of the contract.[74] If, in a different transaction, ExchangeCoin plc sells 1.5 units of bitcoin currency to an investor, Ivan, for £40,000, then the £40,000 of sterling currency is the money price. ExchangeCoin and Ivan treat the bitcoin currency as an investment commodity rather than as money. This illustrates how the legal status of a cryptocurrency as money or a commodity depends on how the parties treat it. It has no absolute status in law.

INTEREST AND LATE PAYMENT

8.38 Suppose a debtor does not pay at the contractually agreed time. Delay by the debtor in making punctual payment (*mora debitoris*) is a form of breach of contract to which special rules apply.[75] Interest does not generally run on the unpaid sum until a judicial demand is made, which is why most craves or conclusions for payment provide for the payment of interest from the date of citation.[76] At common law it is really only banking contracts on which interest may be due implicitly.[77] Many contracts therefore provide expressly from when, and at what rate, interest will be due. For contracts for the supply of goods and services, however, the Late Payment of Commercial Debts (Interest) Act 1998 (the 1998 Act) provides two remedies.

8.39 First, it is an implied term that 'simple' interest runs on any 'qualifying debt' created by the contract.[78] Interest runs from the day after the 'relevant day'. The 'relevant day' will normally be the day agreed by the parties in their contract or, if there is no agreed payment day, at the end of the relevant thirty day period.[79] Interest is generally 8 per cent over the official dealing rate.[80]

8.40 Secondly, once statutory interest begins to run, fixed sums of compensation are due by reference to the qualifying debt: (a) £40 for a debt less than £1,000; (b) for a debt of more than £1,000 but less than £10,000, the sum of £70; and (c) for a debt of £10,000 or more, the sum of £100.[81] Although the fixed sums may sound modest, in a case of multiple qualifying debts,

74 See para. 8.16 above.

75 Bell, *Commentaries* I, 646: 'Since . . . the Reformation, the law of Scotland has been settled, that breach of contract, or *mora* in payment, raises this claim without any inquiry into the actual damage, and estimating all loses arising from this case by the same rule, viz. according to the legal rate of interest'.

76 *Wilson v Dunbar Bank plc* [2008] CSIH 27, 2008 SC 457 at [22]–[32] per Lord Reed.

77 *National Bank of Greece SA v Pinios Shipping Co No. 1* [1990] 1 AC 637 at 681–684. It is also only in banking contracts that a right to compound interest will be implied.

78 1998 Act, s. 1(1). The 1998 Act was amended on a number of occasions in order to implement EU Directives on late payment, the last being 2011/7/EU.

79 1998 Act, s. 4(2A). The leading case on the 1998 Act is *Ruttle Plant Hire Ltd v Secretary of State for the Environment, Food and Rural Affairs (No. 2)* [2009] EWCA Civ 97, [2010] 1 All ER (Comm) 444.

80 1998 Act, s. 6 and Late Payment of Commercial Debts (Rate of Interest) (Scotland) Regulations 2002 (SSI 2002/336), art. 4. There are two reference periods: for interest which starts to run between 1 July and 31 December, the rate is 8 per cent over the official dealing rate in force on the preceding 30 June; or, where interest starts to run between 1 January and 30 June, the rate is 8 per cent over the official dealing rate on the preceding 31 December.

81 1998 Act, s. 5A(1) and (2).

they may be significant. Moreover, if the reasonable costs of the supplier in recovering the debt are not met by the fixed sum, the supplier is also entitled to a sum equivalent to the difference between the fixed sum and those costs.[82] The obligation to pay a fixed compensation sum or an additional sum are also to be treated as part of the term implied into the contract creating the debt.[83] Importantly, however, any attempts to contract out of the implied terms are subject to strict statutory control: contract terms are void to the extent that they purport to exclude the right to statutory interest in relation to the debt, unless there is a substantial contractual remedy for late payment of the debt.[84] Express contractual terms on interest are, however, subject to judicial control to protect against penal rates or bases of calculation.[85]

DISCHARGE OF DEBTS

Express discharges

Most contractual obligations are discharged by performance. Take the example of the homeowner, Jess. Jess obtains a loan for £100,000 payable over twenty years from Banca d'Italia. She grants the bank a standard security in 'all sums' terms. After twenty years she has repaid both capital and interest. On first principles, therefore, the security is now empty of all content: there is no principal debt for the security to secure. But because the security is in 'all sums' terms, Jess will wish an express discharge from the bank of both her indebtedness and the security. In the case of all sums securities, discharge of a debt does not discharge the security; while discharge of the security alone only discharges the debt if the only basis for the debt was the undertaking contained in the security (as in a bond and floating charge[86] or a Form A standard security[87]). Discharge of a Form B standard security,[88] in contrast, discharges only the security: in principle, any outstanding personal obligation would remain undisturbed. In the case of standard securities, the 1970 Act provides a form of discharge for registration.[89] Discharges are also of relevance in the law of insolvency since the giving up of a valuable claim by a creditor, for no consideration, may amount to a gratuitous alienation. **8.41**

82 1998 Act, s. 5A(2A).
83 1998 Act, s. 5A(3).
84 1998 Act, s. 8.
85 Debts Securities (Scotland) Act 1856, s. 5, which confers an express power on the court to modify. This easily overlooked provision remains in force and the statutory power to modify extends to money obligations other than bonds: *Cavendish Square Holding BV v Makdessi Parking Eye Ltd* [2015] UKSC 67, [2016] AC 1172 at [252] and [283].
86 See n 13 above.
87 Conveyancing and Feudal Reform (Scotland) Act 1970, Sch. 2. A Form A security contains both the security and the obligation to pay.
88 Which contains only the security; the obligation to pay is found elsewhere, normally in a separate document.
89 1970 Act (n 121), Sch. 4.

Good faith payment

8.42 Sometimes a debtor pays the wrong person. Suppose an individual takes out a life insurance policy. The proceeds are to be held by their testamentary trustees for the benefit of a dependent child. The insured dies. The trustees are all dead. Someone appears and claims the money from the insurance company. As the insurance company is checking the claimant's identity another person appears also claiming to be the person entitled to payment. The insurance company's obvious remedy is to raise a multiplepoinding:[90] a debtor in double distress or holding in a representative capacity with doubt about who is properly entitled to be paid, may raise an action, offer to consign the money, allowing the claimants to the fund (the fund *in medio*) to fight it out, and seek a decree of exoneration and discharge.[91] But it is also a general principle that where a debtor makes payment:

> '*bona fide* to him who had not the true right, but where there was another with a preferable right, which the defender neither did, nor was obliged to know: and therefore the law secures the payer, without prejudice to the pursuer to insist against the obtainer of the payment'.[92]

8.43 Without a judicial process such as a multiplepoinding, however, a fund holder may have a practical difficulty in demonstrating that payment to the wrong creditor was made in good faith.

Prescription

8.44 A classic method by which obligations are discharged is as a result of the creditor doing nothing. Once the prescriptive period has elapsed the debtor's obligation is extinguished. There are two relevant periods: the short negative prescription (five years)[93] and the long negative prescription (twenty years).[94] Most of the obligations referred to in this chapter are subject to the five-year prescription.[95]

Waiver

8.45 At common law, it may be possible to establish that a creditor, by its actions, must be taken to have waived its right to performance. Waiver may arise in two ways. The first is by facts from which the inference can be drawn that the creditor has abandoned their right. The debtor need not demonstrate that they have acted to their detriment in reliance upon the acts or omissions

90 As in *Carmichael v Carmichael's Executrix* 1920 SC (HL) 195.

91 See Bell, *Commentaries* II, 277.

92 Stair, *Institutions* 4.40.33; for further references, see R G Anderson, *Assignation* (Edinburgh: Edinburgh Legal Education Trust, 2008), para. 7–01.

93 Prescription and Limitation (Scotland) Act 1973, s. 6 and Sch. 1. The five-year period is sometimes known as the *quinquennium*. D Johnston, *Prescription and Limitation*, 2nd edn (Edinburgh: W. Green, 2012) is the indispensable guide.

94 Prescription and Limitation (Scotland) Act 1973 (n 127), s. 7 and Sch. 3.

95 Cf e.g. the obligation arising from the issue of a bank note which is subject to the long negative prescription: Prescription and Limitation (Scotland) Act 1973 (n 127), Sch. 1, para. 2(b).

indicating abandonment.[96] The second is a type of personal bar:[97] where the creditor has acted, or omitted to act, in such a way as to allow it properly to 'be inferred . . . that the defenders were abandoning their right, and whether the pursuers had acted in reliance upon a belief induced by the conduct of the defenders'.[98]

NOVATION AND DELEGATION

Obligations, as has been seen, have a positive end (the creditor's claim) and a negative end (the debtor's obligation). The circulation of creditors' claims is considered below. The debtor's position under an obligation cannot be transferred without the consent of the creditor. Where the content of the obligation, between the original debtor and creditor, is altered by consent, this is known as novation. An agreement between A and B that B's obligations will be performed by C and B will be discharged is known as delegation. Lawyers often speak of the assignation of 'contracts'. But that expression is normally a shorthand for the assignation of the creditor's claims and the discharge of the debtor's obligations in return for a transferee undertaking a new obligation. Sometimes legislation provides for the transfer of a whole contractual positions.[99] Sometimes certain 'transfers' of positions under financial contracts are said to take place by way of novation. These are discussed below.[100] **8.46**

These principles can be important in business transfer cases. Suppose Camus SA has a contract with Kafka GmbH to supply office equipment on a monthly basis. Kafka GmbH's trading name in Scotland is 'Metamorphosis'. Kafka GmbH sells its assets, including its business name and contractual rights, to Stevenson Ltd. Stevenson Ltd carries on the business as before. No notice of the transfer is given to Camus SA which continues to supply the goods, as before, to the Metamorphosis business premises in terms of the contract it has with Kafka GmbH. Stevenson Ltd accepts the goods and pays for them. Stevenson Ltd then becomes insolvent. The question arises: who is Camus SA's debtor or debtors? There are at least two possibilities. One is that Kafka GmbH has been replaced by Stevenson Ltd, Stevenson Ltd in that case being known as an *exprommisor*. For that situation to arise, however, it would have been necessary for Camus SA to have consented to Kafka GmbH's discharge. An alternative analysis, and one favoured in recent case law, is that Stevenson Ltd is an *adprommisor*, an additional debtor. Camus SA can therefore sue either Kafka GmbH or Stevenson Ltd or both.[101] **8.47**

96 *Presslie v Cochrane McGregor Group Ltd* 1996 SC 289 at 291 per Lord Morison; *Armia Ltd v Daejan Developments Ltd* 1979 SC (HL) 56.

97 See E C Reid and J Blackie, *Personal Bar* (Edinburgh: W. Green, 2006).

98 *Lousada & Co Ltd v JE Lesser (Properties) Ltd* 1990 SC 178 at 189 per Lord Justice-Clerk Ross. Lord Hodge summarises the law in the context of a share purchase agreement in *McMullen Group Holdings Ltd v Harwood* [2011] CSOH 132, [69]–[76].

99 Rights and obligations are often transferred by statute, such as the Acts of Parliament used to restructure banks and other juristic persons. Employment contracts may transfer in their entirety on the transfer of an undertaking: Transfer of Undertakings (Protection of Employment) Regulations 2006 (SI 2006/246).

100 See para. 8.71.

101 *MRS Distribution Ltd v D S Smith (UK) Ltd* 2004 SLT 631.

CONFUSION

8.48 Confusion (sometimes also known in English as 'merger')[102] is a doctrine that operates on two levels. The first, and most common, effect relates to the effect of creditor succeeding to the debtor's position in an obligation or the debtor succeeding to the creditor's position. This may happen by succession, as where a child is indebted to a parent; the parent dies; and the child inherits the parent's claim against the child. There are also many corporate examples, as where a company buys back its own shares[103] or bonds. The general principle of confusion of debtor and creditor, from which there are exceptions, is that confusion leads to discharge.

8.49 Finding clear statements of the law is not, however, easy. The Draft Common Frame of Reference (DCFR) position may thus be gratefully adopted: 'An obligation is extinguished if the same person becomes debtor and creditor in the same capacity'. The caveat about capacity relates to a case where, for instance, a sole trustee expends money from their private patrimony on trust affairs. The trustee is entitled to be reimbursed for their expenses from the trust estate. But there is only one legal person, the trustee. The claim is held by the trustee (in their private capacity) against themselves (in their capacity as trustee).

8.50 The second level on which confusion may operate is that of creation of an obligation. Andrea cannot enter into a contract with herself. Again, there is an exception where Andrea is acting in different capacities. And it is quite common in the corporate sphere for single persons to act in all sorts of different capacities. Trusts have already been mentioned. Another example is the case of the one-person company: Andrea may be shareholder, director and creditor of the company. She may pass resolutions as shareholder; as director; or enter into a service contract, *qua* director, with the company, which requires her own express approval *qua* shareholder; or grant the company loans for which the company will grant her security.[104] In such circumstances it is important that good records are kept, essentially recording Andrea's own thought processes.[105]

SET-OFF

General

8.51 'Set-off' is not a term of art in Scots law. But it is useful general expression covering various institutions each of which implement the same general principle. The principle is simple and, indeed, common sense. Suppose Alan owes Stéphanie £10,000. Stéphanie owes Alan £8,000. The various rules of set-off allow Alan, if required by Stéphanie to pay £10,000, to pay that debt in part

102 As in DCFR art. III.–6:201.
103 See Companies Act 2006, s. 690 onward.
104 See the facts of *Salomon v A Salomon & Co Ltd* [1897] AC 22.
105 See, for instance, *Neptune (Vehicle Washing Equipment) Ltd v Fitzgerald* [1996] Ch 274.

by setting-off Stéphanie's liability to Alan of £8,000. Alan is, in principle, bound to pay only £2,000.

Compensation

Compensatio is regulated by the Compensation Act 1592, which remains in force.[106] The Act provides (in its entirety): **8.52**

> 'Oure soverane lord and estaitis of parliament statutis and ordanis that ony debt de liquido ad liquidum instantlie verifiet be wreit or aith of the partie befoir the geving of decreit be admittit be all jugis within this realme be way of exceptioun, bot not eftir the geving thairof in the suspensioun or in reductioun of the same decreit.

[Our sovereign lord and estates of parliament statutes and ordains that any debt *de liquido ad liquidum* instantly verified by writing or oath of the party before decree be admitted by all judges within this realm by way of exception, but not after the giving thereof in the suspension or in reduction of the same decree].'[107]

Most contract debts for a fixed amount are 'liquid' claims; a claim for damages, in contrast, is the classic illiquid claim. The Compensation Act 1592 applies only to liquid claims. There must be an element of mutuality of obligation between the parties in order for compensation to apply (there must be, to use the Latin, a *concursus debiti et crediti*). In the above example, for instance, there is mutuality of obligation between Alan and Stéphanie. But it would not be possible for Alan to seek to plead compensation because Stéphanie's sister happened to owe him money. If Alan assigns his claim against Stéphanie to Jack, Stéphanie can plead such defences she had against Alan (including compensation) up to the moment when she receives intimation of the assignation in favour of Jack. **8.53**

In some circumstances, the court retains an equitable discretion to allow an illiquid claim for damages to be pled in defence of an admitted debt, where the illiquid claim can be rapidly quantified.[108] A defence of compensation need not arise out of the same or related contractual relationship out of which the pursuer seeks payment.[109] So claims on unrelated contracts may found compensation. **8.54**

A defender cannot refuse a claim by compensating a claim the pursuer owes to the defender in a different capacity. So if Peter sues Paul for £100 but Peter is indebted to Paul for £100 in the latter's capacity as trustee for the Third Lanark Supporters' Trust, Paul cannot refuse payment. There is *concursus* of legal personalities, but no *concursus* of patrimonies.[110] This principle must not, however, be taken too far. **8.55**

106 RPS 1592/4/83; APS III, 573, c 61.

107 In *Donaldson v Donaldson* (1852) 14 D 849 at 855, Lord Cunninghame described the Compensation Act as 'a just and positive statute, most creditable to the wisdom and sound views of the ancient Scottish legislature'.

108 *Inveresk plc v Tullis Russell Papermakers Ltd* 2010 SC (UKSC) 106 at [58], [71], [81], [89] and [107] per Lord Rodger.

109 *Turner v Inland Revenue Commissioners* 1994 SLT 811.

110 See para. 1.30 above.

8.56 Take the truster-as-trustee trust. Suppose Hamburg Bank loans €10m to Alba Heritable Investments Limited. Alba has other current accounts in credit with the Bank to the tune of €5m. And suppose the bank sues for payment of the €10m. All other things being equal, Alba could compensate that claim with their liquid counterclaim of €5m. The bank cannot cut out that claim by declaring a trust of the claim to the €10m, at least where the declaration has not been intimated to Alba and Alba's counter-claims arose before intimation.[111] The interposition of a trust does, however, prevent compensation being pled in respect of claims that arise in Alba's favour against the bank subsequent to notice of the declaration of trust.[112]

8.57 Similarly, compensation cannot be pled against a claim for repayment of a fund which has been specifically appropriated to a particular purpose; so, where a firm of accountants had collected debts owed to a company and held them in an account which the client company was free to utilise, the firm could not seek to compensate against those funds its claim for payment of fees.[113] And where money on deposit with a bank is held in the name of A and B, the bank cannot refuse to pay A on the basis of B's outstanding indebtedness.[114] Where, however, Alpha Ltd is in administration and the administrator sues a debtor, Bravo Ltd, Bravo Ltd may still plead compensation.[115]

8.58 Compensation is not automatic; it has to be pled and sustained in court: compensation, it has been said, is the 'the operation of the judge rather than the law'.[116] This rule allows a creditor to choose whether or not to exercise a right of compensation and, if so, in respect of which debt. For example, suppose a B is indebted to A on contract one, but holds claims against A on contracts two and three. The B holds security in respect A's indebtedness on account two. The indebtedness on contract three is unsecured. B can compensate its liability on contract one against contract three, leaving only a secured balance.

8.59 Because compensation is the operation of the judge, it cannot be pled against a charge for payment following on a decree or a document registered in the Books of Council and Session for execution: the effect of registration is the equivalent of a court decree.[117] There are special rules for set-off of debits and credits with HMRC.[118]

111 Cf *Royal Insurance (UK) Ltd v Amec Construction Scotland Ltd* 2008 SC 201.

112 Cf *Johnston v Johnston* (1875) 2 R 986 at 997 per Lord President Inglis.

113 *Mycroft, Petr* 1983 SLT 342; *Melville Dundas Ltd v Hotel Corporation of Edinburgh Ltd* 2007 SC 12 at [24]. See further G L Gretton, 'Scotland' in W Swadling (ed), *The Quistclose Trust: Critical Essays* (Oxford: Hart Publishing, 2004), pp. 169, 172.

114 *Anderson v Northern Bank of Scotland Ltd* (1901) 4 F 49 at 55 per Lord McLaren.

115 This is important because, in terms of the Insolvency Act 1986, Sch. B1, para. 4(6), the consent of the court or the administrator is required to institute legal proceedings against a company in administration. But there is nothing to stop a defender pleading compensation, or, indeed, balancing of accounts in bankruptcy, in defence to a claim brought by a company in administration.

116 Erskine, *Institute* 3.4.12. For the background, see R G Anderson, *Assignation* (2008), para. 8–43 onward.

117 *McLauchlin, Petr* [2010] CSIH 24, at [7]. This decision also deals with the important question of quantification of a claim due under a document of debt.

118 Finance Act 2008, ss. 130–134.

Contractual set-off

8.60 The careful draftsperson of a corporate or financial contract, however, does not wish to leave matters of mutual debit and credit to the vagaries of subsequent litigation. Contracts thus make bespoke provision for set-off. The principle of contractual set-off is so self-evident that it is rarely discussed.[119] The whole point of contractual set-off provisions is to entitle the parties to the contract to achieve the effects of compensation by declaration or notice or some other contractually specified procedure.

Insolvency set-off: 'balancing of accounts in bankruptcy'

8.61 The general principles of compensation are the subject of an equitable extension on insolvency:[120] this is the law of 'balancing of accounts in bankruptcy'.[121] On insolvency a debtor to the insolvent estate may withhold payment of its debt on the basis of a claim against the insolvent estate that is neither liquid nor even presently due;[122] as long as the claim existed prior to insolvency (assuming the debt that the insolvency administrator seeks to recover is also a pre-insolvency debt). A claim that the proponer would otherwise be able to rank on the insolvent's estate is certainly covered.[123] But so too are defences that the defender would have had to any claim for payment made by the insolvent. Contingent claims are covered.[124] A balancing of accounts under Scots law, like compensation, must be asserted; it does not occur automatically.[125] The general principles of balancing of accounts apply also on corporate insolvency whether liquidation, receivership or administration.[126] The right can be invoked by an insolvent debtor as well as by a creditor against an insolvent debtor.[127] The general principles applies too on the insolvency of credit institutions, although within a special framework of provisions applicable to those institutions.[128]

119 See R G Anderson, 'Security over bank accounts in Scots law' (2010) 4 Law and Financial Markets Review 593.

120 *Atlantic Engine Co (1920) Ltd (in liquidation) v Lord Advocate* 1955 SLT 17 at 20 per Lord President Cooper (Ordinary); *Secretary of State for Trade and Industry v Frid* [2004] 2 AC 506 at [32] per Lord Hope of Craighead.

121 The classic discussion is in Bell, *Commentaries* II, 118–120.

122 *Scott's Tr v Scott* (1887) 14 R 1043 at 1051 per Lord President Inglis.

123 *Secretary of State for Trade and Industry v Frid* [2004] 2 AC 506 at [32] and [34] per Lord Hope of Craighead.

124 W A Wilson, *The Scottish Law of Debt*, 2nd edn (Edinburgh: W. Green, 1991), para. 13.10 and authorities there cited.

125 *Westminster Bank Ltd v Halesowen Presswork & Assemblies Ltd* [1972] AC 785 at 822D–822G per Lord Kilbrandon.

126 *Integrated Building Services Engineering Consultants Ltd v Pihl UK Ltd* [2010] CSOH 80 at [21] and [34] per Lord Hodge (Ordinary), pointing out that Lord Hope of Craighead's *dicta* in *Melville Dundas Ltd v George Wimpey UK Ltd* 2007 SC (HL) 116 at [33], that a balancing of accounts is available only on bankruptcy or liquidation, were not intended to be definitive. See too *Joint Administrators of Connaught Partnerships Ltd (in administration) v Perth & Kinross District Council* [2013] CSOH 149.

127 *Borthwick v Scottish Widows' Fund and Life Assurance Society* (1862) 2 M 595 at 599 per Lord Mackenzie (Ordinary). See the full treatment in D Mackenzie-Skene, *Bankruptcy* (Edinburgh: W. Green, 2018), para. 16–78.

128 *Joint Administrators of Heritable Bank plc (in administration) v Winding Up Board of Landsbanki Islands HF* 2012 SC 209 affd 2013 SC (UKSC) 201.

Netting

8.62 'Netting' is the name for contractual set-off on a grand scale, millions of banking transactions that occur every day as a result of a consumer purchases, mortgage payments, bank withdrawals and so on. In so far as these are carried out with bank money, cash rarely, if ever, moves. The payments are effected by multiple account entries between the respective banks of the parties. This is the process of 'netting'. The process is of fundamental importance to finance transactions on regulated market exchanges. Under the regulations, netting is defined thus:[129]

> '"netting" means the conversion into one net claim or obligation of different claims or obligations between participants resulting from the issue and receipt of transfer orders between them, whether on a bilateral or multilateral basis and whether through the interposition of a clearing house, central counterparty or settlement agent or otherwise'.

8.63 Netting may be by novation or by contract consolidation; by settlement, or by payment; or by 'close-out' netting:[130] the conversion of non-monetary obligations into money claims through the exercise of a right to cancel or close out transactions. Settlement or payment netting is not subject to the usual mandatory insolvency rules such as, for example, those that would normally prevent the holder of a collateral security from enforcing it where the security giver is in administration;[131] nor the rule that pre-insolvency debts cannot be set-off against post-insolvency debts and vice versa.[132]

CIRCULATING CREDIT (AND ACCESSORY RIGHTS)

Assignation

8.64 Contracts are at least bilateral and many are multilateral. The creditor in any claim arising out of the contract (like most other creditors) is entitled to transfer their claim to performance without the consent of the debtor. The transferor is called the cedent or assignor; the transferee is the assignee. Transfer to the assignee occurs, however, only on intimation of the assignation to the debtor. Intimation must be in writing and, if it is to comply with the terms of the legislation,[133] should include a copy of at least the operative terms of the assignation and the cedent's signature. But the courts have showing a willingness to accord latitude to the formalities for a valid intimation.[134] It is likely that intimation will be abolished as a constitutive requirement for assignations if the alternative of registration is employed.[135] But intimation is

129 Financial Markets and Insolvency (Settlement Finality) Regulations 1999 (SI 1999/2979), reg. 2(1), reflecting Settlement Finality Directive (1998/26/EC), art. 2(k). 'Transfer order' is separately defined.

130 See the Financial Collateral Arrangements (No. 2) Regulations 2003 (SI 2003/3226), reg. 3.

131 Settlement Finality Directive (1998/26/EC, as amended), implemented in the UK by 1999 Regulations (n 166), reg. 13.

132 Settlement Finality Directive, art. 3(1) (as amended).

133 Transmission of Moveable Property (Scotland) Act 1862 (19 & 20 Vict, c 60), s. 2.

134 See, e.g. *Christie Owen and Davies plc v Campbell* [2009] CSIH 26, 2009 SC 436.

135 Moveable Transactions (Scotland) Bill which followed the Scottish Law Commission's

always important for practical purposes, such as to provide a cut-off date for the debtor's defences; to prevent the debtor paying the assignor in good faith, and thus destroying by performance the asset for which the assignee has paid good money.

The general principle is that the debtor cannot be prejudiced by the assignation. A doctrinal reason for that general principle is that the assignee merely exercises the cedent's rights. This is the rule known as *assignatus utitur iure auctoris*. It is but a positive formulation of the well-known negative formulation much referred to in property law: *nemo dat quod non habet.*[136] As a result, the debtor can raise all defences against a claim by the assignee that they could have raised, prior to intimation, against the cedent. One important defence is that of compensation.[137] Generally speaking, contractual prohibitions on assignation render any assignation in breach of that prohibition ineffective.[138] An exception to that rule may arise where the contract gives rise to a payment obligation that amounts to a receivable due under a contract for the supply of goods and services, which is not a financial contract.[139] As a general principle, and in the absence of any express provision to the contrary, the cedent warrants that the debt is due and owing at the date they grant the assignation, but not the debtor's solvency.[140] That principle does not apply where the assignation is gratuitous; or where the cedent is acting in a representative capacity, such as *qua* executor or *qua* trustee. **8.65**

Some patrimonial rights are dependent on the existence of another right. Such dependent rights are known as 'accessory rights'. Both personal rights and real rights may be accessory. The classic example of an accessory right is a security right. That security right may be personal (such as that arising out of a cautionary obligation) or real (such as that arising out of a pledge). The principal obligation is normally a personal obligation to render some performance. The accessory principle has a number of aspects. The first is that it is not possible to constitute a properly accessory obligation without the existence of a principal obligation. The second is that discharge of the principal leads to discharge of the accessory. And the third is that wherever the principal goes, so too does the accessory. Assignation of securities is a specialised subject of considerable practical importance. In short, the assignation of a standard security is effective only on registration in the Land Register;[141] an assignation **8.66**

Report on Moveable Transactions (Scot. Law Com. No. 279, 2017) and *Discussion Paper on Moveable Transactions* (Scot. Law Com. DP No. 151, 2011).

136 See para. 3.97 onward above.

137 See para. 8.52 above.

138 *Linden Gardens Trust Ltd v Lenesta Sludge Disposal Ltd* [1994] 1 AC 85, followed in *Apollo Engineering Ltd v James Scott Ltd* 2000 SC 228.

139 Small Business, Enterprise and Employment Act 2015, s. 1. The only regulations made under s. 1, however, are the Business Contract Terms (Assignment of Receivables) Regulations 2018 (SI 2018/1254) which appear to apply, at least by implication, only in England and Wales and Northern Ireland. But reg. 1(4) provides that the regulations apply also to a contract term applying the law of Scotland 'where the term appears to the court or arbitrator or arbiter to have been imposed wholly or mainly for the purpose of enabling the party imposing it to evade the operation of these Regulations'.

140 This is known as 'warrandice *debitum subesse*': see *Reid v Barclay* (1879) 6 R 1007.

141 Conveyancing and Feudal Reform (Scotland) Act 1970, s. 14. For detailed discussion, see A J M Steven, 'Accessoriness and security over land' (2009) 13 Edin LR 387.

of a floating charge is effective on intimation of the assignation to the debtor.[142] In the standard security case, however, intimation to the debtor remains a practical requirement.

8.67 Two examples demonstrate some of the issues that arise. Suppose Jim grants an all sums standard security to Maria but primarily in respect of a twenty-year term loan for £150,000. In year five, Maria decides she wishes the capital now, so she 'sells' her claim against Jim to Nina, who pays Maria £130,000 in consideration of an assignation of the claim and the security. The assignation is registered in the Land Register and intimated to Jim. Jim, however, needs additional finance. Nina is willing to make further advances to Jim of £50,000. One difficulty is that, in year three, Jim granted another all sums security to Fenster Finance LLP when he bought new double glazing for his flat in respect of a debt to Fenster of £25,000. Nina will make the further advance of £50,000 only if the further advance is covered by the first ranking security.

8.68 There are two points to make. First, it is sometimes said that the assignation must specify the sum for which the standard security is assigned with the consequence that the effect of assignation of an all sums standard security is to crystallise the amount due under the security.[143] But the need to specify arises because it is possible, in principle, (although rarely encountered in practice) for Maria to retain her all sums security but assign part of a claim against Jim, say £50,000 with part of the security, i.e. to the extent of £50,000.[144] But it is sufficient specification, where an all sums security is to be assigned, to indicate that the amount for which an all sums security is being assigned is for 'all sums'.[145]

8.69 The second issue is whether the debtor's consent is required to the assignation of a standard security. As a matter of general principle, the whole point of assignation is that it is effective without the debtor's consent. And that general principle applies where there is a standard security granted in respect of the claim. It should be remembered too that the granter of a standard security is not always the debtor in the obligation. So if Beth takes a loan for £100,000, it may be that her husband, Peter, will grant a standard security limited to £100,000 over a property he owns, but with no personal obligation on his part. Beth need not consent; neither need Peter.

142 *Libertas-Kommerz GmbH v Johnson* 1977 SC 191; see too *Joint Liquidators of Simclar (Ayrshire) Ltd v Simclar Group Ltd* [2011] CSOH 54, 2011 SLT 1131.

143 The pioneering analysis of this difficult subject is G L Gretton, 'Assignation of all sums standard securities' 1994 SLT (News) 207. See too R G Anderson, 'Assignation of All-Sums Securities' in F McCarthy, J Chalmers and S Bogle (eds), *Property and Conveyancing: Essays for Professor Robert Rennie* (Cambridge: Open Book Publishers, 2015).

144 These issues tend to arise when the transfer is implied as a result of the doctrine of catholic and secondary creditors (for which see para. 8.92 below), or to effect a cautioner's relief (for which, see para. 8.83).

145 Conveyancing and Feudal Reform (Scotland) Act 1970, s. 14(1) provides that the effect of registration of an assignation of a security is 'to vest the security in the assignee as effectually as if the security . . . had been granted in the assignee's favour'. Had an all sums security originally been granted in favour of an assignee for all sums, it would be effective to cover sums acquired by the original grantee by assignation.

There are difficulties with the assignation of an all sums security where the assignee wishes to make further advances.[146] But whatever those difficulties may be, an all sums security – at the risk of stating the obvious – is an all sums security: there is thus nothing to prevent the secured creditor taking assignations of the unsecured claims held by other creditors, with the result that a claim originally unsecured becomes secured. 8.70

Obligations: transfer by novation

Only rights or claims, and not liabilities, may be assigned. Assignation is effective without the debtor's consent. Where a debtor wishes to effect a transfer of a liability, however, this can occur only with the creditor's consent. There are two functional ways in which this can be done. The first is by novation or delegation (their effects are similar). The second is by 'transfer of a contractual position'. 8.71

In financial practice, novations are common. The whole law of syndicated lending, for instance, presupposes that the banks participating in the nominal lender's position, after the funds have been advanced, will change. The market standard documentation (written under English law) refers to transfers by novation. Novation is used because it is often the case that even the lenders have obligations under the contract that they would wish to transfer. For a valid novation, it will be recalled, the consent of the counterparty – in the case of a loan, the borrower – is required. In most syndicated loan contracts, however, the borrower will consent in advance to 'transfers by novation' of the positions of other parties to the loan or other structured finance agreement, even if that involves those parties effectively 'transferring' their obligations.[147] 'Transfer by novation' is sometimes also encountered in relation to the transfer of company shares. In private companies, shares are transferable only with the consent of the directors of the company in which the shares are held. Where the shares are certificated, transfer of the share involves cancellation of the transferor's certificate and the re-issue of a new share certificate to the transferee. This procedure is described in standard English works as 'transfer by novation'.[148] 8.72

Subject to the terms of the parties' agreement, the effect of a novation is to discharge the original obligations and replace them with a new obligation. There is no reason in principle, however, why the law should not admit the transfer of full contractual positions, without the need for the formality of discharge and constitution, providing the original parties to the contract, together with the proposed transferee, all consent.[149] 8.73

146 See Gretton (n 143) and Anderson (n 143).

147 See, e.g. *The Argo Fund Ltd v Essar Steel Ltd* [2006] 1 All ER (Comm) 56; *Habibsons Bank Ltd v Standard Chartered Bank (HK) Ltd* [2011] QB 943; *McKillen v Maybourne Finance Ltd* [2012] EWCA Civ 864.

148 L Gullifer, *Goode and Gullifer on Legal Problems of Credit and Security*, 6th edn (London: Sweet & Maxwell, 2017), para. 3–10 admits also of the 'mortgage by novation'.

149 The idea is recognised in both UNIDROIT Principles of International Commercial Contracts, art. 9.3 onward and the Draft Common Frame of Reference, art. III.–5:302. These provisions apply *mutatis mutandis* the principles of transfer of obligations whereby the

Selling debt

8.74 In the same way that there may be a contract to acquire the real right of ownership of land, parties to a commercial transaction can contract to acquire personal claims, such as receivables. Receivables are what, in a corporate balance sheet, is recorded under the heading 'debtors'. The moneys owed to the company by those debtors represent assets. Suppose, then, Utopia SA seeks to raise finance by 'selling' its receivables to Caledonia Bank Ltd. The parties enter into a contract of sale. Caledonia Bank Ltd agrees to purchase, and Utopia SA agrees to sell, a specified portfolio of receivables. The effect of the sale agreement is to give Caledonia Bank Ltd a personal right under the purchase agreement to transfer of Utopia SA's personal rights against its debtors: Caledonia Bank Ltd has a personal right to personal rights. Whether Caledonia Bank Ltd, in fact, ever seeks transfer of the receivables by intimated assignation is a matter for Caledonia Bank Ltd. Until Caledonia Bank Ltd intimates an assignation Caledonia Bank Ltd is at risk of Utopia SA's insolvency. There are a number of markets for receivables financing depending on which party bears the risk of non-payment.[150]

Securitisation

8.75 Securitisation is often complex[151] but the basic underlying legal concepts are not. Securitisation involves the sale of a portfolio of receivables to a corporate vehicle specially incorporated for the purpose (SPV). The SPV pays for the portfolio by issuing financial instruments on the capital markets, using the proceeds of the issue to fund the purchase and/or ring-fencing the asset pool.[152] The originator (the bank) gets a large capital sum today on a portfolio of loans that may have a term of twenty-five years. The SPV obtains the rights to payment under the original loan contracts and uses those repayments to service its own obligations to the holders of the financial instruments it has issued. And the holders of the instruments are, in theory, able to secure an investment in a particular asset that they consider desirable.

8.76 Nonetheless, despite the simplicity of the basic legal construct, elaborate corporate structures and documentation can give rise to all sorts of intricate legal questions, which go well beyond the scope of this chapter.[153] The sale of the receivables under Scots law is problematic because intimation remains a con-

transferee becomes an additional rather than a substitute debtor unless the original debtor is discharged.

150 See H Beale et al. (eds), *The Law of Security and Title-Based Financing*, 3rd edn (Oxford: Oxford University Press, 2018), paras 7.103–7.132.

151 *Re Sigma Finance Corporation (in administration)* [2009] UKSC 2, [2010] 1 All ER 571 did not concern a securitisation but provides for the student a useful insight into the voluminous nature of structured finance documentation.

152 See the Regulated Covered Bonds Regulations 2008 (SI 2008/346) as amended for a regulated securitisation structure sometimes employed by banks. There are other securitisation structures that are not encompassed by this regulatory regime.

153 A flavour of the documentation can be found in *Citibank NA, MBIA Assurance SA v QVT Financial LP* [2007] EWCA Civ 11. For a helpful overview, see Beale (n 150), paras 7.130–7.139.

stitutive requirement for a completed assignation.[154] If a portfolio of receivables comprises tens of thousands of loans, it is not practicable to intimate the sale to the debtors under each individual loan, not least because the income streams are to continue to be paid to the originator. In practice, therefore, the standard Scots law structure is for the originator to declare a trust over the portfolio in question in favour of the SPV.[155]

Financial collateral

8.77 National law on concepts such as assignation must, however, yield to principles applicable to transnational financial markets where financial assets are involved. The Financial Collateral Regulations[156] apply to such arrangements where the parties choose to invoke the regime. The Regulations implement for the UK the EU Financial Collateral Directive.[157] Neither the Directive nor the Regulations are easy to understand.[158] Financial collateral means 'financial instruments', 'cash' or 'credit claims'. The key concepts are 'control' and 'appropriation'. The idea of the Directive is to allow financial collateral arrangements – such as repurchase agreements – to have effect according to the terms without disruption from local EU laws of insolvency or set-off.

PLURALITY OF DEBTORS AND CREDITORS

General

8.78 Contractual matrices are often very deliberately constructed in order to take advantage of the basic principle of privity of contract: unless there is a third party right[159] only parties to the contract may sue on it.[160] A contract presupposes at least two parties. But contracts may have many more than two parties. Where there are multiple debtors and creditors, plurality of debtors and creditors apply.

154 The Scottish Law Commission, *Report on Moveable Transactions* (2017) proposes that registration in an online register becomes an alternative to intimation as a constitutive requirement of a transfer by assignation.

155 See discussion at para. 11.91 below.

156 Financial Collateral Arrangements (No. 2) Regulations 2003 (SI 2003/3226).

157 Financial Collateral Directive 2002/47/EC (as amended).

158 See generally G L Gretton, 'Financial collateral and the fundamentals of secured transactions' (2006) 10 Edin LR 209. The main appellate consideration of the Regulations has been in two British Virgin Islands appeals to the Privy Council: *Cukurova Finance International Ltd v Alfa Telecom Turkey Ltd* [2009] UKPC 19, [2009] Bus LR 1619 and [2013] UKPC 2, [2016] AC 923 and discussion in Beale (n 150), Ch. 3.

159 Contract (Third Party Rights) (Scotland) Act 2017. For the background, see Scottish Law Commission, *Review of Contract Law: Discussion Paper on Third Party Rights in Contract* (DP No. 157, 2014).

160 Cf 'collateral warranties' provided to persons not otherwise party to the contract in terms of which the original warranties are given: *The Scottish Coal Company Ltd v Trustees of Firm Timber Growth Fund III* [2009] CSOH 30; for the assignation of collateral warranties, see *Scottish Widows Services Ltd v Harmon/CRM Facades Ltd (in liquidation)* 2010 SLT 1102, affd 2012 SLT 68. Cf. *Royal Bank of Scotland plc v Carlyle* 2015 SC (UKSC) 93.

Plurality of debtors

8.79 There are three introductory general principles:

(a) In Scots law, 'joint' liability means that each debtor is liable, pro rata, for their own share. 'Several' liability, in contrast, means that each debtor is liable for the whole amount.[161] So if Jack and Jill are 'jointly' liable to Christine for 100, Jack is liable for fifty and Jill is liable for fifty. Where Jack and Jill are 'severally' liable for 100, Christine can sue either Jack or Jill for 100. To confuse matters, the words 'joint' and 'several' are used in precisely opposite senses in English law.
(b) The most common form of liability, however, is 'joint and several' liability, otherwise known as liability *in solidum*. In short, obligants who are jointly and severally liable in this way (co-obligants) are potentially liable to the creditor for the full amount and liable among themselves pro rata (i.e. for their own share). So, again, if Jack and Jill are jointly and severally liable to Christine for 100, Christine can sue either Jack or Jill for the full 100. If she recovers 100 from, say, Jill, it is for Jill to seek relief from Jack for his share.
(c) Joint and several liability may arise either in contract or in delict; or where one debtor is liable in delict and the other in contract, providing the events contributed to producing the same legal wrong and loss.[162]

Plurality of creditors

8.80 The law of joint and several creditors in Scots law is underdeveloped and it is not easy to find a concise statement of the law.[163] The statements in the international instruments provide a useful systematic benchmark of what the law ought to be in the absence of authority.[164]

8.81 In the absence of express terms, the common law draws the analytical distinction between performances which are divisible and those which are indivisible. But the distinction is more easily stated than applied in practice. The general principles are best illustrated by examples. Suppose Primus, Secundus and Tertius own land in common. They sell the land to David for £90,000. The contract may provide that David shall pay each of them £30,000. Alternatively, the contract may provide that David's debt is owed to Primus, Secundus and Tertius *in solidum* (or, more commonly, 'jointly and severally'). In that case, David can choose which of the creditors to pay. Payment of the whole amount to any of the entitled creditors discharges David.

161 See generally W W McBryde, *The Law of Contract in Scotland*, 3rd edn (Edinburgh: W. Green, 2007), para. 11–01.

162 See the discussion in *Grunwald v Hughes* 1965 SLT 209 and *Ruddy v Chief Constable of Strathclyde Police* [2012] UKSC 57, 2013 SC (UKSC) 126 at [33]. Cf *Fleming v McGillivray* 1946 SC 1.

163 See, e.g. Gloag, *Contract*, 2nd edn (Edinburgh: W. Green, 1929), pp. 202–204; McBryde, *Contract* (2007), para. 11–24; *Trayner's Latin Maxims*, 4th edn (Edinburgh: W. Green, 1894), s.v. *correi credendi*.

164 See, e.g. the Draft Common Frame of Reference, art. III.–4:201–207 and UNIDROIT Principles of International Commercial Contracts, art. 11.2.1. See generally S Meier, 'Introduction before Art 10:201', in N Jansen and R Zimmermann (eds), *Commentaries on European Contract Laws* (Oxford: Oxford University Press, 2018), p. 1603 onward.

8.82 One case of solidarity among creditors is found where creditors are trustees. Each trustee is empowered to discharge the debtor or assign the claim against the debtor without first obtaining the consent of the other trustees.[165] Another case is the joint bank account. Subject to the express terms on which the account is to be operated, the bank is discharged if it complies with an instruction from either of the account holders without reference to the other account holder's consent. In each of these cases, a single co-creditor who receives payment of the whole amount may be obliged to account for that money to their fellow creditors. From the creditors' perspective, however, where the performance is indivisible, in order to protect each creditor, it is normally necessary for each creditor to join in any action to enforce the obligation.[166]

RIGHTS OF RELIEF

General

8.83 Commercial contracts, we have seen, are often not just bilateral, but multilateral. It is also common in commercial situations for complex contractual matrices to be formed by chains of multiple bilateral contracts. The interaction of these contracts, in determining which party bears the ultimate risk for a loss incurred, may be a matter of some complexity. A party who is primarily liable may have various bases for a right of relief against another party, which, in turn, may have a right of relief against another party still. And so on. For more than 2,000 years, Lord Rodger of Earlsferry memorably pointed out, lawyers have been wrestling with questions of 'legal eternal triangles'.[167]

Legal bases for rights of relief

8.84 Commercial contracts are often about allocating risks. Where risks materialise and liability is incurred, there is a question of working out which party is ultimately liable. So the driver of a car who culpably injures another road user is primarily liable in delict to pay damages to the injured party. But in most cases the driver will have a right of relief against their insurers: although the driver is primarily liable *in delict* to the injured party, the insurer is primarily liable to the driver *in contract*.[168]

8.85 A right of relief may be based on an express contractual provision; on an implied contractual provision; in unjustified enrichment; in *negotiorum gestio*; in subrogation; or in an assignation. Rights of relief based on contractual provisions are self-explanatory; difficulties arise not with express rights of relief,

165 Trusts (Scotland) Act 1961, s. 2.

166 *Detrick & Webster v Laing's Patent Overhead Handstitch Sewing Machine Co Ltd* (1885) 12 R 416.

167 *Heaton v Axa & Law Assurance Society plc* [2002] 2 AC 329 at [85].

168 There is a statutory right for someone injured by the insured driver of a motor vehicle to sue the insurer directly: European Communities (Rights against Insurers) Regulations 2002 (SI 2002/3061), reg. 3.

but with the express exclusion of a liability that would otherwise have formed the basis of an action for relief in the context of contribution.[169]

8.86 Both unjustified enrichment and *negotiorum gestio* may be taken together. Rights of relief arise in a three-party situation. So, suppose Paula pays David's debt to Claire. David's debt having been discharged, Paula has a claim against him in order to prevent David being unjustifiably enriched.[170]

Contribution

8.87 This doctrine is best illustrated by example. Suppose Nicola, while cycling to work along the Broomielaw, is hit by a car driven by Andrew. She is injured and sues Andrew for damages. Andrew's position, however, is that the accident was wholly or partially caused by the fault and negligence of Richard, whose careless driving required Andrew to take evasive action, as a result of which, says Andrew, he hit Nicola. Andrew can convene Richard as an additional defender to the civil action by way of a 'third party notice'.[171] Suppose, however, that, when Nicola's personal injuries action comes to court, Andrew has not (yet) been able to identify Richard. If Andrew has to pay the full amount to Nicola he (or his insurers) may subsequently seek contribution from Richard,[172] even in the event that the decree obtained by Nicola against Andrew was essentially of consent.[173]

8.88 In a commercial context, difficult questions can arise where there the contracts regulating the parties' relationships contain indemnity, exclusion or limitation clauses.[174] Suppose a ship owner, Farstad, which chartered a ship to ASCO. ASCO engaged Enviroco to clean Farstad's ship. Enviroco's negligence causes a fire. Enviroco argues that ASCO was also at least partially responsible for the fire. In terms of the charterparty between Farstad and ASCO, Farstad indemnified ASCO for any losses or liabilities that ASCO might incur in relation to loss or damage caused to the vessel even as a result of ASCO's negligence. The question arises whether, despite the contractual provision in the charterparty, Enviroco can seek contribution from ASCO, leaving ASCO to obtain its relief from Farstad. Lord Hodge, in a judgment upheld by the Supreme Court, answers the question in the negative: a contractual arrangement entered into in good faith (prior to the loss or damage incurred), which excludes the liability of a party who has caused the loss (here ASCO) to the party who has suffered the loss (here Farstad), means that ASCO could not

169 See para. 8.87 below.

170 See generally H L MacQueen, 'Payment of Another's Debt' in D E L Johnston and R Zimmermann (eds), *Unjustified Enrichment: Key Issues in Comparative Perspective* (Cambridge: Cambridge University Press, 2002).

171 RCS, r. 26.1; OCR, r. 20.1.

172 Law Reform (Miscellaneous Provisions) (Scotland) Act 1985, s. 3.

173 *Comex Houlder Diving Ltd v Colne Fishing Co Ltd* 1987 SC (HL) 88. On the facts of that case, however, contribution was disallowed because the pursuer had paid pursuant to a foreign action which, the House of Lords held, was not covered by the 1985 Act.

174 The facts of this example are taken from *Farstad Supply A/S v Enviroco Ltd* 2008 SLT 703, revd 2009 SC 489, revd 2010 SC (UKSC) 87. The commendably concise opinion of the Lord Ordinary, Lord Hodge, ultimately upheld in the Supreme Court, is the most lucid treatment of this difficult area.

have been sued by Farstad. And, because ASCO could not have been sued by Farstad, Enviroco could not seek contribution from ASCO.[175]

Assignation

Where a cautioner pays the principal debtor's debt, the cautioner has a right of relief against the principal debtor.[176] The basis for the right of relief may be mandate, *negotiorum gestio*, unjustified enrichment or assignation. **8.89**

One difficulty with a cautioner's right of relief being based on unjustified enrichment is that the enrichment arises only because the principal debtor's debt has been discharged. But if the debt has been discharged, there is nothing to assign and, importantly, any accessory securities must have been discharged. Even if the security is non-accessory – as with the 'all sums' security – an assignation of it is pointless since, *ex hypothesi*, the claim it secured has been discharged. The underlying rationale for the 'benefit of the cession of actions', therefore, is to provide a doctrinal basis for explaining why the payer's right of relief extends to securities. On this analysis, therefore, on payment of another's debt, the payer is conceived of having bought the creditor's rights against the principal debtor: the claim is transferred, with accessory securities, not discharged.[177] **8.90**

SUBROGATION

Where an insurer indemnifies an insured for losses caused by a third party, the insurer is entitled to be 'subrogated' to the insured's rights of action against the third party.[178] One difficulty is the English cases are based on its own peculiar historical developments, which did not easily recognise assignments of claims. It is probably for this reason that, although subrogation appears to effect a transfer of the insured's right of action, the insurer *must* nonetheless bring subrogated claims in the name of the insured.[179] **8.91**

CATHOLIC AND SECONDARY CREDITORS[180]

Gloag and Irvine describe this doctrine in this way:[181] **8.92**

> 'Where a party has granted to one creditor a right in security over two or more subjects, and to another creditor a postponed right over one of such subjects, these rights are known as catholic and secondary securities, and the holders thereof as

175 2008 SLT 703, [19] per Lord Hodge (Ordinary), approved 2010 SC (UKSC) 87, at [40] and [43] per Lord Hope of Craighead.

176 See W M Gloag and J M Irvine, *Law of Rights in Security* (Edinburgh: W. Green, 1897), p. 796 onward; and Chapter Ten: Conventional Security: Cautionary Obligations below.

177 *Caledonia North Sea Ltd v London Bridge Engineering Ltd* 2000 SLT 1123 at 1140 per Lord President Rodger affd 2002 SC (HL) 117.

178 *Simpson & Co v Thomson* (1877) 5 R (HL) 40.

179 *Esso Petroleum Co Ltd v Hall Russell & Co Ltd* 1988 SLT 874 HL at 878H per Lord Goff.

180 See, generally Bell, *Commentaries* II, 417; Gloag and Irvine, (n 176), p. 61.

181 Gloag and Irvine (n 176), p. 58.

catholic and secondary creditors. The rules which regulate the rights of parties holding this relation are the same, whether the subjects of security are all heritable, or partly heritable and partly moveable . . .'

8.93 Suppose Delta Ltd is indebted to each of the Caledonian Bank and the Bank d'Ecosse. The Caledonian Bank has a first ranking standard security over Delta Ltd's retail premises. The Bank d'Ecosse has a second ranking standard security over the same property. The Caledonian Bank also has a first ranking standard security over the company's warehouse, which is the only security over the warehouse. This is known as the 'catholic' security. Generally speaking, a secured creditor can exercise their rights in any manner they choose to facilitate the recovery of their debt. But where the effect of this course of action would be to prejudice the secondary creditor's rights, for example, by first exhausting the estate over which there is a secondary security so as to render the secondary creditor's rights worthless, then the doctrine of catholic and secondary creditors operates in favour of the secondary creditor.

8.94 In our example, therefore, the Caledonian Bank must first seek to recover their debt out of a sale of the warehouse. Only once the warehouse has been sold and indebtedness of Delta remains outstanding, can the Caledonian Bank seek to enforce the standard security against the retail premises. The right arises in favour of the secondary creditor from the date that the catholic security is constituted:

> '[t]he right did not come first into existence when the catholic creditor proceeded to sell. It existed from the date of completion of the security, although its operation was suspended till there could be occasion to act on it. It was a right all along vested in the secondary creditor, that, whenever the catholic creditor should proceed to sell, the secondary creditor might require him to respect his interests, so far as not injurious to himself'.[182]

8.95 The right in favour of the secondary creditor operates *ex lege*:

> 'Nor is actual assignation by the catholic creditor indispensable for the protection of the secondary creditor, for the law implies it, and would give effect to it in any process of distribution. That is clear, and is the simple doctrine as between the catholic and secondary creditors themselves.'[183]

8.96 The doctrine of catholic and secondary creditors applies to all rights in security,[184] except floating charges.[185]

182 *Littlejohn v Black* (1855) 18 D 207 at 227 per Lord Deas. *Littlejohn* was cited with approval in *Szepietowski v National Crime Agency* [2013] UKSC 65, [2014] AC 338 at [81]-[84] per Lord Reid.

183 *Littlejohn v Black* at 218 per Lord Ivory. This passage is cited by Gloag and Irvine (n 176), p. 61 for the proposition that: 'Such an assignation will be assumed in any process for the distribution of the balance remaining after the catholic debt is paid'.

184 See Chapter Eleven: Non-judicial Real Security below.

185 *Forth & Clyde Construction Co Ltd v Trinity Timber & Plywood Co* 1984 SC 1. For application of the doctrine to the landlord's hypothec, see *Butter v Sir James Riddel* (1790–1792) Bell's Octavo Cases 154.

Chapter Nine

Payment Obligations

Matteo Solinas

This chapter deals with the concept of payment and introduces the fundamental distinction between payment made in discharge of money obligations and different forms of payment promise. The focus is on negotiable instruments and, in particular, on bills of exchange where the (intangible) right to payment is embodied in a tangible instrument. Students often find the law of negotiable instruments to be a set of dry, arcane and technical rules and question its relevance in commercial practice. It is the aim of this chapter to contribute to the understanding of its intricate contents and to clarify its historical and current commercial significance. **9.01**

INTRODUCTION

Payment is essentially an act accepted in performance of money obligations. It is the outcome of a claim for debt, for a definite sum of money established in an agreement between the parties in return for the performance of an obligation by one party to the other.[1] All issues relating to payment depend on the terms of the obligations originally undertaken as amended and/or discharged according to subsequent mutual agreement by the parties.[2] **9.02**

With the exception of cash, various highly technical (statutory, contractual and market) rules govern the creation, processing, clearing and settlement of the payment instructions in the UK. An introductory discussion of payment methodologies or even a detour on the structure of clearing and settlement of the payment system is a complex exercise well beyond the scope of this chapter.[3] **9.03**

This chapter will, rather, highlight the distinction between payment and the acceptance of a payment promise and, in particular, the acceptance of a payment promise represented by a negotiable instrument. While it is the layman's view to characterise the transaction where the debtor gives their creditor a negotiable instrument as a 'payment' of the debt, a distinction has to be drawn from payment made in discharge of money obligations. This is because, in the case of a negotiable instrument, there is technically only a payment promise **9.04**

1 C Proctor and V Dixon, *Goode on Payment Obligations in Commercial and Financial Transactions*, 3rd edn (London: Sweet & Maxwell, 2016), p. 12.
2 See Chapter Two: General Principles of Contract Law.
3 See Bank of England, *Payment and Settlement* (2021), *https://www.bankofengland.co.uk/payment-and-settlement* (last accessed 3 September 2021).

and the creditor is not allowed to sue the debtor until the maturity of the instrument:[4] as will be clarified in the sections below, even if the creditor has taken the negotiable instrument the original debt still exists and their right on the underlying obligation is preserved.

9.05 This chapter is structured as follows. First, it considers the legal nature and peculiar elements of negotiable instruments, explaining the relevance of the historical and comparative perspective in understanding the current legal framework, commercial advantages and future use. Secondly, it addresses the legal nature, modes of circulation, liabilities and ways of enforcement of some of the most relevant types of negotiable instruments. Particular attention is focused on the bill of exchange, as its regulation provides a set of default rules that apply to most negotiable instruments. Reference is also made to other widely used types of negotiable instruments and, in particular, to cheques, promissory notes, bankers' drafts and travellers' cheques.

NEGOTIABLE INSTRUMENTS

Nature and essential characteristics

9.06 A negotiable instrument is a document that embodies a monetary obligation capable of being transferred by endorsement and delivery, free from defects in the title of prior parties. In essence, with a negotiable instrument an undertaking to pay a sum of money[5] or an order to pay a sum of money to the person giving the order or to a third person[6] are locked up in a document,[7] which remains distinct from the obligation that determined the issuance of the instrument. This is different from other documents commonly employed for commerce where physical possession does not confer ownership rights on the embodied obligation, nor does it involve any entitlement to claim money.[8]

9.07 In the absence of an *ad hoc* statutory definition of negotiable instruments, three fundamental features can be singled out from the common law, as shaped by the evolution of medieval mercantile custom and usage:

(a) The possession of the document confers on the holder[9] the right of action.
(b) As the contractual right itself does not exist independently of the document, the modes of circulation are different (and less cumbersome) from the rules on assignation.[10] When the instrument is payable to the bearer, it

4 That is, the payment is therefore 'conditional' until the instrument is due.
5 For example, promissory note. See para. 9.48 below.
6 For example, bill of exchange. See para. 9.24 below.
7 A mere receipt for money is not a negotiable instrument: see *Akbar Khan v Attar Singh* [1936] 2 All ER 545 (PC).
8 For example, bill of lading, which is a document of title to goods carried as cargo: see *Simmons v London Joint Stock Bank* [1891] 1 Ch 270 (CA).
9 That is. the payee, the indorsee or the bearer of the instrument, as defined in the Bills of Exchange Act 1882, s. 2.
10 That is, there is no need for intimation to the debtor: *Connal & Co v Loder* (1868) 6 M 1095 at 1102 per Lord Neaves; *Grigor Allan v Urquhart* (1887) 15 R 56.

can be transferred by mere delivery. When it is payable to order, transfer is effected by its holder's indorsement, followed by delivery.

(c) In contrast to the rights acquired by an assignee under a contract, the delivery of the instrument (when complete and regular on its face) to a purchaser in good faith and for value confers on the transferee 'a right of action better than the right of him under whom he derives title'.[11] More accurately, the *bona fide* holder for value transferee acquires good title to the document and to the embodied rights, notwithstanding any defect in title of the party[12] from whom they took it.[13]

It follows from the above that a negotiable instrument enjoys a dual nature: it is a specific item of property capable of being possessed, transferred and destroyed like any other moveable, but it embodies an autonomous contractual right to payment of a certain sum of money enforceable by the holder of the document in their own name. The explanation for this is rooted in the evolution of commercial law as shaped by merchant practice in England, where there was a historical prohibition on assignment of *choses* in action[14] at common law.[15] In *Picker v London & County Banking Co Ltd*, Bowen LJ stated that 'at common law in general a *chose* in action is not transferable. Therefore, the right of action can only pass by delivery of the instrument where the instrument is negotiable or clothed by statute with the attributes of a negotiable instrument'.[16] This has never been the case in Scots law where in principle all personal rights have always been capable of transfer by assignation and intimation,[17] unless assignation was expressly prohibited.[18] **9.08**

To sum up with a definition approved by the authorities, where an instrument is: **9.09**

> 'by the custom of the trade transferable like cash, by delivery, and is also capable of being sued upon by the person holding it *pro tempore*, it is entitled to the name of a

11 *Dixon v Bovill* (1856) 3 Macq 1 at 16 per Lord Cranworth.

12 This is different from the ordinary rule *assignatus utitur jure auctoris* according to which the transferee does not acquire better rights than their transferor: see *Scottish Equitable Life Assurance Society v Buist* (1876) 3 R 1078.

13 *Whistler v Forster* (1863) 143 ER 441, 14 CB 248 at 257 per Willes J. In general, see D V Cowen, *The Law of Negotiable Instruments in South Africa*, 5th edn (Claremont, Juta Legal and Academic Publishers, 1985), p. 52.

14 Under English law, a *chose* in action (a *chose* being a French word meaning 'thing') 'describes all personal rights of property which can only be claimed or enforced by action, and not by taking physical possession': *Torkington v Magee* [1902] 2 KB 427 at 439 per Channell J.

15 Historically, at common law the general rule was that a *chose* in action could not be assigned or otherwise transferred as the right to bring a personal action enforcing a right was founded on the personal relationship between obligor and obligee and in order to prevent the maintenance of actions (i.e. the possible oppression of the obligor by an assignee more powerful than the obligee). See M Smith and N Leslie, *The Law of Assignment*, 3rd edn (Oxford: Oxford University Press, 2018), pp. 213–223.

16 (1887) 18 QBD 515 (CA) at 519. See also *Master v Miller* (1791) 100 ER 1042, 4 TR 320 at 340 per Buller J.

17 Erskine, *Institute* III, 5, 2: 'The general rule is, that whoever is in the right of any subject, though it should not bear to assignees, may at pleasure convey it to another, except where he is barred either by the nature of the subject or by immemorial custom'.

18 For example, rights strictly personal into which an element of *delectus personae* enters as in the case of rights which are alimentary by nature. See R G Anderson, *Assignation* (Edinburgh: Edinburgh Legal Education Trust, 2008), paras 10–31–10–32.

negotiable instrument, and the property in it passes to a *bona fide* transferee for value, though the transfer may not have taken place in the market overt.[19] But that if either of the above requisites be wanting i.e., if it be either not accustomably transferable, or, though it be accustomably transferable, yet if its nature be such as to render it incapable of being put in suit by party holding it *pro tempore*, it is not a *negotiable instrument*, nor will delivery of it pass the property of it to a vendee, however *bona fide*, if the transferor himself have not a good title to it, and the transfer be made out of market overt'.[20]

9.10 The law on negotiable instruments is today primarily regulated under the Bills of Exchange Act 1882 (the BoEA) and, to a limited extent, by the Cheques Act 1957 and associated case law. The very title of the BoEA refers to a negotiable instrument rarely used in inland trade: the bill of exchange. But cheques, share warrants[21] and debentures – probably among the most common negotiable instruments in commercial practice – can only be understood with some knowledge of the provisions on bills of exchange. This explains why the law of negotiable instruments is still largely dominated by the study of bills of exchange and it explains the space in this chapter dedicated to the analysis of this particular instrument.

Historical evolution

9.11 It is generally agreed among historians that negotiable instruments originated and developed in the thirteenth century from a variation of certain Italian notarial exchange contracts and the contract of *cambium*, as effected under the machinery of the bill of exchange (the *tratta*).[22] In essence, the *tratta* consisted of an instrument specifically devised by the 'sedentary merchants' for long distance trade in order to obviate the risk of the physical transport of money from one fair to another or from one country to another.[23] According to medieval commercial practice, in its infancy the *tratta* involved four parties, as it was easier for creditors who wished to collect, and debtors who wished to pay, to appoint exchangers to do it for them.[24] The letter was:

'addressed by B [the drawer – often an exchanger[25]] to C [the drawee/acceptor – often an exchanger], asking C to pay to a third person D [the payee] a sum of money,

19 That is, on an open market. The doctrine of market overt in English law provided that sale of goods made on an open market was binding not only on the parties involved, but also on third parties. According to the Sale of Goods Act 1979, s. 22(1) (repealed in 1994), the purchaser in good faith of stolen goods in market overt acquired a valid title against the true owner. The section did not apply in Scotland.

20 J W Smith, *A Selection of Leading Cases on Various Branches of the Law* (London: A. Maxwell, 1837), p. 259, cited with approval by Blackburn J in *Crouch v Credit Foncier of England* (1873) LR 8 QB 374 (CA) at 381.

21 UK companies have been prohibited from issuing share warrants to bearer since 26 May 2015: Companies Act 2006, s. 779(4).

22 See R De Roover, *L'Evolution de la Lettre de Change XIV–XVIII siècles* (Paris: Armand Colin, 1953).

23 See N S Gras, *Business and Capitalism, an Introduction to Economic History* (New York: F S Crofts & Co, 1939), pp. 37–44.

24 In general, see E Jenks, 'The early history of negotiable instruments' (1893) LQR 70 at 74.

25 That is, a merchant engaged in the business of paying out one currency in exchange for an equivalent amount of another, charging a commission for the service.

which A [the payer] has entrusted to B for this purpose. This letter is handed by B to A, who sends it on to D; and D presents it for payment to C'.[26]

Briefly, the instrument provided that the drawee (C) who had accepted the bill was bound to the instruction of the drawer (B) and the payee (D) could sue the drawee.

From the picture above, it should be clear that some of the peculiar characteristics of the current forms of negotiable instruments were not yet present in the earlier schemes. Namely: **9.12**

(a) the payee (D) could not assign their rights under the bill to a third party;
(b) the drawee (C), even if they had accepted the bill, could successfully plead the fact that they had not received funds from the drawer (B) as a defence against the payee (D); and, above all,
(c) the drawee (C) could exploit any other defence against the payee that could have been adopted by the drawer.

The *tratta*, in its infancy, was therefore a letter of payment, a mandate by a written command to pay.[27] That the *tratta* at that stage possessed full negotiability is largely a myth. It was freely transferable, but not fully negotiable, as it did not protect a *bona fide* acquirer for value of the instrument (the 'holder in due course'[28]) in the absence of title in their author.

The *tratta* was occasionally received in British mercantile practice as early as the fourteenth century, but it was not until about the middle of the fifteenth century that instruments similar to the bills of exchange were used by English merchants.[29] The need in Britain for an instrument suited to the settlement of foreign accounts, such as the bill of exchange, was primarily determined in the fifteenth century by the unprecedented growth of foreign trade. When English merchants became the principal dealers in commodities (wool and cloth exports), they found a very efficient and reliable model already existing in international market practice. Hence, when they became the principal dealers in exchanges, they imported the scheme of the bill of exchange adopted by the Italian banking houses.[30] **9.13**

Negotiability developed in Britain only at the end of the eighteenth century, probably in response to the business practice of employing negotiable instruments in the credit system to raise finance and to accommodate the needs of those who were unable to secure credit directly from banks.[31] Bills of exchange were often discounted by their holders: 'the trader who needed cash could indorse his bill to a bank or discount house, which would charge the seller a sum representing interest on the time remaining before the bill was to be paid, **9.14**

26 W S Holdsworth, *A History of English Law* (London: Sweet & Maxwell, 1925) Vol. VIII, p. 131.
27 M M Postan 'Private Financial Instruments in Medieval England' in Postan (ed), *Medieval Trade and Finance* (Cambridge: Cambridge University Press, 1973), p. 57.
28 For the meaning of holder in due course, see BoEA, s. 29.
29 J M Holden, *The History of Negotiable Instruments in English Law* (London: The Athlone Press, 1955), p. 22.
30 Postan, 'Private Financial Instruments' (n 27) 63.
31 J S Rogers, *The Early History of the Bills and Notes* (Cambridge: Cambridge University Press, 1995) p. 121.

as well as a commission'.[32] An alternative explanation is that negotiability developed in Britain from the growth in the market for investment securities. This view is supported by the case law where the most frequent examples involving the concept of negotiability[33] are about government bonds rather than bills of exchange.[34]

9.15 The history of negotiable instruments and their origin in mercantile custom in Scotland is not distant from the English evolution up to the drafting of the BoEA in 1882. The proposal to apply the law only in England and Ireland because of the possible differences with Scots law was rejected, as it was found that these were insignificant.[35] More accurately, as will be clarified below, there are only three points on which Scots and English law differ materially under the BoEA: the application of the English doctrine of consideration;[36] the fact that in Scotland the bill operates as an assignment of the sum for which it is drawn in favour of the holder, provided that the drawee of a bill (other than a cheque)[37] has in their hands funds available for the payment;[38] and the fact that summary diligence is available following registration of a protest for non-acceptance or non-payment, as the case may be, in the books of court.[39]

9.16 Documents can be recognised as negotiable either by statute or by mercantile usage.[40] Agreement between the parties alone is not *per se* sufficient to make an instrument negotiable.[41] Whether an instrument is negotiable in accordance with merchant law depends on the custom and must be proved,[42] with the exception of the obvious circumstances where the court will simply take judicial notice of it,[43] and unless the instrument expressly states that it should not be negotiable.[44]

32 M Lobban, 'Commercial Law' in Cornish, Anderson, Cock, Lobban, Polden and Smith (eds), *The Oxford History of the Laws of England Volume XII 1820–1914 – Private Law* (Oxford: Oxford University Press, 2010), p. 729.

33 See *Goodwin v Robarts* (1876) 1 App Cas 476 and *Crouch v Credit Foncier of England* (1873) LR 8 QB 374.

34 The leading case (the same rule was later applied to other instruments including government bonds) is *Miller v Race* (1758) 97 ER 398, 1 Burr 452 at 457 per Lord Mansfield where it was established that although bank notes were not goods, nor securities, nor documents for debts, they were 'treated as money, as cash, in the ordinary course and transaction of business, by the general consent of mankind; which gives them the credit and currency of money, to all intents and purposes'.

35 Following the evidence taken from Sheriff Dove-Wilson of Aberdeen, who pointed out the similarities with Scotland and the advantages of a code for the mercantile community. See R Ferguson, 'Legal ideology and commercial interest: the social origin of Commercial Law Codes' (1977) 4 British Journal of Law and Society 18.

36 BoEA, s. 27.

37 The principle has been abolished in relation to cheques in Scotland by the Banking Act 2009, s. 254(2).

38 BoEA, s. 53(2).

39 BoEA, s. 98, retains existing Scots law and practice on summary diligence, they key provision for which is the Bills of Exchange (Scotland) Act 1772, s. 42.

40 *Dixon v Bovill* (1856) 3 Macq 1 at 16 per Lord Cranworth and *Edelstein v Schuler & Co* [1902] 2 KB 144 at 154 per Bigham J.

41 *Crouch v Credit Foncier of England* (1873) LR 8 QB 374 at 386 per Blackburn J.

42 *Bechuanaland Exploration Co v London Trading Bank Ltd* [1898] 2 QB 658 (QBD) at 666 per Kennedy J.

43 *Edelstein v Schuler & Co* [1902] 2 KB 144 at 155 per Bigham J.

44 *London & County Banking Co Ltd v London and River Plate Bank Ltd* (1888) LR 20 QBD 232 at 239 per Manisty J.

Instruments negotiable by virtue of a statutory provision often confirm judicial acceptance of a mercantile use of the instrument as negotiable. This has been, for example, the case of bills of exchange and cheques that qualified as negotiable instruments even before the statutory consolidation under the BoEA.[45] However, it is worth noting that the law merchant rarely ceases to operate altogether after a statutory consolidation, but that it continues to apply save in so far as it is inconsistent with the rules set out in the statute.[46] 9.17

There is not a final comprehensive list of the various types of negotiable instruments. The list is not closed, as: 9.18

> 'the law merchant is not a closed book, nor is it fixed or stereotyped . . . Practices of men change, and courts of law in giving effect to the dealings of the parties will assume that they have dealt with one another on the footing of any relevant custom or usage prevailing at the time in the particular trade or class transaction'.[47]

The indirect corollary is that a relatively short period of usage is not generally a bar to negotiability, even if it is also true that the custom must have prevailed for some time in order to achieve certainty and notoriety.[48]

Finally, there are circumstances where the law expressly restricts the sphere of application of negotiable instruments, i.e. the extent to which negotiable instruments can be used for making payment or for giving security. For example, under s. 123 of the Consumer Credit Act 1974, outside non-commercial agreements,[49] a creditor or owner shall not take a negotiable instruments (other than a bank note or a cheque) in discharge of any sum payable by the debtor under a regulated consumer credit agreement[50] and consumer hire agreements[51] in discharge of a sum payable by the debtor or hirer can be enforced only on an order of the court.[52] Any person taking a negotiable instrument in contravention of s. 123 is not a holder in due course and is not entitled to enforce the instrument.[53] 9.19

Advantages and foreseeable decline in use

In English law, until 1875,[54] negotiable instruments had a crucial importance in commercial practice: an assignee had to join the assignor as a party when seeking to enforce their rights against the debtor[55] and, therefore, the only way 9.20

45 M D Chalmers, 'An experiment in codification' (1886) 3 LQR 125. For an historical enquiry on the subject, see Holden, *The History of Negotiable Instruments* (n 29), p. 199.
46 For example, BoEA, s. 97(2) and the interpretation offered in *Bank of England v Vagliano Bros* [1891] AC 107.
47 *Bank of Baroda Ltd v Punjab National Bank Ltd* [1944] 1 AC 176 at 183 per Lord Wright.
48 *Edelstein v Schuler & Co* at 154 per Bigham J and, generally, see Holden, *The History of Negotiable Instruments* (n 29), pp. 251–256.
49 That is, an agreement not made by the creditor or owner in the course of a business carried on by them. See Consumer Credit Act 1974, s. 123(5) and s. 189(1).
50 Consumer Credit Act 1974, s. 8.
51 Consumer Credit Act 1974, s. 15.
52 Consumer Credit Act 1974, s. 124(1).
53 Consumer Credit Act 1974, s. 125.
54 When s. 25(6) of the Supreme Court of Judicature Act 1873 came into force. The provision was repealed, but substantially re-enacted by the Law of Property Act 1925, s. 136.
55 The relevance of the change is addressed in *Re Westerton* [1919] 2 Ch 104 at 133 per Sargant J and *Marchant v Morton, Down & Co* [1901] 2 KB 829 at 832 per Channell J.

to assign a promise to pay money at common law was by the use of negotiable instruments. The scenario was different in Scotland where claims to payment, by their nature, were freely assignable whether or not reified into moveable bonds.[56] In other words, assignation of rights was settled in Scotland before and independently of the advent of the doctrine on *procuratio in rem suam* as accepted by the decisions of the Court of Session in the nineteenth century.[57] It follows that the growth of negotiable instruments in Scotland has to be primarily explained by the possibility of avoiding the formalities of intimation and the *assignatus* rule[58] in commercial transactions and the availability of summary diligence.[59]

9.21 Notwithstanding the above-mentioned statutory interventions in England and the case law development in Scotland, together with the constant decline in commercial practice for bills in inland trade,[60] negotiable instruments are still widely popular in Britain. In particular, today bills are mainly used in the context of credit lines granted by banks to their customers and as a method of making payment in international sales and in domestic trade, as transferability facilitates discount. With forfaiting,[61] for example, a seller-exporter will be able to raise medium term finance, allowing a period of credit to the buyer-importer (who could use or resell the goods before having to pay for them) and avoiding the risk of the buyer-importer's default. The transaction works as follows: the seller draws on the buyer (no recourse)[62] bills on its own order and the buyer accepts them. If the bills bear an unconditional guarantee from the buyer bank,[63] the seller is then able to discount them without recourse through their own bank[64] and does not have to wait for the buyer's payment. When the instrument at maturity is presented to the buyer and if it is dishonoured, it is for the buyer bank that issued an unconditional guarantee to pay.[65]

56 This is the conventional doctrinal position: see Luig, 'Assignation' in Reid and Zimmermann (eds), *A History of Private Law in Scotland* (Oxford: Oxford University Press, 2000), p. 419 and R G Anderson, *Assignation* (2008), para. 5–01 onward.

57 *Carter v McIntosh* (1862) 24 D 925 per Lord Justice-Clerk Inglis and *British Linen Company Bank v Carruthers and Fergusson* (1883) 10 R 926 per Lord President Inglis.

58 That is, the rule according to which the transferee does not acquire better rights than their transferor.

59 See Bell, *Principles*, §§ 342–344; R G Anderson, *Assignation* (2008), paras 4–49 and 5–01 onward.

60 As defined under BoEA, s. 4(1). The decline was primarily due to the strengthening of the banking system with the granting of overdraft facilities for which the bankers could routinely consent to renewal rather than discounting bills (not to mention the costs associated with *ad valorem* stamp duty on bills). See Holden, *The History of Negotiable Instruments* (n 29), pp. 294–303 and P Mathias, 'Capital, credit and enterprise in the Industrial Revolution' (1973) 2 Journal of European Economic History 121 at 136.

61 This is a type of non-recourse finance, which assists the export seller's cash flow (i.e. the seller receives an immediate payment of the cash value of the bill without recourse in case the buyer defaults on payment) whilst giving the buyer a period of credit: see A Ripley, *Forfaiting for Exporters* (London: Thomson Business Press, 1996).

62 That is, the bill excludes recourse on the seller if the buyer does not pay.

63 Or an *aval* (in substance a guarantee for the payment of the debt) available in the legal systems that have adopted the Geneva Uniform Law on Bills of Exchange and Promissory Notes 1930 and that may take effect as an anomalous indorsement under BoEA, s. 56 in the UK: see *G & H Montage GmbH v Irvani* [1990] 1 WLR 667.

64 That is, to negotiate the bills in return for a payment slightly lower than the face value.

65 Or an *aval*: see n 63. On this issue, in general, see A G Guest, *Chalmers and Guest on Bills of Exchange and Cheques*, 17th edn (London: Sweet & Maxwell, 2009), para. 2–109.

It has recently been argued that the simple forms of circulation of negotiable instruments together with the strong protection of the innocent purchaser for value are largely anachronistic: the focus on transfer is not helpful as today most negotiable instruments (e.g. cheques and promissory notes) do not pass from person to person outside the banking system.[66] **9.22**

The autonomy of the payment obligation from any contract, which caused negotiable instruments to be regarded as equivalent to cash, is also generally considered as out of date under the current electronic payment system. The explanation for that is simply that the law of negotiable instruments developed before the formation of the modern currency and banking systems, and a system of transfer of claims was essential for the creation of an efficient payment system. The same idea of (indispensable) reification of claims into paper documents has been questioned under modern commercial practice of money transfer, as has been the case for the circulation of securities held by intermediaries.[67] As remarked with an extreme formulation, the law of negotiable instruments 'is a museum of antiquities – a treasure house crammed full of ancient artefacts whose use and function have long since been forgotten'.[68] **9.23**

BILLS OF EXCHANGE

Definition

As suggested earlier, the fundamental source of the law on bills of exchange (and on negotiable instruments in general) is the BoEA. According to the BoEA s. 3(1), a bill of exchange is and can only consist of:[69] **9.24**

> 'an unconditional order in writing, addressed by one person to another, signed by the person giving it, requiring the person to whom it is addressed to pay on demand or at a fixed or determinable future time a sum in money to or to the order of a specified person, or to the bearer'.

Before examining the elements of the definition and the modes of circulation, an illustration of the way in which a bill of exchange is drawn and an outline of some basic terms are offered. In particular, below is an example of a bill of exchange drawn in Glasgow on 14 December 2020 that contains an unconditional order ('pay') in writing addressed by A Ltd (the 'drawer'), to Bank B Ltd (the 'drawee'), signed on behalf of A Ltd by a director, requiring the drawee to pay at a fixed or determinable future time ('sixty days after sight') a sum in money (£50,000) to the order of a specified person (C), the 'payee' of the bill. It could also be possible that the order requires Bank B Ltd to pay the

66 J S Rogers, *The End of Negotiable Instruments – Bringing Payment Systems Law Out of the Past* (Oxford: Oxford University Press, 2012).

67 J S Rogers, 'Policy perspectives on revised UCC Article 8' (1996) 43 UCLA Law Review 1431.

68 G Gilmore, 'Formalism and the law of negotiable instruments' (1979) 13 Creighton L Rev 441.

69 An instrument which does not comply with the conditions set up under BoEA, s. 3(1) or which requires an additional act to be done is not a bill of exchange: see BoEA, s. 3(2).

sum specified in the bill not to the order of C (a named payee – 'order bill'), but to whoever is in possession of the bill ('bearer bill').

Glasgow, 14 December 2020

£50,000

at sixty days after sight pay to the order of C the sum of fifty thousand pounds drawn under Bank B Ltd.

To Bank B Ltd — for and on behalf of A Ltd

(signed) a director of A Ltd

Hence,

(a) The person who draws the bill[70] is known as the 'drawer'. They are primarily liable on the bill before the bill is accepted.
(b) The person on whom the bill is drawn[71] is termed the 'drawee' and – it will be clarified below – if they have funds available to pay it, the bill operates as an assignment to the holder of the sum for which it was drawn without need of acceptance (an 'intimated assignation').[72] The position is different in England and Wales where a drawee is not strictly a party to the bill and does not incur any liability on the bill until they agree to comply with the instructions and honour the bill on maturity to the payee or to the holder (becoming, therefore, the 'acceptor').[73]
(c) The person in whose favour the bill is payable is known as the 'payee'.
(d) A payee[74] who warrants to a transferee that the bill will be honoured by signing their name in the back of the instrument qualifies as 'indorser' and the person to whom it is indorsed is the 'indorsee'. The indorser's position is very similar to that of the drawer and several cases have suggested that the indorser is, in effect, a new drawer who gives a new order as to the payment of the bill to the drawee.[75]
(e) The payee who physically retains the bill, or the transferee who obtains possession of it by indorsement completed by delivery or by mere delivery, is known as the 'holder'.

9.25 As stated in the definition above, the order to the drawee[76] does not have to be in a specified form, but it must be imperative,[77] it must be in writing,[78] signed

70 That is, the one who gives the unconditional order.
71 That is, the one who is the subject of the drawer's order.
72 BoEA, s. 53(2).
73 BoEA, s. 17(2)(a). As suggested below, it follows that in England and Wales, if the drawee does not accept the bill (or in Scotland if the drawee does not have funds available to pay it), the bill becomes dishonoured 'by non-acceptance' and the payee has an immediate right of action against the drawer under BoEA, s. 43(2).
74 And, similarly, the following transferees.
75 *Steele v McKinlay* (1880) 7 R (HL) 85, 5 App Cas 754.
76 The drawee must be named or otherwise indicated with reasonable certainty: see *Gray v Milner* (1819) 129 ER 571, 8 Tauton 739.
77 That is, it cannot be a precative request or a mere invitation to pay. An instrument reading 'Bank B Ltd, please let the bearer have £50,000, and place it to my account and you will oblige. A director of A Ltd (signed)' is not a bill of exchange, as it does not contain an order made by one party having a right to call on the other to pay: see *Hamilton v Spottiswoode* (1849) 154 ER 1182 and *Little v Slackford* (1828) 173 ER 1120, 1 M&M 171.
78 Not necessarily written in English: see *Arab Bank Ltd v Ross* [1952] 2 QB 216.

by the drawer[79] and not be subject to any qualifications or limitations (i.e. it must be 'unconditional').[80] Moreover, the obligation must be exclusively[81] for a certain sum of money[82] with no ambiguity as regards its date of payment:[83] a bill is valid only if payable on demand (at sight, on presentation or if no time for payment is mentioned in it)[84] or at fixed date or, in any case, at an ascertainable future date.[85] Finally, it must be payable either to a specified person (the payee)[86] or to the bearer.[87]

Apart from the case of an unsigned document,[88] an instrument which fails to comply with all the requirements of BoEA, s. 3(1) (i.e. an 'inchoate instrument') may still be converted to a bill of exchange by the transferee who has *prima facie* authority to fill it up as a complete bill and rectify any omission of any material particular,[89] provided that this is done within a reasonable time, and strictly in accordance with the authority given.[90] **9.26**

Transfer

This section deals with the rules governing the transfer of bills between holders. Subject to the contrary explicit wish of a drawer who creates a bill of exchange without allowing for its transfer,[91] the method by which a bill is transferred is termed 'negotiation'. It involves the circulation 'from one person to another in such a manner as to constitute the transferee the holder of the bill'.[92] When the bill is negotiable, it continues to be so until it is restrictively indorsed[93] or 'discharged by payment or otherwise'.[94] The law distinguishes between the actual mode of transfer depending on whether the bill is a bearer bill or is payable to order. **9.27**

79 In the absence of the drawer's signature, the acceptor is not liable on the bill: see *M'Call v Taylor* (1865) 144 ER 803, 19 CB (NS) 301.
80 BoEA, s. 11(2) provides that if the instrument is conditional, such defect cannot be cured by the happening of the event in question.
81 The order should not require the drawee to do any other act: see *Dickie v Singh* 1974 SLT (Notes) 3.
82 A sum is certain within the meaning of BoEA, even if the amount is not designated in English currency or if it has to be paid with interest or in instalments: see BoEA, s. 9. If A Ltd writes and sends to Bank B Ltd the following order: 'Bank B Ltd, please pay to C the proceeds of a sale value about £50,000', the order is not a bill of exchange, the sum not being certain: see *Jones v Simpson* (1823) 107 ER 402, 2 B&C 318.
83 See *Korea Exchange Bank v Debenhams (Central Buying) Ltd* [1979] 1 Lloyd's Rep 100.
84 BoEA, s. 10(1).
85 BoEA, s. 11(2). If the bill is undated, it is still valid and the holder may insert the date: see BoEA, s. 3(4)(a) and s. 20, respectively.
86 Or, possibly, several payees either as joint or alternative payees: see BoEA, s. 7(2).
87 A bill is payable to the bearer when it is explicitly written in the document or when the 'only or last indorsement is an indorsement in blank': see BoEA, s. 8(3). Moreover, according to BoEA, s. 7(3) a bill is payable to bearer 'where the payee is a fictitious or not existing person'.
88 Which cannot be cured by the holder.
89 BoEA, s. 20(1).
90 BoEA, s. 20(2). See *Mckeekin v Russell* (1881) 8 R 587.
91 That is, the bill can only be enforced by the original payee: see BoEA, s. 8(3).
92 BoEA, s. 31(1).
93 That is, when the drawer instructs the drawee that payment should only made to a specified payee and further negotiation is prohibited: BoEA, s. 35(1)(2).
94 BoEA, s. 36. That is, cancellation, renunciation or when the acceptor has themselves become a holder: see BoEA, ss. 61–63.

Bearer bills

9.28 Bearer bills are transferred by (actual or constructive[95]) delivery of the instrument from one person to another, and the rights under them will vest in the holder.[96] A signature is not required to negotiate a bearer bill.[97] Once the bill passes to the hands of a holder in due course, 'a valid delivery of the bill by all parties prior to him so as to make them liable to him is conclusively presumed'.[98] This simply means that there will be no flaw in the title of the holder in due course even if the delivery was unauthorised. Bearer bills are payable when it is expressly so established,[99] when the last indorsement is in blank[100] or when the payee is a fictitious or non-existing person.[101] That said, these instruments are rarely used in practice because of the potential risks involved for the holder in losing the possession of the document *vis-à-vis* the right of the acceptor in good faith and without notice of a defect in title always to achieve a good discharge by payment of the bill.[102]

Order bills

9.29 When the bill is payable to order, it is transferable by indorsement and delivery of it.[103] To qualify as a valid indorsement, the indorsement must be written on the instrument, signed by the indorser[104] and must be for 'the entire bill'.[105] Delivery without indorsement still allows the transferee to sue on the bill in their own name, but not to become a holder in due course.[106] A transferee of an unindorsed bill will therefore acquire the bill in the same position as an assignee.[107] Order bills are payable when it is so expressly established in the document (and there are no words suggesting that it should not be transferable)[108] or when the only or last indorsement is in blank[109] and the holder converts the blank indorsement into a special indorsement 'by writing above the indorser's signature a direction to pay the bill to or to the order of himself or some other person'.[110]

95 For example, when a person holding a bill as owner agrees to transfer ownership to a third party, but continues to hold the bill as agent of that other person.
96 BoEA, s. 31(2).
97 BoEA, s. 58(2).
98 BoEA, s. 21(2).
99 BoEA, s. 8(3).
100 BoEA, s. 8(3).
101 BoEA, s. 7(3). See *Bank of England v Vagliano Bros* [1891] AC 107 and *Clutton & Co v Attenborough* [1897] AC 90.
102 BoEA, s. 59.
103 BoEA, s. 31(3).
104 BoEA, s. 32(1).
105 BoEA, s. 32(2).
106 *Hood v Stewart* (1890) 17 R 749.
107 That is, subject to any defects in the right of the transferor to obtain payment: see *Whistler v Forster* (1863) 143 ER 441, 14 CBNS 248 per Willes J.
108 BoEA, s. 8(4).
109 That is, it consists of the simple signature of the indorser, but no indorsee is identified: see BoEA, s. 34(1).
110 BoEA, s. 34(4).

Entitlement to benefit from the obligation on the bill

When a bill is issued and negotiated, it circulates through the hands of 'holders'. It follows that the right to enforce payment of a bill belongs to the holder who, as mentioned above, is 'the payee or indorsee of a bill or note who is in possession of it, or the bearer thereof'.[111] According to the combination of ss. 27 and 38 of the BoEA, three types of holder can be identified: the mere holder, the holder for value and the holder in due course. **9.30**

Mere holder

The mere holder has not given value for the bill, but they still enjoy a number of important rights. They can sue on the bill in their own name,[112] convert a blank indorsement on an order bill into a special one,[113] negotiate an order bill[114] and provide good discharge to an acceptor in good faith and without notice of the defect in title. However, the drawee can raise a number of defences against an action brought by a mere holder based on defect in title of prior parties,[115] with the exception, possibly, of the absence of consideration under s. 27 BoEA for the enforcement of an obligation, as this doctrine does not form part of Scots law,[116] and the presumption is that 'onerosity of a bill is to be assumed'.[117] That said, non-onerosity may possibly be pleaded in evidence when the bill is regarded to be invalid on other grounds such as fraud, error, undue influence or illegality. **9.31**

Holder for value

A holder for value is a holder who has provided valuable consideration for the bill consisting of any consideration sufficient to support a simple contract or an antecedent debt or liability.[118] A holder for value may also be someone who did not give value themselves, so long as value was given by some other party in the chain between the holder and the acceptor.[119] As suggested above, because the defence of absence or failure of consideration is irrelevant in Scotland, the position of the holder for value is similar to that of a mere holder,[120] as they do not acquire better title than their transferor. **9.32**

111 BoEA, s. 2.
112 BoEA, s. 59(1).
113 BoEA, s. 34(4).
114 BoEA, s. 31(3).
115 BoEA, s. 38(2).
116 In England, old authorities have clearly established that a mere holder who does not give consideration for the bill (i.e. a mere holder who is not a holder for value) cannot succeed in their claim against an immediate or a remote party. The absence of consideration therefore has been held to be a valid defence against the holder in *Forman v Wright* (1851) 138 ER 560, 11 CB 451 at 492 and *Milnes v Dawson* (1850) 155 ER 413, 5 Exch 948 at 950.
117 *Law v Humphrey* (1876) 3 R 1192 at 1193 per Lord President Inglis and reference to BoEA, s. 30(1).
118 BoEA, s. 27(1).
119 BoEA, s. 27(2).
120 *Nova (Jersey) Knit Ltd v Kammgarn Spinnerei GmbH* [1977] 1 WLR 713.

Holder in due course

9.33 The holder in due course enjoys advantages not available to other holders. They hold the bill free from any defects of title of prior parties, as well as from mere personal defences available to prior parties among themselves.[121] Every holder of a bill is *prima facie* deemed to be a holder in due course, unless it is proven that the requirements set out in the definition under BoEA, s. 29(1) are not met. In particular, a holder in due course must be a holder of the bill other than the payee[122] who has taken it without notice of defect in title,[123] in good faith and for value.[124] Moreover, the bill must not be overdue[125] at the time of transfer[126] and must be complete and regular on its face.[127] Finally, contrary to the case of the holder for value,[128] in order to be a holder in due course it is necessary to give valuc pcrsonally.[129]

Liabilities of the parties on the bill

9.34 Having considered what amounts to a bill complete with all the necessary parties and the way it is negotiated, this section looks at how far the parties involved may incur liability on the bill. A drawer, acceptor or indorser who has no capacity to contract is not liable on the bill[130] and will be liable only if they have signed it in such a capacity[131] (or if the bill has been signed by an agent in a representative capacity on their behalf).[132] Where a signature on a bill is forged or placed on it without the authority of the person whose signature it purports to be,[133] such signature is inoperative and no title to the bill can be derived from it, unless the party against whom it is sought to retain it or enforce payment of the bill is personally barred from raising the question of forgery or want of authority.[134] This applies also to a company, which will make itself liable as a drawer, acceptor or indorser of a bill only if it is compe-

121 BoEA, s. 38(2).

122 That is, they can only be a subsequent possessor of a bearer bill or an indorsee in possession of an order bill: BoEA, s. 29(1)(b). See the description of the exceptions to the *nemo dat* rule offered in *Whistler v Forster* (1863) 143 ER 441 14 CB 196 per Willes J.

123 BoEA, s. 29(2)(a), i.e. actual notice of a fact that constitutes defect in title. See *Raphael v Bank of England* (1855) 139 ER 1030, 17 CB 161.

124 BoEA, s. 29(2)(b). BoEA, s. 90 suggests that a thing is deemed to be done in good faith 'where it is in fact done honestly, whether it is done negligently or not'. On the interpretation of the provision, see *Jones v Gordon* (1877) 2 App Cas 616 at 628 per Lord Blackburn.

125 That is, already matured.

126 BoEA, s. 29(1).

127 BoEA, s. 29(1). This is the case of an inchoate instrument or a bill that contains on its face an irregular indorsement. See *Arab Bank Ltd v Ross* [1952] 2 QB 216 and *Lombard Banking Ltd v Central Garage & Engineering Ltd* [1963] 1 QB 220.

128 BoEA, s. 27(2).

129 See Guest, *Chalmers and Guest on Bills of Exchange and Cheques* (n 65), para. 4–057.

130 BoEA, s. 22(1).

131 BoEA, s. 23.

132 For example, signature by procuration. In other words, an agent will not be personally liable on the bill if they sign it as drawer, indorser of an acceptor and adds words to their signature indicating that they sign for or on behalf of a principal: see BoEA, s. 26(1).

133 Unless the unauthorised signature has been ratified: see BoEA, s. 24(2).

134 In other words, the party barred must have led the other party to believe that the signature was in order and the other party must have acted as if the bill was fully valid: see BoEA, s. 24 and s. 54(2)(a).

tent to do so under the law relating to corporations.[135] However, the lack of capacity to contract does not release other parties from liability on the bill.[136] For example, a transferor of a bearer bill by mere delivery may face liability outside the bill for breach of warranty on the fact that the bill is genuine to a transferee (provided that the transferee is a holder for value).[137] Liability of specific parties on the bill is as follows.

Liability of the drawer

The drawer promises that the bill will be accepted and paid according to the terms of their promise written on the instrument (its tenor) when presented to the drawee. If the drawee dishonours the bill by not accepting or not paying it, and provided that the holder has given notice of dishonour, then the drawer is in a position similar to the one of a joint guarantor and they will be obliged to compensate the holder or an indorser who was compelled to pay it.[138] **9.35**

Liability of the drawee (and of the acceptor)

In England and Wales the drawing of a bill creates no obligations upon the drawee to accept or pay the bill.[139] In Scotland, while a bill does constitute an assignation of funds, which the drawer has in the hands of the drawee in favour of the holder,[140] the drawee is not liable on the bill without acceptance by signature.[141] However, once the bill is accepted, the acceptor is liable to pay in accordance with the terms of their acceptance[142] and, among other things, they cannot deny to a holder in due course 'the existence of the drawer, the genuineness of his signature, and his capacity and authority to draw the bill'.[143] **9.36**

Liability of an indorser

The liability of the indorser is similar to that of the drawer of a bill. They promise that the bill will be accepted and paid according to its tenor and that should the bill be dishonoured (and provided that the holder has given notice of dishonour), they will have to compensate the holder or a subsequent indorser.[144] No dispute on the 'genuineness and regularity in all respects of the drawer's signature and all the previous indorsements'[145] is allowed when **9.37**

135 BoEA, s. 22(2). Note that the strict rule according to which the capacity of the company depended on the powers conferred in the articles has been relaxed with the abolition of the *ultra vires* rules in relation to third parties under the Companies Act 2006, s. 39.

136 For example, *Wauthier v Wilson* (1912) 28 TLR 239 where a father was found liable on note made jointly by himself and his minor son.

137 BoEA, s. 58(3).

138 BoEA, s. 55(1).

139 See *Credit Lyonnais Bank Nederland NV v Export Credits Guarantee Department* [1998] 1 Lloyd's Rep 19 at 39 per Hobhouse J.

140 BoEA, s. 53(2). See *Williams v Williams* 1980 SLT (Sh Ct) 25 and *British Linen Company Bank v Carruthers and Fergusson* (1883) 10 R 923 at 928 per Lord Shand.

141 BoEA, s. 23.

142 BoEA, s. 54(1).

143 BoEA, s. 54(2)(a).

144 BoEA, s. 55(2)(a).

145 BoEA, s. 55(2)(b).

the other party satisfies the criteria for a holder in due course. However, as suggested above, the indorser called to make a payment on a bill, which has been dishonoured, is in a position similar to a joint guarantor and they will have the right to be repaid by the drawer.[146]

Exemptions

9.38 It is possible for the drawer or for an indorser to exclude or limit the liability that would ordinarily fall on them to guarantee the drawee by express stipulation, after the signature in the bill, of the words *sans recours* (or its English equivalent 'without recourse').[147] However, this device is not available to an acceptor who may only mitigate their liability by qualified acceptance under BoEA, s. 19(2).

Enforcement

9.39 A demand bill matures immediately and the payee (or other holder) simply presents for payment to the drawee. Unless the terms of the bill so require[148] or it is necessary to fix the maturity date of the instrument,[149] the presentation of the bill for acceptance is not essential,[150] as the holder of an unaccepted bill may still act against the drawer (or any prior indorser).[151] The failure to pay a demand bill duly presented for payment amounts to dishonour by non-payment[152] with slightly different procedures following the refusal depending on whether it is a foreign or inland bill.[153] This is different from the term bill where the bill must first be presented and accepted by the drawee.[154] If the bill is dishonoured by non-acceptance, the holder can enforce their rights against the drawer (and any prior indorser) without waiting for the maturity of the bill.[155] Where the bill is accepted, presentation for payment on its maturity is necessary to establish dishonour of non-payment[156] and drawer/indorser liability.[157]

146 BoEA, s. 55(1)(a).
147 BoEA, s. 16(1).
148 BoEA, s. 39(2).
149 BoEA, s. 39(1).
150 BoEA, s. 39(3).
151 BoEA, ss. 42 and 43(2).
152 BoEA, s. 47(1).
153 In the case of a foreign bill (i.e. a bill which is not drawn and payable within the British Islands or it is drawn within the British Islands by a non-resident person), notice is not sufficient to preserve the holder's right of recourse. The bill must be also noted and protested: see BoEA, s. 51(2). While noting is an act preliminary to protest consisting in the making of a note or minute on the face of the bill, protest is a solemn declaration made by a notary public that a bill has been dishonoured. Protest in Scotland is required also in the case of inland bills for the purpose of summary diligence (i.e. the procedure for obtaining warrant for diligence might be done on a bill of exchange without first resorting to a court action): see BoEA, s. 98 and Bills of Exchange (Scotland) Act 1772, s. 42 (as amended by the Debtors (Scotland) Act 1987).
154 BoEA, s. 45(1).
155 BoEA, s. 43(2).
156 BoEA, s. 45.
157 BoEA, s. 47(1).

Drawers' (and prior indorsers') liability on the bill is based not only on the fact that the bill has been dishonoured for non-acceptance or non-payment, but also on the fact that the holder has given them notice of dishonour within a reasonable time.[158] Similar rules to notice of dishonour by non-acceptance apply to dishonour by non-payment.[159] This is subject to the important Scottish qualification mentioned above under s. 53(2) of the BoEA whereby presenting a bill for acceptance or for payment has the effect of assigning the drawer's funds (held by the drawee) to the holder.[160] 9.40

Discharge

There are various ways according to which a bill may be discharged so that no party can sue or be sued on the instrument. The obvious one is the payment at or after maturity of the bill by or on behalf of the drawee (or acceptor) to the holder in good faith and without notice that their title to the bill is defective ('payment in due course').[161] A bill may also be discharged where the acceptor of a bill becomes the holder at or after its date of maturity;[162] when the holder, after maturity, waives their rights against the acceptor either in writing or by delivering the bill to them;[163] where the bill is intentionally and clearly cancelled[164] by the holder or their agent;[165] where materially altered, it is avoided against any party who did not assent to the alteration;[166] and, where applicable, via a five-year prescription starting from the date on which the obligation under the instrument becomes enforceable.[167] 9.41

CHEQUES

Definition and distinguishing elements

Cheques are probably one of the most common forms of negotiable instruments: they operate as an order from the drawer directed to a drawee bank (the paying bank) to make a payment to the holder of the cheque. The law relating to cheques is to be found in the BoEA Part 3 (ss. 73–81) and in the Cheques Acts 1957 and 1992, together with the associated case law. In essence, a cheque is 'a bill of exchange drawn on a banker and payable on demand'[168] and the rules set out for bills of exchange apply to cheques as 9.42

158 BoEA, s. 48.
159 BoEA, s. 49.
160 See *British Linen Company Bank v Carruthers and Fergusson* at 926 per Lord President Inglis; *Kirkwood & Sons v Clydesdale Bank* 1908 SC 20; *Sutherland v Royal Bank of Scotland plc* 1997 SLT 329.
161 BoEA, s. 59(1). And the bill ceases to be negotiable: BoEA, s. 36(1).
162 BoEA, s. 61.
163 BoEA, s. 62(2).
164 BoEA, s. 63(1); *Bank of Scotland v Dominion Bank* [1891] AC 592.
165 BoEA, s. 63(1).
166 BoEA, s. 64(1). See *Hong Kong and Shanghai Banking Corporation v Lo Lee Shi* [1928] AC 182 (PC); *Smith v Lloyd's TSB Group* [2001] QB 541 at 556 per Pill LJ.
167 Prescription and Limitation (Scotland) Act 1973, s. 6(3) and Sch. 1(1)(e).
168 BoEA, s. 73.

default rules, unless otherwise provided under the BoEA.[169] However, apart from the necessary involvement of a banker, there are certain substantial operational differences between the two,[170] including the fact that by nature a cheque is not intended to be a credit instrument (it is payable on demand) and the fact that in commercial practice it is not usually discounted or sold by the payee.

Crossed cheques

9.43 A crossing is essentially an instruction given to a banker to pay the proceeds of a cheque not in cash to the person who presents the cheque, but to the holder's own account. This is a common arrangement in many cheque forms today and it is aimed at reducing the risk of loss, particularly when the cheque is sent through the post: if the cheque is crossed, it will be difficult for a finder who does not have a bank account to collect and the proceeds will be easier to monitor/trace. More accurately, when two parallel transverse lines are drawn across its face to which may be added the words 'and the company' or 'not negotiable'[171] or both, the cheque is 'crossed' and must be presented for payment through a bank account (general crossing),[172] unless the crossing bears the name of the bank to whom the payment is to be made and in that case the cheque must be presented for payment through the designated bank (special crossing).[173] Apart from the drawer,[174] a holder may also cross an uncrossed cheque or make the instrument more restrictive, but not less.[175] Finally, when a cheque bears either a general or special crossing and it has not been altered,[176] the drawee bank will be liable to the 'true owner' of the cheque for any loss incurred.[177]

9.44 A crossed cheque that bears across its face the words 'account payee' or 'a/c payee', either with or without the word 'only' cannot be passed by negotiation and is only valid as between the drawer and the drawee.[178] In essence, this type of crossing amounts to a direction to the collecting bank that the proceeds of the cheque should not be collected for a person other than the nominated payee.[179] As matters stand, it is questionable whether following the changes for the transferability of crossed cheques brought about by the Cheques Act 1992,[180] cheques should be regarded as negotiable instruments. It is not possible to do summary diligence on non-payment of a cheque.[181]

169 BoEA, s. 73.
170 See *Ramchurn Mullick v Luchmeechund Radakissen* (1954) 9 Moo PCC 46 at 69 per Parke B.
171 In the words of Lindley LJ, 'everyone who takes a cheque which is marked "non negotiable" takes it at his own risk, and his title to the money is as defective as his title to the cheque itself'; *Great Western Railway Co v London and County Banking Co* [1901] AC 414 at 424.
172 BoEA, s. 76(1).
173 BoEA, s. 76(2).
174 BoEA, s. 77(1).
175 BoEA, s. 77(2), (3) and (4).
176 BoEA, ss. 64 and 78.
177 BoEA, s. 79(2). See *Phillip v The Italian Bank* 1934 SLT 78.
178 BoEA, s. 81A(1).
179 *National Bank v Silke* [1891] 1 QB 435.
180 BoEA, s. 81A.
181 *Glickman v Linda* 1950 SC 18.

The clearing system

Until 2018 the cheque could only be physically presented for payment to the branch of the paying bank on which it was drawn.[182] Given the huge volume of cheques that circulated every day through the banking system, this operation was simplified by the use of a centralised clearing system that favoured the process of presentation for payment of cheques in bulk between banks, with the aim of achieving only a single balance among participating banks. Cheques were not therefore individually paid, but only a balance was transferred between the two banks at the end of each trading day. The standardised maximum time-limits for the clearing of customers' cheques were the '2-4-6' commitments.[183] Under one of the most common scenarios, when the drawer and the payee had their accounts with different banks and the cheque was paid in the branch where the payee had their account, it was encoded in magnetic ink and a computerised credit entry was made on the payee's account before being sent together with the other cheques drawn on the drawer's bank to the central clearing department of the payee's bank. Once all the cheques had been verified with the encoded details, they were delivered to the central clearing department of the drawer's bank where a balance in the drawer's account was taken and a provisional settlement between the total amount of cheques presented between the two banks each day was performed. The cheque was finally forwarded to the drawer's bank branch and, unless the account's funds were not adequate (and the bank resolved to dishonour the cheque), it was paid. This elaborate process of collecting a cheque has today changed with the advent of 'cheque imaging', aimed at cutting down cheque clearing times from a possible six days to one day by sending a digital image of the cheque for clearing, rather than the paper cheque itself. The innovation was introduced by s. 13 of the Small Business, Enterprise and Employment Act 2015, which amended the BoEA by inserting Part IVA (ss. 89A–89F). Part IVA BoEA is supplemented by the Electronic Presentment of Instruments (Evidence of Payment and Compensation for Loss) Regulations 2018[184] to ensure the absence of detrimental impact of the image clearing system on the existing position for cheque users. **9.45**

Protection of the collecting bank

Among the functions of the banker is to collect the proceeds of cheques paid in by the customer and to credit them to their account. In this capacity a bank acts as the agent of the customer, whereas a bank that discounts a cheque (rare now that most cheques are crossed) acts as principal on its own behalf. If the customer does not have good right to the cheques, the law protects **9.46**

182 BoEA, s. 45(3) and *Barclays Bank plc v Bank of England* [1985] 1 All ER 385 at 392.

183 That is, the proceeds of a cheque to a customer's account for the purpose of earning interests are credited on the second working day following the cheque being deposited in that account; customers can withdraw funds from the account on the fourth working day following the cheque's deposit; and six days following the deposit assure the customer that the cheque will not be dishonored by the drawee bank. See Cheque and Credit Clearing and the Image Clearing System (2021) *History of the Cheque*, *The 2-4-6 agreement* (*https://www.chequeand-credit.co.uk/information-hub/history-cheque* (last accessed 3 September 2021)).

184 SI 2018/832.

the banker from liability for the value of the cheque to the true owner by means of the 'holder in due course' doctrine. In particular, if the instrument is complete and regular on its face and it is taken by the banker in good faith, for value and without notice that it has been dishonoured,[185] then the banker can claim to be the true owner of the instrument as against any former true owner.[186] Other than in the cases where the banker cannot claim the holder in due course status,[187] a banker who has acted in good faith and without negligence in receiving payment for a customer or, having credited the customer's account, receives payment for themselves, is no longer protected by s. 4 of the Cheques Act 1957 and, outside the cases of gross negligence or fraud, may liable to the true owner of the instrument by reason only of having received payment thereof, even if the customer has no title or a defective title to the cheque.[188]

Protection of the paying bank

9.47 A paying banker shall not be responsible or incur any liability, nor shall the payment be questioned if, in the ordinary course of business, they pay a crossed cheque (even if crossing has not been altered)[189] or analogous instrument in good faith and without negligence in accordance with the appearance of the instrument.[190] Apart from the case of cheques crossed 'account payee', which are not transferable,[191] a banker who pays a (crossed or uncrossed) cheque payable to order to the wrong person because an indorsement has been forged is also protected from liability.[192] Lastly, and specifically aimed at reducing time spent in checking indorsement, when a banker 'in good faith and in the ordinary course of business pays a cheque which is drawn on him which is not indorsed or is irregularly indorsed' they do not, in doing so, incur any liability by reason only of the absence of, or irregularity in the indorsement, and the bank is deemed to have paid the cheque in due course.[193]

OTHER NEGOTIABLE INSTRUMENTS

Promissory notes

9.48 While a bill of exchange is essentially an unconditional order addressed by one person to another requiring the person to whom it is addressed to pay on demand or at a fixed or determinable future time a sum certain in money to the order of a specified person, or to the bearer, a promissory note is simply a

185 BoEA, s. 29.
186 Cheques Act 1957, s. 2.
187 This occurs frequently since most cheques nowadays are crossed 'a/c payee' and not discounted, with the result that a bank rarely becomes a holder in due course.
188 The Electronic Presentment of Instruments (Evidence of Payment and Compensation for Loss) Regulations 2018, reg. 5.
189 BoEA, s. 79(2).
190 BoEA, s. 80.
191 BoEA, s. 81A(1).
192 BoEA, s. 60.
193 Cheques Act 1957, s. 1.

promise made by one person, known as 'the maker' to another.[194] Once this difference is taken into account, the law governing promissory notes under Part IV of the BoEA (ss. 83–89) is very similar to the law of bills of exchange and, unless otherwise expressly provided,[195] the rules on bills of exchange apply with few necessary adjustments to promissory notes.[196] In particular, in applying these rules, the maker of the note[197] is deemed to correspond with the acceptor of the bill, and the first indorser with the drawer of an accepted bill payable to their own order.[198]

The definition of a promissory note under BoEA follows that of a bill of exchange and, quite interestingly, many of the cases that are used to describe and explain the sections of the bills of exchange are promissory note cases.[199] According to the BoEA s. 83(1): **9.49**

> 'a promissory note is an unconditional promise in writing made by one person to another, signed by the maker, engaging to pay, on demand or at a fixed or determinable future time, a sum certain in money, to, or to the order of, a specified person or to bearer'.

A promissory note is not mere evidence of indebtedness (such as an IOU), but it involves an explicit promise on the face of the document to be negotiable.[200] Moreover, in order to establish the liability of the maker of a formally complete document it must be delivered to the payee or bearer.[201] The liability of the maker is similar to that of an acceptor of a bill of exchange: the maker promises that they will pay the note according to its tenor[202] and they are precluded from denying to a holder in due course the existence of the payee and their capacity to indorse.[203] **9.50**

Presentation for payment of notes is regulated differently in the BoEA from the corresponding provisions relating to bills of exchange. In the case of notes payable on demand, once the note has been indorsed, it must be presented for payment within reasonable time of the indorsement and if this is not done, the indorser is discharged.[204] This is different from the case of a bill of exchange where the delay in presenting the bill for payment also releases the drawer:[205] in that case both the drawer and the indorser are under a joint guarantee. In all other circumstances, and similarly to the case of bills of exchange, **9.51**

194 In English law simple promises are not enforceable whereas in Scots law they are. See Chapter Two: General Principles of Contract Law.
195 For example, the provisions relating to presentment for acceptance and to acceptance. See BoEA, s. 89(3).
196 BoEA, s. 89(1).
197 That is, the party primarily liable.
198 BoEA, s. 89(2).
199 For example, *Williamson v Rider* [1963] 1 QB 89.
200 That is, not subject to the rules on assignation, but transferable by delivery or delivery and indorsement.
201 BoEA, s. 84.
202 BoEA, s. 88(1).
203 BoEA, s. 88(2). An interesting comparison can be made with the preclusions concerning the acceptor of the bill under BoEA, s. 54.
204 BoEA, s. 86.
205 BoEA, s. 45.

presentation for payment to the maker is a necessary precondition to establish the indorser's liability.[206]

Bankers' drafts

9.52 A banker's draft is generally used (especially where large sums of money are involved) to overcome the risks inherent in the possibility that an ordinary cheque is dishonoured by a drawer with insufficient funds in the account. In essence, it is the result of an action taken by the customer of the bank who transfers to the bank funds equivalent to the amount of the draft and instructs the bank to issue the draft as an undertaking to pay in a way that is *de facto* the same as cash.[207] More accurately, a banker's draft is a document drawn by a branch of a bank on its head office or on another branch and as such it cannot be qualified as a bill of exchange (or a cheque) under s. 3(1) of the BoEA. However, it can be used by the holder as a bill of exchange or as a promissory note within the definition of s. 5(2) of the BoEA:[208] in the first case the bank is protected under s. 4(2) of the Cheques Act 1957 and in the case of a crossed draft by the provisions of BoEA[209] relating to crossed cheques.

Travellers' cheques

9.53 Travellers' cheques are means by which a person travelling can acquire cash from overseas banks in the course of a journey abroad. Even if they take a variety of forms (and not all of them will closely resemble negotiable instruments), travellers' cheques are usually purchased by a customer of the bank and signed before an official of the bank either as an order from the issuing bank to other banks to pay the cheques, or as an order from the customer to the bank to pay themselves as payee or another payee whose name is left in blank (not dissimilar in these two cases to the structure of a bill of exchange) or, possibly, as a promise by the issuing bank to repay the paying bank that cashes the cheque for the payee (not dissimilar to the structure of a promissory note). Given that the cheques need to be signed before the issuing bank and countersigned by the same customer before the paying bank, it has been suggested that the payment order or promise is conditional and, therefore, the instrument, even if treated as a negotiable instrument by modern mercantile custom, cannot technically be regarded as negotiable within the meaning of ss. 3(1), 73 and 83 of the BoEA.

206 BoEA, s. 87(1). This means that the person under the primary liability must have been unsuccessfully approached.

207 Cheques Act 1957, s. 5.

208 See *Abbey National plc v JSF Finance & Currency Exchange Ltd* [2006] EWCA Civ 328.

209 BoEA, ss. 79 and 80.

Chapter Ten

Conventional Security: Cautionary Obligations

Paul McClelland

GENERAL

Concept of a cautionary obligation

'A cautionary obligation or guarantee is granted by way of security for the fulfilment of some primary obligation on the part of a principal debtor, who, as such, remains liable.'[1] There are, accordingly, at least three parties involved with any cautionary obligation: a creditor; a debtor; and a cautioner. **10.01**

Cautionary obligations often relate to debts owed by a debtor, such as a sum due under a bank loan. It is also possible to create cautionary obligations in respect of the performance of non-monetary obligations. All insolvency practitioners, for instance, are required to provide a bond of caution. **10.02**

Dependent and independent obligations

There is generally no distinction between the terms 'guarantee' and 'caution'.[2] In English law, a cautioner is sometimes known as a 'surety'. Not all agreements that carry the label 'guarantee' are cautionary obligations in the technical sense. Cautionary obligations arise where an agreement is accessory to, or dependent on, a principal obligation. Sometimes a document that is called a 'guarantee' is so drafted that it is, in form, a principal obligation whereby the guarantor becomes a principal obligant with the principal debtor. **10.03**

The distinction between a cautionary obligation and a separate principal obligation depends on the proper construction of the obligation, since they are almost invariably in writing. An important factor is whether the parties intend the second obligation to be conditional on the debtor's breach of the principal obligation. If so, the second obligation is cautionary; if they do not, it is a separate principal obligation. Labels do not matter. A purported cautionary obligation that mentions the principal debt generally but is otherwise 'totally unconnected'[3] with the existence[4] or extent[5] of that principal debt will likely be considered independent rather than cautionary.[6] In practice, the **10.04**

1 W M Gloag and J M Irvine, *Law of Rights in Security* (Edinburgh: W. Green, 1897), p. 644; Erskine, *Institute* 3.3.61.
2 *Aitken's Trs v Bank of Scotland* 1944 SC 270 at 281 per Lord Mackay.
3 *Sutton & Co v Grey* [1894] 1 QB 285 at 288 per Lord Esher MR.
4 *Yeoman Credit Ltd v Latter* [1961] 1 WLR 828.
5 *Goulston Discount Co Ltd v Clark* [1967] 2 QB 493.
6 *Wilson v Tait* (1840) 1 Rob App 137.

classification of an obligation as a cautionary obligation or as a separate principal obligation will often depend on the particular facts of the case, making an abstract test quite difficult.

10.05 The courts will consider whether the terms of the agreement are consistent with a cautionary obligation.[7] This may be the case, for example, because of an exclusion of the cautioner's common law privileges, such as its rights of recourse, or by specifically derogating from the rule that the cautioner's liability can be no greater than that of the principal obligation.

Privileges of the cautioner

10.06 The common law privileges of the cautioner that are implicit in a cautionary obligation are: (1) that cautioner shall be bound for the whole debt; (2) that the principal debtor shall be required to perform before the cautioner's obligation is triggered (the so-called benefit of discussion); (3) satisfaction of the principal obligation discharges the cautioner; (4) the cautioner shall have a right of relief against the principal debtor and may require the creditor to assign to the cautioner the creditor's rights (including accessory securities) against the principal debtor.

10.07 As discussed below, some of these common law rights have been modified by legislation or subsequent decision.

Proper and improper caution

10.08 Within the category of cautionary (as opposed to independent) obligations, a further distinction may be made between proper caution and improper caution.

10.09 Proper caution arises where the cautioner is bound explicitly as a cautioner for the debts of a named debtor.[8]

10.10 Improper caution arises where a cautioner appears on the face of the document creating the obligation to be bound to the creditor as a co-debtor in the principal obligation, but the co-obligant's rights against the principal debtor are reserved.

10.11 In such a case, the creditor can proceed against the co-obligants on a joint and several basis; that is to say, the creditor can seek to recover the full amount from any one of the co-obligants, leaving the co-obligant who pays to seek to recover from their co-obligants in the agreed proportions.

7 See, e.g. *Buchan Biogas Ltd v BSC Civil Engineering Ltd* [2020] CSOH 42.
8 Bell, *Principles*, 4th edn (1839), § 246; Erskine, *Institute* 3.3.61.

CONSTITUTION AND VALIDITY

Promise or contract

Cautionary obligations may be constituted by unilateral obligations (a promise from the cautioner to the creditor), bilateral obligations (between the cautioner and creditor), or tripartite contracts (principal debtor-creditor-cautioner). Many cautioners are commercial undertakings (banks or insurance companies) who provide the guarantee or bond of caution for a fee. Such obligations undertaken in the course of business do not have to be in writing, although in practice they usually are. **10.12**

Sometimes cautioners act gratuitously, such as where one family member guarantees the obligations of a child or partner. A cautionary obligation constituted gratuitously as a unilateral obligation requires to be in writing.[9] These are the types of obligations that might typically be undertaken informally. As a result, the law seeks to protect those who, acting gratuitously, may be prone to rash or impulsive promises.[10] It is sometimes unclear from the dealings between the parties whether the cautioner offers to enter a contract of guarantee, requiring acceptance, or whether the cautioner simply promises to pay if the debtor fails, requiring only communication to the promisee. This should be decided according to the normal rules of interpretation.[11] **10.13**

Formal validity

With two exceptions, cautionary obligations need not be reduced to writing. **10.14**

The first exception is where, as mentioned above, a cautionary obligation is constituted as a unilateral obligation, otherwise than in the course of business.[12] The second exception is where the obligation relates to a regulated credit agreement.[13] **10.15**

If an agreement is constituted in writing, the written terms are presumed to represent the entire agreement on that matter, subject to extrinsic evidence of additional terms.[14] Parties may not lead extrinsic evidence for the purpose of seeking to vary the written terms, unless the document fails to accurately express the common intention of the parties and the court is being asked to rectify the document.[15] However, the subsequent words or conduct of the parties entitled to the benefit of obligations under the agreement may personally **10.16**

9 Requirements of Writing (Scotland) Act 1995, s. 1(2)(a)(ii).
10 K G C Reid, *Greens Annotated Acts: Requirements of Writing (Scotland) Act 1995*, 2nd edn (Edinburgh: W. Green, 2015), p. 8.
11 Cf S Eden, 'Cautionary Obligations and Representations as to Credit', *Stair Memorial Encyclopaedia* (Edinburgh: LexisNexis, 1994) (SME) Vol. 3, paras 882–884.
12 Requirements of Writing (Scotland) Act 1995, s. 1(2)(a)(ii).
13 Consumer Credit Act 1974, ss. 105, 106 (a cautionary obligation may fall within the definition of either 'security' or 'surety' or both. The relevant regulations are the Consumer Credit (Guarantees and Indemnities) Regulations 1983 (SI 1983/1556)).
14 Contract (Scotland) Act 1997, s. 1.
15 Law Reform (Miscellaneous Provisions) (Scotland) Act 1985, s. 8.

bar that person from insisting on the rights contained in the written document, if those words or conduct are inconsistent with the existence of the right.[16]

10.17 There are no particular words that must be used, except where the cautionary obligation relates to a regulated credit agreement, in which case it must be constituted in the prescribed written form, otherwise it may be enforced only by an order of the court.[17]

Substantive validity

10.18 Cautionary obligations are subject to the normal rules of capacity, error, misrepresentation, fraud, force and fear, undue influence, facility and circumvention, and illegality.

Wrongs by the debtor against the cautioner

10.19 Misrepresentation, undue influence, facility and circumvention, or fraud by the principal debtor on the cautioner will not generally have any effect on the validity of a cautionary obligation. Caution is constituted by a contract between cautioner and creditor, or by a promise by the cautioner to the creditor, subject to privity of contract, so the creditor is not normally responsible for the conduct of the principal debtor unless the debtor can be said to be acting as agent for the creditor.[18]

10.20 Nonetheless, a cautionary obligation may be indirectly vulnerable to a wrong committed by the principal debtor against the cautioner. Where the cautioner's relationship with the principal debtor is such that there may be a risk of undue influence or a particular reason to suspect a misrepresentation, and the caution is given gratuitously, the creditor has an obligation: (a) to ensure that the cautioner has sufficient information about the nature of the obligation being entered into; and (b) to promote taking independent legal advice.

10.21 This rule, based on a limited requirement of good faith, was established in *Smith v Bank of Scotland*.[19] The wife of a bank's debtor entered into a standard security with her husband in favour of the bank over their matrimonial home, securing sums due by the husband's partnership to the bank. The wife was therefore a cautioner to the partnership's debt. She averred that her husband had misrepresented the indebtedness to her. The House of Lords held that the standard security should be set aside. This was not because, as in England, the bank was to be clothed with constructive knowledge of the misrepresentation, but because it had not discharged its duty of good faith to the wife. It had failed to warn her of the consequences of entering into the security or to advise her to take separate legal advice.

10.22 Subsequent cases have affirmed the effect of the decision, although not always its basis in the principles of Scots contract law. In particular, *Smith* did not

16 *Gatty v Maclaine* 1921 SC (HL) 1.

17 Consumer Credit Act 1974, s. 105(7) and the Consumer Credit (Guarantees and Indemnities) Regulations 1983 (SI 1983/1556).

18 See *Young v Clydesdale Bank* (1889) 17 R 231.

19 1997 SC (HL) 111. *Smith* was followed in *Cooper v Bank of Scotland plc* [2014] CSOH 16.

clarify whether a failure of good faith alone was sufficient to allow a cautioner to escape liability, or whether lack of good faith needed to be coupled with an actionable wrong by the debtor. An actionable wrong was required in *Royal Bank of Scotland plc v Wilson*,[20] where the pursuers had been legally represented. The court in *Wilson* also added that the rule in *Smith* is relevant only where the obligation is gratuitous. The term 'gratuitous', however, was given a wide meaning. A joint security which covers all sums due to the creditor by either party would not be 'gratuitous' for present purposes, as both parties would have the benefit of the other's potential liability for their debt.

There is no closed group of relationships to which the rule in *Smith* applies. The requirement is simply that there is some objective risk of wrongdoing by virtue of the nature of the relationship between debtor and cautioner. This risk exists in practically all non-commercial cases,[21] and would therefore include relationships between a parent and child, husband and wife, and cohabitees. **10.23**

On the basis of the above, it is suggested that a cautioner may seek reduction of a cautionary obligation where: (a) there was an objective risk of wrongdoing by the debtor against the cautioner by virtue of their non-commercial relationship; (b) the caution is granted gratuitously; (c) the creditor failed to take steps to mitigate that risk; and (d) the debtor did in fact commit an actionable wrong against the cautioner. **10.24**

One exception to the general rule that a debtor cannot directly affect the validity of a cautionary obligation is force and fear. If a debtor induces a cautioner to enter into a cautionary obligation by force and fear, the resulting cautionary obligation is void by lack of consent, despite the good faith of the creditor.[22] **10.25**

Wrongs by the creditor against the cautioner

The Inner House has suggested that the meaning to be accorded to the underlying requirement of good faith in a cautionary obligation is that 'there must be perfect fairness of representation on the part of the creditor in the constitution of the contract'.[23] The rules about concealment and half-truths must also be applied rigorously.[24] The creditor must disclose all material risks within its knowledge if the cautioner is 'excusably ignorant'.[25] Further, as discussed above, the creditor must not act in bad faith. Thus, if the creditor is aware that the cautioner misunderstands the facts or the nature of the transaction, the creditor cannot remain silent. **10.26**

Where the creditor makes a positive representation, the cautioner may seek reduction of the obligation should the representation prove to be materially false, provided the cautioner would not have entered the contract on the basis **10.27**

20 2004 SC 153.

21 *Royal Bank of Scotland plc v Etridge (No. 2)* [2001] UKHL 44, [2002] 2 AC 773 at [89] per Lord Nicholls.

22 *Hislop v Dickson Motors (Forres) Ltd* 1978 SLT (Notes) 73.

23 *Royal Bank of Scotland plc v O'Donnell* [2014] CSIH 84, 2015 SC 258 at [43] per Lord Drummond Young, citing Gloag and Irvine, *Rights in Security* (n 1), p. 706.

24 *O'Donnell* (n 23) at [43].

25 *Smith* (n 19) 117–118 per Lord Clyde.

of the true circumstances.[26] Positive representations may include false statements, partial truths or concealment when a duty to speak exists.[27] Damages may also follow if the misrepresentation was fraudulent or negligent.[28]

Error

10.28 An error as to the essentials of the contract will render the cautionary obligation void, regardless of the actions or inactions of the debtor or cautioner.[29] Thus where the cautioner erroneously grants a guarantee under essential error as to identity of the debtor, or believing the guarantee to be a different kind of obligation altogether,[30] the cautionary obligation may be void. However, as a general rule, the cautioner will not be released because of a misunderstanding of the terms of the guarantee or the extent of the indebtedness of the debtor, unless that error was induced by the creditor.[31] In these latter cases – depending on the terms of the caution – there is still consent, albeit the outcome of giving that consent has turned out to be different from what the cautioner expected.

10.29 Where the cautionary obligation is a unilateral gratuitous obligation (whether or not given in the course of business), it may be susceptible to reduction on the ground of unilateral essential error, without needing to show that the error was induced.[32]

Gratuitous alienations

10.30 Upon the insolvency of a cautioner, his or her creditors, trustees in bankruptcy, administrators or liquidators (as appropriate) may apply to the court to reverse a gratuitous alienation made by the insolvent party. Gratuitous alienations may, under statute, be reversed only if they were made in the previous two years. However, if the transaction was for the benefit of an 'associate' of the insolvent party, the time limit is extended to five years.[33] Cautionary obligations can be particularly susceptible to challenge on this ground, as by their nature there will frequently be no consideration given for them by the creditor.

10.31 If a caution is challenged, the creditor may object on the grounds that: (a) the cautioner's assets were greater than their liabilities immediately after or at any time following the grant of the guarantee; or (b) that the guarantee was granted for adequate consideration.[34]

26 See *Ritchie v Glass* 1936 SLT 591; *Lees v Todd* (1882) 9 R 807.
27 For example, *Railton v Mathews and Leonard* (1844) 6 D 536.
28 *Bryson & Co Ltd v Bryson* 1916 1 SLT 361. For negligent misrepresentation, see Law Reform (Miscellaneous Provisions) (Scotland) Act 1985, s. 10.
29 Stair, *Institutions* 1.10.13.
30 For example, *Ellis v Lochgelly Iron and Coal Co Ltd* 1909 SC 1278.
31 *Stewart v Kennedy* (1890) 17 R (HL) 25; see also para. 10.24 above.
32 *Hunter v Bradford Property Trust Ltd* 1970 SLT 173.
33 Insolvency Act 1986, s. 242(2); Bankruptcy (Scotland) Act 2016, s. 98(4).
34 Insolvency Act 1986, s. 242(3); Bankruptcy (Scotland) Act 2016, s. 98(6).

Consumer protection

Pre-contractual duties

Pre-contractual duties in relation to cautionary obligations are regulated by common law, as discussed above at para. 10.20, where it was seen that creditors must take steps to ensure that, in practically all non-commercial transactions, the cautioner has been advised to take independent legal advice.[35] **10.32**

It may be that 'non-commercial' is a narrower definition than 'consumer', as it can conceivably exclude commercial consumers. In practice, corporate lenders are likely to supply the same information to commercial consumers granting cautionary obligations as they are to non-commercial guarantors.[36] **10.33**

Unfair terms

The Consumer Rights Act 2015 is probably applicable to cautionary obligations where: (a) both the debtor and the cautioner enter into their respective obligations as consumers; and (b) the cautioner has been unable to influence the substance of the agreement.[37] **10.34**

It was at one time thought that cautioners could not be considered as consumers for the purposes of the regulations, because the creditor could not be considered as a supplier to the cautioner.[38] The argument went that it was impossible to be categorised as a supplier where the only supply was by the cautioner to the creditor. In other words, that the creditor was the recipient of services, not the supplier of them. However, discussing the Distance Selling Directive,[39] the Court of Justice of the European Union decided that there was no need for the consumer to be the person to whom such services were supplied in order for the protections to apply.[40] This decision was based on the nature of cautionary obligations as subsidiary to a relevant supply of services (i.e. the credit extended to the debtor), and therefore the regulations may not apply to independent obligations. No case has yet settled the matter in Scots law, although it is expected that a Scottish court would follow the English decision in *Barclay's Bank*.[41] **10.35**

The Unfair Contract Terms Act 1977 also applies to cautionary obligations. In particular, the Act restricts specific types of unreasonable contract terms where either: (a) the cautioner is a consumer and the creditor is not; or (b) the cautionary obligation is in standard form. As the 1977 Act does not require **10.36**

35 See *Etridge (No. 2)* (n 21).

36 See also *Bankers Trust International plc v PT Dharmala Sakti Sejahtera (No. 2)* [1996] CLC 518.

37 Consumer Rights Act 2015, s. 63. See, e.g. the discussion of the now-repealed Unfair Terms in Consumer Contracts (Regulations) 1999 in *Barclays Bank plc v Kufner* [2008] EWHC 2319 (Comm), [2009] 1 All ER (Comm) 1.

38 *Bank of Scotland v Singh* 17 June 2005, QB Div (unreported, referred to in *Williamson v Governor of the Bank of Scotland* [2006] EWHC 1289 (Ch)).

39 Directive 85/577/EEC.

40 Case C-45/96 *Bayerische Hypothetken-und Wechselbank AG v Dietzinger* [1998] ECR I-1199.

41 *Barclays Bank* (n 37).

a link with a 'supply', there is no need for the debtor to be a consumer, in contrast with the 2015 Act.

LIABILITY OF CAUTIONER

Amount and limits

10.37 Cautionary obligations are accessory to liability for a principal debt. It follows that, unless expressly provided for, a cautioner is liable only to the extent of the principal debt, plus interest and expenses.[42] Unless otherwise specified, the cautioner will be liable for the full extent of the loss sustained by the creditor resulting from the debtor's default. This is also called the principle of co-extensiveness. Any express liability over this amount might indicate that the obligation is not a cautionary obligation but an independent obligation, as discussed above. If a specific limit is provided for then naturally the creditor cannot recover more than that agreed amount from the cautioner.

10.38 It follows from the principle of co-extensiveness that any repayment of debt will reduce the cautioner's liability accordingly. Where the caution is for a fixed debt, liability will not be affected by further advances. However, where the guarantee is a continuing guarantee, further advances may increase the cautioner's liability.[43]

10.39 Where a limit is placed on the cautioner's liability, it is a matter of construction as to the effect of that limit. Either the cautioner guarantees part of the debt, or guarantees the whole debt up to a particular limit on liability.[44] In the former case, in the event of the debtor's bankruptcy, the cautioner is entitled to share in any dividends or securities, thus reducing liability proportionately.[45] So if the debt is £1,000, and the cautioner guarantees £100, a dividend of £500 from the debtor's bankruptcy will reduce the cautioner's liability to £50. If liability is for the whole amount, subject to a limit, then the creditor can seek recovery up to that limit ignoring any dividends paid from the bankrupt estate.

10.40 Repayment of the principal obligation can be made either by the debtor, or by the cautioner. If the latter repays the debt, the cautioner may then seek recovery of that expenditure from the debtor, as discussed below.[46]

Further advances

10.41 A cautioner may guarantee specific obligations, past debts, or future debts. Where additional debts have been incurred after the creation of the cautionary obligation, it is a matter of construction of the agreement whether these further advances are to be included in the guarantee. If so, the guarantee is sometimes referred to as a continuing guarantee. If not, and the cautioner has agreed to be held liable only for debt that existed or was in the contem-

42 *Struthers v Dykes* (1847) 9 D 1437.
43 See paras 10.41–10.42 below.
44 See *Veitch v National Bank of Scotland Ltd* 1907 SC 554.
45 *F W Harmer & Co v Gibb* 1911 SC 1341.
46 At para. 10.55.

plation of the cautioner at the time the cautionary obligation was created,[47] any credit extended subsequently will not be secured by the prior cautionary obligation.

Where further advances are made and the debtor later makes a payment to the creditor, it is necessary to determine whether this payment goes towards reducing the secured or the unsecured portion of the debt. In the first instance, it is open to the debtor to specify which portion should be reduced – this is called appropriation. Failing an appropriation by the debtor, it is open to the creditor to make the decision.[48] **10.42**

If neither the debtor nor creditor makes the appropriation, the presumption is that the payment will be set against the earliest outstanding indebtedness. In effect, the cautioner's liability will be reduced first before the (unsecured) further advances. Thus, if a debtor borrows £100 in respect of which a cautionary obligation is granted, then later borrows a further £50, any repayment will be notionally attributed to the debt of £100 first, until that debt is extinguished and only £50 remains. This is sometimes referred to as the rule in *Clayton's Case*.[49] **10.43**

Assignation of the principal debt

It is a general principle that an assignee of a principal debt may call upon the cautioner to make payment.[50] **10.44**

ENFORCEMENT

Default of the principal

Cautionary obligations are guarantees that, should the principal debtor fail to perform obligations owed to the creditor, the cautioner will perform instead. It follows that the debtor must have breached the principal obligation before the creditor may seek to enforce the caution. Non-payment of a debt is often called 'default', although this is not a term of art. Typically, commercial facilities will expand the definition of default to include, for example, the commencement of formal insolvency proceedings against the debtor, or the debtor's breach of any financial covenants. Furthermore, in practice, many guarantees state that the guarantor will perform the principal obligations 'on demand', regardless of whether the debtor is in default, which might indicate that such guarantees are separate principal obligations rather than cautionary obligations. **10.45**

47 *Scott v Mitchell* (1866) 4 M 551.
48 *Jackson v Nicoll* (1870) 8 M 408.
49 *Devaynes v Noble* (1816) 35 ER 781.
50 See, e.g. *Promontoria (RAM) Ltd v Moore* [2017] CSOH 88, 2018 SCLR 299 at [49].

Debt must be proved

10.46 A creditor cannot sue a cautioner unless the principal debt has been proved. A debt may be proved by obtaining a decree for payment, by probative deed, or by the debtor's admission. It is no longer possible to prove a debt by oath.[51]

RIGHTS OF A CAUTIONER

Generally

10.47 Unless expressly agreed, cautionary obligations include certain implied terms that reflect the special position the law affords a cautioner. These equitable rights are: the benefit of discussion; division; relief; and assignation of the creditor's rights. It is open to the parties to modify or exclude these rights, and so they should not be regarded as a package of rights afforded in all circumstances but as context-sensitive specialties of cautionary obligations.

Right to benefit of discussion

10.48 At common law, a proper cautioner is entitled to expect that the creditor will exhaust all potential legal methods of recovering from the debtor before seeking to enforce the caution – sometimes called the benefit of discussion. By Act of Parliament, the benefit of discussion no longer applies to caution for monetary debts.[52] This means that a creditor may now proceed against the cautioner of a monetary obligation immediately upon the default of the debtor.

Right to division

10.49 Where several proper cautioners are bound jointly as co-cautioners, each co-cautioner is liable for only a pro rata share of the debt – provided that the debt is capable of division. Therefore, a co-cautioner can refuse to pay until the other co-cautioners are called to pay.[53]

10.50 The right of division is subject to an exception if one of the joint cautioners is insolvent. In this case, the solvent cautioners can be required to increase their pro rata share as if the insolvent cautioner did not exist, subject to any agreed limit on liability.[54] So, for example, if only one cautioner out of five remains solvent, then that single cautioner can be held liable for the whole debt. That cautioner may then attempt to exercise their right of relief. This is discussed in more detail below.[55]

51 Requirements of Writing (Scotland) Act 1995, s. 11; see *Royal Bank of Scotland plc v Malcolm* 1999 SCLR 854.

52 Mercantile Law Amendment Act Scotland 1856, s. 8; Gloag and Irvine (n 1), p. 788. It remains possible for the benefit of discussion to be included as an express term of the contract of cautionary.

53 Bell, *Principles*, § 62; SME Vol. 3, para. 927.

54 Erskine, *Institute* 3.3.63.

55 At paras. 10.51–10.54.

Right of relief

The right of relief has two elements. First, the cautioner has a right to be relieved, based on the implied mandate between the debtor and the cautioner. The idea is that the debtor has impliedly commissioned the cautioner to pay on his or her behalf.[56] Like any other agent, a cautioner is entitled to be relieved of obligations incurred as an agent. **10.51**

The right to relief based on implied mandate arises when the cautioner is put in distress – that is, where the creditor takes legal steps against the cautioner to enforce the caution[57] – or where the debtor is on the brink of becoming insolvent. Once this right arises, the cautioner does not need to perform the obligations under the cautionary obligation before demanding that the debtor either obtain the cautioner's discharge or repay the debt. In appropriate circumstances the cautioner may be able to protect their position by exercising the right of retention or compensation over money due to the principal debtor.[58] **10.52**

There are also certain occasions where the cautioner does not need to be put in distress before pressing the debtor for relief. Where the caution is for an indefinite period of time, the cautioner may at any time after the principal debt has become due take proceedings to compel the debtor to pay the debt, 'it being unreasonable that a man should always have a cloud hanging over him'.[59] **10.53**

On the basis of this implied mandate, the cautioner is entitled to a lien over any assets belonging to the debtor that may be in the cautioner's possession.[60] **10.54**

Right to assignation from creditor

The cautioner is entitled on payment to an assignation from the creditor of the creditor's claims (and accessory securities) against the debtor,[61] as well as an assignation of any diligence that has been executed by the creditor.[62] In effect, the cautioner who has paid fully should be put in the shoes of the creditor. Whether the security was held without the cautioner's knowledge, or was obtained after creation of the cautionary obligation, is irrelevant.[63] **10.55**

56 *Smithy's Place Ltd v Blackadder & McMonagle* 1991 SLT 790 at 795 per Lord Cameron of Lochbroom.
57 Erskine, *Institute* 3.3.65.
58 See Chapter Two: General Principles of Contract Law.
59 *Ranelagh v Hayes* (1683) 23 ER 405 at 406 per Sir Francis North, cited with approval by Gloag and Irvine, p. 801.
60 *McPherson v Wright* (1885) 12 R 942.
61 *Smithy's Place Ltd* (n 56) at 795 per Lord Cameron of Lochbroom; *Sligo v Menzies* (1840) 2 D 1478; Bell, *Principles*, § 558.
62 Bell, *Principles*, § 255.
63 *Duncan, Fox & Co v New South Wales Bank* (1880) 6 App Cas 1; *Forbes v Jackson* (1882) 19 Ch D 615.

TERMINATION

Extinction of principal obligation

10.56 The existence of a proper caution entirely depends on the existence of a principal debt. Should the agreement from which the principal debt flows be found to be void as a result of operation of the principles of contract law, for example as a result of essential error or illegality, the cautioner will be released from any obligation: there is nothing for the caution to support.[64] This is called the accessory principle. Similarly, if the principal obligation is voidable, and is subsequently reduced, the cautionary obligation will come to an end.

10.57 As a caveat to this rule, it may be the case that a cautionary obligation will be unaffected by voidness resulting from a lack of capacity[65] or a defect in form[66] on the part of the principal debtor. In such cases, the cautioner must have been aware of the debtor's lack of capacity if the cautioner is to remain bound when the debtor is not. The reason for this is variously ascribed to the operation of personal bar or to the nature of the risk underwritten by the cautioner.[67] There may be a presumption that the cautioner is aware of the debtor's condition.[68]

10.58 Since full repayment of a debt extinguishes that debt, full repayment of the principal debt will release the cautioner from liability.

Material alterations

10.59 Just as total extinction of the principal debt releases the cautioner, so too will material alteration to the principal debt without the consent of the cautioner. A material alteration to the obligation that is being guaranteed means that it is no longer the same thing as the original debt upon which the cautionary obligation was entirely dependent.[69]

10.60 The impact that variation of the principal debt can have on a cautionary obligation can be explained in several ways, which largely depend on how the guaranteed liability is defined in the particular cautionary obligation in question. If the guarantee secures a particular and definite obligation (e.g. '*this* debt'), the novation of that obligation effectively amounts to frustration of the guarantee because the debt that has been guaranteed no longer exists.[70] Where the terms of the guarantee are more general (e.g. '*the* debt'), an alteration of the principal debt may be prejudicial to the cautioner, thus permitting relief.[71] Of course, the terms of the guarantee may even permit alteration to the debtor's liability, but in such cases the accessory principle must be at least partially ignored – which may suggest an independent rather than cautionary obligation.

64 *Garrard v James* [1925] Ch 616.
65 *Stevenson v Adair* (1872) 10 M 919.
66 Erskine, *Institute* 3.3.64.
67 SME Vol. 3, para. 838.
68 Erskine, *Institute* 3.3.64.
69 Cf J J Gow, *The Mercantile and Industrial Laws of Scotland* (Edinburgh: W. Green, 1964), p. 323.
70 *Calder & Co v Cruikshank's Tr* (1889) 17 R 74.
71 *N G Napier Ltd v Crosbie* 1964 SLT 185.

It is thought that giving time, as discussed below, may also constitute a material alteration depending on the terms of the cautionary obligation at hand. 10.61

Prejudicial conduct

No general duty to act reasonably

From time to time it is suggested that a creditor owes a cautioner a duty to act reasonably in exercising rights under the cautionary obligation. While case law does not necessarily support this proposition as a general principle, there are certainly instances where the unreasonable actions of a creditor can release the cautioner from the cautionary obligation. Rather than asserting that a creditor owes the cautioner a duty to act reasonably, it is perhaps more accurate to state that the creditor cannot act in a manner that is prejudicial to the cautioner and later insist upon the caution.[72] The meaning of prejudicial conduct has been elaborated upon by the courts, and while the list is never closed, it is possible to identify particular types of conduct that are likely to be classed as prejudicial. 10.62

Giving time

Giving time happens where the creditor legally binds him or herself (for example, by agreement) not to demand immediate payment of the principal debt when it falls due.[73] It is thought to be prejudicial to the rights of the cautioner,[74] because it may temporarily restrict or remove some of the cautioner's rights of relief – for example, the right to call on the debtor to repay the debt. However, it may be that the existence of prejudice is merely ancillary to the fact that, by giving time, the creditor has materially altered the principal debt.[75] As we have seen above, a material alteration to the principal debt will release the cautioner without consideration of prejudice. 10.63

A distinction should be made between situations in which the creditor becomes legally disabled from demanding payment, and situations in which the creditor simply fails to press for immediate payment. An example of the former may be agreeing to accept repayment in instalments rather than a lump sum; an example of the latter may be neglecting to immediately demand payment when it falls due. The latter does not affect the existence of the original obligation, nor does it alter the nature of the obligation. 10.64

Discharging securities

The release of real security rights (for example, standard securities, pledges, liens) can have a significant impact on the risk and extent to which the cautioner will be called upon to perform. Furthermore, the release of a security would be prejudicial to the cautioner's right to assignation of securities. For these reasons, a cautioner is entitled to assume that the creditor will not 10.65

72 *Lord Advocate v Maritime Fruit Carriers Co Ltd* 1983 SLT 357.
73 See, e.g. *Rouse v Bradford Banking Co* [1894] AC 586.
74 For example, *C and A Johnstone v Duthie* (1892) 19 R 624 at 627 per Lord McLaren.
75 *Richardson v Harvey* (1853) 15 D 628.

voluntarily release securities securing the debt. Discharge of a security interest will release the cautioner, but only to the extent of the security released.

10.66 The same effect will result where a security interest is lost due to the negligence or omission of the creditor. *Fleming v Thomson*[76] illustrates the potentially severe consequences for a legal practitioner involved in secured lending. In that case, the solicitors for the creditor failed to properly register a bond and disposition in security (a form of heritable security since replaced by the standard security[77]) in the General Register of Sasines. Not only was the security ineffective for want of registration, but the cautioner was released too.

Discharging a co-cautioner

10.67 Where caution has been granted by multiple co-cautioners, releasing one cautioner from his or her cautionary obligations will automatically release the others.[78] It does not matter whether the co-cautioners are liable severally (in other words, separately) rather than jointly or jointly and severally. It is thought that the reason behind this is that each co-cautioner is entitled to assume that the others will remain bound: their release has substantially the same effect as the discharge of a real security.

10.68 There is one potential exception or limit to this rule. Where each of the cautioners is bound severally for less than the whole debt, discharge of one will have no effect on the others.[79]

10.69 In practice, the procedural aspects of releasing co-cautioners will be set out in the agreement. The consent of the other cautioners to the discharge of one of their number will prevent such problems arising.

Discharge of the cautioner

By agreement

10.70 It is open to the parties to a cautionary obligation, as with any other contract, to simply agree that their respective obligations shall be at an end.

10.71 Where the cautionary obligation is reduced to writing, it is good practice to obtain the discharge in writing too – although it is no longer the case that it must be.[80] Even if writing is required for some reason, the creditor may, by words or conduct, become personally barred from insisting on the caution.[81]

Revocation by the cautioner

10.72 Provided that doing so will not breach the terms of the cautionary obligation, a cautioner may give notice to the creditor that further advances will not be

76 (1826) 2 W & S 277.
77 Conveyancing and Feudal Reform (Scotland) Act 1970, s. 9(3).
78 Mercantile Law Amendment Act Scotland 1856, s. 9.
79 *Morgan v Smart* (1872) 10 M 610.
80 Requirements of Writing (Scotland) Act 1995, s. 1; Cf *Charles and James McPherson v John and James Reid Haggart* (1881) 9 R 306.
81 *Gatty v Maclaine* 1921 SC (HL) 1.

guaranteed – in effect withdrawing from future liability. In such cases the cautioner will continue to be held liable for advances made prior to the notice. The cautioner is then, as at any other time, free to call upon the principal debtor to repay the debt and obtain a discharge of the caution from the creditor.

It is implied that a cautioner may revoke liability for further advances where liability is on a continuing basis, whether or not there is a cap on the amount the cautioner can be held liable for.[82] The terms of the cautionary obligation may, and frequently do, expressly override this implied term. No such implied term exists where the cautionary obligation is for a definite period of time, or for the finance of a particular transaction. **10.73**

Operation of law

Prescription

Prescription of liability under the cautionary obligation will release the cautioner. The relevant period is five years from the time at which the cautionary obligation becomes enforceable.[83] In the absence of contrary agreement, a cautionary obligation becomes enforceable upon default of the principal obligation, meaning that the cautionary obligation and principal debt both prescribe together. **10.74**

In practice, it is common to state that the guarantee will become enforceable 'on demand'. If this is the case, then the date of demand is the relevant date for the purposes of prescription, regardless of the date of default.[84] **10.75**

Death

The death of the cautioner will, upon notice being given to the creditor, have the same effect as revocation of the obligation, i.e. to relieve the cautioner from any future obligation. As noted above, revocation is not possible where it would contradict the terms of the guarantee, in which case the cautioner's estate remains bound in relation to any further advances. Notice of the death must be given to the creditor. In the absence of notice, it does not appear to be relevant whether the creditor was in fact aware of the cautioner's death. However, it is possible that knowledge of the death coupled with a failure by the creditor to notify the cautioner's estate of the cautionary obligation will bar claims as to further advances. **10.76**

Death of the creditor or debtor will generally determine the obligation, thereby preventing future liabilities, but not liability for previously incurred debts.[85] **10.77**

82 Bell, *Principles*, § 266.
83 Prescription and Limitation (Scotland) Act 1973, s. 6.
84 See, e.g. *Royal Bank of Scotland v Brown* 1982 SC 89.
85 *Woodfield Finance Trust (Glasgow) Ltd v Morgan* 1958 SLT (Sh Ct) 14.

Insolvency

Generally

10.78 Insolvency of any of the parties has certain effects on cautionary obligations established between them but does not generally terminate or otherwise alter their obligations. Instead, it is better to think of insolvency as influencing the way in which the creditor and cautioner may enforce their respective rights under the cautionary obligation.

Of the debtor

10.79 Upon the insolvency of the debtor, the creditor may elect to rank in the insolvency for the debt. Typically, the creditor will be paid a dividend representing a percentage of the debt if there is any payment at all. Once the dividend is paid, the creditor is then free to seek recovery of the balance of the debt from the cautioner. A co-obligant is not discharged by the discharge of a co-obligant following bankruptcy.[86] However, because the debt has been settled in full as far as the insolvent estate is concerned the cautioner cannot seek to rank in the insolvency after assignation[87] and is therefore left without a remedy.

10.80 On the other hand, the creditor may seek to enforce against the cautioner directly and bypass the debtor's insolvency. If the debt is settled in full, the cautioner, exercising the rights of relief, is then entitled to rank in the insolvency.

10.81 Complications can arise where the caution is limited by amount. As a matter of construction, it must be established whether the guarantee was: (a) for the whole debt, subject to a limit; or (b) for part of the debt only. In the first case, should the creditor choose to rank in insolvency, the cautioner will be precluded from doing so as discussed above. This is because the cautioner would effectively be ranking on the insolvent estate for the same debt, thus counting it twice – so called 'double ranking'. The agreed limit will still apply. In the second case, should the cautioner repay the guaranteed part of the debt in full, both the creditor and the cautioner may rank in insolvency: the cautioner for the part of the debt guaranteed, and assigned by virtue of the rights of relief discussed below; the creditor for the parts of the debt not covered by the guarantee.[88]

Of the cautioner

10.82 Should the cautioner become bankrupt before the cautionary obligation becomes enforceable, the creditor is entitled to rank in the cautioner's insolvency on a contingent basis. After the obligation is enforceable, the creditor may simply rank on the cautioner's insolvent estate for the debt. If there are co-cautioners, the creditor may only rank for the cautioner's pro rata

86 Bankruptcy (Scotland) Act 2016, s. 206.
87 See *Mackinnon v Monkhouse* (1881) 9 R 608.
88 *Veitch v National Bank of Scotland Ltd* 1907 SC 554.

liability of the debt, leaving the creditor to recover the balance from the other co-cautioners.

Of the principal debtor and co-cautioners

If the principal debtor and some, but not all, of the co-cautioners become insolvent, the creditor is again entitled to choose between two options. First, the creditor may rank on the insolvent estates for the full debt, thereafter seeking the balance from the solvent cautioners.[89] This would have the effect of preventing the solvent cautioners from ranking on the insolvent estates for the same debt.[90] Alternatively, the creditor may recover the full amount from the solvent cautioners, leaving them to rights of relief against the insolvent estates. In this case, the solvent cautioners are entitled to rank on the debtor's estate for the full amount they have paid, but may rank on the insolvent co-cautioners' estates only for the extent to which they have paid more than their pro rata share.[91] **10.83**

89 See *Morton's Trs v Robertson's Judicial Factor* (1892) 20 R 72.
90 See para. 10.79 above.
91 Bell, *Commentaries* I, 354.

Chapter Eleven

Non-judicial Real Security

John MacLeod

INTRODUCTION

Why grant or seek rights in security?

11.01 Personal rights are only as valuable as the person who owes the correlative obligation. If that person is unwilling or unable to pay or perform, the value of the right will be seriously diminished. The expense and hassle of enforcing a small debt may mean that it is not worth pursuing if the debtor resists. Even if a creditor successfully obtains a decree for payment and does diligence, expenses may not cover the full cost of recovery. Further, the debtor may not have sufficient assets to pay the creditor. A right to payment of £500 against a solvent debtor will be worth more than one for £5,000 against an insolvent one, if the so-called dividend which the insolvency official pays out to the insolvent debtor's creditors is less than 10p for every pound owed.[1]

11.02 Creditors have a strong interest in protecting themselves against these risks before giving credit to debtors. The mechanisms which allow them to do so are known as rights in security. Rights in security take two forms: personal security (known in Scots law as caution); and real or proprietary security. Personal security gives the creditor a secondary personal right: the basic idea is that, if the debtor does not pay the creditor, another person will (thus the term personal security). In real security, the creditor's secondary right is not against a different person but against a thing, a *res* (thus the term real security). The thing over which the right is granted is sometimes referred to as the object of the right in security or the security subjects.

11.03 As discussed in Chapter Twelve, certain forms of diligence enable a creditor to acquire a real right in the debtor's property, which allows the value of the asset to be realised and applied to payment of the debt. For that reason, diligence is sometimes referred to as judicial security. This chapter is concerned with non-judicial real security. Judicial security is discussed in Chapter Twelve. Rights in security may be granted in respect of obligations other than debts but debts are the most common form of secured obligation and, for the sake of simplicity, the rest of this chapter will proceed on the assumption that the secured obligation is a debt.

11.04 The reasons why a creditor might want a right in security are obvious, but why would the debtor be willing to grant one? Without them a creditor might

1 See generally Chapters Thirteen and Fourteen.

not be willing to lend at all or might only advance credit at a much higher rate of interest. Given the possibility of diligence and insolvency processes where debts are not paid, granting a right of security does not really put the debtor at greater risk of losing the asset. The assets will be sold off one way or another anyway. Those who are really prejudiced by rights in security are the other creditors of the person who gives security because the security holder's real right will entitle them to preferential access to the asset in question but they have no say in the granting of the right.

Timing and parties

While the grant of the right in security is usually contemporaneous with the creation of the debt, this need not be the case. It is perfectly permissible to grant a right in security to secure the payment of a pre-existing debt. **11.05**

Also, while the right in security will usually be granted by the debtor, this need not be the case. A third party may well be willing to grant a right in security for another's debt. David may want to borrow money from Carol but she is unwilling to lend it to him without security. David has no suitable assets, so he asks Oliver to put up security for him. Oliver agrees and pledges his antique clock in security for David's debt. In that situation, if David does not pay the debt, Carol could sue David for the price. She could also sell the clock (although she might have to apply to the court for authority to do so) so the proceeds could be applied to satisfaction of the debt. She could not, however, sue Oliver for the price. Oliver's clock is, in a manner of speaking, liable for the debt but Oliver has no personal liability. **11.06**

In order to keep things simple, the rest of this chapter has been written on the assumption that the right in security has been granted by the debtor but it should be borne in mind that the rules discussed are equally applicable where the right in security is granted by a third party. Unless a specific case is being discussed, debtors and the owners will be referred to using the masculine pronoun and creditors will be referred to using the feminine pronoun. **11.07**

Granting a right of security for someone else's debt is one reason why someone might own an asset burdened by a right in security without being liable to pay the relevant debt. The other reason is transfer of the burdened asset. Since rights in security are real rights, they affect the asset even after transfer. **11.08**

Types of real security

Scots law recognises a wide range of real rights in security. The key examples are given below. They may be subdivided into conventional rights and tacit or automatic rights. Those in the former category are created as a result of a juridical act by the debtor and creditor; those in the latter are created by operation of law, without the need for any juridical act on the part of either owner or security holder. Real rights in security may also be subdivided into possessory and non-possessory security rights. For the former, the creditor must take possession of the object of the right, while this is not necessary for the latter. **11.09**

Voluntary rights in security

11.10 • Pledge: a possessory right in security over corporeal moveables.
- Standard security: a non-possessory security over heritable property constituted by registration.
- Floating charge: a non-possessory right in security that can only be granted by companies and a small number of other types of juristic person.[2]
- Aircraft mortgage: a non-possessory security over aircraft.
- Ship mortgage: a non-possessory security over ship.

Tacit rights in security

11.11 • Lien: a right to retain property until the discharge of the secured obligation where the property has not come into the creditor's possession for the purpose of constituting a right in security.
- Landlord's hypothec: a non-possessory right securing the right to rent over corporeal moveables belonging to the debtor which are on the property that has been let out.
- Solicitor's lien or hypothec (more properly a hypothec): a solicitor's right in security over an award of expenses against her client to secure her right to payment for the conduct of the litigation.
- Maritime lien or hypothec: a right in security over the ship for seamen's wages, for the price of foreign repairs and for damage done by the ship.

In English law, the term 'charge' is sometimes used to mean a right in security. Sometimes English lawyers use the term charge in contradistinction to a mortgage to refer to a particular type of right in security. English influence on Scots law means that the term charge is sometimes used in Scotland too. In Scotland, a charge is a right in security.

GENERAL PRINCIPLES APPLICABLE TO RIGHTS IN SECURITY

11.12 Scots law recognises a number of different kinds of right in security. The appropriate right in security will vary depending on the nature of the thing that is being used as security, the granter of the security and the circumstances in which it arises. However, there are certain principles that are applicable to most kinds of right in security.

Nemo plus iuris ad alium transfere potest quam ipse haberet

11.13 The general rule that no one can grant a greater right than they have themself applies to the grant of rights in security as much as it does to the creation of other real rights. This means that, while the debtor and the owner of the object of the security right need not be the same person, the granter of the security right requires to be the owner of the object of the security right. There are some exceptions to this, however.

2 As discussed below, the floating charge does not confer a real right prior to attachment.

The protection that ss. 24 and 25 of the Sale of Goods Act 1979 gives to those who buy goods from non-owning sellers or buyers who are nonetheless in possession of the goods was discussed in Chapter Three.[3] This protection also extends to pledges: Sam sells some machinery to Bertha and remains in possession. By virtue of s. 17 of the Sale of Goods Act 1979, ownership has passed to Bertha. Sam needs to borrow some money and pledge's Bertha's machinery in security for the loan. Section 24 of the 1979 Act means that, provided the pledgee is in good faith, the pledge will be validly constituted and thus effective even against Bertha. **11.14**

Prior tempore potior iure

Multiple rights in security may be granted in the same object. If the object is of sufficient value to pay all of the security holders then this is unproblematic. Where the asset is not sufficiently valuable to satisfy all of security holders, it become necessary to rank the rights in security to determine who has first call on the proceeds of the object of the right in security and who has to wait until others have been paid. **11.15**

As might be expected, given that they are real rights, rights in security rank according to their date of creation. Colin lends £100,000 to Doreen, which is initially unsecured. Later she borrows £50,000 from Carol and grants to her a standard security over her flat. Colin becomes concerned about the debt that Doreen owes him. To calm him down, Doreen grants him a right in security over the flat. Doreen defaults so the standard securities are enforced and the flat is sold. The sale raises £100,000 after the expenses have been paid. Who gets what? Colin was the first lender but that is not what matters. What matters is who has the prior real right. Carol has the prior real right, so she will be paid first, leaving only £50,000 for Colin. **11.16**

It is open to the holders of rights in security to vary the *prior tempore* rule by a ranking agreement. **11.17**

Publicity principle

Because rights in security are real rights, third parties need to be aware of dealings with them. For this reason, as with other real rights, the creation, modification or transfer of a right in security requires some means of publicity. Broadly speaking, this publicity is achieved by transfer of possession where the right in security is possessory and by registration when it is not. In most cases the relevant publicity is a constitutive requirement, so the right in security will not be created until the publicity step has been taken. **11.18**

Additional publicity is required for rights in security over property owned by companies.[4] When a right in security other than a pledge is granted by a company, 'particulars' giving the basic details of the right in security must be **11.19**

3 See paras 3.111–3.123.

4 There are some cases where registration is not required so as to facilitate financial market transactions: rights in security held by central banks such as the Bank of England (Banking Act 2009, s. 252) and rights in security granted as part of financial collateral arrangements (Financial Collateral Arrangements (No. 2) Regulations 2003 (SI 2003/3226), reg. 4(4)).

submitted for registration in the charges section of the entry for the relevant company in the Companies Register, within twenty-one days.[5] Failure to do so will prevent the security holder from relying on it in a dispute with an insolvency official or other creditor.[6] This means that, if a company grants a standard security or a ship mortgage, it must be registered twice: once in the Land Register or the Merchant Shipping Register in order to constitute the right in security and once in the charges section of the Company Register. It is open to the Secretary of State to make an order under s. 893 of the Companies Act 2006 which would avoid the need for double registration by requiring the keeper of the "special register" (such as the land or merchant shipping register) to communicate relevant registrations to the Registrar of Companies. Thus far, no s. 893 order has been made.

Accessoriness principle

11.20 Rights in security exist to ensure the payment of debts or the fulfilment of other obligations. For this reason, the right in security is said to be accessory to the relevant debt or other obligation. The idea behind the principal of accessoriness is that the right in security depends for its existence on the existence of the debt. The most important implications of the principle of accessoriness are that the right in security cannot be enforced if the debt is not enforceable[7] and that rights in security are extinguished by payment the debt in question.[8]

11.21 The accessoriness principle is not enforced with the full rigour that might be used: it is possible to grant a security for sums that are yet to be lent or for all sums due or to become due. In the former case, the right in security exists but only becomes enforceable when the money is advanced. In the latter, payment of everything that is owed to the creditor at a particular moment suspends, but does not extinguish, the security because it remains in force to secure any further debts which become due to the security holder.

Obligations on the party in possession

11.22 Rights in security are subordinate real rights. The existence of a subordinate real right means that there are at least two persons with an interest in the object of the right: the owner and the holder of the security right. Only one of the two parties with an interest can be in possession of the object. For this reason, certain obligations are imposed on the party in possession to protect the other party's interest in the object not being harmed. The detail varies depending on the particular right in security.

Transfer of rights in security

11.23 In principle, rights in security are assets which may be transferred by the right-holder. However, a right in security is worth nothing without the right whose performance it secures. It might be thought that, because rights in security are

5 Companies Act 2006, s. 859A.
6 Companies Act 2006, s. 859H.
7 *Nisbet's Creditors v Robertson* (1791) Mor 572.
8 Bell, *Commentaries* I, 711.

accessory, they should follow the right which they secure automatically. So, if Adam has a right to payment secured by a right in security and he assigns the right to payment to Eve, both the personal right to payment and right in security would pass to Eve when the assignation of the right to payment was intimated to the debtor. This idea is sometimes expressed by the maxim *accessorium sequitur principale.*

However, there is a potential conflict between the publicity principle and the principle of accessoriness in such a case. The latter might suggest that the right in security should follow the right to which it is accessory. On the other hand, the publicity principle suggests that any change to a right in security should be accompanied by some form of publicity. In the case of the standard security, the publicity principle prevails, so the right in security can only be transferred by registration of the relevant deed in the Land Register.[9] Thus it may lag behind the right to payment, which may be transferred by intimation of the assignation. The position regarding the transfer of other rights in security is mixed. A floating charge may be assigned[10] but there is doubt as to when and whether the right of pledge may be assigned. If assignation of the right of pledge is possible, it appears to require transfer of possession from the assignor to the assignee.[11] **11.24**

The requirement of publicity for transfer of a right in security raises the possibility of a security being held by the assignor when the right to payment has already passed to the assignee. Can the right in security survive such a separation, given that it is accessory to the right to payment? The drafters of the legislation governing the standard security appear to have assumed that it could. Were this not the case, we might expect to see some provision that holds back the transfer of the right to payment until the assignation of the right in security has been registered. **11.25**

Sale by the security holder

In most cases the right in security is enforced by sale of its object. This sale is effected by or on behalf of the first ranking security holder, who has a duty to get as a high a price as can reasonably be obtained.[12] Although the security holder is not the owner, she has the power to make the buyer owner. The transfer also has the effect of discharging any security rights (including those arising from diligence) that rank alongside or below that of the selling security holder.[13] The proceeds are used to pay the expenses of the sale and the debt due to the security holder. Any surplus proceeds must be remitted to security holders with lower rankings (if there are any) and then (if anything is left) to the owner of the object of security right.[14] **11.26**

9 Conveyancing and Feudal Reform (Scotland) Act 1970 (CFR(S)A 1970), s. 14(1).

10 There is no statutory provision for assignation of floating charges but it is possible as a matter of general principle and has been recognised by the court: *Libertas-Kommerz GmbH v Johnson* 1977 SC 191.

11 A J M Steven, *Pledge and Lien* (Edinburgh: Edinburgh Legal Education Trust, 2008), paras 4-18–4-27.

12 For example, CFR(S)A 1970, s. 25.

13 For example, CFR(S)A 1970, s. 26(1).

14 For example, CFR(S)A 1970, s. 27(1).

11.27 Imagine that Derek owns a factory. He borrows money from Ellie and grants a standard security over the factory to her. She registers it promptly. A few months later, he grants a second standard security to Felicity (who also registers). Unfortunately, Derek does not pay either of them and Ellie takes the relevant steps to enforce the security.[15] Ellie sells the factory to Betty for a price that is greater than the total amount due to her and to Felicity. The grant by Ellie is effective to make Betty the owner and to discharge both standard securities. Ellie has a duty to pay Felicity with the money left over after her expenses and the debt due to her have been paid. The surplus left over after Felicity has been paid must be given to Derek.

Extinction

11.28 The two main reasons for extinction of a security right have already been discussed: payment of the secured debt and enforcement of the security or of a prior ranking security. A right in security will also be extinguished if the security holder discharges the right or if the object of the security ceases to exist. So, if flour that has been pledged is used to make bread, the security right in the flour will cease to exist because the flour has been destroyed by specification.

Some attention will now be given to the detailed rules governing the most important rights in security.

VOLUNTARY RIGHTS IN SECURITY

Pledge

11.29 Giving a pledge is the most basic way of granting real security: giving something to the creditor that she is entitled to hold on to until the obligation is fulfilled. Only corporeal moveables may be pledged: the requirement for delivery means that pledge of incorporeals is impossible and the only right in security that can be granted over heritable property is the standard security.[16] So a car or antique painting can be pledged.

Creation

11.30 Pledge is effected by delivery to the creditor together with an agreement that the object is to secure the debts.[17] Delivery is necessary to satisfy the requirement of publicity and the pledge only subsists while possession is maintained.[18] The agreement is considered as a real contract (real because it does not come into effect until the thing (*res*) is delivered). The agreement usually does not need to be in writing.[19]

15 Discussed below, in paras 11.41–11.56.
16 CFR(S)A 1970, s. 9(3).
17 Bell, *Principles*, § 1363.
18 Bell, *Principles*, § 1364; *Wolifson v Harrison* 1977 SC 384.
19 Requirements of Writing (Scotland) Act 1995, s. 1(1).

The exception to this rule is a pledge under an agreement regulated by the Consumer Credit Act 1974 (the 1974 Act).[20] The only creditors permitted to take pledges which are covered by the 1974 Act are those authorised by the Financial Conduct Authority: pawnbrokers.[21] Therefore, while the pledge agreement need not normally be in writing, it does need to be in writing if the creditor is a pawnbroker. **11.31**

Obligations

The security holder has possession of the pledged object but is not entitled to use it or take its fruits unless this is necessary for the care of the object or the parties have agreed otherwise.[22] The security holder is obliged to take ordinary care of the pledged object but is entitled to payment of reasonable expenses for costs incurred as a result.[23] The owner is entitled to return of the property on payment of the debt. **11.32**

Enforcement

Where the 1974 Act does not apply, the common law continues to govern security holder's right to enforce a pledge. The default rule at common law is that authority to sell must be obtained from a sheriff before the sale can be effected.[24] However, it is open to the parties to agree that the security holder should have the power to sell without needing to go to court.[25] **11.33**

Where an object has been pawned, i.e. pledged under a regulated consumer credit agreement, and the debtor defaults, the security holder is entitled to enforce without recourse to the courts. There are two possible enforcement mechanisms: one for small, short-term debts and the other for other debts. **11.34**

The small debt rule applies where the period for repayment is six months (the statutory minimum for consumer loans secured by pledge[26]), the debt secured is £75 or less and the pledged object was not already in the possession of the security holder by virtue of a prior pledge. If the small debt rule applies, ownership of the pledged object passes to the security holder on the debtor's default.[27] Where the small debt rule does not apply, the pawnbroker has the power to sell the pledged object.[28] **11.35**

The small debt rule is less favourable to debtors because, where there is no sale, there is no chance of a price greater than the debt being obtained generating a surplus that is payable to the debtor.[29] The rule is poorly drafted: it **11.36**

20 Consumer Credit Act 1974, s. 114.
21 Consumer Credit Act 1974, s. 8(3) with Financial Services and Markets Act 2000, s. 19 and Financial Services and Markets Act 2000 (Regulated Activities) Order 2001 (SI 2001/544), art. 60B(3).
22 Bell *Principles*, § 206; *Moore v Gledden* (1869) 7 M 1016.
23 Bell *Principles*, § 206; Erskine 3.1.33.
24 Bell, *Principles*, § 207.
25 *North-Western Bank Ltd v Poynter, Son & Macdonalds* (1894) 22 R (HL) 1.
26 Consumer Credit Act 1974, s. 116.
27 Consumer Credit Act 1974, s. 120(1)(a).
28 Consumer Credit Act 1974, s. 120(1)(b).
29 Consumer Credit Act 1974, s. 121(3).

depends on the value of the debt secured rather than on the value of the item pledged. If David pledged a watch worth £1,000 for a debt of £50 repayable within six months, it will be forfeited if he fails to pay within the allotted time. If, however, the loan had been for £100 rather than £50, the creditor would have had a simple power of sale and so David would have received around £900. (The precise amount would depend on the expenses of the sale.) A fairer rule would depend on the value of the item that has been pledged rather than on the debt which is secured.

Standard security

11.37 If pledge is the most basic right in security, the standard security is arguably the most important. It is the only right in security which can be granted over heritable property.[30] In many cases, the most valuable asset that can be used as a security is land. This is subject to a slight caveat because a floating charge can also cover heritable property but only certain kinds of person can grant a floating charge.[31]

11.38 Standard securities are usually granted over land but they can also be granted over any real right in land.[32] In practice, the most important application of this rule is that standard securities can be granted over registered leases.

Creation

11.39 Since a standard security is a real right in land, it requires to be granted by formal writing.[33] It also requires to be registered in the Land Register.

Obligations

11.40 In contrast to pledge, the object of the standard security is not in the creditor's possession. Therefore, the most important obligations that apply while the security subsists protect the creditor's interest by controlling what the owner can do with the property. These obligations are set out in the 'conditions' of the standard security. Schedule 3 of Conveyancing and Feudal Reform (Scotland) Act 1970 (the CFR(S)A 1970) sets out standard conditions which, by default, apply to every standard security. It is open to the parties to vary these conditions. The default rules contain the obligations which might be expected for the protection of the value of the object of the security, for example: to keep the property in good repair;[34] a prohibition on alterations without the consent of the creditor;[35] to insure the property;[36] and not to let the property without the creditor's consent.[37]

30 CFR(S)A 1970, s. 9(3).
31 See para. 11.58.
32 CFR(S)A 1970, s. 9(2).
33 Requirements of Writing (Scotland) Act 1995, s. 1(2)(b).
34 CFR(S)A 1970, Sch. 3, para. 1.
35 CFR(S)A 1970, Sch. 3, para. 2.
36 CFR(S)A 1970, Sch. 3, para. 5.
37 CFR(S)A 1970, Sch. 3, para. 6.

Enforcement

As well as containing rules on what can be done to the security subjects, the standard conditions contain rules about the enforcement of the standard security. Where the debtor fails to pay the debt, the creditor must serve a calling up notice on the debtor.[38] The calling up notice gives the debtor two months to pay the debt.[39] Failure to do so puts the debtor in default in terms of standard condition 9(1)(a). That, in turn, enables the creditor to sell the security subjects.[40] **11.41**

If the property is used for residential purposes, significant further procedural requirements apply. Notification of the calling up notice must be given to the relevant local authority.[41] This notification allows the local authority to make provision for housing anyone evicted from the property. Further, before the property can be sold the creditor requires either a court order or written consent to the sale and certification that the subjects are unoccupied from the debtor, the owner (if that is a different person) and anyone with family law occupancy rights.[42] The requirement of consent means that any of the people on the list can force the creditor to obtain a court order. **11.42**

A court will not grant warrant to sell a residential property unless the 'pre-action requirements' have been complied with.[43] The pre-action requirements are set out in s. 24A of the CFR(S)A. Essentially, the requirements are threefold. First, there are information duties: the creditor must provide the debtor with information about the obligations which are unfulfilled and the consequences of not fulfilling them.[44] Further information must be given about sources of advice and assistance for debt management.[45] Secondly, there is a duty to encourage the debtor to make contact with the relevant local authority (so that emergency housing can be arranged).[46] Thirdly, there are duties aimed at a consensual outcome: the creditor must make reasonable efforts to agree a plan of action with the debtor that will remedy the defaults[47] and the creditor is barred from making an application for warrant to sell if the debtor is taking reasonable steps towards dealing with the defaults.[48] Further detail on the content of these pre-action requirements can be found in the Applications by Creditors (Pre-Action Requirements) (Scotland) Order 2010.[49] **11.43**

Once the pre-action requirements have been complied with, the creditor can go to court for her warrant, but she must give notification of her application to the debtor, the owner and the occupier of the security subjects (often these will **11.44**

38 CFR(S)A 1970, s. 19; *Royal Bank of Scotland plc v Wilson* [2010] UKSC 50, 2011 SC (UKSC) 66.
39 CFR(S)A 1970, Sch. 6, Form A.
40 CFR(S)A 1970, s. 20(2); Sch. 3, para. 10(2).
41 CFR(S) Act 1970, s. 19B.
42 CFR(S) Act 1970, ss. 20(2A) and 23A.
43 CFR(S)A 1970, ss. 24(1A)–(1D).
44 CFR(S)A 1970, s. 24A(2).
45 CFR(S)A 1970, s. 24A(5).
46 CFR(S)A 1970, s. 24A(6).
47 CFR(S)A 1970, s. 24A(3).
48 CFR(S)A 1970, s. 24A(4).
49 SSI 2010/317.

all be the same person) and give notification to the local authority.[50] Section 24 also contains guidance on when warrant to sell should be granted. The court must consider not only whether the debtor is in default and whether the pre-action requirements have been complied with but also whether warrant to sell is reasonable in all the circumstances.[51]

11.45 In determining whether the warrant is reasonable, subs. (6) and (7) of s. 24 direct that the court must have regard to the nature and reasons for the default, the debtor's ability to address the problem within a reasonable time, what the creditor has done to help, participation by the debtor in a statutory debt payment programme and the ability of the debtor or other occupants of the security subjects to find alternative accommodation. Sections 24B and 24C give 'entitled residents' the right to make an application to the court about the warrant to sell. Essentially, this gives the owner, spouses, civil partners, cohabitants and the parents of children who live in the property the right to a say about whether the warrant to sell should be granted.

11.46 If it proves impossible to find a buyer willing to pay a price that would cover the debt secured by the standard security and any other securities ranking alongside or below it in the two months after the property was first advertised for sale, the creditor can apply for a decree of foreclosure.[52] When such an application is made, the court may either grant the decree or order that the property should be re-exposed for sale at a price fixed by the court.[53] If the decree of foreclosure is granted, it must then be registered. On registration of the decree, the creditor becomes the owner and her security along with all rights in security that rank alongside or below hers are extinguished.[54]

All sums due securities

11.47 As discussed above, sale may be by private bargain or public auction and the price to be applied to paying secured creditors according to their ranking. Ordinarily, standard securities rank according to the rule *prior tempore potior iure*. However, some special rules are necessary to deal with standard securities which secure 'all sums due or to become due' to the creditor from the debtor. This means that every debt owed by the debtor to the creditor is secured by the standard security, even if the debt is created after the right in security has been granted. Such securities present a challenge to potential second ranking security holders.

11.48 Imagine that David has borrowed £75,000 from Bank of Shetland Ltd and granted a standard security for all sums due or to become due. Later he needs another loan and he approaches Bank of Orkney Ltd. Bank of Orkney is not keen to lend because of the prior ranking security but David produces documents proving that only £25,000 of the debt to Bank of Shetland is still outstanding and that his house is worth £250,000. This should reassure Bank of Orkney but it is worried because Bank of Shetland's security is for all sums

50 CFR(S)A 1970, s. 24(3).
51 CFR(S)A 1970, s. 24(5)(b).
52 CFR(S)A 1970, s. 28(1).
53 CFR(S)A 1970, s. 28(4).
54 CFR(S)A 1970, s. 28(6).

due and ranks first. What if Bank of Shetland later lent David £250,000? Would Bank of Orkney then find itself ranking behind a security that would use up the whole value of the property?

Bank of Orkney's concern is addressed by s. 13 of the CRF(S)A. It allows a lower ranking security holder to freeze the amount which can be covered by a prior ranking all sums due standard security by notifying the prior ranking holder of the creation of the lower ranking security. So if Bank of Orkney obtains a standard security from David, it can notify Bank of Shetland of that fact. After that notification, Bank of Shetland's prior ranking will be limited to the amount that is outstanding at the time of notification and interest on that sum together with any further sum which they are obliged to advance to David under their contract with him.[55] In that way, Bank of Orkney can be reasonably confident there will be enough value in the house to secure its loan as well. **11.49**

The same procedure can be used if the security subjects are sold. Usually, the seller will obtain a discharge of any standard security burdening the property but this is not necessarily the case. Instead of borrowing from Bank of Orkney, David may sell the property to Betty. Even if some of the price Betty pays to David is used to clear the last £25,000 of the loan, the security will not be extinguished because it is for all sums due and to become due. However, Betty can prevent David from borrowing on the security of her house by notifying Bank of Shetland that the house now belongs to her. Since there is no debt outstanding, Betty will only be at risk if Bank of Shetland is obliged to advance further sums to David. **11.50**

Floating charges

Pledge is not a very convenient mechanism for granting security over corporeal moveable property. It requires that the pledged items be in the possession of the security holder. That means that the debtor cannot use them. It also means that the creditor has to find somewhere to put them. Further, businesses whose major assets are corporeal moveables often want to be able to sell them and buy others frequently: their stock in trade is continually turning over. Even if the problems surrounding possession could be overcome, this would present another challenge to pledge as a security mechanism. Those who buy from the debtor would want to get an unburdened right but it would not be convenient to get a release of the security right from the creditor in every case. Furthermore, creditors did not want the administrative burden of accepting the grant of a security right for each new item of stock. **11.51**

These concerns led to pressure for the introduction of a security device which could cover corporeal moveables, was non-possessory and could handle rotating stock. English law appeared to have developed just such a security: the floating charge. Although the floating charge was the product of case law development in the English, it was introduced by statute in Scotland. **11.52**

The floating charge is part of equity in English law. Broadly speaking, equity recognises the transfer or creation of property rights more readily than either common law rules in England or Scots property law. English law has a set **11.53**

55 CFR(S)A 1970, s. 13(1).

of rules which deal with what happens when there is a conflict between the common law rules and those in equity. Scots law does not have a division between law and equity and therefore does not have rules that deal with the relationship between law and equity. Indeed, such a division makes little sense in the context of a civilian system of property law. For this reason, certain aspects of the floating charge have made it a rather poor fit in Scots law, causing some anomalous results and conceptual difficulties.[56]

The basic idea

11.54 Two key concepts distinguish the floating charge from other kinds of security in Scots law: it is a global security; and there is a gap between creation of the charge and its attachment.

11.55 As a global security, the floating charge can be granted 'over all or any part of the property which may from time to time be comprised in its property and undertaking'.[57] So the floating charge is not limited to corporeal moveables: heritable property and incorporeals can also be subject to a floating charge. Further, while a floating charge over a particular asset or particular class of assets might be granted,[58] the most common is the global security which covers the company's whole property and undertaking. Traditional voluntary rights in security cover particular assets; the floating charge can cover everything in the company's 'property and undertaking'.

11.56 The key concept in the floating charge is the gap between creation of the charge and its attachment. While other rights in security give the creditor a real right as soon as they are created, this is not the case with the floating charge.

11.57 As the name suggests the charge floats over the company's assets. While the charge is floating, the creditor has no real right in them. This means that, when an asset that is under the shadow of the charge is transferred, the acquirer takes it free of any right in security. When a new asset is acquired, it falls under the shadow of the charge and thus becomes liable to be affected by the charge if it attaches. When the charge attaches, it has effect 'as if the charge were a fixed security'.[59] This has generally been taken to mean that, from the moment of attachment, the chargeholder has a real right in security over the assets which are subject to the charge.[60]

56 For an extensive discussion of these issues, see A D J MacPherson, *The Floating Charge* (Edinburgh: Edinburgh Legal Education Trust, 2020).

57 Companies Act 1985, s. 462(1). Cf Bankruptcy and Diligence etc. (Scotland) Act 2007, s. 38(1), which is not yet in force.

58 See para. 14.87 onward below.

59 Companies Act 1985, s. 463(1) and (2) (liquidation); Insolvency Act 1986, s. 53(7) (receivership), Sch. B1, para. 115(1B) and (3) (administration).

60 For example, *Sharp v Thomson* 1995 SC 455 at 488 per Lord Coulsfield. MacPherson casts doubt on this view, pointing to the absence of direct enforcement mechanism, the limitations on enforcement (and priority) in the context of corporate insolvency processes, the apparent unity of the attached charge and questions around the possibility of real rights in personal rights: MacPherson, *The Floating Charge* (2020), Ch. 5, esp. paras 5–32–5–35. He suggests that the attached floating charge is a *sui generis* right rather than a real right. While it is certainly the case that the detailed rules in the legislation to which MacPherson refers must certainly be applied in preference to any general conceptual principles about the operation of

Creation

Floating charges can only be granted by companies and a small number of other juristic persons (notably limited liability partnerships).[61] There is no specific legislative requirement that the charge be in writing. In practice, charges are always made in writing as this greatly facilitates registration of the 'particulars' of the charge in the Companies Register. Since the floating charge can only be granted by companies or other entities subject to their publicity regime, all floating charges require to be registered in accordance with the special regime for publicity of rights in security granted by companies.[62] **11.58**

As discussed above,[63] the companies registration regime is different from registration in the Land Register: registration is retrospective rather than constitutive. It is not something which needs to be done in order to create the right in security. Rather, it is something which requires to be done once a right in security has been created. In contrast to other rights in security, the floating charge is created by a private act between the parties: delivery of the signed deed granting the charge to the creditor.[64] This is dangerous because it means that there is a twenty-one day 'blind period' during which the floating charge exists but third parties have no notice of it. **11.59**

If Part 2 of the Bankruptcy and Diligence etc. (Scotland) Act 2007 (the 2007 Act) is ever brought into force, this will change. It requires registration of a subscribed document granting the floating charge in a new Register of Floating Charges. Only once that step has been completed would the charge come into existence.[65] There is no immediate prospect of Part 2 of the 2007 Act being brought into force. **11.60**

Attachment and enforcement

Only once a floating charge has attached does the chargeholder have a real right in security and thus the right to the value of the items affected by the charge. When does attachment occur? For a long time, the principal mechanism for enforcing a floating charge was the appointment of a receiver. If the debtor defaulted on his obligations, the chargeholder was entitled to appoint a receiver.[66] The appointment of the receiver triggered the attachment of the charge and the receiver took control of the assets covered by the charge and sold them to pay off the debt.[67] Since the charge usually covered all of the company's 'property and undertaking', the receiver had effective control of the company. These receivers were known as administrative receivers. However, **11.61**

real rights, conceptualisation of the attached charge as a real right continues to provide the clearest starting point for thinking about its operation.

61 Companies Act 1985, s. 462(1); Limited Liability Partnership (Scotland) Regulations 2001 (SSI 2001/128), reg. 3.

62 There are some cases where registration is not required: see above n 4.

63 See para. 11.19.

64 *AIB Finance Ltd v Bank of Scotland* 1993 SC 588; Companies Act 2006, s. 859E(1).

65 2007 Act, s. 38(3). Again, there are some exceptions for central banks and financial collateral arrangements: 2007 Act, s. 38(3A)–(3B).

66 Insolvency Act 1986, ss. 51–52.

67 Insolvency Act 1986, ss. 53(7), 55 and Sch. 2.

the power to appoint receivers has been significantly restricted by statute. The basic rule is that, if the floating charge was granted after 15 September 2003, the holder of the floating charge cannot appoint an administrative receiver.[68] It remains competent to appoint receivers to enforce charges whose scope is limited to particular assets.

11.62 Does this mean that the chargeholder is now left without a mechanism for enforcement? No. Instead of being entitled to appoint a receiver, the chargeholder can appoint an administrator.[69] There are two important differences between the appointment of a receiver and of an administrator: first, the administrator must act for the benefit of the company's creditors as a whole rather than just for the benefit of the chargeholder;[70] secondly, appointment of the administrator does not automatically trigger the attachment of the floating charge.

11.63 If a company goes into administration, the charge only attaches when the administrator delivers a para. 115 notice to the registrar of companies.[71] This is a notice which says that the only way the administrator will be able to pay out to unsecured creditors is by invoking the 'carve out' provision in s. 176A(2)(a) of the Insolvency Act 1986.[72] The 'carve out' rule is discussed below but the basic import of such a notice is that the company's secured debts are greater in value than its assets.

11.64 The third trigger that can cause a floating charge to attach is the company going into liquidation.[73]

Ranking: other rights in security

11.65 Once a charge has attached, it becomes necessary to determine how the floating charge ranks. The basic principles discussed above would suggest that the floating charge should rank ahead of unsecured creditors who have a merely personal right, and that it should rank with other rights in security according to whether they were created before or after attachment, when the chargeholder gets her real right. Unfortunately, the picture is not quite that simple.

11.66 The rules just stated are the starting point[74] but there are some important variations. The first of these is the so-called negative pledge clause. The document creating the floating charge may contain a clause which forbids or restricts the grant of other rights in security that would rank prior to or equally with the floating charge.[75] If such a pledge is included, the floating charge will rank ahead of any right in security created after the floating charge comes into

68 Insolvency Act 1986, s. 72A. A number of exceptions are set out in ss. 72B–72GA, preserving the right to appoint administrative receivers for certain classes of debtor. These are limited to public sector activity and financial and capital markets.
69 Insolvency Act 1986, Sch. B1, para. 14(1).
70 Insolvency Act 1986, Sch. B1, para. 3(2).
71 Insolvency Act 1986, Sch. B1, para. 115(3).
72 Insolvency Act 1986, Sch. B1, para. 115(2).
73 Companies Act 1985, s. 463(1).
74 Companies Act 1985, s. 464(4); Insolvency Act 1986, s. 60, Sch. B1, para. 116.
75 Companies Act 1985, s. 464(1)(a).

existence.[76] This applies despite the fact that these rights in security have been granted before the floating charge has attached and thus before the charge-holder has a real right.

Imagine that Bust Co Ltd grants a floating charge over its whole property and undertaking to Bank of Shetland on 14 June, which is duly registered. On 31 August, it grants a standard security to Bank of Orkney, which is registered the same day. On 2 September, the charge attaches. The respective ranking depends on whether a negative pledge clause has been included in the floating charge or not. If there is such a clause, then Bank of Shetland's floating charge will rank ahead of Bank of Orkney's standard security. If there is no such clause, Bank of Orkney's standard security will rank ahead of Bank of Shetland's floating charge. **11.67**

As might be expected, nearly all floating charges include a negative pledge clause. If Part 2 of the 2007 Act comes into force, the default rule will be changed so that no security granted after the floating charge was created will rank ahead of it.[77] This will render negative pledge clauses unnecessary. **11.68**

The negative pledge clause is effective to prevent the debtor from making grants of rights in security that will rank ahead of it but it has no effect against involuntary securities. Thus, the charge will rank behind 'effectually executed diligence' (i.e. diligence done properly and not struck down by insolvency law rules) and tacit securities such as lien and the landlord's hypothec.[78] **11.69**

Floating charges rank among themselves according to their date of registration in the Companies Register.[79] If a floating charge has been granted to cover future advances, the amount secured by the charge may be frozen by giving notification of a subsequent floating charge in a manner very similar to that which applies to standard securities that secure future advances.[80] If Part 2 of the 2007 Act comes into force, the power to freeze the debt secured will also be available to subsequent grantees of other rights in security.[81] **11.70**

Ranking: unsecured creditors

The second major variation on the normal rules of ranking is that the floating charge is subject to rights of certain unsecured creditors. First, the floating charge ranks behind 'preferential debts'.[82] These cover certain obligations owed to employees, contributions to occupational pension schemes and levies on coal and steel production.[83] Secondly, the chargeholder's right is subject to the prescribed part under s. 176A of the Insolvency Act 1986. **11.71**

76 Companies Act 1985, s. 464(1A).
77 2007 Act, s. 40(2).
78 Companies Act 1985, s. 463(1); Insolvency Act 1986, s. 60(1)(b). On the interpretation of the phrase 'effectually executed diligence', see *MacMillan v T Leith Developments Ltd* [2017] CSIH 23, 2017 SC 642 at [56]–[59] per Lord President Carloway.
79 Companies Act 1985, s. 464(4)(b).
80 Companies Act 1985, s. 464(5).
81 2007 Act, s. 40(5)(b).
82 Companies Act 1985, s. 464(6); Insolvency Act 1986, ss. 60, 175 and Sch. B1, para. 116.
83 Insolvency Act 1986, s. 386.

11.72 The prescribed part carves out a portion of what would otherwise be payable to the chargeholder for the benefit of unsecured creditors. The prescribed part was introduced because of concerns that the global nature of the floating charge meant that the chargeholder would 'scoop the pool' and leave nothing for unsecured creditors.

11.73 Whether a carve out is made, and the size of the carve out, depends on the size of the company's 'net property', which is the property left for the satisfaction of the chargeholder once prior ranking security holders and preferential debts have been paid.[84] If the net property is less than £10,000, then the carve out is only made if the liquidator, administrator or receiver thinks that the benefit of making it would outweigh the cost.[85] Even if the net property is £10,000 or more, the liquidator, administrator or receiver can apply to the court for an order that the carve out should not be made on the basis that thc cost would outweigh the benefit.[86]

11.74 Assuming that a carve out is to be made, the next step is to determine how big it should be. If the net property is £10,000 or less, the prescribed part is 50 per cent of that net property. If the net property is more than £10,000, the prescribed part is £5,000 plus 20 per cent of the surplus above £10,000.[87] The prescribed part is subject to an upper limit of £800,000.[88] So if, the net property is £7,000, the prescribed part would be £3,500 because that is half of the net property. If the net property is £15,000, the prescribed party would be £6,000: £5,000 plus 20 per cent of £5,000, which is the amount by which the net property exceeds £10,000. No matter how big the net property is, the prescribed part will never be more than £800,000.

Floating charges and purchasers

11.75 As noted above, the floating charge was the product of equity in English law. For the purposes of equity, a buyer who has paid for property and taken possession is considered to be the owner, although some of the necessary formalities have still to be completed. That means that, even if the charge granted by the seller attaches before the disposition has been registered, the buyer who has paid and taken possession is safe.

11.76 In *Sharp v Thomson*,[89] this set of circumstances arose under a Scottish floating charge. The purchasers had paid the price, obtained possession of the property and received delivery of the disposition but not registered the disposition when the charge attached. An orthodox Scots property law analysis suggested that the chargeholder should prevail over the purchaser in these circumstances: the seller was the owner of the property when the charge attached. However, the House of Lords found in favour of the purchasers. The best explanation of the result is that the term 'property and undertaking' as it is used in the

84 Insolvency Act 1986, s. 176A(6).
85 Insolvency Act 1986, s. 176A(3), Insolvency Act 1986 (Prescribed Part) Order 2003 (SI 2003/2097), art. 2.
86 Insolvency Act 1986, s. 176A(5).
87 Insolvency Act 1986 (Prescribed Part) Order 2003, art. 3(1).
88 Insolvency Act 1986 (Prescribed Part) Order 2003, art. 3(2).
89 1997 SC (HL) 66.

floating charge legislation does not quite cover everything which the granter of the charge owns.[90] The *Sharp* exception has not been applied in any other case and appears to be restricted to cases where payment has been made for an asset but the transfer has not been completed when the charge attaches.

TACIT RIGHTS IN SECURITY

The rights in security considered hitherto occur as a result of a grant by debtor. However, some rights in security occur automatically, without the need for any grant. They are known as tacit rights in security. **11.77**

Lien

The simplest tacit right in security is lien. It can be thought of as the tacit security equivalent of pledge. Like pledge, lien is a possessory right in security. In contrast to pledge, it may be possible to have a lien of land as well as of corporeal moveable property.[91] **11.78**

Special and general liens

Liens are either special or general. Special liens arise on the basis of mutuality of obligations. The creditor has an obligation to deliver the debtor's property but that obligation is conditional on the debtor fulfilling his obligation to her.[92] It can arise in any case where a creditor finds herself in possession of the debtor's property as a result of the same transaction which gave rise to the debtor's obligation to the creditor. This personal right to retain the property is fortified by the real right of lien, so it is effective even in insolvency. Thus, where ownership passes to the buyer before delivery, the seller has a lien for the price.[93] Similarly, a repairer has a lien entitling her to retain possession of the repaired item until the owner pays for the repair.[94] **11.79**

General liens are broader in scope than the special lien: it is not necessary for the creditor to show that her position and the debtor's obligation to her arise from the same transaction. They arise by reason of usage in relation to particular professions. The most important instances are the general lien of the solicitor,[95] the factor (a commercial agent in possession the principal's goods),[96] the broker (a commercial agent who does not have possession of the principal's goods)[97] and the banker.[98] In these cases, the creditor is entitled to maintain possession of items acquired in the course of acting in the relevant capacity for rights to payment accrued in that capacity. Thus a solicitor who **11.80**

90 *Sharp v Thomson* read with *Burnett's Tr v Grainger* 2004 SC (HL) 19.
91 A J M Steven, 'Property issues in lien' (2010) 14 Edin LR 455. Cf *McGraddie v McGraddie* [2010] CSOH 60.
92 Bell, *Principles*, § 1419.
93 Sale of Goods Act 1979, s. 41.
94 *Lamonby v Foulds, Ltd* 1928 SC 89.
95 For example, *Liquidator of Grand Empire Theatres v Snodgrass* 1932 SC (HL) 73.
96 For example, *Mackenzie v Cormack* 1950 SC 183.
97 For example, *Glendinning v Hope & Co* 1911 SC (HL) 73.
98 For example, *Clydesdale Bank Ltd v Liquidators of James Allan Senior & Son Ltd* 1926 SC 235.

holds title documents which relate to the debtor's house may exercise a lien over them because the debtor has yet to pay the solicitor for acting on his behalf in litigation. In the case of a solicitor, banker or broker, the items will often be documents rather than items of inherent value.

Enforcement and extinction

11.81 Like pledge, the right in security is lost if possession is lost (unless creditor is deprived of possession by undue means).[99] Also like pledge, the general rule is that court sanction is required for sale.[100] In contrast with pledge, however, there is little scope for a power of sale to be agreed by the parties. Lien is subject to equitable control by the courts. If its exercise is inappropriate, the court may order the property to be handed over, sometimes on condition that the debt in question be consigned to the court.[101]

Landlord's hypothec

11.82 The other important tacit right in security in Scots law is the landlord's hypothec. It gives the landlord a right in security over corporeal moveables belonging to the tenant that are to be found on the leased premises[102] for rent that is due and unpaid.[103] Certain moveables are excluded: notably cash; documents of debt; or clothes.[104] The hypothec does not apply to residential or agricultural leases.[105] In effect, that means that it only applies to commercial leases.

11.83 Someone who acquires property subject to the hypothec from the debtor takes it free from the hypothec if the acquirer is in good faith.[106] If there is reason to fear that the tenant will attempt to defeat the hypothec by removing or disposing of property, the landlord can obtain an interdict prohibiting such actions. If the tenant disposes of property in breach of such an interdict then the acquirer must not only be in good faith but must also have given value in order to be safe from the hypothec.[107]

11.84 The landlord's hypothec has no specific mechanism for enforcement.[108] It is open to the landlord to do diligence or to rely on the hypothec in insolvency proceedings.

99 Bell, *Principles*, § 1415.
100 Bell, *Principles*, § 1417.
101 *Onyvax Ltd v Endpoint Research (UK) Ltd* [2007] CSOH 211.
102 2007 Act, s. 208(2)(a). See A Sweeney, *The Landlord's Hypothec* (Edinburgh: Edinburgh Legal Education Trust, 2021).
103 2007 Act, s. 208(8).
104 Bell, *Principles*, § 1276.
105 2007 Act, s. 208(3).
106 2007 Act, s. 208(5)(a).
107 2007 Act, s. 208(5)(b).
108 2007 Act, s. 208(1).

FUNCTIONAL SECURITIES

The security devices discussed so far are proper rights in security: that is to say they are legal institutions whose specific function is to secure performance of obligations. However, certain other institutions can be used in a way which closely mirrors the effect of a right in security. Often these are resorted to because of perceived deficiencies in the proper rights in security. **11.85**

Assignation in security

It does not appear to be possible to grant a right in security over incorporeal property in Scots law. It is likely (although the point is disputed) that the diligence of arrestment gives the arresting creditor a judicial right in security in a right that is arrested[109] and the attachment of a floating charge which covers incorporeal property seems to create a right in security in that incorporeal property. But there is no equivalent to pledge or the standard security for incorporeals. **11.86**

Instead, a debtor who wants to use incorporeal property as collateral for a loan must use an assignation in security. As the name suggests, this is a transfer of the relevant property to the creditor. As such, it must comply with the usual formalities for such a transfer (intimation in case of personal rights, registration in case of registered intellectual property rights). The difference between assignation in security and normal assignation is that the creditor has an obligation to retransfer the assigned property when the debt is paid off. Of course, this transfer must also be done in the usual way. **11.87**

Thus assignation in security differs from a proper right in security in two important ways: the security taker becomes the owner of the claim assigned and payment of the debt does not bring the security arrangement to an end automatically. Since the security giver has a mere personal right to the return of the property, there is also the risk that it will be transferred to a third party by the creditor.[110] **11.88**

Retention of title

Buyers of goods often require to be able to use them before they can pay for them. One way of allowing this to happen which protects the seller is to use a retention of title clause. Section 17 of the Sale of Goods Act 1979 provides that, where there is a contract for the sale of goods, ownership passes when the parties intend that it should. That leaves it open to the parties to agree that, although the goods have been delivered, the seller will remain the owner until the price is paid. Indeed, there is nothing to stop the parties from agreeing that ownership does not pass until the buyer has paid all sums due by it to the seller (even if some of the debts arise from completely separate contracts). **11.89**

109 Cf *MacMillan v T Leith Developments Ltd* [2017] CSIH 23, 2017 SC 642 at [56]–[57] per Lord President Carloway. For arrestment, see paras 12.27–12.34.
110 See generally A D J MacPherson, *The Floating Charge* (2020), Ch. 9.

11.90 There were some suggestions that arrangements of this kind circumvented the rules on publicity for rights in security, because the seller has a real right while the buyer has possession and there is no public register. This argument was correctly rejected by the House of Lords in *Armour v Thyssen Edelstahlwerke AG.*[111] A true right in security over property involves someone giving the creditor a real right in his property so that she can have recourse to it if the debt is not paid. In retention of title, the creditor merely keeps something which already belongs to her (ownership of the goods); she acquires no new real right.

Trusts

11.91 As discussed in Chapter Three, assets held in trust are protected from the trustee's insolvency and from diligence by the trustee's personal creditors. Trusts can also be created with minimal formalities and no publicity and it is possible to have a truster-as-trustee trust, whereby the owner of property declares that he holds property for the benefit of some third party rather than for his own benefit. Furthermore, any kind of asset can be held in trust: be it heritable or moveable, corporeal or incorporeal. There is no restriction on who can create a truster-as-trustee trust. It is open to sole traders and partnerships as well as to companies and limited liability partnerships.

11.92 All of these factors combine to make the trust very tempting as a functional security device. The basic idea is straightforward: Alf declares that he holds certain assets in trust and that his creditor, Betty, is the beneficiary. Alf retains possession and can carry on using the assets. If Alf becomes insolvent, his other creditors will have no access to the assets because they are held in trust. This is not a problem for Betty, however, because she is a beneficiary of the trust as well as being Alf's creditor. As beneficiary of the trust, she is entitled to satisfaction from the trust assets.

11.93 There is some authority for the validity of using trusts in this way.[112] However, it remains rather controversial.[113] Commercial trusts often appear to have little in the way of trust purposes. Trust purposes are essential to the constitution of a trust because the point of a trust is to allow certain assets to be dedicated to a particular use. The insolvency protection might be regarded as ancillary to this function: the main point is that the trustee administers the assets in accordance with the trust purposes and the insolvency protection is just there to deal with the unfortunate – and hopefully unusual – case of a trustee who gets into financial difficulties.

11.94 In a commercial trust, this order of priorities is reversed. The main reason for using the trust is to take advantage of the insolvency protection. Connected to that is the concern that there is little in the way of a 'divesture' by the truster. The parties will rarely envisage that the debtor will use the trust assets for the benefit of the creditor or that she will have any particular right in respect of the trust assets prior to the debtor's insolvency. He will simply continue to do

111 1990 SLT 891.
112 *Tay Valley Joinery Ltd v CF Financial Services Ltd* 1987 SLT 207.
113 See *Clark Taylor & Co Ltd v Quality Site Development (Edinburgh)* 1981 SC 111.

his usual business with them (although this may generate profits which can be used to pay the creditor). The truster/trustee continues to use the assets as before and the only purpose of the trust is to avoid sharing the asset with other creditors in insolvency.

Another objection to the use of trusts as security devices relates to one of their main attractions: they are private. Since a trust can be created without the publicity of registration, delivery or intimation which normally attends the creation of a right in security or an assignation in security, it might be argued that the use of trusts in this way subverts the publicity principle. **11.95**

REFORM

Certain aspects of the Scots law of rights in security have been subject to sustained criticism. There has been particular dissatisfaction with the absence of a non-possessory right in security over corporeal moveables or a proper right in security over incorporeals. The floating charge addresses these concerns to some degree but it can only be granted by certain kinds of debtor and there are concerns about how well it fits with the rest of Scots property law. **11.96**

In light of these pressures, the Scottish Law Commission undertook a project on the reform of rights in security over moveable property.[114] The proposed reforms would permit the creation of a new form of security known as the 'statutory pledge'. This would be a non-possessory, real right in security, created by registration in a new Register of Statutory Pledges and ranking from the date of registration.[115] **11.97**

The statutory pledge could be granted by any person rather than just by companies and limited liability partnerships. It could be granted over both corporeal moveables and certain classes of incorporeals, namely financial instruments (such as shares or bonds) and intellectual property.[116] **11.98**

Non-consumer debtors would be able to burden classes of asset as well as individually-specified items of property. They would also be able to burden future assets so that they become subject to the pledge as soon as they are acquired by the debtor.[117] These two rules address concerns about the administrative cost of taking security over moveable assets. In many cases, individual assets are not particularly valuable so a security device that requires them to be dealt with or identified individually is less attractive than a security device that can cover classes of asset. **11.99**

However, such wide-ranging security rights create potential problems for freedom of commerce. The low value of particular moveable assets means it is unreasonable to expect that those considering buying them will check a register to see if they are subject to a security right. For that reason, the proposed **11.100**

114 *Report on Moveable Transactions Volume 2: Security over Moveable Property* (Scot. Law Com. No. 249, 2017).

115 Draft Moveable Transactions (Scotland) Bill (in *Report on Moveable Transactions Volume 3*), ss. 43 and 64

116 Draft Moveable Transactions (Scotland) Bill, s. 47.

117 Draft Moveable Transactions (Scotland) Bill, s. 46.

rules would make extensive protection for good faith acquirers of property which is subject to a statutory pledge.[118] The basic effect of these protections is to allow such an acquirer to take the property free of the pledge and the presence of the pledge on the register is not enough to put the acquirer in bad faith.

11.101 The Scottish Law Commission's proposal would also provide a common set of rules for enforcement of pledges whether possessory (traditional) or statutory. The new scheme would commence with the service of a pledge enforcement notice on the debtor.[119] It defines when a court order is needed (essentially to protect consumer debtors)[120] and gives the enforcing creditor rights to take possession of the property subject to the pledge or certificates of financial instruments and to sell the pledged property.[121]

11.102 The Commission's scheme would address many of the concerns which have been raised about the Scots law of security over moveable property.

11.103 Having proposed a comprehensive overview of security over moveable property, the Scottish Law Commission is currently undertaking a project on heritable securities.[122] A comprehensive review of the operation of standard securities is being undertaken but the focus of the project is on simplifying and clarifying the rules on enforcement, ensuring a fair balance in the rules between the interests of creditor and debtor and examining the appropriateness of the standard security to secure non-pecuniary obligations.[123] It is not expected that the reforms proposed in relation to heritable security will be as radical as those proposed in relation to security over moveable property.[124] The basic need for a non-possessory, real right in security has already been met. The focus of the reform will be on refining that institution so that it works as well as possible.

118 Draft Moveable Transactions (Scotland) Bill, ss. 54–57.

119 Draft Moveable Transactions (Scotland) Bill, s. 69.

120 Draft Moveable Transactions (Scotland) Bill, s. 70.

121 Draft Moveable Transactions (Scotland) Bill, ss. 71–73.

122 *Discussion Paper on Heritable Securities: Pre-default* (Scot. Law Com. DP No. 168, 2019).

123 *Discussion Paper on Heritable Securities: Pre-default* (Scot. Law Com. DP No., 2019), paras 1.8–1.10.

124 *Discussion Paper on Heritable Securities: Pre-default* (Scot. Law Com. DP No., 2019), paras 1.19–1.20.

Chapter Twelve

Judicial Security: Diligence

Frankie McCarthy

INTRODUCTION

What is diligence?

Diligence is the term used in Scots law to describe attachment of the debtor's assets to force the debtor to provide security for, or to implement, a judgment or document of debt.[1] A creditor will 'do diligence' in order to obtain repayment of an obligation by exercising particular remedies against the debtor's property. Imagine that Anna owes Brian £5,000. Despite his polite requests, she has refused to pay it back. If Anna had consented to grant Brian a right in security when they agreed the loan contract, Brian could now recover his money by exercising that right, sometimes known as a 'conventional' or 'voluntary' security, against Anna's property.[2] However, in this example, imagine that no such voluntary security was granted. Instead, Brian can ask the court to create a right in security now without Anna's consent. This is sometimes referred to as a 'judicial' or 'involuntary' security. Brian will again recover his money by exercising that right against Anna's property. The process by which Brian asks the court for a judicial security, and the range of rights it is possible for the court to grant him, are known as diligence. **12.01**

Which diligence?

There are a number of different types of diligence. Which diligence a creditor chooses will depend on the nature of the assets the debtor has in their patrimony. For example, where a debtor owns corporeal heritable property such as land or buildings, the creditor may use the diligence of inhibition or alternatively the diligence of adjudication. Where the debtor owns corporeal moveable property, the creditor may use attachment. The application of each type of diligence is explained below. The creditor must know or make an educated guess as to what property is within the debtor's patrimony in order to work out which diligence is likely to be effective. This will normally have been done before the creditor incurred the expense of litigation to obtain a decree. There is no point inhibiting a debtor who does not own heritable property, for example. **12.02**

1 Cf J Graham Stewart, *A Treatise on the Law of Diligence* (Edinburgh: W. Green, 1898), p. 1.
2 Chapters Ten and Eleven.

12.03 Diligences can also be divided into two categories – seize diligences and freeze diligences – based on their effect on the debtor's property. A seize diligence enables the creditor to transfer property out of the debtor's patrimony without the debtor's consent. The creditor may transfer the property into their own patrimony in satisfaction of the debt. Alternatively, the creditor may transfer the property by sale to a third party, using the proceeds of the sale to satisfy the debt. In either case, the purpose of the transfer is repayment of the debt. Attachment is an example of a seize diligence. A freeze diligence, on the other hand, prevents the debtor transferring property out of their patrimony or granting subordinate real rights in respect of it without the creditor's consent. The creditor will normally consent only if the debtor agrees to repay the debt with the proceeds of the transfer or grant. Inhibition is the main example of a freeze diligence.[3]

12.04 A creditor may use more than one type of diligence in respect of the same debt. If Anna owned a car worth £2,500 and had savings in a bank account of £2,500, Brian might seek both to attach the car and to arrest the savings in the bank account. Together, these two processes might enable him to recover the full £5,000 that Anna owes him. Alternatively, a creditor may use more than one type of diligence in respect of the same item of property. The most obvious example of this is in relation to heritable property, where a creditor might first use the freeze diligence of inhibition to prevent the debtor selling the property, and then use the seize diligence of adjudication to transfer rent money paid for the property from the debtor's tenants to the creditor in repayment of the debt.

General principles

12.05 Some general principles of property law are particularly relevant to the law of diligence. In the first place, diligence can only be effected against assets in the debtor's personal patrimony. If Anna is a trustee, Brian cannot do diligence against assets in the trust patrimony. Only assets in Anna's personal patrimony are available for diligence processes. (It is possible for a trustee to have incurred debts in their capacity as trustee. In this situation, the creditor could do diligence against the assets in the trust patrimony, but not against assets in Anna's personal patrimony).[4]

12.06 Any right the creditor receives from the debtor as a result of diligence can be no better than the right held by the debtor in the first place. This is an application of the principle *nemo plus juris ad alium transferre potest, quam ipse haberet*, discussed above.[5] Where the creditor acquires a personal right held by the debtor, they acquire it on the same terms as the debtor.[6] For example, imagine Anna has £5,000 in a bank account. Anna deposited the money some

3 Freeze diligences are nonetheless effectual and potentially powerful: *MacMillan v T Leith Developments Ltd* [2017] CSIH 23, 2017 SC 642.

4 Even where Anna has incurred debt for the trust, unless she has expressly limited her liability to the trust assets, the assets in her personal patrimony may be liable to diligence from the trust creditors: *Muir v City of Glasgow Bank* (1879) 6 R (HL) 21 and discussion in para. 1.31 above.

5 At para. 3.97 above.

6 In this context, the *nemo plus* principle is expressed by the equivalent maxim *assignatus utitur iure auctoris*.

months ago subject to an agreement that she would not withdraw it for two years, in return for which she would obtain a higher than normal rate of interest. Brian can acquire a right in Anna's bank account by way of arrestment. However, he cannot oblige the bank to pay the funds over to him any earlier than they would have paid the funds over to Anna. His right is subject to the same restrictions as Anna's right. Similarly, if Brian acquires a real right in Anna's property, it will be acquired subject to any existing subordinate real rights.[7]

Diligence works on a 'first come, first served' basis. Where a debtor has several creditors, the first to effect diligence on a particular asset is able to recoup his debt in full before the second creditor has any claim. Imagine that, in addition to owing Brian £5,000, Anna also owes Dorothy £5,000. Anna has savings in a bank account of £7,500. Brian arrests these savings on 1st May. Dorothy arrests them two days later. Since Brian obtained his arrestment first, he is entitled to recover his £5,000 in full. Dorothy will only be able to obtain the remaining £2,500 of savings towards repayment of her debt. In this situation, it does not matter which creditor loaned money to Anna first, or which creditor has been waiting the longest for repayment. All that matters is which creditor was first to obtain a right via diligence. This is an application of the principle *prior tempore, potior iure* discussed above.[8] **12.07**

Procedure

The effect of diligence in execution is to expropriate the debtor of their assets without their consent. Such expropriation is a significant interference with the debtor's property rights. For that reason, the procedural rules governing how diligence is carried out must be adhered to strictly in order to ensure that the debtor is fairly treated; that is to say, that any expropriation is in accordance with law.[9] Where even a small mistake is made, the whole procedure is likely to be invalidated, meaning the creditor must begin again from the start. **12.08**

Diligence can only be used with warrant from a court to enforce debts, either in execution or on the dependence. The first step in any diligence procedure is to establish that the debt exists. In most cases, this requires the creditor to raise a court action. The claim may already be in debt, e.g. for repayment of a loan. Or the claim may be for damages which, if successful, will also seek a decree for a fixed sum of money. In either case, if the factual basis for any court action is disputed, there may need to be a proof (trial). At the end of the day, if decree is awarded to the pursuer, it will authorise 'all lawful execution'.[10] **12.09**

Parties have the option to avoid the expense and inconvenience of court action by agreeing in the contract to an expedited enforcement procedure known **12.10**

7 It is sometimes said that a creditor doing diligence takes *tantum et tale*, but it is not clear that this maxim correctly applied is anything other than a restatement of the *nemo plus* principle. For discussion, see *Burnett's Trustee v Grainger* 2004 SC (HL) 19 and J A MacLeod, *Fraud and Voidable Transfer* (Edinburgh: Edinburgh Legal Education Trust, 2020), Ch. 8.

8 At para. 3.34.

9 See the comments of Lord President Roger in *Atlas Appointments Ltd (No. 2) v Tinsley* 1997 SC 200 at 210.

10 RCS, r. 7.10; OCR, r. 30.7.

as summary diligence.[11] Where a contract contains a clause stating that the parties 'consent to registration for execution' or 'consent to registration for summary diligence', they are effectively consenting to a court decree coming into existence without the need to go to court. The consent takes effect when the document is registered in the Books of Council and Session. In this situation, the registered document is proof of existence of the debt equivalent to a court decree. A form of summary diligence is also available where the right to payment is embodied in a negotiable instrument.[12] The creditor in this instance can instruct a notary public to present the bill to the debtor[13] and, if payment is refused, the notary can issue a formal certificate protesting the bill for non-payment.[14] A negotiable instrument noted and protested for non-payment is also proof of the existence of a debt equivalent to a court decree.

12.11 Once decree[15] is obtained, the creditor must arrange for it to be served on the debtor[16] accompanied by a 'charge for payment', a formal final notice demanding payment of the debt within a fourteen-day period known as the 'days of charge.'[17] If the days of charge expire without payment of the debt, the creditor is entitled to proceed with an appropriate type of diligence. Diligence must follow within two years of the date of service of the charge.[18] On expiry of the days of charge, it may also be possible to petition for the debtor's sequestration.[19]

12.12 Where the debtor is a natural person, it will also usually be necessary to provide them with a debt advice and information package (DAIP) before diligence can be enforced. The DAIP is a booklet prepared by the Accountant in Bankruptcy on behalf of the Scottish Government[20] that sets out the debtor's rights in relation to legal proceedings, gives advice on how the debt might be managed and suggests where further support and guidance might be sought within the debtor's local area.[21] For most forms of diligence, a set period of time must elapse after provision of the DAIP before the diligence can proceed. The details will be discussed with reference to each of the specific forms of diligence below.

11 Summary diligence is not competent for debts arising under a regulated consumer credit agreement: Consumer Credit Act 1974, s. 93A.
12 For an explanation of negotiable instruments, see paras 9.06–9.09.
13 A debtor is usually referred to as a 'drawee' in this context: see para. 9.24.
14 Bills of Exchange Act 1882, s. 51.
15 Decree is defined in Debtors (Scotland) Act 1987 (the 1987 Act), s. 73A(4); Debt Arrangement and Attachment (Scotland) Act 2002, s. 10(5); Bankruptcy and Diligence etc. (Scotland) Act 2007, s. 221.
16 Service will be carried out by officers of court, namely sheriff officers in the case of a sheriff court decree, or messengers-at-arms in the case of a Court of Session decree. Officers of court are regulated by their professional body, the Society of Messengers-at-Arms and Sheriff Officers (SMASO), in line with the Officers of Court's Professional Association (Scotland) Regulations 2011 (SSI 2011/90).
17 The period of payment will be fourteen days if the debtor is within the UK. It is increased to twenty-eight days if the debtor is outside the UK or their whereabouts are unknown: 1987 Act, s. 90(3).
18 1987 Act, s. 90(5).
19 See para. 13.07.
20 Debt Arrangement and Attachment (Scotland) Act 2002, s. 10(5).
21 A copy of the DAIP can be found on the AIB website at *https://www.aib.gov.uk/debt/deal-debt/debt-advice-and-information-package* (last accessed 5 September 2021).

Protection from diligence

The Scottish Government operates a voluntary Debt Arrangement Scheme ('DAS') available to natural persons resident in Scotland.[22] An individual with debt problems may contact a DAS money adviser who will liaise with creditors on the debtor's behalf and support the debtor to apply for a debt payment programme (DPP).[23] A DPP usually enables the debtor to make repayments over a longer period of time than initially agreed without incurring additional interest, and may even allow for some discount on the amount to be repaid. A creditor is not obliged to consent to a DPP, but the Accountant in Bankruptcy, acting as the DAS administrator, has the authority to overrule the creditor's refusal if the proposal is, in their view, 'fair and reasonable'.[24] Where a DPP is in operation, it is not competent for creditors to take other steps to enforce the debt, such as diligence.[25] **12.13**

A debtor is also protected from diligence where a 'time to pay' direction or order is in effect. A debtor may ask the court for a period of time to repay in manageable instalments with reference to their financial situation. An application for a time to pay direction can be made at any point prior to decree;[26] an application for a time to pay order may be made after a charge for payment has been served, an arrestment executed or an action for adjudication for debt has been commenced.[27] Where a time to pay direction is in effect, the right of any creditor to serve a charge for payment or do diligence is suspended.[28] **12.14**

ATTACHMENT

The diligence of attachment gives the creditor the right to seize and sell the debtor's corporeal moveable property at auction in order to recoup the debt. Prior to the introduction of the Debt Arrangement and Attachment (Scotland) Act 2002 (the 2002 Act), this type of diligence was known as poinding (pronounced 'pinding') and warrant sale. Poinding was considered a harsh and humiliating experience for a debtor and a sustained political campaign for its abolition was led by then-MSP Tommy Sheridan. Attachment, which is poinding in attenuated form, was introduced by the 2002 Act, ss. 10–57. **12.15**

22 Authority for the scheme is set out in Part 1 of the Debt Arrangement and Attachment (Scotland) Act 2002, with detailed provision in the Debt Arrangement Scheme (Scotland) Regulations 2011 (SSI 2011/141). DAS is also available to partnerships, trusts or unincorporated bodies.

23 Further information can be found on the DAS website at *https://www.aib.gov.uk/debt-arrangement-scheme* (last accessed 5 September 2021).

24 Debt Arrangement Scheme (Scotland) Regulations 2011, reg. 25.

25 Debt Arrangement and Attachment (Scotland) Act 2002, s. 4. Where a debtor applies for a DPP, a moratorium on diligence for up to six weeks is imposed from the date of registration of the application in the DAS Register, or earlier if the debtor advises the AIB of an intention to propose a DPP: Bankruptcy (Scotland) Act 2016, ss. 195–198.

26 1987 Act, s. 1. The rules are contained in the Act of Sederunt (Proceedings in the Sheriff Court under the Debtors (Scotland) Act 1987) 1988 (SI 1988/2013). The sheriff may allow a debtor to be represented by a party other than a solicitor or advocate: r. 70.

27 1987 Act, ss. 5(1), 6(3) and 8.

28 1987 Act, s. 9.

Procedure

12.16 A creditor seeking to use the diligence of attachment must first serve a charge. Where the debtor is a natural person, the creditor must also provide the debtor with a DAIP. When the days of charge have expired,[29] or in the case of a natural debtor no earlier than twelve weeks after the DAIP was provided,[30] the creditor can execute the attachment by instructing officers of court to attend any premises where the debtor has goods. The officers will make up a schedule identifying every asset owned by the debtor and estimating the value of that item.[31] A copy of the schedule must be served on the debtor.[32] The officer of court must give a signed report to the sheriff within fourteen days of executing the attachment including the schedule and specifying whether anyone other than the debtor asserted ownership of any of the listed goods.[33] Once the report is received, the officer has six months in which to arrange for the goods to be removed from the debtor's premises[34] and sold at public auction.[35] The proceeds of goods sold are acquired by the creditor in satisfaction of the debt.[36] If the auction raises funds in excess of the debt, the surplus must be returned to the debtor.[37] Ownership of any goods not sold is transferred to the creditor, who again must pay the debtor the value of any surplus in excess of the debt.[38] The officer then makes a report of the auction to the sheriff, which brings the attachment to an end.[39]

12.17 Any person interfering with an attached article, for example by giving it away or destroying it, between execution of the attachment and the auction may be found in contempt of court and will incur personal liability to the creditor for the value of the item.[40]

Limitations on attachment

12.18 The attachment process can only be carried out from Monday to Saturday between the hours of 8am and 8pm, avoiding public holidays, unless the creditor has a court order authorising officers of court to operate outside these times.[41] A significant number of goods are exempt from attachment. Most importantly, the creditor has no right to attach articles inside the debtor's dwellinghouse without obtaining an exceptional attachment order, discussed below. Further exemptions are listed in s. 11 of the 2002 Act. These include: tools of the trade or other equipment used in the debtor's profession, trade or

29 2002 Act, s. 10(3).
30 2002 Act, s. 10(3)(c).
31 2002 Act, s. 13A.
32 2002 Act, s. 13A(3).
33 2002 Act, s. 17. The forms and procedural rules are found in the Act of Sederunt (Debt Arrangement and Attachment (Scotland) Act 2002) (SSI 2002/560).
34 2002 Act, s. 19.
35 2002 Act, ss. 27–30. The traditional Scots law term is 'roup'.
36 2002 Act, s. 31(1)(b).
37 2002 Act, s. 31(1)(c).
38 2002 Act, s. 31(2).
39 2002 Act, s. 32.
40 2002 Act, s. 21.
41 2002 Act, s. 12; Act of Sederunt (Debt Arrangement and Attachment (Scotland) Act 2002) (n 33), reg. 7.

business; any vehicle reasonably required by the debtor not exceeding £1,000 in value; a mobile home that is the debtor's only or principal residence; and money, which must be dealt with by the separate diligence of money attachment.[42]

Only assets owned by the debtor may be attached.[43] The fact that the debtor is in possession of the goods gives rise to a presumption of ownership.[44] Third party owners may overturn this presumption by making representations to the officers of court or, later, to the sheriff.[45] Goods owned in common by the debtor and a third party may be attached,[46] with the third party entitled to receive their share of thc proceeds from the sale of the item.[47] **12.19**

Exceptional attachment

Where a creditor wishes to attach goods inside the debtor's dwellinghouse, they must seek an exceptional attachment order from the court.[48] The exceptional circumstances in which such an order may be granted are detailed in the 2002 Act, s. 48 – essentially, there must be no other way for the creditor to recoup their debt, and it must be reasonably clear that there are sufficient assets in the debtor's dwellinghouse to make the order worthwhile. Even where the order is granted, the creditor may only attach 'non-essential' assets as defined in Sch. 2 to the 2002 Act, which excludes clothing, most household goods and furnishings, articles required for the care or upbringing of a child, educational articles such as books and medical aids or equipment.[49] Exceptional attachment is therefore effectively limited to luxury goods inside the debtor's home. **12.20**

MONEY ATTACHMENT

A specific attachment procedure applies where the property the creditor wishes to obtain is money. The precise legal definition of 'money' is complex,[50] but for the purposes of this diligence, it is interpreted as cash (in other words, coins and banknotes) and banking instruments (such as cheques, money orders, promissory notes and postal orders) in any currency.[51] Money attachment is regulated by the Bankruptcy and Diligence etc. (Scotland) Act 2007 (the 2007 Act), ss. 174–198 and Sch. 3. **12.21**

42 See paras 12.21–12.26 below.
43 2002 Act, s. 10(2).
44 2002 Act, s. 13, restating the position at common law.
45 2002 Act, s. 34.
46 2002 Act, s. 10(2).
47 2002 Act, ss. 35–36.
48 2002 Act, s. 46.
49 2002 Act, s. 47.
50 See Chapter Eight: Money and Debt.
51 2007 Act, s. 175.

Procedure

12.22 The procedure follows a similar pattern to that of attachment of goods. A creditor must serve a charge and provide a DAIP where the debtor is a natural person. When the days of charge expire,[52] and no earlier than twelve weeks after the DAIP was provided,[53] the creditor can instruct officers of court to attend the debtor's premises,[54] attach any money belonging to the debtor up to the value of the debt and remove it from the premises.[55] A schedule of money removed must be prepared by the officers of court and served on the debtor.[56] Any foreign currency removed must be converted into sterling[57] and all cash must be deposited in a bank account.[58] Banking instruments should be valued by the officer at their open market value and stored in a secure place.[59] The officer must give a signed report to the sheriff within fourteen days of executing the attachment.[60] Once the report is received, the creditor has fourteen days in which to apply to court for a payment order, authorising transfer of the attached money to the creditor up to the value of the debt.[61] If no application is made for a payment order within the time limit, the attachment is terminated and the money restored to the debtor.[62] If a payment order is applied for and granted, the officers of court will realise any banking instruments and pay over the money to the creditor.[63] The officer then makes a final statement to the sheriff, which brings the money attachment to an end.[64]

12.23 Any attempt by the debtor to frustrate money attachment, for example by inducing someone to cancel an attached cheque made out to the debtor and issue a new cheque in its place, is unlawful and may be dealt with as a contempt of court.[65]

Limitations on money attachment

12.24 As with attachment of goods, the money attachment process can only be carried out from Monday to Saturday between the hours of 8am and 8pm, avoiding public holidays, unless the creditor has a court order authorising officers of court to operate the process outside these times.[66] The creditor has no right to attach money kept in a dwellinghouse.[67] Cash or instruments which have 'an intrinsic value greater than any value it may have as a medium of exchange' – for example, a gold coin, which is valuable because it is made of

52 2007 Act, s. 174(2)(a)–174(c).
53 2007 Act, s. 174(2)(d).
54 Excluding their dwellinghouse: 2007 Act, s. 174(3). See para. 12.24 below.
55 2007 Act, s. 177.
56 2007 Act, s. 179.
57 2007 Act, s. 177(3).
58 2007 Act, s. 177(5).
59 2007 Act, s. 177(7)–177(8).
60 2007 Act, s. 182.
61 2007 Act, s. 183.
62 2007 Act, s. 187.
63 2007 Act, s. 184.
64 2007 Act, s. 189.
65 2007 Act, s. 193.
66 2007 Act, s. 176.
67 2007 Act, s. 174(3).

gold, as opposed to a £50 note, which is valuable for what it represents rather than the paper it is printed on – are also exempt from attachment.[68]

Only money owned by the debtor may be attached, although as with attachment of goods, possession gives rise to a presumption of ownership.[69] Third party owners may overturn this presumption by making representations to the officer of court or, later, the sheriff.[70] Money owned in common by the debtor and a third party may be attached, although the third party may apply for relief where the attachment is unduly harsh.[71] The third party is entitled to receive their share of the proceeds, for example where a banking instrument owned in common is realised.[72] 12.25

It is open to the debtor to apply for release of the money attachment prior to a payment order being made on the grounds that it is unduly harsh.[73] 12.26

ARRESTMENT

The diligence of arrestment covers two types of assets. First, and most importantly, it may be used to attach incorporeal moveable property of the common debtor. In other words, the assets that are found in a set of accounts under 'debtors'. A common example are the funds held on a credit balance in a bank account. Secondly, arrestment may be used to seize corporeal moveable property owned by the debtor, but in the possession of a third party. For example, the creditor may arrest furniture belonging to the debtor that is being kept in a storage facility. The rules of arrestment are based in the common law, but extensively modified by ss. 73A–73T of the Debtors (Scotland) Act 1987 (the 1987 Act). The creditor using the arrestment is known as the 'arrester'; the debtor against whom decree has been obtained and whose assets the creditor is seeking to arrest, is known as the 'common debtor'; and the party in whose hands the arrestment is served is known as the 'arrestee'. The schedule of arrestment will therefore be served in the hands of the creditor's debtor's debtor. 12.27

Procedure

The creditor must first serve a charge for payment on the debtor. At present, there is no requirement to provide a DAIP where the debtor is a natural person – provision is made for this requirement in the 1987 Act, s. 73D but the section is not in force. On expiry of the days of charge,[74] the creditor instructs officers of court to serve a 'schedule of arrestment' on the arrestee – the third party who has possession of the debtor's property.[75] The schedule is a formal notice advising the arrestee that: (i) funds held by them on behalf of the debtor 12.28

68 2007 Act, s. 175(1).
69 2007 Act, s. 178, restating the position at common law.
70 2007 Act, s. 183.
71 2007 Act, s. 191.
72 2007 Act, s. 192.
73 2007 Act, s. 185.
74 1987 Act, s. 73A.
75 1987 Act, s. 73B.

up to the value of the debt; and/or (ii) all moveable property held by them on behalf the debtor have been arrested, meaning the arrestee is prohibited from releasing the property from their possession.[76] The arrestee is then obliged to send a form of disclosure to the creditor, the debtor and anyone else who claims ownership of the arrested property.[77] The form sets out the nature and value of any items arrested. It must be sent out within three weeks of service of the schedule of arrestment, or else the arrestee may be subject to a financial penalty.[78] The arrestee must release funds to the arrestor fourteen weeks after service of the schedule if the debt has not been repaid, or earlier on receipt of a mandate by the debtor authorising release.[79] Where goods have been arrested, the creditor must raise an action of furthcoming, by which the arrestee will be ordered to sell the goods and transfer the sale proceeds to the arrestor. Once the arrested property has been released to the creditor, the arrestment is at an end.[80]

Arrestable property

12.29 Corporeal moveable property owned by the debtor but in the possession of a third party can be arrested.[81] It is also competent to arrest ships.[82] But the most common type of arrestment is in respect of personal rights owed to the debtor by a third party.[83] Money in a bank account falls into this category, since strictly speaking this is an obligation owed by the bank to the debtor. Suppose Brian loans Anna £5,000 repayable in twelve months. At the term, Anna does not pay. Assuming Brian has obtained a decree with a warrant for all lawful execution, Brian can arrest credit claims held by Anna against her debtors. If Anna had loaned £500 to Felix, Brian can serve an arrestment on Felix and thereby arrest the obligation to repay owed by Felix to Anna. Similarly, if Brian serves arrestments in the hands of the high street banks, these will catch any credit balances that those banks owe to Anna. In each case, Anna's debtors, on the expiry of fourteen weeks,[84] will be required to pay Brian rather than Anna.

12.30 Two important exceptions exist to these general principles. One is that benefit payments cannot be arrested, whether in the hands of the relevant government

76 The form of the schedule is prescribed by the Diligence (Scotland) Regulations 2009 (SSI 2009/68), Sch. 7.

77 1987 Act, s. 73G. The form of disclosure is prescribed by the Diligence (Scotland) Regulations 2009, Sch. 8. The arrestee is under no obligation to provide a nil return if it holds no property capable of arrestment: *ME III Ltd v Carlin* [2018] SC EDIN 6, 2018 Hous LR 29.

78 1987 Act, s. 73H.

79 1987 Act, s. 73J. The sum to be released is specified in s. 73K. The court may make an order preventing automatic release of funds in certain circumstances: see ss. 73L–73N. The debtor may apply to the court to release certain funds or property from the arrestment where it is 'unduly harsh': ss. 73Q–73R.

80 An arrestee who releases fund to the wrong person in good faith is protected per 1987 Act, s. 73P.

81 *Moore and Weinberg v Ernsthausen Ltd* 1917 SC (HL) 25.

82 Ships arrests are subject to detailed common law, statutory and procedural rules: see para. 12.34 below.

83 *Caldwell v Hamilton* 1919 SC (HL) 100 at 109; *Boland v White Cross Insurance Association* 1926 SC 1066.

84 See n 79 above.

authority,[85] or after payment into the common debtor's bank account.[86] The other is that funds held by a bank or other financial institution are subject to a minimum amount protected from arrestment, known as the protected minimum balance (PMB), currently £529.90.[87] The PMB does not apply where the account is held in the name of a company, LLP, partnership or unincorporated association.[88]

Earnings arrestment

A person's employer becomes their debtor at the point in the week or month where wages fall due. It is therefore open to the employee's creditor to arrest earnings in the hands of the employer.[89] As with the example of Anna and Felix above, the employer in this case will pay the wages over not to their employee, but to their employee's creditor. In practice, earnings arrestment is often likely to be the most useful form of diligence available to the creditor of a natural person. **12.31**

Specific rules for arrestment of earnings are set out in the 1987 Act, ss. 46–50, although the procedure is broadly the same as for any other arrestment. The creditor first serves a charge on the debtor. Where the debtor is a natural person, a DAIP must also be provided. On expiry of the days of charge,[90] or no earlier than twelve weeks after provision of the DAIP,[91] the creditor serves an earnings arrestment schedule[92] on the employer specifying the amount of the debt. The employer must provide the creditor with details of how, when and how much the debtor is paid in wages.[93] The employer must then make deductions from the debtor's net earnings on every pay day and transfer the funds to the creditor until the debt is paid off. Regulations set out the amount to be deducted, dependent on the debtor's earnings and whether they are paid weekly or monthly.[94] Where an employer fails to comply with an earnings arrestment, they may be held personally liable for the sums due to the creditor.[95] **12.32**

The legislation also provides for two other forms of diligence against earnings. Where two or more creditors seek to arrest their common debtor's earnings in the hands of their employer at the same time, the provisions on a *conjoined arrestment order* will apply.[96] Where the diligence is used to enforce a court **12.33**

85 See, e.g. the Social Security Administration Act 1992, s. 187(1) and the Tax Credits Act 2002, s. 45(1).
86 *North Lanarkshire Council v Crossan* 2007 SLT (Sh Ct) 169, reversed on appeal by Temporary Sheriff Principal Kearney (Airdrie SC, 2 May 2008, unreported).
87 1987 Act, s. 73F and Sch. 2.
88 1987 Act, s. 73F(2)(a).
89 1987 Act, s. 47.
90 1987 Act, s. 90.
91 1987 Act, s. 47(3).
92 The form of the earnings arrestment schedule is prescribed in the Act of Sederunt (Proceedings in the Sheriff Court under the Debtors (Scotland) Act 1987) 1988 (SI 1988/2013), art. 38 and Schedule (Form 30).
93 1987 Act, s. 70A.
94 1987 Act, s. 49 and Sch. 2.
95 1987 Act, s. 57.
96 1987 Act, ss. 60–66.

award of maintenance, because the debtor has defaulted on an order to make periodical payments of aliment in respect of their child, for example, the provisions on a *current maintenance assessment* will apply.[97] Both schemes operate in much the same way as an earnings arrestment.

Admiralty arrestment

12.34 It is possible to arrest a 'ship' and the cargo on board where the debtor has a real right in the ship.[98] A ship may be arrested in the hands of its owners. The effect is usually to prevent the ship sailing until the debt is repaid. Admiralty arrestment is regulated by the Administration of Justice Act 1956, as amended by the 2007 Act.[99] There are specific provisions dealing with arrestments on the dependence.

INHIBITION

12.35 Inhibition is a diligence against real rights in land.[100] It is a 'freeze' diligence, which prevents the debtor from, for example, selling a piece of land, or granting a lease over it, without the creditor's consent. Normally the creditor will consent only if the proceeds of the debtor's transaction with the property will be used to repay the debt. Inhibition might therefore be viewed as a bargaining tool employed by the creditor to persuade the debtor to repay their debt 'voluntarily', as opposed to a 'grab' diligence like attachment described above, where the creditor simply takes property from the debtor in satisfaction of the debt. Inhibition is now largely regulated by the 2007 Act, ss. 146–168.

Procedure

12.36 A creditor may begin the process of inhibition by instructing officers of court to serve a 'schedule of inhibition' on the debtor. The schedule is a formal notice advising the debtor that they are being inhibited, accompanied by extract of the court decree in respect of the debt.[101] Where the debtor is a natural person, the schedule must be accompanied by a DAIP.[102] The schedule of inhibition, along with a certificate of execution (certifying that the schedule was served on the debtor), must then be registered in the Register of Inhibitions and

97 1987 Act, ss. 51–59.

98 For these purposes, a ship means 'includes any description of vessel used in navigation not propelled by oars': Administration of Justice Act 1956, s. 48. This definition thus covers, for instance, semi-submersible rigs or remotely operated vehicles.

99 Administration of Justice Act 1956, s. 47 onward. For a fuller account, see *Stair Memorial Encyclopaedia*, Vol. 8, paras 322–327.

100 Strictly speaking, the form of inhibition discussed in this section is known as inhibition in execution. Two other forms of inhibition are competent: inhibition on the dependence, discussed at paras 12.57–12.61 below, and the rare process of inhibition on a document of debt, for which see *Stair Memorial Encyclopaedia*, Vol. 8, paras 134 and 138A. The procedure and effect of inhibition on a document of debt are largely the same as those described here.

101 The form of the schedule is prescribed by the Diligence (Scotland) Regulations 2009, reg. 3(1)(a) and (2) and Sch. 1.

102 2007 Act, s. 147.

Adjudications, also known as the Personal Register.[103] Unlike other forms of diligence, there is no need for the creditor to wait for expiry of the days of charge before registering the inhibition. The inhibition takes effect from the beginning of the day on which it is registered.[104]

A variation on this procedure is available to creditors who worry that the debtor, once alerted to the fact an inhibition is shortly to be registered, will attempt to dispose of their property quickly before the inhibition can take effect. A creditor with this concern may begin the process of inhibition by registering a 'priority notice'[105] in the Register of Inhibitions. The priority notice is effectively a statement that the creditor intends to register a schedule of inhibition in the near future. Officers of court would then serve the schedule on the debtor as outlined above. The schedule and certificate of execution must then be registered within twenty-one days of the priority notice being registered. If this time limit is adhered to, the effect of the inhibition will be backdated to the beginning of the day on which the schedule was served.[106] Accordingly, any attempted disposal of the property by the debtor after the schedule was served would be caught by the inhibition nevertheless. **12.37**

Once registered, the inhibition remains in effect for five years, at which time it prescribes.[107] Alternatively, the inhibition may be discharged by the creditor, in full or in relation to a specific property only. The inhibition will also be brought to an end where the debtor satisfies their obligation to the creditor, normally by repaying the debt in full.[108] **12.38**

Effect of inhibition

Inhibition affects all heritable property in Scotland within the debtor's patrimony.[109] The creditor need not specify what property the debtor has in their patrimony – the creditor may not even know what heritage the debtor owns. In other words, the inhibition affects a specific person, rather than specific property. **12.39**

Inhibition does not give the creditor any real rights in respect of the debtor's heritage. Instead, it has a 'freeze' effect on the debtor's capacity to interact with their property. It prohibits the debtor from voluntarily conveying their heritage to a third party, and from voluntarily granting subordinate real rights in their heritage.[110] If the debtor proceeds to convey property or grant a subordinate real right despite the inhibition, the creditor can reduce that transaction.[111] In **12.40**

103 This will be renamed the Register of Inhibitions if and when the abolition of adjudication provided for in the 2007 Act is brought into force: see para. 12.46 below.

104 Titles to Land Consolidation (Scotland) Act 1868, s. 155.

105 Referred to somewhat confusingly in the statute as a 'Notice of Inhibition': Titles to Land Consolidation (Scotland) Act 1868, s. 155(2)(a).

106 Titles to Land Consolidation (Scotland) Act 1868, s. 155(2)–155(3).

107 Conveyancing (Scotland) Act 1924, s. 44(3).

108 2007 Act, ss. 157–158.

109 2007 Act, s. 150.

110 2007 Act, s. 160.

111 Where the grantee of the transaction acquires ownership or another real right in good faith and for adequate consideration, protection is provided under the 2007 Act, s. 159. Since the inhibition must be registered, the circumstances in which a grantee could, in good faith, be

practice, this means the debtor will be unable to transact with their heritage without the creditor's consent.

12.41 Inhibition only strikes at voluntary actions by the debtor. If, for example, heritage is transferred out of the debtor's patrimony by a bank exercising its power of sale under a standard security, that is not a voluntary action on the debtor's part. Similarly, if the debtor is under a personal obligation which predates the inhibition to transfer property to a third party, the debtor's actions in fulfilment of that obligation will not be considered voluntary.[112] Imagine that Anna owns a house. On 3 May, she concludes missives to sell the house to Evan. On 4 May, she is inhibited by Brian. On 5 May, Anna delivers the disposition in respect of the house to Evan, who registers it in the Land Register, resulting in ownership of the house transferring to Evan. Although the property is transferred out of Anna's patrimony after the inhibition takes effect, Anna's actions are not voluntary: she could not have refused to deliver the disposition to Evan without breaching her personal obligation to him.[113]

12.42 Inhibition does not affect heritage acquired by the debtor after the date of inhibition.[114] However, a person is said to acquire property for the purposes of this rule at the beginning of the day on which the deed conveying or otherwise granting a real right in the property is delivered.[115] Imagine Anna has concluded missives for the purchase of a cottage from Zoe. On 5 May, Zoe delivers the disposition in respect of the cottage to Anna. On 6 May, Brian registers his inhibition against Anna in the Personal Register. On 7 May, Anna registers her title to the cottage in the Land Register. Ownership of the house does not transfer to Anna until the moment the title is registered. However, the cottage will nevertheless be caught by the inhibition because the disposition – the deed transferring the real right to Anna – had been delivered prior to the inhibition taking effect. Anna now owns the house but cannot transfer it or grant any subordinate real rights in it without breaching the inhibition.

ADJUDICATION

12.43 Like inhibition, adjudication is a form of diligence against heritable property.[116] Unlike inhibition, adjudication allows the creditor to obtain a real right in security over the property. The rules of adjudication are based largely in the common law.

unaware of its existence are unusual, but cases may arise: see *Commodity Solution Services Ltd v First Scottish Searching Services Ltd* 2018 SLT (Sh Ct) 117, affd at 2019 SLT (Sh Ct) 63 and the connected decision on damages at 2020 GWD 22-293.

112 This is thought to be a correct statement of the law, although the 2007 Act introduced some scope for doubt: see the discussion of *Playfair Investments Ltd v McElvogue* 2013 SLT 225 in K G C Reid and G L Gretton, *Conveyancing 2012* (Edinburgh: W. Green, 2013).

113 *Halifax Building Society v Smith* 1985 SLT (Sh Ct) 25; *Playfair Investments Ltd v McElvogue* 2013 SLT 225.

114 Titles to Land Consolidation (Scotland) Act 1868, s. 157. Property acquired after the date of the inhibition is referred to as 'acquirenda'.

115 2007 Act, s. 150(3).

116 Strictly speaking, the form of diligence discussed in this section is known as 'adjudication for debt'. Other forms of adjudication are discussed below: see paras 12.48–12.51.

Procedure

Unlike other diligences, a creditor cannot simply proceed to adjudication once they have obtained decree in respect of the debt.[117] Instead, they must raise a second action of adjudication, competent only in the Court of Session. In practice, they will usually have inhibited the debtor first, although this is not required. The summons in the action for adjudication must specify the particular property the creditor wishes to adjudge, including the title sheet number if the property is in the Land Register.[118] Unless the debtor has a relevant defence (which is unlikely, since any defence which could be made out would have been used in response to the earlier action for repayment), the court will pronounce a decree of adjudication including details of the property in question. The creditor must then register the extract decree against the title to the property in the Land Register or Register of Sasines. **12.44**

Effect of adjudication

Once the creditor has registered extract decree of adjudication against title to the property concerned, they have a right in security over that property. Unlike a standard security, adjudication does not confer on the creditor a power to sell the heritage. Instead, the adjudger has the power to eject the debtor from the property if necessary,[119] grant leases over the property and keep the rent paid by the tenants in satisfaction of the debt.[120] If the debt has not been repaid at the end of ten years – known as 'expiry of the legal' – the adjudger may raise another court action seeking declarator of expiry of the legal. This decree, if granted, can be registered in the Register of Sasines or the Land Register with the effect that ownership of the property is transferred to the adjudger. If the value of the property exceeds the amount of the debt remaining, any surplus must be paid to the debtor.[121] **12.45**

Abolition of adjudication and replacement with land attachment

The 2007 Act contains provisions abolishing adjudication[122] and introducing in its place a new diligence of land attachment.[123] The new diligence will work in a similar way to attachment of moveables, discussed above,[124] but focused on a specific piece of heritable property. The creditor will first serve a charge on the debtor. When the days of charge have expired, the creditor will register a notice of land attachment against the title to the property in the Land Register or Register of Sasines, and against the name of the debtor in **12.46**

117 See para. 12.09 above.
118 Land Registration etc. (Scotland) Act 2012, ss. 26(1) and 113(1).
119 Heritable Securities (Scotland) Act 1894, s. 5. If the property is 'used to any extent for residential purposes', the additional protective provisions in ss. 5A–5F will apply. Most importantly, these provide that the court may grant decree of ejection only if it is reasonable in all the circumstances, taking into account various factors including the ability of the debtor and any other person residing at the property to secure reasonable alternative accommodation.
120 Heritable Securities (Scotland) Act 1894, ss. 6–7.
121 *Hull v Campbell* 2011 SLT 881.
122 2007 Act, s. 79.
123 2007 Act, ss. 81–128.
124 See paras 12.15–12.20.

the Register of Inhibitions.[125] One registered, the creditor will obtain a right in security over the property.[126] After six months have elapsed, if at least £3,000 of debt remained outstanding, the creditor could apply to the court for a warrant to sell the property.[127] The debt outstanding could be recouped from the sale proceeds and any surplus returned to the debtor.[128]

12.47 It is unclear at present when, if ever, these provisions will be brought into force.

Other forms of adjudication

12.48 Lawyers tend to use the broad term 'adjudication' to refer to what is in fact only one form of adjudication process, namely adjudication for debt. This is the process outlined above. Other forms of adjudication do exist, although they are virtually unknown in practice nowadays. For the sake of completeness, three of these will be mentioned here.

Adjudication in security

12.49 Adjudication in security is akin to diligence on the dependence, discussed below.[129] An action of adjudication in security can be brought by a creditor before the debt is due to be repaid in circumstances where the creditor has reasonable grounds to suspect that the debtor is on the verge of insolvency. If granted, decree has the same effect as in adjudication for debt. This form of adjudication will be abolished by s. 172 of the 2007 Act, if ever brought into force.

Adjudication in implement

12.50 Adjudication in implement is not a form of diligence, despite sharing the same name. This is a mechanism by which a buyer of heritable property could obtain specific implement of an obligation to deliver a valid disposition.[130] In modern practice, the pursuer often seeks the ordinary contractual remedy of specific implement of the obligation, which failing for authority to the clerk of court to execute the deed.[131] That remedy is not limited to dispositions.

Declaratory adjudication

12.51 Declaratory adjudication is also not a form of diligence. This is a mechanism by which the court can confer title to land on the adjudger when the identity

125 2007 Act, ss. 81(3) and 83.
126 2007 Act, s. 81(5).
127 2007 Act, s. 92.
128 2007 Act, s. 116.
129 See paras 12.57–12.61.
130 See J Graham Stewart, *A Treatise on the Law of Diligence* (Edinburgh: W. Green, 1898), p. 667. Titles to Land Consolidation (Scotland) Act 1868, s. 62.
131 *Mackay v Campbell* 1966 SC 237; *Boag, Ptr* 1967 SLT 275; *Hoey v Butler* 1975 SC 87. For the sheriff court, see Courts Reform (Scotland) Act 2014, s. 87 and OCR, r. 34.12; and, for the Scottish Land Court, see *Gains v Gifford's Exrs* 2016 SLCR 86.

of the previous owner is not known and cannot be discovered. This remedy is unheard of in modern practice.

OTHER DILIGENCES

For the sake of completeness, brief mention is made here of some other forms of diligence. These diligences are little used, obsolete or have been abolished. **12.52**

Where a debtor has died, the diligence of *confirmation as executor-creditor* is available to their creditor(s). The creditor will take charge of the deceased's estate and recoup their debt from any assets. This diligence remains competent although it is seldom used in practice.[132] **12.53**

At common law, it was possible to imprison debtors for wilful or neglectful refusal to pay, considered a diligence directed against the person rather than their property. *Civil imprisonment for debt* is no longer possible,[133] except in enforcement of a limited class of alimentary debts, including child support.[134] **12.54**

The diligence of *mails and duties* is available to heritable creditors where the security subjects have been let. Where the diligence is used, the tenant will make rent payments directly to the creditor rather than the landlord-debtor. The diligence is not available to standard security holders, rendering it effectively obsolete in modern practice. It will be abolished by s. 207 of the 2007 Act, if brought into force. A related diligence, known as *poinding of the ground* or *real poinding*, allowed a heritable creditor to recoup their debt by poinding (attaching) corporeal moveables on the security subjects belonging to the debtor or the debtor's tenant. This diligence was abolished alongside all other forms of poinding.[135] **12.55**

The diligence of *sequestration for rent*, formerly a mechanism for enforcement of the landlord's hypothec, has also been abolished.[136] A landlord seeking to enforce the hypothec may now be required to instigate a formal insolvency process, though the position is unclear.[137] **12.56**

DILIGENCE ON THE DEPENDENCE

Diligence on the dependence is not a specific form of diligence, but rather a way in which many of the diligences explained above can be used. When a pursuer raises a court action, often the ultimate goal will be to obtain money from the defender, perhaps in implement of a contract (as with an action for repayment of debt), perhaps in damages for a delictual loss and so on. A devious defender who suspects that they are likely to lose the case may seek to **12.57**

132 For a fuller account, see *Stair Memorial Encyclopaedia*, Vol. 8, paras 350–358.
133 Debtors (Scotland) Act 1880, s. 4.
134 For a fuller account, see *Stair Memorial Encyclopaedia*, Vol. 8, paras 347–349.
135 2002 Act, s. 58.
136 2007 Act, s. 208.
137 For discussion, see S Skea and A J M Steven, 'The landlord's hypothec: difficulties in practice' 2010 SLT (News) 120 and A Sweeney, *The Landlord's Hypothec* (Edinburgh: Edinburgh Legal Education Trust, 2021).

frustrate the pursuer by ridding themselves of their assets. If the defender does so successfully, the pursuer's eventual court decree will be worthless, since a decree cannot be enforced against a person with no property. As the adage says, you can't get blood from a stone.[138]

12.58 The law seeks to prevent this evasion of the judicial process by allowing a pursuer in an action with a financial conclusion to carry out certain forms of diligence 'on the dependence of the action'. The diligence process takes effect when the court action is first raised, or at some point during the life of the case, and prevents the defender disposing of their assets whilst the action is ongoing. If the pursuer wins the case, the diligence can then be fully enforced if necessary to obtain payment in terms of the court decree. If the pursuer loses the case, the diligence is discharged and the defender's assets remain with them.

12.59 The forms of diligence that can be used in this way are inhibition,[139] arrestment[140] and attachment[141] (referred to in this context as 'interim attachment').

12.60 It used to be the case that diligence on the dependence would be granted automatically by the court if requested by a pursuer seeking a sum of money. However, the effect on the defender can be quite severe – a large part of the defender's assets can effectively be frozen for years if the case is complicated or there are delays in the court process – so that an automatic grant of diligence on the dependence was eventually found to be in violation of the defender's right to peaceful enjoyment of their possessions under art. 1 of the first Protocol to the ECHR.[142] The automatic nature of diligence on the dependence was considered the heart of the violation. An order granted after the court had been addressed on why the diligence was necessary in a particular case, where the defender had an opportunity to make arguments against the grant of diligence, would not contravene the defender's Convention rights.[143]

12.61 The Convention-compliant approach to diligence on the dependence was put on a statutory footing in 2008 by virtue of amendments to the 1987 Act.[144] The court will grant warrant for diligence on the dependence if satisfied: (i) that the pursuer has a *prima facie* case on the merits of the action. This is a 'substantial hurdle', which requires a 'good arguable case';[145] (ii) that there is a 'real and substantial' risk that any decree obtained by the pursuer will be unenforceable because the defender is on the verge of insolvency or is likely to dispose of their assets; and (iii) it is reasonable in all the circumstances of the case.[146]

138 A defender in this situation is sometimes referred to as 'judgment proof'. See L M LoPucki, 'The Death of Liability' (1996) 106 Yale Law Journal 1.

139 1987 Act, s. 15A(1)(b).

140 1987 Act, s. 15A(1)(a).

141 2002 Act, s. 9A.

142 *Karl Construction Ltd v Palisade Properties plc* 2002 SC 270; *Fab-Tek Engineering Ltd v Carillion Construction* 2002 SLT (Sh Ct) 113.

143 2002 SLT (Sh Ct) 113.

144 1987 Act, ss. 15A–15N.

145 *Gillespie v Toondale Ltd* 2006 SC 314 at [12]–[13]. See too *Scottish Ministers v MacDonald* 2016 SC 528.

146 1987 Act, s. 15F. See, e.g. *McCormack v Hamilton Academical Football Club Ltd* 2009 SC 313; *Bain v The Rangers Football Club plc* [2011] CSOH 158.

Special rules apply to admiralty arrestments on the dependence. In brief terms, these rules implement international conventions on ship arrests. It is a remedy that may be used only for a limited number of listed claims on the dependence of which the arrest is sought.[147] These provisions can be very important practically, and are often used in support of litigation outside of Scotland.[148] **12.62**

147 Administration of Justice Act 1956, s. 47. See, e.g. *Fish & Fish Ltd v Sea Shepherd UK* [2011] CSOH 122, 2012 SLT 156.

148 It is possible to obtain interim measures in one jurisdiction in the UK in support of proceedings in another: Civil Jurisdiction and Judgments Act 1982, s. 27.

Chapter Thirteen

Insolvency: Bankruptcy

Frankie McCarthy

INTRODUCTION

13.01 Insolvency describes a situation in which a legal person is unable to meet their obligations to creditors. In certain circumstances, the law allows the creditors of a debtor in this position to seize the debtor's assets and sell them off in satisfaction of the debts. The creditors will receive a percentage of what is owed. The remainder of the debts are written off, and the debtor is able to start afresh. Where the debtor is a company or limited liability partnership, the relevant insolvency process may be receivership, administration or liquidation. These processes are discussed in Chapter Fourteen. Where the debtor is a natural person, trust, partnership, body corporate or unincorporated association, the relevant insolvency process is sequestration, otherwise known as bankruptcy. This chapter sets out the rules of sequestration: when it can happen, the legal effect and the results for both debtor and creditors.

13.02 Personal insolvency processes have existed in Scotland for centuries.[1] At the time of its introduction, the Bankruptcy (Scotland) Act 1985 represented a substantial revision and restatement of that earlier law. However, rapidly evolving economic factors resulted in the 1985 Act itself being subject to a number of significant pieces of amending legislation over the following thirty years.[2] A further consolidation was carried out in the Bankruptcy (Scotland) Act 2016 (the '2016 Act'),[3] which is now the key piece of legislation in this area.[4]

Why have insolvency law?

13.03 Imagine that Gordon owes money to four different creditors. The debts amount to £100,000, with interest continuing to accrue. When the loans were taken out, Gordon was a sole trader and his business was doing well, and he was confident he could repay on the agreed terms. Since then, a recession has struck, and Gordon's business is failing. Despite using all of his meagre income towards his debt repayments, there is not enough to make his

1 For the history, see D Mackenzie-Skene, *Bankruptcy* (Edinburgh: W. Green, 2018), Ch. 2.

2 The key pieces of legislation were the Bankruptcy (Scotland) Act 1993, the Bankruptcy and Diligence etc. (Scotland) Act 2007 and the Bankruptcy and Debt Advice (Scotland) Act 2014.

3 The 2016 Act followed on the recommendations of the Scottish Law Commission in its *Report on the Consolidation of Bankruptcy Legislation in Scotland* (Scot. Law Com. No. 232, 2013).

4 Various procedural rules are contained in the Bankruptcy (Scotland) Regulations 2016 (SSI 2016/397).

minimum payments. Each month, he borrows more money to service existing debts, which puts him only further into debt. It is hard to see how Gordon will ever recover.

The law allows sequestration to happen in this context for two reasons. In the first place, the law aims to ensure creditors are treated equally. It is not possible for Gordon to repay them all. Each creditor could individually attempt diligence in respect of their debts,[5] but there are not sufficient assets for them all to be repaid – it would be a case of 'first come, first served'. This is considered unfair on the creditors who were slower to act, especially those who delayed taking action in a spirit of compassion towards Gordon. Four creditors doing diligence also means four times the amount of time and money spent, and court time used, which is inefficient. Insolvency gives creditors the option to cut their losses in an efficient and equitable manner. The law also seeks to protect Gordon in this situation. His debts have arisen through a combination of bad judgment and bad luck. Gordon took a risk when starting his business – if no one was prepared to take that risk, a country's economy would never grow. Enabling Gordon to escape from his debts is therefore both a humane recognition that people make mistakes and an economic second chance that may allow Gordon to become a financially contributing member of society once again. 13.04

Different types of insolvency

The word insolvency can be used to describe a range of situations which have different legal consequences. Where a debtor is unable to pay their debts as they fall due, this is referred to as simple or practical insolvency, and does not necessarily indicate that a debtor is in real financial trouble. If Gordon owns a shop premises worth £500,000, and his only debt is a credit card bill of £500, his financial situation is very healthy. However, if his credit card bill must be paid today and there is no cash in his bank account to pay it, he will be practically insolvent. This is a short-term problem: he will be able to obtain the money he needs, perhaps by asking the bank for an overdraft secured against his house. In business, this kind of liquidity problem often arises because clients are late in paying their bills, which in turn leaves the business owner unable to pay their own creditors. Sequestration would not usually be necessary or sensible here. 13.05

Absolute insolvency, alternatively referred to as 'balance sheet insolvency', describes the situation where a debtor's total liabilities exceed their total assets. A debtor in this situation will not inevitably be sequestrated. Some absolutely insolvent debtors continue to operate for long periods, by borrowing money to pay off the most immediate debts in the hope or expectation that their overall financial health will improve. This type of solution cannot continue indefinitely, however, and eventually the creditors may wish to take action. 13.06

Apparent insolvency is the critical test for sequestration. This is a term created by the bankruptcy legislation to describe a number of situations in which the debtor's financial situation is deemed sufficiently precarious to give creditors 13.07

5 For a discussion of diligence, see Chapter Twelve: Judicial Security: Diligence.

grounds for sequestration. The 2016 Act, s. 16 provides that a debtor's apparent insolvency shall be constituted where:

- The debtor gives written notice to their creditors that they have ceased to pay their debts in the ordinary course of business.[6] In other words, the debtor gives notice that they are practically insolvent.
- The debtor grants a trust deed (a kind of negotiated sequestration, discussed below).[7]
- The debtor is served with a charge and the days of charge expire without payment;[8] or a decree of adjudication is granted against any part of their estate;[9] or a debt payment programme is revoked.[10] Apparent insolvency will not be constituted by any of these events if either of the circumstances in s. 16(2) exist, the most practically important of which is that the debtor can demonstrate that they were practically solvent at the time the event occurred.[11]
- A creditor in respect of a liquid debt of £1,500 or more has served on the debtor a formal notice requiring payment or security for the debt,[12] and three weeks have passed without payment being made, security being provided or the debtor formally denying the existence of the debt.[13]
- The debtor's estate has been sequestrated in Scotland or subjected to an equivalent bankruptcy process in England and Wales or Northern Ireland.[14] In this situation, rather than insolvency triggering sequestration, it is the sequestration that constitutes apparent insolvency. This might happen where the sequestration is initiated by the debtor, discussed below.[15]

13.08 Where the debtor is a partnership, in addition to the situations outlined above, apparent insolvency will be constituted where any of the partners is apparently insolvent for a debt of the partnership.[16] Where the debtor is an unincorporated body, apparent insolvency will be constituted where any person who represents the body or holds property on behalf of the body in a fiduciary capacity is apparently insolvent for a debt of the body.[17]

6 Bankruptcy (Scotland) Act 2016, s. 16(1)(c).

7 2016 Act, s. 16(1)(e). A trust deed is a mechanism by which a debtor voluntarily transfers all their assets to a third party trustee to distribute to their creditors in satisfaction of their debts: see paras 13.72–13.75.

8 2016 Act, s. 16(1)(f). Service of a charge is the first formal step in enforcing a court decree for repayment of debt: see the discussion at paras 12.09–12.12.

9 2016 Act, s. 16(1)(g). Adjudication is a form of diligence directed against a debtor's heritable property which enables the creditor to take rents paid in respect of any lease over the property. See the discussion at paras 12.43–12.45.

10 2016 Act, s. 16(1)(h). A debt payment programme is an agreement between debtor and creditor negotiated through the government Debt Arrangement Scheme, usually on favourable terms to the debtor. See para. 12.13.

11 2016 Act, s. 16(2)(a).

12 2016 Act, s. 16(1)(i).

13 2016 Act, s. 16(3).

14 2016 Act, s. 16(1)(a) and (b).

15 See paras 13.14–13.16.

16 2016 Act, s. 16(4)(b).

17 2016 Act, s. 16(5).

Equalisation of diligence

Apparent insolvency, of itself, has important consequences for creditors. Creditors using arrestments or attachments within sixty days prior to the debtor's apparent insolvency or within four months following apparent insolvency rank *pari passu*.[18] Since apparent insolvency is often a precursor to sequestration, these rules, when combined with the rules on equalisation of diligence on the eve of bankruptcy can have important practical consequences for creditors who may otherwise consider that they have secured a preference successfully doing diligence.[19] **13.09**

THE SEQUESTRATION PROCESS

The process of sequestration generally goes through the following stages: **13.10**

(a) an application is made for sequestration by the debtor, a creditor or another person qualified to petition the court;
(b) an award of sequestration is made, including the appointment of a trustee in sequestration to deal with the debtor's estate;
(c) the trustee investigates the debtor's estate, establishing their assets and liabilities and challenging any recent transactions designed to defeat the sequestration process;
(d) the trustee realises the debtor's assets, distributing property or funds amongst the creditors of the estate. Creditors will generally receive a percentage of what they are owed, referred to as their 'dividend' from the estate; and
(e) the sequestration is terminated and the debtor is discharged, free of debt.

This chapter will look at each of these stages in detail.

The role of the Accountant in Bankruptcy

The Accountant in Bankruptcy (AiB) is a government agency set up to oversee the operation of personal insolvency law in Scotland.[20] The AiB operates from an office in Kilwinning staffed by civil servants with legal qualifications, accountancy qualifications or various other skills. One of its main functions is to supervise the performance of those administering the insolvency process, including insolvency lawyers. This means providing guidance to practitioners on law and procedure, in addition to investigating complaints from debtors or creditors about the administration of a sequestration in which they were involved. The AiB also has a record-keeping role, with responsibility for maintaining the Register of Insolvencies.[21] In a limited range of situations, the AiB **13.11**

18 2016 Act, s. 233 and Sch. 7. See generally Mackenzie-Skene (n 1), para. 15–07 onward.

19 *Stewart v Jarvie* 1938 SC 309. See generally Mackenzie-Skene (n 1), para. 15–19 onward.

20 The key powers and functions of the AiB are now set out in the 2016 Act, ss. 199–205.

21 A public register containing details of all sequestrations awarded by the Scottish courts, in addition to information on protected trusts deeds for creditors and details of limited companies in receivership or liquidation. It can be consulted at *https://roi.aib.gov.uk/roi/Security/Home/Landing* (last accessed 7 September 2021).

can step in to act as the trustee itself. More information on the AiB's role and functions can be found on its website.[22]

13.12 The chief executive of the agency holds the statutory post of Accountant in Bankruptcy, an officer of the court. At the time of writing, the post is held by Richard Dennis.

APPLYING FOR SEQUESTRATION

Who can be sequestrated?

13.13 Provision as to which legal persons are liable to sequestration is made in the 2016 Act, Part 1. In the first place, the estate of a natural person can be sequestrated, whether that person is alive[23] or dead.[24] In addition, it is competent to sequestrate the estate belonging to or held by or for: a trust in respect of debts incurred by the trust;[25] a partnership or limited partnership, including a dissolved partnership or dissolved limited partnership;[26] a body corporate other than a company or LLP;[27] and an unincorporated body.[28]

Obtaining a sequestration

13.14 A debtor who is a living person can apply to the AiB to sequestrate their own estate. A trust, partnership, body corporate or unincorporated body is known as an 'entity debtor'. Such a debtor can apply to the AiB to sequestrate its estate with the concurrence of a creditor. Alternatively, creditors and other qualified persons can petition the court to make an award of sequestration in respect of the estate of a debtor.

Application by debtor

13.15 A living person is permitted to apply for sequestration of their own estate[29] as a 'standard' case or a 'low asset' case. The standard case conditions are set out in s. 2(8). Under these, the debtor may apply if the total amount of their debts is not less than £3,000, there has been no award of sequestration made against them within the five years prior to the application, they have obtained the advice of a money adviser and have given various undertakings.[30] In addition,

22 Accountant in Bankruptcy, *https://www.aib.gov.uk/* (last accessed 7 September 2021).
23 2016 Act, s. 2.
24 2016 Act, s. 5.
25 2016 Act, s. 6(1)(a).
26 2016 Act, s. 6(1)(b) and (d). A limited partnership (LP) is different from a limited liability partnership (LLP), as discussed at para. 1.25 onward. An LP can be sequestrated; an LLP cannot: 2016 Act, s. 6(2)(b). For the application of the 2016 Act to LPs, see further Bankruptcy (Scotland) Regulations 2016, reg. 31.
27 2016 Act, s. 6(1)(c) and (2).
28 2016 Act, s. 6(1)(d).
29 2016 Act, s. 2(1)(a). Where the debtor is deceased, an application can be made on their behalf by the executor of their estate, or by a person entitled to be appointed as executor: s. 5(a).
30 2016 Act, s. 2(8)(a)–(d).

the debtor must be apparently insolvent,[31] or have been granted a 'certificate of sequestration',[32] or have granted a trust deed that cannot be converted into a protected trust deed.[33] The 'low asset' conditions are set out in s. 2(2). Under these, the debtor may apply if the total amount of their debts is not less than £1,500 and not more than £25,000, the total value of their assets (excluding liabilities) on the date of the application does not exceed £2,000, they have no single asset worth over £1,000 and they do not own land.[34] In addition, the debtor must have been granted a certificate of sequestration,[35] and no award of sequestration can have been made against them in the past ten years under the 'low asset' route,[36] or in the past five years under any other route.[37] A 'low asset' application will only be competent where the debtor has been in receipt of prescribed welfare benefits for at least six months prior to the application,[38] or where the debtor has been assessed by the AiB as requiring to make zero debtor's contribution.[39]

Entity debtors may also apply for sequestration of their own estates. The majority of trustees must make the application with the concurrence of a qualified creditor for the sequestration of a trust estate in respect of debts incurred by the trust.[40] Where the debtor is a partnership, an application may be made where it is apparently insolvent,[41] or with the concurrence of a qualified creditor.[42] For bodies corporate and unincorporated, a person authorised to act on behalf of the body must make the application.[43] **13.16**

A debtor makes their or its application to the AiB.[44] The application must specify the name and address of the money adviser consulted by the debtor in advance of the application, and include a declaration by the money adviser that advice has been given.[45] Along with the application, the debtor must send the AiB a statement of assets and liabilities, and a statement of undertakings.[46] A material misstatement or failure to disclose a material fact in either statement is a criminal offence.[47] If the AiB is satisfied that the debtor meets the conditions set out in the statute, it will award sequestration forthwith.[48] The **13.17**

31 2016 Act, s. 2(8)(e)(i). See para. 13.07.
32 2016 Act, s. 2(8)(e)(ii). This certificate can be granted by authorised persons who have reviewed the debtor's financial statements and confirmed that the debtor is unable to pay their debts as they fall due: 2016 Act, s. 9.
33 2016 Act, s. 2(8)(e)(iii): see para. 13.72–13.75.
34 2016 Act, s. 2(2)(b)–(e) as amended by the Bankruptcy (Miscellaneous Amendments) (Scotland) Regulations 2021 (SSI 2021/148).
35 2016 Act, s. 2(2)(f).
36 2016 Act, s. 2(2)(g).
37 2016 Act, s. 2(2)(h).
38 2016 Act, s. 2(2)(a)(ii).
39 2016 Act, s. 2(2)(a)(i). Debtor's contributions are discussed below at para. 13.30.
40 2016 Act, s. 6(3)(a). For the meaning of 'qualified creditor', see para. 13.17.
41 2016 Act, s. 6(4)(a).
42 2016 Act, s. 6(4)(b).
43 2016 Act, s. 6(7)(a).
44 2016 Act, s. 8(1).
45 2016 Act, s. 8(2).
46 2016 Act, s. 8(3).
47 2016 Act, s. 8(4).
48 2016 Act, s. 22(1).

AiB must also send a copy of the AiB's determination of the application to the Keeper of the Register of Inhibitions for recording in that register.[49]

Petition to the sheriff

13.18 A qualified creditor is one who, at the date of the petition, is owed at least £3,000 by the debtor in question, or more than one creditor whose debts add up to at least £3,000.[50] A qualified creditor can petition the sheriff to award sequestration[51] in respect of the estate of a living debtor,[52] trust estate,[53] partnership,[54] limited partnership,[55] body corporate or unincorporated body[56] that is apparently insolvent,[57] and that apparent insolvency was constituted within four months of the date of the petition.[58] If a living person, the creditor must provide the debtor with a Debt Advice and Information Package not less than fourteen days and not more than twelve weeks before the petition is made.[59] A qualifying creditor may petition for the sequestration of a deceased debtor's estate not earlier than six months after the death unless the debtor was apparently insolvent at some point in the four months preceding their demise.[60] A petition in respect of a deceased debtor's estate may alternatively be made by the executor.[61] The different methods of service for each debtor are set out in the regulations.[62]

13.19 A petition for sequestration can also be presented to the sheriff in respect of any debtor's estate by a trustee acting under a trust deed in respect of that estate.[63]

13.20 A copy of any petition made to the sheriff must be sent to the AiB.[64] The sheriff will cite the debtor to a hearing between six and fourteen days after the petition was presented.[65] The purpose of the hearing is to ascertain whether the defender can show cause why the petition should not be granted. They may argue that the procedural formalities in respect of the petition have not been carried out correctly, or that the applicant was not entitled to petition the court because the debts were not due or the debtor was not apparently insolvent. If good cause is shown, or if the debtor pays or secures the debt, the petition will be dismissed.[66] The court may continue the petition in cer-

49 2016 Act, s. 26(2).
50 2016 Act, s. 7. For information on the DAIP, see para. 12.12.
51 The form petition is found in the Act of Sederunt (Sheriff Court Bankruptcy Rules) 2016 (SSI 2016/313), Sch. 1.
52 2016 Act, s. 2(1)(b)(i).
53 2016 Act, s. 6(3)(b)(iii).
54 2016 Act, s. 6(4)(c)(iv).
55 2016 Act, s. 11(3)(a).
56 2016 Act, s. 6(7)(b)(iii).
57 2016 Act, s. 2(1)(b)(i).
58 2016 Act, s. 13(2)(a) and s. 13(3)(a) in respect of limited partnerships.
59 2016 Act, s. 3. The time limits are currently set out in the Bankruptcy (Scotland) Regulations 2016 (n 4), reg. 11.
60 2016 Act, s. 5(b) and 13(4).
61 2016 Act, s. 5(a) and 13(4)(b)(i).
62 Bankruptcy (Scotland) Regulations 2016 (n 59), reg. 6.4.
63 2016 Act, s. 13(4)(b)(ii).
64 2016 Act, s. 13(1).
65 2016 Act, s. 22(3)–(4).
66 2016 Act, s. 23(1).

tain circumstances if it appears matters can be resolved without the need for sequestration.[67] Otherwise, sequestration must be awarded forthwith.[68] The sheriff clerk must send a copy of the order granting the sequestration to the Keeper of the Register of Inhibitions for recording in that register, to the AiB, and where the debtor was participating in a debt payment programme,[69] to the Debt Arrangement Scheme administrator.[70]

CONSEQUENCES OF THE AWARD OF SEQUESTRATION

In the case of debtor application, the date of sequestration is the date on which the award was made by the AiB.[71] Where sequestration has been awarded by the court following on a petition, the date of sequestration is backdated to the date on which warrant to cite the debtor in respect of the petition was first granted by the sheriff.[72] An award of sequestration has several immediate consequences. In the first place, a trustee in sequestration is appointed to deal with the debtor's estate. Secondly, the debtor's estate immediately vests in the trustee. Thirdly, diligence is equalised. Finally, a sequestrated debtor is subject to certain legal restrictions. **13.21**

The trustee in sequestration

On making an award of sequestration, the AiB or the sheriff must appoint a person to act as the trustee in sequestration. This person must be a qualified insolvency practitioner (almost invariably a lawyer) and consent to taking on the role.[73] It is normally the case that the application or petition will nominate someone to act as trustee,[74] failing which the AiB will take on the role.[75] In the unusual situation where an 'interim trustee' has been appointed to safeguard the debtor's assets whilst the application for sequestration is ongoing,[76] the same person will usually continue into the role of trustee in sequestration.[77] Where the debtor has applied through the 'low asset' route, the AiB must act as the trustee.[78] **13.22**

The trustee's functions are set out in the 2016 Act, s. 50. In summary, these are: **13.23**

- to recover, manage and realise the debtor's estate, wherever situated;
- to distribute the estate amongst the creditors according to their respective entitlements;

67 2016 Act, s. 23(2)–(3).
68 2016 Act, s. 22(5).
69 See the discussion of the Debt Arrangement Scheme at para. 12.13.
70 2016 Act, s. 26(1).
71 2016 Act, s. 22(7)(a).
72 2016 Act, s. 22(7)(b).
73 2016 Act, s. 51(1)(b) and (2)(a) for petitions and s. 51(8)(b) and (9) for debtor applications.
74 2016 Act, s. 51(1)(a) for petitions and s. 51(8)(a) for debtor applications.
75 2016 Act, s. 51(3).
76 2016 Act, s. 54.
77 2016 Act, s. 51(4)–(7).
78 2016 Act, s. 51(11)–(12).

- to ascertain the reasons for the debtor's insolvency and the circumstances surrounding it; and
- to ascertain the state of the debtor's liabilities and assets.

These duties should be performed only in so far as, in the trustee's view, it would be of financial benefit to the estate of the debtor and in the interests of creditors to do so.[79] The trustee also has a responsibility to ensure accurate records of the sequestration are maintained and supplied to the AiB, and to keep all interested parties up to date on progress.[80]

13.24 In practice, the trustee's first duties on being appointed will be to secure the debtor's estate as necessary[81] (by requiring the debtor to physically hand over assets, for example) and to prepare a statement of the debtor's financial affairs.[82] The debtor is required to provide the trustee with a list of assets and liabilities to assist the trustee in preparation of their statement.[83] The debtor is under a broad statutory duty to co-operate with the trustee, with failure to do so a criminal offence.[84]

13.25 The trustee also has the option to call a 'statutory meeting' of creditors,[85] at which the creditors vote to approve the appointment of a trustee (or replace them)[86] and submit claims on the estate.[87] This used to be a compulsory but ill-attended aspect of the sequestration process, which is little used since the law was amended to make the meeting optional. If the trustee wishes to call a meeting, they must do so within sixty days of being appointed.[88]

13.26 At the statutory meeting, or any other meeting, it is open to creditors to elect up to five of their number as 'commissioners' whose task it is to oversee the trustee's dealings with the estate.[89] In practice, this tends not to happen except in particularly large or complex sequestrations. Commissioners have a responsibility to supervise and provide guidance to the trustee on their management of the estate,[90] although they are not obliged to follow their advice. Commissioners will also audit a trustee's accounts and determine what payment in respect fees and outlays they are entitled to in any accounting period.[91] Commissioners must act gratuitously and owe fiduciary duties to the debtor and other creditors.

79 2016 Act, s. 50(9).
80 2016 Act, s. 50(1)(e)–(g).
81 2016 Act, s. 108. Where an interim trustee is appointed, see 2016 Act, s. 39.
82 2016 Act, s. 42.
83 2016 Act, s. 41.
84 2016 Act, s. 215.
85 2016 Act, ss. 43–44.
86 2016 Act, s. 49.
87 2016 Act, s. 46.
88 2016 Act, s. 44(3).
89 2016 Act, ss. 76–77.
90 2016 Act, s. 76.
91 2016 Act, s. 133.

Vesting of the estate

On appointment, the whole estate of the debtor is transferred out of their patrimony and vested in the trustee for the benefit of the creditors.[92] The estate is said to vest in the trustee *tantum et tale*, meaning the trustee acquires no better right to the property than the debtor had.[93] If the debtor owned property subject to a right in security, the trustee's ownership will also be subject to that right in security.[94] **13.27**

In respect of moveable property, the trustee acquires any personal rights held by the debtor, such as a right to repayment of debt from a third party. However, the trustee does not automatically acquire any onerous obligations owed by the debtor, such as the obligations they may owe as a tenant under a lease. The trustee will not be liable for such obligations unless they specifically adopt the relevant contract.[95] Where delivery, possession or intimation would normally be required to complete title to a piece of moveable property, this will be deemed to have occurred by virtue of the trustee's appointment.[96] **13.28**

In respect of heritable property, 'vesting' does not make the trustee owner.[97] As a matter of general property law principle, the trustee must register their title to the property in the Land Register or Register of Sasines in order to acquire a real right in that property. This cannot be done until at least twenty-eight days after the sequestration has been recorded in the Register of Inhibitions.[98] The twenty-eight-day window was introduced to avoid the situation where the disposition in respect of the sale of a house by the debtor was delivered prior to the award of sequestration, but not registered until afterwards, leaving the prospective house buyer without the sale price, the house or any effective remedy against the debtor or the trustee.[99] **13.29**

Certain property is exempt from vesting. Property that the debtor holds in trust is specifically excluded.[100] Property exempt from attachment, such as household goods and tools of the debtor's trade,[101] do not vest in the trustee.[102] Protected tenancies, including assured or Scottish secure tenancies, are excluded.[103] **13.30**

92 2016 Act, s. 78(1); *O'Boyle's Tr v Brennan* [2020] CSIH 3, 2020 SC 217.
93 It is not clear that the maxim *tantum et tale* correctly applied is anything other than a restatement of the *nemo plus* principle. See *Burnett's Trustee v Grainger* 2004 SC (HL) 19 and J A MacLeod, *Fraud and Voidable Transfer* (Edinburgh: Edinburgh Legal Education Trust, 2020), Ch. 8. The *nemo plus* principle is explained in detail at para. 3.97 onward.
94 2016 Act, s. 88(3).
95 If there is no express adoption, the trustee is deemed not to have adopted: 2016 Act, s. 110(10).
96 2016 Act, s. 78(8).
97 *Joint Liquidators of The Scottish Coal Co Ltd v Scottish Environment Protection Agency* 2014 SC 372 at [111]–[113].
98 2016 Act, s. 78(4).
99 See *Burnett's Tr v Grainger* 2004 SC (HL) 19.
100 2016 Act, s. 88(1)(c).
101 For a full discussion, see paras 12.18–12.19.
102 2016 Act, s. 88(1)(a)–(b).
103 2016 Act, s. 79(2)–(3).

13.31 More broadly, the rules on vesting apply to assets and not to income, so any income received by the debtor will not vest unless it has been derived from assets already vested in the trustee.[104] Dividends paid on shares owned by the debtor will therefore vest in the trustee. Wages or periodical payments from a pension fund will not. However, account will still be taken of the debtor's income in the sequestration process. Using the common financial tool,[105] the AiB must assess the appropriate amount of any contribution to be made by the debtor from their income,[106] and make a 'debtor contribution order' in every case.[107] Where the debtor has little income, the contribution will be fixed at zero.[108] The order may require payment of the contribution by the debtor or a third party with money due to the debtor,[109] for example the debtor's employer, who may be required to pay over a portion of the debtor's wages. The order will generally require payments to be made at regular intervals for a period up to forty-eight months from the time when the first payment is made.[110]

13.32 Property acquired by the debtor up to four years after the date of sequestration but prior to them being discharged,[111] known as *acquirenda*, will vest in the trustee.[112] A debtor must immediately inform the trustee of any *acquirenda* or they commit a criminal offence.[113]

Equalisation of diligence

13.33 Once an award of sequestration has been made, it is no longer competent for creditors to enforce their right to repayment of debt through diligence against the estate of the debtor vested in the trustee.[114] This is because sequestration has the same effect as if the trustee had carried out all relevant forms of diligence against the debtor's estate for the benefit of all creditors.[115] The law also does not wish to incentivise creditors to aggressively pursue debts at a time when the debtor is close to bankruptcy, since this is considered unfair both

104 2016 Act, s. 85(1).
105 The 'common financial tool' is a set of rules on how to assess a debtor's income and expenditure used across a range of statutory debt processes: see Bankruptcy (Scotland) Regulations 2016 (SSI 2016/397), regs. 15–17.
106 2016 Act, ss. 89 and 90(3).
107 2016 Act, s. 90(1).
108 2016 Act, s. 90(4).
109 2016 Act, s. 90(6).
110 2016 Act, s. 91.
111 For an explanation of the procedure for discharge of the debtor from the sequestration, see paras 13.65–13.69.
112 2016 Act, ss. 79(5) and 86(4)–(5).
113 2016 Act, s. 87(1)–(3).
114 *Sinclair v Edinburgh Parish Council* 1909 SC 1353. That no preference is created by diligence after sequestration follows from first principles and, for arrestment and attachment, from the express words of the 2016 Act, s. 24(6). A creditor cannot do diligence against post-sequestration income that vests in the debtor rather than the trustee: 2016 Act, s. 86(1). For more detail on the process and effect of diligence, see Chapter Twelve: Judicial Security: Diligence. Where a debtor applies for sequestration, a moratorium on diligence applies for six weeks from the date on which they first give written notice to the AiB of their intention to apply for sequestration (2016 Act, ss. 195 and 196) with potential to extend the time limit if the application takes longer to process (2016 Act, s. 198).
115 2016 Act, s. 24(2).

on the debtor and other creditors. To this end, any diligence process started in the period sixty days prior to the award of sequestration will not create a preferential right in favour of the creditor who performed the diligence.[116] Any right or asset obtained by a creditor through a diligence process started during this period must be handed over to the trustee to be shared amongst creditors with the rest of the estate.[117] Any right of inhibition obtained by a creditor during this period must be assigned to the trustee to exercise for the benefit of all creditors.[118] This is known as equalisation of diligence, since the creditor's rights are equalised with those of the trustee and other creditors.

Personal consequences for the debtor

In addition to being divested of their assets, the debtor is also subject to certain legal restrictions as a result of the sequestration. They are not permitted to obtain credit over a value of £2,000, or of any amount where their outstanding debts amount to £1,000 or more, without advising the creditor about the sequestration.[119] If outside Scotland, they must return when ordered to do so by the court for any purposes connected with the administration of the estate.[120] They are not permitted to act as a director of a company or to be involved in the promotion, formation or management of a company without the leave of the court.[121] Breach of any of these restrictions is a criminal offence. In addition, an undischarged bankrupt is not entitled to practise as a solicitor[122] or in various other professions, and may not become an MP or take up various other public offices.[123] **13.34**

INVESTIGATING THE ESTATE

Although the estate automatically vests in the trustee at the date of sequestration, they must take practical steps to ingather it. The trustee is given power to take possession of the estate and any document in the debtor's possession related to their assets or business and financial affairs.[124] The trustee is also entitled to access such documents in the hands of a third party and to require delivery of title deeds or documents belonging to the debtor in the hands of a third party.[125] In order to obtain information necessary for their investigation of the estate, the trustee may request the debtor or any other person to appear before them for questioning in respect of the debtor's assets, and may apply for a court order compelling attendance if a person will not comply.[126] A person who fails to attend commits a criminal offence.[127] **13.35**

116 2016 Act, s. 24(6).
117 2016 Act, s. 24(7).
118 2016 Act, s. 24(3)–(5).
119 2016 Act, s. 218(13).
120 2016 Act, s. 218(5).
121 Company Directors Disqualification Act 1986, s. 11(1).
122 Solicitors (Scotland) Act 1980, s. 18(1).
123 Insolvency Act 1986, s. 427.
124 2016 Act, s. 108(1).
125 2016 Act, s. 108(3)–(5).
126 2016 Act, ss. 118 (private examination) and 119 (public examination).
127 2016 Act, ss. 118(7) and 119(8).

13.36 The trustee is also given powers to manage the debtor's estate as necessary for the discharge of their functions. Specifically, they are empowered to: carry on or close down any business of the debtor's; bring, defend or continue any legal proceedings related to the debtor's estate; create a right in security over any part of the estate; make payments or incur liabilities in order to acquire property that is the subject of a right or option; borrow money; and effect or maintain insurance policies.[128] Additionally, the trustee may adopt or decline to adopt any contract entered into by the defender prior to sequestration, or enter into new contracts, if they consider it would be beneficial for the administration of the debtor's estate.[129]

CHALLENGEABLE TRANSACTIONS

13.37 Another aspect of the trustee's role in investigating the estate is to counteract any steps the debtor may have taken during the run up to the sequestration in an attempt to defeat their creditors. Return to the example of our businessman, Gordon. As the only person with full knowledge of his financial situation, he is aware that he is insolvent some time before any of his creditors come to realise that fact. Gordon suspects bankruptcy is on the horizon. He does not want his shop to be taken from him and sold to pay off his creditors, so he decides to 'sell' it to his brother Graeme for a small amount of money. The brothers agree privately that, once the sequestration is over and Gordon has been discharged, Graeme will 'sell' the shop back to Gordon for the same nominal sum. This would allow Gordon to write off his debts and yet still hold on to one of his biggest assets. The law does not consider this to be fair. Accordingly, the trustee has the power to investigate transactions entered into by the debtor in the period prior to the sequestration, and to undo steps taken to defeat the interests of creditors.

13.38 The two most significant types of challengeable transaction are gratuitous alienations and unfair preferences. The trustee is also empowered to challenge financial orders on divorce, excessive pension contributions and extortionate credit transactions. Each of these will be discussed below.

Gratuitous alienations

13.39 The essence of a gratuitous alienation is that the debtor has simply given away part of their estate. Section 98 of the 2016 Act sets out what is required for a transaction of this type to be challenged. In the first place, there must have been an alienation, meaning the debtor must have transferred property out of their estate.[130] This would include the debtor making a cash payment, or renouncing a right or preference. The transfer must have been made within the two years prior to the date of sequestration,[131] unless it was made to an

128 2016 Act, s. 109(5).
129 2016 Act, s. 110.
130 2016 Act, s. 98(1)(a).
131 2016 Act, s. 98(1) and (4)(b). Where the debtor is deceased, the alienation must have been made within two years prior to their death, and their estate sequestrated within twelve months after their death: s. 98(1)(b)(iii).

associate of the debtor, in which case any transfer within five years prior to the sequestration is potentially challengeable.[132] 'Associate' is defined to include spouses and civil partners, relatives and in-laws, business partners, the debtor's employee or employer and a company controlled by the debtor alone or with associates.[133] It does not include a friend of the debtor. The transfer will be considered to have taken place on the date on which it became effectual;[134] so, on the date of registration for transfer of heritable property, for example. If all these requirements are met, the alienation can be challenged by the trustee or any creditor.[135]

Three defences are available to a debtor where a transaction has been challenged on this basis. First, if the debtor can show that at any time after the alienation their assets exceeded their liabilities, the transaction will stand.[136] Secondly, if the debtor can prove that the transaction was for adequate consideration (in other words, was not 'gratuitous'), this will be a defence to a challenge.[137] What will be considered adequate consideration is a question of fact, although the court has indicated that it need not mean 'the best possible price which could have been achieved' so long as the price actually paid was reasonable.[138] Attempts to argue that consideration was given by the transferee in separate transactions are unlikely to find favour with the court, as with the husband who claimed that the transfer of his house to his wife had been paid for by a number of gifts given to him in the past.[139] Thirdly, if the debtor can demonstrate that the alienation was a permitted gift such as a Christmas present or a charitable donation (made to someone other than an associate of the debtor), the transaction will stand.[140] The debtor must show that a gift of this type was reasonable at the time it was made, which may be difficult to do if the debtor was in financial difficulties at that point. **13.40**

If the debtor is unable to defend the transaction, the court must grant decree: (a) of reduction; or (b) for such other restoration of property to the debtor's estate, or such other redress, as may be appropriate.[141] Previously these provisions had been read to suggest that property should be restored to the estate wherever possible, with no discretion available to the court to address any resulting loss to the recipient of the alienation because, for example, the property had increased in value in the time between the alienation and the court order,[142] or the recipient had used the property in question to pay some of the debtor's obligations.[143] Although the recipient would normally have a **13.41**

132 2016 Act, s. 98(1) and (4)(a). Where the debtor is deceased, the alienation must have been made within five years prior to their death, and their estate sequestrated within twelve months after his death: s. 98(1)(b)(iii).
133 2016 Act, s. 229.
134 2016 Act, s. 98(3).
135 2016 Act, s. 98(2). A trustee under a trust deed is also entitled to make a challenge under this subsection.
136 2016 Act, s. 98(6)(a).
137 2016 Act, s. 98(6)(b).
138 *Lafferty Construction v McCombe* 1994 SLT 858.
139 *Matheson's Tr v Matheson* 1992 SLT 685. See also *McFadyen's Tr v McFadyen* 1994 SC 416.
140 2016 Act, s. 98(6)(c).
141 2016 Act, s. 98(5).
142 *Short's Trustee v Chung (No. 1)* 1991 SLT 472.
143 *Cay's Trustee v Cay* 1998 SC 780.

claim against the debtor for their loss in situations of this kind, such a claim is likely to result in little or no payment from a bankrupt debtor's estate. In *MacDonald v Carnbroe Estates*,[144] however, the Supreme Court took the view that the court has power to devise a remedy in which credit can be given in some way for consideration that a bona fide recipient has paid.[145] In this case, the defenders had purchased for £550,000 a property valued on the open market at £1,200,000. Under the statute, the court had the discretion to order, for example, that payment of the purchase price by the insolvency practitioner to the seller was a condition of the restoration of the property to the insolvent estate.[146]

13.42 The statute also makes clear that a third party who has acquired property in good faith and for value from the recipient of a gratuitous alienation should not be prejudiced by a challenge to that alienation.[147] So, where a debtor has gifted property to their wife, and their wife has sold that property on to a good faith third party for value, the court cannot order the property to be restored to the estate. The appropriate remedy in this situation would be for the wife to return the proceeds of the sale to the estate.

13.43 In addition to the statutory regime, it remains possible for a challenge to be made to a gratuitous alienation at common law.[148] This right, originally available only to creditors, is extended to the trustee under the 2016 Act.[149] In order to make a successful common law challenge, the challenger faces a somewhat heavier burden of proof than in the statutory regime, having to demonstrate all three of the following components. First, the alienation must have been gratuitous in the sense described above. Secondly, it must have had a prejudicial effect on creditors. Thirdly, the debtor must have been absolutely insolvent at the time the alienation was made, or else have been rendered absolutely insolvent by the alienation and remained so until the challenge to the transaction was made. This should be contrasted with a statutory challenge, in which the onus of proof would be on the debtor to show that they were *not* insolvent in order to defend the transaction. If a common law challenge can be successfully made out, the advantage to the challenger is that any alienation can be challenged without limit of time. The common law route also enables a creditor to bring a challenge outwith the sequestration process, although a creditor may be unwilling to take on this difficulty and expense when a successful challenge would only lead to the property being restored to the debtor for diligence at the hands of any creditor.

144 [2019] UKSC 57, 2020 SC (UKSC) 23.
145 This case concerned the equivalent statutory provision for gratuitous alienations in corporate insolvencies: Insolvency Act 1986, s. 242(a).
146 *MacDonald v Carnbroe Estates Ltd* [2019] UKSC 57, 2020 SC (UKSC) 23 at [69] per Lord Hodge.
147 2016 Act, s. 98(7).
148 Bell, *Commentaries* II, 170.
149 2016 Act, s. 98(11). A trustee under a trust deed is also entitled to make a challenge under this section.

Unfair preferences

A preference is unfair if the debtor has given it to one creditor at the expense of the others. Imagine that Gordon, on the verge of bankruptcy, decides he wishes to maintain a good relationship with his creditor, Heather, so that she will lend him money once again after the sequestration has been dealt with. He grants her a standard security over his shop, which is his principal asset, in respect of debts which have been outstanding for several years. In the sequestration proceedings which follow, Heather as a secured creditor will have a preference since sequestration does not affect the rights of secured creditors.[150] Gordon and Heather are happy, but the other creditors are out of pocket. The law considers this to be inequitable, so such preferences are challengeable. **13.44**

Grant of a security to a creditor is one example of a preference which could be unfair. Paying off a debt before it falls due, particularly when other debt payments are overdue, is another example. Any action by the debtor that favours one creditor over the others may fall within this category. **13.45**

The statute allows a challenge to be made to any unfair preference granted to a creditor within the six months prior to the date of sequestration.[151] A challenge can be brought by the trustee or any creditor.[152] **13.46**

The statute also sets out four categories of transactions that cannot be challenged as creating an unfair preference: **13.47**

(a) a transaction in the ordinary course of trade or business.[153] This would include paying a debt as it fell due, or performing any other obligation under a contract at the required time;
(b) a payment in cash for a debt which had fallen due, unless the transaction was collusive with the purpose of prejudicing the general body of creditors;[154]
(c) a transaction where the debtor and creditor undertake reciprocal obligations.[155] Again, this exception does not apply where there was collusion to defeat the interests of other creditors; or
(d) the grant of a mandate by the debtor to pay over arrested funds.[156]

As with gratuitous alienations, if the debtor is unable to defend the transaction, the court has three options: to order reduction of the deed effecting the preference, as with the grant of a standard security; to order restoration of the property to the estate, as with early payment of a debt; or to grant 'such other redress as may be appropriate'.[157] Where a creditor transfers property **13.48**

150 2016 Act, s. 88(3) and s. 129(9).
151 2016 Act, s. 99(1). Where the debtor is deceased, the preference must have been granted within the six months prior to their death and their estate sequestrated within twelve months after their death.
152 2016 Act, s. 99(5). A trustee under a trust deed is also entitled to make a challenge under this section.
153 2016 Act, s. 99(2)(a).
154 2016 Act, s. 99(2)(b) and (3).
155 2016 Act, s. 99(2)(c) and (3).
156 2016 Act, s. 99(2)(d). For the rules of arrestment, see paras 12.27–12.30.
157 2016 Act, s. 99(6).

acquired via an unfair preference to a third party, the third party's title will be protected so long as the transfer was in good faith and for value.[158]

13.49 Fraudulent preferences can also be challenged at common law.[159] This right, originally available only to creditors, is extended to the trustee under the 2016 Act.[160] Despite the use of the word 'fraudulent', it is not necessary for a challenger to demonstrate a fraudulent intention on the part of the debtor or the creditor in receipt of the preference.[161] What the challenger must prove is that the debtor carried out a voluntary act[162] which preferred one creditor to the prejudice of others, at a time when they were absolutely insolvent and knew themselves to be so.[163] It is irrelevant whether the creditor was aware of the debtor's state of solvency.

13.50 It has been said that the first three statutory defences outlined above will also operate as a defence against a common law fraudulent preference claim. McBryde argued[164] that these are only examples of situations in which a defence might be made out: the real question is whether the defender can show their act was not voluntary, they were not insolvent, or they did not know themselves to be insolvent. If that is the case, a wider range of potential defences is available to the debtor at common law. The advantage of a successful common law challenge here, as with gratuitous alienations, is that preferences granted at any time can be challenged, not just those granted within the six-month statutory time limit. Additionally, an interested creditor need not wait until sequestration proceedings are underway in order to bring their challenge.

Recall of financial orders on divorce

13.51 On divorce or dissolution of civil partnership, the court can make a number of financial orders to ensure that both parties leave the relationship with a fair share of the property. A party can be ordered to pay a capital sum to their former spouse or civil partner,[165] to transfer specific property,[166] or to share rights in a pension fund.[167] The trustee may ask the court retrospectively to reconsider an order of this kind[168] in the following circumstances:

158 2016 Act, s. 99(7).

159 Bell, *Commentaries* II, 170.

160 2016 Act, s. 99(8). A trustee under a trust deed is also entitled to make a challenge under this section.

161 The fraud is 'insolvency fraud' in the sense used in Stair, *Institutions* I.9.15; *M'Gowan v Wright* (1853) 15 D 494; *Dryburgh v Scotts Media Tax Ltd (in liquidation)* [2014] CSIH 45, 2014 SC 651 at [30] per Lord Drummond Young.

162 *Nordic Travel Ltd v Scotprint Ltd* 1980 SC 1.

163 See, e.g. *Liquidator of Letham Grange Development Co Ltd v Foxworth Investments Ltd* [2014] UKSC 41, 2014 SC (UKSC) 203.

164 W W McBryde, *Bankruptcy*, 2nd edn (Edinburgh: W. Green, 1995), p. 317.

165 Family Law (Scotland) Act 1985, s. 8(1)(a) and (2).

166 1985 Act, s. 8(1)(aa) and (2).

167 1985 Act, s. 8(1)(baa) and (2).

168 2016 Act, s. 100(2). A trustee under a trust deed is also entitled to make a challenge under this section.

- on the date the order was made, the party subject to the order was absolutely insolvent, or was rendered absolutely insolvent as a result of the order;[169] or
- within five years of the order being made, the party subject to the order was sequestrated.[170]

The court has the power to order the debtor's former spouse or civil partner to return any or all property or capital transferred. However, it can only do so after having regard to all the circumstances of the case, including the financial circumstances in which the debtor's former spouse or civil partner now finds themselves.[171]

Recovery of excessive pension contributions

Any share the debtor may have in an approved pension scheme is excluded from the debtor's estate vesting in the trustee.[172] Payments received from a pension fund are classed as income and remain with the debtor.[173] For this reason, a debtor who fears bankruptcy may choose to make substantial contributions to their pension fund in order to keep the funds out of reach of their creditors. If the trustee considers that the debtor's pension contributions have unfairly prejudiced their creditors, they may make an application to court for an order restoring the position to what it would have been had the contributions not been made.[174] The court, having satisfied itself that the contributions were excessive in the circumstances and designed to put assets beyond the reach of creditors,[175] may make such order as it thinks fit. This is likely to include ordering the pension fund administrators to restore some or all of the pension contributions to the debtor's estate, and to adjust the benefits the debtor or any dependent is entitled to receive from the pension fund.[176] **13.52**

Extortionate credit transactions

A debtor in a difficult financial position may find themselves borrowing money on extremely uncompetitive terms. If a debtor has entered into a credit transaction within three years prior to the sequestration on terms which the trustee considers extortionate,[177] they can apply to court to have the transaction varied or set aside, and for funds or property paid over in respect of the transaction to be restored to the estate.[178] The statute defines an extortionate transaction as one which required 'grossly exorbitant' payments to be made or otherwise **13.53**

169 2016 Act, s. 100(1)(b).
170 2016 Act, s. 100(1)(c). Where the debtor is deceased, they must have died within five years of the order being made and the estate must have been sequestrated within twelve months after their death: s. 100(1)(c)(iii).
171 2016 Act, s. 100(3).
172 Welfare Reform and Pensions Act 1999, ss. 11 and 12 (as read with s. 13) and the Occupational Pension Schemes (Bankruptcy) (No. 2) Regulations 2002 (SI 2002/836), regs 2 and 11.
173 2016 Act, s. 85(1); *Cook v Accountant in Bankruptcy* 2020 SLT (Sh Ct) 1 (lump sum payment considered to be income).
174 2016 Act, s. 101(1) and (3).
175 2016 Act, s. 101(2) and (7).
176 2016 Act, s. 102(1).
177 2016 Act, s. 209(1)–(2).
178 2016 Act, s. 209(5).

'grossly contravened' the principles of fair dealing.[179] Where the trustee makes an application under this section of the statute, it will be presumed that the transaction was extortionate, with the onus of proof resting on the credit provider to demonstrate the terms were fair and reasonable.[180]

REALISING THE ESTATE

13.54 Once the trustee has ascertained the contents of the estate and restored any property to which the creditors are entitled in terms of the challengeable transactions outlined above, their next task will be to realise the property in order that it can be paid over to creditors.[181] In addition to the management powers outlined above[182] that enable the trustee to take possession of the estate, the trustee is empowered to sell off any part of it by public sale or private bargain.[183] Estate property cannot, however, be bought by the trustee, any associate of theirs or any commissioner.[184]

13.55 Where the estate contains heritable property subject to a security, both the secured creditor and the trustee have power to sell.[185] The trustee cannot exercise their power here without the agreement of the secured creditor, unless it is clear that the sale proceeds will pay off the debt to that creditor in full. Once either party indicates an intention to sell, the other party cannot take steps to do so. Where one party has commenced sale proceedings, the other is entitled to seek a remedy from court if the sale is unduly delayed.[186]

13.56 As an exception to the general rule on heritable property, the trustee does not have an automatic right to sell the debtor's family home, defined to mean a place in which the debtor and/or their current or former spouse or civil partner and/or any child of the family was resident on the day immediately preceding the sequestration.[187] The trustee must seek consent to the sale from the spouse or civil partner. If there is no spouse or civil partner, but the debtor lives in the home with a child of the family, the trustee must seek the consent of the debtor.[188] If consent is not given, the trustee can apply to court for authority to make the sale.[189] The court can give or refuse authority subject to any appropriate conditions after having regard to all the circumstances of the case, including the needs and financial resources of any resident of the house, and the interests of the creditors.[190] If the trustee does not exercise the power of sale within three years of the date of sequestration, the family home will reinvest in

179 2016 Act, s. 209(3).
180 2016 Act, s. 209(4).
181 2016 Act, s. 50(1)(a)–(b).
182 See para. 13.23.
183 2016 Act, ss. 50(1)(a) and 109(6).
184 2016 Act, s. 109(11). For an explanation of the role of commissioner, see para. 13.26.
185 2016 Act, s. 109(7).
186 2016 Act, s. 109(7)(c).
187 2016 Act, s. 113(1) and (7).
188 2016 Act, s. 113(1)(a) and (7).
189 2016 Act, s. 113(1)(b).
190 2016 Act, s. 113(2). For discussion, see *Accountant in Bankruptcy v Brooks* [2020] SAC Civ 15, 2020 GWD 38-488.

the debtor.[191] It should be noted that where a secured creditor seeks to sell the family home, they are not subject to the conditions outlined above, although they will have to comply with the usual protections available to a debtor where a home is sold under a standard security.[192]

PAYMENT OF CREDITORS

Having realised the estate, the trustee must then arrange to pay the creditors and eventually bring the sequestration to an end. **13.57**

Submission of claims

Any creditor who believes they have a right in the sequestration must submit a claim to the trustee.[193] Where a statutory meeting has been held, claims will normally have been submitted in advance since, without a claim, a creditor has no right to vote at the meeting.[194] Otherwise, a claim must be submitted not later than 120 days after the trustee has invited submissions, or the creditor will not be entitled to share in dividend payments made by the trustee at the end of that accounting period.[195] So long as a claim has been submitted once, it will be included in every subsequent dividend paid out by the trustee.[196] The form of the claim is prescribed by statute, which requires the creditor to provide details of each debt owed to them and any security held in respect of that debt, as well as an account or voucher as evidence that the debt exists.[197] A creditor who submits a false claim or evidence in support of it commits an offence.[198] **13.58**

A creditor is entitled to claim the amount owed plus interest due at the date of sequestration.[199] Where the debt is secured, unless the creditor wishes to surrender the security for the benefit of the estate, the value of the security must be deducted from their claim.[200] If a creditor has not exercised their rights under a security within twelve weeks of the date of sequestration, they can be compelled to transfer the security to the trustee in exchange for payment of the secured debt.[201] Where the debtor has previously been ordered by the court to pay aliment or a periodical allowance to a spouse, civil partner or child, or where they undertook to make such payments in a formal written agreement, a claim can be made in respect of any arrears.[202] A claim can also be made in respect of a contingent debt: that is, a debt that may come into existence at **13.59**

191 2016 Act, s. 112.
192 See the discussion at paras 11.35–11.48.
193 2016 Act, s. 122.
194 2016 Act, ss. 122(1) and 128.
195 2016 Act, ss. 122(4)–(5) and 128.
196 2016 Act, s. 122(8). In other words, it is not necessary to resubmit the claim in every accounting period.
197 2016 Act, s. 122(9).
198 2016 Act, s. 124.
199 2016 Act, Sch. 2, para. 1(1).
200 2016 Act, Sch. 1, para. 4(1).
201 2016 Act, Sch. 1, para. 2.
202 2016 Act, Sch. 1, para. 3.

some future point.[203] For example, if the debtor is defending a court action at the date of sequestration and may be ordered to make a damages payment at the conclusion of the proceedings, the pursuer may wish to submit a claim in respect of that potential future payment. A creditor in this situation has the option to submit a claim at the time of sequestration, the value of which will be estimated by the trustee, or alternatively to wait until the debt comes into existence and make the claim at that stage (the risk being that the whole estate may already have been paid out by then).

Adjudication of claims

13.60 When the trustee has funds available to make payment, they will accept or reject every claim submitted in respect of the estate,[204] and determine where a claim should rank in the order of priority.[205] They are entitled to ask the creditor or any relevant person for further evidence in support of the validity or value of a claim if they consider it necessary.[206] Where a claim is rejected, the trustee must give the claimant written reasons for the rejection[207] and the claimant is entitled to appeal the decision to the AiB, and thereafter to the sheriff.[208] The debtor may also appeal any acceptance or rejection of claims against their estate.[209]

Distribution of estate

13.61 The trustee will pay the claims they have accepted in the order of priority set out by the statute.[210] It should be recalled that secured debts do not form part of this list, since the security can be exercised outside of the sequestration process, or surrendered to creditors in exchange for full repayment of the secured debt.[211] Broadly speaking, priority is given to the expenses of the sequestration itself, which is why a creditor is unwise to apply for sequestration if the debtor's estate is limited. After the expenses are paid, the order of payment is as follows:

(a) outlays and remuneration of the interim trustee, if appointed;
(b) outlays and remuneration of the trustee;
(c) deathbed and funeral expenses of the debtor if appropriate, and expenses reasonably incurred in administering the deceased's estate;
(d) expenses incurred by a creditor who petitioned for sequestration;
(e) ordinary preferred debts (primarily debts owed to employees including arrears of pension contributions, holiday pay and wages up to four months prior to the date of sequestration, up to a prescribed amount per employee, currently £800);[212]

203 2016 Act, Sch. 1, para. 3. See also *Crighton v Crighton's Tr* 1999 SLT (Sh Ct) 113.
204 2016 Act, s. 126(1).
205 2016 Act, s. 126(7).
206 2016 Act, s. 123.
207 2016 Act, s. 126(6).
208 2016 Act, s. 127.
209 2016 Act, s. 127.
210 2016 Act, s. 129.
211 See para. 13.58.
212 2016 Act, s. 129(1)(e) and Sch. 3.

(f) secondary preferred debts;[213]
(g) ordinary non-preferential debts, followed by secondary and tertiary non-preferential debts;[214]
(h) interest on preferred debts and ordinary debts accrued after the date of sequestration; and
(i) postponed debts (including repayment of a loan made to a debtor by their spouse or civil partner, and any payment owed to the transferee in respect of a gratuitous alienation successfully challenged by the trustee).[215]

Each category of debts will be paid in full before the next category is entitled to any payment at all. For example, if the whole value of the estate is required to cover the expenses of the sequestration (categories (a)–(d) above), preferred creditors and everyone below them on the list will receive nothing. **13.62**

Where there are insufficient funds to pay every creditor within a particular category in full, each creditor in that category will be paid a rateable portion of what they are owed.[216] So, imagine that Gordon owes £1,500 of ordinary non-preferential debt, of which Ian is owed £500 and Isabel is owed £1,000. Once all prior ranking creditors in the sequestration have been paid, only £750 remains in the estate – half of what is needed to pay all the ordinary debts. Accordingly, each ordinary creditor receives half of what they are owed, meaning Ian is paid £250 and Isabel is paid £500. Any creditor ranked lower than an ordinary creditor will receive nothing at all. **13.63**

In the highly unlikely event that surplus funds remain in the estate once all debts are paid in full, those funds will be paid over to the debtor.[217] **13.64**

TERMINATING THE SEQUESTRATION

Once the estate has been paid out to creditors, the sequestration can be brought to an end. This requires both the debtor and the trustee to be discharged. **13.65**

Discharge of debtor

Once at least twelve months has passed since the date of sequestration, the debtor may be discharged by the AiB. Where the AiB is not the trustee in sequestration, it must consider a report from the trustee[218] on the sequestration proceedings and the debtor's conduct,[219] together with any representations from creditors in respect of the same,[220] before determining whether the discharge should be granted.[221] Where the AiB is the trustee in sequestration, it must prepare a report on the same matters[222] when determining whether the **13.66**

213 Certain types of consumer deposit, set out in the 2016 Act, Sch. 3, paras 7–8.
214 Defined in the 2016 Act, s. 129A.
215 2016 Act, s. 129(4).
216 2016 Act, s. 129(5).
217 2016 Act, s. 129(6).
218 2016 Act, s. 137(4).
219 2016 Act, s. 137(5).
220 2016 Act, s. 137(3)(b).
221 2016 Act, s. 137(1)–(3).
222 2016 Act, s. 138(3).

discharge should be granted.[223] In both cases, a copy of the report must be provided to the debtor and every known creditor.[224] The trustee (if not the AiB), the debtor and any creditor may apply for a review of the decision to the AiB[225] and thereafter to the sheriff.[226]

13.67 Where a sequestration has followed on an application by the debtor under the 'low asset' route,[227] the debtor is discharged automatically six months after the date of sequestration.[228]

13.68 Discharge of the debtor has two main effects. First, the various restrictions to which the debtor was subject as a result of the sequestration are lifted.[229] Secondly, the debtor is discharged from all debts due at the date of the sequestration with a few limited exceptions.[230] Discharge of the debtor does not bring the sequestration itself to an end, so the debtor remains under an obligation to co-operate with the trustee.[231]

13.69 Where the debtor has not co-operated with the trustee, or otherwise failed to conduct themselves appropriately during the sequestration process,[232] the AiB can make a bankruptcy restrictions order, or apply to the sheriff to do the same.[233] The effect of such an order is that the debtor remains subject to some or all of the legal restrictions that affected them during the sequestration for a further period of time.

Discharge of the trustee

13.70 It is not mandatory for the trustee to seek a discharge from the sequestration, but in most cases they will wish to do so, as discharge signals an end to their liability to debtors and creditors in respect of their dealings with the estate.[234] The trustee can apply to the AiB for discharge once they have made a final division of the debtor's estate amongst the creditors and provided the AiB with final audited accounts for the sequestration proceedings.[235] The debtor and creditors are entitled to inspect the accounts and make written representations to the AiB as to the trustee's application for discharge.[236] The AiB may then grant or refuse the application.[237] A separate procedure is set out for situations where the AiB acted as trustee.[238]

223 2016 Act, s. 138(1)–(2).
224 2016 Act, ss. 137(6)(a), 138(3)(c) and 138(6)(c).
225 2016 Act, s. 139(1)–(2).
226 2016 Act, s. 139(6).
227 See para. 13.14.
228 2016 Act, s. 140.
229 See para. 13.34.
230 2016 Act, s. 145.
231 2016 Act, s. 215(6).
232 2016 Act, s. 156.
233 2016 Act, s. 155(1).
234 2016 Act, s. 148(7).
235 2016 Act, s. 148(1).
236 2016 Act, s. 148(4).
237 2016 Act, s. 148(5).
238 2016 Act, s. 151.

In the overwhelming majority of cases, discharge of the trustee marks a practical end to the sequestration process. If, following the discharge of the trustee but within five years of the date of the sequestration, it is discovered that the debtor had further assets in their estate at the time of the sequestration, it is possible for a new trustee to be appointed to deal with the new assets, however.[239] 13.71

TRUST DEED FOR CREDITORS

A debtor and their creditors may seek to avoid the expense and administrative burden of sequestration by agreeing amongst themselves that the debtor will transfer some or all of their estate to a trustee to administer on the creditors' behalf. In addition to being less expensive, a voluntary arrangement of this sort allows for greater flexibility than formal sequestration, meaning the debtor may negotiate to retain particular assets, perhaps in exchange for a contribution from their income for a set period of time, for example. If the voluntary arrangement ceased to function effectively, it would remain open to parties to instigate formal sequestration proceedings. 13.72

A simple trust deed is essentially a private arrangement, regulated under the general law of trusts. In this situation, the trustee would not be able to make use of the statutory powers enabling a formal trustee in sequestration to investigate the estate or challenge transactions unless these were explicitly provided for in the trust deed. The major drawback to an ordinary trust deed, however, is that it can only bind creditors who expressly agree to its terms, meaning other creditors are not prevented from performing diligence or raising sequestration proceedings. 13.73

If a trust deed meets certain requirements, however, it will be deemed a protected trust deed that binds all creditors.[240] The principal requirements are that the debtor must be a person who could be sequestrated and who has debts not less than £5,000;[241] the trustee is a person who would not be disqualified from acting as a trustee in a formal sequestration process;[242] the deed provides for vesting in the trustee of all assets that would vest in a formal sequestration process;[243] the deed provides for payment of a debtor's contribution in appropriate circumstances;[244] the deed is published in the Register of Insolvencies;[245] and a copy of the trust deed and other relevant information is sent to every creditor known to the trustee.[246] Unless a majority of creditors by number or a third of the creditors by value object to the trust deed in writing within five weeks, all creditors will be deemed to have agreed to its terms.[247] The trustee then sends copies of the relevant information to the AiB, who will record the 13.74

239 2016 Act, s. 152.
240 2016 Act, ss. 163 and 172.
241 2016 Act, s. 164.
242 2016 Act, s. 165.
243 2016 Act, s. 167.
244 2016 Act, s. 168.
245 2016 Act, s. 169.
246 2016 Act, s. 170(1).
247 2016 Act, s. 170(2).

details in the Register of Insolvencies.[248] One registered, the trust deed will be protected.[249]

13.75 Where a trust deed is protected, it prevents a creditor from petitioning for sequestration or performing diligence, even where they were not aware of the deed or objected to it.[250] It also allows the trustee or any creditor to challenge certain transactions as outlined above.[251]

248 2016 Act, s. 171.
249 2016 Act, s. 171.
250 2016 Act, s. 172.
251 See paras 13.37–13.50.

Chapter Fourteen

Corporate Insolvency

Ross Anderson and Elisabeth Roxburgh

INTRODUCTION

This chapter deals with the dissolution of juristic persons. The paradigm juristic person is the company and the focus of this chapter is the Scots law of corporate insolvency as applied to companies. A major reason for dissolution is insolvency and the greater part of this chapter is concerned with those rules. But insolvency does not necessarily mean dissolution; and dissolution, like the death of natural persons, may occur for reasons other than insolvency. 14.01

The Scots law of corporate insolvency is not always easy to access. The principal legislation is the Insolvency Act 1986 (the 'IA 1986'). Some rules are found in the Companies Act 2006. Although the corporate insolvency provisions no longer cross-refer to the rules on personal bankruptcy, the IA 1986 cannot be read in isolation. It must be considered together with the provisions of the Insolvency (Scotland) (Company Voluntary Arrangements and Administration) Rules 2018 (the 'CVA and Administration Rules');[1] the Insolvency (Scotland) (Receivership and Winding-up) Rules 2018 (the 'Winding-up Rules');[2] or, in some cases still, the Insolvency (Scotland) Rules 1986.[3] 14.02

In addition, it is necessary to consider the domestic legislation in the context of the retained version of the Recast EU Insolvency Regulation, which applies following implementation period (IP) completion day.[4] All this must also be considered in the context of an extensive case law interpreting those provisions, setting out various common law rules and decided within the framework of the applicable rules of court.[5] 14.03

A long-overdue consolidation of personal bankruptcy law took place in the Bankruptcy (Scotland) Act 2016.[6] There appears to be no prospect of Scots corporate insolvency law being set down in consolidated form. 14.04

1 Insolvency (Scotland) (Company Voluntary Arrangements and Administration) Rules 2018 (SI 2018/1082).
2 Insolvency (Scotland) (Receivership and Winding-up) Rules 2018 (SSI 2018/347).
3 The Insolvency (Scotland) Rules 1986 (SI 1986/1915) continue to apply where an LLP is subject to an insolvency proceeding: see para. 14.44 below.
4 Retained Recast EUIR (2015/848) as amended by the Insolvency (Amendment) (EU Exit) Regulations 2019 (SI 2019/146). See further para. 14.8 below.
5 The principal court rules are found in the Act of Sederunt (Sheriff Court Company Insolvency Rules) 1986 (SI 1986/2297) and the RCS, Ch. 74.
6 See Chapter Thirteen: Bankruptcy.

GENERAL PRINCIPLES OF INSOLVENCY

Pari passu principle

14.05 Insolvency is, by definition, unfair: where liabilities exceed assets, creditors must lose out.[7] In those circumstances, Scots law, like most legal systems, favours egalitarian over individual equity.[8] The principle is known in the IA 1986 as the '*pari passu* principle'.[9] Each unsecured creditor receives the same *pro rata* dividend from the insolvent estate: a general creditor, A, with a claim of £1m will receive the same dividend as B, a general creditor for £100: if the dividend is 5p in the pound (5 per cent) A receives £50,000 and B £5. Scots law is particularly reluctant to listen to individual creditors who argue for special treatment.

Ranking

14.06 In general terms, whereas the unsecured or general creditors rank *pari passu*, secured creditors are entitled to look to the particular asset over which they hold a security. A bank, holding a standard security over an insolvent company's ownership of land, is entitled to sell the land and pay itself from the proceeds. Take the example of the standard security, for the purposes of corporate insolvency law it is a 'fixed charge'. Fixed charges are essentially proper rights in security.[10] Fixed charges may be contrasted with 'floating' charges. Floating charges have been dealt with in the context of rights in security; it is important to emphasise, however, that floating charges play a central role in corporate insolvency law: their function is as much a tool for taking control of a restructuring or insolvency procedure, since a 'qualifying floating charge' (QFC)[11] confers on the holder the power to appoint an administrator.

14.07 The differences between fixed and floating charges are important in relation to ranking. In principle, a fixed charge ranks ahead of a floating charge. That principle is often inverted in practice, however, because almost all floating charges contain a negative pledge clause.[12] Holders of fixed or floating charges are each secured creditors[13] and, in principle, secured creditors rank ahead of unsecured creditors. In the case of the floating charge, however, particularly where the assets are insufficient, there are a number of exceptions to that principle.

7 G L Gretton, 'Ownership and Insolvency' (2004) 8 Edin LR 389–395.

8 *Mansfield v Walker's Tr* (1833) 11 S 813 at 828 per Lord Craigie: 'It is a rule established, beyond all memory, that there are no [individual] equities in competitions among creditors' (affd (1835) 1 Sh & McL 203, 3 Ross LC 139). In the litigation arising out of the fraudulent scheme concocted by one Carlo Pietro Giovanni Guglielmo Tebaldo Ponzi (the original 'Ponzi Scheme'), *Cunningham v Brown* (1924) 265 US 1 (68 L Ed 873) at 13 (877), Taft CJ observed that '[this] is a case the circumstances of which call strongly for the principle that equality is equity, and this is the spirit of the bankrupt law'.

9 IA 1986, s. 107; *Re Nortel GmbH (in administration)* [2013] UKSC 52, [2014] AC 209, at [35] per Lord Neuberger.

10 See Chapter Eleven: Non-judicial Real Security.

11 IA 1986, Sch. B1, para. 14(2) and (3): see para. 14.49 below.

12 See para. 14.82, n 244 below.

13 IA 1986, s. 248(b).

The practical result, therefore, in general terms, means the order of ranking (subject always to the facts of the case, sufficiency of assets and the application of the actual provisions applicable to the applicable insolvency proceeding(s)) tends to look more like this: 14.08

(a) Fixed chargeholders (although secured creditors usually do not claim).[14]
(b) A1 moratorium debts.[15]
(c) Expenses.[16]
(d) Preferential creditors.[17]
(e) Prescribed part (where it applies).[18]
(f) Floating chargeholders.
(g) Unsecured creditors.[19]

Where a creditor seeks to rank their claim in the insolvency of a company, this is sometimes known, according to the English terminology, as 'proving' in the liquidation: the creditor has to adduce evidence to the liquidator or administrator that the debt exists.[20] The process of adjudication is intended to be relatively light touch and is provisional in that the proving creditor and any other dissatisfied creditor may seek to appeal the ruling.[21] 14.09

Expenses[22]

Insolvency practitioners – normally chartered accountants – charge significant professional fees. The remuneration of insolvency practitioners and their advisors is a subject of importance. Suffice it to say for present purposes that the insolvency practitioner's fees may be authorised either by the company's creditors or by the court, with the result that many reported insolvency cases deal with questions of remuneration.[23] Where the assets of the company are insufficient to satisfy the liabilities, the court may make an order as to the 14.10

14 Winding-up Rules (n 2), r. 7.24; CVA and Administration Rules (n 1), r. 3.113.

15 IA 1986, s. 174A; Sch. B1, para. 64A. For the A1 moratorium, see para. 14.64 below.

16 IA 1986, Sch. B1, paras 64A, 65, 99, and 116 (administration); IA 1986, s. 60 (receivership); IA 1986, s. 115 (voluntary liquidation).

17 IA 1986, s. 175 as read with Companies Act 1985, s. 464(4); Sch. B1, para. 65.

18 IA 1986, s. 176A(6): see para. 14.89 below.

19 Winding-up Rules (n 2), rr. 7.24 and 7.27(4) is subject to s. 175; CVA and Administration Rules (n 1), rr. 3.113 and 3.115(4) is subject to s. 175.

20 Although this requirement to provide documentary evidence may be dispensed with: see Winding-up Rules (n 2), r. 7.16(2); CVA and Administration Rules (n 1), r. 3.105(2).

21 *Michael J Lonsdale Ltd v Bresco Electrical Services Ltd* [2020] UKSC 25, [2020] Bus LR 1140 at [32] per Lord Briggs.

22 Winding-up Rules (n 2), r. 7.28; for administration expenses, see CVA and Administration Rules (n 1), r. 3.116.

23 The conduct of professional advisors was criticised in *Joint Administrators of Martin Groundland & Co Ltd, Petrs* [2011] CSOH 14; *Liquidator of St Margaret's School Edinburgh Ltd, Noter* [2013] CSOH 4, 2013 SLT 241 and *Quantum Distribution (UK) Ltd (in liquidation)* [2012] CSOH 191, 2013 SLT 211. A summary of the normal procedure – which, for the uninitiated, is not immediately obvious from the face of the legislation – is contained in Lord Glennie's opinion in *Joint Liquidators of Park Gardens Investments Ltd, Petrs* 2011 SC 243; see further *Liquidator of Exchange Trading Ltd, Noter* 2018 SLT 710; and *Thomas Auld & Sons Ltd (in Liquidation)* [2019] CSOH 83.

payment of the expenses incurred in the winding up out of the assets of the company in such order of priority as the court thinks just.[24]

Preferential creditors

14.11 There are detailed provisions on preferential debts.[25] Preferential debts are essentially contributions to occupational pension schemes and remuneration of employees;[26] levies on coal and steel production;[27] and debts owed to the financial services compensation scheme.[28] These are known collectively as the 'ordinary preferential debts'.[29] In addition, other deposits[30] and certain debts due to HMRC are also preferential debts.[31] These are 'secondary preferential debts'.[32]

Prescribed part

14.12 Since the Enterprise Act 2002, the IA 1986 also makes provision for a fund – the 'prescribed part' – for unsecured creditors.[33] The prescribed part applies to liquidation (including where there is a provisional liquidator), administration, and receivership. The rules relating to the prescribed part are dealt with more fully below.[34]

Contracting out and ranking agreements

14.13 The courts have always been alive to creditors seeking to improve their position on the insolvency of a debtor. A creditor is, subject to rules attacking transactions entered into on the eve of insolvency, entitled to seek security to improve its position. However, the court will not allow parties to contract out of the operation of insolvency law. So suppose A Ltd has a contract with B Ltd. The contract provides that, on A Ltd suffering an 'insolvency event', B Ltd shall have no obligation to pay anything to A Ltd and that A Ltd may not enforce any rights that A Ltd may have against B Ltd. Such a provision is invalid because it is an attempt to contract out of the operation of insolvency law on A's assets. Similarly, any contractual provision designed to transfer A Ltd's assets to another company, where the transfer is intended to take effect after the commencement of a winding up, is void.[35] The rule against contracting out is also the rationale for what is known in English law as the

24 IA 1986, s. 156 and see *Joint Liquidators of Doonin Plant Ltd* [2018] CSOH 89 2019 SLT 195 for an example of such an order being granted.
25 IA 1986, ss. 175(3), 386 and Sch. 6.
26 IA 1986, s. 386 and Sch. 6, paras 8–15. The maximum amount prescribed under paras 9 and 12 for remuneration is £800 per person: Insolvency Proceedings (Monetary Limits) Order 1986 (SI 1986/1996), art. 4.
27 IA 1986, s. 386 and Sch. 6, para. 15A.
28 IA 1986, s. 386 and Sch. 6, paras 15AA and 15B.
29 IA 1986, s. 386(1A).
30 IA 1986, s. 386 and Sch. 6, paras 15BA–15BB.
31 IA 1986, s. 386(1) and Sch. 6, para. 15D.
32 IA 1986, s. 386(1B).
33 IA 1986, s. 176A.
34 See paras 11.71 above and 14.89 below.
35 IA 1986, s. 127(1).

'anti-deprivation' principle:[36] Alexandra cannot agree with Brian that, on the event of Alexandra's bankruptcy, certain of Alexandra's assets will become Brian's property. The 'anti-deprivation' principle has always been of more limited importance in Scotland since, at common law, it has never been possible to transfer patrimonial rights *solo consensu*. The important point is that the various rules described seek to implement a general public policy: to prevent a fraud on the insolvency statutes.[37] Fraud, in this sense, means insolvency fraud.[38]

Commercial agreements, such as intellectual property licences, or finance leases, entered into in good faith with no intention to deprive the insolvent estate, but which contain resolutive conditions, bringing the contract to an end on specified events, such as insolvency events, do not therefore normally offend the principle.[39] However, in 2020 statutory provisions were introduced that went further than the common law and prevented the enforcement of certain standard clauses found in commercial agreements. The provisions apply in relation to contracts for the supply of goods or services and provide that any terms which automatically terminate the contract, or give the supplier the option to terminate, on an insolvency event, 'cease to have effect'.[40] If the supplier wishes to terminate the contract, it will require to obtain the consent of the insolvency practitioner appointed to the company or the permission of the court.[41] Whilst a number of the provisions brought into force at the commencement of the COVID-19 pandemic have since been revoked, this provision remains in force. 14.14

A ranking agreement (sometimes known by its English name, an 'intercreditor') does not amount to contracting out of insolvency law. Suppose Alpha Ltd is a first ranking creditor by virtue of an all sums floating charge containing a negative pledge. Bravo sarl is a second ranking creditor but it holds a fixed security over particular heritable assets in Scotland. It is possible for Alpha and Bravo to agree between themselves as to how they exercise their rights *qua* secured creditors. 14.15

Pre-insolvency and post-insolvency debts

It has been seen that the general principle is that unsecured creditors of an insolvent company rank *pari passu*. That principle is rudimentary. But the principle assumes that it is possible to identify who is actually a creditor of the 14.16

36 See *British Eagle International Airlines Ltd v Compagnie Nationale Air France* [1975] 1 WLR 758 and R M Goode, 'Perpetual Trustee and Flip Clauses in Swap Transactions' (2011) 127 *LQR* 1.

37 *Belmont Park Investments Pty Ltd v BNY Corporate Trustee Services Ltd* [2011] UKSC 38, [2012] 1 AC 383 at [102]–[106] per Lord Collins; [121] per Lord Walker (founding on *R v J* [2005] 1 AC 562, [64] per Lord Rodger of Earlsferry); and [159]–[165] per Lord Mance. Cf the dictum of Lord Coalston quoted at (n 324) below.

38 *Belmont Park* (n 37) at [151] per Lord Mance. For the Scottish authorities on fraud on insolvency, see para. 14.97 below.

39 See, e.g. *Granor Finance Ltd v Liquidator of Eastore Ltd* 1974 SLT 296; *EFT Commercial Ltd v Security Change Ltd* 1992 SC 414.

40 IA 1986, s. 233B (inserted by the Corporate Insolvency and Governance Act 2020).

41 IA 1986, s. 233B(5).

company. Identifying who is a creditor may be more difficult than might be imagined, especially in relation to contingent liabilities:[42]

> 'A fundamental principle that underlies insolvency law is that all creditors as at the date of bankruptcy or winding up are entitled to share equally in the debtor's funds. If a person is a creditor at that date, even if he is merely a contingent creditor, he is entitled to share equally with the other creditors. If, however, he is not a creditor in any sense at that date, he cannot participate in the division of the assets among the creditors. Thus a person who has a mere *spes obligationis* would have no locus to participate in such a division.'

Future liabilities and contingent liabilities

14.17 On insolvency – including, for these purposes, working out whether a company is insolvent at all[43] – it is often necessary to consider future or contingent liabilities. As Bell put it, 'debts are either presently due; or due at a future day certain; or due provisionally, in a certain event. The first are called pure; the second, future; the last, contingent debts'.[44] Future obligations are presently owed, but are payable only in the future (*debitum in praesenti, solvendum in futuro*). A sum due on someone's death will become due sometime (under the law of mortality). Contingent obligations, in contrast, may never become due. A sum due only on a person marrying may never become due because not everyone marries. The law on contingent debts is of general importance: debts presently due, though payable in the future, may be arrested; a contingent obligation, where the contingency has not yet been purified, may not be.[45] The Supreme Court considered the position of contingent debts arising from statutory obligations under the English insolvency rules in the case of *In re Nortel GmbH*.[46] Lord Neuberger concluded that, in order for a company to have incurred a relevant obligation prior to insolvency three requirements must be satisfied. First, the company must have taken, or been subjected to, some step or combination of steps that had some legal effect. Secondly, those steps must have resulted in the company being vulnerable to the specific liability in question, such that there would be a real prospect of that liability being incurred. Thirdly, it would have to be consistent with the regime under which liability was imposed to conclude that the step or combination of steps gave rise to a contingent obligation. For insolvency purposes, contingent liabilities may be very relevant where a court has to consider whether a company is balance sheet insolvent.

42 *Liquidator of Ben Line Steamers Ltd, Noter* [2010] CSOH 174, 2011 SLT 535 at [30] per Lord Drummond Young.

43 IA 1986, s. 123(1)(e), for which, see para. 14.34 below.

44 Bell, *Commentaries* I, 332. See too Erskine, *Institute* 3.1.6 approved by the House of Lords in *Re Sutherland* [1963] AC 235 at 248 per Lord Reid.

45 *Costain Building and Civil Engineering Ltd v Scottish Rugby Union plc* 1993 SC 650 at 661 per Lord President Hope (a decision of five judges).

46 [2013] UKSC 52, [2014] AC 209.

EU INSOLVENCY REGULATIONS AND EU WITHDRAWAL

EUIR and Recast EUIR Regimes

The UK left the EU on 31 January 2020.[47] A transition period ended at 11pm on 31 December 2020 (IP completion day).[48] But it is likely to be necessary to understand the operation of the European regime, which provides the framework for recognition and enforcement of insolvency proceedings throughout the EU, for years to come. There are two fundamental instruments of EU law which deal with insolvency proceedings: **14.18**

- for insolvency proceedings opened before 26 June 2017, the EU Insolvency Regulation (the 'EUIR');[49] and
- for insolvency proceedings opened on or after 26 June 2017 but before 31 December 2020, the Recast EUIR.[50]

The Recast EUIR will continue to apply to main insolvency proceedings opened in the UK in the course of the transition period which ended on IP completion day, on 31 December 2020.[51] In all applications for opening insolvency proceedings in the UK prior to 31 December 2020, whether they had an EU element or not, the applications had to state whether, for the purposes of the EUIR, they were 'main' or 'territorial' or 'secondary' proceedings.[52] The idea behind the EUIR and Recast EUIR is to avoid conflicts between courts in different Member States. **14.19**

In general terms, the Recast EUIR, like the EUIR, provides that the courts of the Member State, where the insolvent person (the 'debtor') has its 'centre of main interests' ('COMI'), have jurisdiction to open main insolvency proceedings.[53] In the case of legal persons, the presumption is that the debtor's COMI is in the Member State in which it has its registered office.[54] There is a considerable body of case law, domestic and with the Court of Justice of the European Union, on how a company's COMI is to be determined.[55] Locating a company's COMI in the UK extends, for the purposes of administration, to a company with its COMI in Gibraltar.[56] Main proceedings opened in Scotland **14.20**

47 European Union (Withdrawal Agreement) Act 2020 and Council Decision (EU) 2020/135 of 30 January 2020 [2020] OJ L29/1, each adopting the Agreement on the Withdrawal of the United Kingdom of Great Britain and Northern Ireland from the European Union and European Atomic Energy Community (the 'Withdrawal Agreement').
48 European Union (Withdrawal Agreement) Act 2020, s. 39(1).
49 Council Regulation (EC) 1346/2000 on insolvency proceedings.
50 Regulation (EU) 2015/848. For both the EUIR and the Recast EUIR, see generally D Mackenzie-Skene, *Bankruptcy* (Edinburgh: W. Green, 2018), para. 25–19 onward.
51 Withdrawal Agreement, art. 67(3)(c) which is given effect by the Insolvency (EU Exit) (Scotland) (Amendment) Regulations 2019 (SSI 2019/94), reg. 9(2) (as amended by the Insolvency (Amendment) (EU Exit) (Scotland) Regulations 2020 (SSI 2020/337)).
52 EUIR, arts 3 and 17; Recast EUIR art. 3(1), (2) and (3). For a useful summary of the issues to be considered when drafting pleadings, see W W McBryde, 'Insolvency Jurisdiction' 2004 SLT (News) 185.
53 Recast EUIR, art. 3(1).
54 EUIR, art. 3(2); Recast EUIR, art. 3(1): '. . . That presumption shall only apply if the registered office has not been moved to another Member State within the 3-month period prior to the request for the opening of insolvency proceedings'.
55 Case C-341/04 *Eurofood IFSC Ltd* [2006] Ch 508 (ECJ).
56 *Re Nektan (Gibraltar) Ltd* [2020] EWHC 65 (Ch), under reference to the definition of

pre-IP completion day and the insolvency practitioners appointed pursuant to those proceedings, are entitled to automatic recognition by all courts in the EU.[57] Those UK insolvency proceedings, which, pre-IP completion day, were recognised throughout the EU are listed in Annex A to the EUIR:

- Winding up by or with the supervision of the court.
- Creditors' voluntary winding up (with confirmation by the court).[58]
- Administration (including appointments made by filing prescribed particulars with the court).[59]
- Voluntary arrangements under insolvency legislation (for Scottish purposes, company voluntary arrangements (CVAs)).
- Bankruptcy or sequestration.

14.21 The officers appointed pursuant to these pre-IP completion day proceedings – liquidators (including provisional liquidators), CVA supervisors, administrators, trustees in sequestration (and, for Scottish purposes, a judicial factor[60]) – were all recognised throughout the EU.[61] Importantly, it should be emphasised that receivership was not recognised under the EUIR as an insolvency procedure.[62]

EU withdrawal: the RR EUIR

14.22 Following EU withdrawal, two key issues arise for the purposes of corporate insolvencies in Scotland. The first is when, as a matter of Scots law, the Scottish courts will have jurisdiction to open insolvency proceedings in respect of a company. The second is when those insolvency proceedings will be recognised in other countries. As far as Scots law is concerned, following IP completion day, the jurisdiction of the Scottish courts is governed by the Insolvency (Amendment) (EU Exit) Regulations 2019.[63] Those regulations contain a modified version of the Recast EUIR (the 'RR EUIR'). In short, they omit almost all of the Recast EUIR but retain amended versions of arts 1–4. The RR EUIR applies to each of the proceedings mentioned in para. 14.20 above.[64]

14.23 There is jurisdiction under the RR EUIR to open any of those proceedings for the purposes of rescue, adjustment of debt, reorganisation or liquidation where: (a) the centre of the debtor's main interests is in the UK; or (b) the centre of the debtor's main interests is in a Member State and there is an establishment in the UK.[65] The first case just mentioned is known as 'COMI

'company' in IA 1986, Sch. B1, para. 111. The Court of Session has also wound-up companies registered in Gibraltar.

57 EUIR, art. 16(1); Recast EUIR, art. 19.
58 A members voluntary winding up is not included because it can occur only where a company is solvent.
59 So-called 'out of court' appointments.
60 Recast EUIR, Annex B.
61 Recast EUIR, Annexes A and B.
62 Cf the domestic UK position referred to below (n 71).
63 Insolvency (Amendment) (EU Exit) Regulations 2019 (SI 2019/146). These regulations have themselves been amended.
64 RR EUIR, arts 1 and 1B.
65 RR EUIR, art. 1A.

proceedings'; in the second, as 'establishment proceedings'.[66] In practical terms, what this means is that, where application is made to open insolvency proceedings in Scotland, it will be necessary to state: (i) whether or not the COMI of the debtor is situated in the UK or in a Member State (other than Demark); (ii) whether or not the company possesses an establishment in the UK; and (iii) whether there are insolvency proceedings elsewhere in respect of the company.[67] COMI is now defined in RR EUIR art. 3 as follows:

(1) The COMI shall be the place where the debtor conducts the administration of its interests on a regular basis and which is ascertainable by third parties.
(2) In the case of a company or legal person, the place of the registered office shall be presumed to be the centre of its main interests in the absence of proof to the contrary. That presumption shall only apply if the registered office has not been moved from the UK to a Member State or to the UK from a Member State within the three-month period prior to the request for the opening of insolvency proceedings.
(3) In the case of an individual exercising an independent business or professional activity, the COMI shall be presumed to be that individual's principal place of business in the absence of proof to the contrary. That presumption shall only apply if the individual's principal place of business has not been moved [from the UK to a Member State or to the UK from a Member State] within the three-month period prior to the request for the opening of insolvency proceedings.
(4) In the case of any other individual, the COMI shall be presumed to be the place of the individual's habitual residence in the absence of proof to the contrary. This presumption shall only apply if the habitual residence has not been moved [from the UK to a Member State or to the UK from a Member State] within the six-month period prior to the request for the opening of insolvency proceedings.

The question of whether those proceedings will be recognised in other Member **14.24**
States is less straightforward. UK insolvency proceedings that commence after IP completion day no longer benefit from automatic recognition throughout the EU. Whether a particular legal system within the EU will recognise the powers of an insolvency practitioner appointed to a company by the Scottish courts is a matter for that legal system. The Insolvency Service has produced guidance identifying the applicable frameworks in the different Member States within the EU.[68] However, the document is not comprehensive. Ultimately, recognition of Scottish insolvency proceedings will be a matter for the domestic law of the foreign legal system concerned.

66 Winding-up Rules (n 2), rr. 1.2 and 1.8; CVA and Administration Rules (n 1), rr. 1.2 and 1.8.
67 AS (Sheriff Court Company Insolvency Rules) 1986 (n 5), r. 10 (administration), r. 18 (winding-up orders); RCS, r. 74.10 (administration), r. 74.21 (winding-up).
68 The Insolvency Service, *https://www.gov.uk/government/publications/cross-border-insolvencies-recognition-and-enforcement-in-eu-member-states/cross-border-insolvencies-recognition-and-enforcement-in-eu-member-states* (last accessed 7 September 2021).

Intra-UK insolvency

14.25 The IA 1986 confers jurisdiction on the courts of the country where a company is incorporated: Scottish courts for Scottish companies and English courts for English companies.[69] In the event of a Scottish registered company, with its COMI in, say, London, the IA 1986 nonetheless confers jurisdiction on the Scottish courts. The converse also holds true: an English-registered company with its COMI in Edinburgh is nonetheless to be wound-up by the English courts.[70] Under the 1986 Act, although not under the Recast EUIR or RR EUIR, a reference to a company's 'insolvency' covers administrative receivership.[71]

International elements in non-EU cases

14.26 The Scottish courts are reluctant to subject foreign companies to Scottish insolvency proceedings,[72] especially if those companies have no assets in Scotland. However, the court retains a power to wind-up 'unregistered companies',[73] where either the company has its principal place of business in Scotland, or the company has assets subject to a floating charge and the court is satisfied that the security of the creditor is in jeopardy. In those circumstances, the court may exercise its discretion to place the company into liquidation in Scotland under the provisions in the IA 1986 dealing with unregistered companies.[74]

14.27 There are also provisions for the mutual recognition of certain insolvency proceedings outside of the EU.[75] Where the insolvency proceedings are abroad, the UK courts have powers to assist foreign insolvency practitioners and courts.[76]

69 IA 1986, s. 120.

70 IA 1986, s. 117 and s. 120. See *Bank Leumi (UK) plc, Petr* [2017] CSOH 129, 2017 SLT 1281.

71 IA 1986, s. 247(1).

72 *Banco Nacional de Cuba v Cosmos Trading Corp* [2000] BCLC 813 at 819 quoted with approval by Lord Hodge in *HSBC Bank plc, Petr* [2009] CSOH 147, 2010 SLT 281.

73 IA 1986, s. 220: 'For the purposes of this Part "unregistered company" includes any association and any company, with the exception of a company registered under the Companies Act 2006 in any part of the United Kingdom'.

74 IA 1986, s. 221(3) and (7). See too s. 51(1)(b) discussed at (n 253) below in the context of receivership.

75 Cross-Border Insolvency Regulations 2006 (SI 2006/1030), implementing the UNICTRAL Model Law, for which see D Mackenzie-Skene, *Bankruptcy* (2018), para. 25–165 onward; L Chan Ho, *Cross-Border Insolvency: A Commentary on the UNCITRAL Model Law*, 4th edn (London: Globe Business Publishing, 2017); and the Foreign Judgments (Reciprocal Enforcement) Act 1933 (for certain commonwealth countries), discussed in *Rubin v Eurofinance SA* [2012] UKSC 46, [2013] 1 AC 236.

76 IA 1986, s. 426, for which see *Re HIH Casualty & General Insurance Ltd* [2008] UKHL 21, [2008] 1 WLR 852 and *Rubin* (n 75).

THE CORPORATE INSOLVENCY PROCEEDINGS

Introduction

In this chapter, the following procedures are considered: 14.28

- Liquidation (or 'winding up').
- Receivership and administrative receivership.
- Administration.
- Part A1 moratorium with a monitor.
- Company voluntary arrangements (CVAs).
- Schemes of arrangement.
- Section 110 reorganisation.

LIQUIDATION

'Liquidation' is used in the Companies Acts and the IA 1986 in the same sense as it might be used by a totalitarian state security service: to liquidate is to kill. A synonym for liquidation is 'winding up' and this latter term better describes the process, which may be swift but may, in some cases, be tortuous. Death of a company comes only with the expiry of the three month period following publication of a notice of dissolution in the register of companies at the end of the winding up process.[77] The date of commencement of the liquidation is either on the date of the resolution to wind up (in a members' or creditors' voluntary liquidation)[78] or on the date of a petition (in the case of a creditors' winding up), as the case may be.[79] But for companies, liquidation may not be the end: companies, unlike mortal men and women, are potential revenants and, by the process of 'restoration to the register', may be brought back from the dead.[80] 14.29

Liquidation types

The first distinction in the types of liquidation is between voluntary and compulsory liquidation. A voluntary liquidation is one instigated by the company itself, normally by a special resolution of the members;[81] a compulsory liquidation, in contrast, is instigated by court procedure. The result is that there are three types of winding up: 14.30

- Members' voluntary winding up.
- Creditors' voluntary winding up.
- Compulsory winding up.

77 IA 1986, s. 205(2).
78 IA 1986, s. 86.
79 IA 1986, s. 129(2). It is possible for an administration to be converted into a creditors voluntary liquidation by the administrators filing a conversion notice with the Registrar: IA 1986, Sch. B1, para. 83. In such a case, the liquidation is deemed to have commenced from the date that the company went into administration: Sch. B1, para. 83(8)(b).
80 See para. 14.129 below.
81 IA 1986, s. 84(2). The other basis is the example of a joint venture company, which is formed for a specific purpose and that purpose has been fulfilled: s. 84(1)(a).

Voluntary winding up

14.31 A members' voluntary liquidation (MVL) can occur only where the company is solvent.[82] A creditors' voluntary liquidation (CVL) may involve insolvency. Otherwise, the distinction between MVL and CVL depends upon whether the directors have delivered a statement of solvency: such a statement is a pre-requisite for an MVL.[83] In a CVL the creditors, in practice, will appoint the liquidator.[84] On a resolution to wind up the company voluntarily, the company must cease to carry on its business, except in so far as may be required for its beneficial winding up.[85] An important difference between a CVL and a compulsory winding up is that, in the case of a CVL, the liquidator is able to exercise many of their powers without court sanction;[86] and such a liquidator has the power to sell heritable property free of an inhibition.[87]

Compulsory winding up

14.32 Insolvency is perhaps the most common ground for a compulsory winding up.[88] But insolvency is not the only ground on which a company may be wound up by the court. The other reasons that tend to arise in practice are that: (a) there has been a special resolution of members that the company be wound up by the court; (b) the company has not commenced business within a year of incorporation; (c) the limited CVA moratorium has come to an end without a CVA being put in place;[89] or (d) because it is 'just and equitable' to do so. Of these four examples, in all except (c), the company will be solvent.[90]

14.33 It remains competent for a floating chargeholder to enforce its floating charge by petitioning to have the company wound up.[91] The basis for doing so is that the floating chargeholder's security will otherwise be placed in 'jeopardy'; and the court is satisfied that events have occurred – or are about to occur – which render it unreasonable for the company to retain the power to dispose of the property subject to the floating charge.[92]

Insolvency: timings and duties

14.34 In practice, the most common reason that a company is wound up at the instance of a creditor is because that company is unable to pay its debts.[93] There are four distinct bases on which a creditor can demonstrate the company's inability to pay its debts:

82 IA 1986, s. 89: the directors must deliver to the Registrar of Companies a statutory declaration of solvency within fifteen days.
83 IA 1986, s. 90.
84 IA 1986, s. 100(2).
85 IA 1986, s. 87(1).
86 IA 1986, s. 166(2) and (3).
87 IA 1986, s. 166(1A).
88 IA 1986, s. 122(1)(f).
89 IA 1986, s. 122(1)(fa).
90 IA 1986, s. 122.
91 IA 1986, s. 122(2).
92 IA 1986, s. 122(2).
93 IA 1986, s. 122(f).

(i) A statutory demand to pay a sum exceeding £750 has been served on the company at its registered office and the company has neglected to pay that sum for three weeks thereafter or to secure or compound for it to the reasonable satisfaction of the creditor ('apparent insolvency').[94]
(ii) The *induciae*[95] of a charge for payment on an extract decree, or an extract registered bond, or an extract registered protest, have expired without payment being made ('apparent insolvency').[96]
(iii) If it is proved to the satisfaction of the court that the company is not paying its debts as they fall due ('practical insolvency').[97]
(iv) It is proved to the satisfaction of the court that the value of the company's assets is less than the amount of its liabilities, taking account of prospective and contingent liabilities ('balance sheet insolvency').[98]

The expiry, without payment, of a statutory demand, or charge for payment, provides the clearest basis for a creditor to petition for a winding up. Often, however, matters are more complicated because the basis of the creditor's claim relates to the viability of the company. Both practical insolvency and balance sheet insolvency have been elaborated upon in the case law. A failure by a company to pay a debt which is undisputed gives rise to an inference that a company is unable to pay its debts as they fall due.[99] It follows that, where practical insolvency is the basis for presentation of a petition, difficulties may arise where the company disputes that the creditor's claim is due at all.[100] A claim in respect of which there is a genuine and good faith defence to liability is not a claim that will found a winding up petition. That is because the court will not draw the inference that the company is unable to pay its debts. Conversely, however, if the claim on which the petition is based is one to which the company does not, or cannot, substantially dispute, and which has not been settled, that will form the basis of an inference that the company is unable to pay its debts as they fall due even where the company can show that it has funds to pay the debt in question.[101] The shortcomings of the practical insolvency test (otherwise known as the 'cash-flow' test), particularly in relation to future liabilities, have been explained by the Supreme Court thus:[102] **14.35**

> 'the 'cash-flow' test is concerned, not simply with the petitioner's own presently-due debt, nor only with other presently-due debt owed by the company, but also with debts falling due from time to time in the reasonably near future. What is the reasonably near future, for this purpose, will depend on all the circumstances, but especially on the nature of the company's business . . . The express reference to

94 IA 1986, s. 123(1)(a).
95 G Watson (ed), *Bell's Dictionary and Digest of the Law of Scotland*, 7th edn (Edinburgh: Bell & Bradfute, 1890) '*induciae legales*': 'the days which intervene between the citation of a defender and the day of appearance in the action or process; or the days which are allowed to a debtor to obey a charge or decree'. The standard period of notice for a charge for payment is fourteen days: Debtors (Scotland) Act 1987, s. 90(3).
96 IA 1986, s. 123(1)(c).
97 IA 1986, s. 123(1)(e).
98 IA 1986, s. 123(2).
99 *Blue Star Security Services (Scotland) Ltd* 1992 SLT (Sh Ct) 80.
100 *MacPlant Services Ltd v Contract Lifting Services (Scotland) Ltd* 2009 SC 125.
101 *Cornhill Insurance plc v Improvement Services Ltd* [1986] 1 WLR 114.
102 *BNY Corporate Trustee Services Ltd v Eurosail-UK 2007-3BL plc* [2013] UKSC 28, [2013] 1 WLR 1408 at [37]–[38] per Lord Walker.

> assets and liabilities is in my view a practical recognition that once the court has to move beyond the reasonably near future (the length of which depends, again, on all the circumstances) any attempt to apply a cash-flow test will become completely speculative, and a comparison of present assets with present and future liabilities (discounted for contingencies and deferment) becomes the only sensible test. But it is still very far from an exact test . . .'

14.36 In relation to balance sheet insolvency, meanwhile, the Supreme Court has emphasised that the correct test is whether, on the balance of probabilities, the petitioner has satisfied the court that a company has insufficient assets to be able to meet all its liabilities, including prospective and contingent liabilities.[103] In that case, the Supreme Court specifically rejected the test of whether the company had reached the 'point of no return'.

14.37 In order to qualify as a contingent creditor, the creditor need show only that the obligation has a basis at common law or statute at the date of the winding up petition, though it may be subject to a contingency that will be purified only at some later stage.[104] But a company that is managing to pay its debts as they fall due may nonetheless be insolvent, as where a company is able to pay debts that fall due only by borrowing.[105] Lord Hodge has said of the balance sheet test that:[106]

> 'It is clear that when the court looks at balance sheet insolvency under section 123(2) it is not simply taking a snap shot of the balance between a company's assets and it liabilities then and there. It is not concerned with temporary imbalances. Rather in considering that balance the court looks to the future and asks whether it is clear in practical terms that because of an incurable deficiency in its assets it will not be able to meet its future or contingent liabilities. In other words, the section allows the court to have regard to the interests of contingent or prospective creditors (the latter being creditors with existing debts which are not yet due for payment) and form a judgment whether it has been established that the company cannot reasonably be expected to meet those liabilities . . .'

14.38 The various tests that provide a basis for petitioning for a company's winding up may be relevant in other contexts. A debtor of a company in financial difficulties, as has been seen, may refuse to pay on the basis of the defence of 'balancing of accounts in bankruptcy'.[107] For such a case to be made out, however, in cases where the company is not yet in formal insolvency proceedings, very clear averments of insolvency are required.[108]

Publicity

14.39 A voluntary winding up is deemed to commence at the time of the passing of the special resolution to wind up.[109] As soon as a resolution is passed, there is a duty on the officers of the company to publicise it in the *Edinburgh Gazette*

103 *Eurosail* (n 102) [2013] UKSC 28, [2013] 1 WLR 1408 at [48].
104 *Liquidator of Ben Line Steamers Ltd, Noter* [2010] CSOH 174, 2011 SLT 535.
105 *Re Casa Estates (UK) Ltd (in Liquidation)* [2014] EWCA Civ 383.
106 *Joint Building Society Special Administrators of Dunfermline Building Society v FM Front Door Ltd* [2011] CSOH 175 at [25].
107 See para. 8.61 above.
108 See, e.g. *J & A Construction (Scotland) Ltd v Windex Ltd* [2013] CSOH 170.
109 IA 1986, s. 86.

within fourteen days,[110] and to lodge it with the Registrar of Companies,[111] and the Accountant in Bankruptcy, within fifteen days.[112] In the case of a winding up by the court, the winding up is deemed to commence at the time of the presentation of the petition.[113] A copy of the court order must be forwarded to the Registrar of Companies and Accountant in Bankruptcy 'forthwith'.[114] As a result, they are entered on the Register of Insolvencies held by the Accountant in Bankruptcy. The appointment of administrators should be intimated to the Keeper of the Register of Inhibitions and Adjudications (the Personal Register).[115]

Effect of winding up

On the court making a winding up order, the person appointed is known as the 'interim' liquidator. Within twenty-eight days of their appointment they must seek nominations from the company's creditors and contributories for the purpose of appointing a liquidator (who may be, and often is, the interim liquidator).[116] The most important practical consequence of liquidation is that legal proceedings may be commenced against a company in liquidation (including provisional liquidation) only with the consent of the court.[117] The court has worldwide jurisdiction over the assets of the company.[118] **14.40**

Liquidation, unlike sequestration, does not result in the vesting of the company's assets in the liquidator. Corporate insolvency uses the law of legal personality rather than the law of property to effect collective procedure for realisation of the company's assets: the liquidator replaces the company's directors as the person able to bind the company.[119] But care is needed with the word 'vesting'. For although there is no automatic 'vesting' of the company's **14.41**

110 IA 1986, s. 85.
111 IA 1986, s. 84(3) and Companies Act 2006, ss. 29 and 30.
112 IA 1986, s. 84(3) and Companies Act 2006, ss. 29 and 30 read with Scotland Act 1998, Sch. 8, para. 23.
113 IA 1986, s. 129(2). Where the court makes a winding-up order by virtue of Sch. B1, para. 13(1)(e) (on application for administration), the winding up is deemed to commence on the making of the order.
114 IA 1986, s. 130(1). Where liquidation is to follow from administration on the basis of a conversion notice under IA 1986, Sch. B1, para. 83(2), the administrator must send a notice to the Registrar and, 'as soon as is reasonably practicable', file a copy of the notice with the court and send copies to creditors.
115 CVA and Administration Rules (n 1), r. 3.27(3)(e).
116 IA 1986, s. 138(2) and (3).
117 IA 1986, s. 130(2). In *Jervis v Pillar Denton Ltd* [2014] EWCA Civ 180, [2015] Ch at [31], Lewison LJ said that 'the precise scope of [these sections] is still to some extent uncertain'. But the prohibition on proceedings without the consent of the court extends to proceedings brought against the company elsewhere in the EU: *Re ARM Asset Backed Securities SA* [2014] EWHC 1097. For creditors' voluntary liquidations, the court, on the application of the liquidator, may direct that proceedings can be brought against the company only with the leave of the court: IA 1986, s. 113.
118 *Bilta (UK) Ltd (No. 2) v Nazir* [2016] AC 1 at [109] per Lord Sumption and [213]–[218] per Lords Hodge and Toulson. Compare the situation where a Scottish registered company has been placed into liquidation abroad: *Hooley Ltd, Petr* [2016] CSOH 141, 2017 SLT 58 (revd on procedural grounds *sub nom Hooley Ltd v Ganges Jute Private Ltd* [2019] CSIH 40, 2019 SC 632).
119 IA 1986, s. 91(2) (members' voluntary), s. 103 (CVL) and s. 169(2) (compulsory). The same is true on administration: Sch. B1, para. 64(1). But the board retains a residual power

assets in the liquidator, the respective positions of a trustee in sequestration and a liquidator are similar.[120] Neither the trustee nor the liquidator is owner of immoveable property unless they are registered as such. Both can do so in theory, although the power of a trustee in sequestration is now limited.[121] The liquidator can do so by deducting title in favour of themselves,[122] or by virtue of an order of the court,[123] although such orders are, in practice, unknown. Such an order takes effect only when an extract has been recorded or registered as the case may be.[124]

14.42 A company must publicise the fact that it is in liquidation in all business correspondence.[125] Any disposition of the company's property and any transfer of shares or alteration in the status of the company's members made after commencement of the winding up is, unless the court otherwise orders, void.[126] Where the company has granted a floating charge, liquidation causes the floating charge to attach.[127]

ADMINISTRATION

Outline

14.43 It was as a result of the Enterprise Act 2002 that administration was given the primacy that it now enjoys in corporate insolvency practice. The amendments introduced by the 2002 Act are now mainly found in Sch. B1 to the IA 1986. There were also consequential amendments to the Insolvency (Scotland) Rules then in force. The relevant rules are now found in the Insolvency (Scotland) (Company Voluntary Arrangements and Administration) Rules 2018.[128]

14.44 It is possible for LLPs to enter administration. The Limited Liability Partnerships Act 2000 made provision for regulations to deal with the insolvency of LLPs by application of certain parts of the 1986 Act. The provisions of Sch. B1 to the IA 1986 in relation to administrations are applied to LLPs subject to modifications,[129] as are other specified parts of the IA 1986,[130] again,

to challenge the appointment of a provisional liquidator, receiver or administrator, as the case may be: *Stephen, Petr* [2011] CSOH 119.

120 G L Gretton, 'The Title of a Liquidator' (1984) 29 *JLSS* 357 summarised in G L Gretton and A J M Steven, *Property, Trusts and Succession*, 4th edn (London: Bloomsbury Professional, 2021), para. 8.16. *Joint Liquidators of The Scottish Coal Company Ltd* [2013] CSIH 108, 2014 SC 372, at [111]–[113].

121 Bankruptcy (Scotland) Act 2016, s. 78.

122 Titles to Land Consolidation (Scotland) Act 1868, s. 25. The Scottish Law Commission has proposed that this provision be repealed: *Report on Sharp v Thomson* (Scot. Law Com. No. 208, 2007), paras 4.3–4.6.

123 IA 1986, s. 145.

124 Conveyancing (Scotland) Act 1924, ss. 4 and 4A.

125 IA 1986, s. 188.

126 IA 1986, s. 127.

127 Companies Act 1985, s. 463(1).

128 See n 1 above.

129 IA 1986, s. 8 and the Limited Liability Partnerships Regulations 2001 (SI 2001/1090) (as amended) (the 'LLP Regulations'), reg. 5(1).

130 LLP Regulations (n 129), reg. 2A(1)(b).

subject to certain modifications.[131] However, the CVA and Administration Rules 2018 do not apply to the administration of an LLP.[132] Instead, the Insolvency (Scotland) Rules 1986 continue to apply to LLPs.[133]

An administration must have a statutory objective, selected by the administrator according to a threefold statutory hierarchy: **14.45**

(a) to rescue the company as a going concern;
(b) to achieve a better result for the company's creditors as a whole than would be likely if the company were wound up (without first being in administration); or
(c) to realise property in order to make a distribution to one or more secured or preferred creditors.[134]

The procedure is intended to be quick and efficient.[135] The general rule is that administrators are under a duty to have regard to the interests of the company's creditors as a whole.[136] On occasion, that duty may involve the subordination of one creditor's interests to the greater good.[137] It is under (b) that there may be a transfer of the company's undertaking. 'One of the main advantages of administration over liquidation', the Court of Appeal has remarked: **14.46**

> 'is precisely that administrators have power to continue the insolvent company's business, protected (unlike the company's directors) by the moratorium on the pursuit of claims by creditors, so that it can be prepared and marketed for sale as a going concern, and the proceeds of sale distributed to the company's creditors, either by the administrators themselves, or (less commonly now) in a subsequent liquidation . . . continuation of the company's business is commonly a prerequisite of a beneficial sale. Once a business is closed down, its value rapidly declines to an amount no greater than the aggregate of the forced sale value of its constituent assets'.[138]

Purpose (c), however, is available only when (a) and (b) are not viable options. Administrators may therefore seek to realise property for the purposes of making a distribution to a secured creditor only if rescuing the company as a going concern or achieving a better result for the creditors as a whole is not reasonably practicable and realising the property for the purposes of making a distribution to a secured creditor does not unnecessarily harm the interests of the general creditors.[139] **14.47**

An administrator may be appointed by: (a) the court; (b) the company (i.e. a resolution of the members) or the directors (i.e. the managers); or (c) the **14.48**

131 LLP Regulations (n 129), reg. 5(3) and Sch. 4.
132 CVA and Administration Rules (n 1), Sch. 2, para. 12.
133 The Limited Liability Partnerships (Scotland) Regulations 2001 (SI 2001/128), reg. 6(1).
134 IA 1986, Sch. B1, para. 3. These provisions were introduced by the Enterprise Act 2002. Prior to that Act, administrators were not able to make distributions to creditors.
135 IA 1986, Sch. B1, para. 4. Cf Sch B1, para. 52(1).
136 IA 1986, Sch. B1, para. 3(2).
137 *Joint Administrators of Rangers Football Club plc, Noters* 2012 SLT 599 at [57]–[59] and [62] discussed by G L Gretton, 'The Laws of the Game' (2012) 16 Edinburgh Law Review 414.
138 *Kavanagh v Crystal Palace FC 2000 Ltd* [2013] EWCA Civ 1410, [2014] ICR 251, at [19]–[20] per Briggs LJ.
139 IA 1986, Sch. B1, para. 3(4).

holder of a qualifying floating charge.[140] A little more will be said about each in turn.

Appointment by QFC holder

14.49 Appointment may be made either by petitioning the court or 'out of court' by filing a notice of appointment with the court. A floating charge 'qualifies' where it is created by an instrument which states that para. 14 of Sch. B1 to the IA 1986 applies to it; or purports to confer on the holder of the charge a power to appoint an administrator; or purports to confer on the holder the power to appoint a receiver or administrative receiver.[141] In addition, the charge must relate to the whole or substantially the whole of the company's property.[142] The question whether a floating charge is in respect of the whole of the property of the company is determined by reference to the wording of the floating charge itself.[143] The power of a QFC holder to appoint is likely to be limited only if there is a prior QFC in place in favour of another creditor. Where such a prior QFC does exist, at least two business days' notice must be given to the prior QFC holder, by way of a filing of a 'notice of intention to appoint'.[144]

14.50 A QFC holder has a power to appoint an administrator only when the floating charge is enforceable.[145] This requirement precludes the appointment of an administrator unless and until there occurs a default on the company's part or some other event that entitles the chargeholder to make such an appointment. The provision does not have a wider application.[146] It has been held that a dispute regarding the enforceability of the charge does not mean that the charge is unenforceable.[147] However, a creditor who appoints in those circumstances runs the risk that the appointment may subsequently be found to be invalid. In practical terms, one of the great attractions of the out of court procedure is that it can be done quickly and cheaply. If necessary, it can be done in the middle of the night, by sending the appropriate forms to the court.[148] Nonetheless, care must be taken in following the procedures as a failure to do so may result in the appointment of the administrator being invalid.[149]

140 IA 1986, Sch. B1, para. 2.

141 IA 1986, Sch. B1, para. 14(2). The conditions in para. 14(2) are alternatives, so a floating charge need satisfy only one of the conditions to be characterised as a QFC: *Stephen, Petr* [2011] CSOH 119.

142 IA 1986, Sch. B1, para. 14(3)(a).

143 *Hooley Ltd, Petr* (n 118) 2017 SLT 58.

144 IA 1986, Sch. B1, para. 15.

145 IA 1986, Sch. B1, para. 16.

146 *Hooley Ltd, Petr* (n 118) 2017 SLT 58 at [40].

147 *BCPMS (Europe) Ltd v GMAC Commercial Finance plc* [2006] EWHC 3744 (Ch) followed in *Hooley Ltd, Petr* (n 118) 2017 SLT 58 at [40].

148 CVA and Administration Rules (n 1), rr. 3.20–3.22.

149 See *Re Skeegs Beef Ltd* [2019] EWHC 2607 (Ch), [2020] BCC 43; *NMUL Realisations Ltd (in administration)* [2021] EWHC 94 (Ch).

Moratorium

The most important practical consequence of administration is the moratorium. A company in administration is protected from attempts by creditors to enforce any contractual rights or rights in security against the company, whether by litigation, diligence or other enforcement.[150] A company must publicise on all business documents, including websites, that it is in administration.[151] **14.51**

Power to deal with company's property

On administration, subject to limited exceptions, the floating charge does not attach. The administrator is empowered to deal freely with the company's property, which would otherwise fall within the charge, without the chargeholder's consent. The power extends to disposing of the property, as by sale.[152] So if an administrator sells the company's stock, the buyer takes free from the charge and the price becomes an asset of the company. Property which is subject to a fixed security is in a different position. The administrator cannot dispose of that property without the consent of either the chargeholder or the court.[153] A court will supply consent only on the condition that the proceeds are used to pay the secured creditor[154] and that the sale leaves the secured creditor, *qua* secured creditor, no worse off than if the secured creditor had itself sold the secured assets.[155] Similar rules apply to goods held by the company subject to hire purchase agreements.[156] The court can supply consent to a disposal only of assets which are the property of the company.[157] **14.52**

Business and employees

These powers allow an administrator to continue the company's business. But, as Briggs LJ (as he then was) has explained, the economic realities will often make any trading difficult and, in practice, it is often necessary for the administrators to make employees redundant:[158] **14.53**

> 'An administrator's ability to continue the business pending sale is inevitably constrained by acute economic considerations. The company will not be in administration unless it is insolvent and, indeed, hopelessly insolvent, in the sense that the directors had reached the view that, without protection from its creditors, the company could not realistically expect to trade out of its difficulties. In most cases, that insolvency will have arisen because of the manner in which the company had been conducting its business. Thus, leaving aside pre-packs, administrators will typically need urgently to reform and economise upon the manner in which the business is being conducted immediately prior to their appointment, both to maximise the

150 IA 1986, Sch. B1, para. 43, explained in *Re Globespan Airways Ltd* [2013] 1 WLR 1122 at [6] per Arden LJ.
151 IA 1986, Sch. B1, para. 45.
152 IA 1986, Sch. B1, para. 70.
153 IA 1986, Sch. B1, para. 71.
154 IA 1986, Sch. B1, para. 71(3).
155 Cf *O'Connell v Rowlings* [2014] EWCA Civ 639 at [70] per Kitchin LJ.
156 IA 1986, Sch. B1, para. 72 and see para. 111(1) for the expansive definition of hire purchase agreements.
157 *Re Business Environment Fleet Street Ltd (in administration)* [2014] EWHC 3540 (Ch), [2015] 1 WLR 1167.
158 *Kavanagh v Crystal Palace FC 2000 Ltd* [2013] EWCA Civ 1410, [2014] ICR 251 at [22].

period before a lack of resources compels closure, and to make the business more attractive to purchasers. Dismissal of employees is, unfortunately for them, a principal method by which the administrators can achieve the economies necessary for those two purposes. Those who are kept on have to be paid their wages and salaries in full, as a prior claim on the limited funds available to the administrators.'

Pre-pack administrations

14.54 Insolvency carries considerable stigma and, at all events, even the suspicion that a company may be on the verge of insolvency can lead to a crisis of confidence among the company's creditors. Credit may be withdrawn. The company's goodwill may be irretrievably damaged. The most efficient way for an administrator to realise a company's assets in order to achieve the purposes of administration is often, therefore, as Lord Briggs indicated in the passage quoted in the previous paragraph, to sell the assets before creditors know about the insolvency event. This is the practice of the 'pre-pack' sale of the company's business. The details of the sale are negotiated with the buyer prior to appointment of the administrator. Normally, the accountant advising on the sale is also appointed as the administrator. When the sale is due to complete, the administrator is appointed out of court and the sale is completed on the same day. The driver behind the sale will be the QFC holder. Other creditors are not consulted prior to the sale. Pre-packs are particularly important for small businesses where the only prospective buyers are likely to be the management of the old company (OldCo).

14.55 The legal basis for the whole scheme is the power of an administrator, as agent of the company,[159] to do anything necessary or expedient for the management of the affairs, business and property of the company.[160] Unless the administrator proposes to dispose of property subject to a fixed security without the consent of the fixed security holder,[161] the court's consent is not required.[162] The practice had proved controversial because of the lack of scrutiny of the administrators' role, the fees charged,[163] and the general result that unsecured creditors receive nothing. There is now mandatory independent scrutiny of such sales.[164] There are special statements of insolvency practice to regulate how administrators must act in these circumstances.[165]

159 IA 1986, Sch. B1, para. 69.

160 IA 1986, Sch. B1, para. 59(1).

161 See n 153 and n 154 above.

162 See *Re Transbus International Ltd (in liquidation)* [2004] 1 WLR 2654; *Re Kayley Vending Ltd* [2009] EWHC 904 (Ch), [2009] BCC 578; *Clydesdale Financial Services Ltd v Smailes* [2009] EWHC 1745 (Ch), [2009] BCC 810.

163 For the need for disclosure and approval of pre-administration costs incurred by the creditors, see CVA and Administration Rules (n 1), rr. 3.35–3.37.

164 Administration (Restrictions on Disposal etc. to Connected Persons) Regulations 2021 (SI 2021/427).

165 See, e.g. Statement of Insolvency Practice 13 (Scotland): Disposal of Assets to Connected Persons in an Insolvency Process (30 April 2021); Statement of Insolvency Practice 16 (Scotland): Pre-Packaged Sales in Administrations (30 April 2021). Both are available from *https://www.icas.com/* (last accessed 7 September 2021).

Business names and phoenixing

A company subject to an insolvency proceeding undergoes a mandatory change of name to include, in its corporate name, an indication that it is 'in administration' or 'in liquidation' as the case may be. These facts must be disclosed on all of the company's business correspondence and websites.[166] One of the primary rationales for a pre-pack sale, as has been seen, is to preserve the goodwill of the business by effecting a sale before the insolvency is publicised. Goodwill is accessory to a business name.[167] The purchasers under a pre-pack sale, therefore, will often wish to carry on the new business under the same trading name as before. The purchaser may want the new entity to take the corporate name of the seller or be able to exercise registered trademarks or unregistered business names of the seller. **14.56**

But there is a major legal catch to giving effect to such an arrangement: the rules against phoenixing.[168] 'Phoenixing' is the phenomenon whereby an insolvent OldCo sells its business and assets to a new company (NewCo), perhaps for an undervalue;[169] the NewCo trades on debt free under the same name as the OldCo previously traded, while the OldCo is placed into insolvent liquidation. Section 216 of the IA 1986 was introduced to deal with this phenomenon. Section 216(3) prohibits someone who has been a director of a company in the twelve months prior to its insolvent liquidation, from being concerned in any way with the carrying on of a business using the same or similar name as was used by the insolvent company. The prohibition lasts for a period of five years following the liquidation. The name under which OldCo carried on its business is the 'prohibited name'.[170] The sanctions for breach are severe: criminal penalties plus personal liability for such debts and other liabilities of the NewCo company as are incurred at a time when the former director of OldCo was involved with management of NewCo.[171] It is important to recognise that s. 216 does not, in terms, expressly apply to administration. But s. 216 has important practical implications for the sale of a business by an administrator, particularly in a pre-pack situation, for two reasons. First, at one stage it was thought that around 60 per cent of pre-packs were to connected parties, such as to former directors;[172] and, secondly, following such a sale, the OldCo will **14.57**

166 IA 1986, s. 188 (liquidation); Sch. B1, para. 45 (administration).

167 *Commissioners of Inland Revenue v Muller & Co's Margarine Ltd* [1901] AC 217 at 224 per Lord Macnaghten; *Drummond v Assessor for Leith* (1888) 13 R 540 at 541.

168 See C Wilson, 'Prohibited Names and Phoenix Companies' 2005 SLT (News) 207.

169 For which see para. 14.114 below. Careful consideration should be given to the value paid for the goodwill and intellectual property transferred: *Western Intelligence Ltd v KDO Label Printing Machines Ltd* [1998] BCC 472.

170 IA 1986, s. 216(2)(a) refers to the name 'by which the liquidating company was known'. That may be its corporate name or its trading name; s. 216(2)(b) covers a name that is so similar as to suggest an association with the insolvent company. In *Advocate General v Reilly* [2011] CSOH 141, Lord Bannatyne held that 'Aquaseal UK Ltd' was sufficiently similar to the liquidating company's name of 'Aqua Seal IT Ltd' to be a prohibited name.

171 IA 1986, s. 217(1)(a). See *ESS Production Ltd (in administration) v Sully* [2005] EWCA Civ 554. The right of action is personal to creditors; a liquidator has no right of action: *Re Prestige Grinding Ltd* [2006] BCC 421.

172 L Graham, *Graham Review into Pre-Pack Administration* (2014), para. 7.50. The words 'connected with' are defined in IA 1986, s. 249. 'Associate', for these purposes, is defined in s. 435.

normally be placed into insolvent liquidation. The OldCo directors, if concerned with the management or with the carrying on of the NewCo business, may thereby incur liability under s. 217 for NewCo's debts.

14.58 The prohibition in s. 216 is, however, subject to three exceptions. First, s. 216(3) is expressed to be subject to the leave of the court.[173] An application for leave of the court may be sought prior to the OldCo's insolvent liquidation or within seven days. Where such an application is made, the director in question may carry on a business under the prohibited name until the court decides to grant leave or for six weeks, whichever is the earlier.[174] Secondly, there is no breach of s. 216(3) where the company that goes into insolvent liquidation had been known by that name for the whole of the twelve month period ending with the company's liquidation and which, during that time, had not been dormant.[175] Finally, there is an exception for a director who has acted in terms of s. 216(3) where 'the whole or substantially the whole' of the business of the OldCo has been acquired from an insolvency office holder such as an administrator or liquidator. In order to invoke this exception, notice must be given in a prescribed form to the creditors of the company and published in the *Edinburgh Gazette* within twenty-eight days of the completion of the sale.[176] The purpose of this provision is not so much to support the rescue of a business but to ensure that the 'phoenix' company is disclosed as such.[177] But difficult questions may arise where only part of the business is acquired (as where the underperforming part of the business is left behind) and there is uncertainty as to whether 'the whole or substantially the whole' of the business has been acquired. Careful thought is thus needed in advance in order to decide which exception may be invoked. The whole area is now subject to additional statutory control and independent scrutiny.[178]

14.59 One example where s. 216 and s. 217 were triggered is *Glasgow City Council v Craig*.[179] The defenders operated two business from adjacent units. One business, operated by a company called Arigo Ltd, was an Italian restaurant. The other, a wine bar, was operated by a company called Degreefresh Ltd. Degreefresh also operated other businesses from other addresses. At the end of 2004, Degreefresh took an assignation of Arigo Ltd's lease. Degreefresh Ltd then operated the Italian restaurant business, named Arigo, as before. In January 2005, Arigo Ltd was placed into insolvent liquidation. Degreefresh Ltd, in January 2005, wrote to the local authority acknowledging that it was now liable for payment of the domestic rates for both shop units. Degreefresh Ltd paid the rates for both properties until it itself was placed in insolvent liquidation in September 2007. The local authority therefore sought to recover all the unpaid rates, for both units, from the directors personally on the basis of s. 217.

173 1986 Act, s. 216(3) and Winding-Up Rules (n 2), r. 12.1.
174 Winding-Up Rules (n 2), r. 12.6 (the 'second excepted case').
175 Winding-Up Rules (n 2), r. 12.7 (the 'third excepted case').
176 Winding-Up Rules (n 2), r. 12.4 (the 'first excepted case').
177 *Penrose v Secretary of State for Trade and Industry* [1996] 1 WLR 482 at 489 per Chadwick J, approved by the Court of Appeal in *ESS Production Ltd* (n 171) above.
178 See nn 164 and 165 above.
179 [2008] CSOH 171, 2009 SC 185.

The defenders accepted that none of the exceptions in the insolvency rules applied.[180] The Lord Ordinary accepted that Arigo was a prohibited name for the purposes of s. 216(2). The question arose for decision whether the directors were liable for the rates in respect of both Arigo and Degreefresh or just for the debts of Degreefresh that arose in respect of the latter's use of the Arigo name. Lord Glennie held, as a general principle, that liability under s. 217 may be incurred even where only part of NewCo's business is carried on under OldCo's name. But Parliament did not intend to extend liability beyond the liabilities incurred by Degreefresh while carrying on business under the prohibited name, for there is no warrant for imposing personal liability on directors who have carried on a business under a name that is not prohibited. The 'relevant debts' under s. 217 are thus limited to those 'incurred by the company while carrying on business under a prohibited name'.[181] **14.60**

In addition to the provisions of the IA 1986 regarding phoenix trading, the Finance Act 2020 introduced new provisions which apply where a director has been involved with two or more companies that have entered insolvency in the previous five years with specified levels of unpaid taxes. Where the provisions apply, and the director is involved in the management of a company that carries on a similar trade or business to the two insolvent companies, HMRC may issue a notice that will cause the director to become jointly and severally liable for the tax liabilities of the NewCo.[182] **14.61**

Exiting administration

All other things being equal, administration automatically comes to an end after one year.[183] The company's creditors may agree to extend the administration for one year; or the administrator may apply to the court to extend the administration.[184] Prior to the Enterprise Act 2002, where an administration failed to rescue a company, it was expected that the company would be wound-up. An administrator may make the distributions to the company's secured creditors avoiding the need for a winding up.[185] That objective having occurred, where the administrator 'thinks' that the purpose[186] of the administration has been achieved, the administrator can bring the administration to an end without winding up.[187] This decision is effective only on notice to both the Registrar and the court, but the court's consent is not required.[188] **14.62**

A company may exit administration by being wound up in a creditors' voluntary liquidation. This can be done seamlessly by the administrators filing a **14.63**

180 See n 173 to n 176 above.
181 *Glasgow City Council v Craig* (n 179) at [21].
182 Finance Act 2020, s. 100 and Sch. 13.
183 IA 1986, Sch. B1, para. 76(1).
184 IA 1986, Sch. B1, para. 76(2). The court may extend the period of administration for longer than twelve months.
185 IA 1986, Sch. B1, para. 3(1)(c). Distributions to unsecured creditors may be made only: (i) where the distribution is made under the prescribed part; or (ii) with the permission of the court: Sch. B1, para. 65(3).
186 IA 1986, Sch. B1, para. 80.
187 *Re Kaupthing Singer & Friedlander Ltd (in administration)* [2010] EWCA Civ 518 at [7]–[8] per Etherton LJ; *Nortel* (n 9) at [34] per Lord Neuberger.
188 *Joint Administrators of Station Properties Ltd* [2013] CSOH 120.

notice to that effect. The notice takes effect on registration.[189] In the liquidation that follows, creditors, whose debts existed prior to the administration, and who remain undischarged, may rank in the liquidation, with their claims calculated from the date of the administration.[190] Otherwise, it is possible for a company, following administration, to be dissolved without going into liquidation; dissolution taking place at the end of the period of three months beginning with the date of registration of the notice.[191]

PART A1 MORATORIUM WITH A MONITOR

14.64 Where businesses are in difficulties, often what they require is breathing space from creditors. Under the administration regime, a moratorium was available following registration of a notice to appoint administrators, even if no administrator was in fact appointed. The Corporate Insolvency and Governance Act 2020 now inserts some fifty-five new provisions to the first part of the IA 1986 in Part A1. These govern what is now called the Part A1 moratorium. These provisions allow certain types of company to seek protection from creditors by way of a moratorium without going into a formal insolvency proceeding. The moratorium is only available to a company where an insolvency practitioner, acting as monitor, forms the view that it is likely that a moratorium will result in the rescue of the company.[192] Where the moratorium is obtained, the procedure involves the directors of the company continuing to run the business with an insolvency practitioner acting in the role of monitor overseeing matters.[193] In very broad terms, the moratorium enables a company to continue to trade without making payments of outstanding debts, providing that it meets all further debts that it incurs as they fall due.

14.65 Not all companies are eligible for the moratorium procedure. In terms of status, the general requirement is that the company must be incorporated under the Companies Acts or be an unregistered company that could be wound up under the 1986 Act. Thereafter, particular categories of companies, such as banks and insurance companies, are identified as being ineligible.[194] A company will also be ineligible for a moratorium where it has been subject to specified insolvency procedures in the previous twelve months.[195]

14.66 Provided that a company is not identified as ineligible, a moratorium will be available to a company when: (i) the directors state that the company is, or is likely to become, unable to pay its debts;[196] and (ii) the monitor is of the view that a moratorium would be likely to result in the rescue of the company as

189 IA 1986, Sch. B1, para. 83(3) and (8)(b); *Cartwright v Register of Companies* [2012] EWCA Civ 1159; *Re Globespan Airways Ltd* [2013] 1 WLR 1122.
190 IA 1986, Sch. B1, para. 83(6)(b) and *Re Kaupthing Singer & Friedlander Ltd (in administration)* [2010] EWCA Civ 518 at [7]–[8] per Etherton LJ and Winding Up Rules, r. 7.22(5) and r. 7.27(2)(b).
191 IA 1986, Sch. B1, para. 84(1) and (6).
192 IA 1986, s. A6.
193 IA 1986, ss. A34 and A35. The monitor can require the directors to provide information: s. A36.
194 IA 1986, s. A2 and Sch. ZA1.
195 IA 1986, Sch. ZA1, para. 2.
196 IA 1986, s. A6(1)(d).

a going concern.[197] It is important to note that it is the company itself, rather than its business, which must be capable of rescue.

There are two ways in which a company may enter a moratorium. The first is by filing specified documents with the court in what is referred to as the 'out-of-court process'.[198] This process is not available where the company is subject to an outstanding liquidation petition. The second is by making an application to the court. Where the company is subject to an outstanding liquidation petition, the court may not make the order for a moratorium unless it is satisfied that a moratorium would be likely to achieve a better result for creditors than if the company were wound up (without first being subject to a moratorium).[199] **14.67**

Where the moratorium takes effect, it subsists for twenty business days[200] unless it is extended, or is subject to early termination.[201] The directors may seek an initial extension of twenty business days without creditor consent.[202] Thereafter, any further extensions will require either the consent of the creditors or an order of the court.[203] The moratorium will only last for so long as the monitor remains of the view that it is likely that the company will be rescued as a going concern. If the monitor ceases to hold that view, the moratorium will be brought to an end.[204] **14.68**

For the purposes of the provisions dealing with moratoriums, the company's debts are divided into moratorium debts and pre-moratorium debts.[205] A moratorium debt is one that is incurred during the course of the moratorium. In contrast, a pre-moratorium debt is a debt incurred before the moratorium. Pre-moratorium debts are further subdivided into those for which the company has a payment holiday and those for which there is no payment holiday. The legislation sets out specific categories of pre-moratorium debt for which there is no payment holiday. These include pre-moratorium debts that fell due before the moratorium and which are payable in respect of: **14.69**

(i) the monitor's remuneration or expenses;
(ii) goods or services supplied during the moratorium;
(iii) wages or salary;
(iv) redundancy payments;
(v) rent in respect of a period during the moratorium; and
(vi) debts or other liabilities arising under a contract or other instrument involving financial services.[206]

All pre-moratorium debts which are not specified as being without a payment holiday are pre-moratorium debts with a payment holiday.[207] Those debts do not fall to be paid during the moratorium. Both moratorium debts and **14.70**

197 IA 1986, s. A6(1)(e).
198 IA 1986, s. A3.
199 IA 1986, s. A4.
200 IA 1986, s. A9(1) and (2).
201 IA 1986, s. A9.
202 IA 1986, s. A10.
203 IA 1986, ss. A11 and A13.
204 IA 1986, s. A38.
205 IA 1986, s. A53.
206 IA 1986, s. A18(3).
207 IA 1986, s. A18(3).

pre-moratorium debts for which there is no payment holiday must be paid as they fall due.

14.71 A Part A1 moratorium prevents anyone other than the company's directors applying to open insolvency proceedings with respect to the company.[208] Subject to certain exceptions, creditors are also prevented from seeking to enforce their rights whether by court action and diligence against the company.[209] Floating chargeholders are prevented from appointing administrators.[210] Provisions of a floating charge which purport to impose restrictions on the disposal of the company's property or crystallise the charge on a moratorium being obtained are void.[211]

14.72 The company is also restricted in respect of some of the acts which it can undertake. In particular, restrictions are placed on the company's ability: to obtain credit of more than £500;[212] to grant security;[213] to enter into specified financial transactions;[214] to dispose of property;[215] and to make repayment of pre-moratorium debts.[216] With the exception of the prohibition on entering specified financial transactions, the restrictions are not absolute and the actions can be undertaken if specified criteria are met.

14.73 One point of some significance is that debts or other liabilities arising under a contract or other instrument involving financial services are classified as pre-moratorium debts without a payment holiday. Accordingly, if a company has borrowing that is repayable on demand, a lender will remain entitled to demand repayment of the loan during the moratorium. If that were to occur, it seems likely that a monitor would be forced to conclude that the company could not be rescued, which would require the moratorium to be brought to an end. It follows that a moratorium is unlikely to prove effective unless the company has the support of its lenders.

14.74 The moratorium will come to an end if it is not extended. It will also come to an end if terminated by the monitor, if it is terminated by order of the court or if the company enters another insolvency process.

14.75 Where the company enters into administration or liquidation within twelve weeks of the end of the moratorium the legislation provides for unpaid moratorium debts and certain pre-moratorium debts without a payment holiday (defined as priority pre-moratorium debts) to have priority of ranking in the subsequent insolvency.[217]

208 IA 1986, s. A20 and s. A24. LLPs may be subject to a Part A1 moratorium: Limited Liability Partnerships Act 2000, s. 14(1), and Limited Liability Partnerships Regulations 2001 (SI 2001/1090), reg. 5(1)(a) and Sch. 3 (as amended).
209 IA 1986, s. A21.
210 IA 1986, s. A22.
211 IA 1986, s. A52.
212 IA 1986, s. A25.
213 IA 1986, s. A26.
214 IA 1986, s. A27.
215 IA 1986, s. A29.
216 IA 1986, s. A28.
217 1986 Act, s. 174A (winding-up); Sch. B1, para. 64A (administration).

COMPANY VOLUNTARY ARRANGEMENTS

The law on CVAs is found in Part 1 of, and Sch. A1 to, the IA 1986 and in Part 2 of the CVA and Administration Rules 2018.[218] The procedure is designed to allow a company to come to an arrangement with its creditors which will allow it to continue trading. The company need not be insolvent.[219] But a CVA is often combined with other procedures, such as administration. It is a hybrid procedure: a cross between a scheme of arrangement and a private contract. Subject to the CVA terms, the directors may remain in control. A CVA looks like a contractual document and, according to the terms of the Act, binds all those who voted for or against it, as well as those that would have been entitled to vote on it had they known about it.[220] It is a standard term of a CVA that no legal proceedings may be brought against the company. **14.76**

INTERACTIONS

Provisional liquidation and administration

A creditor petitioning for a winding up may seek the appointment of a provisional liquidator.[221] This is a draconian power which has been described in England as the nuclear weapon of the Companies Court.[222] The court may appoint a provisional liquidator before the petition to wind up has been heard. A provisional liquidator's purpose is to take control of the company's business and assets, normally with a view to their preservation and prevention of their dissipation. Since the appointment of a provisional liquidator, however, has much the same practical effect of a liquidator being appointed, the court will only do so if it is satisfied that it is likely that a liquidator will, indeed, be appointed when the petition is heard.[223] **14.77**

A hearing is bound to be required.[224] The general rule is that presentation of a liquidation petition prevents the company or the directors seeking to appoint an administrator.[225] But it may be impossible to obtain the appointment of a provisional liquidator in the face of a QFC holder who has caveats in place.[226] On being alerted that there is to be a hearing on the appointment of a provisional liquidator, the QFC holder may proceed to file a notice of appointment, **14.78**

218 CVA and Administration Rules 2018 (n 1) above.
219 IA 1986, s. 1(1).
220 IA 1986, s. 5(2)(b).
221 IA 1986, s. 135.
222 *Re a company (No. 007070 of 1996)* [1997] 2 BCLC 139 at 142 per Harman J (where the order was granted on the application of the Secretary of State in relation to alleged fraud on the public in relation to the taking of orders for casks of well-known Scotch whiskies).
223 Cf *Revenue and Customs Commissioners v Rochdale Drinks Distributors Ltd* [2011] EWCA Civ 1116.
224 Cf *Teague, Petr* 1985 SLT 469 and, in England, *Practice Direction (Ch D: Companies Court: Appointment of Provisional Liquidator)* [1997] 1 WLR 3.
225 IA 1986, Sch. B1, para. 25.
226 'Caveat' in this context is a notice filed with the court that prevents interim orders being granted against a party who has lodged such a caveat without a hearing: *Bell's Dictionary* (n 95) 'caveat'.

which suspends the liquidation petition.[227] Once a provisional liquidator has been appointed it is not possible for the QFC holder to appoint an administrator by the out of court route.[228] However, the floating charge holder can apply to court to have an administration order granted and the provisional liquidator removed from office.[229]

Administration and liquidation

14.79 On the presentation of a winding up petition, the standard period of notice is eight days.[230] Given an administrator may be appointed by the holder of a QFC 'out of court', that is to say, by filing forms with the appropriate court, there is a potential for conflict. So where, during the period allowed by the court for intimation of the winding up petition, a notice of appointment of an administrator is filed with the court, the winding up petition is immediately suspended on the filing of the notice.[231] Following the making of a winding up order, the court can make an administration order on the application of a QFC holder. Where this is done, the winding up order is discharged.[232]

ENFORCING FLOATING CHARGES: RECEIVERSHIP

Fixed and floating charges

14.80 Under the Companies Acts, where a company grants a right in security, such as a standard security in respect of Scottish land, the charge must be registered at Companies House within twenty-one days of its creation.[233] In the English law jargon of the Companies Acts, a right in security granted by a company is a 'charge'. In Scots law, the provisions on registration of company charges have long been problematic, not least because, in Scotland, they were generally unnecessary: it was already a general principle of Scots law that rights in security could be created only with some form of publicity.[234] The registration of company charges regime thus leads, with one exception, to a system of dual publicity for all rights in security granted by bodies corporate. The exception is the floating charge, which is registered only at Companies House.[235] A standard security granted by a company and registered in the

227 IA 1986, Sch. B1, para. 40(b).
228 IA 1986, Sch. B1, para. 17(a). Appointment by the company or the directors is prevented by the general rule Sch. B1, para. 25.
229 *Ultimate Invoice Finance Ltd, Petr* 2017 SLT 791 and the commentary thereon: D McKenzie-Skene 2017 Bus LB (148), pp. 3–8,
230 RCS, r. 74.22(2). That rule, however, is subject to RCS, r. 14.6(2) which allows for the period of notice to be shortened.
231 IA 1986, Sch. B1, para. 40(1)(b).
232 IA 1986, Sch. B1, para. 37.
233 Companies Act 2006, Part 25, as amended.
234 For all this, see G L Gretton, 'The Registration of Company Charges' (2002) 6 Edin LR 146 and A D J MacPherson, 'Registration of Company Charges Revisited: New and Familiar Problems' (2019) 23 Edin LR 153.
235 All charges created by a company must also be registered in the granter company's own statutory registers: that is to say, the file of prescribed information that must be kept at the company's registered office and available for inspection: Companies Act 2006, s. 859P.

Land Register may therefore be 'invalid against a liquidator' if the charge is not registered at Companies House within twenty-one days of its registration in the Land Register. In transactional practice, the twenty-one day rule is of central importance. If the period for registration is missed, an application can be made to the court to extend the period.[236]

Floating charges, in Scots law, are creatures of statute.[237] As in the US prior to the introduction of the Uniform Commercial Code,[238] floating charges are not recognised at common law.[239] They were introduced to Scots law by legislation[240] in terms of which certain bodies corporate – which today means, in practice, companies, LLPs and co-operative and community benefit societies – are permitted to grant floating charges.[241] Prior to attachment, the status of a floating charge is difficult to explain conceptually. But despite the constant conceptual problems floating charges have caused, the importance of the floating charge in daily financial practice cannot be overstated. Just two aspects of its importance can be mentioned here. 14.81

The first relates to its ranking with other 'fixed' rights in security. In principle, a floating charge ranks behind prior fixed securities.[242] But a floating charge is also allowed to contain a so-called negative pledge clause: that is to say, a clause prohibiting the company from creating any subsequent security ranking prior to, or *pari passu* with, the floating charge.[243] In other words, a floating charge containing such a clause, as they ordinarily do, ranks ahead of any fixed rights in security, other than those arising by operation of law, which are created after the floating charge has been executed but before the floating charge has attached. Since the clause takes effect as soon as the floating charge has been executed but remain latent for twenty-one days, it may prejudice a subsequent *bona fide* third party creditor who takes a standard security in good faith.[244] 14.82

Example: suppose, on day one, Alpha Limited executes a floating charge, containing a negative pledge, in favour of Bank of Bermuda SA. On day four, Alpha Limited grants a standard security in favour ABC Banking Corporation Inc. On day seven the standard security is registered in the Land Register. On day ten both the floating charge and the standard security are registered at Companies House. On first principles, because the standard security has been created as a subordinate real right prior to enforcement of the floating charge, the standard security ought to prevail over the

236 Companies Act 2006, s. 859F.
237 See generally A D J MacPherson, *The Floating Charge* (Edinburgh: Edinburgh Legal Education Trust, 2020).
238 *Benedict v Ratner* 268 US 353 (1925).
239 *Carse v Coppen* 1951 SC 233 at 239 per Lord President Cooper: 'a floating charge is utterly repugnant to the principles of Scots law and is not recognised by us as creating a security at all'.
240 Companies (Floating Charges) (Scotland) Act 1961.
241 Companies Act 1985, s. 462 (companies), applied to LLPs by the Limited Liability Partnerships (Scotland) Regulations 2001, reg. 3 and Sch. 1; and Co-operative and Community Benefit Societies Act 2014, ss. 62–64.
242 Companies Act 1985, s. 463(1)(b).
243 Companies Act 1985, s. 464, for which see para. 11.66 above.
244 *AIB Finance Ltd v Bank of Scotland* 1993 SC 588.

floating charge. Because the floating charge contained a negative pledge, however, the effect is to invert the ordinary ranking.[245]

14.83 The second important aspect of floating charges is their role in corporate insolvency. Indeed, under the modern law, one of the main rationales for taking an all-encompassing floating charge may have less to do with its effect as a security instrument and more to do with the control it provides to a creditor and, in particular, the right it confers on the holder to appoint an administrator.

Receivership and administrative receivership

14.84 Prior to 1972, the only way to enforce a floating charge in Scotland was to kill the company by liquidation. Receivership was thus introduced as a method for enforcing floating charges in 1972.[246] Receivership allows enforcement by way of an appointment by the floating chargeholder of an insolvency practitioner on an event of default under the instrument creating the floating charge.[247] A receiver whose appointment covered the 'whole or substantially the whole of the company's property and undertaking' was known as an administrative receiver.[248] Other receivers – such as those appointed in respect of specific assets – are plain receivers. The distinction is crucial because, for floating charges executed after September 2003,[249] it is generally no longer possible to appoint an 'administrative receiver'.[250] But it remains possible to appoint a receiver who is not an administrative receiver, such as where a receiver is appointed in respect of a particular asset.

14.85 In either case, however, a receiver's primary duties were owed to the floating chargeholder rather than to the general creditors. Floating charges are generally only held by sophisticated creditors, such as banks. One view, widely held, was that administrative receivership allowed a bank to appoint a receiver, instigate a fire sale of the assets and take whatever could be realised. The unsecured creditors, in contrast, often unsophisticated, usually unrepresented and always ignored, received nothing. It was dissatisfaction with the operation of administrative receivership that led to its abolition for most companies. The abolition of administrative receivership means that, in practice, by far the most important insolvency proceedings are administration (where the business might be saved) and liquidation (where there may be little or nothing left to save).

Abolition of administrative receivership

14.86 The Enterprise Act 2002 was introduced in order to promote a rescue culture. A prescribed part for unsecured creditors was introduced. And the general position is that a floating chargeholder's only option is to place the company

245 IA 1986, Sch. B1, para. 116(f).
246 Floating Charges and Receivers (Scotland) Act 1972.
247 IA 1986, s. 52. The receiver is subject to the Winding-Up Rules (n 2).
248 IA 1986, s. 259(b).
249 When IA 1986, s. 72A came into force.
250 IA 1986, s. 72A. For the exceptions, see (n 252) below.

into administration: a procedure that, generally speaking,[251] prevents all creditors from enforcing rights in security. It has not been possible to appoint an administrative receiver under a floating charge executed after 30 September 2003 – at least in respect of most private companies.[252]

Remnants of receivership

It is still possible to have a receivership that is not an administrative receivership, as where the receiver is not to be appointed over the 'whole or substantially the whole' of the company's property and undertaking. It is also now competent to appoint a receiver in respect of Scottish-based assets pursuant to a Scottish floating charge created by a company that is not registered in Scotland and which the Court of Session would not have jurisdiction to wind up.[253] The IA 1986 allows a receiver to be appointed to a company 'in respect of which a court of a Member State has under the EU Regulation jurisdiction to open insolvency proceedings'.[254] **14.87**

When a receiver is appointed, all business documents, including websites, must publicise the fact that the company is in receivership.[255] A receiver is deemed to be the agent of the company in respect of such property of the company as is attached by the floating charge under which they have been appointed.[256] But the receiver may be personally liable on such contracts as they conclude while holding office, unless they expressly qualify their liability.[257] **14.88**

The prescribed part

One of the many criticisms of administrative receivership was that the receiver acted solely in the interests of the creditor in the strongest position, namely the floating chargeholder. When administrative receivership was abolished, one of the amendments that was introduced was the introduction of the prescribed part: that is to say, a proportion of the assets that would otherwise be paid to the floating chargeholder would be carved out to form a fund for the payment of something to the unsecured creditors. The prescribed part applies, however, only where the company's net property, that would otherwise be available to the floating chargeholder, exceeds £10,000.[258] In so far as the company's net property exceeds £10,000, the prescribed part represents £5,000 of the first **14.89**

251 See para. 14.51 above.

252 But there are a host of exceptions where floating charges have been granted in respect of major financial transactions: see IA 1986, s. 72B–72GA. For a reported example where an administrative receiver was appointed under s. 72E: see *Cabvision Ltd v Feetum* [2006] Ch 585.

253 IA 1986, s. 51(1)(b) and (2), as a result of amendments introduced in 2011. For the background to the amendments, see H Patrick, 'Receivership of Foreign Based Companies' 2010 SLT (News) 177.

254 IA 1986, s. 51(1)(b).

255 IA 1986, s. 64.

256 IA 1986, s. 57(1). The receiver's powers are set out in 1986 Act, Sch. 2.

257 IA 1986, s. 57(2). But even if they are personally liable, they are entitled to an indemnity from the funds subject to the charge: s. 57(3). There are special provisions dealing with employment contracts: s. 57(2A)–57(2C).

258 IA 1986, s. 176A(3)(a) read with Insolvency Act (Prescribed Part) Order 2003 (SI 2003/2097), art. 2.

£10,000; and 20 per cent of the company's net property thereafter.[259] From April 2020, the maximum value of the prescribed part is £800,000 unless the first ranking floating charge was created prior to that date. In those circumstances, the maximum value of the prescribed part will remain at £600,000.[260]

14.90 Where the company has net property that would be available to a floating chargeholder that is less than the prescribed minimum (currently £10,000); and the liquidator, administrator or receiver 'thinks that the cost of making a distribution to the unsecured creditors would be disproportionate to the benefits',[261] then the prescribed part does not apply. Separately, and in any event, it is possible for the administrator or liquidator to ask the court to disapply the prescribed part.[262] One common reason in practice for seeking to disapply is that the prescribed part will be small relative to the expense that would be involved in adjudicating on the unsecured creditors' claims. But the court has a discretion. The mere fact that the dividend to individual unsecured creditors will be small is not, of itself, enough to justify the disapplication of the prescribed part.[263] The prescribed part may be disapplied only in general terms: it is not possible to seek its disapplication in relation only to specific creditors.[264]

REALISING ASSETS: POWERS

14.91 The powers of the various office holders are set out in various schedules to the IA 1986:

(i) The powers of an administrator are contained in Sch. 1.
(ii) The powers of a Scottish receiver are contained in Sch. 2.
(iii) The powers of a liquidator are contained in Sch. 4.

14.92 The exercise of these powers has sometimes been controversial in relation to the assignation of rights of action held by the company in favour of a particular creditor. Although it had long been tolerably clear that office holders do have such a power,[265] the Small Business, Enterprise and Employment Act 2015 introduced various amendments to the IA 1986 to make it clear – particularly for English law – that liquidators and administrators may assign claims that otherwise they alone were able to bring: such as claims for fraudulent or wrongful trading; unfair preferences or gratuitous alienations.[266]

259 2003 Order (n 258) above, art. 3. See further paras 11.71–11.72 above.
260 2003 Order (n 258) above, art. 3(2) as amended by the Insolvency Act 1986 (Prescribed Part) (Amendment) Order 2020 (SI 2020/211).
261 IA 1986, s. 176A(3)(b).
262 IA 1986, s. 176A(5).
263 See, e.g. *Administrators of QMD Hotels Ltd, Noters* [2010] CSOH 168 and the subsequent guidance from Lord Doherty in *Joint Administrators of Castlebridge Plant Ltd, Noters* [2017] BCC 87.
264 *Joint Administrators of Courts plc (in Liquidation)* [2008] EWHC 2339 (Ch).
265 IA 1986, Sch. 1, para. 2; *Norglen v Reeds Rains Prudential Ltd* [1999] 2 AC 1 at 11E–12E and at 16H–17B per Lord Hoffmann.
266 IA 1986, s. 246ZD.

INSOLVENCY REMEDIES: DIRECTORS AND TRANSFEREES

Personal liability and directors' disqualification

Directors of companies in financial difficulties may be subject to personal liability. Under s. 212 of the IA 1986, an officer[267] of a company who has 'misapplied or retained, or become accountable for, any money or other property of the company, or been guilty of any misfeasance or breach of any fiduciary or other duty in relation to the company' may be examined and, on the application of a liquidator or a creditor, be required: (a) to repay, restore or account for the money or property or any part of it, with interest at such rate as the court thinks just; or (b) to contribute such sum to the company's assets by way of compensation in respect of the misfeasance or breach of fiduciary or other duty as the court thinks just.[268] Section 212 does not add anything to existing common law remedies, but s. 212(3) confers discretion on the court concerning the remedy to be awarded once liability is established.[269] **14.93**

Sections 213 (fraudulent trading) and 214 (wrongful trading) of the IA 1986, in contrast, provide statutory rights of action. The two sections are materially different. Section 213 deals with fraudulent trading, which is also a criminal offence.[270] It may lead to liability being imposed on 'any person' who has 'carried on the business of the company with intent to defraud creditors of the company or creditors of any other person, or for any fraudulent purpose'. It is worldwide in its scope.[271] Section 214, in contrast, applies to persons who are, or who have been, directors of the company. In terms of s. 214(4), the court will take into account both: (a) the general knowledge, skill and experience that may reasonably be expected of a person carrying out the same functions as are carried out by that director in relation to the company; and also (b) the general knowledge, skill and experience that that director has. Part (b) of this test refers to actual knowledge which the director has over and above the minimum to be expected of an ordinarily competent director. Part (b) of the test is of particular importance to qualified professionals – such as lawyers and accountants – who act as company directors. For whereas part (b) of the test may increase the standard of care incumbent on the director, it will never lower the standard below that set out in part (a). Sections 213 and 214 are of real concern in practice, although reported case law involving applications under those sections is limited. **14.94**

267 Officer, in this context, includes, in principle, *de facto* or shadow directors: *Revenue and Customs Commissioners v Holland* [2010] UKSC 51, [2010] 1 WLR 2793 at [51] per Lord Hope of Craighead.

268 See, e.g. *Trustees of the Dyglen Engineering Ltd Pension Scheme (No. 2) v Russell* 2014 GWD 1-6 (Sh Ct).

269 *Stone & Rolls Ltd (in liquidation) v Moore Stephens (a firm)* [2009] 1 AC 1391 at [110]–[111] per Lord Scott. There are other aspects of this decision (particularly with regard to attribution) which can no longer be regarded as authoritative: see *Singularis Holdings Ltd (in liquidation) v Daiwa Capital Markets Europe Ltd* [2019] UKSC 50, [2020] AC 1189 at [34].

270 Companies Act 2006, s. 993(1): 'If any business of a company is carried on with intent to defraud creditors of the company or creditors of any other person, or for any fraudulent purpose, every person who is knowingly a party to the carrying on of the business in that manner commits an offence'.

271 *Bilta (UK) Ltd (No. 2) v Nazir* [2016] AC 1.

14.95 Finally, it should be mentioned that an insolvency practitioner is required to investigate into, and report to, the Secretary of State the conduct of all persons who were directors of the company in the three years prior to insolvency.[272] The Secretary of State will consider these reports and decide whether a particular director is someone against whom disqualification proceedings under the Company Directors Disqualification Act 1986 should be instigated. Where proceedings are brought under s. 6 of that Act, the court must make a disqualification order of between two and fifteen years against a director if it is satisfied that their conduct as a director of that company makes them unfit to be concerned in the management of a company.[273] In considering whether the director's conduct amounts to unfitness, the court requires to determine whether the director's conduct had fallen below the standards of probity and competence appropriate for persons fit to be directors of companies.[274]

14.96 On an application by the Secretary of State, the court has the power to grant a compensation order against an individual who has been disqualified from acting as a director of a company. The order can be made where the person who is subject to the disqualification order or undertaking has caused loss to one or more creditors of an insolvent company of which the person has, at any time, been a director.[275]

Fraudulent breach of trust and embezzlement

14.97 Bell used the term 'embezzlement' to describe the acts of an insolvent debtor that prefer particular creditors.[276] The term has proved evocative and its effect enduring. Under the law of prescription, for example, the prescriptive period is interrupted where the creditor is induced to refrain from making a relevant claim in relation to the obligation by the debtor's fraud;[277] while claims to make reparation or restitution for 'fraudulent breach of trust' are imprescriptible.[278] It is necessary to say something of these two elements: what must be demonstrated in order to satisfy the 'fraudulent' aspect; and, secondly, what is meant by 'trust' in this context.

Fraudulent breach of trust

14.98 It is often said in civil proceedings that any allegations of fraud must be specific.[279] But the specification indicated – identity of alleged perpetrator

272 Company Directors Disqualification Act 1986, s. 7A; Insolvent Companies (Reports on Conduct of Directors) (Scotland) Rules 2016 (SI 2016/185).

273 Company Directors Disqualification Act 1986, ss. 1, 6, 12C and Sch. 1.

274 See, e.g. *Re Sevenoaks Stationers (Retail) Ltd* [1991] Ch 164 at 176; *Re Grayan Building Services Ltd* [1995] Ch 241 at 255 and *Secretary of State for Business, Innovation and Skills v Khan* 2012 SLT 1090.

275 Company Directors Disqualification Act 1986, ss. 15A–15C. For judicial consideration of these provisions see *Re Noble Vintners Ltd* [2019] EWHC 2806 (Ch).

276 Bell, *Commentaries* II, 170 (quoted at (n 325) below).

277 Prescription and Limitation (Scotland) Act 1973, s. 6(4).

278 Prescription and Limitation (Scotland) Act 1973, Sch. 3, para. (e)(ii).

279 *Royal Bank of Scotland plc v Holmes* 1999 SLT 563 at 569 per Lord Macfadyen: 'It is in my view essential for the party alleging fraud clearly and specifically to identify the act or representation founded upon, the occasion on which the act was committed or the representation made, and the circumstances relied on as yielding the inference that that act or

and specification of the allegedly fraudulent acts – is little different than the specification that ought to be required for any action. In Scots law, insolvency fraud has never required proof of the transferee's dishonesty.[280] In Bankton's strikingly modern phrase, insolvency fraud is a form of 'statutory presumptive fraud'.[281] Indeed, it was early established in the nineteenth century that, in attacking an unfair preference under the Bankruptcy Act 1696 it was not necessary to prove fraud.[282]

As has been seen, claims for 'fraudulent breach of trust' are imprescriptible.[283] **14.99** 'Trust' language is, for this reason, often banded around in corporate insolvencies. Sometimes it is said, based on an imaginative reading of the legislation,[284] that the company is a trustee for its creditors; sometimes that the directors of the insolvent company are trustees for the company's creditors. But it is only the company that can reasonably be described as a trustee for its creditors; and, even then, as Lord President Emslie has pointed out, only in a general and non-technical sense.[285] Not all breaches of fiduciary duty by a company director, however, amount to a breach of trust.[286] The remedy for breach of trust is normally damages or restitution. Clear averments are required for any case based on constructive trust.[287] In England it has been held that claims based on constructive trust are subject to the ordinary law of limitation and do not fall within a similar exception for claims based on a fraudulent breach of trust.[288] But those provisions would apply to a company director who made unlawful distributions.[289]

representation was fraudulent. It is also, in my view, essential that the person who committed the fraudulent act or made the fraudulent misrepresentation be identified'.

280 *M'Gowan v Wright* (1853) 15 D 494 approved in *Dryburgh v Scotts Media Tax Ltd (in liquidation)* [2014] CSIH 45, 2014 SC 651 at [30] per Lord Drummond Young. More generally, see D Reid, 'The Doctrine of Presumptive Fraud in Scots Law' (2013) 34 *Journal of Legal History* 307.

281 Bankton, *Inst* I, 264, 85.

282 *Speir v Dunlop* (1827) 5 S 729 at 731 per Lord Justice Clerk Boyle, followed in *Mitchell v Rodger* (1834) 12 S 802 at 810 per Lord President Hope: 'After the case of *Speir*, it is in vain to contend that fraud is an essential element in a reduction on the [Bankruptcy Act 1696] . . .'. For the crime of embezzlement, see *HM Advocate v City of Glasgow Bank Directors* (1879) 4 Coup 161; *Moore v HMA* [2010] HCJAC 26, 2010 SCCR 451; *McCraw v Murphy* [2016] HCJAC 20, 2016 SCL 383.

283 Prescription and Limitation (Scotland) Act 1973, Sch. 3, para. (e)(ii).

284 1986 Act, s. 130(4).

285 *Nordic Travel Ltd v Scotprint Ltd* 1980 SC 1 at 10: 'There are no doubt certain acts which, in the interests of all his creditors . . . an insolvent person is obliged not to do, but to say that he is, literally, a trustee for his creditors is unwarranted in authority and wholly misleading'. The idea, in English law, of an insolvent company holding its assets in trust for creditors is set out in *Ayerst v C & K (Construction) Ltd* [1976] AC 167. But as Lord Hoffmann has pointed out, 'it is a special kind of trust . . . The creditors have only a right to have the assets administered by the liquidator in accordance with the provisions of the Insolvency Act 1986': *Buchler v Talbot* [2004] 2 AC 298 at [28].

286 Cf *Dryburgh v Scotts Media Tax Ltd* [2011] CSOH 147 revd [2014] CSIH 45, 2014 SC 651.

287 *Ross v Morley and Williamson* [2013] CSOH 175; *Ted Jacob Engineering Group Inc v Matthew* [2014] CSIH 18, 2014 SC 579 at [98]–[101] per Lord Drummond Young. Cf N Whitty, 'The "No Profit from Another's Fraud" Rule and the Knowing Receipt Muddle' (2013) 17 Edin LR 37.

288 *Williams v Central Bank of Nigeria* [2014] UKSC 10, [2014] 2 WLR 355. For a consideration of the issues in Scots law, see *King's Trs v King* [2020] CSOH 101.

289 *Burnden Holdings (UK) Ltd v Fielding* [2018] UKSC 14, [2018] AC 857.

Maintenance of capital and unlawful distributions

14.100 In corporate insolvency there is an overlap between the rules of insolvency law with the substantive rules of company law designed to protect creditors. As a general rule, company law imposes conditions on the circumstances in which a company may deal with its capital (the 'maintenance of capital' principle).[290] Companies may make distributions, by way of dividends, only out of profits available for distribution. The Companies Acts expressly prohibit, for instance, distributions of capital that have not been properly declared as a dividend (the 'unlawful distributions rule');[291] and at common law disguised returns of capital to shareholders are prohibited, even where the recipients are not shareholders, but corporate vehicles controlled, directly or indirectly, by the same person who controls the company making the distribution.[292]

EFFECT OF INSOLVENCY ON PATRIMONIAL RIGHTS

Introduction

14.101 Insolvency, in the general sense, means that the insolvent company cannot meet its liabilities. But there are a number of legal principles which regulate how the insolvency administrator can deal with the company's property and existing contractual relationships. It is often difficult to find a modern statement of these principles in the case law so it makes sense to explain some of the vocabulary sometimes encountered: adoption and judicial rescission, abandonment and disclaimer.

General principle

14.102 On insolvency, a company remains the holder of its patrimonial rights: it remains creditor of its receivables, owner of its immoveable and corporeal moveable properties, and holder of its other patrimonial rights such as intellectual property rights. Conversely, the company remains the debtor in respect of its liabilities and remains liable for the performance of its obligations even after a liquidator, or other insolvency practitioner, has been appointed.[293] The effect of appointment of an insolvency practitioner is rather to invest the insolvency practitioner with the power to manage the company and the authority to enter into contracts on behalf of the company. Unless otherwise expressed, however, an insolvency practitioner is considered as acting independently after appointment: creditors, with whom the insolvency practitioner contracts, in the absence of express limitations on the insolvency practitioner's liability, are entitled to look to the personal credit of the insolvency practitioner (and,

290 The *locus classicus* is *Trevor v Whitworth* (1887) 12 App Cas 409 at 423–424 per Lord Watson.

291 Companies Act 2006, s. 847.

292 *Aveling Barford Ltd v Perion* (1989) 5 BCC 677; *Progress Property Co Ltd v Moore* [2010] UKSC 55, [2011] 1 WLR 1.

293 *Smith v Lord Advocate (No. 1)* 1978 SC 259 at 270–271 per Lord President Emslie.

on ordinary principles of agency, the professional firm which the insolvency practitioner represents).[294]

Adoption

An insolvency practitioner, such as a liquidator, is not liable to perform the insolvent company's obligations. But the liquidator is entitled, where they consider it in the interests of the creditors to do so, to 'adopt' certain contracts, procure the performance of the company's outstanding obligations, and then claim the benefits of that performance for the company's creditors. This is the general process known as 'adoption'.[295] **14.103**

A liquidator has the power to carry on the business so far as necessary for the beneficial winding up;[296] an administrator has the power to do anything necessary or expedient for the management of the affairs, business and property of the company, together with a long list of specific powers.[297] Many of the older Scottish authorities deal with trustees in sequestration. The rules as they apply to trustees in sequestration have been reformed. The position is that the trustee now has twenty-eight days to decide to adopt a contract of the bankrupt's. If the trustee does not respond to a written request to adopt, the trustee is deemed to have refused to adopt the contract.[298] **14.104**

The rationale for adoption is that the bankrupt's contract may be profitable for the bankrupt's estate and thus benefit the general creditors. Adoption applies only to the bankrupt's liabilities under the contract. By adoption, the trustee assumes (personal) liability for the bankrupt's liabilities under the contract. In a personal bankruptcy, the trustee is already vested in the bankrupt's claims under the contract. **14.105**

On a corporate insolvency, the company remains creditor in respect of its own debtors, and it remains liable for its debts. Like the trustee in sequestration, therefore, a liquidator or administrator has the power to adopt any outstanding liabilities the company has under the contract, in order to obtain the counter-performance owed to the insolvent company. The effect of the administrator or liquidator as the case may be adopting, is that the company's liability under the contract ranks as an insolvency expense. **14.106**

A contract is not adopted by the mere fact of the insolvency administrator claiming an accrued debt.[299] Special provisions apply to employment contracts and there are strict time limits in which an insolvency practitioner must decide whether the employees are to be retained and the contracts adopted.[300] A receiver cannot 'cherry-pick' the obligations adopted under a contract **14.107**

294 *Smith* (n 293) at 270 and 272 per Lord President Emslie.

295 Cf *Edinburgh Heritable Security Co Ltd v Stevenson's Tr* (1886) 13 R 427 at 428 per Lord McLaren (Ordinary).

296 IA 1986, s. 165(2), 167(1) and Sch. 4.

297 IA 1986, Sch. B1, paras 59–60 and Sch. 1.

298 Bankruptcy (Scotland) Act 2016, s. 110(1) and (10). See para. 13.28 above.

299 *Sturrock v Robertson's Tr* 1913 SC 582; *Craig's Tr v Lord Malcolm* (1900) 2 F 541.

300 IA 1986, s. 57(5) and Sch. 2. para. 11 (receivers); Sch. B1, para. 59 and Sch. 1, para. 11 (administrators), for which see *Kavanagh v Crystal Palace FC 2000 Ltd* (n 138); IA 1986, Sch. 4, paras 12 and 13 (liquidators) (no express power in relation to employees).

of employment.[301] But a liquidator[302] or an administrator[303] may decline to adopt an onerous personal obligation.

14.108 An insolvency practitioner may be deemed to have adopted contracts where they have taken post-insolvency benefits, such as where an administrator has retained 'beneficial occupation' by the company of leased premises. The rent under such leases becomes an insolvency expense. This is sometimes known as the '*Lundy Granite* principle'.[304] So where administrators had continued to possess under a lease and had, as part of a restructuring, purported to grant a sub-lease (in breach of the terms of the lease), the landlords were held entitled to require the administrators to treat the rent as an expense of the administration.[305] In England, there is continuing controversy about whether rent payable in advance – as where the quarter day on which the rent is payable falls before the date of administration – falls within the principle. The cases impose a 'pay-as-you-go' principle: such rent too is to be treated as an expense of the administration in so far as the administrator remains in beneficial occupation.[306] In Scotland, an insolvency practitioner who has not caused the company to remain in beneficial occupation of the leased premises is not liable for the rent. It should be remembered that the landlord retains a fixed security for unpaid rent by virtue of the landlord's hypothec, but in practice there may be limited corporeal moveables belonging to the company of value.

Rescission

14.109 All other things being equal, insolvency has no effect on existing contracts. But most professionally drafted contracts contain 'events of default' provisions, the result of which normally confers various rights on the solvent counter-party, such as accelerating the date for performance of the insolvent party's liabilities under the contract.[307] Such provisions may be the subject of judicial scrutiny.[308] The solvent party normally has an option, but not the obligation, to rescind. It is open to the solvent party to claim the amounts due under the contract as a debt. Where the solvent party wants to rescind but has no contractual right to terminate the contract with the insolvent company, the solvent party may ask the court to terminate the contract judicially.[309]

301 *Powdrill v Watson* [1995] 2 AC 394 at 449.

302 *Joint Liquidators of The Scottish Coal Co Ltd* 2014 SC 372 at [124] per Lord Justice Clerk Carloway.

303 *Joint Administrators of Rangers Football Club plc, Noters* 2012 SLT 599 at [53] per Lord Hodge.

304 *Re Lundy Granite Company, ex parte Heavan* (1871) LR 6 Ch App 462 at 466 per James LJ, explained in *Re Toshoku Finance UK plc* [2002] 1 WLR 671 at [27] and [29] per Lord Hoffmann; and *Re London Bridge Entertainment Partners LLP (in administration)* [2019] EWHC 2932 (Ch).

305 *Cheshire West and Chester Borough Council, Petr* [2010] CSOH 115.

306 *Jervis v Pillar Denton Ltd* [2014] EWCA Civ 180, [2015] Ch 87.

307 Although see para. 14.14 above.

308 See *Belmont Park* (n 37).

309 IA 1986, s. 186.

Abandonment

In principle, any solvent person, natural or juristic, may abandon ownership of corporeal moveables.[310] At common law, the Crown acquires ownership of such abandoned objects.[311] But there is now a statutory procedure which must be followed by the finder of lost or abandoned corporeal moveable property.[312] Solvent creditors too may 'abandon' personal rights held against debtors by discharging the debtors or by doing nothing and allowing the period for negative prescription to expire. **14.110**

Ownership of land is morc difficult. A trustee in sequestration may 'abandon' property so as to re-vest the property in the bankrupt.[313] But there is no recognised procedure for the registration of a unilateral abandonment of ownership of immoveable property without a disposition in favour of another person.[314] Assets held by a company that is dissolved, including ownership of immoveable property, vest as *bona vacantia* in the Queen's and Lord Treasurer's Remembrancer.[315] **14.111**

Disclaimer of onerous property

The IA 1986 contains bespoke provisions allowing the liquidators of English companies to 'disclaim onerous property'.[316] That provision applies to the company's property wherever situated. There is no equivalent express provision in the IA 1986 for liquidators of Scottish companies. The IA 1986 applies to Scottish companies the general principles of bankruptcy and insolvency law and a liquidator is given the same powers as the trustee of a bankrupt estate.[317] Adoption, as has been seen, is a power conferred on a trustee in sequestration, administrator or liquidator. The power to adopt is also a power to refuse to adopt. But whereas the power to adopt relates to the company's liabilities, disclaimer is a power which relates to the company's assets.[318] It is useful to make this distinction at the outset as it is not one that is otherwise made in the Scottish cases that do mention a power to disclaim.[319] **14.112**

310 See K G C Reid, *The Law of Property in Scotland* (Edinburgh: LexisNexis, 1996), paras 540 and 547–552.
311 Reid, *The Law of Property in Scotland* (n 310), paras 540 and 547.
312 Civic Government (Scotland) Act 1982, ss. 67–79.
313 Bankruptcy (Scotland) Act 2016, s. 87(8) and (9).
314 *Joint Liquidators of The Scottish Coal Co Ltd* 2014 SC 379 at [124].
315 Companies Act 2006, s. 1012, for which see *ELB Securities Ltd v Love* 2016 SC 77.
316 IA 1986, s. 178.
317 IA 1986, s. 169(2).
318 The rather different evolution of English law in this area is charted in *Hindcastle Ltd v Barbara Attenborough Ltd* [1997] AC 70 at 89H–96D per Lord Nicholls of Birkenhead. But Lord Nicholls too, in the context of the effect of disclaimer on a lease, at the outset of his speech carefully distinguishes the respective rights and obligations of the parties to a lease: 85B–85D. In England, a liquidator's power to disclaim is today statutory: 1986 Act, s. 178; but there is no equivalent power for an administrator: *Re Nortel GmbH* (n 9) at [104] per Lord Neuberger.
319 For example, *Crown Estate Commissioners v Liquidators of Highland Engineering Ltd* 1975 SLT 58 at 59 per Lord Keith.

14.113 In *Joint Liquidators of The Scottish Coal Co Ltd, Noters*,[320] the liquidators applied to the court for directions on whether they were entitled to abandon on behalf of the company the ownership of various coalmines to which significant environmental liabilities attached. The Inner House held that although it is possible for a Scottish insolvency administrator to refuse to adopt liabilities under contracts or leases, or to abandon assets in the form of ownership of corporeal moveables, Scots law does not recognise any power in an owner of land to 'abandon' ownership.[321] Similarly an administrator cannot 'disclaim' the company's ownership of immoveable property situated in Scotland.[322]

CHALLENGEABLE TRANSACTIONS[323]

Introduction

14.114 'Wherever there is commerce, there must be bankrupts', the eighteenth century judge, Lord Coalston, once observed; adding that, 'wherever there are bankrupts, there will be attempts to disappoint the law'.[324] Transactions entered into by an insolvent verging on insolvency (*vergens ad inopiam*) to the detriment of his creditors are challengeable at common law, as well as under statute. As Bell observed:

> 'From the moment of insolvency a debtor is bound to act as the mere trustee, or rather as the *negotiorum gestor*, of his creditors, who thenceforward have the exclusive interest in his funds. He may, as long as he is permitted, continue his trade, with the intention of making gain for his creditors and for himself; but his funds are no longer his own, which he can be entitled secretly to set apart for his own use, or to give away as caprice or affection may dictate. This is the great principle on which the creditors of an insolvent debtor are, by the law of Scotland, entitled to proceed in detecting embezzlement.'[325]

14.115 Two classic examples of fraudulent transactions voidable at the instance of a creditor or the liquidator or administrator,[326] as the case may be, are gratuitous alienations and unfair preferences. It is worth emphasising, however, that such transactions remain capable of challenge at common law.[327] And, unlike under the statutory provisions, there are no time limits for challenging transactions

320 [2013] CSOH 124.

321 [2013] CSIH 108, 2014 SC 372.

322 For subsequent cases, see *Joint Liquidators of Doonin Plant Ltd, Noters* [2018] CSOH 89, 2019 SLT 195; and *Administrator of Dawson International plc, Noter* [2018] CSOH 52, 2018 SLT 1000 (land in England owned by Scottish company).

323 The creditors' right to challenge can be traced to the *actio Pauliana* of Roman law and the term is often used internationally to describe equivalent actions in other legal systems: e.g. *l'action paulienne* or *Paulianische Anfechtung*. For the history, see the opinion of the Advocate General in Case C-339/07 *Seagon v Deko Marty Belgium NV* [2009] ECR I-767, [2009] 1 WLR 2168.

324 *Mansfield, Hunter & Co v Macilmun* (1770) Mor 'Bill of Exchange' App 1, No. 1, Hailes 350 at 351. Cf *Belmont Park Investments* (n 37) above per Lord Walker.

325 Bell, *Commentaries* II, 170, approved in *Nordic Travel Ltd* (n 285) and in *Johnston v Peter H Irvine Ltd* 1984 SLT 209.

326 IA 1986, s. 242(1) and (7) (gratuitous alienations); and s. 243(4) and (6) (unfair preferences).

327 See ss. 242(7) and 243(6) and *Bank of Scotland, Petrs* 1987 SC 234, affd 1988 SC 245.

at common law: this is consistent with the rule that obligations arising out of fraudulent breach of trust are imprescriptible[328] and to which a discharge from bankruptcy does not extend.[329]

Gratuitous alienations

A gratuitous alienation is the classic 'attempt to disappoint the law'. A company, seeing the writing on the wall, seeks to transfer assets, often to connected persons, without adequate consideration. Any pre-insolvency creditor, or a liquidator, or an administrator, is therefore entitled to reduce such transactions as being prejudicial to the general body of creditors for whose benefit these assets, or their proceeds, ought to have been retained. There are two periods during which gratuitous alienations may be challenged. The standard period is two years. But where the transferee is an 'associate',[330] the relevant suspect period in respect to which the liquidator or administrator may examine alienations is five years. If the alienation became 'completely effectual' within one of those periods, it was made on a 'relevant day'. In terms of the IA 1986, all 'alienations' (which terms includes a transfer, discharge or renunciation of a patrimonial right belonging to the company) on a relevant day are challengeable. A court will grant reduction or an order for restoration unless the defender can demonstrate that one of the defences has been fulfilled. The defences are that: (a) the company assets were greater than its liabilities; or (b) the alienation was made for adequate consideration; or (c) the alienation was a conventional or charitable gift which, in all the circumstances, it was reasonable for the company to make.[331] Importantly, in a case where there has been consideration for a transfer, but the consideration is inadequate, the court has an inherent power to modify the remedy of reduction so as to protect the transferee who, *ex hypothesi*, has paid some consideration, as by making it a condition for the decree of reduction that the liquidators paid back the consideration; or to make an order against the transferee to pay a specified sum to the liquidators.[332] **14.116**

The relevant date is calculated from the date on which the suspect transaction became 'completely effectual'.[333] For example, suppose a company disponed heritable property on 20 January 2007 to an associate company for no consideration. That disposition was registered on 10 January 2009. The transferor company is wound up on 5 January 2014. The liquidator would be able to seek reduction of the disposition because the disposition became 'completely effectual' only on registration and registration was within the five year period. **14.117**

328 See para. 14.97.

329 Bankruptcy (Scotland) Act 2016, s. 145(3)(e).

330 Defined in Bankruptcy (Scotland) Act 2016, s. 229 for natural persons to mean 'relative', the spouses of relatives or relatives of spouses; in broad terms, a company is an associate of another company if it is controlled by the same person: s. 229(11)–(15). Cf IA 1986, s. 435(6).

331 IA 1986, s. 242(4).

332 *MacDonald v Carnbroe Estates Ltd* [2019] UKSC 57, 2020 SC (UKSC) 23 at [65]–[69] per Lord Hodge.

333 IA 1986, s. 242(3). See, e.g. *Craiglaw Developments Ltd v Gordon Wilson & Co* 1997 SC 356; *Jackson v Royal Bank of Scotland plc* 2002 SLT 1123; *Accountant in Bankruptcy v Orr* 2005 SLT 1019.

An action of reduction is brought at the instance of the liquidator or administrator as the case may be, and by action not petition.[334] Where the legal basis of a payment is reduced, the liquidator or administrator will be able to seek either repayment from the transferee on the basis of unjustified enrichment[335] or an order under the IA 1986 for restoration of the property.[336] An alienation is normally a transfer of an asset. However the discharge, without consideration of patrimonial value,[337] of a good security or personal right to payment held by the company may also amount to an alienation. The relevant date for considering whether there was a shortfall in patrimonial value is the date on which the attacked transaction was entered into;[338] where the consideration is represented by the transferee undertaking an obligation, it can only constitute consideration if it is undertaken as the counterpart of the alienation.[339] Agreements to pay, 'as soon as I have money'[340] or 'when funds are available' or 'with the consent of the debtor' are not normally considered to amount to an enforceable obligation to pay on which a defence to an action of reduction may be founded.

Unfair preferences

14.118 The law on unfair preferences is said to be based on the notional distinction between formal insolvency (such as commencement of winding up or administration) and constructive insolvency which is deemed, by statute, to have occurred at any earlier date.[341] This is often referred to as the 'suspect period'. Under s. 243(1), the suspect period is the six months before the commencement of the winding up. An unfair preference often involves the payment of a genuine debt to a genuine creditor. The transaction is attacked rather because, in the suspect period, that creditor has received payment of their debt before it was actually due. So in a case where a director of a company transferred £9,000 to themselves in their capacity as a creditor of the company and, on the same day, resolved to wind up the company, it is likely that, in the absence of documentary evidence demonstrating that this was indeed a cash payment in respect of a presently due debt, it would amount to an unfair preference.[342] Similarly, where a director has acted as cautioner for a company and been called upon to pay the company's debts, payments made during the suspect period to the director in relief of their cautionary obligation are likely

334 *Joint Administrators of Prestonpans (Trading) Ltd, Petrs* [2012] CSOH 184, 2013 SLT 138.

335 *Stak Realty Group Co Ltd (in administration) v McKenna* [2010] CSOH 29; *Joint Administrators of Questway Ltd v Simpson* [2012] CSOH 107.

336 See, e.g. *Joint Administrators of Oceancrown Ltd v Stonegale Ltd* [2013] CSOH 189 at [48] (affd [2015] CSIH 12 and 2016 SC (UKSC) 91).

337 *MacFadyen's Trustee v MacFadyen* 1994 SC 416 at 421–422 per Lord McCluskey; *Matheson's Tr v Matheson* 1992 SLT 685 at 686G–686H per Lord Marnoch (Ordinary): 'the giving of "consideration" involve[s] either the discharge of an existing obligation or an exchange of new obligations'.

338 *Liquidator of Letham Grange Development Co Ltd v Foxworth Investments Ltd* [2013] CSIH 13, 2013 SLT 445 at [75] per Lady Paton revd (n 339) below.

339 *Liquidator of Letham Grange Development Co Ltd v Foxworth Investments Ltd* [2014] UKSC 41, 2014 SC (UKSC) 203 at [25] per Lord Reed.

340 *Rose v Falconer* (1868) 6 Macph 960.

341 Cf Bell, *Commentaries* II, 193.

342 *Liquidator of 3G Design Engineering Ltd v White* [2012] CSOH 124 revd [2013] CSIH 20.

to amount to a preference.[343] There may be an overlap between s. 242 and s. 243.

Payments in cash, ordinary course of trade and *nova debita*

The general rule in s. 243 is that, in the suspect period, a company may not confer preferential treatment in favour of a creditor to the prejudice of the general body of creditors. Section 243(2) contains a number of exceptions: (a) transactions in the ordinary course of trade or business; (b) a payment in cash for a debt which, when it was paid, had become payable, unless the transaction was collusive; and (c) a transaction whereby the parties to it undertake reciprocal obligations (sometimes known as the *nova debita* principle);[344] (d) the granting of a mandate by a company authorising an arrestee to pay over arrested funds to an arrester. **14.119**

The onus is on any defender seeking to demonstrate that any of the above exceptions apply. A pursuer may not even need to lead any evidence if little in the way of evidence is offered by the defender, since the defender will thus fail to discharge the evidential burden.[345] A major difficulty is that in many, perhaps most, cases where the defences are pled, they cannot be made out because neither the insolvent company nor the transferees kept any records documenting the transactions which, later, those selfsame parties, when called as defenders, seek to set up. It is often on insolvency that failures by former directors of a company to comply with their statutory obligation to keep proper records is thrown into sharp focus. The courts are generally unsympathetic to after-the-event attempts by such directors to place a commercially justifiable construction on the attacked transactions.[346] The statutory exceptions will not provide a defence if the party pursuing the action can show that the transaction in question was collusive. Knowledge of insolvency will not of itself be sufficient to evidence collusion.[347] It is necessary to show that there has been a scheme that was intended to benefit one creditor to the prejudice of the general body of creditors.[348] **14.120**

Floating charges as preferences

The IA 1986 also contains provisions on the enforceability of floating charges granted within the relevant suspect period.[349] The relevant suspect period is two years prior to the onset of insolvency where the floating charge is created in favour of connected persons; and twelve months from the onset of insolvency where the person in whose favour the charge is created is not **14.121**

343 *Mitchell v Rodger* (1834) 12 S 802 followed in *Anderson v Dickens* [2008] CSOH 134, 2009 SCLR 609 at [73] and [93] per Sir David Edward QC. See too *Baillie Marshall Ltd (in Liquidation) v Avian Communications Ltd* 2002 SLT 189.

344 In *Nicoll v Steelpress (Supplies) Ltd* 1992 SC 119, the Inner House held that nothing less than full patrimonial value would found a relevant *novum debitum* defence.

345 Cf *McLuckie Brothers Ltd v Newhouse Contracts Ltd* 1993 SLT 641; and *Stak Realty Group Co Ltd (in administration) v McKenna* [2010] CSOH 29.

346 See, e.g. authorities cited in (n 335) above.

347 *Coutt's Tr & Doe v Webster* (1886) 13R 1112.

348 *Nordic Travel Ltd v Scotprint Ltd* 1980 SC 1 at 11.

349 IA 1986, s. 245. This provision applies to Scots and English law alike.

a connected person. Where the person in whose favour the charge is granted is not a connected person the charge may be avoided only where, at the time the charge was created, the company was unable to pay its debts in terms of s. 123; or became unable to pay its debts within the meaning of s. 123 as a result of the creation of the charge.[350] There is no statutory definition of 'floating charge' and it thus 'bears the meaning attributed to it by judicial decision'.[351] Avoidance under s. 245 is partial rather than catholic in effect. The charge is 'invalid except to the extent of the aggregate of':[352] (a) the value of so much of the consideration for the creation of the charge as consists of money paid, or goods or services supplied, to the company at the same time as, or after, the creation of the charge; (b) the value of so much of that consideration as consists of the discharge or reduction, at the same time as, or after, the creation of the charge, of any debt of the company; plus (c) interest.

14.122 In order to understand what the words, 'at the time of or subsequently to the creation of . . . the charge' mean, a practical example is required. In *Re Shoe Lace Ltd*[353] a Jersey company, Shoe Lace, had sought financial support from its parent company. The parent provided payments of £300,000 in April, £50,000 in May, £75,000 in June and £11,500 in July 1990. A debenture (including a floating charge) was created in July and particulars were registered at Companies House within twenty-one days in August 1990. Shoe Lace Ltd resolved that it was unable to pay its debts in September, sold its entire business and undertaking to a new company, Shoe Hut, and used the proceeds to pay, among others, all the debts due to its parent as floating chargeholder. Shoe Lace went into liquidation in November 1990. The liquidator sought repayment of the sums paid to the parent company on the basis that the floating charge was invalid to the extent of the payments made in April, May, June and July. The directors of the company argued that the sums advanced to Shoe Lace and the indebtedness it incurred, representing the consideration for the charge, occurred 'at the same time as' the charge was created. Hoffmann J said this:[354]

> 'The degree of contemporaneity which such words connote must depend upon the context. It might not be unreasonable to say that two species of dinosaur became extinct "at the same time" when millions of years separates their last known representatives. On the other hand, one would not say that the winner of a 100 metres race crossed the tape at the same time as the runner who came second, even though they were separated by less than a tenth of a second. The question, I think, is whether a businessman having knowledge of the kind of time limits imposed by the Insolvency and Companies Acts and using ordinary language would say that the payments had been made at the same time as the execution of the debenture. In my judgment no businessman would use such language of the payments made in this case.'

14.123 That view was affirmed by the Court of Appeal which held that Parliament included the words 'at the same time as, or after' in the legislation 'for the purpose of excluding from the exemption moneys paid to the company before

350 IA 1986, s. 245(3) and (4). For s. 123, see para. 14.25 above.
351 *Re Spectrum Plus Ltd (in liquidation)* [2005] 2 AC 680 at [98] per Lord Scott.
352 IA 1986, s. 245(2).
353 *Re Shoe Lace Ltd* [1992] BCC 367.
354 [1992] BCC 367 at 369–370.

the creation of the charge, even though they were paid in consideration for the charge'.[355]

The courts have given consideration to the question of when money is paid to the company for the purposes of this section: 14.124

> 'It appears from these cases that the general purpose of the provision is to prevent a company, which is on its last legs, from creating a floating charge to secure past debts or to secure moneys which do not go to swell its assets and become available for creditors . . . The question in each case is whether, in all the circumstances, the payment is in substance to the company for its benefit. If the effect of a payment, which is in form made to the company, is merely to substitute a secured debt for an unsecured debt, then the payment is not in substance a payment to the company.'[356]

Clayton's Case and insolvency

Suppose, at January 2021, a company has a bank overdraft of £100,000. The overdraft is unsecured. The bank is concerned about the position and, in June 2021, the company creates a floating charge in favour of the bank. In July, the company pays £40,000 into the account. A few days later, the company instructs a payment out of the account of £40,000. In November 2021 the company goes into insolvent liquidation. In an application of the rule in *Clayton's Case*,[357] it has been held that the company's payment into the account of £40,000, after the floating charge was created, must be taken to have extinguished the earliest debit; moreover, the post-floating charge advance by the bank of £40,000 is permitted post-floating charge consideration. In the result, therefore, the floating charge may be considered to be invalid under s. 245 only in respect of the remaining £60,000.[358] 14.125

It has been suggested that the new value provided by the bank post-floating charge has benefitted the business and the bank should be entitled to enjoy, to that extent, the benefit of the floating charge.[359] Nonetheless there is force in the view that the rule in *Clayton's Case* is based on an outdated understanding of a current account;[360] a floating charge for pre-creation indebtedness of £100,000, having been struck at by s. 245, cannot be saved retrospectively by an application of *Clayton's Case* to post-creation payments; while the very grant of the floating charge, on the facts given in the example, may be considered to be an unfair preference, with the result that the floating charge would fall to be reduced.[361] 14.126

355 [1993] BCC 609 at 619 per Sir Christopher Slade.

356 *Re Fairway Magazines Ltd* [1992] BCC 924 at 932 per Mummery J.

357 *Devaynes v Noble* (1816) 35 ER 781, for which see paras. 8.25–8.26 above.

358 *Re Yeovil Glove Co Ltd* [1965] Ch 148.

359 Goode (n 377), para. 13.112.

360 D Fox, *Property Rights in Money* (Oxford: Oxford University Press, 2008), para. 7.64: '[if] it is accepted that a current account with a bank does not consist in a sequence of individuated debts, the foundation for applying the rule in *Clayton's Case* . . . can no longer stand'.

361 IA 1986, s. 243(5).

PARTNERSHIPS

14.127 The IA 1986 provisions which cover unregistered companies apply also to associations.[362] Those provisions alone, however, cannot be invoked to confer on a Scottish court jurisdiction to wind up a partnership or limited partnership under the Act.[363] A conscious decision has been taken to subject Scottish partnerships and limited partnerships to the bankruptcy regime.[364] Nonetheless there are exceptions that do allow Scottish partnerships and limited partnerships, which are regulated by the Financial Conduct Authority (FCA), to be wound up on a petition by the FCA under the IA 1986 regime for unregistered companies.[365]

14.128 A judicial factor may be appointed in respect of any 'estate', including over the estate of a company,[366] partnership or limited partnership or trust.

RESTORATION TO THE REGISTER

14.129 Companies and LLPs are subject to various filing obligations. Failure to comply may result in the Registrar of Companies assuming that the company or LLP is not carrying on business and striking it from the register.[367] It is possible for the registrar to fulfil their information obligations but the company or LLP or its officers are somehow not informed of the dissolution. In such a case, an application may be made to restore the company or LLP to the register. In other cases, an application for restoration may need to be made because, some time after the company or LLP has been wound up, a creditor – often a personal injuries claimant, such as a former employee of a company who, many years later, develops an industrial disease – wishes to sue the company or its insurers; or a company in a group has been wound up, but it has subsequently been established that the company continued to hold assets at the date of dissolution which had not been dealt with in the liquidation.

14.130 There are two procedures available for restoring the company to the register: (a) the administrative procedure; and (b) the court procedure. The administrative procedure is available only on the application of (former) members or directors of the company. There are three conditions: (i) immediately prior to dissolution the company was carrying on business; (ii) Crown consent is obtained where property has vested in the Crown as *bona vacantia*; and (iii) delivery of all necessary documentation and records.[368] Under both the

362 IA 1986, s. 220: 'For the purposes of this Part "unregistered company" includes any association and any company, with the exception of a company registered under the Companies Act 2006 in any part of the United Kingdom'.

363 *Smith, Petr* 1999 SLT (Sh Ct) 5.

364 Bankruptcy (Scotland) Act 2016, s. 6(1); Bankruptcy (Scotland) Regulations 2016 (SSI 2016/397), reg. 31.

365 Financial Services and Markets Act 2000, s. 367 and Insolvency Act 1986, s. 220.

366 See, e.g. *Fraser, Petr* 1971 SLT 146 approved in *Weir v Rees* 1991 SLT 345 (which involved a public company). See too *McGuiness v Black (No. 2)* 1990 SC 21.

367 Companies Act 2006, s. 1000.

368 Companies Act 2006, s. 1025.

administrative and the judicial procedure, the application should be made within six years of the company having been dissolved.[369]

The judicial procedure is more flexible. The general ground for seeking restoration is that it is just to do so.[370] The application may be brought by anyone appearing to the court to have an interest.[371] As a general rule, the six year time limit also applies.[372] But there is an important exception to that rule where the purpose of the restoration is in order to bring an action for damages for personal injuries: in that case there is no time limit for bringing a restoration application.[373] **14.131**

'The general effect of an order by the court for restoration to the register is that the company is deemed to have continued in existence as if it had not been dissolved or struck off the register.'[374] In other words, the order has retrospective effect. Providing an order has been made restoring the company to the register, therefore, any acts purportedly done by the company will be deemed to have been done by the company;[375] similarly any actions raised against the company before the order for restoration will be deemed to have been raised against the company.[376] **14.132**

RESTRUCTURING: SCHEMES OF ARRANGEMENT

General

A scheme of arrangement (SoA) is a useful restructuring tool,[377] given the wide powers of the court.[378] It is not limited to insolvent restructuring and is often used in cases of solvent restructuring too.[379] The law is now found in Part 26 of Companies Act 2006,[380] as supplemented by the provisions in Part 26A,[381] introduced in 2020, making provision for arrangements and reconstructions of companies in financial difficulty (RSoA). These provisions **14.133**

369 Companies Act 2006, s. 1024(4).
370 Companies Act 2006, s. 1031(1)(c). See *MCR Oil Tools LLC v Spex Offshore (UK) Ltd* [2020] CSOH 5, 2020 SLT 607 affd [2020] CSIH 23, [2020] BCC 679.
371 Companies Act 2006, s. 1029(2). Express mention is made, for example, of those with a 'potential legal claim against the company'; of the trustees of any employee pension fund; and of the holders of an interest in land which is burdened by a right held by the company or which benefited from an obligation owed by the company: s. 1029(2)(d). A party who would be liable to indemnify a restored defender, has an interest to oppose restoration: *City of Edinburgh Council, Petr* [2010] CSOH 20.
372 Companies Act 2006, s. 1030(4).
373 Companies Act 2006, s. 1030(1) and (4).
374 Companies Act 2006, s. 1032(1).
375 Such as presentation of particulars for registration of a charge: *Hounslow Badminton Association v Registrar of Companies* [2013] EWHC 2961 (Ch).
376 *Joddrell v Peaktone Ltd* [2012] EWCA Civ 1035, [2013] 1 WLR 784.
377 Only an outline may be given here. For fuller treatment, see, e.g. P L Davies and S Worthington (eds), *Gower and Davies: Principles of Modern Company Law*, 11th edn (London: Sweet & Maxwell, 2021), Ch. 29; K van Zweiten, *Goode's Principles of Corporate Insolvency Law: Student Edition*, 5th edn (London: Sweet & Maxwell, 2019), para. 12–12 onward.
378 Companies Act 2006, s. 900. The equivalent provision under Part 26A is s. 901J.
379 As in *Scottish Lion Insurance Co Ltd, Petitioner* 2010 SC 349.
380 Companies Act 2006, s. 895 onward.
381 Companies Act 2006, s. 901A onward.

apply too, with modifications, to LLPs[382] and to co-operative and community benefit societies.[383] The legislation is quite skeletal: there is nothing in the legislation that prescribes the content of a scheme. It is for the company's lawyers to draft the scheme which will be presented to the court to approve. Interested parties must receive notice of the proposed scheme and they must consent to it. But consent is not required from those whose interests the SoA does not affect: thus, for example, a SoA which gives effect to a takeover offer to the shareholders and which has no effect on the creditors does not require the consent of the creditors.

14.134 The crucial point about a SoA, which explains why a company may wish to go to the expense of presenting one, is that majority support may be obtained with the consent of only 75 per cent of each class of members or creditors required.[384] Once 75 per cent is obtained and the court approves the scheme, the minority is bound. Importantly, however, there must be a 'meeting' of the class. A 'meeting' at which only one member of the class purports to attend and vote is not, however, a meeting at all.[385]

14.135 A SoA has three distinct stages. The first is an application to the court to call the requisite meetings of members or creditors or both as the case may be (known in England as the convening hearing).[386] The second is the meetings where the members or creditors vote on the proposed scheme. The third stage is for the petitioning company to apply to the court to sanction the scheme (the sanction hearing).[387]

14.136 The Companies Act 2006 contains no detailed procedural provisions about notice of, and procedure to be adopted at, meetings and the like. So the requisite notice periods will depend on the content of the scheme.[388] Depending on the resolutions required, the notice periods set out in the articles of association must ordinarily be complied with;[389] as must other notice periods set out in the Companies Act 2006, if these provisions are invoked. So if the SoA proposes,

382 Limited Liability Partnerships (Application of Companies Act 2006) Regulations 2009, regs. 45 and 45A.

383 Co-operative and Community Benefit Societies and Credit Unions (Arrangements, Reconstruction and Administration) Order 2014 (SI 2014/229), art. 2.

384 Companies Act 2006, s. 899. The classic definition of a 'class' is found in *Sovereign Life Assurance Co Ltd (in liquidation) v Dodd* [1892] 2 QB 573 at 583 per Bowen LJ: 'those persons whose rights are not so dissimilar as to make it impossible for them to consult together with a view to their common interest'. For an application of that definition to modern documentation, see *Redwood Master Fund Ltd v T D Bank Europe Ltd* [2006] 1 BCLC 149.

385 *Re Altitude Scaffolding Ltd* [2006] BCC 904.

386 Companies Act 2006, s. 896 (SoA); s. 901C (RSoA).

387 *Re The British Aviation Insurance Co Ltd* [2006] BCC 14 at [54] per Lewison J and *Premier Oil plc and Premier Oil UK Ltd, Petrs* [2020] CSOH 39 at [34] and [35] where Lady Wolffe sets out a summary of the procedure in Scotland and the ways in which it differs from the position in England and Wales.

388 But see the English Practice Statement (Companies: Schemes of Arrangement under Part 26 and Part 26A of the Companies Act 2006) (June 2020) which contains useful guidance, *inter alia*, on the matters to be considered prior to any hearing seeking orders for convening meetings. The previous version [2002] 1 WLR 1345 was referred to with approval in Scotland: *Scottish Lion Insurance Co Ltd, Petitioner* 2011 SC 534 at [5].

389 So if the SoA proposes a change to the articles, the notice periods for proposing a resolution to change the articles – set out in s. 307 and s. 307A Companies Act 2006 – must be complied with.

as part of the scheme, that the company's share capital is to be reduced, the notice periods set out in the Companies Act 2006 for securing a reduction of capital must be complied with.[390] Any notice of a meeting to consider the terms of a proposed SoA must be accompanied by an explanatory statement setting out the proposed scheme and its effects.[391] Where a SoA is proposed before the end of the period of twelve weeks beginning with the day after the end of any Part A1 moratorium, and the creditors with whom the SoA envisages a compromise or arrangement include creditors of a moratorium debt or a priority moratorium debt, the court cannot sanction a SoA if it includes provision in respect of any relevant creditor who has not agreed to it.[392]

A SoA can be between: 14.137

- a company and its members;
- a company and its creditors; or
- a company and its members and its creditors

The SoA must, however, be in the nature of a 'compromise or arrangement' with creditors or members. Neither term is defined in the CA 2006, although it is accepted that the two terms are not synonyms.[393] An arrangement which does not involve members giving up any rights may still be an 'arrangement' for SoA purposes between the members and the company because, for instance, it is proposed that the membership, on the SoA being approved, will change.[394] But if members or creditors are to give up their rights, they cannot do so for no consideration: there must be 'some element of accommodation' or 'give and take' on each side.[395] The scheme may extend to releasing a third party guarantor, not otherwise party to the scheme, from its obligations.[396] 14.138

Court sanction of SoA

The final stage in the process – the sanction hearing – itself normally has at least two aspects. The first is a question of jurisdiction: have the statutory formalities been complied with in such a way as to confer a jurisdiction on the court to consider the scheme? If the formalities have not been complied with, it may not be competent for the court even to consider sanctioning the scheme. The second stage for consideration assumes that the court does have jurisdiction. At this stage the court addresses the question of whether, in broad terms, the scheme is fair and does not oppress those who did not vote for it.[397] In deciding whether to approve the SoA, the court will consider:[398] 14.139

- whether the scheme is reasonable;
- whether those voting were representative of each class; and
- whether each class voted in good faith.

390 Companies Act 2006, s. 641 onward.
391 Companies Act 2006, s. 897 (SoA); s. 901D (RSoA).
392 Companies Act 2006, s. 899A(5).
393 *Re Guardian Assurance Co* [1917] Ch 341.
394 *Re Savoy Hotel Ltd* [1981] Ch 351.
395 *Re NFU Development Trust Ltd* [1972] 1 WLR 1548 at 1555C per Brightman J.
396 *Re La Seda de Barcelona SA* [2010] EWHC 1364, [2011] 1 BCLC 555.
397 *Re British Aviation Insurance Co Ltd* [2006] BCC 14.
398 *Re Anglo-Continental Supply Co Ltd* [1922] 2 Ch 723.

14.140 Difficulties can arise with the valuation of the claim of contingent creditors. This may be a matter of considerable practical importance given that the value of a creditor's claims is likely to determine its voting rights.[399] A SoA becomes effective only on the delivery of the court order to the Registrar of Companies.[400]

Part 26A RSoAs

14.141 RSoAs build on the basic framework contained in Part 26 for the SoA.[401] The English practice statement, a previous version of which was referred to with approval by the Court of Session, also covers RSoAs.[402] A Part 26A RSoA is only available where two conditions are satisfied: (a) the company has encountered, or is likely to encounter, financial difficulties that are affecting or will or may affect, its ability to carry on its business as a going concern; and (b) the purpose of the arrangement is in order to 'eliminate, reduce or prevent, or mitigate' the effect of the company's financial difficulties on its ability to carry on business as a going concern.[403] However, it is not a requirement that the scheme will preserve the company's business as a going concern. If a company's financial difficulties are such that it is no longer able to carry on business as a going concern, with the consequence that its creditors will receive only a small dividend on their claims, a RSoA, which provides for a slightly enhanced dividend on those claims, should be treated as mitigating the effect of those financial difficulties, irrespective of whether or not there is any intention for the company to continue to carry on its business as a going concern.[404]

14.142 The main differences between an ordinary SoA and RSoA are:[405]

(i) Every creditor whose rights are affected by the compromise or arrangement has a statutory entitlement to participate in a meeting unless the court determines that none of the members of the class have a genuine economic interest in the company: s. 901A(3) and (4).

(ii) The statutory voting majority was 75 per cent by value of creditors present and voting (s. 901F); there is no requirement for a majority by number.

(iii) Most significantly, s. 901G permits 'cross-class cram down' of a dissenting class where none of the dissenting class would be any worse off than they would be in the event of a relevant alternative (s. 901G(3), also called condition A). The relevant alternative is defined by s. 901G(4) to mean whatever the court considers would be most likely to occur if the compromise or arrangement were not to be sanctioned. Where that is established, and the compromise or arrangement has been agreed by a class the members of which would receive a payment or have a genuine

399 *Scottish Lion Insurance Co Ltd, Petitioner* 2011 SC 534.

400 2006 Act, s. 899(4).

401 *Re Virgin Atlantic Airways Ltd (No. 1)* [2020] EWHC 2191 (Ch), [2021] 1 BCLC 87 at [17] onward per Trower J.

402 Practice Statement (Companies: Schemes of Arrangement under Part 26 and Part 26A of the Companies Act 2006)(n 388).

403 Companies Act 2006, s. 901A.

404 *Re DeepOcean 1 UK Ltd* [2020] EWHC 3549, [2021] Bus LR 632.

405 *Re Virgin Atlantic Airways Ltd (No. 1)* [2020] EWHC 2191 (Ch), [2021] 1 BCLC 87 at [44] per Trower J.

economic interest in the company in the event of the relevant alternative (s. 901G(5), also called condition B), the fact that that dissenting class has not agreed a compromise or arrangement does not prevent the court from sanctioning it under s. 901F.

There are similar provisions to SoA dealing with Part A1 moratorium creditors.[406] As with a SoA, a RSoA becomes effective only on delivery of the court order to the Registrar of Companies.[407] **14.143**

SECTION 110 REORGANISATION

The 1986 Act, s. 110 allows a company, or LLP,[408] on liquidation, to transfer all or part of its business and undertaking to another company, in consideration of shares in the transferee company. Sometimes this is used as a form of 'de-merger' restructuring. As the specialist texts point out, however, 'it rarely has anything to do with insolvency, because the creditors have to be paid in full and almost invariably the winding up is a members' voluntary winding up'.[409] **14.144**

406 Companies Act 2006, s. 901H.
407 Companies Act 2006, s. 901F(6).
408 IA 1986, s. 110(1)(b).
409 *Goode's Principles* (n 377), para. 1.51; see too Gower and Davies (n 377), para. 29.17.

Chapter Fifteen

Alternative Dispute Resolution

Ross Anderson and Alexander Sutherland

INTRODUCTION

15.01 This chapter deals with the different forms of alternative dispute resolution (ADR). There is no single definition of ADR. The types of ADR that are covered in this chapter are arbitration, adjudication, expert determination, and mediation.

ARBITRATION

What is arbitration?

15.02 Arbitration is a form of dispute resolution procedure whereby the parties to a dispute agree to submit their differences to a third party for a binding decision. The party on whom jurisdiction is conferred to determine the dispute was traditionally known in Scotland as the 'arbiter', but that person is now known by the internationally recognised term, 'arbitrator'.[1] Certain characteristic elements of arbitration may be identified:

(i) Arbitration is based on party autonomy:[2] parties to a dispute are free to agree the bases and parameters on which they will be bound by the decision of an arbitral tribunal.
(ii) The parties are free to choose their arbitrator(s).
(iii) A valid agreement to arbitrate, if founded upon, will normally prevent court action from proceeding. 'If the parties have contracted to arbitrate, to arbitration they must go.'[3]

1 Arbitration (Scotland) Act 2010, s. 36(6). The following provides only a general overview. For further reading, see: F Davidson, *Arbitration*, 2nd edn (Edinburgh: W. Green, 2012) and D Bartos and H Dundas, *Greens Annotated Acts: Arbitration (Scotland) Act 2010*, 2nd edn (Edinburgh: W. Green, 2014); and D Parratt and P Foreman, *Scottish Arbitration Handbook*, 2nd edn (Edinburgh: Edinburgh University Press, 2021). There are many international works. See, e.g. *Redfern and Hunter on International Arbitration*, 6th edn (Oxford: Oxford University Press, 2015).

2 J Paulsson, *The Idea of Arbitration* (Oxford: Oxford University Press, 2013), p. 1: 'The idea of arbitration is that of binding resolution of disputes accepted with serenity by those who bear its consequences because of their special trust in chosen decision-makers.'

3 *A Sanderson & Son v Armour & Co Ltd* 1922 SC (HL) 117 at 126 per Lord Dunedin.

(iv) The court will not intervene in the arbitration except where expressly permitted to do so by the law of the seat;[4] but the court will assist the arbitration where permitted.
(v) Arbitration is, as a default rule, private and confidential.
(vi) Arbitration gives rise to a final and binding determination of the matters submitted to the arbitrator, which are contained in the arbitrator's 'award'. The grounds of challenge are limited.
(vii) Subject to the limited grounds of challenge, the arbitrator's award will be recognised and enforced by the courts in Scotland and, in very many cases, internationally.

Each of these aspects will be considered further below.[5]

The legal framework

Arbitration has been said to be as old as Scots law itself.[6] A legislative framework that was rooted in the language of late seventeenth century Scotland, and various perceived deficiencies in the common law rules, led to the passing of the principal legislation which today regulates the law of arbitration in Scotland: the Arbitration (Scotland) Act 2010 (the '2010 Act').[7] The 2010 Act is heavily influenced by both the English Arbitration Act 1996[8] and the benchmark international instrument, the UNCITRAL Model Law on International Commercial Arbitration (the 'Model Law').[9] **15.03**

The 2010 Act comprises the main body of the act, together with the Scottish Arbitration Rules (abbreviated in this chapter to 'SAR'). which are contained in Sch. 1 to the 2010 Act. The SAR govern every arbitration seated in Scotland.[10] The SAR contain rules which are designated as being either 'mandatory' or 'default' rules. The mandatory rules cannot be modified or disapplied in relation to a Scottish-seated arbitration.[11] The parties may modify or disapply the default rules.[12] Where the parties agree for some other rules to apply to the arbitration, the default rules are to be treated as being disapplied or modified to the extent that those rules are inconsistent with the default **15.04**

4 Arbitration (Scotland) Act 2010, s. 1(c); Model Law, art. 5.
5 The present chapter is concerned with contractual arbitration. Sometimes, however, legislation provides that disputes arising under the legislation will be determined by arbitration. The 2010 Act applies with modifications to such disputes too: 2010 Act, s. 16. Statutory arbitrations will not be further considered here.
6 J M Bell, *Law of Arbitration in Scotland*, 2nd edn (Edinburgh: T & T Clark, 1877) 2. The pre-2010 Scottish legislative framework included: 25th Act of the Articles of Regulation 1695 (now disapplied to arbitration: 2010 Act, s. 28); the Arbitration (Scotland) Act 1894; and the Administration of Justice (Scotland) Act 1972, s. 3. The latter two enactments are also repealed by the 2010 Act.
7 The 2010 Act applies irrespective of the date of the arbitration agreement, following the repeal of s. 36(3) of the 2010 Act by SSI 2016/435. Appropriate translations of terminology used in enactments and arbitration agreements which pre-date the 2010 Act are contained in the 2010 Act, s. 36.
8 See *Arbitration Application No. 3 of 2011* [2011] CSOH 164, 2012 SLT 150.
9 United Nations Commission on Trade Law, *https://uncitral.un.org/en/texts/arbitration/modellaw/commercial_arbitration* (last accessed 9 September 2021).
10 2010 Act, s. 7.
11 2010 Act, s. 8.
12 2010 Act, s. 9.

rules. The rules are each designated '(D)' or '(M)' to identify whether the rule is a mandatory or default rule.

Founding principles

15.05 The founding principles, set out in s. 1 of the 2010 Act, are:

(a) The object of arbitration is to resolve disputes fairly, impartially and without unnecessary delay or expense.
(b) The parties should be free to agree how to resolve disputes subject only to such safeguards as are necessary in the public interest.
(c) The court should not intervene in an arbitration except as provided by the 2010 Act.

Domestic and international arbitration

15.06 There is a long history of arbitration in Scotland, much of it entirely domestic. But one of the attractions of arbitration is its application to international disputes. Following the UK's exit from the EU, judgments of the courts in Scotland or from the UK's other courts no longer enjoy automatic recognition and enforcement throughout the EU under the Recast Brussels I Regulation. However, arbitral awards are generally the subject to international recognition and enforcement in terms of the United Nations Convention on the Recognition and Enforcement of Foreign Arbitral Awards (1958), commonly known as the 'New York Convention' and to which some 168 countries are parties.[13]

The arbitration agreement

15.07 The foundational basis for an arbitration is the arbitration agreement. Such an agreement may be very simple, such as:

> 'If any dispute or difference of any kind whatsoever shall arise between the parties to the contract in relation to any matter or thing arising out of or in connection with the contract the same shall be referred to and settled by arbitration under the Arbitration (Scotland) Act 2010.'

An arbitration agreement may be self-standing (concluded after a dispute arose) or, more usually, form one of the provisions of a contract which was agreed in advance of any dispute arising. In Scotland, arbitration agreements are very commonly found in standard commercial contracts such as construction contracts, commercial leases and in deeds of conditions,[14] or in the constitutions of clubs and associations.[15] Arbitration agreements are almost invariably in writing, even if the writing is contained in multiple, perhaps electronic, documents, although Scots law does not expressly require that the agreement be in writing.[16] The arbitration agreement may be incorporated in

13 United Nations Commission on Trade Law (last accessed 23 February 2022), *https://www.newyorkconvention.org/english*.

14 *Arbitration Application No. 2 of 2011* [2011] CSOH 186, 2011 Hous LR 72.

15 *Arbitration Appeal No. 2 of 2017* [2018] CSOH 12.

16 2010 Act, s. 4. Cf Model Law, art. 7, option I and option II. The Requirements of Writing (Scotland) Act 1995 does not require arbitration agreements to be in writing.

a contract by reference. An arbitration agreement may be severed from the contract of which it forms part.[17] Formalities, in short, are limited.

It is for the arbitrator to rule on matters of his or her own jurisdiction under the arbitration agreement.[18] The interpretation of an arbitration clause should start from the assumption that the parties intended any dispute arising out of the relationship into which they have entered or purported to enter to be decided by the same tribunal.[19] Arbitration clauses are therefore to be liberally construed. The 'golden rule' is that if the parties wish to have issues as to the validity of their contract decided by one tribunal and issues as to its meaning or performance decided by another, they must say so expressly.[20] **15.08**

Suppose in a dispute under a contract containing an arbitration clause, one of the parties raises proceedings in the Court of Session. There is no obligation in the rules of court to make averments about arbitration clauses which confer jurisdiction on an arbitrator.[21] However, it is open to the defender served with those proceedings to plead that the proceedings should be sisted for arbitration.[22] A party who seeks to bring legal proceedings in breach of an arbitration agreement may be interdicted from so doing. To bring such court proceedings may be a breach of other rules to which the party is subject. But the right to invoke the arbitration clause may be lost if the party which seeks to invoke the arbitration clause has taken any step in the legal proceedings to answer the substance of the claim or otherwise acted in a manner indicating a desire to have the dispute resolved in court.[23] **15.09**

The seat (*lex arbitri*) and applicable law

The seat of the arbitration determines its 'curial law';[24] that is to say, the law which governs the arbitration and which sets the standards external to the arbitration agreement and the wishes of the parties for the conduct of the arbitration. The arbitration will be subject to the mandatory rules of the law of the seat. The law of the seat governs the definition and form of the agreement to arbitrate, arbitrability, grounds of challenge, interim measures, court assistance of the arbitration, the form of the award and the court's supervisory jurisdiction.[25] The seat of the award will normally determine where the award is made for the purposes of recognition and enforcement,[26] as under the New York Convention. The parties are free to agree the seat, the law applicable to the arbitration agreement and the law applicable to their substantive dispute. **15.10**

17 2010 Act, s. 5.
18 SAR, r. 19(a) (M).
19 *Fiona Trust and Holding Corporation v Privalov* [2007] UKHL 40, [2007] Bus LR 1719 at [13] per Lord Hoffmann.
20 *Fiona Trust* (n 19) at [26] per Lord Hope of Craighead. See further *Mozambique v Credit Suisse International* [2021] EWCA Civ 329.
21 RCS, r. 13.2.
22 2010 Act, s. 10. *Fraserburgh Harbour Commissioners v McLaughlin & Harvey Ltd* [2021] CSIH 58.
23 2010 Act, s. 10. See generally, *Heart of Midlothian Football Club plc v Scottish Professional Football League Ltd* [2020] CSOH 68, 2020 SLT 736.
24 *James Miller & Partners Ltd v Whitworth Street Estates (Manchester) Ltd* [1970] AC 583.
25 *Paul Smith Ltd v H & S International Holding Inc* [1991] 2 Lloyd's Rep 127 at 130.
26 See, e.g. Model Law, art. 31(3).

15.11 The arbitration agreement may be governed by a different law to that which governs the substance of the dispute.[27] Under the 2010 Act where there is no express choice of law but the parties have agreed that the arbitration is to be seated in Scotland then, unless the parties otherwise agree, the arbitration agreement is to be governed by Scots law.[28]

15.12 The seat of an arbitral tribunal is not the same as the physical place where hearings may be conducted. A Scottish-seated tribunal may sit outside Scotland.[29] An award made in a Scottish-seated arbitration is treated as having been made in Scotland even if it is signed at, or delivered to or from, a place outwith Scotland.[30]

Arbitrability

15.13 A party considering arbitration needs to consider at the outset whether an arbitrator can competently provide the desired remedy. The first issue is arbitrability: whether the dispute that has arisen is capable of being submitted to arbitration. It is not every dispute that is capable of being arbitrated and nothing in the 2010 Act innovates on the common law in this regard.[31] The point is important because an award may not be enforceable in so far as it purports to determine matters that were not arbitrable.[32] Nonetheless, most civil and commercial matters may be submitted to arbitration, including disputes alleging unfair prejudice in a company,[33] or disputes already before a statutory tax tribunal.[34] The main examples of disputes that are not arbitrable are those which relate to:

- matters of personal status;
- employment tribunal claims;[35]
- terms in consumer contracts 'requiring the consumer to take disputes exclusively to arbitration not covered by legal provisions';[36]
- grants of patents or trade marks; and

27 See, e.g. *Enka Insaat ve Sanayi AS v OOO Insurance Company Chubb* [2020] UKSC 38, [2020] 1 WLR 4117 at [170].

28 2010 Act, s. 6.

29 SAR, r. 29. Cf *Enka Insaat ve Sanayi AS v OOO Insurance Company Chubb* [2020] UKSC 38, [2020] 1 WLR 4117 at [68]; *Bay Hotel and Resort Ltd v Cavalier Construction Co Ltd* [2001] UKPC 34 (hearings in USA, *lex arbitri* and proper law of contracts the law of the Turks and Caicos Islands); *Braes of Doune Wind Farm (Scotland) Ltd v Alfred McAlpine Business Services Ltd* [2008] EWHC 426 (TCC), [2008] 1 CLC 487 (hearings in Glasgow, but *lex arbitri* held to be English law); *Shagang South-Asia (Hong Kong) Trading Co Ltd v Daewoo Logistics* [2015] EWHC 194 (Comm), [2015] 1 All ER (Comm) 545 (hearings in Hong Kong, but *lex arbitri* English law); cf. *Kabab-JI (Lebanon) v Kout Food Group* [2021] UKSC 48 (hearings in Paris, but arbitration agreement subject to English law).

30 SAR, r. 52 (D).

31 2010 Act, s. 30.

32 New York Convention, art. V(1)(a).

33 *Fulham Football Club (1987) Ltd v Richards* [2011] EWCA Civ 855, [2012] Ch. 333.

34 Tribunal Procedure (First-tier Tribunal) (Tax Chamber) Rules 2009 (SI 2009/273), r. 3.

35 See Employment Rights Act 1996, s. 203 and *Irwell Insurance Co Ltd v Watson* [2021] EWCA Civ 67.

36 Consumer Rights Act 2015, Sch. 2, para. 20. But an agreement in writing to submit present or future differences to arbitration is not to be regarded as excluding or restricting any liability for the purposes of ss. 31(4), 47(4), 57(6).

• competition law.

It is important to recognise, however, that an arbitral award will not normally bind those who were not parties to the arbitration; arbitration is therefore not well suited to disputes about matters that affect the rights of persons who are not parties to the arbitration.[37] Although insolvency is the classic case where third party interests arise, there are a number of express statutory provisions dealing with arbitration. An administrator or receiver has the power to refer to arbitration any question affecting the company.[38] Otherwise an arbitral claim may be instituted or continued against a company in administration only with the consent of the administrator or the permission of the court.[39] An arbitral claim may be brought against, or continued with, against a company in liquidation only with the consent of the court.[40] A trustee in sequestration may refer to arbitration any claim or question arising in the course of a sequestration.[41] **15.14**

Orders

As a summons or writ begins with conclusions or craves, it is important to consider whether an arbitrator can provide the desired remedy. An arbitral tribunal may grant orders for payment of a sum of money (including in respect of damages in any currency,[42] with interest),[43] declarator, interdict, specific performance, rectification or reduction of any deed to the extent permitted by the law governing the deed or document.[44] These orders are usually made in an 'award'. An award ordering reduction or rectification of a deed or other document is of no effect in so far as it would adversely affect the interests of any third party acting in good faith.[45] It is also possible to ask the arbitrator to grant any of the orders it could grant on a permanent basis on a provisional or interim basis.[46] Such orders are normally contained in a 'provisional award'. A provisional award will be superseded by any final award. **15.15**

Commencing arbitration proceedings and prescription

There is no standard form for commencing arbitration proceedings. It is normally done by the serving of a 'notice of arbitration' on the other party. The notice should identify the parties, the arbitration agreement, the dispute and the claims made against the respondent(s). The terms of such a notice commencing arbitration are important, particularly for the purposes of prescription and limitation.[47] In order for there to be 'judicial interruption' of a **15.16**

37 Cf *Bridgehouse (Bradford No. 2) Ltd v BAE Systems plc* [2020] EWCA Civ 759, [2020] Bus LR 2025; *Riverrock Securities Ltd v International Bank of St Petersburg Joint Stock Co* [2020] EWHC 2483 (Comm), [2020] 2 Lloyd's Rep 591.
38 Insolvency Act 1986, Sch. 1, para. 6 (administrator), Sch. 2, para. 6 (receiver).
39 Insolvency Act 1986, Sch. B1, para. 43(6).
40 Insolvency Act 1986, s. 130(2).
41 Bankruptcy (Scotland) Act 2016, s. 216.
42 SAR, r. 48 (M).
43 SAR, r. 50 (M).
44 SAR, r. 49 (D).
45 2010 Act, s. 11(2).
46 SAR, r. 53 (D).
47 Prescription and Limitation (Scotland) Act 1973, ss. 4 and 9.

prescriptive period by way of an arbitration, the relevant claim must be made in 'appropriate proceedings', which means 'any arbitration in Scotland in respect of which an arbitrator (or panel of arbitrators) has been appointed' or 'any arbitration in a country other than Scotland, being an arbitration an award in which would be enforceable in Scotland'.[48] The date of judicial interruption, where the claim is made in an arbitration, is the date on which the arbitration begins.[49] An arbitration begins when the parties to the arbitration agree that it begins, or, in the absence of agreement, in accordance with SAR, r. 1,[50] which provides: '[a]n arbitration begins when a party to an arbitration agreement (or any person claiming through or under such a party) gives the other party notice submitting a dispute to arbitration in accordance with the agreement'.

Constitution of the tribunal: the arbitrator(s)

15.17 It is for the parties to agree on the appointment of the tribunal. An arbitrator must be an individual.[51] An arbitrator has to be paid and it is good practice for the parties to have agreed terms and conditions of appointment with the arbitrator at the time of appointment. A common difficulty is that the claimant cannot obtain the agreement of the respondent. Another is that the procedure provided for in the arbitration agreement for constitution of the tribunal fails. In those cases, it is open to either party to refer the matter to an arbitral appointments referee, which will appoint the tribunal. The referees who may be asked to appoint an arbitrator are:[52]

- Agricultural Industries Confederation Limited.
- Chartered Institute of Arbitrators.
- Dean of the Faculty of Advocates.
- Institution of Civil Engineers.
- Law Society of Scotland.
- Royal Incorporation of Architects in Scotland.
- Royal Institution of Chartered Surveyors.
- Scottish Agricultural Arbiters and Valuers Association.

15.18 Where a party objects to the arbitral appointments referee making an appointment, the appointments referee fails to make an appointment within twenty-one days, or the parties agree not to refer the matter to an appointments referee, an application may be made to the court to make the necessary appointment.[53] The default position under the SAR is that the tribunal will consist of a single arbitrator.[54] But the parties are free to modify this position. In international arbitrations, larger tribunals are more common.[55]

48 1973 Act, s. 4(2).
49 1973 Act, s. 4(3).
50 1973 Act, s. 4(4). See generally D Johnston, *Prescription and Limitation*, 2nd edn (Edinburgh: W. Green, 2012), para. 5.07 onward.
51 SAR, rr. 3 (M) and 6 (D).
52 Arbitral Appointments Referee (Scotland) Order 2010 (SSI 2010/196).
53 SAR, r. 7(6). See, e.g. *Tolland v Scottish Squash and Racketball Ltd* 2016 SLT (Sh Ct) 141.
54 SAR, r. 5 (D).
55 Under Model Law, art. 10, the default position is a tribunal of three arbitrators.

A Court of Session judge may act as an arbitrator in commercial disputes with the consent of the Lord President.[56] That provision may be of particular use in cases where proceedings have been raised in the court but the defender moves the judge to sist for arbitration.[57] Appointment of a judge as an arbitrator is, however, to be distinguished from the Court of Session procedure known as a 'summary trial', which bears some of the hallmarks of arbitration, but will result in a decree of the Court of Session and not an arbitral award.[58] **15.19**

Arbitrator's duties

The tribunal must be impartial and independent. It must treat the parties fairly. It must conduct the arbitration without unnecessary delay and without incurring unnecessary expense.[59] Arbitrators have a legal duty to make disclosure of facts and circumstances which would or might reasonably give rise to the appearance of bias.[60] **15.20**

Procedure and practicalities

Preliminaries

It is for the tribunal to determine the procedure to be followed in an arbitration and the admissibility, relevance, materiality and weight of any evidence.[61] It is possible to have a 'documents only' arbitration where the entire procedure is written. In such a case there may be no hearings. But the more normal course is for a preliminary meeting or hearing to be fixed in order to determine the procedure to be adopted in the arbitration and a procedural timetable. There is no fixed vocabulary to describe the hearings or meetings. The arbitrator or the parties may circulate in advance of the hearing a draft 'procedural order No. 1' in order to provide an agenda of sorts of the matters to be addressed and to allow the parties to make representations on that first order. The meeting may be in person or it may take place online. **15.21**

Seat and applicable law

There are certain preliminary matters which the arbitrator should confirm in his or her first procedural order. An arbitration must have a seat. As with jurisdiction and choice of law in the courts, it is possible for an arbitral tribunal with a Scottish seat to have to apply a foreign law to the merits of the dispute. If such a foreign law applies, it is useful for that to be identified at the outset and some consideration given to how that law will be addressed. Assuming **15.22**

56 2010 Act, s. 25.

57 See, e.g. *The New Saints FC Ltd v The Football Association of Wales Ltd* [2020] EWHC 1838 (Ch), at [9] where, given the urgency, the parties agreed to appoint the judge as the arbitrator.

58 RCS, r. 77. The aspects of this procedure which might be said to be hallmarks of arbitration are speed (hearing within six weeks where facts agreed); privacy (potential for proof in chambers): RCS, r. 77.4(3)(a) and (b); and finality: RCS, r. 77.9.

59 SAR, r. 24(1) (M).

60 *Halliburton Co v Chubb Bermuda Insurance Ltd* [2020] UKSC 48, [2020] 3 WLR 1474.

61 SAR, r. 28 (D).

that Scots law applies, then it will ordinarily be the Scots law of evidence that applies at any evidential hearings.

Confidentiality and communications

15.23 One of the fundamental incidents of arbitration is that, unlike the open justice principle which applies to the courts,[62] the default rule is that arbitration is private and confidential.[63] The tribunal should address at the outset of the arbitration the obligations that the rule on confidentiality imposes.[64] Because it is a default rule, it is possible that the parties may be content that the arbitration should not be confidential. But where the default rule on confidentiality applies, it is in principle an actionable breach of confidence for the arbitrator or a party to disclose information relating to the arbitration. There are express exceptions to that rule, which are obvious and necessary.[65] A disclosure may be permitted where:

(a) it is authorised expressly or impliedly by the parties;
(b) it is required by the tribunal;
(c) it may be required: (i) in order to comply with the any enactment or rule of law; (ii) for the proper performance of the discloser's public functions; (iii) in order to enable any public body or office holder to perform public functions properly;
(d) it can reasonably be considered as being needed to protect a party's lawful interests;
(e) it is in the public interest;
(f) it is necessary in the interests of justice; or
(g) it is made in circumstances in which the discloser would have absolute privilege had the disclosed information been defamatory.

15.24 There are obvious examples where disclosures falling within the above provisions will have to be made. Companies will often have to disclose the existence and progress of arbitration proceedings to their auditors. Documents relating to the arbitration may have to be produced pursuant to an order of the court.[66] Disclosure for the purposes of recognition or enforcement of an award will ordinarily be necessary in the interests of justice.[67]

15.25 A practical incident of the obligation of confidentiality, especially in non-institutional arbitrations, is how the parties and the tribunal are to communicate with each other and how documents are to be lodged or curated, often electronically. The general rule is that any correspondence which one party has with the tribunal, or which the tribunal has with a party, should always be copied to the other parties to the arbitration or their representatives.

62 *A v Secretary of State for the Home Department* [2014] UKSC 25, 2014 SC (UKSC) 151; *MH v Mental Health Tribunal for Scotland* 2019 SC 432; *Cape Intermediate Holdings Ltd v Dring* [2019] UKSC 38, [2020] AC 629.
63 SAR, r. 26 (D).
64 SAR, r. 26(3) (D).
65 SAR, r. 26(1) (D).
66 *Gray Construction Ltd v Harley Haddow LLP* [2012] CSOH 92, 2012 SLT 1035.
67 *Associated Electric and Gas Insurance Services Ltd v European Reinsurance Co of Zurich* [2003] UKPC 11, [2013] 1 WLR 1041 at [20].

Challenges to jurisdiction

An arbitrator's powers are limited to those conferred upon the tribunal by the arbitration agreement. The arbitration agreement delineates the boundaries of the tribunal's jurisdiction. A party which disputes the jurisdiction of the tribunal has two principal options. First, the party who considers the tribunal has no jurisdiction at all may elect not to participate and then seek to challenge any award. There is obviously some risk involved in that approach. Secondly, the party may object to the tribunal that the tribunal does not have, or has exceeded its, jurisdiction in relation to any matter.[68] An objection that the tribunal has no jurisdiction at all should be raised at the outset. As a general rule, a party which actively participates in an arbitration will be deemed to have waived its objection.[69] **15.26**

Where the objection is that the tribunal is exceeding its jurisdiction (which may arise only later) the objection should be made as soon as reasonably practicable.[70] Where the tribunal sustains an objection it must end the arbitration in so far as it relates to a matter over which the tribunal has ruled that it does not have jurisdiction, and set aside any provisional or part award that has already been made in relation to such a matter.[71] Where the tribunal rules on its own jurisdiction, there is an appeal to the Outer House of the Court of Session. The party appealing must do so no later than fourteen days after the tribunal's decision on the objection.[72] In so far as the tribunal has found that it continues to have jurisdiction, the arbitration may continue pending determination of the appeal.[73] The Outer House decision on that matter is final.[74] **15.27**

Instead of asking the tribunal to rule on its own jurisdiction, the default rule is that either party may seek to have the question of jurisdiction decided by the Outer House.[75] Where that default rule applies, such an application to the Outer House may be made only where: (a) the parties agree; or (b) the tribunal has consented and the court is satisfied that: (i) determining the question is likely to produce a substantial saving in expenses; (ii) the application was made without delay; and (iii) there is good reason why the question should be determined by the court.[76] The arbitration can in principle continue pending the court's determination of the application. The Outer House's determination of the question of whether the application is valid and, if it is, the question of jurisdiction, is final.[77] **15.28**

68 SAR, r. 20 (M).
69 SAR, r. 76 (M). Cf Model Law, art. 4.
70 SAR, r. 20 (M). Cf Model Law, art. 16.
71 SAR, r. 20(3) (M).
72 SAR, r. 21 (M).
73 SAR, r. 21(2) (M).
74 SAR, r. 21(3) (M).
75 SAR, r. 22 (D).
76 SAR, r. 23(2) (M).
77 SAR, r. 23(4) (M).

Duties on the tribunal and the parties

15.29 In general terms, the rules of natural justice and the right of a party to be heard apply in arbitration. The rules expressly provide that treating the parties fairly includes giving each party a reasonable opportunity to put its case and to deal with the other party's case.[78] A breach of that rule is likely to give rise to a challenge on the grounds of procedural irregularity. The parties, for their part, are also required to ensure that the arbitration is conducted without unnecessary delay and without incurring unnecessary expense.[79]

Directions, provisional and part awards

15.30 It is for the arbitrator to fix procedure. Incidental procedural applications may result in the arbitrator issuing directions, with which the parties must comply.[80] Such directions are often contained in 'procedural orders'. Where a party fails to comply with a direction or any obligation imposed by the arbitration agreement or the rules, the tribunal can order the party to comply.[81] Where the party so ordered fails to comply, the tribunal may direct that the party is not entitled to rely on any allegation or material which was the subject matter of the order; draw adverse inferences from the non-compliance; proceed with the arbitration and make its award; and make such provisional award (including an award on expenses) as it considers appropriate in consequence of the non-compliance.[82]

15.31 Where interim orders or relief is sought from the arbitrator in terms that may require enforcement, such orders are likely to be embodied in a provisional award. A provisional award is not final, and it is binding only to the extent specified or until it is superseded by a subsequent award.[83] The arbitrator has a power to order a party making a claim to give security for expenses, which failing to dismiss that party's claim.[84] The arbitrator may cap a party's liability for expenses.[85]

15.32 The arbitrator may direct that preliminary issues should be addressed first (as in the form of a debate), or that issues of liability should be addressed separately from quantum. Where such a discrete aspect of the procedure takes place, the arbitrator's decision will normally be embodied in a 'part award'.[86] Often the substantive resolution of a dispute will be in a part award because the arbitrator may have reserved certain matters, such as expenses.

78 SAR, r. 24(2) (M); Model Law, art. 18.
79 SAR, r. 25 (M).
80 SAR, r. 31 (D).
81 SAR, r. 39(1) (D).
82 SAR, r. 39(2) (D).
83 2010 Act, s. 11(4).
84 SAR, r. 64 (D).
85 SAR, r. 65 (D).
86 SAR, r. 54 (M).

Clerks and experts

The tribunal may appoint a clerk and such other agents, employees or other persons as it thinks fit to assist in the conduct of the arbitration. But the parties' consent is required for any appointment in respect of which significant expenses are likely to arise.[87] It is common for arbitrators to appoint a clerk. The appointment of agents may arise in the case of an arbitrator who is not a lawyer considering that he or she needs advice on how to deal with points of law. The tribunal may also obtain expert opinion on any matter arising in the arbitration. But the parties must be given a reasonable opportunity to make representations about any written expert opinion, and to hear any oral expert opinion and ask questions of the expert giving it.[88] **15.33**

Property and documents

The tribunal may direct a party to allow the tribunal, an expert or another party to inspect, photograph, preserve or take custody of any property which that party owns or possesses that is the subject of the arbitration (or as to which any question arises in the arbitration); or to take samples from or conduct an experiment on any such property. The tribunal may direct a party to preserve any document or other evidence which the party possesses or controls.[89] That rule, which is widely worded, would appear to give the tribunal authority to order parties to the arbitration to disclose or produce documents, or to appoint a commissioner to deal with any production or recovery exercise as between the parties to the arbitration. **15.34**

Court support

General

The court has extensive powers to grant orders to assist an arbitration:[90] **15.35**

(a) To appoint a person to safeguard the interest of any party lacking capacity.
(b) To order the sale of any property in dispute in the arbitration.
(c) To make an order securing any amount due in the arbitration.
(d) To make an order under s. 1 of the Administration of Justice (Scotland) Act 1972.
(e) To grant warrant for arrestment or inhibition.
(f) To grant interdict or interim interdict.
(g) To grant any other interim or permanent order.

Pre-arbitration orders

Before an arbitration has commenced, it is possible to make an application to the court for an order under s. 1 of the Administration of Justice (Scotland) Act 1972 for: **15.36**

87 SAR, r. 32 (D).
88 SAR, r. 34 (D).
89 SAR, r. 35 (D).
90 SAR, r. 46(1) (D).

> 'the inspection, photographing, preservation, custody and detention of documents and other property (including, where appropriate, land) which appear to the court to be property as to which any question may relevantly arise in any existing civil proceedings before that court or in civil proceedings which are likely to be brought, and to order the production and recovery of any such property, the taking of samples thereof and carrying out of any experiment thereon or therewith'.

'Civil proceedings' has been held to extend to arbitration.[91]

After commencement of arbitration

15.37 The standard practice is to seek such orders from the arbitrator in the first instance,[92] not least because the court can grant the above orders only with the consent of the tribunal or where it is satisfied that the case is one of urgency.[93] Where there is non-compliance with the arbitrator's order, or where, for instance, recovery of documents is sought from a third party not subject to the jurisdiction of the arbitrator, it will be necessary to apply to the court to assist. Even in respect of third party havers who are not parties to the arbitration, however, the application should still be made in the first instance to the arbitrator.[94] An application can then be made to the court and intimation will be made to those parties from which recovery is sought.[95]

15.38 In relation to witnesses, a tribunal can administer oaths or affirmations to witnesses who attend.[96] But the arbitrator cannot compel the attendance of witnesses or disclosure of evidence. As a result, an application may be made to the court by the tribunal or any party for assistance.[97]

Referral of point of law: SAR, r. 41 (D)

15.39 The default position (often excluded) is that any party may refer any point of Scots law to the Outer House for determination. But such an application may be made only if the parties have agreed that it be made, or the tribunal has consented and the court is satisfied that: its determination is likely to produce a substantial saving in expenses; that the application was made without delay; and that there is a good reason why the question should be determined by the court.[98] The Outer House decision on the question is final.

Default and non-participation

15.40 The tribunal can bring an arbitration to an end if the claimant delays in pursuing its claim. Where the tribunal considers that there is no good reason for the delay and is satisfied that the delay: (a) either gives rise to a substantial risk that it will not be possible to resolve the issues in the claim fairly,

91 *Anderson v Gibb* 1993 SLT 726. See too SAR, r. 46(4) (D).
92 *SGL Carbon Fibres Ltd, Petr* [2013] CSOH 21, 2013 SLT 307.
93 SAR, r. 46(2) (D).
94 *SGL Carbon Fibres Ltd, Petr* [2013] CSOH 21, 2013 SLT 307.
95 SAR, r. 45 (M).
96 SAR, r. 36 (D).
97 SAR, r. 45 (M). See *Heart of Midlothian Football Club plc v Scottish Professional Football League Ltd* [2020] CSOH 68, 2020 SLT 736.
98 SAR, r. 42 (M).

(b) or has caused serious prejudice to the other party, the tribunal must end the arbitration in so far as it relates to the subject matter of the claim and may make such award, including on expenses, as it considers appropriate.[99] Where a respondent unnecessarily delays in submitting a defence and the tribunal considers that there is no good reason for the delay, the tribunal must proceed with the arbitration. Since the absence of a defence does not amount to an admission of anything,[100] the tribunal cannot make a substantive award based only on default. It should proceed to consider the merits of the claim and any evidence so that the appropriate findings can be made and reasons provided which are necessary for the making of the award. A similar provision applies where a party fails to attend a hearing or produce a document ordered by the tribunal.[101]

Date and form of award

As a matter of form, the award must state the seat of the arbitration, when the award is made and when it takes effect, the reasons for the award, and whether any previous provisional or part award has been made, superseded or confirmed.[102] The award must be signed by all the arbitrators.[103] An award is 'made' by delivering it to each of the parties in accordance with the rules on formal communications.[104] That date is important for the purposes of the tight time limits within which any challenges to the award need to be brought. Because an arbitrator can withhold delivery of the award pending payment of the arbitrator's fees, ordinarily the period for any appeal should not begin to run until the award has in fact been delivered to the parties. **15.41**

Expenses

Arbitration expenses include the arbitrator's fees and expenses, the tribunal's expenses, the parties' other legal expenses and the fees of any arbitral appointments referee.[105] The parties are severally liable to pay the arbitrator's fees and expenses, subject to the arbitrator allocating liability between the parties for these, if given the power to do so by the parties after the dispute has arisen.[106] The tribunal must have regard to the principle that expenses follow success.[107] The amount of the arbitrator's fees and expenses is to be agreed between the parties and the arbitrator or, failing such agreement, to be determined by the auditor of the Court of Session.[108] In relation to legal expenses ('other arbitration expenses'), the arbitrator may either summarily assess the amount or arrange for the auditor of the Court of Session to determine that amount.[109] **15.42**

99 SAR, r. 37(1) (D).
100 SAR, r. 37(2) (D). The rule largely reflects the terms of the Model Law, art. 25.
101 SAR, r. 38 (D).
102 SAR, r. 51(2) (D).
103 SAR, r. 51(1) (D).
104 SAR, r. 51(3) (D). Delivery has to be in accordance with SAR, r. 83 (D).
105 SAR, r. 59 (D).
106 SAR, r. 60 (M). The power to make awards of legal expenses is found in SAR, r. 61(2) (D) 'other arbitration expenses'.
107 SAR, r. 62(2) (D).
108 SAR, r. 60 (3) and (4) (M).
109 SAR, r. 61(2) (D).

15.43 The Outer House of the Court of Session has power on the application of a party when the arbitrator's tenure has ended to make orders regarding the arbitrator's fees which include the amount, whether any should be repaid or, where the arbitrator has resigned, about their liability in respect of 'acting as arbitrator'.[110]

Arbitrator liability

15.44 Neither the tribunal nor any arbitrator is liable for anything done or omitted to be done in the performance or purported performance of the tribunal's functions.[111] A similar immunity is extended to any body appointing an arbitrator[112] and to any clerk, agent, employee or other person who assisted the tribunal. The exceptions to the immunity are: (a) if the act or omission is shown to have been in bad faith; and (b) any liability arising from the arbitrator's resignation.[113] Otherwise, every person who participates in the arbitration as an expert, witness or legal representative has the same immunity in respect of acts or omissions as the person would have if the arbitration were civil proceedings.[114]

Settlement

15.45 It may be that the parties agree to settle their differences in the course of the arbitration. In such a case, the parties may request the arbitrator to make an award reflecting the terms of the settlement.[115]

Effect of an award

15.46 A part award or final award is final and binding on the parties.[116] A provisional award that may have been issued is, by definition, provisional or interim and not final.[117] Any final award, therefore, must confirm or recall any provisional awards. Once the tribunal has issued its final award, including dealing with fees and expenses, the arbitrator is *functus officio*. He or she has no power to do anything further in the arbitration except to correct a typographical or other error in the award that was an accident or omission or is required to clarify an ambiguity in the award.[118] This can only be done within twenty-eight days of the award or later with leave of the court.

110 SAR, r. 16 (M).
111 SAR, r. 73 (M).
112 SAR, r. 74 (M).
113 SAR, r. 73(2) (M).
114 SAR, r. 75 (M). For expert witness liability, see *Jones v Kaney* [2011] UKSC 13, [2011] 2 AC 398.
115 SAR, r. 57 (D).
116 2010 Act, ss. 11 and 19(1).
117 2010 Act, s. 11(4).
118 SAR, r. 58. This has been described as 'the slip rule': *Arbitration Application No. 1 of 2013* [2014] CSOH 83 at [15]. For a case where an application was made to the court to require the tribunal to correct its award, see *Arbitration Appeal No. 2 of 2019* [2020] CSOH 51.

Challenging an award: appeals

General

The general principle is that there is no appeal on the merits of an arbitration tribunal's decision, except in the limited circumstances set out in the rules. There are three types of appeal: jurisdiction, serious irregularity and legal error. Each will be addressed in turn below. But there are some rules of general application.[119] **15.47**

Appeal is to the Outer House of the Court of Session. The appeal, and any application for leave, is made by petition, which will be heard by a nominated arbitration judge. In any such appeal, the appellant can seek anonymity by seeking an order prohibiting the disclosure of the identity of the party in any report of the proceedings.[120] The court must grant the application for anonymity unless one of the exceptions applies.[121] If the application is granted, the court proceedings on appeal are heard in private.[122] Unless a s. 15 order is granted, all applications and appeals under the 2010 Act will be held in public.[123] **15.48**

An appeal is competent only if the appellant has exhausted any available arbitral process of appeal or review, including asking the tribunal to correct obvious errors or clarify any ambiguity in the award.[124] An appeal must be made no later than twenty-eight days after the later of: (a) the date on which the award being appealed against is made; (b) if the award was the subject to a process of correction under SAR, r. 58, the date on which the tribunal decided whether to correct the award; or (c) if there has been an arbitral process of review or appeal, the date on which the appellant was notified of the result of that process.[125] The award is 'made' by delivering it to each of the parties in accordance with SAR, r. 83.[126] Applications for leave are normally dealt with on the papers.[127] **15.49**

A serious irregularity or a legal error appeal, if successful, may involve remitting to the arbitrator to reconsider the award and either make a new award or confirm its original award within three months.[128] In other words, even if a ground of appeal is successful, it may be possible for the tribunal to confirm its award. In any appeal, the appellant can be required to find caution (security) for the expenses of the appeal.[129] There is an appeal from the Outer House to the Inner House, but only with leave of the Outer House. The Outer House decision on whether to grant leave is final;[130] there is no appeal to the Inner **15.50**

119 SAR, r. 71 (M).
120 2010 Act, s. 15; RCS, r. 100.9.
121 2010 Act, s. 15(2).
122 RCS, r. 100.9(2).
123 RCS, r. 100.9(3).
124 SAR, r. 71(2). For review, see SAR, r. 58.
125 SAR, r. 71(4).
126 SAR, r. 51(3) (D).
127 See, e.g. *Arbitration Appeal No. 2 of 2016* [2017] CSOH 23.
128 SAR, r. 72(1) (M).
129 SAR, r. 71(10) (M).
130 SAR, r. 71(13)–(16) (M).

House on the question of leave. If leave is granted, the decision of the Inner House is final;[131] in other words, there is no appeal in Scottish arbitration cases to the Supreme Court.

Jurisdiction: SAR, r. 67 (M)

15.51 A party may appeal to the Outer House against an award on the ground that the arbitrator did not have jurisdiction to make the award. This is known as a 'jurisdictional appeal'. Given the terms of SAR, r. 19 and r. 76, a jurisdictional challenge to an award may be most likely to occur either where an early objection to the jurisdiction of the tribunal was taken but the tribunal decided to postpone its decision on that matter until it considered the merits; where the challenge is to the tribunal's jurisdiction to some part of the award; or where the party seeking to challenge jurisdiction did not participate. Another example is that the claimant was not in fact a party to the arbitration agreement.

Serious irregularity: SAR, r. 68 (M)

15.52 A serious irregularity is defined as an irregularity of any of the following kinds which has caused or will cause substantial injustice to the appellant:

'(a) the tribunal failing to conduct the arbitration in accordance with—
  (i) the arbitration agreement,
  (ii) these rules (in so far as they apply), or
  (iii) any other agreement by the parties relating to conduct of the arbitration,
(b) the tribunal acting outwith its powers (other than by exceeding its jurisdiction),
(c) the tribunal failing to deal with all the issues that were put to it,
(d) any arbitral appointments referee or other third party to whom the parties give powers in relation to the arbitration acting outwith its powers,
(e) uncertainty or ambiguity as to the award's effect,
(f) the award being—
  (i) contrary to public policy, or
  (ii) obtained by fraud or in a way which is contrary to public policy,
(g) an arbitrator having not been impartial and independent,
(h) an arbitrator having not treated the parties fairly,
(i) an arbitrator having been incapable of acting as an arbitrator in the arbitration (or there being justifiable doubts about an arbitrator's ability to so act),
(j) an arbitrator not having a qualification which the parties agreed (before the arbitrator's appointment) that the arbitrator must have, or
(k) any other irregularity in the conduct of the arbitration or in the award which is admitted by—
  (i) the tribunal, or
  (ii) any arbitral appointments referee or other third party to whom the parties give powers in relation to the arbitration.'

15.53 Some assistance as to what is meant by 'substantial injustice' can be found in some of the commentary of the English Arbitration Act 1996 from which the concept is drawn. 'It is designed as a long stop only available in extreme cases where the tribunal has gone so wrong in its conduct of the arbitration

131 SAR, r. 71(17) (M).

that justice calls out for it to be corrected.'[132] To the extent that a party has been aware of such an irregularity during the arbitration and has not made timeous objection, that party may not raise that objection in such an appeal.[133] If the Outer House allows the appeal, the court may require the arbitrator to reconsider the award or any part of it, or the court may set aside the award or any part of it.

Error of law: SAR, r. 69 (D)

SAR, r. 69, which deals with legal error appeals, is a default rule. It may therefore be disapplied. The mere reference in an arbitration agreement to the arbitrator's award being final and binding between the parties is not likely to be sufficient to exclude the application of legal error appeals.[134] Importantly, unless there has been a major error on the part of the arbitrator, any appeal on the grounds of an error of law will have to proceed on the basis of the findings in fact made by the arbitrator.[135] **15.54**

Legal error appeals are made to the Outer House of the Court of Session. They may be brought only with the agreement of the parties or with leave of the Outer House.[136] A legal error appeal is treated as having been made for the purposes of the twenty-eight day time limit if an application for leave is made.[137] Leave will be given only if the Outer House is satisfied:[138] **15.55**

(a) deciding the point will substantially affect a party's rights;
(b) the tribunal was asked to decide the point; and
(c) on the basis of the findings of fact in the award (including any facts which the tribunal treated as established for the purpose of deciding the point) the tribunal's decision on the point:

    (i) was obviously wrong; or
    (ii) where the court considers the point to be of general importance, is open to serious doubt.

An application for leave is valid only if it identifies the point of law concerned, and states why the applicant considers leave should be granted.[139] The test for leave has been said to be the same as that applied in England, so English authorities may be relevant.[140] The test for demonstrating that the arbitrator was obviously wrong is high:[141] **15.56**

132 The Departmental Advisory Committee on Arbitration (DAC) Report 1996, para. 280. See *Arbitration Application No. 1 of 2013* [2014] CSOH 83; *Arbitration Appeal No. 2 of 2017* [2018] CSOH 12.
133 SAR, r. 76 (M).
134 *Arbitration Appeal No. 4 of 2020* [2021] CSOH 14.
135 SAR, r. 70(3)(c) (M).
136 SAR, r. 70(2) (M).
137 SAR, r. 70(4) (M).
138 SAR, r. 70(3) (M).
139 SAR, r. 70(4) (M).
140 *Arbitration Application No. 3 of 2011* [2011] CSOH 164, 2012 SLT 150.
141 *Arbitration Appeal No. 1 of 2019* [2019] CSOH 60, 2019 SLT 1309 at [13] and [17] per Lord Bannatyne.

'[13] I consider that it is clear from the well established line of authority I earlier set out that the test of "obviously wrong" creates a very high hurdle for the petitioner to surmount. Thus, I may consider that the arbitrator is on balance wrong. However, that is not sufficient to hold that he is "obviously wrong" and to grant leave. It is necessary for the court to seek to find on the part of the arbitrator "a major intellectual aberration" (see: *Braes of Doune Wind Farm (Scotland) Ltd*[142] at para.31 per Aikenhead J). Or to use the words of Lord Diplock in *Antaios Compania Naviera* (p.206)[143] the court is required to search for a view of the arbitrator which is "so obviously wrong as to preclude the possibility that he might be right".'

[17] It appears to me that the arguments advanced on behalf of the petitioner in their proposed grounds of appeal fail to reach the level of a manifest legal error which could cause the court to apprehend there is anything 'obviously wrong' in the approach and reasoning of the arbitrator and in the decision they have reached.'

The application for leave must be made within twenty-eight days.[144] If leave is granted, the appeal must then be brought within seven days.[145]

Enforcement

15.57 Application can be made to the court for an order that an arbitral award can be enforced as if it were an extract registered decree bearing a warrant for execution granted by the court.[146] That applies also to awards made elsewhere in the world in respect of which enforcement is sought in Scotland.[147] If the arbitration agreement is itself registered, or contained in a document registered, in the Books and Council of Session or sheriff court books for execution, then any arbitral award may also be registered for execution.[148] In the case of international awards, the duly authenticated original award (or a duly certified copy of it), plus the original arbitration agreement (or a duly certified copy of it) must be provided, together with a translation, in any application for recognition or enforcement.[149] The court rules contain specific rules for making applications for enforcement.[150] The grounds for refusal of recognition or enforcement of New York Convention awards are limited.[151]

ADJUDICATION

Framework

15.58 Adjudication can be used when a dispute arises between parties to a construction contract. Section 108(1) of the Housing Grants, Construction and

142 *Braes of Doune Wind Farm (Scotland) Ltd v Alfred McAlpine Business Services Ltd* [2008] EWHC 426 (TCC), [2008] 1 CLC 487.
143 *Antaios Compania Naviera SA v Salen Rederierna AB* [1985] AC 191.
144 See para. 15.49 above.
145 SAR, r. 70(7) (M).
146 2010 Act, s. 12.
147 2010 Act, s. 12(6).
148 2010 Act, s. 12(5) and s. 19(2).
149 2010 Act, s. 21.
150 RCS, r. 100.10 (domestic) and r. 62.57 (recognition of Convention award) and r. 62.58 (registration of Convention award in the Books of Council and Session).
151 2010 Act, s. 20.

Regeneration Act 1996 (the 1996 Act) provides that 'a party to a construction contract has the right to refer a dispute arising under the contract for adjudication under a procedure complying with this section'. Furthermore, the 1996 Act provides that all construction contracts must contain provisions:

> '(a) enabling a party to give notice at any time of their intention to refer a dispute to adjudication;
> (b) providing a timetable with the object of securing the appointment of the adjudicator and referral of the dispute to them within seven days of that notice;
> (c) requiring the adjudicator to reach a decision within twenty-eight days of referral or such longer period as is agreed by the parties after the dispute has been referred;
> (d) allowing the adjudicator to extend the period of twenty-eight days by up to fourteen days, with the consent of the party by whom the dispute was referred;
> (e) imposing a duty on the adjudicator to act impartially; and
> (f) enabling the adjudicator to take the initiative in ascertaining the facts and the law.'[152]

There must also be provision in writing: (i) that the decision of the adjudicator is binding until the dispute is finally determined by legal proceedings, arbitration or agreement; and (ii) that the adjudicator is not liable for anything done or omitted in the discharge or purported discharge of their functions as adjudicator unless the act or omission is in bad faith. If the construction contract fails to comply with s. 108, the adjudication provisions of the scheme for construction contracts apply.[153] The adjudication provisions can be found in Part I of the Schedule to the Scheme for Construction Contracts (Scotland) Regulations 1998 (SCCS).[154] **15.59**

Rough and ready justice

In *Macob Civil Engineering Ltd v Morrison Construction Ltd* Dyson J summarised as follows: **15.60**

> 'The intention of Parliament in enacting the [1996] Act was plain. It was to introduce a speedy mechanism for settling disputes in construction contracts on a provisional interim basis, and requiring the decisions of adjudicators to be enforced pending the final determination of disputes by arbitration, litigation or agreement . . .'[155]

As it is designed to produce a provisionally binding decision in rapid time, adjudication has been described as a kind of rough justice. It is, however, a kind of justice born out of the judicially recognised reality that cash flow is the lifeblood of the construction industry.[156] It is a short and sharp, if rough and ready, means to obtain a provisionally binding decision.[157] That roughness **15.61**

152 Housing Grants, Construction and Regeneration Act 1996, s. 108(2); 'construction contract' is defined in s. 104(1).
153 Housing Grants, Construction and Regeneration Act 1996, s. 108(5).
154 Scheme for Construction Contracts (Scotland) Regulations 1998 (SI 1998/687).
155 [1999] CLC 739 at [14].
156 *Gilbert-Ash (Northern) Ltd v Modern Engineering (Bristol) Ltd* [1974] AC 698 at 718 per Lord Diplock, citing Lord Denning MR in the Court of Appeal. That said, the construction industry is not unique in respect of the importance of cash flow.
157 *NKT Cables A/S v SP Power Systems Ltd* 2017 SLT 494 at [90] per Lady Wolffe.

and readiness is offset by the fact that the disgruntled party has a remedy, i.e. litigation or arbitration on the merits.[158]

15.62 Adjudication does not interrupt the running of a prescriptive period. It does not constitute the making of a 'relevant claim' for the purposes of s. 9 of the Prescription and Limitation (Scotland) Act 1973. If the end of the quinquennium is nigh, the referring party can raise an action and then seek to have it sisted.[158A]

Procedure under the Scheme for Construction Contracts

15.63 The process is commenced by the referring party giving a notice of intention to refer a dispute to adjudication (the notice of adjudication). The notice of adjudication is sent to every other party to the construction contract. It must set out the nature of the dispute, the details of where and when the dispute has arisen and the nature of the redress sought.[159] The adjudicator will be the person (if any) specified in the contract, chosen by nominating body (if any) specified in the contract or chosen by an adjudicator nominating body.[160] After an adjudicator has been chosen, the referring party refers the dispute in writing to them by means of a referral notice.[161]

15.64 Paragraph 12 provides that the adjudicator must act impartially and reach a decision in accordance with the law and avoid incurring unnecessary expense. Paragraph 13(1) provides that '[t]he adjudicator may take the initiative in ascertaining the facts and the law necessary to determine the dispute, and shall decide on the procedure to be followed in the adjudication'. The procedure to be followed is the adjudicator's prerogative. Parties must comply with any requests or directions of the adjudicator.[162] Subject to any agreement to the contrary, parties may be assisted or represented by whom they wish, legally qualified or not.[163]

The adjudicator's decision

15.65 Under the Scheme for Construction Contracts, the adjudicator must reach their decision not later than: (i) twenty-eight days after the date of the referral notice; (ii) forty-two days after the date of the referral notice, if the referring party consents; or (iii) such period exceeding twenty-eight days as parties may agree.[164]

15.66 The adjudicator must determine the matters which have been validly referred for their determination; no more, and certainly no less.[165] The scope of the

158 *Hochtief Solutions AG v Maspero Elevatori SpA* 2021 SLT 528 at [20] per Lord Woolman, delivering the opinion of the court.

158A *Greater Glasgow Health Board v Multiplex Construction Europe Ltd* [2021] CSOH 115 at [28]–[36] per Lord Tyre.

159 SCCS, para. 1.

160 SCCS, para. 2(1). An adjudicator nominating body is defined in para. 2(3).

161 SCCS, para. 7(1).

162 SCCS, para. 14.

163 SCCS, para. 16(1).

164 SCCS, para. 19(1).

165 Cf SCCS, para. 20(1).

adjudication is delineated by the initiating documents and includes any ground founded on by the responding party.[166] The adjudicator must deal with any lines of defence raised by the responding party,[167] although it is not necessary for the adjudicator to reach a decision on each and every point raised. The adjudicator does not have to provide reasons for the decision unless requested to do so by one of the parties.[168]

Parties must comply with the adjudicator's decision immediately on its delivery.[169] Even if the adjudicator's decision is wrong, whether based on a legal error, factual error or both, it remains an enforceable decision on the issue referred.[170] **15.67**

The adjudicator's jurisdiction ceases on the expiry of the time limit for making the decision. The time limit may be that prescribed by statute or may be a longer one, as agreed between the parties. If the adjudicator issues a decision after the expiry of the time limit, it is of no effect.[171] **15.68**

Enforcement of the adjudicator's decision

A party can apply to the court for enforcement of an adjudicator's decision. The summons will conclude for (or the initial writ will crave) decree in terms of the order made by the adjudicator.[172] The objective of the Housing Grants, Construction and Regeneration Act 1996, and the Scheme for Construction Contracts, requires the courts to respect the adjudicator's decision unless it is plain that the question decided by the adjudicator was not referred or the adjudicator has gone about their task in an obviously unfair manner. Only rarely will the courts interfere by refusing to enforce an adjudicator's decision.[173] **15.69**

In summary, enforcement can be resisted on the grounds: (i) that the adjudicator has either exceeded or failed to exhaust their jurisdiction (either decided more than or decided less than the matters validly referred); or (ii) that there has been a material breach of the rules of natural justice (a clear example of the adjudicator's going about their task in an obviously unfair manner). A failure to exhaust jurisdiction does not have to be deliberate to render the decision unenforceable.[174] Natural justice requires that the adjudicator be impartial and give each side a fair opportunity to present its case.[175] **15.70**

An example of an adjudicator being found to have breached the rules of natural justice is *Highlands and Islands Airports Ltd v Shetland Island Council*,[176] **15.71**

166 *Hochtief Solutions AG v Maspero Elevatori SpA* 2021 SLT 528 at [26]–[27].
167 *Joint Administrators of the Connaught Partnership Ltd v Perth & Kinross Council* 2014 SLT 608 at [19] per Lord Malcolm.
168 SCCS, para. 22.
169 SCCS, para. 21.
170 *Macob Civil Engineering Ltd v Morrison Construction Ltd* [1999] CLC 739 at [19].
171 *Ritchie Brothers (PWC) Ltd v David Philp (Commercials) Ltd* 2005 1 SC 384.
172 If the adjudicator has awarded a sum or sums totalling £100,000 or less, and the party wishes to seek decree in terms of that order, the action for enforcement must be brought in the sheriff court: Courts Reform (Scotland) Act 2014, s. 39(2).
173 *Barhale Ltd v SP Transmission plc* [2021] CSOH 2, 2021 SLT 852 at [26].
174 *Barhale Ltd v SP Transmission plc* [2021] CSOH 2, 2021 SLT 852.
175 *Costain Ltd v Strathclyde Builders Ltd* 2004 SLT 102 at [7] per Lord Drummond Young.
176 [2012] CSOH 12.

where the adjudicator sought advice from senior counsel as to the proper construction of a contractual clause, but did not advise parties what the advice was or afford them an opportunity to make submissions on it.

EXPERT DETERMINATION

15.72 Parties to a contract may agree to expert determination. In other words, a third party will determine (specific) issues arising under the contract. While it may be most obviously suited to technical valuations (for example, the valuation of a private company), it is used more widely than that. In *Macdonald Estates plc v National Car Parks Ltd*,[177] Lord Reed observed:

> 'Expert determination, understood as an alternative to arbitration, has taken root in Scottish legal practice, as a consequence of its attractiveness to the commercial community as a relatively quick and informal means of resolving matters of disagreement or potential disagreement. It is now a well-recognised means of resolving disputes in almost every area of commercial life, and owes its success to the fact that it generally works well and is found to be commercially useful.'

As regards the difference between an arbitrator and an expert, he observed:

> 'Although the use of the word "expert" is not conclusive, phrases such as "acting as an expert and not as an arbiter" denote a concept which is clear in its general effect. A person who sits in a judicial or quasi-judicial capacity, as an arbiter ordinarily does, decides matters on the basis of submissions and evidence put before him, whereas an expert, subject to the provisions of his remit, is entitled to carry out his own investigations and come to his own conclusion regardless of any submissions or evidence adduced by the parties themselves.'[178]

15.73 A referral to expert determination does not interrupt the running of a prescriptive period. Procedure will depend on the clause in the contract, as will the identity of the expert and the expert's remit. The clause may specify criteria (e.g. a particular amount of professional experience in a particular area) for appointment. It will likely provide a timescale (normally tight) within which the expert is expected to make their decision. As for procedure, it may simply provide that all relevant information is to be passed to the expert, who will carry out their own analysis and investigations and reach a decision. The decision can be made without the benefit of submissions by the parties. If it is not set out in the clause, procedure will have to be agreed between the parties and the expert.

15.74 The clause will likely provide that the decision will be binding on the parties. If it provides that the decision will be binding in the absence of 'manifest error', that is a reference to oversights and blunders so obvious and obviously capable of affecting the determination as to admit of no difference of opinion[179] or 'a glaring mistake that jumps off the page'.[179A] The clause should specify whether the expert is required to provide reasons for the decision.

177 2010 SC 250 at [22].
178 2010 SC 250 at [21].
179 *Veba Oil Supply & Trading GmbH v Petrotrade Inc* [2001] EWCA Civ 1832 at [33] per Simon Brown LJ.
179A *Eastern Motor Co Ltd v Grassick* [2021] CSIH 67 at [41] per Lord Pentland

Challenging the expert's determination

The law was considered in *Eastern Motor Co Ltd v Grassick*.[180] Lord Tyre observed that the starting point in English law was an observation by Lord Denning MR in *Campbell v Edwards*:[181] **15.75**

> 'It is simply the law of contract. If two persons agree that the price of property should be fixed by a valuer on whom they agree, and he gives that valuation honestly and in good faith, they are bound by it. Even if he has made a mistake they are still bound by it. The reason is because they have agreed to be bound by it. If there were fraud or collusion, of course, it would be very different. Fraud or collusion unravels everything.'

Lord Tyre considered the distinction drawn by Dillon LJ in *Jones v Sherwood Computer Services plc* between, on the one hand, a material departure by an expert from their instructions and, on the other, a mistake made by the expert while doing what he was asked to do.[182] The law was summarised by Simon Brown LJ in *Veba Oil Supply & Trading GmbH v Petrotrade Inc*: **15.76**

> 'Under the modern law the position is the same as it was with regard to a departure from instructions, different with regard to mistakes. As Lord Denning explained in *Campbell v Edwards*, if an expert makes a mistake whilst carrying out his instructions, the parties are nevertheless bound by it for the very good reason that they have agreed to be bound by it. Where, however, the expert departs from his instructions, the position is very different: in those circumstances the parties have not agreed to be bound.'[183]

In summary, an expert's determination cannot be challenged merely on the ground that it is wrong. The expert must have departed from their instructions. To borrow from the language of adjudication, the expert must have either exceeded or failed to exhaust their jurisdiction. The departure from instructions must be material, in the sense of not being trivial or *de minimis*.[184] As the expert's jurisdiction derives from the terms of their appointment,[185] the court must look to the contract to assess what the instructions were and therefore what the jurisdiction of the expert was. **15.77**

MEDIATION

Adjudication and expert determination are both forms of adjudicative alternative dispute resolution, i.e. they involve a third party reaching a binding decision. Mediation is the most commonly used form of non-adjudicative alternative dispute resolution. In mediation a third party assists parties to a dispute to negotiate a settlement. **15.78**

180 2021 SLT 340.
181 [1976] 1 WLR 403 at 407.
182 [1992] 1 WLR 277 at 287.
183 [2001] EWCA Civ 1832, [2002] 1 All ER 703 at [26].
184 *Veba Oil Supply & Trading GmbH v Petrotrade Inc* [2001] EWCA Civ 1832, [2002] 1 All ER 703 at [26] per Simon Brown LJ.
185 *Redding Park Development Company Ltd v Falkirk Council* [2011] CSOH 202 at [42] per Lord Menzies.

15.79 While a mediator has no authority to make a decision on the merits of a dispute, they may choose to express a view on the merits. That may assist parties to reconsider their respective positions. Where the mediator expresses a view, the process has been described as 'evaluative' mediation.[186] It stands in contrast to 'purely facilitative' mediation, where the mediator expresses no view.[187] All power remains with the parties. It is they, and not a third party, who must resolve the dispute. To that extent, it is a consensual process.

15.80 A successful mediation will almost certainly be less costly than either litigation or arbitration. It may also prevent the irretrievable breakdown of the parties' relationship. The focus of mediation is not on parties' *legal rights*, but on parties' *interests*.

15.81 There is no statute governing how mediation must operate. The Cross-Border Mediation (Scotland) Regulations 2011[188] implemented in part Directive 2008/52/EC of the European Parliament and of the Council of 21 May 2008 on certain aspects of mediation in civil and commercial matters (the 'Mediation Directive'). They applied where there was a cross-border dispute between parties in which at least one of the parties was domiciled or habitually resident in an EU Member State other than that of any other party on the date on which, *inter alia*, parties agreed to use mediation or mediation was ordered by a court. The Mediation Directive covered the quality of mediation (requiring EU Member States to encourage mediators to adhere to voluntary codes of conduct), the enforceability of agreements resulting from mediation, the confidentiality of mediation and the effect of mediation on prescriptive periods. The 2011 Regulations were revoked as a result of the UK's departure from the EU.

15.82 Like adjudication, mediation does not interrupt the running of a prescriptive period. The 2011 Regulations had amended the Prescription and Limitation (Scotland) Act 1973 in relation to cross-border disputes, extending in certain cases the prescriptive period where parties to a cross-border dispute were using, or had used, mediation. The relevant provisions have been repealed.

When to mediate

15.83 Parties can agree to mediate at any time. A contract may prescribe mediation as a particular stage in a process of dispute resolution. They can mediate before or during litigation or arbitration. Mediation may be used in tandem with arbitration. In arbitration-mediation (arb-med) the arbitrator makes an award, which is kept confidential, and then parties seek to mediate the dispute. The award is used as a prompt to settlement. If no settlement is negotiated, the arbitrator's award takes effect.[189] In mediation-arbitration (med-arb) the third party acts first as mediator and, if parties cannot reach an agreement, then as arbitrator.[190]

186 S Shipman, B Waters, W Wood, H Brown, *Brown & Marriott's ADR Principles and Practice*, 4th edn (Edinburgh: W. Green, 2019), para. 2–033.
187 *Brown & Marriott's ADR Principles and Practice* (2019), para. 2–034.
188 SSI 2011/34.
189 *Brown & Marriott's ADR Principles and Practice* (2019), para. 2–026.
190 *Brown & Marriott's ADR Principles and Practice* (2019), para. 2–027.

How to mediate

Assuming that parties have agreed to mediate, the next step is to appoint a mediator. If mediation is prescribed in a contract, the contract may stipulate how the mediator is to be appointed. Parties may agree on an individual. Otherwise, parties may approach a body, such as Scottish Mediation,[191] to find a mediator. Notably, there is no single body responsible for accreditation of mediators. **15.84**

How the mediation is conducted is a matter for the mediator. An agenda may be agreed in advance. The mediation is likely to consist of the mediator moving between the parties, holding private conversations with each. This could take place by parties congregating in a building or by the use of 'breakout rooms' online. Any number of parties can take part in a mediation, the number being constrained only by common sense and feasibility. Parties may represent themselves at a mediation or a representative may attend on their behalf. Whoever they are, those attending the mediation must have full authority to settle the dispute. **15.85**

It is common for parties to sign an agreement to mediate before the mediation begins. The agreement to mediate may cover, *inter alia*: (i) the identity of the mediator; (ii) where and when the mediation will take place; (iii) the duties of parties and of the mediator; (iv) procedure; (v) confidentiality; and (vi) expenses.[192] It will likely include provision that either party may withdraw from the mediation at any time. **15.86**

If they succeed in negotiating a settlement, parties will normally draw up and sign an agreement recording the terms of the settlement. **15.87**

(Non-adjudicative) alternative dispute resolution and the courts

As regards commercial actions in the Court of Session, the court requires that, before litigation is commenced, both parties 'consider carefully and discuss whether all or some of the dispute may be amenable to some form of alternative dispute resolution'.[193] Failure to comply with that requirement may sound in an adverse award of expenses. Resort to alternative dispute resolution should also be considered as the litigation progresses.[194] Expectations are much the same in sheriff courts where commercial actions may be raised. **15.88**

While they may request that parties consider alternative dispute resolution, judges and sheriffs are not empowered to refer cases subject to ordinary procedure in the Court of Session or the sheriff court to alternative dispute resolution. It is not wholly clear whether the same is true in cases subject to commercial procedure. Rule 47.11(1)(e) of the Rules of the Court of Session allows the judge, at the preliminary hearing, to make 'such . . . order as he **15.89**

191 Scottish Mediation, *https://www.scottishmediation.org.uk/find-a-mediator/* (last accessed 10 September 2021).
192 For a sample agreement to mediate, see M Mantle, *Mediation: A Practical Guide for Lawyers*, 2nd edn (Edinburgh: Edinburgh University Press, 2017), pp. 120–123.
193 Practice Note No. 1 of 2017, para. 11.
194 Practice Note No. 1 of 2017, para. 20(c).

thinks fit for the speedy determination of the action'. Referring a case to alternative dispute resolution would not be an order for the speedy determination *of the action*. However, r. 40.12(3)(m) of the Ordinary Cause Rules allows the sheriff, at the case management conference, to make 'any order which the sheriff thinks will result in the speedy resolution of the action (including the use of alternative dispute resolution)'. The Simple Procedure Rules enable a sheriff to refer cases to alternative dispute resolution.[195] Only cases worth £5,000 or less are subject to simple procedure.

195 Simple Procedure Rules, rr. 7.6(1)(a), 7.7(3), 12.3(1). Rule 1.4(3) requires the sheriff to encourage negotiation and alternative dispute resolution. The rules are contained in the Act of Sederunt (Simple Procedure) (SSI 2016/200).

Index

EU Authorised Representative:
Easy Access System Europe Mustamäe tee 50, 10621 Tallinn, Estonia
gpsr.requests@easproject.com

Printed and bound by CPI Group (UK) Ltd, Croydon, CR0 4YY
14/09/2026
02216780-0008